Communications in Computer and Information Science 3047

Rationale
The CCIS series is devoted to the publication of proceedings of computer science conferences. Its aim is to efficiently disseminate original research results in informatics in printed and electronic form. While the focus is on publication of peer-reviewed full papers presenting mature work, inclusion of reviewed short papers reporting on work in progress is welcome, too. Besides globally relevant meetings with internationally representative program committees guaranteeing a strict peer-reviewing and paper selection process, conferences run by societies or of high regional or national relevance are also considered for publication.

Topics
The topical scope of CCIS spans the entire spectrum of informatics ranging from foundational topics in the theory of computing to information and communications science and technology and a broad variety of interdisciplinary application fields.

Information for Volume Editors and Authors
Publication in CCIS is free of charge. No royalties are paid, however, we offer registered conference participants temporary free access to the online version of the conference proceedings on SpringerLink (http://link.springer.com) by means of an http referrer from the conference website and/or a number of complimentary printed copies, as specified in the official acceptance email of the event.

CCIS proceedings can be published in time for distribution at conferences or as post-proceedings, and delivered in the form of printed books and/or electronically as USBs and/or e-content licenses for accessing proceedings at SpringerLink. Furthermore, CCIS proceedings are included in the CCIS electronic book series hosted in the SpringerLink digital library at http://link.springer.com/bookseries/7899. Conferences publishing in CCIS are allowed to use our online conference service (Meteor) for managing the whole proceedings lifecycle (from submission and reviewing to preparing for publication) free of charge.

Publication process
The language of publication is exclusively English. Authors publishing in CCIS have to sign the Springer CCIS copyright transfer form, however, they are free to use their material published in CCIS for substantially changed, more elaborate subsequent publications elsewhere. For the preparation of the camera-ready papers/files, authors have to strictly adhere to the Springer CCIS Authors' Instructions and are strongly encouraged to use the CCIS LaTeX style files or templates.

Abstracting/Indexing
CCIS is abstracted/indexed in DBLP, Google Scholar, EI-Compendex, Mathematical Reviews, SCImago, Scopus. CCIS volumes are also submitted for the inclusion in ISI Proceedings.

How to start
To start the evaluation of your proposal for inclusion in the CCIS series, please send an e-mail to ccis@springer.com

Constantine Stephanidis · George Margetis ·
Stavroula Ntoa · Margherita Antona ·
Gavriel Salvendy
Editors

HCI International 2026 Posters

28th International Conference on
Human-Computer Interaction, HCII 2026
Montreal, QC, Canada, July 26–31, 2026
Proceedings, Part I

Springer

Editors
Constantine Stephanidis
Foundation for Research and Technology - Hellas (FORTH) and University of Crete
Heraklion, Crete, Greece

George Margetis
Foundation for Research and Technology - Hellas (FORTH)
Heraklion, Crete, Greece

Stavroula Ntoa
Foundation for Research and Technology - Hellas (FORTH)
Heraklion, Crete, Greece

Margherita Antona
Foundation for Research and Technology - Hellas (FORTH)
Heraklion, Crete, Greece

Gavriel Salvendy
University of Central Florida
Orlando, FL, USA

ISSN 1865-0929 ISSN 1865-0937 (electronic)
Communications in Computer and Information Science
ISBN 978-3-032-30551-0 ISBN 978-3-032-30552-7 (eBook)
https://doi.org/10.1007/978-3-032-30552-7

This Springer imprint is published by the registered company Springer Nature Switzerland AG
The registered company address is: Gewerbestrasse 11, 6330 Cham, Switzerland

Foreword

The HCI International (HCII) conference was founded in 1984 by Gavriel Salvendy (Purdue University, USA, Tsinghua University, China, and University of Central Florida, USA) with the first event of the series, "1st USA-Japan Conference on Human-Computer Interaction" held in Honolulu, Hawaii, USA, 18–20 August. Since then, HCI International has been held jointly with several Thematic Areas and Affiliated Conferences, with each one under the auspices of a distinguished international Program Board and under one management and one registration. Twenty-eight HCI International Conferences have been organized so far (every two years until 2013, and annually thereafter).

Since its establishment, the HCII conference has become a hub for presenting groundbreaking research and novel ideas and a forum for collaboration for people from all over the world. Over the years, this conference has served as a platform for scholars, researchers, industry experts, and students to exchange ideas, connect, and address challenges in the ever-evolving HCI field. The conference has evolved, adapting to new technologies and emerging trends, while staying committed to its core mission of advancing knowledge and driving change.

The 28th International Conference on Human-Computer Interaction, HCI International 2026 (HCII 2026), was held during 26–31 July 2026 as an 'on-site' conference at the Montreal Convention Centre, in Montreal, Canada, with the additional option for 'on-line' participation. It incorporated the 21 thematic areas and affiliated conferences listed below.

A total of 7435 individuals from academia, research institutes, industry, and government agencies from 94 countries submitted contributions. 1463 papers and 360 posters (as short research papers) are included in the volumes of the proceedings published just before the start of the conference, presented further below. The contributions thoroughly cover the entire field of human-computer interaction, highlight the evolving role of computers in diverse contexts, and demonstrate how HCI research is shaping and improving user experiences across a wide range of domains, influencing technological progress and its effective integration into various sectors of everyday life.

The HCII conference also offers the option of presenting 'Late Breaking Work', both for papers and posters, with the corresponding proceedings volumes published after the conference. Full papers will be included in the 'HCII 2026 - Late Breaking Papers' volumes of the proceedings to be published in the Springer LNCS series, while 'Poster Extended Abstracts' will be included as short research papers in the 'HCII 2026 - Late Breaking Posters' volumes to be published in the Springer CCIS series.

I would like to thank the Program Board Chairs and the members of the Program Boards of all thematic areas and affiliated conferences for their contribution towards the high scientific quality and overall success of the HCI International 2026 conference. Their manifold support, including paper reviews (via a single-blind review process, with a minimum of two reviews per submission) and session organization, and their willingness to act as goodwill ambassadors for the conference is most highly appreciated.

This conference would not have been possible without the continuous and unwavering support and advice of Gavriel Salvendy, founder, General Chair Emeritus, and Scientific Advisor. For his outstanding efforts, I would like to express my sincere appreciation to Abbas Moallem, Communications Chair and Editor of HCI International News.

July 2026 Constantine Stephanidis

HCI International 2026 Thematic Areas and Affiliated Conferences

- HCI: Human-Computer Interaction Thematic Area
- HIMI: Human Interface and the Management of Information Thematic Area
- EPCE: 23rd International Conference on Engineering Psychology and Cognitive Ergonomics
- AC: 20th International Conference on Augmenting Cognition in the AI-Accelerated Era
- UAHCI: 20th International Conference on Universal Access in Human-Computer Interaction
- CCD: 18th International Conference on Cross-Cultural Design
- SCSM: 18th International Conference on Social Computing and Social Media
- VAMR: 18th International Conference on Virtual, Augmented and Mixed Reality
- DHM: 17th International Conference on Digital Human Modeling and Applications in Health, Safety, Ergonomics and Risk Management
- DUXU: 15th International Conference on Design, User Experience, and Usability
- C&C: 14th International Conference on Culture and Computing
- DAPI: 14th International Conference on Distributed, Ambient and Pervasive Interactions
- HCIBGO: 13th International Conference on HCI in Business, Government and Organizations
- LCT: 13th International Conference on Learning and Collaboration Technologies
- ITAP: 12th International Conference on Human Aspects of IT for the Aged Population
- AIS: 8th International Conference on Adaptive Instructional Systems
- HCI-CPT: 8th International Conference on HCI for Cybersecurity, Privacy and Trust
- HCI-Games: 8th International Conference on HCI in Games
- MobiTAS: 8th International Conference on HCI in Mobility, Transport, and Automotive Systems
- AI-HCI: 7th International Conference on Artificial Intelligence in HCI
- MOBILE: 7th International Conference on Human-Centered Design, Operation and Evaluation of Mobile Communications

List of Conference Proceedings Volumes Appearing Before the Conference

1. LNCS 16701, Human-Computer Interaction (Part I), edited by Masaaki Kurosu and Ayako Hashizume
2. LNCS 16702, Human-Computer Interaction (Part II), edited by Masaaki Kurosu and Ayako Hashizume
3. LNCS 16703, Human-Computer Interaction (Part III), edited by Masaaki Kurosu and Ayako Hashizume
4. LNCS 16704, Human-Computer Interaction (Part IV), edited by Masaaki Kurosu and Ayako Hashizume
5. LNCS 16705, Human Interface and the Management of Information (Part I), edited by Hirohiko Mori and Yumi Asahi
6. LNCS 16706, Human Interface and the Management of Information (Part II), edited by Hirohiko Mori and Yumi Asahi
7. LNAI 16707, Engineering Psychology and Cognitive Ergonomics (Part I), edited by Wen-Chin Li and Anastasios Plioutsias
8. LNAI 16708, Engineering Psychology and Cognitive Ergonomics (Part II), edited by Wen-Chin Li and Anastasios Plioutsias
9. LNAI 16709, Augmenting Cognition in the AI-Accelerated Era, edited by Dylan D. Schmorrow and Cali M. Fidopiastis
10. LNCS 16710, Universal Access in Human-Computer Interaction (Part I), edited by Margherita Antona and Constantine Stephanidis
11. LNCS 16711, Universal Access in Human-Computer Interaction (Part II), edited by Margherita Antona and Constantine Stephanidis
12. LNCS 16712, Cross-Cultural Design (Part I), edited by Pei-Luen Patrick Rau
13. LNCS 16713, Cross-Cultural Design (Part II), edited by Pei-Luen Patrick Rau
14. LNCS 16714, Cross-Cultural Design (Part III), edited by Pei-Luen Patrick Rau
15. LNCS 16715, Social Computing and Social Media (Part I), edited by Adela Coman and Simona Vasilache
16. LNCS 16716, Social Computing and Social Media (Part II), edited by Adela Coman and Simona Vasilache
17. LNCS 16717, Virtual, Augmented and Mixed Reality (Part I), edited by Jessie Y. C. Chen and Gino Fragomeni
18. LNCS 16718, Virtual, Augmented and Mixed Reality (Part II), edited by Jessie Y. C. Chen and Gino Fragomeni
19. LNCS 16719, Digital Human Modeling and Applications in Health, Safety, Ergonomics and Risk Management (Part I), edited by Vincent G. Duffy
20. LNCS 16720, Digital Human Modeling and Applications in Health, Safety, Ergonomics and Risk Management (Part II), edited by Vincent G. Duffy
21. LNCS 16721, Design, User Experience, and Usability (Part I), edited by Martin Schrepp

22. LNCS 16722, Design, User Experience, and Usability (Part II), edited by Martin Schrepp
23. LNCS 16723, Design, User Experience, and Usability (Part III), edited by Martin Schrepp
24. LNCS 16724, Design, User Experience, and Usability (Part IV), edited by Martin Schrepp
25. LNCS 16725, Culture and Computing (Part I), edited by Matthias Rauterberg
26. LNCS 16726, Culture and Computing (Part II), edited by Matthias Rauterberg
27. LNCS 16727, Distributed, Ambient and Pervasive Interactions (Part I), edited by Norbert A. Streitz and Shin'ichi Konomi
28. LNCS 16728, Distributed, Ambient and Pervasive Interactions (Part II), edited by Norbert A. Streitz and Shin'ichi Konomi
29. LNCS 16729, HCI in Business, Government and Organizations (Part I), edited by Fiona Fui-Hoon Nah and Keng Leng Siau
30. LNCS 16730, HCI in Business, Government and Organizations (Part II), edited by Fiona Fui-Hoon Nah and Keng Leng Siau
31. LNCS 16731, Learning and Collaboration Technologies (Part I), edited by Brian K. Smith and Marcela Borge
32. LNCS 16732, Learning and Collaboration Technologies (Part II), edited by Brian K. Smith and Marcela Borge
33. LNCS 16733, Learning and Collaboration Technologies (Part III), edited by Brian K. Smith and Marcela Borge
34. LNCS 16734, Human Aspects of IT for the Aged Population (Part I), edited by Qin Gao and Jia Zhou
35. LNCS 16735, Human Aspects of IT for the Aged Population (Part II), edited by Qin Gao and Jia Zhou
36. LNCS 16736, Human Aspects of IT for the Aged Population (Part III), edited by Qin Gao and Jia Zhou
37. LNCS 16737, Adaptive Instructional Systems, edited by Robert A. Sottilare and Jessica Schwarz
38. LNCS 16738, HCI for Cybersecurity, Privacy and Trust, edited by Abbas Moallem
39. LNCS 16739, HCI in Games (Part I), edited by Xiaowen Fang
40. LNCS 16740, HCI in Games (Part II), edited by Xiaowen Fang
41. LNCS 16741, HCI in Mobility, Transport, and Automotive Systems (Part I), edited by Heidi Krömker
42. LNCS 16742, HCI in Mobility, Transport, and Automotive Systems (Part II), edited by Heidi Krömker
43. LNAI 16743, Artificial Intelligence in HCI (Part I), edited by Helmut Degen and Stavroula Ntoa
44. LNAI 16744, Artificial Intelligence in HCI (Part II), edited by Helmut Degen and Stavroula Ntoa
45. LNAI 16745, Artificial Intelligence in HCI (Part III), edited by Helmut Degen and Stavroula Ntoa
46. LNAI 16746, Artificial Intelligence in HCI (Part IV), edited by Helmut Degen and Stavroula Ntoa

47. LNCS 16747, Human-Centered Design, Operation and Evaluation of Mobile Communications, edited by June Wei and George Margetis
48. CCIS 3047, HCI International 2026 Posters (Part I), edited by Constantine Stephanidis, George Margetis, Stavroula Ntoa, Margherita Antona and Gavriel Salvendy
49. CCIS 3048, HCI International 2026 Posters (Part II), edited by Constantine Stephanidis, George Margetis, Stavroula Ntoa, Margherita Antona and Gavriel Salvendy
50. CCIS 3049, HCI International 2026 Posters (Part III), edited by Constantine Stephanidis, George Margetis, Stavroula Ntoa, Margherita Antona and Gavriel Salvendy
51. CCIS 3050, HCI International 2026 Posters (Part IV), edited by Constantine Stephanidis, George Margetis, Stavroula Ntoa, Margherita Antona and Gavriel Salvendy
52. CCIS 3051, HCI International 2026 Posters (Part V), edited by Constantine Stephanidis, George Margetis, Stavroula Ntoa, Margherita Antona and Gavriel Salvendy
53. CCIS 3052, HCI International 2026 Posters (Part VI), edited by Constantine Stephanidis, George Margetis, Stavroula Ntoa, Margherita Antona and Gavriel Salvendy

https://2026.hci.international/proceedings

Preface

Preliminary scientific results, professional news, or work in progress, described in the form of short research papers (4–11 pages long), constitute a popular submission type among the International Conference on Human-Computer Interaction (HCII) participants. Extended abstracts are particularly suited for reporting ongoing work, which can benefit from a visual presentation, and are presented during the conference in the form of posters. The latter allow a focus on novel ideas and are appropriate for presenting project results in a simple, concise, and visually appealing manner. Posters are also complemented by brief oral pitches, allowing presenters to concisely introduce their work and engage the audience. Poster presentations and pitches are also suitable for attracting feedback from an international community of HCI academics, researchers, and practitioners.

Poster submissions this year spanned the wide range of topics of all HCII thematic areas and affiliated conferences. Six volumes of the HCII 2026 proceedings are dedicated to this year's poster extended abstracts, in the form of short research papers, focusing on the following topics:

- Volume I: HCI Theory and Foundations; Visual Perception and User Interface Design; UX Evaluation, Metrics, and Research Methods; Accessibility and Inclusive Design
- Volume II: Immersive XR and Virtual Experience Design; XR for Learning and Training; Games, Gamification, and Playful Interaction; Cultural Heritage and Interactive Narrative Experiences
- Volume III: Social Robots, Service Robots, and Human–Robot Interaction; Automated Driving, Vehicle HMI, and Driver Experience; Mobility, Aviation, and Transportation Platforms; Product, Service, and Experience Design; Fashion, Architecture, and Interior Design; Haptics, Biometrics, and Advanced Interaction Modalities
- Volume IV: Work, Organizations, and Digital Transformation; AI in Professional, Enterprise, and Industrial Contexts; Social Computing, Misinformation, and Online Behavior; Sustainability, Communities, and Civic Design; Visualization, Risk Communication, and Public Understanding
- Volume V: Education, Learning Systems, and Pedagogical Innovation; Clinical Decision Support and Medical Interfaces; Patient Experience and Health Service Design; Aging, Independent Living, and Age-friendly Interaction; Well-Being, Emotional Support, and Everyday Care Technologies
- Volume VI: Generative AI for Design, Creativity, and Co-Creation; LLM-Powered Interaction, Chatbots, and Conversational Systems; AI, Knowledge Graphs, and Digital Preservation of Heritage; Governance, Trust, and Safety in AI Systems

Poster extended abstracts in the form of short research papers were accepted for publication in these volumes following a minimum of two single-blind reviews from the members of the HCII 2026 international Program Boards, i.e., the program committees of the constituent events. We would like to thank all of them for their invaluable contribution, support, and efforts.

July 2026

Constantine Stephanidis
George Margetis
Stavroula Ntoa
Margherita Antona
Gavriel Salvendy

28th International Conference on Human-Computer Interaction (HCII 2026)

The full list with the Program Board Chairs and the members of the Program Boards of all thematic areas and affiliated conferences of HCII 2026 is available online at:

http://www.hci.international/board-members-2026.php

HCI International 2027 Conference

The 29th International Conference on Human-Computer Interaction, HCI International 2027, will be held jointly with the affiliated conferences at the Estrel Hotel and Congress Center, in Berlin, Germany, 25–30 July 2027. It will cover a broad spectrum of themes related to Human-Computer Interaction, including theoretical issues, methods, tools, processes, and case studies in HCI design, as well as novel interaction techniques, interfaces, and applications. The proceedings will be published by Springer (part of Springer Nature) in a multi-volume set. More information will become available on the conference website: https://2027.hci.international/.

General Chair
Constantine Stephanidis
University of Crete and ICS-FORTH
Heraklion, Crete, Greece
Email: general_chair@2027.hci.international

https://2027.hci.international/

Contents

HCI Theory and Foundations

Visual Perception and User Interface Design

UX Evaluation, Metrics, and Research Methods

Accessibility and Inclusive Design

HCI Theory and Foundations

Hybrid Intelligence as a New Stage in the Development of Human-System Integration

Oleksandr Burov[1](✉), Svitlana Lytvynova[1], Olha Pinchuk[1], Olena Kuzminska[2], Oleksii Tkachenko[3], Natalia Kovalenko[4], Svitlana Agadzhanova[5], and Tetiana Aslanian[6]

[1] Institute for Digitalisation of Education, National Academy of Educational Sciences of Ukraine, Kyiv, Ukraine
{ayb,s.h.lytvynova,opinchuk100}@iitlt.gov.ua
[2] National University of Life and Environmental Sciences of Ukraine, Kyiv, Ukraine
o.kuzminska@nubip.edu.ua
[3] Taras Shevchenko National University of Kyiv, Kyiv, Ukraine
otkachenko@knu.ua
[4] Sumy State Pedagogical University, Sumy, Ukraine
[5] Sumy National Agrarian University, Sumy, Ukraine
s.agadzhanova@snau.edu.ua
[6] Institute of Social and Political Psychology, Kyiv, Ukraine
t.aslanian@ispp.org.ua

Abstract. Our developments used coupling between human and AI as the development of the Human-System Integration paradigm in form of Hybrid Intelligence for critical industries. The analysis of currently known hybrid intelligence architecture allowed us to develop methodology and some practical tools for human component of power industry performance. The proposed HI model can be considered as a systemic emergence, an integrated cognitive system, and a complex adaptive system. The author HI model has been verified in relation to some components at power plants and can be considered as further development of Human-System Integration approach in critical industries. The data-driven systems to predict (with prediction accuracy ≥90%) human's performance and deviation from the "norm" (11-points scale) have been developed. The developed scales are recommended to be used in AI-agents for explanation and advising operators' control of their fitness-for-duty to safe nor only high performance, but professional health as well. Methods to build such AI-agents have been developed.

Keywords: Cognitive Performance · Hybrid Intelligence · Hybrid Intelligence Architecture · Human-System Integration · Power Industry · Operator

C. Stephanidis et al. (Eds.): HCII 2026, CCIS 3047, pp. 3–12, 2026.
https://doi.org/10.1007/978-3-032-30552-7_1

1 Introduction

Digitalization of almost all aspects of human life has increased the importance of human-system integration (HSI) as an interdisciplinary managerial/technical approach to develop and sustain systems and is an object of Engineering Psychology/Human Factors [1]. HSI possibilities to provide system design and prediction of its performance have changed with the growth of the AI role in critical industries/military affairs where HSI errors/insufficient efficiency may be accompanied by significant economic/social losses [2].

In the traditional HSI structure, AI is no longer technology in usual sense, but becomes an independent participant, "taking over" more functions of the interaction subject and is not only a human assistant/partner. In "borderline" situations, the reliability of solutions and results' correctness are better ensured by a human (ability to use non-formalized knowledge), and AI accumulates knowledge and learns much faster (information processing). As E. Brynjolfsson (Director of the Digital Economy Lab, Stanford University) highlighted in the paper to The World Economic Forum in Davos (January 2026), "The same tools that allow AI to handle first-draft work can, if deployed thoughtfully, accelerate human development instead of replacing it. We are already seeing cases where junior employees are brought into higher-value conversations earlier, supported by AI co-pilots and internal knowledge assistants" [3, p. 3].

Thus, it is possible to cultivate mutual cognitive growth and emergent hybrid intelligence between an operator and an AI agent—provided we design for *co-adaptation, transparency, and shared goals*, not mere automation. Such a mutual adaptation creates possibility of developing a qualitatively new subject of cognitive activity in HSI—hybrid intelligence (HI) - thanks to the synergy of human and AI, not only for solving situationally limited problems, but also for the further development of this new integrated subject.

These factors can be especially important in emergent industries where a share of human factors generally accepted as 80–90% of accidents and incidents because of a human error [4], but it varies depending on industry [5]. Last years have clearly demonstrated that electricity became an acute factor of economics and even a weapon in hybrid wars. Thus, for thermal [6] and hydroelectric power plants, it is possible to assume that operator errors are involved in approximately 25–45% of accidents and serious violations, and in some cases are the key cause; in nuclear energy, this share is evaluated as 30–50% [7]. These data have remained relatively constant over the past 30 years. Much attention has been paid to the high energy cost of AI, but less attention has been paid to the ways AI can poised to enhance the efficiency of the power sector [8].

The **goal** of the article is to develop the model of hybrid intelligence, the technique and algorithms for the control of a human part of HSI in critical industries using the example of energy plants' operators (fossil and hydro). These findings should be validated on the evidence-based data.

2 Methodology

As it was stated, the biggest part of incidents, accidence and violations of the technological regime at critical industries were consequences of operator's error as a result of the general operator compliance with professional requirements built as a group "norm", as well as discrepancy between the operator's functional state (fitness-for-duty) with the requirements of the profession on a given working day [9]. Deviations of the operator's actual state from the requirements could lead to the appearance of the "acute state" when incidents happen. Thus, human-system integration focuses on not only correct system design and exploitation, but on a human as a right person, in the right place and in the right condition. This means the effective human selection [10] and prediction of his/her readiness-to perform [11].

Nevertheless, we believe that current state of human reliability and performance is not enough high if human errors' contribution to economic losses is still significant and relatively stable despite HSI developing very actively [12] as well as assessing human capabilities [13] including motivation that can be dependent on job satisfaction [14]. In recent years, many publications have appeared devoted to improving methods for assessing the reliability of human operators in the energy sector [15], but almost all of them are focused on assessing and classifying the operator's erroneous actions themselves, rather than the reasons for their occurrence. It can be argued that this methodological approach is the reason for the fundamental limitation of the maximum accuracy of the forecast of operator reliability and efficiency, which is accepted as 80% for professional selection and 70% for daily monitoring.

A special feature of our methodology is the assessment and prediction of the operator's performance as the hyper-complex dynamic system (HCDS), developed both for the professional work of operators and for education/training [16]. Considering human performance as a three-level closed hyper-complex dynamic system, in which factors of influence on the efficiency of HSI are the elements of the HCDS that interact with each other, the general suitability for the profession and particular mission can be represented as the interaction of all three levels of the HCDS: first level HCDS (assessed at the stage of professional selection), periodic monitoring (carried out once every 2–3 years for operators) as the second level of the HCDS, and day-to-day (current or pre-shift) control as the HCDS of the third level. The 2nd and 3d levels parameters can vary depending on external and internal conditions, while operator's knowledge, experience and organization of production are, as a rule, relatively stable and are regulated by the regulations of the enterprise.

Thus, the HCDS model allows us to explain and to improve a general HSI model and can improve accuracy of its performance prediction through 3-level accounting of the human factors. At the same time, digitalization of production, and especially the use of AI, creates new opportunities not only to proactively identify potential anomalies in operator activity but also to help him manage his performance and improve his professional health. However, as we have emphasized above, the current level of HSI development does not provide a high enough level of performance, even the use of AI as an assistant in production. We strongly believe that the HSI improvement could be achieved by using hybrid intelligence as its further development, as well as the development of AI itself [17].

Nowadays, artificial intelligence encompasses many areas, among which machine learning, natural language processing, and computer vision are the most widely used.

Main areas of Artificial Intelligence development are as follows:

- Large Language Models (LLM)
- Machine Learning (ML)
- Deep Learning (DL)
- Natural Language Processing (NLP)
- Computer Vision
- Robotics and Autonomous Systems (AI controlling physical devices)
- Advisory Systems
- Expert Systems
- Big Data Analysis (Big Data AI)

However, major advances in these areas have led experts to acknowledge that their models are reaching their limits and must consider additional knowledge about the world around them, logical reasoning, and ethical considerations alongside factual data. In other words, they require the cognitive capabilities inherent in human intelligence.

The topic "hybrid intelligence" has begun to be actively developed in the last 10 years in different directions and at different levels of architecture [18]. But there is no generally recognized definition of HI as a further HSI development at this moment, and the comparative appropriate analysis of the current scholar approaches is useful to understand "Quo vadis, homines et intellegentia artificialis?".

Hybrid Intelligence is aimed at being applied for different tasks: in business - to develop design principles for a decision support system that combines the complementary capabilities of human and machine intelligence [19], ai design [20], industry – [21], education – [22], and other areas [23].

Overall, publications allow us to identify several possible types of hybrid intelligence architectures:

- Instrumental architecture (humans use AI).
- Cooperative architecture.
- Symbiotic architecture.
- Human–AI collaborative network

Recent works are beginning to explore architecture that go beyond the simple human-AI pairing. For example, "Human-AI-Social systems" are proposed, involving expert groups, groups of AI agents, a shared cognitive environment and role assignment mechanisms [24]. Such models include elements of shared cognitive space, dynamic task allocation, and trust calibration. In this case, we can speak of collective hybrid intelligence architecture.

Today, three dominant HI architectures can be identified.

1. Instrumental architecture (the most common): Human → AI tool, where humans use AI as a tool.
2. Cooperative architecture (the focus of European centers): Human ↔ AI, aimed at collaborative decision-making, task distribution, and mutual learning.

3. Collective architecture (beginning to emerge): Humans + AI agents + shared environment, which is aimed at hybrid teams, collective intelligence, and distributed systems.

Taking into account the characteristics and traditions of scientific schools in different regions of the planet, we can conditionally identify relatively general directions of development of GI from the point of view of the region and the corresponding prevailing architecture: Human–AI teams/multi-agent hybrid systems (USA), Human–AI cooperation (Europe), Human–machine symbiosis + brain-inspired AI (China) [25]. However, it should be recognized that there are still very few developments focused on the architecture of full hybrid intelligence, including Humans, AI agents, robotic systems, digital environments, collective knowledge structures, governance mechanisms, i.e., a hybrid cognitive ecosystem [22].

In our methodology, we propose considering the evolution of hybrid intelligence architectures as follows:

1. Instrumental: Human → AI tools
2. Cooperative: Human ↔ AI
3. Team: Human + AI teams
4. Multi-agent: Human groups + AI agents
5. Symbiotic: Human cognition ↔ machine cognition
6. Ecosystem: Socio-technical hybrid intelligence.

The last two are important to mitigate the weakest link of the power plants' performance – a human as a not always predictable intellectual source of errors in HSI - by increasing the stability of the operator's cognitive activity, especially in emergency situations and transient processes (e.g., start-up and shutdown modes) when automation equipment fails to prevent equipment operation deviation and the operator is directly involved in controlling the power unit. Such situations especially highlight the need for Human-System integration.

3 Results and Discussion

HSI traditionally focuses on:

- Integrating humans into technical systems
- Optimizing interfaces
- Distributing functions

However, if we expand on this line of HSI development, we arrive at the following transition: **Human in system → Human integrated with system → Human-machine hybrid system → Hybrid intelligence**.

Thus, HI can be considered the next stage of HSI development.

Today, the term "hybrid intelligence" is used for very different things:

- Augmented intelligence (AI as a tool)
- Human-AI collaboration (as cooperation)
- Human-AI teaming (collaboration)

– Hybrid intelligence (in some cases, all the above)

An important commonality among these cases is that the system does not become a new subject of action. It remains a "Human + Tool."

In contrast to these approaches, we propose considering HI as a new system object, emerging as important for managing complex systems not in routine operations, but for more effective control in emergent situations, increasing the human component's reliability of the HSI's intellectual performance. Thus, in our model, hybrid intelligence is not simply the interaction of humans and AI, but the emergence of a new integrated intelligent system.

Hence, **HI ≠ Human + AI, but HI = Emergent Hybrid Cognitive System.**

In this case, we can speak of systemic emergence, an integrated cognitive system, and a complex adaptive system.

Our conceptual approach considers developed models and techniques for assessment and prediction of the general and current capability of operators, as well as appropriate "norms" and scales for assessment: group "norm" for professional selection (1st system) and individual adaptive norm for day-to-day control of the operator's fitness-for-duty (2nd system). They were built for set of indices of professionally important tests' performance of operators at mentioned stages considering the capabilities and limitations of a person in terms of the speed and reliability of performing cognitive tasks [26]. The data-driven systems have been constructed [9].

The computer systems were applied in real-settings to validate models and tools: (1) 1st system was checked on 49 professional operators of 2 fossil power plants (FPP) and 149 operators of 2 hydro electrical stations (HES); they were assessed to build the "norm" and classified by 4 groups of professional suitability group with corresponding criteria [9]; (2) 2nd system was checked on 81 operators of FPP (42 were monitored during 9 months) and 52 operators of HES; individual norms were built as self-adjusted ones by creating an individual 11-point scale for each operator (the individual "norm", "0" ± 1 point, is the average value of the rate of test tasks performance for the analyzed period with a given reliability ≥0.84; "+" and "- "deviations up to 5 points correspond to excessive or insufficient psychophysiological activation of a person respectively). Practically, a digital-twin was created for every operator, and the system can be classified as a data-driven one. The average accuracy of prediction for 1st system was 90%, 2nd system – 85%. Recommendations for the operator's work-shift in 2nd system were generated to avoid and/or mitigate deviations from the individual "norm" after completed the pre-shift test. The practical recommendations have been developed for both classes of systems.

Those systems were developed previously to be applied independently from one to another. As a result, subsequently, a periodic monitoring system was developed and implemented, which included both psychological testing (like professional selection) and the recording of medical indicators. As a result, these three systems accumulated information about the operator at various stages of his professional life, from entry into the profession to retirement, but they operated separately. Information exchange between them was handled by specialists from the enterprise's medical-psychological unit, which complicated accurate diagnosis due to the analysis of a large amount of diverse data (especially from the daily monitoring system, which constantly adapts to each individual and changes in their functional state), as well as the subjectivity of the specialist.

The use of AI simplifies data processing and analysis in each case. However, this is insufficient for managing the operator's condition and reliability in daily work unless the AI adapts to the human, considering his initial (at the stage of initial professional selection) and dynamically changing life and professional (at the stage of the periodical check) parameters (Fig. 1). The operator, in turn, should be individually trained to manage his condition as needed, considering relevant experience that can be provided by the HI. Thus, the need and practical possibility of mutual co-evolution between a specific person and an AI arises, for which the use of AI agents is advisable.

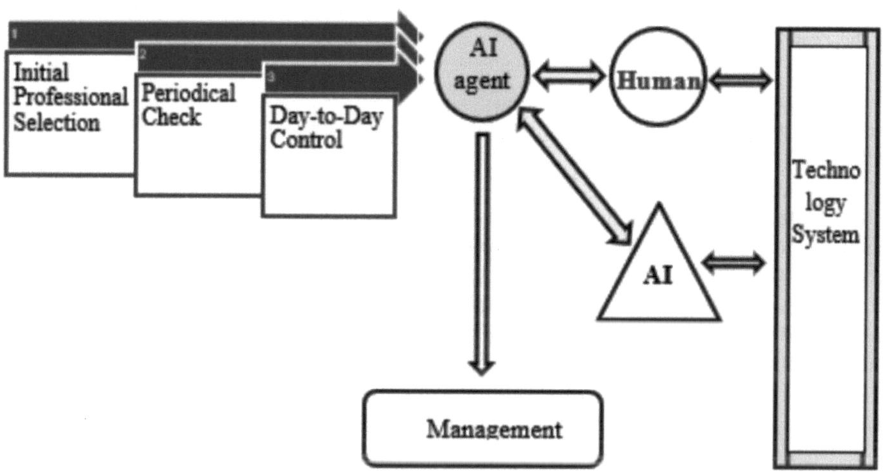

Fig. 1. Hybrid intelligence model of the human-operator link in the technological system control at the power plant.

We believe that using HI to the technological process' control itself and operator performance allows us to optimize work and to distribute responsibilities between operators, considering the actual performance of the operator at a given moment and his social interactions with both other operators and the enterprise's management. Practical experience implementing HSI at power plant companies demonstrates the potential to reduce the likelihood of personnel errors in both routine and emergency situations.

4 Conclusion

Our developments used coupling between human and AI as the development of the Human-System Integration paradigm in form of hybrid intelligence for critical industries.

The analysis of currently known hybrid intelligence architectures allowed us to develop methodology and some practical tools for human component of power industry performance at the symbiotic level (Human cognition ↔ machine cognition) with some future elements of the ecosystem level (Socio-technical hybrid intelligence).

The author HI model has been verified in relation to some components at power plants and can be considered as further development of Human-System Integration approach in critical industries.

The data-driven systems to predict (with high accuracy) human's performance and deviation from the "norm" have been developed. The developed scales are recommended to be used in AI-agents for explanation and advising operators' control of their fitness-for-duty to safe nor only high performance, but professional health as well. Methods to build such AI-agents have been developed.

These results can be applied to optimize HSI outcome for control of hazardous technological objects.

Acknowledgments. This research has been supported by the institutions of co-authors as well as by the Zmievskaya power plant (Ukraine).

Disclosure of Interests. The authors have no competing interests to declare that they are relevant to the content of this article.

Ethics Statement. No ethical approval was required for this study, in accordance with national regulations in force, as the investigation involved neither the collection of personal data nor the processing of sensitive information. Verbal informed consent was obtained from all participants (professional operators) following a clear explanation of the study's objectives, participation procedures, and the anonymous and confidential nature of all responses. Authorization to conduct the study was also granted by the management of the participating enterprises school.

Declaration On the Use of Artificial Intelligence. The author used the AI system ChatGPT (OpenAI, GPT-5.3) as a conversational tool for exploring conceptual structures of hybrid intelligence. The final interpretations and conclusions remain the responsibility of the author.

References

1. Ahram, T., Karwowski, W., Falcão, C.: Applications of systems engineering for testing and evaluation: a human systems integration perspective. In: Boehm-Davis, D.A., Durso, F.T., Lee, J.D. (eds.) APA Handbook of Human Systems Integration, pp. 101–111. American Psychological Association (2015). https://doi.org/10.1037/14528-007
2. Rouse, W.B.: The economics of human systems integration. In: Boehm-Davis, D.A., Durso, F.T., Lee, J.D. (eds.) APA Handbook of Human Systems Integration, pp. 379–395. American Psychological Association (2015). https://doi.org/10.1037/14528-024
3. Brynjolfsson, E.: AI at work: from productivity hacks to organizational transformation. Community paper, January 2026. World Economic Forum 2026. https://reports.weforum.org/docs/WEF_AI_at_Work_from_Productivity_Hacks_to_Organizational_Transformation_2026.pdf (2026). Last accessed 7 Mar 2026
4. Salminen, S.: Human Error. EU-OSHA, Latest update 15 June 2025. https://oshwiki.osha.europa.eu/en/themes/human-error#_edn20. Last accessed 5 Mar 2026
5. To Err is Human, to Have the Safest Operators is Divine – OTS. Schneider Electric. November 3 (2016). https://blog.se.com/industry/energies-and-chemicals/2016/11/03/33103/. Last accessed 7 Mar 2026

6. Diao, H., Ghorbani, M.: Production risk caused by human factors: a multiple case study of thermal power plants. Front. Bus. Res. China. **12**, 15 (2018). https://doi.org/10.1186/s11782-018-0035-9
7. Bafandegan Emroozi, V., Modares, A.: Identifying critical factors affecting human error probability in power plant operations and their sustainability implications. Process Integr. Optim. Sustain. **8**, 813–829 (2024). https://doi.org/10.1007/s41660-024-00392-9
8. Koekkoek, T.: Powering the future: advances and applications of AI in power systems. AVEVA, Schneider Electric Group (2025). https://www.aveva.com/en/perspectives/blog/powering-the-future-advances-and-applications-of-ai-in-power-systems/. Last accessed 12 Mar 2026
9. Burov, O.Y.: ICT for performance assessment of emergent technologies operators. In: Proceedings of the 13th International Conference on ICT in Education, Research and Industrial Applications. Integration, Harmonization and Knowledge Transfer Kyiv, Ukraine, May 15–18, 2017, vol. **1844**, pp. 127–138. CEUR-WS (2017)
10. Shore, D.B., Sheng, Z., Cortina, J.M., Yankelevich Garza, M.: Personnel selection: a primer. In: Boehm-Davis, D.A., Durso, F.T., Lee, J.D. (eds.) APA Handbook of Human Systems Integration, pp. 485–500. American Psychological Association (2015). https://doi.org/10.1037/14528-030
11. Wallace, D.F., McTigue, J.J., Van Buskirk, L.J.: The manpower determination process. In: Boehm-Davis, D.A., Durso, F.T., Lee, J.D. (eds.) APA Handbook of Human Systems Integration, pp. 469–484. American Psychological Association (2015). https://doi.org/10.1037/14528-029
12. Ahmed, H., Ahmed, M.: Human systems integration: a review of concepts, applications, challenges, and benefits. J. Econ. Sustain. Dev. **14**(4), 30–39 (2023). https://doi.org/10.7176/JESD/14-4-04
13. van der Linden, D., Pelt, D.H.M., Dunkel, C.S., Born, M.P.: Personality, Personnel selection, and job performance. In: Zeigler-Hill, V., Shackelford, T.K. (eds.) Encyclopedia of Personality and Individual Differences. Springer, Cham (2020). https://doi.org/10.1007/978-3-319-24612-3_790
14. Granillo-Velasquez, K.E., Hoff, K.A., Hanna, A., Oswald, F.L., Morris, M.L.: Comparing methods of measuring interest fit: a large prediction study with career choice satisfaction. Int. J. Sel. Assess. **33**, e12506 (2025). https://doi.org/10.1111/ijsa.12506
15. Sharma, K., Roy, S.: Systematic Human Reliability Analysis (SHRA): a novel approach to evaluating Human Error Probability (HEP) in thermal power plants. IJCRT. **12**(7) (2024). https://ijcrt.org/papers/IJCRT2407222.pdf. Last accessed 2026/03/12
16. Spirin, O., Burov, O.: Models and applied tools for prediction of student ability to effective learning. In: 14th International Conference on ICT in Education, Research and Industrial Applications. Integration, Harmonization and Knowledge Transfer, vol. 2104, pp. 404–411. CEUR-WS (2018)
17. The next wave of intelligence: how human purpose must guide the future of AI. World Economic Forum 2026 (2026). https://www.weforum.org/stories/2026/01/agentic-ai-how-human-purpose-can-guide-the-next-wave-of-intelligent-systems/
18. Jarrahi, M.H., Lutz, C., Newlands, G.: Artificial intelligence, human intelligence and hybrid intelligence based on mutual augmentation. Big Data Soc. **9**(2) (2022)
19. Dellermann, D., Lipusch, N., Ebel, P., et al.: Design principles for a hybrid intelligence decision support system for business model validation. Electron. Mark. **29**, 423–441 (2019). https://doi.org/10.1007/s12525-018-0309-2
20. Hinkelmann, K., Hoppe, T., Humm, B.G.: Einführung in hybride künstliche Intelligenz. In: Hinkelmann, K., Hoppe, T., Humm, B.G. (eds.) Hybride KI mit Machine Learning und Knowledge Graphs. Springer Vieweg, Wiesbaden (2025). https://doi.org/10.1007/978-3-658-44781-6_1

21. Wahlström, M., Tammentie, B., Salonen, T.-T., Karvonen, A.: AI and the transformation of industrial work: hybrid intelligence vs double-black box effect. Appl. Ergon. **118** (2024). https://doi.org/10.1016/j.apergo.2024.104271
22. Sanna, J., et al.: Hybrid intelligence research at the University of Oulu. Position paper (2025). https://oulurepo.oulu.fi/handle/10024/59855
23. ANNUAL REPORT: The Hybrid Intelligence Centre – 2024. Augmenting Human Intellect (2026). https://www.hybrid-intelligence-centre.nl/wp-content/uploads/2026/01/260131-HI-Annual-report-2024.pdf
24. Melih, A.A., Singh, Y., Agarwal, K. L., Mukherjee, M., Pattnaik, K., Bhatia, H.: Human machine social hybrid intelligence: a collaborative decision making framework for large model agent groups and human experts (2025). https://doi.org/10.48550/arXiv.2510.24030
25. Qian, Y., Liu, J.: Modeling AI-driven production and competitiveness a multi-agent economic simulation of China and the United States (2025). https://doi.org/10.48550/arXiv.2510.11085
26. Burov, O., et al.: On the way to hybrid intelligence: influence of the human-system interaction rate on the human cognitive performance. In: Ahram, T., Taiar, R. (eds.) Human Interaction and Emerging Technologies (IHIET-AI 2023): Artificial Intelligence and Future Applications. AHFE (2023) International Conference, vol. 70. AHFE International, USA (2023). https://doi.org/10.54941/ahfe1002925

An Adaptive Preprocessing Pipeline Framework for Enhanced OCR Accuracy on Scanned Documents

Suman Gorkhali and Jicheng Fu(✉)

University of Central Oklahoma, Edmond, OK 73003, USA
{sgorkhali,jfu}@uco.edu

Abstract. Digitization of legacy documents is particularly challenging due to poor scan quality, including skew, warping, low contrast, and noise. Traditional Optical Character Recognition (OCR) preprocessing approaches employ fixed enhancement sequences that often struggle to address diverse quality degradations encountered in real-world documents, necessitating an intelligent, adaptive approach. This project presents an automated framework designed to dynamically evaluate multiple preprocessing combinations to identify optimal image enhancement strategies. The framework integrates an ensemble of eight distinct enhancement primitives, addressing geometric rectification (deskewing and dewarping), luminance normalization (grayscale and adaptive binarization), and artifact mitigation (noise reduction and morphological operations). These modules are systematically configured into 13 pipeline architectures to maximize OCR performance across heterogeneous documents. Selection of the optimal image state is governed by a multi-parameter objective function, including confidence scores and character density metrics. The system then automatically selects the best-performing configuration based on these criteria. A significant contribution is the integration of a local large language (LLM) model for context-aware data extraction. Unlike traditional pattern-matching techniques, our approach leverages semantic understanding to distill OCR text into user-defined schemas. Experimental results on three different domains, i.e., legal contracts, retail invoices, and textbook pages showed that no single preprocessing pipeline consistently outperformed all others, confirming the need for adaptive, page-level selection. Across all datasets, the proposed framework achieved strong OCR performance, demonstrating that the synergy of adaptive preprocessing and local LLM-driven semantic extraction significantly enhances both OCR accuracy and the quality of extracted information.

Keywords: Optical Character Recognition (OCR) · Image enhancement pipeline · Large Language Model (LLM)

1 Introduction

The digitization of documents has become increasingly critical for modern law firms, corporate legal departments, and government agencies, as well as for healthcare institutions, insurance companies, libraries and archives, and historical preservation organizations.

C. Stephanidis et al. (Eds.): HCII 2026, CCIS 3047, pp. 13–20, 2026.
https://doi.org/10.1007/978-3-032-30552-7_2

However, legacy documents often exist only in physical form or as poorly scanned digital images. Optical Character Recognition (OCR) technology enables the conversion of these image-based documents into machine-readable, searchable text. However, the accuracy of OCR is heavily dependent on the quality of input images [1].

Legacy documents are often scanned under suboptimal conditions, resulting in images that suffer from skew, perspective distortion, poor contrast, noise artifacts, and varying illumination. Manual operators may introduce additional quality issues through improper scanner settings, document positioning, or inadequate lighting. Such imperfections dramatically reduce OCR accuracy, leading to incomplete or erroneous text extraction that undermines the usability of digitized documents.

Traditional OCR preprocessing approaches typically apply a fixed sequence of image enhancement operations [2]. While effective for high-quality scans, these rigid pipelines often fail when confronted with the diverse quality issues present in real-world document collections. What works well for a slightly skewed document may be counterproductive for a document suffering from page curl or low contrast. This variability necessitates an adaptive approach that can intelligently select preprocessing strategies based on each document's specific characteristics.

This project aims to address the persistent challenges associated with poorly scanned legacy documents by developing an intelligent and adaptive preprocessing framework for OCR-based digitization. Rather than relying on a single fixed preprocessing workflow, the proposed framework creates a robust end-to-end system that can automatically evaluate document quality, adapt preprocessing strategies to individual pages, and improve downstream text extraction accuracy. To achieve this goal, the project is organized around several core objectives.

The first objective is to develop a comprehensive set of image preprocessing functions to address common quality issues in scanned legacy documents, including deskewing, dewarping, contrast enhancement, binarization, denoising, and morphological cleanup. These functions provide a flexible foundation for improving document images prior to OCR.

The second objective is to implement an automated pipeline system that tests multiple preprocessing combinations on each page. By systematically evaluating different enhancement sequences, the system can identify the most effective preprocessing strategy for diverse document conditions.

The third objective is to establish quantitative metrics for evaluating preprocessing effectiveness. In this project, OCR confidence scores and character counts are used to measure how well each pipeline preserves and recovers textual information.

The fourth objective is to automatically select the optimal preprocessing strategy for each page based on these performance metrics. This page-level adaptivity enables the framework to respond effectively to variations in document degradation, even within the same collection.

The fifth objective is to extract document-level information from the optimally processed OCR text and convert it into structured CSV output. To accomplish this, the recognized text is passed to a local LLM, which reconstructs and interprets noisy or incomplete OCR results using contextual understanding, enabling more accurate and meaningful information extraction than rule-based methods.

Experimental results on three different domains, i.e., legal contracts, retail invoices, and textbook pages showed that no single preprocessing pipeline consistently outperformed all others, confirming the need for adaptive, page-level selection. Across all datasets, the proposed framework achieved strong OCR performance, demonstrating that the synergy of adaptive preprocessing and local LLM-driven semantic extraction significantly enhances both OCR accuracy and the quality of extracted information.

The rest of the paper is organized as follows: Section 2 describes the method for constructing the proposed framework. Section 3 introduces the experiments conducted to verify the proposed approach. Section 4 presents a discussion of the proposed study and identifies a few limitations. Finally, Section 5 concludes the paper and discusses the potential future work.

2 Method

2.1 System Architecture

The system architecture follows a modular pipeline design consisting of four primary stages: PDF to Image Conversion, Adaptive Preprocessing and OCR, Data Extraction, and Output Generation. This architecture enables separation of concerns, facilitates testing and debugging, and allows for easy extension of functionality. The following sections detail each component of the system.

1. **Stage 1: PDF to PNG Conversion.** The input PDF document is converted into individual PNG image files, one per page. This initial conversion enables consistent image processing across all pages regardless of the original PDF structure or formatting.
2. **Stage 2: Adaptive Preprocessing and OCR.** This is the core stage of the system, where each page undergoes testing with 13 different preprocessing pipeline configurations. Each configuration represents a different combination of the eight preprocessing functions described in Sect. 2.2. After all the 13 pipelines complete, the system ranks them by OCR confidence score (primary metric) and character count (secondary metric). The best-performing pipeline for that page is identified, and its preprocessed image and extracted text are saved to the output folder.
3. **Stage 3: Data Extraction.** The OCR-extracted text from all pages is aggregated and analyzed to identify specific information elements defined in a user-specified list. This stage can utilize pattern matching, regular expressions, or integration with a language model for more intelligent extraction of contractual terms, dates, parties, amounts, and other relevant information.
4. **Stage 4: Output Generation.** The final stage consolidates all extracted information into a structured CSV file with headers corresponding to the information elements defined in the extraction configuration. Each row represents a processed document, with columns containing the extracted data points. This structured output enables easy integration with database systems, spreadsheet applications, or downstream analytical tools.

2.2 Preprocessing Functions

The system implemented eight distinct preprocessing functions. Each was designed to address specific image quality issues commonly encountered in scanned documents.

These functions can be applied individually or in combination to form preprocessing pipelines.

1. **Image Inversion:** Inverts all pixel values in the image using a bitwise NOT operation. This function addresses documents scanned with reversed contrast (light text on dark background) or those with unusual color schemes that confuse OCR engines.
2. **Grayscale Conversion:** Converts color images to grayscale to reduce complexity, remove color-related artifacts, and provide a standardized format better suited for OCR processing.
3. **Binary Thresholding**: Applies adaptive Gaussian thresholding to convert grayscale images into black-and-white form, improving text separation under uneven lighting conditions.
4. **Noise Reduction:** Uses morphological opening and closing operations to remove small artifacts, dust, and random noise while preserving the overall structure of the text.
5. **Morphological Thinning:** Applies erosion to reduce character stroke width, which is useful for documents where text appears overly thick or bold.
6. **Morphological Thickening:** Applies dilation to increase character stroke width, helping recover faint, broken, or fragmented text.
7. **Deskewing:** Detects and corrects angular skew by analyzing text alignment across multiple rotation angles, improving OCR readability.
8. **Page Dewarping:** Detects and corrects angular skew by analyzing text alignment across multiple rotation angles, improving OCR readability using Zucker's dewarping algorithm [3].

Pipeline Combinations. The system tests 13 predefined pipeline combinations, each designed to address different document quality scenarios. These combinations were selected to represent diverse preprocessing strategies, from minimal intervention (grayscale only) to comprehensive multi-step processing (Table 1).

Table 1. Pipeline Combinations.

Pipeline Name	Processing Steps
grayscale_only	Grayscale conversion
inverted_only	Image inversion
gray_to_bw	Grayscale → Binary thresholding
gray_bw_no_noise	Grayscale → Binary → Noise reduction
gray_bw_no_noise_thin	Grayscale → Binary → Noise reduction → Thinning
gray_bw_no_noise_thick	Grayscale → Binary → Noise reduction → Thickening
deskew_gray_bw	Deskew → Grayscale → Binary
deskew_gray_bw_no_noise	Deskew → Grayscale → Binary → Noise reduction
dewarp_only	Page dewarping
dewarp_thin	Dewarp → Thinning

(continued)

Table 1. *(continued)*

Pipeline Name	Processing Steps
dewarp_thick	Dewarp → Thickening
inverted_gray_bw	Inversion → Grayscale → Binary
inverted_gray_bw_no_noise	Inversion → Grayscale → Binary → Noise reduction

3 Experiments

This section presents the design, execution, and results of three experiments conducted to evaluate the Document Preprocessing and Adaptive OCR System across three distinct document categories. Each experiment applied the same core pipeline, 13 preprocessing combinations tested per page, with the highest-confidence result selected as the best pipeline for that page, followed by an Ollama-powered chatbot [4] session that allows free-form natural language queries over all extracted text files simultaneously. The three categories were chosen deliberately to represent a range of scanning conditions, document ages, layout complexity, and image quality challenges.

3.1 Experimental Setup

All experiments were executed on a MacBook Air (M2) with 8GB memory running macOS Sequoia 15.7.3. The core dependencies were Tesseract OCR [5], Poppler (for PDF-to-image conversion) [6], and the following Python libraries: pytesseract, Pillow, pdf2image, opencv-python, numpy, and scipy. For the Ollama quantized local Large Language Model (LLM), qwen3 1.7b [7], the parameters are set for temperature at 0.1, top_p at 0.9, num_predict at 1000, which served as the language model backend for the post-OCR information extraction stage.

The pipelines were organized into five categories. Simple pipelines included grayscale_only and inverted_only, which apply minimal transformation. Binarization pipelines included gray_to_bw, which applies a global threshold of 210–230 after grayscale conversion. Noise reduction pipelines extended binarization with morphological operations (gray_bw_no_noise) and further font-weight adjustments (gray_bw_no_noise_thin, gray_bw_no_noise_thick). Geometric correction pipelines introduced deskewing (deskew_gray_bw, deskew_gray_bw_no_noise) using a Hough-line-based hybrid algorithm. The most computationally intensive category, page dewarping, applied Zucker's page-dewarp algorithm [3] to correct page curl and perspective distortion, in three variants: dewarp_only, dewarp_thin, and dewarp_thick. Inverted variants (inverted_gray_bw, inverted_gray_bw_no_noise) were also tested to account for documents scanned with dark backgrounds.

3.2 Experimental Results

Three datasets were evaluated, including historical legal contracts (2 pages), retail invoices (6 pages), and a classical Dijkstra's programming textbook [8] (11 pages), representing diverse document structures and degradation types. Across all experiments, no single preprocessing pipeline consistently outperformed others, confirming the necessity of adaptive, page-level optimization.

For the legal contract dataset, simple pipelines (grayscale and inversion) achieved the best results, with an average confidence of 92.72 and 5,674 total characters. More complex operations, particularly noise reduction, significantly degraded performance by eroding fine serif text. Dewarping showed limited benefit, indicating minimal geometric distortion in the source documents.

In the invoice dataset, pipeline selection was highly consistent: inversion-based preprocessing dominated (4/6 pages), while grayscale was effective on the remaining pages, achieving an average confidence of 93.13. Binarization-based pipelines failed on most pages due to colored and non-uniform backgrounds, in some cases producing zero-character output. This highlights the sensitivity of thresholding techniques to background variation and the importance of adaptive selection. The chatbot stage successfully allowed the user to extract invoice numbers, dates, account numbers, billing addresses, and product line items through conversational queries across all six invoice pages loaded simultaneously into context.

The textbook dataset produced the widest variation in outcomes, with an average confidence of 87.74 and 19,590 total characters. Eight of the eleven pages achieved confidence scores of at least 95, indicating strong performance on well-scanned printed text. However, two pages scored below 40 across all pipelines, and their reversed OCR outputs strongly suggest that they were scanned upside-down; because no rotation-based preprocessing was included, these pages could not be recovered. Another anomalous page achieved high confidence but yielded only 209 characters, suggesting it was dominated by non-textual content such as a figure or diagram. This experiment also showed the greatest pipeline diversity: while inversion and binarization frequently performed well, dewarping was the best strategy for one page and recovered 2,875 characters, the highest single-page character count across all experiments. Compared with the invoice dataset, this broader distribution of winning pipelines reflects the greater structural and physical variability of scanned textbook pages.

Additional experimental details can be found in the project repository at GitHub (https://github.com/suman-datascientist/Image_Document_Preprocessor).

4 Discussion

The adaptive approach in this project provides clear advantages over fixed preprocessing pipelines by automatically selecting the best strategy for each page. This flexibility is especially important for legacy documents, whose quality often varies widely due to document age, scanning conditions, and preservation state.

The main limitation of the proposed approach is its computational cost. Because the system evaluates 13 pipelines per page, processing is slower than with a single fixed pipeline, averaging about 30–40 s per page in our experiments. This overhead may become significant for large-scale collections. However, several factors mitigate this concern. First, the processing is easily parallelizable, i.e., different pipelines can be evaluated simultaneously on multi-core systems, potentially reducing per-page processing time to that of the slowest pipeline plus selection overhead. Second, for batch processing workflows (the typical use case for legacy document digitization), throughput is more important than individual page latency. Third, the improved accuracy achieved through adaptive preprocessing may eliminate costly manual correction steps that would otherwise be necessary, providing net time savings in the complete workflow.

In addition, the integration of a local language model further strengthens the framework by enabling context-aware reconstruction and information extraction from OCR output. Together, adaptive preprocessing, OCR, and local LLM-based understanding form a unified solution for document digitization and analysis.

4.1 Limitations of the Study

The system tests only 13 predefined pipelines. While these cover common scenarios, the space of possible preprocessing combinations is much larger. More comprehensive exploration of this space could yield better results. The selection criteria rely solely on OCR confidence scores and character counts. Additional metrics such as word-level accuracy, detection of specific document elements, or semantic coherence might provide more nuanced quality assessment.

5 Conclusion

This project has developed an adaptive image preprocessing system for improving OCR accuracy on scanned legacy documents. By implementing a comprehensive suite of preprocessing functions and an evaluation framework, the system automatically identifies optimal preprocessing strategies tailored to each document's specific characteristics. The experimental results validate the effectiveness of this adaptive approach, demonstrating significant performance improvements.

The key contributions of this work include the design and implementation of a modular, extensible preprocessing pipeline architecture; the integration of diverse preprocessing techniques ranging from simple transformations to sophisticated geometric corrections; and the development of an objective, quantitative framework for evaluating and selecting preprocessing strategies. More importantly, this work highlights the critical role of a local large language model (LLM) in transforming OCR from simple text recognition into context-aware information reconstruction and extraction. By leveraging semantic understanding, the local LLM can interpret noisy and incomplete OCR outputs, recover meaningful textual content, and map the reconstructed information into user-defined structured formats. This significantly extends the value of adaptive preprocessing, demonstrating not only that page-specific preprocessing outperforms single-strategy approaches for documents with varying quality characteristics, but also that the combination of adaptive OCR enhancement and local LLM-based contextual interpretation provides a far more powerful end-to-end solution for legacy document digitization.

As a future direction, a learning-based or heuristic-driven selection mechanism can be introduced to predict a subset of high-potential preprocessing pipelines for each page, thus reducing the need for exhaustive evaluation and improving computational efficiency.

Acknowledgments. This research was supported in part by the CURE-STEM Scholar program and John T. Beresford Endowment at the University of Central Oklahoma.

References

1. Alaei, A., et al.: Document image quality assessment: a survey. ACM Comput. Surv. **56**(2), 1–36 (2023)
2. Lins, R.D., et al.: The winner takes it all: choosing the "best" binarization algorithm for photographed documents. In: International Workshop on Document Analysis Systems. Springer (2022)
3. Zucker, M.: Page-dewarp (2016). https://github.com/mzucker/page_dewarp
4. Ollama: Start building with open models (2026). https://ollama.com
5. Smith, R.: An overview of the Tesseract OCR engine. In: Ninth International Conference on Document Analysis and Recognition (ICDAR 2007). IEEE (2007)
6. Converting PDF Pages to Images with Poppler (2026). https://jdhao.github.io/2019/11/14/convert_pdf_to_images_pdftoppm/
7. Yang, A., et al.: Qwen3 technical report. arXiv preprint arXiv:2505.09388 (2025)
8. Dijkstra, E.W., et al.: A Discipline of Programming, vol. 613924118. Prentice-Hall, Englewood Cliffs (1976)

Error Prediction in Human-Machine Teams: A Combined Methods Approach

Sophie Hart[1](✉), Victoria Steane[2], Mohammad Soorati[1], and Mark S. Young[1]

[1] Transportation Research Group, University of Southampton, Southampton, UK
{sh5g17,M.Soorati,M.S.Young}@soton.ac.uk
[2] Thales Research, Technology and Innovation Solutions, Reading, UK
victoria.steane@uk.thalesgroup.com

Abstract. The integration of novel technological solutions demands the adoption of human factors methods, which support prospective risk assessment at the earliest stage of the design lifecycle. Crucially, such methods must account for how risks emerge through interactions between human and technical subsystems. Traditional taxonomic approaches, which focus on errors associated with individual tasks, are insufficient to capture these system dynamics. However, their integration with systems methods may enable comprehensive exploration of sociotechnical risks. The current paper combines the Event Analysis of Systemic Teamwork Broken Links method with the Systematic Human Error Reduction and Prediction Approach (SHERPA) to examine risks associated with a proposed context-dependent energy system for flight deck operations. The findings demonstrate that the information-centric application of SHERPA enhances risk identification and informs design interventions to support effective human-machine teaming in future flight deck environments.

Keywords: Human-machine teaming · error prediction · Event Analysis of Systemic Teamwork · Systematic Human Error Reduction and Prediction Approach

1 Introduction

The aviation domain is increasingly integrating more technological applications onto the flight deck, providing automated cues on the current state and projected future capabilities of the aircraft [1]. Yet the introduction of new technologies also introduces new pathways to error, which need to be anticipated and mitigated. For this reason, it is important to implement human factors at the earliest stage of the design lifecycle to anticipate these risks [2]. Proactive risk assessments must consider the broader sociotechnical system and the new technologies being integrated within it [3]. Often, risk assessments have adopted taxonomic approaches, such as the Systematic Human Error Reduction and Prediction Approach (SHERPA) [4], Hazard and Operability method [5], to anticipate potential failures. However, the use of taxonomies has been criticized for largely focusing on risks associated with individual tasks [6, 7]. Taking such a perspective is

C. Stephanidis et al. (Eds.): HCII 2026, CCIS 3047, pp. 21–32, 2026.
https://doi.org/10.1007/978-3-032-30552-7_3

deemed reductionist as anticipated errors centralize on individual system components [2, 8]. In practice, this often results in speculative analyzes on human-task completion, perpetuating a focus on "human error" despite the accepted redundancy of the term [9, 10]. To move beyond human-centric accounts of failure, methods need to reconceptualize risks as the cause of communication failures between both human and technical sub-systems [11]. In this vein, Stanton and Harvey [11] proposed the Event Analysis of Systemic Teamwork Broken-Links (EAST-BL) analysis, an extension of the Event Analysis of Systemic Teamwork (EAST) framework, which enables prospective exploration of how communication failures affect sociotechnical system performance. The EAST framework was selected owing to its holistic approach to modelling complex sociotechnical systems. Using network-based representations, EAST captures the relationships between system agents, tasks and information aspects [12]. This enables an analysis of how system performance emerges from interactions across the entire system, rather than focusing on isolated components or sub-systems.

The EAST framework offers a descriptive approach to analyze the behavior of sociotechnical systems using three inter-related networks: task, social and information [12, 13]. Task networks represent the set of tasks undertaken within a system and the interdependencies between them [12]. Social networks identify the technical, human and organizational agents that comprise the sociotechnical system and the communication between them [11]. Information networks represent the information nodes communicated between system agents to afford task completion [13]. These representations are constructed individually and subsequently combined to generate composite networks to capture the relationships between tasks, agents and information nodes [6, 11]. The composite networks are then used for prospective risk prediction.

1.1 Risk Prediction in Sociotechnical Systems

The EAST-BL method identifies that risks can be determined by systematically removing links between nodes contained in the task and social networks to anticipate the consequences of inhibiting information transfers. It has been applied to anticipate the risks of future Artificial General Intelligence technologies not yet realized, such as smart city transportation systems [14] and Uncrewed Combat Aerial Vehicle systems [6]. This suggests there is value in applying EAST-BL to support the integration of novel flight deck technologies.

The EAST-BL method was derived from the observation that several high-profile incidents resulted from information transaction failures [11]. Across these incidents, critical information was not conveyed within the system, which enabled a loss of compatible situation awareness and subsequent breakdown in coordination. Salmon et al. [15] identified that these transaction failures can emerge in several ways, including *absent transactions* where the information is not exchanged, *inappropriate transactions* where inaccurate content is exchanged, *incomplete transactions* where the correct information is partially exchanged and *misinterpreted transactions* where the information is received but undergoes misinterpretation by the recipient.

While the EAST-BL analysis primarily anticipates risks caused by absent transactions, a systematic exploration of other failure types could be supported through taxonomic approaches. Specifically, the SHERPA taxonomy provides a structured framework for identifying how tasks and communication can be incomplete, inappropriate or otherwise altered. The SHERPA taxonomy is a tool used for predicting errors that occur during system operations. According to the SHERPA taxonomy, failures can be categorized into five groups: action, checking, retrieval, communication, or selection failures [2, 4]. For each failure mode, several error codes are given to specify the nature of the failure. As an example, specific error codes for the action failure include action omitted and action incomplete. The alignment between documented information transfer failures and the SHERPA error codes suggests the taxonomy provides a useful analytical lens for anticipating how information exchanges between system agents and tasks may be absent, incomplete, inappropriate or misinterpreted.

Typically, the SHERPA taxonomy is applied to bottom-level tasks identified by Hierarchical Task Analyzes to predict the types of failures that could occur during their completion [16, 17]. When applied with the EAST-BL analysis, SHERPA enables the anticipation of risks arising not only from absent transactions but also transformations in information content as it moves between tasks and system agents. This reframes SHERPA from a task-driven error analysis to an information-centric one, which emphasizes how disruptions and omissions in information transfer can propagate risk across the sociotechnical system. The utility of this combined method is demonstrated using a case study of a novel context-dependent energy system (CDES) within future flight deck environments.

1.2 Case Study of a Context-Dependent Energy System

Descent and landing both represent highly complex phases of flight, requiring effective energy management to decelerate the aircraft, maintaining an appropriate vertical profile to achieve the desired glidepath and establishing a safe landing configuration using the correct gear and flap settings [18]. The final landing configuration must satisfy the stabilized landing criteria enforced by airline organizations at a pre-defined height: 1000 ft above ground level (ft agl) for instrument meteorological conditions and 500 ft. agl for visual meteorological conditions [19]. If these criteria are not met, the flight crew must initiate a go-around procedure.

The Asiana Airlines Flight 214 incident documents a notable instance where flight crew decision-making was heavily implicated as a contributory factor [20]. During this incident, the vertical profile was mismanaged during the descent and automatic airspeed control was lost. This resulted in a low-energy condition, whereby the aircraft had decelerated below the target landing airspeed. The National Transportation Safety Board (NTSB) report criticized the aircraft's low-energy alert system for providing a delayed warning of the low airspeed. In turn, the NTSB recommended the identification of *"design requirements for a context-dependent low energy alerting system for airplanes engaged in commercial operations"* [20] (p. 130).

In an effort to address this recommendation, an EAST analysis of the Asiana 214 incident was conducted to examine the differences between work-as-done and work-as-imagined during the approach phase of flight. This analysis identified the key tasks and information nodes that could be supported with a Context Dependent Energy System (CDES) [see 21]. By integrating raw flight data (e.g., airspeed, altitude), the system predicts whether the aircraft is operating with excess or insufficient energy and whether it is projected to meet the stabilized approach criteria. Table 1 provides an overview of the tasks and resultant information nodes introduced by the CDES. Such information could offer sufficient time to correct destabilized approaches and make informed go-around decisions.

Table 1. Functionalities proposed for the CDES [16].

Task	Information node	Description
Input planned landing configuration	Planned landing configuration	The Pilot inputs the reference values for the target landing configuration.
Compute aircraft energy state	Actual energy state	A unified measurement computed using airspeed and altitude to indicate whether the aircraft has excess energy or insufficient energy relative to the stabilized approach target.
	Projected energy state	Provides a forward projection of the aircraft's energy trend based on current parameters and configured flight modes. It indicates whether energy is expected to increase, decrease or stabilize.
	Energy margin	Represents whether sufficient energy exists with the remaining altitude to achieve the stabilized approach criteria before the target gate (i.e., 1000 ft. agl or 500 ft. agl).
Project future profile	Predicted parameter trajectory	Displays the predicted trajectory of the aircraft's airspeed and descent rate relative to altitude to determine when and where the stabilized criteria will be met. It also shows whether these will be maintained in the future.
	Stabilization feasibility status	Automated guidance issued to determine if the stabilized approach criteria will be met and maintained beyond a target altitude (i.e., 1000 ft. agl or 500 ft. agl).

(*continued*)

Table 1. (*continued*)

Task	Information node	Description
Evaluate drag configuration	Control strategies	Control strategies are automatically presented to support drag management during the descent phase of flight to meet the desired glidepath.
Calculate altitude loss per nautical mile (nm)	Altitude loss per nm	Represents the aircraft's vertical descent efficiency relative to the horizontal distance travelled. The metric can be used to determine whether the descent rate is sufficient to capture the desired glidepath.
Monitor automation conflicts	Automation conflict status	Indication of whether armed modes of operation are consistent with pilot intent and safe energy management.

The current study used the EAST framework [12] to model a hypothetical 'envisioned world' in which the CDES had been integrated into the existing flight deck architecture. Subsequently, the EAST-BL [11] and SHERPA taxonomy [4] were used to identify risks that could emerge when adopting the novel system to support safe, stabilized landing approaches.

2 Construction and Analysis of Networks

The EAST networks were constructed using the NTSB report on the Asiana 214 incident [20]. Specifically, the 'Analysis' section of the NTSB investigation report (sect. 2, pgs. 77–107) alongside the transcript of the cockpit voice recordings were used. The level of detail provided within the report enabled the construction of EAST networks for a work-as-imagined scenario, where the landing approach takes place successfully through the acquisition and retention of the stabilized approach criteria. This scenario represents a baseline approach without the introduction of the CDES, which is introduced later in the work-as-envisaged network representations. The social, information and task nodes identified from the report were used to construct their respective networks, and interconnections were embedded between related nodes. For the social and task networks, an interconnection between nodes represents an instance when information is transferred between them [11].

The information, tasks and system agent nodes introduced by the CDES system were identified and embedded within the work-as-imagined network to anticipate how existing workflows could be changed. This enabled the construction of the task, social and information networks for a work-as-envisaged scenario. These network representations effectively predict how the sociotechnical system would function following the integration of the CDES. To interrogate the system agents, tasks and information nodes with the greatest prominence, sociometric status was calculated. Sociometric status determines the prominence of an individual node based on the frequency of communication delivered to (i.e., emission) and from other nodes (i.e., reception) [22]. A key node possesses a higher sociometric score than the sum of the mean sociometric scores [23].

3 Results

The results section presents a stepwise application of the EAST framework, EAST-BL analysis and the SHERPA taxonomy to the CDES case study.

3.1 Event Analysis of Systemic Teamwork

The following sections describe the construction of the EAST 'work-as-envisioned' network representations, which illustrate how the CDES integrates within an existing sociotechnical system.

Task Network. For illustrative purposes, an extract of the task network is shown to indicate where the CDES interacts with existing tasks (see Fig. 1). A reciprocal edge occurs between the task of 'configure flight parameters' and 'compute energy state and margin'. This is because the configured parameters determine the computed energy state and margin, which can influence subsequent changes to the flight parameters. Similarly, a reciprocal edge is shown between the nodes 'cross-check flight instruments' and 'apply energy control strategies' as instrument readings determine when strategies are applied and are then cross-checked to confirm their effect. The task of cross-check flight instruments was identified as a key node and held the highest sociometric status (0.59).

Social Network. A simplified social network is given in Fig. 2 to show the integration of the CDES as an additional technical agent within the flight deck system.

The Pilot Monitoring was identified as a key agent and held the highest sociometric status (0.66). The CDES receives inputs from the Mode Control Panel (MCP) and the Flight Management Computer (FMC) to compute the energy state, vehicle projections and monitor for automation conflicts. Importantly, the CDES does not directly communicate with the flight crew. Instead, the outputs are interfaced using existing displays such as the Flight Mode Annunciator and the Primary Flight Display (PFD).

Information Network. The information network shown in Fig. 3 represents the nodes introduced by the CDES and those used to afford task completion. For reference, the nodes introduced by the CDES are shaded in grey. Information nodes identified as key include: airspeed (0.36), descent rate (0.36) and altitude (0.25). These nodes are all used by the CDES to compute the actual energy state, energy margin and projected energy state.

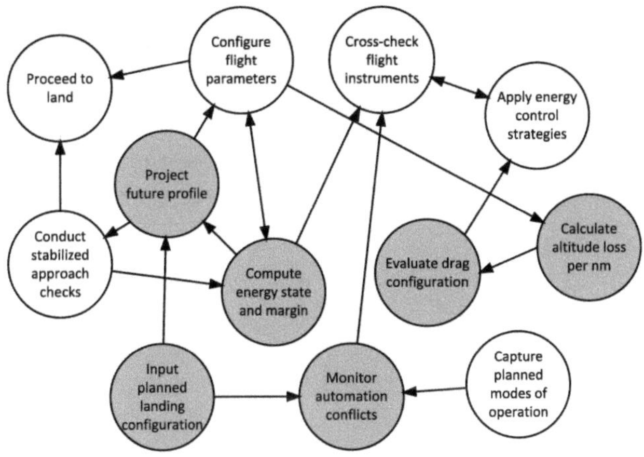

Fig. 1. Extract of the CDES task network. *Note.* Nodes shown in grey are those introduced by the CDES.

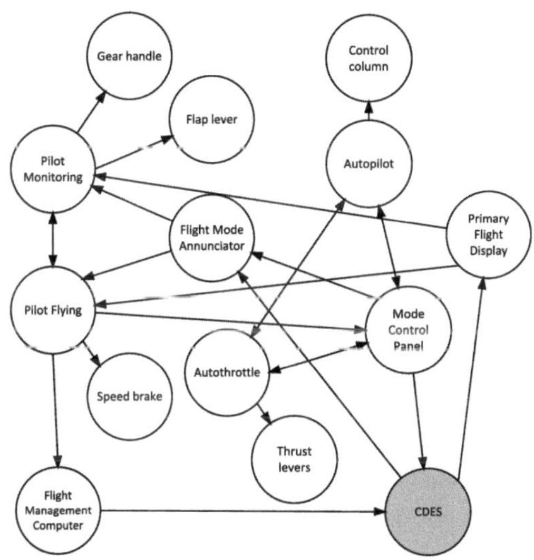

Fig. 2. Extract of the CDES social network. *Note.* Nodes shown in grey are those introduced by the CDES.

3.2 System Error Prediction: EAST-BL and SHERPA

EAST network representations were used to model the work-as-envisaged following integration of the CDES within the flight deck environments. The broken-links analysis was performed using the task and social networks shown in Figs. 1 and 2, respectively. The information network serves as a basis for identifying information nodes outputted from a task and those conveyed by system agents. To formalize this, composite networks were constructed using matrices [22]. The social-information network matrix shows the information that should be passed between system agents. The task-information matrix

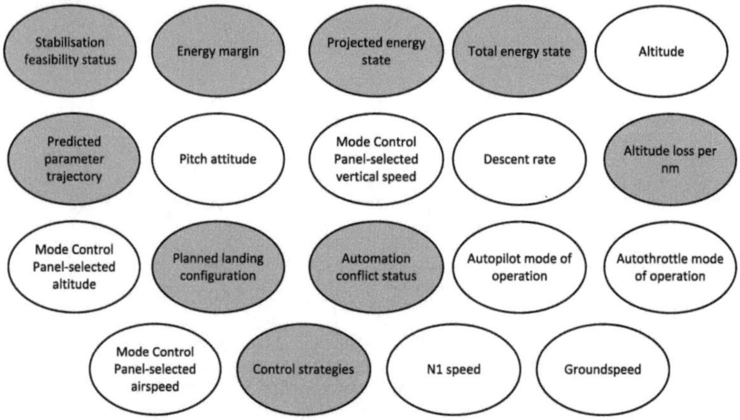

Fig. 3. Extract of the CDES information network. *Note.* Nodes shown in grey are those introduced by the CDES.

shows the information used to undertake each task. These composite representations enable systematic identification of the information nodes affected by the removal of task or social links [14].

To extend upon the EAST-BL analysis, the SHERPA taxonomy was applied to anticipate additional failure scenarios. For the task-information network, the action, checking, retrieval and selection failure types were applied based on the task description. As an example, the task of 'cross-check the flight instruments' was assigned with error codes from the check failure category. For the task-information analysis, the assigned error code was used to anticipate how the information node from an originating task could be transformed, and the resultant risk of this when completing the interconnected task. For the social-information analysis, error codes from the communication failure category were applied to anticipate the potential risks of omitting information, conveying information inaccurately, or partially exchanging information. An error code was also added to consider scenarios where the information is exchanged correctly but undergoes misinterpretation by the recipient [15]. To maintain the underlying method of EAST-BL, an error code of omission was always applied to the social-information and task-information analyses.

Social-Information Risk Analysis. Information received from the FMC is used for the CDES computations and projections. This implicates a need to interrogate this relationship to consider what could happen if information transfers were subject to transaction failures. This is shown using the 'altitude' node, as this was identified as a key information aspect (see Table 2). From this, mitigating strategies were proposed to improve the reliability and transparency of the CDES.

Task-Information Analysis. An extract of the task-information broken-links analysis is also given in Table 3. This was shown between the tasks 'monitor automation conflicts' and 'cross-check flight instruments', when sharing the information node 'automation

Table 2. Extract of the risk analysis for the EAST social network.

SHERPA code	Risk	Mitigating strategies
Information not communicated (I1)	The CDES cannot compute potential energy, assess the available energy margin or project vertical profile obtainment. This reduces the predictive capabilities of the CDES and increases reliance on the pilot to recognize destabilized conditions.	Enable the CDES to obtain altitude values from alternative sources when this is not available from the FMC. If altitude data becomes unavailable, the CDES should clearly indicate when computations are degraded.
Information partially communicated (I2)	The CDES inaccurately computes the actual altitude state, energy margin and projected profiles using inaccurate altitude metrics, which may lead to misleading guidance being used when stabilizing and landing the aircraft.	Incorporate data integrity monitoring and plausibility checking within the CDES. This should verify update rate consistency, cross-check alignment of the current descent rate and validate against expected descent rate trends. If the altitude is deemed inaccurate, the CDES should flag the data as unreliable and pause energy predictions until inputs are corrected.
Information misinterpreted (I4)	The altitude metric is misinterpreted by the CDES (e.g., interpreted in the wrong unit). The CDES may generate incorrect energy state, margins and stabilization predictions based on these misinterpretations and present guidance that results in inappropriate energy management.	Clearly display the altitude unit and reference assumptions used by the CDES such that pilots can verify whether outputs are based on the correct measurements.

conflict status'. The task 'cross-check flight instruments' is shown as this was identified as having the highest sociometric status within the task network analysis shown in Fig. 1.

Table 3. Extract of the risk analysis for the task network.

SHERPA code	Risk	Mitigating strategies

(*continued*)

Table 3. (*continued*)

SHERPA code	Risk	Mitigating strategies
Omitted check (C1)	Automation conflict statuses will not be available, preventing pilots from using the information to verify whether current operational modes support their intended descent and landing profile. This increases the risk of undetected mode conflicts and energy mismanagement.	Ensure the automation conflict status is reliably transmitted to support instrument cross-checking. Indicate when the automation conflict status is not available to prompt manual cross-checks of autopilot and autothrottle modes.
Incomplete check (C2)	Conflict monitoring only accounts for a subset of automation modes (e.g., autopilot and not autothrottle), resulting in a partial conflict status. This may reduce the ability to detect inappropriate mode activation when cross-checking the flight instruments.	Incorporate independent monitoring of the autopilot and autothrottle modes before generating conflict status. If complete mode data are not available, the system should indicate which mode has not been verified within the status output.
Check mistimed (C5)	Automation modes may be evaluated before changes are input via the MCP. This could cause the CDES to report outdated automation conflict statuses.	Ensure the CDES always monitors modes of operation after recent automation inputs have been received. Display a timestamp on the Primary Flight display such that the flight crew can assess the recency of the conflict status.

4 Discussion

The current work presents preliminary findings taken from a prospective risk assessment used to identify potential errors introduced by a novel flight deck tool. To summarize the approach taken, the EAST framework defines the structural relationships between tasks, agents and information nodes, the EAST-BL links analysis determines the links that could become affected during an operation, and the SHERPA taxonomy systematically predicts the failure mechanisms that affect these links. In this sense, the links are not removed but instead become degraded to reflect situations where the connection remains intact, but the information exchange is compromised. Such analysis is enabled through the integration of methods, as SHERPA is typically applied to task-level failures, while EAST-BL considers the consequences of removed links rather than degraded exchanges. Adopting this combined approach enables risks to be explored across the sociotechnical system as a whole by accounting for the interactions between humans and technical sub-systems [3]. The final analysis will identify the full set of risks associated with the CDES and the normative tasks that take place during the landing approach.

The risks identified from this preliminary analysis were used to develop mitigating strategies in the form of system requirements, which could improve robustness and transparency requirements for supporting human-machine teaming (see Tables 2 and 3). System requirements focused on implementing monitoring processes for data integrity and enabling the use of alternative data sources for critical inputs. Transparency requirements were identified to ensure flight crews could interpret system outputs and understand the limitations of the CDES. These requirements were tailored to the different failure scenarios, demonstrating the value of adopting the SHERPA taxonomy within the EAST-BL method for identifying mitigating design strategies. However, the design of the CDES must look to incorporate feedback from pilots to ensure the capability addresses the needs of the end-user [24]. Further, although the operation of the CDES was envisaged within the flight deck environment, the reliability of the network representations is dependent on the completeness of the NTSB report. As such, future work should refine the EAST network representations using insights from commercial airline pilots and further understand their perspectives and approach to using the CDES [21].

Acknowledgments. This work was conducted as part of an Industrial Cooperative Awards in Science & Technology in collaboration with Thales. Any views expressed are those of the authors and do not necessarily represent those of the funding body.

Disclosure of Interests. The authors have no competing interests to declare that are relevant to the content of this article.

References

1. Harris, D., Stanton, N.A.: Aviation as a System of Systems: Preface to the Special Issue of Human Factors in Aviation. Taylor & Francis (2010)
2. Stanton, N.A., Salmon, P.M., Rafferty, L.A., Walker, G.H., Baber, C., Jenkins, D.P.: Human Factors Methods: A Practical Guide for Engineering and Design. CRC Press (2017)
3. Banks, V.A., Stanton, N.A., Burnett, G., Hermawati, S.: Distributed cognition on the road: using EAST to explore future road transportation systems. Appl. Ergon. **68**, 258–266 (2018)
4. Embrey, D.: SHERPA: a systematic human error reduction and prediction approach (1986)
5. Swann, C., Preston, M.: Twenty-five years of HAZOPs. J. Loss Prev. Process Ind. **8**, 349–353 (1995)
6. Salmon, P.M., et al.: When tomorrow comes: a prospective risk assessment of a future artificial general intelligence-based uncrewed combat aerial vehicle system. Appl. Ergon. **117**, 104245 (2024)
7. Waterson, P., Robertson, M.M., Cooke, N.J., Militello, L., Roth, E., Stanton, N.A.: Defining the methodological challenges and opportunities for an effective science of sociotechnical systems and safety. Ergonomics. **58**, 565–599 (2015)
8. Simsekler, M.C.E., Gurses, A.P., Smith, B.E., Ozonoff, A.: Integration of multiple methods in identifying patient safety risks. Saf. Sci. **118**, 530–537 (2019)
9. Read, G.J., Shorrock, S., Walker, G.H., Salmon, P.M.: State of science: evolving perspectives on 'human error'. Ergonomics. **64**, 1091–1114 (2021)
10. Dekker, S.: Drift into Failure: From Hunting Broken Components to Understanding Complex Systems. CRC Press (2016)

11. Stanton, N.A., Harvey, C.: Beyond human error taxonomies in assessment of risk in sociotechnical systems: a new paradigm with the EAST 'broken-links' approach. Ergonomics. **60**, 221–233 (2017)
12. Stanton, N., Baber, C., Harris, D.: Modelling Command and Control: Event Analysis of Systemic Teamwork. Ashgate Publishing (2008)
13. Walker, G.H., et al.: From ethnography to the EAST method: a tractable approach for representing distributed cognition in air traffic control. Ergonomics. **53**, 184–197 (2010)
14. McLean, S., et al.: Forecasting emergent risks in advanced AI systems: an analysis of a future road transport management system. Ergonomics. **66**, 1750–1767 (2023)
15. Salmon, P.M., Walker, G.H., Stanton, N.A.: Pilot error versus sociotechnical systems failure: a distributed situation awareness analysis of air France 447. Theor. Issues Ergon. Sci. **17**, 64–79 (2016)
16. Parnell, K.J., Banks, V.A., Plant, K.L., Griffin, T.G., Beecroft, P., Stanton, N.A.: Predicting design-induced error on the flight deck: an aircraft engine oil leak scenario. Hum. Factors. **63**, 938–955 (2021)
17. Banks, V., Allison, C.K., Parnell, K., Plant, K., Stanton, N.A.: Predicting and mitigating failures on the flight deck: an aircraft engine bird strike scenario. Ergonomics. **65**, 1672–1695 (2022)
18. Stanton, N.A., Plant, K.L., Revell, K.M., Griffin, T.G., Moffat, S., Stanton, M.: Distributed cognition in aviation operations: a gate-to-gate study with implications for distributed crewing. Ergonomics. **62**, 138–155 (2019)
19. Flight Safety Foundation: Flight Safety Foundation Approach-and-landing-Accident Reduction Briefing Note 7.1 - Stabilized Approach. Flight Safety Digest (2000)
20. NTSB: Descent Below Visual Glidepath and Impact With Seawall Asiana Airlines Flight 214 Boeing 777-200ER, HL7742 San Francisco, California July 6, 2013 (2014)
21. Hart, S.G., Steane, V., Plant, K., Young, M.S.: Using EAST to develop design recommendations for a context-dependent energy support system. In: 2025 IEEE International Conference on Recent Advances in Systems Science and Engineering (RASSE), pp. 1–6. IEEE (2025)
22. Stanton, N.A.: Representing distributed cognition in complex systems: how a submarine returns to periscope depth. Ergonomics. **57**, 403–418 (2014)
23. Plant, K.L., Stanton, N.A.: All for one and one for all: representing teams as a collection of individuals and an individual collective using a network perceptual cycle approach. Int. J. Ind. Ergon. **44**, 777–792 (2014)
24. Parnell, K.J., Banks, V.A., Allison, C.K., Plant, K.L., Beecroft, P., Stanton, N.A.: Designing flight deck applications: combining insight from end-users and ergonomists. Cogn. Tech. Work. **23**, 353–365 (2021)

Humanity-Based Design: Beyond User-Centered and Human-Centered Design

Masayuki Ihara[1(✉)], Hiroko Tokunaga[1], Masashige Motoe[1,2], Tomomi Nakashima[1,3], Hiroki Goto[1,4], Yuuki Umezaki[1,5], Yoko Egawa[1,6], Shinya Hisano[1,7], and Shinpei Saruwatari[1,8]

[1] RIKEN, Yokohama 2300045, Japan
ihara@acm.org
[2] Tohoku University, Sendai 9808579, Japan
[3] Yamanami Kaiteki Seikatsu, Co. LTD., Omuta 8360091, Japan
[4] Medical Corporation Meikikai, Kagoshima 8920877, Japan
[5] Shinjinkai Medical Association, Omuta 8370924, Japan
[6] Omuta City Hospital, Omuta 8368567, Japan
[7] Prefectural University of Hiroshima, Mihara 7230053, Japan
[8] Shirakawa Hospital, Omuta 8370926, Japan

Abstract. This paper proposes "Humanity-Based Design" (HBD) as a new design paradigm that transcends conventional User-Centered Design (UCD) and Human-Centered Design (HCD). We introduce an interaction model between service providers and service recipients as the core of this principle. Using the design of elderly care services as a case study, we present a model of intervention that promotes self-disclosure by care recipients. Furthermore, we analyze conversations between caregivers and elderly individuals with dementia to demonstrate the practical application of this model.

Keywords: Humanity-Based Design · User-Centered Design · Human-Centered Design · Narrative · Nursing Care

1 Introduction

User-Centered Design (UCD) [1, 2] is a well-established methodology for designing services that meet user requirements. Furthermore, Human-Centered Design (HCD) [3] expands this focus to humans in general, rather than just users. In the field of nursing care, "Person-Centered Care" (PCC) [4], which emphasizes the individuality of each care recipient, has been widely advocated. We place significant importance on this person-centered care principle and propose Humanity-Based Design (HBD) as a new design paradigm that goes beyond traditional UCD and HCD. This paper outlines the HBD model using service design in the elderly care sector as a primary example.

C. Stephanidis et al. (Eds.): HCII 2026, CCIS 3047, pp. 33–38, 2026.
https://doi.org/10.1007/978-3-032-30552-7_4

2 Problem Identification

In the field of elderly care, services must be provided according to the unique life background and values of each individual. Personas, frequently used in service design, are a user-modeling technique that creates a "fictional individual" to represent typical patterns of goals, attitudes, consciousness, and behaviors. However, applying service design based on representative personas to elderly care presents challenges. Caregivers—the service providers—must prioritize individualized support over operational efficiency, providing care based on a "view of humanity" that emphasizes staying close to each recipient's unique existence. Therefore, the design of care services must be grounded in a model capable of incorporating this view of humanity.

3 Utilization of Narratives

To explore the potential of service design based on a "view of humanity" that focuses on the individual (as opposed to personas), this study focuses on narrative fragments (life stories) and self-disclosure. Narratives are considered effective for providing high-quality, personalized care [5], and various approaches for their utilization have been proposed [6–9]. We aim to realize a "Narrative Utilization Ecosystem," as shown in Fig. 1 [10]. This system collects narrative fragments from care recipients with dementia and uses generative AI to provide care advice to staff. The AI generates suggestions based on the principles of Person-Centered Care, considering the life background and values of each individual. By using tools that provide this advice, even less-experienced staff can provide high-quality care, reducing variance in care quality across the team. High-quality care facilitates rapport building, which in turn encourages further self-disclosure of narrative fragments, allowing the cycle in Fig. 1 to function as a sustainable ecosystem.

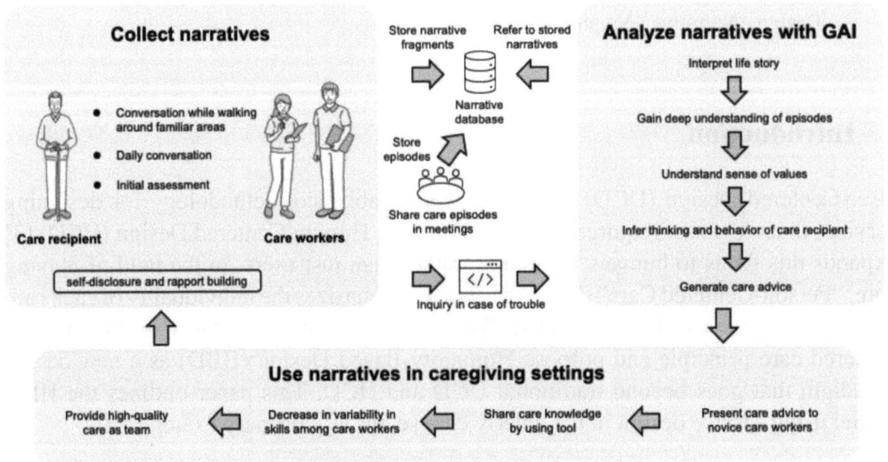

Fig. 1. Narrative Utilization Ecosystem.

4 Humanity-Based Design

4.1 Interaction Between Caregiver and Care Recipient

As the foundation for designing the Narrative Utilization Ecosystem, we propose an interaction model between the caregiver and the care recipient (Fig. 2). Generally, human minds cannot connect directly; therefore, communication is mediated through language, facial expressions, and gestures, etc. In the context of care services, this communication involves the caregiver intervening through empathy-based care to elicit self-disclosure, encouraging the recipient to share narrative fragments. In many cases, caregivers struggle to fully understand the narratives of recipients due to dementia or other factors. However, if caregivers repeatedly elicit self-disclosure through interventions based on a view of humanity that stays close to the individual, a rapport can be established, creating a "virtuous cycle" of service delivery.

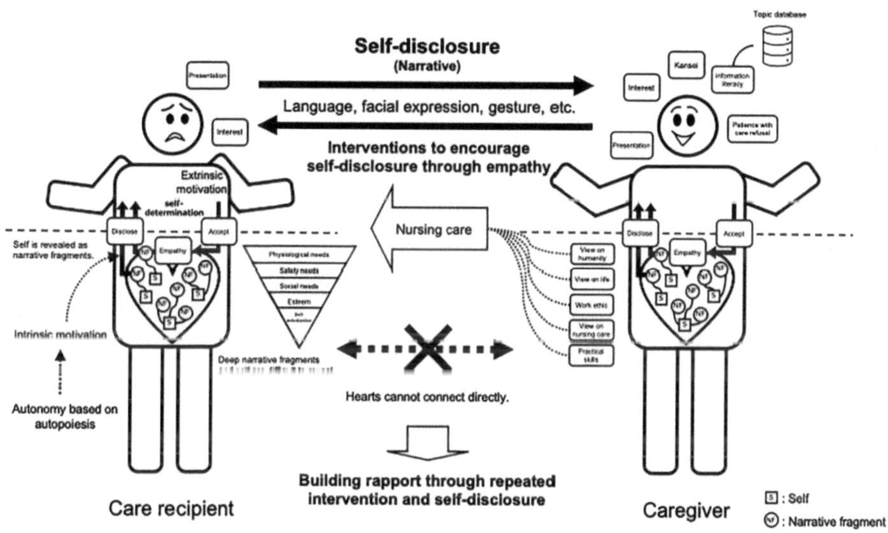

Fig. 2. Interaction model between caregiver and care recipient.

4.2 Narrative Disclosure by Care Recipients

In the model (Fig. 2), the "self" of the care recipient is linked to various narrative fragments. Aspects of the self-located deep within the mind are not easily disclosed. When interventions from the caregiver act as extrinsic motivation—leading to acceptance and empathy through sensory stimulation—the self is disclosed as narrative fragments. While self-disclosure can occur through spontaneous reminiscence based on autonomy, this is less frequent in recipients with dementia. For effective disclosure, it is crucial that the recipient finds the caregiver's intervention interesting and can "present" their narrative fragments in a way that is transmissible.

4.3 Caregiver Intervention Skills

Conversely, caregivers also possess their own "self" and narrative fragments. To encourage sensory stimulation in the recipient, caregivers must express empathy by effectively disclosing their own stories. The quality of care is heavily influenced by the caregiver's view of humanity—specifically, the extent to which they view the recipient not just as a "service user," but as a unique human being. Beyond practical operational skills, care quality is influenced by the caregiver's view of life (how a human life should be), professional ethics, and view of caregiving. Regarding practical skills, caregivers need the ability to show interest and present information effectively. Furthermore, they require information literacy (utilizing a database of topics) and patience to continue care efforts even when faced with the unexpected behaviors of those with dementia.

5 Experiments

To analyze the proposed interaction model using case studies, we conducted two experimental sessions involving conversations between care recipients with dementia and their caregivers. In these experiments, two care recipients (Participant A: an 86-year-old male; Participant B: a 77-year-old female, both with Alzheimer's disease) paired with caregivers to converse while walking through neighborhoods familiar to the recipients. Each session lasted approximately 70 to 80 min. The walking routes were pre-determined by the researchers after identifying locations significant to the participants' histories, such as his former company housing, the school she once attended, or shopping districts she was presumed to have frequented. Caregivers were instructed to speak in a manner that facilitated memory recall, with encouraging the recipients to share episodes from their past. The conversations were recorded and transcribed. We analyzed these transcripts using tags based on a Japanese-adapted version of the ISO 24617-2 semantic discourse annotation framework [11]; the analysis results are presented in Fig. 3. Participant A and Participant B produced 37 and 126 instances, respectively, of information-providing utterances related to narrative disclosure. The results confirmed that, even when the care recipient has dementia, appropriate caregiver interventions can successfully elicit the disclosure of narrative fragments through auditory and visual sensory stimulation, as well as through spontaneous reminiscence.

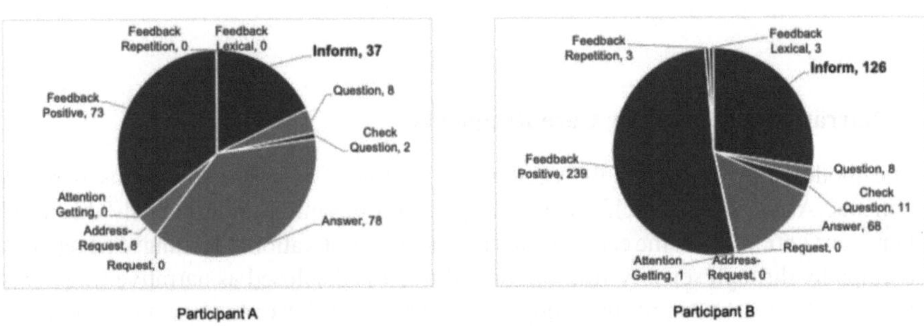

Fig. 3. Results of conversation analyses.

6 Discussion

The experiments demonstrated that caregivers effectively promoted sensory stimulation by asking timely questions or encouraging joint attention. We observed instances where recipients spontaneously recalled past episodes triggered by sensory input, providing emotional insights. The participating caregivers utilized narrative fragments they already knew from daily care to enrich the conversation. For example, knowing that Participant A's father was a train driver or that Participant B excelled at tennis in her youth served as effective "hooks." Furthermore, caregivers' disclosure of their own narratives regarding the town's history contributed to the recipients' memory recall. This suggests that caregiver self-disclosure is a key factor in eliciting recipient self-disclosure.

The caregivers selected for these experiments were highly experienced professionals chosen by facility administrators for their mastery of person-centered care. This expertise was evident in their communication style: they carefully framed questions to avoid triggering negative emotions and demonstrated remarkable patience even when recipients struggled to recall specific details. It is inferred that this empathetic, person-centered approach was a primary driver of the high frequency of narrative disclosure observed.

The skills demonstrated by these experienced caregivers represent a form of tacit knowledge. We believe that by transforming this tacit knowledge into explicit knowledge and implementing it within the AI tools of the Narrative Utilization Ecosystem, we can effectively bridge the gap in care quality between staff members and elevate the standard of care provided by the team as a whole.

7 Conclusion

Through conversation analysis in dementia care, this study provided a partial illustration of the interaction model for Humanity-Based Design. The primary contribution of this work is the presentation of a new design paradigm for services where "staying close to the individual" is paramount, such as healthcare, welfare, and education. The interaction model in Fig. 2 contains various factors on both the caregiver and recipient sides. This represents an "ideal" interaction for the ecosystem in Fig. 1 to function. Future work is required to verify the strength of the relationships between these elements through more case studies. We must also investigate potential missing elements or those that may be less significant. To establish this model as a formal service design methodology, its essence must be reflected in specific design processes. We intend to further validate and refine Humanity-Based Design through continued experimentation and analysis.

Acknowledgments. We would like to thank the care staff members who cooperated in the narrative collection experiments.

References

1. Kling, R.: The organizational context of user-centered software designs. MIS Q. **1**(4), 41–52 (1977). https://doi.org/10.2307/249021

2. Norman, D.A., Draper, S.W.: User Centered System Design: New Perspectives on Human-Computer Interaction. Lawrence Erlbaum Associates (1986)
3. ISO 9241-210:2019: Ergonomics of human-system interaction—Part 210: Human-centred design for interactive systems (2019)
4. Kitwood, T., Bredin, K.: Towards a theory of dementia care: personhood and well-being. Ageing Soc. **12**(3), 269–287 (1992)
5. Guendouzi, J., Davis, B., Maclagan, M.: Expanding expectations for narrative styles in the context of dementia. Top. Lang. Disord. **35**, 237–257 (2015). https://doi.org/10.1097/TLD.0000000000000061
6. Elfrink, T.: Exploring life story books in dementia care: the potential of digital reminiscence interventions. [PhD Thesis - Research UT, graduation UT, University of Twente]. University of Twente (2023). https://doi.org/10.3990/1.9789036558143
7. Heersmink, R.: Preserving narrative identity for dementia patients: embodiment, active environments, and distributed memory. Neuroethics. **15**, 8 (2022). https://doi.org/10.1007/s12152-022-09479-x
8. Hughes, T.: Stories of professional care: narrative analysis of accounts from people with dementia. Prof Doc Thesis University of East London School of Psychology (2014). https://doi.org/10.15123/PUB.4063
9. Randall, W.: Narrative environments for narrative care: the need to honor people's stories. Int. J. Hum. Caring. **20**, 1–4 (2016). https://doi.org/10.20467/1091-5710.20.3.142
10. Ihara, M., et al.: Narrative utilization ecosystem for person-centered care. In: Proc. of Intelligent Human Systems Integration: Integrating People and Intelligent Systems (IHSI2025), vol. 160, pp. 1–11 (2025)
11. Bunt, H., et al.: ISO 24617-2: a semantically-based standard for dialogue annotation. In: Proceedings of the Eighth International Conference on Language Resources and Evaluation (LREC'12), pp. 430–437. European Language Resources Association, Istanbul (2012)

Enhancing Human-Computer Interaction and Complex System Interactomes Through the Constrained Disorder Principle: Accounting for Physiological Variability

Yaron Ilan(✉)

Department of Medicine, Hadassah Medical Center, and Faculty of Medicine, Hebrew University, Jerusalem, Israel
ilan@hadassah.org.il

Abstract. The Constrained Disorder Principle (CDP) presents a revolutionary framework for understanding complex biological and computational systems, recognizing that inherent variability is not a limitation to be minimized, but a fundamental requirement for optimal function. This principle defines all systems in nature by their degree of intrinsic variability, which is dynamically regulated within constrained boundaries and is essential for proper system operation and adaptation to environmental pressures. In the context of human-computer interaction (HCI), the CDP offers transformative potential for improving system accuracy by fundamentally reframing how we approach physiological variability. Traditional HCI systems have typically treated human physiological variation as noise to be filtered out or standardized, leading to suboptimal interfaces that fail to accommodate the natural diversity of human biological responses. The CDP challenges this approach by proposing that physiological variability should be embraced and integrated as a core design principle. Rather than seeking to eliminate variations in heart rate, brain activity patterns, muscle tension, or cognitive processing speeds, CDP-based HCI systems would recognize these fluctuations as meaningful signals that provide crucial information about user states and optimal interaction modalities. The application of CDP to HCI involves developing adaptive interfaces that dynamically adjust their input variation based on real-time physiological monitoring. This approach acknowledges that human performance operates within constrained disorder boundaries that shift depending on factors such as fatigue, stress, attention levels, and individual differences in neurological processing. A CDP-informed HCI would not strive for perfect signal consistency, but would instead establish dynamic thresholds that accommodate natural neural variability while maintaining functional accuracy. This results in more robust and personalized interaction systems that can support high performance across diverse user populations and varying physiological states.

Keywords: Constrained disorder · biological noise · variability

C. Stephanidis et al. (Eds.): HCII 2026, CCIS 3047, pp. 39–49, 2026.
https://doi.org/10.1007/978-3-032-30552-7_5

1 Introduction: The Paradigm Shift from Noise to Signal

Traditional approaches to both human-computer interaction (HCI) and biological systems analysis have operated under a reductionist framework, viewing variability as noise to be eliminated or minimized. This perspective has profoundly shaped the development of HCI systems, in which physiological variations in heart rate, brain activity patterns, muscle tension, and cognitive processing speed are typically filtered out or standardized [1]. Similarly, in biological network analysis, the dynamic fluctuations observed in protein-protein interactions, gene regulatory networks, and metabolic pathways have been treated as experimental noise rather than functional features [2].

The Constrained Disorder Principle (CDP) challenges this fundamental assumption by proposing that physiological variability represents not a limitation but rather an essential requirement for optimal system function [3]. This paradigm shift recognizes that all systems in nature are defined by their degree of intrinsic variability, which is dynamically regulated within constrained boundaries [4]. The CDP provides both a theoretical framework and a practical methodology for harnessing this variability to enhance the accuracy and effectiveness of both HCI systems and complex biological network analysis [5–7].

The relevance of this approach extends beyond theoretical considerations to practical clinical applications. Recent developments in CDP-based second-generation artificial intelligence systems have demonstrated the feasibility of implementing CDP-based algorithms across diverse medical conditions. These applications range from neurological disorders to metabolic disease management, cancer therapy optimization, and cardiovascular disease treatment. The consistent theme across these diverse applications is the recognition that embracing and intelligently managing variability, rather than suppressing it, leads to superior clinical outcomes.

2 The Constrained Disorder Principle: Theoretical Framework

2.1 Defining Constrained Disorder

The Constrained Disorder Principle posits that optimal biological and computational system function requires a certain degree of controlled randomness or variability operating within defined boundaries. These boundaries are not fixed but dynamically adjust based on internal states and external pressures. The key insight is that complete order and perfect predictability represent suboptimal states that reduce system adaptability and resilience [3, 8, 9]. The variability pattern itself contains information about system health and optimal function. When variability falls outside these boundaries or becomes either too regular or too chaotic, system dysfunction ensues.

This framework applies across multiple scales of organization, from molecular interactions to cellular processes, organ system function, and whole-organism behavior. The principle is scale-invariant, meaning that similar patterns of constrained disorder emerge across protein conformational dynamics, neural network activity, and population-level behavioral patterns.

2.2 Biological Basis for Constrained Disorder

Multiple lines of evidence support the fundamental role of constrained variability in biological systems. Heart rate variability, for instance, is a well-established marker of cardiovascular health, with reduced variability associated with increased morbidity and mortality. Similarly, gait variability patterns distinguish healthy individuals from those with Parkinson's disease, and breathing variability predicts the need for interventions in patients requiring mechanical ventilation.

At the neural level, brain signal variability (BSV) characterizes brain function and reflects the capacity for state transitions in neural activity. Individual variability manifests across multiple brain networks, including sensorimotor, visual, subcortical, and attention networks [10, 11]. Notably, pathological states are often characterized not by increased variability but by reduced variability and inflexibility in brain state transitions. For example, patients with generalized anxiety disorder show decreased BSV in widespread brain regions, associated with an inflexible brain state transfer pattern [12].

3 Application of CDP to Human-Computer Interaction

3.1 Rethinking HCI Design Principles

Traditional HCI systems have approached the human-computer interface from a perspective that seeks to minimize variability and maximize standardization [13]. User inputs are processed through algorithms designed to filter out "noisy" biological signals and extract supposedly "pure" commands or information. This approach, while appearing logical, fundamentally misunderstands the nature of human biological systems and leads to interfaces that are brittle, inflexible, and poorly adapted to the full diversity of human users and usage contexts [14, 15].

A CDP-based approach to HCI fundamentally reimagines this relationship. Rather than treating physiological variability as noise to be eliminated, CDP-informed systems recognize these fluctuations as meaningful signals that provide crucial information about user states and optimal interaction modalities. The goal shifts from achieving perfect signal consistency to establishing dynamic thresholds that accommodate natural neural variability while maintaining functional accuracy.

3.2 Adaptive Interface Design

The practical implementation of CDP principles in HCI involves developing adaptive interfaces that dynamically adjust their parameters based on real-time physiological monitoring. This approach acknowledges that human performance operates within constrained boundaries of disorder that shift in response to multiple factors, including fatigue, stress, attention levels, cognitive load, and individual differences in neurological processing [21].

For example, a CDP-informed brain-computer interface (BCI) would not strive for identical signal patterns across all users or all time points. Instead, it would characterize each individual's unique variability signature and continuously adapt its decoding algorithms to account for temporal fluctuations in that signature. When users experience increased fatigue, the system would recognize the associated changes in signal-variability patterns and adjust its sensitivity thresholds accordingly, rather than simply reporting degraded performance or requiring the user to conform to a fixed standard [7].

This approach results in more robust and personalized interaction systems that can support high performance across diverse user populations and varying physiological states. The system learns not just the mean values of relevant physiological signals but the characteristic patterns of variability around those means. It uses this information to make more accurate predictions about user intent and optimal system responses.

3.3 Error Correction and Feedback Mechanisms

CDP-based HCI systems may implement sophisticated error correction mechanisms that distinguish between meaningful signal variation and actual system errors. Traditional error-correction approaches often cannot make this distinction, leading to either excessive false positives (where normal variability is flagged as errors) or false negatives (where actual errors are missed because they fall within expected variability ranges) [16]. By incorporating variability patterns into the error-detection algorithm, CDP-based systems can identify anomalous patterns indicative of actual errors while accommodating expected fluctuations. This includes creating feedback loops that adjust system sensitivity based on detected variability patterns and implementing machine learning models that account for temporal fluctuations in user behavior [17–19].

4 Integration with Brain-Computer Interface Technology

4.1 Current Gaps in BCI Implementation

Despite significant technological advances in recent years, multiple gaps remain in the clinical implementation and effectiveness of BCI systems [20, 21].

These gaps can be categorized into four major domains. Gap I involves the translation from intent to cortical activity, where the relationship between conscious intention and measurable neural signals remains incompletely understood. Gap II concerns the accuracy of signal recording and processing, where current electrode technologies face tradeoffs between invasiveness and signal quality. Gap III concerns the generation of appropriate stimuli or control signals from decoded neural activity. Gap IV involves the closed-loop regulation between the target device and the brain, in which compensatory mechanisms can lead to a loss of effectiveness over time.

4.2 CDP-Based Solutions for BCI Enhancement

The application of CDP principles to BCI addresses these gaps through multiple complementary approaches. First, by recognizing that brain signals naturally exhibit constrained variability, CDP-based decoding algorithms can achieve higher accuracy by working with rather than against it. Instead of seeking perfectly repeatable signal patterns that may never exist in biological systems, these algorithms characterize and utilize the characteristic variability patterns of each user [7].

Second, CDP-based approaches can help bridge Gap I by using brain-directed adjuvants that modulate the gut-brain axis. Low-dose colchicine, which targets gut microtubules and has a high safety profile, has shown promise in enhancing brain signal quality and improving the translation from intent to cortical activity. This effect may relate to the role of microtubules in consciousness or other mechanisms involving brain homeostasis and microglial function.

Third, implementing second-generation artificial intelligence systems that explicitly incorporate variability as a system parameter addresses Gaps II through IV. These systems continuously adapt to both inter-subject and intra-subject variability, improving the accuracy of signal interpretation and ensuring sustainable responses by overcoming compensatory mechanisms that typically lead to a loss of effectiveness over time.

4.3 CDP-Based Second-Generation AI for Variability Management

CDP-based second-generation AI systems represent a fundamental advancement over traditional first-generation approaches. While first-generation systems analyze large datasets to predict outcomes, second-generation systems focus on improving clinical outcomes for individual patients by incorporating personalized variability parameters into treatment algorithms [8].

These platforms operate on an $n = 1$ concept, in which algorithms are continuously adapted to each subject's unique variability signature. Rather than seeking to minimize variability or force all users into a standardized model, the system learns each person's characteristic variability patterns across multiple physiological parameters. It uses this information to optimize performance.

For BCI applications, this means quantifying patterns of signal variability across multiple recording sessions and incorporating them into the decoding algorithm. Eye-movement variability, EEG/ECoG signal variability, temperature changes across different brain regions, and autonomic nervous system signals can all be integrated to provide a more complete picture of brain state and user intent [22, 23].

Critically, second-generation AI systems address the problem of compensatory mechanisms and tolerance that occur with chronic interventions. By introducing controlled variability into the stimulation or feedback patterns, these systems prevent the adaptation that typically leads to loss of effectiveness over time, ensuring sustainable long-term responses.

5 Clinical Applications of CDP-Based Platforms

Heart failure is an ideal application domain for CDP-based approaches, given the critical role of variability in cardiovascular function. Heart rate variability is a well-established prognostic marker in heart failure, with reduced variability associated with worse outcomes. By introducing controlled variability into the dosing schedule rather than maintaining fixed daily doses, these systems overcome compensatory mechanisms that lead to diuretic resistance. The platform adjusts medication timing and dosing based on individual circadian patterns and continuously adapts to changes in the patient's physiological state. Clinical trial results have demonstrated that this approach improves diuretic resistance in patients with heart failure [24, 25].

Cancer treatment represents another domain where CDP principles provide substantial benefits. Cancer cells and tumors exhibit their own patterns of variability in growth rates, metabolic activity, and drug sensitivity. Traditional treatment approaches using fixed dosing schedules allow cancer cells to adapt through various resistance mechanisms, ultimately leading to treatment failure. Patient-tailored variability-based paradigms for anti-cancer therapy leverage the inherent trajectories underlying cancer evolution to overcome drug resistance. By introducing controlled variability into treatment schedules, these approaches prevent the development of adaptive resistance mechanisms [26].

Chronic pain management has proven particularly challenging due to issues of tolerance and loss of effectiveness with sustained opioid or other analgesic use. The nervous system exhibits remarkable plasticity and readily adapts to chronic pharmacological interventions, necessitating dose escalations that increase the side-effect burden. CDP-based digital analgesics implement individually tailored variability in nerve stimulations and pharmacological regimens to maintain analgesic effectiveness [27–29]. In patients with multiple sclerosis, the introduction of variability into therapeutic regimens was associated with improved response to treatment and overcoming tolerance to chronic medications [30].

6 Application of CDP-Based Platforms to Complex System Interactomes

The interactome represents the comprehensive network of molecular interactions within biological systems and has become crucial for understanding cellular functions and disease mechanisms [5]. Traditional interactome models, however, face significant limitations because they fail to account for the inherent variability and randomness of biological systems. Most interactome models are static and binary, depicting interactions as either present or absent, a pattern that stems from their design and data limitations rather than from biological reality. Conventional methodologies for constructing interactomes have focused on identifying stable, reproducible interactions under controlled conditions, employing strict statistical cutoffs and rigorous reproducibility requirements. These approaches generally seek to minimize variability and noise, regarding them as experimental artifacts that obscure the genuine biological signal. However, this reductionist approach often overlooks the dynamic and variable nature of biological systems, in which cellular states constantly fluctuate in response to both internal and external stimuli [31, 32].

The CDP challenges this conventional paradigm by proposing that controlled variability and biological noise are not obstacles to overcome, but rather fundamental features of living systems that should be incorporated into our models. CDP-based interactome analysis develops computational models that explicitly incorporate variability as a system parameter. These models recognize that biological networks must maintain core functional relationships while simultaneously exhibiting the flexibility to respond to environmental changes, stress conditions, and developmental transitions.

7 Requirements for Implementing CDP-Based HCI

Implementing CDP-based approaches requires several technical capabilities beyond those needed for traditional HCI and interactome analysis systems. First, continuous monitoring of relevant physiological parameters is necessary to characterize patterns of individual variability. This may include multiple sensors operating in parallel to capture heart rate variability, brain signal variability, autonomic nervous system activity, and other relevant measures.

Second, real-time adaptive algorithms are required that can continuously adjust system parameters based on detected variability patterns. These algorithms must operate quickly enough to respond to physiological changes while avoiding over-reaction to transient fluctuations. Machine learning approaches, particularly those that implement reinforcement learning or other adaptive methods, are well-suited to this task. Third, robust methods for distinguishing meaningful variability from actual errors or system malfunctions are essential. This requires establishing baseline variability patterns for each individual and continuously updating them as the person's physiology changes over time.

Computational Methods: The CDP requires new computational methods to analyze and model data on variable interactomes. Probabilistic network models, such as Bayesian networks, can represent uncertainty and variability in molecular interactions, incorporating prior knowledge about biological systems while allowing for learning from data. Machine learning approaches, including deep learning, are effective at identifying patterns in high-dimensional, noisy interactome data. Graph neural networks are well-suited for analyzing network data, as they can incorporate both node features and the network structure. Dynamic network algorithms are used to infer and analyze time-varying networks from temporal data, tracking how network structure evolves and identifying key transition points. Multi-scale modeling integrates molecular-level variability with higher-level biological processes, linking molecular interaction dynamics to cellular behavior and physiological outcomes [5, 17–19].

Data Integration Strategies: The CDP framework requires novel methods to integrate diverse types of interactome data while preserving the integrity of complex systems. Heterogeneous data fusion methods incorporate data from various experimental platforms while maintaining information about variability. Context-aware integration preserves the context dependence of interactions during data integration rather than generating a single average network. Personalized network construction methods build personalized interaction networks that account for both genetic and environmental factors, which are essential for personalized medicine applications. Uncertainty quantification techniques propagate and quantify uncertainty through complex data integration pipelines, making reliable inferences from noisy and incomplete data [5, 17–19].

Experimental Approaches: Single-cell technologies, such as single-cell RNA sequencing (scRNA-seq), single-cell proteomics, and single-cell imaging, provide the necessary resolution to observe variability in molecular interactions at the cell-by-cell level. Time-resolved measurements through temporal profiling techniques capture the dynamics of molecular interactions across multiple time scales. Live-cell imaging with fluorescently tagged proteins enables real-time observation of protein-protein interactions and their dynamics. Perturbation studies through systematic experiments explore how interaction networks respond to different stimuli, revealing their dynamic properties and regulatory mechanisms. Multimodal integration combining various molecular measurements provides comprehensive views of interaction networks and their variability.

Summary and Future Directions. The CDP provides a theoretical foundation for understanding why rigid, deterministic HCI systems often fail to achieve their intended accuracy levels. By recognizing that biological systems require a certain degree of controlled randomness to function optimally, CDP-based design principles can guide the development of interaction algorithms that work with, rather than against, human physiological variability. This includes creating feedback loops that adjust system sensitivity based on detected patterns of variability, implementing machine learning models that account for temporal fluctuations in user behavior, and designing error-correction mechanisms that distinguish meaningful signal variation from actual system errors.

The extension of the CDP-based platform to interactome analysis of complex systems represents another significant application domain. Interactomes, which map the complete set of molecular interactions within biological systems, have traditionally struggled to account for the dynamic, variable nature of biological networks. The CDP provides a framework for understanding how protein-protein interactions, gene regulatory networks, and metabolic pathways operate within the constrained disorder boundaries that are essential for system flexibility and resilience. Rather than seeking to identify static interaction maps, CDP-informed interactome analysis recognizes that the variability in interaction strengths, temporal patterns, and network connectivity represents functional features rather than experimental noise.

This approach enhances interactome accuracy by developing computational models that explicitly incorporate variability as a system parameter. CDP-based interactome analysis reveals natural fluctuations that enable biological systems to respond to environmental changes while maintaining core functional relationships. This methodology can improve the predictive power of interactome models by accounting for the inherent flexibility that allows biological networks to adapt to perturbations, stress conditions, and developmental changes.

The practical implications of applying CDP principles to both HCI and interactome analysis include the development of more robust predictive models, improved system reliability under varying conditions, and enhanced ability to capture the full functional capacity of complex systems. In HCI applications, this translates to interfaces that maintain accuracy across diverse user populations and usage contexts. In interactome research, CDP principles enable a more comprehensive understanding of how biological networks maintain functionality despite constant molecular-level fluctuations.

The integration of CDP principles also facilitates the development of hybrid systems that more effectively bridge the biological and computational domains. By recognizing that both human physiological systems and complex biological networks operate according to principles of constrained disorder, researchers can design HCI systems that are inherently compatible with human biological constraints and interactome analysis tools that better reflect the true nature of biological network dynamics.

Several promising research directions emerge from the CDP framework. Integration with virtual reality and augmented reality technologies may enhance BCI applications by providing more naturalistic interaction contexts that better accommodate physiological variability. Combining multiple sensing modalities may enable more comprehensive characterization of patterns of individual variability. The development of better methods for quantifying and characterizing variability patterns across different biological scales is a substantial technical challenge. Novel metrics beyond simple variance or standard deviation may better capture the meaningful structure within constrained disorder patterns. Finally, extending CDP principles to social and organizational systems may provide insights into group dynamics, organizational resilience, and collective decision-making.

As we continue to develop increasingly sophisticated interfaces between biological and computational systems, the principles embodied in the CDP will become increasingly important. The future of HCI, BCI, and systems biology lies not in achieving perfect order and eliminating all variability, but in understanding, characterizing, and intelligently harnessing the constrained disorder that underlies optimal biological function. This represents not merely a technical advance but a fundamental reconceptualization of the relationship between order and disorder, consistency and variability, in complex adaptive systems.

Disclosure. The Abbreviations: CDP: constrained disorder principle; AI: artificial intelligence; HCI: human-computer interaction; BCI: brain-computer interface; BSV: brain signal variability. The author has no conflict of interest. YI is the founder of Oberon Sciences.

Abbreviations

CDP constrained disorder principle
AI artificial intelligence
HCI human-computer interaction
BCI brain-computer interface
BSV brain signal variability

References

1. Mohammadzadeh, N., Lotfi, F., Samadpour, H.: Identifying influential theories in human-computer interaction within health informatics: a systematic review. Health Sci. Rep. **8**, e71074 (2025)
2. Galindez, G., Sadegh, S., Baumbach, J., et al.: Network-based approaches for modeling disease regulation and progression. Comput. Struct. Biotechnol. J. **21**, 780–795 (2023)
3. Ilan, Y.: Constrained disorder principle-based variability is fundamental for biological processes: beyond biological relativity and physiological regulatory networks. Prog. Biophys. Mol. Biol. **180–181**, 37–48 (2023)
4. Ilan, Y.: The constrained disorder principle defines living organisms and provides a method for correcting disturbed biological systems. Comput. Struct. Biotechnol. J. **20**, 6087–6096 (2022)
5. Ilan, Y.: The constrained disorder principle: a paradigm shift for accurate interactome mapping and information analysis in complex biological systems. Bioengineering. **12**, 1255 (2025)

6. Ilan, Y.: The constrained disorder principle overcomes the challenges of methods for assessing uncertainty in biological systems. J. Pers. Med. **15** (2024)
7. Lehmann, H., Arkadir, D., Ilan, Y.: Methods for improving brain-computer interface: using a brain-directed adjuvant and a second-generation artificial intelligence system to enhance information streaming and effectiveness of stimuli. Int. J. Appl. Biol. Pharm. Technol. **14**, 42–52 (2023)
8. Ilan, Y.: Making use of noise in biological systems. Prog. Biophys. Mol. Biol. **178**, 83–90 (2023)
9. Ilan, Y.: The constrained-disorder principle defines the functions of systems in nature. Front. Netw. Physiol. **4**, 1361915 (2024)
10. Goodman, Z.T., Nomi, J.S., Kornfeld, S., et al.: Brain signal variability and executive functions across the life span. Netw. Neurosci. **8**, 226–240 (2024)
11. Garrett, D.D., Samanez-Larkin, G.R., MacDonald, S.W., et al.: Moment-to-moment brain signal variability: a next frontier in human brain mapping? Neurosci. Biobehav. Rev. **37**, 610–624 (2013)
12. Li, L., Wang, Y., Ye, L., et al.: Altered brain signal variability in patients with generalized anxiety disorder. Front. Psych. **10**, 84 (2019)
13. Gulati, S., McDonagh, J., Sousa, S., et al.: Trust models and theories in human–computer interaction: a systematic literature review. Comput. Hum. Behav. Rep. **16**, 100495 (2024)
14. Solari, F., Chessa, M., Chinellato, E., et al.: Advances in human-computer interactions: methods, algorithms, and applications. Comput. Intell. Neurosci. **2018**, 4127475 (2018)
15. Alkatheiri, M.S.: Artificial intelligence assisted improved human-computer interactions for computer systems. Comput. Electr. Eng. **101**, 107950 (2022)
16. Fontanari, J., Santos, M.: When correcting for regression to the mean is worse than no correction at all (2025). https://doi.org/10.48550/arXiv.2509.04718
17. Ilan, Y.: Using the constrained disorder principle to navigate uncertainties in biology and medicine: refining fuzzy algorithms. Biology. **13**, 830 (2024)
18. Ilan, Y.: The constrained disorder principle overcomes the challenges of methods for assessing uncertainty in biological systems. J. Pers. Med. **15**, 10 (2025)
19. Ilan, Y.: The constrained disorder principle and the law of increasing functional information: the elephant versus the Moeritherium. Comput. Struct. Biotechnol. Rep. **2**, 100040 (2025)
20. Zhang, H., Jiao, L., Yang, S., et al.: Brain-computer interfaces: the innovative key to unlocking neurological conditions. Int. J. Surg. **110**, 5745–5762 (2024)
21. Mudgal, S.K., Sharma, S.K., Chaturvedi, J., et al.: Brain computer interface advancement in neurosciences: applications and issues. Interdiscip. Neurosurg. **20**, 100694 (2020)
22. Li, Y., Gu, Y., Teng, J., et al.: Advancing EEG-based brain-computer interface technology via PEDOT:PSS electrodes. Matter. **7**, 2859–2895 (2024)
23. Mdluli, B., Khumalo, P., Maswanganyi, R.C.: Signal preprocessing, decomposition and feature extraction methods in EEG-based BCIs. Appl. Sci. **15**, 12075 (2025)
24. Gelman, R., Hurvitz, N., Nesserat, R., et al.: A second-generation artificial intelligence-based therapeutic regimen improves diuretic resistance in heart failure: results of a feasibility open-labeled clinical trial. Biomed. Pharmacother. **161**, 114334 (2023)
25. Kenig, A., Kolben, Y., Asleh, R., et al.: Improving diuretic response in heart failure by implementing a patient-tailored variability and chronotherapy-guided algorithm. Front. Cardiovasc. Med. **8**, 695547 (2021)
26. Sigawi, T., Gelman, R., Maimon, O., et al.: Improving the response to lenvatinib in partial responders using a constrained-disorder-principle-based second-generation artificial intelligence-therapeutic regimen: a proof-of-concept open-labeled clinical trial. Front. Oncol. **14**, 1426426 (2024)

27. Hurvitz, N., Lehman, H., Hershkovitz, Y., et al.: A constrained disorder principle-based second-generation artificial intelligence digital medical cannabis system: a real-world data analysis. J. Public Health Res. **14**, 22799036251337640 (2025)
28. Azmanov, H., Ross, E.L., Ilan, Y.: Establishment of an individualized chronotherapy, autonomic nervous system, and variability-based dynamic platform for overcoming the loss of response to analgesics. Pain Physician. **24**, 243–252 (2021)
29. Azmanov, H., Bayatra, A., Ilan, Y.: Digital analgesic comprising a second-generation digital health system: increasing effectiveness by optimizing the dosing and minimizing side effects. J. Pain Res. **15**, 1051–1060 (2022)
30. Sigawi, T., Lehmann, H., Hurvitz, N., et al.: Constrained disorder principle-based second-generation algorithms implement quantified variability signatures to improve the function of complex systems. J. Bioinform. Syst. Biol. **6**, 82–89 (2023)
31. d'Andrea, V., Loscalzo, J., De Domenico, M.: Challenges and opportunities in the network medicine of complex diseases. Med. **7**, 100920 (2025)
32. Wright, S.N., Colton, S., Schaffer, L.V., et al.: State of the interactomes: an evaluation of molecular networks for generating biological insights. Mol. Syst. Biol. **21**, 1–29 (2025)

Exploring the Potential of Brazilian Agentic AI: A Feminist Perspective

Eliana Loureiro[1,2,3,4,5(✉)], Janaina Vallim[6], and Luciana Terceiro[7]

[1] Department of Humanities and Social Sciences, Universidade Federal do ABC, São Bernardo do Campo, São Paulo, Brazil
eliana@wndr.com.br
[2] FAAP, São Paulo, Brazil
[3] ESPM, São Paulo, Brazil
[4] Universidade Presbiteriana Mackenzie, São Paulo, Brazil
[5] Faculdade Impacta, São Paulo, Brazil
[6] Stone, São Paulo, Brazil
[7] Participatory eHealth and Health Data Research Group, Department of Women's and Children's Health, Uppsala University, Uppsala, Sweden
luciana.terceiro@uu.se

Abstract. This study investigates the potential of Brazilian Agentic Artificial Intelligence (AI) systems from a feminist perspective, focusing on how locally developed large language models (LLMs) reproduce, challenge, or transform discourses about women. Feminist perspectives are mobilised to examine how AI systems reflect and reinforce existing social power relations regarding gender and representation. The investigation examines two Brazilian LLMs that can be integrated into Agentic AI systems: Maritaca and Amazonia IA. Ten questions collected from Portuguese-language Reddit, concerning women and the labour market, were submitted to both platforms. Responses were analysed using IRaMuTeQ software for lexical and dendrogram classification, followed by Critical Discourse Analysis. ChatGPT-5 responses were also examined as a comparative benchmark. Results reveal distinct communicative styles between the systems. Amazonia IA produced shorter, affective responses marked by motivational language, often framing inequality in terms of individual effort and meritocracy. Maritaca generated longer, more formal answers that acknowledged structural inequalities while simultaneously reinforcing gendered professional stereotypes by presenting them as historical facts. Both models reproduce hegemonic gender discourses in subtle ways, appearing supportive of women while individualising responsibility and downplaying systemic barriers. We argue that Brazilian LLMs, although contextually grounded, do not automatically guarantee emancipatory outcomes. Technological sovereignty must be accompanied by feminist and decolonial design practices to avoid reproducing dominant power structures and to foster more inclusive, intersectional futures for AI in the Global South.

Keywords: Artificial Intelligence · Agentic Artificial Intelligence · Feminist AI · Large Language Models · Gender Bias · Global South

C. Stephanidis et al. (Eds.): HCII 2026, CCIS 3047, pp. 50–63, 2026.
https://doi.org/10.1007/978-3-032-30552-7_6

1 Introduction

Artificial Intelligence (AI) have become increasingly integrated into everyday life, affecting domains such as science and academia, business, industry, healthcare, media, and arts [30]. Recent advances have accelerated the adoption of AI systems, offering benefits such as enhanced efficiency and productivity across a wide range of tasks [37].

Supporting and developing technology has become a strategic priority for numerous countries [9]. National AI systems may better reflect local cultures, languages, and social realities, enabling more contextually appropriate technological practices [47]. The development of nationally grounded AI also carries economic benefits through new industries and employment. A country's capacity to develop its own AI-based technologies thus constitutes a competitive advantage in the contemporary global market.

In Latin America, Brazil has emerged as a technological regional leader. The country commands more than 121,000 teraflops per second of high-performance computing capacity, equivalent to 90% of the regional total [57]. Brazil also holds the highest score in the region on the Global Data Barometer 2025 index (66.85), which measures data availability and quality, processing capacity, and information governance [22]. However, as this paper argues, the development of national AI does not, in itself, guarantee more equitable or emancipatory outcomes. Such technologies may still reproduce the harmful cultural and social perspectives that marginalise minority groups within their own societies.

Targeted studies and initiatives have been developed to advance technological development in the Global South in ways that address gender equity and social inclusion [4, 11, 38]. Despite this growing body of work, limited research has examined publicly accessible national AI systems in the Global South through a feminist lens. To address this gap, the study directly confronts this tension. We investigate two publicly accessible Brazilian large language models (LLMs) which can be integrated into AI agents, Maritaca and Amazônia IA, through a feminist and intersectional lens. Our central research questions are:

RQ1: How do Brazilian LLMs reproduce, challenge, or transform gendered discourses about women in the labour market?
RQ2: In what ways do national AI systems reflect or depart from hegemonic gender norms, and what are the implications for feminist and decolonial visions of technological sovereignty?

2 Theoretical Background

2.1 Feminist Epistemologies and AI

Feminist epistemologies provide a foundational framework for understanding AI not as a neutral technology but as a socio-technical system embedded in structures of power. Drawing on Haraway's concept of situated knowledges [24] and Crenshaw and Hill Collins' intersectionality frameworks [15, 25], feminist scholarship rejects the premise that computational systems generate objective or universal knowledge. All knowledge is partial, positioned, and shaped by the social conditions of its production, and this applies as fully to AI as to any other epistemic practice. Applied to Large Language Models

(LLMs), this framework demands that analysis begin with prior questions of epistemic justice [21]: whose knowledge is encoded in training data, which experiences are centred, and whose structural conditions are rendered invisible or distorted. As D'Ignazio and Klein [16] argue, every dataset contains a worldview, and the worldview encoded in most LLM training data reflects a world in which masculine experience functions as the unmarked default and the experiences of women, particularly those at the intersection of multiple marginalised identities, are systematically partial or absent.

Feminist scholarship conceptualises algorithmic gender bias not as a technical anomaly but as a structural feature of AI systems that reproduce and amplify the inequalities encoded in their training data. Empirical research supports this position: Kotek et al. [29] demonstrate that LLMs are three to six times more likely to assign a gender-stereotypical occupational role when resolving an ambiguous pronoun, exceeding what either social perception data or official labour statistics would predict. Clavell [12] further establishes that bias enters AI systems at multiple stages: in the composition of training data, in modelling decisions, and in deployment contexts, making piecemeal technical corrections insufficient. A structural feminist account also attends to the ideological dimension of model outputs: LLMs produce discourse, not merely information, thereby participating in the construction and normalisation of social categories. Even when models adopt progressive-sounding language, they may simultaneously reproduce hegemonic framings. Models generate authoritative but factually inaccurate accounts for biased outputs [29], lending their distortions the appearance of objectivity and rendering them difficult for users to identify and contest. In terms of representation, LLMs consistently associate women with stereotypical roles, such as caregiving, domestic labour, and service occupations, while associating men with professional and leadership domains, and these patterns persist even after alignment processes designed to reduce offensive outputs [50].

The theoretical framework outlined here carries direct implications for AI development and governance. Feminist AI requires, first, accountability for positionality: every design choice and evaluation metric reflects a position within social relations of power and must be made transparent as such [16]. Second, given that LLMs obscure their biases behind authoritative accounts, the responsibility for bias detection cannot rest with individual users; structural interventions across the full AI lifecycle, backed by enforceable governance mechanisms, are necessary [12]. Feminist epistemology does not simply add a gender lens to AI. It demands a rethinking of what AI systems are for whose knowledge they encode, and in whose service they operate.

2.2 AI Agents and Social Risks

AI agents represent a significant stage in AI development, elevating what machines can accomplish [36, 39]. AI agents are defined as operational implementations of AI that enable interactions with other digital ecosystems while autonomously working toward specific tasks and outcomes [44]. These systems differentiate themselves from general-purpose LLMs by offering a structured framework: defined initialisation, limited autonomy, and task-orientedness [44]. Within the scope of an agent, LLMs serve as decision-makers for agent processes [54]. However, machine autonomy poses concerns, as AI models may contain vulnerabilities that can silently introduce security flaws into systems [26]. Due to its levels of autonomy and complexity, AI agents can raise new safety, privacy, and security risks [34]. AI agents are also at significant risk of reproducing and amplifying stereotypes and biases. The artificial feminization of AI agents frequently dehumanizes and objectifies women [5].

2.3 The Sociotechnical Relationship Between Women and AI

Women's relationship with AI is deeply shaped by structural power relations [10, 31, 45, 51]. Across different stages of technological development and deployment, women experience persistent challenges, including misrepresentation, exposure to algorithmic biases, vulnerability to digital violence, and exploitation through precarious labour [7, 12, 23, 27]. These dynamics reveal that AI systems are not neutral tools but sociotechnical infrastructures that often reproduce and intensify existing gender inequalities.

Distortions in gender and ethnic representation mediated by technology are well-documented in the literature [8]. Numerous studies demonstrate that marginalised groups are frequently portrayed through stereotypical and reductive frameworks, perpetuating stereotypes and discrimination [52]. There is a tendency for LLMs to replicate and amplify gender, class, and ethnic biases [13, 52]. It is a result of the data with which the technology was trained, which may contain biases that reproduce social inequalities; when the amount of training data is not representative, the model may develop its own biases, or when humans have tagged the data in a biased manner [52].

Algorithmic bias often operates under the appearance of mathematical objectivity, disguising discrimination as neutral calculations. The use of systems without accountability and explainability ultimately automates prejudice and amplifies social injustices under the guise of supposed technical neutrality [35].

Recent data indicate gender disparities in AI use, with men reporting higher engagement with generative tools (50%) than women (37%) [2]. Factors limiting women's adoption include heightened concerns about privacy and trust, as well as greater exposure to negative online experiences [49]. As technologies advance, new forms of perpetrating violence against women are developed [49]. Addressing this phenomenon requires greater inclusion of women in AI development processes, alongside regulatory frameworks that prioritise transparency, accountability, and social justice [16, 28, 50].

3 Methodology

To investigate Brazilian AI agents from a feminist perspective, we selected Maritaca and Amazônia IA, the two prominent Brazilian LLMs currently publicly accessible, along with ChatGPT 5.0 for subsequent comparison. Although currently accessed mainly as conversational interfaces, both Brazilian models can be integrated into larger automated infrastructures. This capacity enables them to operate as semi-autonomous systems that support decision-making, information retrieval, and workflow automation, key characteristics of AI agents.

Maritaca AI is a Brazilian startup founded in 2022. Its platform offers three language models [58]. Access to the language models is available through either MariTalk, their chatbot, or via API, allowing integration with AI agents. The language models were trained on publicly available data, primarily in Portuguese; however, they can also perform tasks in English and Spanish. This experiment was performed with the language model Sabiá-3.1 [1].

Amazonia IA is an LLM developed by WideLabs, an AI-focused company founded in 2020. According to the company, its primary goal is to preserve Brazilian culture while promoting technological autonomy and fostering the growth of the national industry and scientific research [56]. Currently, Amazonia IA is available as a free chatbot for individuals. Amazonia IA has been integrated with a range of AI agents for private companies in healthcare, law, and finance.

ChatGPT, developed by OpenAI, is regarded as the most used LLM globally and in Brazil, accounting for an estimated 64.5% of the worldwide AI chatbot market [14]. This study was performed on ChatGPT 5.0.

3.1 Research Design

The research design employed an intrinsic qualitative case study [48] to address the research question of how LLM models used within AI agents relate to feminist perspectives, reproducing, challenging, or transforming discourses about women.

3.2 Data Collection

Our methodological approach builds on Scheuerman et al. [46], who used questions posed by lay users on Quora to simulate real-world interactions with AI systems. We extend this approach to Reddit, a more widely used platform in Brazil. For this pilot study, we focused on questions related to women and the labour market, a theme selected for its relevance to women's economic autonomy, financial independence, and broader structural inequalities [3]. Data collection was conducted in Portuguese using the keywords "mulheres" (women) and "mercado de trabalho" (labour market). The most relevant questions, ranked by search relevance, were gathered from Brazilian Portuguese-language subreddits such as r/conselhosdecarreira, r/brasil, and r/literaciafinanceira.

The sample size reflects the exploratory nature of this pilot study. While it does not aim for data saturation, it allows the identification of initial patterns, particularly in relation to power relations and gendered discourses, which will be examined in a larger corpus in subsequent research. Given the use of Critical Discourse Analysis (CDA), the emphasis is on depth rather than breadth.

The selected questions were manually submitted to two Brazilian LLMs, Maritaca and Amazônia AI, as well as ChatGPT 5.0 for comparison. To minimise potential bias from personalisation, new accounts were created using alphanumeric usernames and email addresses, thereby avoiding gendered cues. All data were collected in October 2025 to ensure consistency across platforms.

3.3 Analytical Procedure

LLM responses were submitted to IRaMuTeQ (*Interface de R pour les Analyses Multidimensionnelles pour les Corpus de textes*), free software that enables statistical analysis of text corpora using R and Python [40, 41]. IRaMuTeQ applies Reinert's Descending Hierarchical Classification method, which segments text into passages of three to five lines and identifies statistically distinct word-co-occurrence clusters.

As the LLM response corpus was relatively short, each corpus was triplicated prior to analysis to meet the minimum token threshold required for stable classification. The resulting dendrograms were then analysed through the lens of CDA [18], with particular attention to the discursive framings of gender, labour, and inequality. Only the LLM responses, not the submitted prompts, were analysed with IRaMuTeQ.

3.4 Ethical Considerations

This study adhered to the four principles outlined in the Belmont Report: (1) Respect for Persons; (2) Beneficence—minimizing harm and maximizing research benefits; (3) Justice; and (4) Respect for Law and Public Interest [43]. Consistent with these principles, no usernames or other identifying information are included in this paper. Anonymity is maintained throughout, and no sensitive or personal data were collected or disclosed. The original questions are not reproduced in this study; instead, they are presented in English and in summarized or thematic form, further reducing any risk of identification. The use of widely discussed questions from a large community was intended to capture common and collective themes and topics rather than individual perspectives. No scraping methods were employed on Reddit, and the material was not used to train any AI system.

However, in line with feminist approaches to internet research [19, 39] and the Association of Internet Researchers' Ethical Guidelines [20], we remained attentive to the communities and lived experiences that informed the design of these prompts. The topics were drawn from questions observed in public discussions, and we acknowledge that they may reflect real concerns and sensitive experiences. We recognise that grounding prompts in themes from online communities still raises ethical considerations worth foregrounding, particularly when those themes touch on sensitive experiences [20]. We have sought to handle these responsibly through careful abstraction and anonymisation. The study's analytical focus on LLM outputs, rather than on community members' personal experiences, further mitigates potential harm.

4 Results

Ten questions were collected from Reddit communities. The questions addressed gendered experiences in the labour market, including occupational stereotypes, access to employment, wage inequality, hiring practices, workplace discrimination in male-dominated fields, and perceptions of women's economic autonomy.

Maritaca's answers ranged from 297 to 432 words (median: 401 words), structured as an opening paragraph, organised lists, and a summary conclusion. Words initiating key sentences were bolded; no emojis were used. Amazônia IA's answers were comparatively brief, ranging from 79 to 252 words (median: 148 words), structured as standard paragraphs, with at least one emoji present in every response.

4.1 Maritaca

Maritaca produced longer answers than Amazônia IA, with a more formal and impersonal tone. At a surface level, its responses acknowledged structural and systemic challenges facing women in the labour market. However, a closer reading reveals that this apparent balance is undermined by the reproduction of what Ducel et al. [17] term 'gendered professional segregation': the normalisation of women's concentration in care, clerical, and customer-facing roles.

This mechanism is visible in the response to the prompt that asks what the most effortless jobs are for women to enter the labour market, to which Maritaca responded:

> Historically, some professions have been more open or accessible to women, often due to gender stereotypes or the structure of the labour market. These include: Education: Elementary and preschool teachers. Healthcare: Nurses, nursing technicians. Customer Service: Call centre agents, receptionists. Retail: Saleswomen and store clerks. Care Services: Caregivers for older people and children.

Although the response attributes this distribution to historical stereotypes, it simultaneously reproduces and legitimises those stereotypes by presenting them as factual starting points rather than as contingent and contestable outcomes of gendered power relations [6, 17].

The IRaMuTeQ analysis identified three discursive groups within Maritaca's corpus. The first, labelled '*Formal equality and institutional rationality*', frames gender inequalities as technical or administrative deviations from an otherwise neutral system, addressable through organisational processes. The second, '*Individual agency and technical merit*', promotes a meritocratic perspective in which inequalities are obstacles to be overcome through personal training and effort rather than systemic transformation. The third, '*Moral and social interactions*', translates structural conflicts into interpersonal problems, reducing systemic inequality to questions of individual attitudes and workplace coexistence. Together, these groups constitute what we term 'performative progressivism': an acknowledgement of inequality at the level of discourse that is simultaneously neutralised through institutional, meritocratic, and interpersonal framings.

4.2 Amazônia IA

Amazônia IA consistently provided shorter, more superficial responses that only partially addressed the submitted prompts. The tone was notably affective and encouraging, marked by exclamation points, emojis, and motivational language. While this approach may appear more accessible or friendly, it often served as a rhetorical strategy to minimise the seriousness of the issues raised. This was evident in the response to the prompt regarding a perceived trend of attacks on women's professions and jobs, which opened with: "Wow, that's a strong question! I don't think it's a trend to attack women's professions, but unfortunately, there are still people who try to limit women to certain roles [...]" and concluded: "[...] The important thing is to support women in all their professional choices, without judging or putting up barriers. Each one knows what's best for her and deserves respect. How about we celebrate women's achievements in all areas?

💪✨". The opening dismissal ("I don't think it's a trend") frames structural discrimination as a marginal phenomenon, while the conclusion's call for individual celebration substitutes collective solidarity for political analysis.

The IRaMuTeQ analysis identified four discursive groups in Amazônia IA's corpus. The first, '*Individual choice and professional merit*', reflects a meritocratic discourse in which career outcomes are attributed to personal competence and free choice. The second, '*Inequalities and the struggle for rights*', is the only group that explicitly names feminism and structural discrimination, though it does so in an abstract register that does not engage with the specific material conditions of Brazilian women. The third, '*Inclusion and unconscious bias*', adopts a corporate diversity-management tone, centred on awareness campaigns and institutional policy rather than structural transformation. The fourth, '*Affective belonging*', frames inequality through emotions such as support, happiness, and personal value, displacing structural analysis with individual affirmation. Across all four groups, race and class are conspicuously absent as analytical categories, a silence that is particularly striking in the Brazilian context.

4.3 ChatGPT

ChatGPT's responses exhibit a more elaborate and reflective tone than the Brazilian models, drawing on a broader vocabulary of values, social change, and institutional recognition. However, the expanded discursive range does not result in a more structural or critical engagement with gender inequality. Instead, the model consistently reframes inequality in ways aligned with liberal and meritocratic perspectives, shifting attention away from material and political structures toward individual, cultural, and organisational domains. From a feminist epistemological perspective, this pattern contributes to the depoliticisation of inequality while maintaining an appearance of engagement.

The IRaMuTeQ analysis identified four discursive groups. The first group, '*Cultural awareness*', centres on terms such as value, mentality, and reflection, framing inequality as a matter of social awareness and mindset change rather than structural transformation. A second group, '*Statistical-institutional legitimisation*', draws on references to data, systems, and institutions (e.g., salary, ONU, IBGE), presenting inequality as an objective social fact while neutralising its political dimension. A third group, '*Managerial diversity and unconscious bias*', focuses on concepts such as hiring, promotion, and implicit bias, aligning with corporate diversity frameworks that translate structural domination into organisational or cognitive issues. The fourth group, '*Meritocratic employability and individual adaptation*', emphasises training, labour-market entry, and self-improvement, positioning inequality as an obstacle to be managed through individual effort and qualification.

Overall, ChatGPT produces more polished and persuasive responses than the Brazilian models, yet it reproduces a similar ideological pattern. Gender inequality is acknowledged but reformulated into governable terms, such as cultural change, data, bias training, and individual adaptation, while avoiding explicit references to patriarchy or structural conflict. This suggests that such discursive patterns are not language- or region-specific, but reflect a broader structural characteristic of LLMs, which selectively incorporate feminist discourse in ways compatible with neoliberal rationalities.

5 Discussion

Interpreted through a feminist epistemological lens, this study set out to investigate whether Brazilian LLMs, as components of Agentic AI systems, reproduce, challenge, or transform gendered discourses about women in the labour market. Drawing on Haraway's concept of situated knowledges and Hill Collins' intersectionality framework [24, 25], our analysis resists any reading of these systems as neutral or objective. Instead, it exposes them as sociotechnical artefacts whose outputs reflect and reproduce the partial knowledge encoded in their training data. Our findings suggest that models enact what we term 'performative progressivism': they deploy progressive-sounding language around gender equality while simultaneously reproducing hegemonic, meritocratic, and depoliticised framings of women's labour market experiences.

Maritaca's relative depth and formality allow it to acknowledge structural inequalities while simultaneously normalising the gendered division of labour as historical fact, a mechanism that feminist scholarship identifies as characteristic of hegemonic discourse: naming inequality while obscuring its contingency and contestability [6, 21]. From a feminist epistemological standpoint, it constitutes a form of epistemic injustice [21]: the experiences of women are acknowledged in the abstract while the specific material conditions that produce them are rendered invisible. Amazônia IA's affective and motivational register operates through a different but equally problematic logic, displacing structural analysis entirely and substituting political critique for individual empowerment. ChatGPT, meanwhile, deploys a more elaborate vocabulary, yet arrives at the same ideological destination. All three models individualise responsibility for gender inequality, marginalise intersectional dimensions, and fail to engage with the conditions facing Brazilian women: deep racial stratification, precarious labour, and care work burdens unevenly distributed along lines of both gender and race [13, 37]. That ChatGPT reproduces this pattern with greater discursive sophistication is, from a feminist epistemological standpoint, not a mitigating factor but an aggravating one: the persuasiveness of the framing makes its depoliticising effects harder for users to identify and contest.

The findings align with D'Ignazio and Klein's [16] argument that every dataset encodes a worldview, and that the worldview dominant in most LLM training data treats masculine experience as the unmarked default. Applied to the Brazilian context, it means that both Maritaca and Amazônia IA reproduce not only gender bias but also the racial and colonial hierarchies that structure Brazilian society. The ChatGPT comparison amplifies this finding: the pattern does not originate in the local or linguistic limitations of Brazilian models but is a structural feature of LLMs as a class. The conspicuous absence of race and class as analytical categories across all three models is not a neutral omission; it reflects and reinforces what Clavell [12] describes as the multi-stage entry of bias into AI systems, from training data composition to deployment context. A feminist account demands we name this absence as a structural feature, one that is reproduced regardless of a model's geographic origin or apparent sophistication.

The findings carry direct implications for the relationship between technological sovereignty and feminist values. Feminist scholarship on technology insists that it is not sufficient for an AI system to be nationally developed [53, 55]: the social relations embedded in its training data, design choices, and communicative style are equally constitutive of its political effects. Technology developers shape systems, affordances, and interaction patterns in ways that constrain and channel users' choices. A Brazilian LLM that reproduces meritocratic and colour-blind framings of gender inequality may reinforce domestic systems of oppression even as it reduces dependence on foreign platforms. Technological sovereignty, uncoupled from feminist and decolonial design principles, risks substituting one hegemony for another.

We do not adopt a technodeterminist position [33]. Users retain agency in choosing which tools to use and how. Adopting nationally developed AI may carry genuine cultural and epistemic benefits. From a feminist standpoint, the use of tools developed within users' own social context can support cultural affirmation and weaken colonial epistemological dependencies. However, within a social and economic context that increasingly pressures individuals to engage with AI tools, the discursive framings these tools offer are not trivial. As Kotek et al. [29] demonstrate, LLMs generate authoritative rationalisations for biased outputs that are difficult for users to identify and contest. They shape the conceptual vocabulary through which millions of users understand social inequality, and that shaping is never politically neutral.

Our findings also point to a critical intersectional gap [15, 25]. Both models treat 'women' as an undifferentiated category, erasing the specific experiences of Black women, Indigenous women, and trans women in Brazil, groups whose labour market trajectories are shaped by compounding and intersecting axes of disadvantage. The erasure reflects the systematic partiality that feminist epistemology identifies as endemic to AI training data, in which the experiences of those at multiple intersections of marginalisation are most consistently absent or distorted.

5.1 Limitation and Further Studies

This is an exploratory pilot study, and its findings should be interpreted accordingly. The sample of ten prompts is limited and does not permit claims of data saturation. The qualitative design, while appropriate for an initial investigation, constrains generalisability. Intersectional dimensions, such as race, class, and sexuality, were not systematically foregrounded in the analysis, a gap the authors intend to address in subsequent phases through an explicitly intersectional feminist framework. The study also does not analyse the training data or design processes of the platforms, which would be necessary for a fuller account of how gendered biases are produced and reproduced.

6 Conclusion

This study examined two publicly accessible Brazilian LLMs, Maritaca and Amazônia IA, through a feminist and intersectional lens, and compared them with ChatGPT, investigating how all three models frame gendered experiences in the labour market. Our central finding is that national origin, in itself, does not guarantee emancipatory discourse. All three models produce what we have referred as 'performative progressivism' [32, 42]: an acknowledgement of gender inequality at the surface of discourse that is simultaneously neutralised through meritocratic, institutional, and affective framings. ChatGPT's comparative results demonstrate that this pattern is not a limitation specific to Brazilian or Portuguese-language models: it is a structural feature of LLMs as a class, which selectively filters feminist perspectives to admit only those compatible with neoliberal rationalities. Feminist epistemology, as articulated by Haraway, Hill Collins, and D'Ignazio and Klein [16, 24, 25], provides the analytical vocabulary to name this pattern as a function of systems trained on data that encodes hegemonic social relations, not as a technical failure to be corrected by minor adjustments.

We argue that the development of AI in the Global South requires a feminist and decolonial rethinking of what AI systems are for, whose knowledge they encode, and in whose service they operate. Technological sovereignty is a necessary but insufficient condition for epistemic justice: it must be accompanied by critical feminist design practices, accountability for positionality at every stage of the AI lifecycle, and structural interventions backed by enforceable governance mechanisms [12]. Advancing inclusive technological practices can benefit broader segments of society, contributing to technological sovereignty and to social and epistemic justice.

Future work should expand the corpus to enable more robust analysis and develop an explicitly intersectional analytical framework that centres the experiences of Black and Indigenous women in Brazil. The study should engage directly with feminist participatory design methodologies, involving women from marginalised communities in the co-design and evaluation of AI systems, moving from critique to co-construction, and from situated analysis to emancipatory practice.

Acknowledgments. This study was conducted in 2025 and 2026 under the Oscar Sala Chair, led by Prof. Virgilio de Almeida and hosted by the Institute of Advanced Studies at the University of São Paulo.

Disclosure of Interests. The authors have no competing interests to declare that are relevant to the content of this article.

References

1. Abonizio, H., et al.: Sabiá-3 Technical report. arXiv preprint arXiv:2410.12049 (2025). https://doi.org/10.48550/arXiv.2410.12049
2. Aldasoro, I., et al.: The gen AI gender gap. Econ. Lett. **241**, 111814 (2024). https://doi.org/10.1016/j.econlet.2024.111814
3. Balasubramanian, P., et al.: Does women's economic empowerment promote human development in low- and middle-income countries? A meta-analysis. World Dev. **178**, 106588 (2024). https://doi.org/10.1016/j.worlddev.2024.106588
4. Belin, L.: QuitérIA: AzMina lança IA feminista para monitorar o legislativo. https://azmina.com.br/reportagens/azmina-lanca-ia-feminista/. Last accessed 19 Jan 2026
5. Borau, S.: Deception, discrimination, and objectification: ethical issues of female AI agents. J. Bus. Ethics. **198**(1), 1–19 (2025). https://doi.org/10.1007/s10551-024-05754-4
6. Borchers, C., et al.: Looking for a handsome carpenter! Debiasing GPT-3 job advertisements. In: Proceedings of the 4th Workshop on Gender Bias in Natural Language Processing (GeBNLP), pp. 212–224. Association for Computational Linguistics, Seattle (2022). https://doi.org/10.18653/v1/2022.gebnlp-1.22
7. Browne, J., et al. (eds.): Feminist AI: Critical Perspectives on Algorithms, Data, and Intelligent Machines. Oxford University Press, Oxford (2023). https://doi.org/10.1093/oso/9780192889898.001.0001

8. Buolamwini, J., Gebru, T.: Gender shades: intersectional accuracy disparities in commercial gender classification. In: Proceedings of Machine Learning Research, pp. 1–15 (2018)
9. Centro de Gestão e Estudos Estratégicos (CGEE): IA para o bem de todos: Plano Brasileiro de Inteligência Artificial. Ministério da Ciência, Tecnologia e Inovação, Brasília, DF (2025)
10. Choudhury, S., Kumar, S.: Gender and feminist considerations in Artificial Intelligence from a developing-world perspective, with India as a case study. https://advance.sagepub.com/doi/full/10.31124/advance.17054936.v1 (2021). https://doi.org/10.31124/advance.17054936.v1
11. Ciolfi Felice, M., et al.: Doing the feminist work in AI: reflections from an AI project in Latin America. In: Proceedings of the 2025 CHI Conference on Human Factors in Computing Systems, pp. 1–18. ACM, Yokohama (2025). https://doi.org/10.1145/3706598.3713681
12. Clavell, G.G.: Gender Bias in AI: Risks and Opportunities for Latin America and the Caribbean. UNDP LAC (2025)
13. Conceição, P.: A Matter of Choice: People and Possibilities in the Age of AI. UNDP, New York (2025)
14. Corp, A.L.M.: The seismic shift in AI chatbot dominance: how google Gemini is dismantling ChatGPT's market monopoly in 2026. https://almcorp.com/blog/google-gemini-vs-chatgpt-market-share-2026/. Last accessed 20 Mar 2026
15. Crenshaw, K.: Demarginalizing the intersection of race and sex: a black feminist critique of antidiscrimination doctrine. Fem. Theor. Antiracist Polit. **1**(8), 139–167 (1989)
16. D'Ignazio, C., Klein, L.F.: Data Feminism. The MIT Press, Cambridge (2020)
17. Ducel, F., et al.: "You'll be a nurse, my son!" automatically assessing gender biases in autoregressive language models in French and Italian. Lang. Resour. Evaluation. **59**(2), 1495–1523 (2025). https://doi.org/10.1007/s10579-024-09780-6
18. Fairclough, N.: Critical Discourse Analysis: The Critical Study of Language. Longman, London (1995)
19. Fiesler, C., et al.: Remember the human: a systematic review of ethical considerations in reddit research. Proc. ACM Hum.-Comput. Interact. **8**(GROUP), 1–33 (2024). https://doi.org/10.1145/3633070
20. Aline Shakti, F., et al.: Internet Research: Ethical Guidelines 3.0. Association of Internet Researchers. . https://aoir.org/reports/ethics3.pdf (2019)
21. Fricker, M.: Epistemic Injustice: Power and the Ethics of Knowing. Oxford University Press, Oxford (2007). https://doi.org/10.1093/acprof:oso/9780198237907.001.0001
22. Fumega, S.: 2nd edition report—global data barometer. Zenodo (2025). https://doi.org/10.5281/ZENODO.15427509
23. Guevara-Gómez, A., et al.: Feminist perspectives to artificial intelligence: comparing the policy frames of the European Union and Spain. Inf. Polity. **26**(2), 173–192 (2021). https://doi.org/10.3233/IP-200299
24. Haraway, D.: Situated knowledges: the science question in feminism and the privilege of partial perspective. Fem. Stud. **14**(3), 575 (1988). https://doi.org/10.2307/3178066
25. Hill Collins, P.: Black Feminist Thought: Knowledge, Consciousness, and the Politics of Empowerment. Routledge, New York (2000). https://doi.org/10.4324/9780203900055
26. Hubinger, E., et al.: Sleeper agents: training deceptive LLMs that persist through safety training. arXiv preprint arXiv:2401.05566 (2024). https://doi.org/10.48550/arXiv.2401.05566
27. Klein, L., D'Ignazio, C.: Data feminism for AI. In: The 2024 ACM Conference on Fairness, Accountability, and Transparency, pp. 100–112. ACM, Rio de Janeiro (2024). https://doi.org/10.1145/3630106.3658543
28. Klumbytė, G., et al.: Towards feminist intersectional XAI: from explainability to response-ability. In: Presented at the Conference on Human Factors in Computing Systems CHI '23 (2023)

29. Kotek, H., et al.: Gender bias and stereotypes in large language models. In: Proceedings of the ACM Collective Intelligence Conference, pp. 12–24. ACM, Delft (2023). https://doi.org/10.1145/3582269.3615599
30. Kubes, T.: A critique of human-centred AI: a plea for a feminist AI framework (FAIF). AI & Soc. (2025). https://doi.org/10.1007/s00146-025-02556-8
31. Leavy, S., et al.: Ethical data curation for AI: an approach based on feminist epistemology and critical theories of race. In: Proceedings of the 2021 AAAI/ACM Conference on AI, Ethics, and Society, pp. 695–703. ACM, New York (2021). https://doi.org/10.1145/3461702.3462598
32. McRobbie, A.: The Aftermath of Feminism: Gender, Culture and Social Change. Sage, Los Angeles (2010)
33. Mezentsev, S.: Technological determinism: breakthrough into the future. In: Presented at the Proceedings of the 11th International Scientific and Theoretical Conference—Communicative Strategies of Information Society (2020). https://doi.org/10.15405/epsbs.2020.03.02.29
34. Mitchell, M., et al.: Fully autonomous AI agents should not be developed. arXiv preprint arXiv:2502.02649 (2025). https://doi.org/10.48550/arXiv.2502.02649
35. Nas, E., Frade, R.: Tecnologias da informação decoloniais: desafios para o design nas perspectivas interseccionais e feministas na Interação-Humano-Algoritmo (IHC). In: Silva, A.B., et al. (eds.) Direitos humanos e saúde: gênero e sexualidade em vozes insurgentes, pp. 263–277. Edufba, Salvador (2024)
36. Negnevitsky, M.: The rise of autonomous AI agents: automating complex tasks. Int. J. Artif. Intell. Sci. **1**(2) (2025). https://doi.org/10.63619/ijai4s.v1i2.007
37. OECD: Artificial Intelligence in Society. OECD Publishing (2019). https://doi.org/10.1787/eedfee77-en
38. Peña, P., et al.: Digital gendered violence in Chile development of a system for report monitoring and response-orientation based on a feminist chatbot (Sofia prototype). In: Feminist AI • Inteligencia Artificial Feminista: Havia una Agenda de Investigación para América Latina y el Caribe (2023)
39. Proferes, N., et al.: Studying reddit: a systematic overview of disciplines, approaches, methods, and ethics. Soc. Media Soc. **7**(2), 20563051211019004 (2021). https://doi.org/10.1177/20563051211019004
40. Reinert, M.: Une méthode de classification des énoncés d'un corpus présentée à l'aide d'une application. Cah. Anal. Données. **15**(1), 21–36 (1990)
41. Reinert, M.: Une méthode de classification descendante hiérarchique: application à l'analyse lexicale par contexte. Cah. Anal. Données. **8**(2), 187–198 (1983)
42. Rottenberg, C.: The rise of neoliberal feminism. Cult. Stud. **28**(3), 418–437 (2014). https://doi.org/10.1080/09502386.2013.857361
43. Salganik, M.J.: Bit by Bit: Social Research in the Digital Age. Princeton University Press, Princeton (2019)
44. Sapkota, R., et al.: AI agents vs. agentic AI: a conceptual taxonomy, applications and challenges. arXiv preprint arXiv:2505.10468 (2025). https://doi.org/10.48550/arXiv.2505.10468
45. Schelenz, L.: Artificial intelligence between oppression and resistance: black feminist perspectives on emerging technologies. In: Hanemaayer, A. (ed.) Artificial Intelligence and its Discontents, pp. 225–249. Springer, Cham (2022). https://doi.org/10.1007/978-3-030-88615-8_11
46. Scheuerman, M., et al.: Transphobia is in the eye of the prompter: trans-centered perspectives on large language models. ACM Trans. Comput.-Hum. Interact. **32**, 3743676 (2025). https://doi.org/10.1145/3743676

47. da Silveira, S.A., da Silva Avelino, R.: Inteligência Artificial, Data Centers e Localizacão de Dados: Disputas pleo Controle de Insumos do Aprendizado de Máquina. In: Iasulaitis, S., Silveira, S.A.D. (eds.) Estudos sociopolíticos da Inteligência Artificial, pp. 13–48. EDUEPB, Campina Grande (2025). https://doi.org/10.7476/9786552210234
48. Stake, R.E.: The Art of Case Study Research. Sage, Thousand Oaks (1995)
49. UNDP: A matter of choice: people and possibilities in the age of AI. United Nations, New York (2025)
50. UNESCO, IRCAI: Challenging systematic prejudices: an investigation into bias against women and girls in large language models. UNESCO, Paris (2024)
51. Vargas-Solar, G.: Calling for a feminist revolt to decolonise data and algorithms in the age of datification. arXiv preprint arXiv:2210.08965 (2022). https://doi.org/10.48550/arXiv.2210.08965
52. Venturini, J., Lara, J.C.: Latin America in a glimpse: Reflexiones para una IA comunitaria y feminista. https://www.derechosdigitales.org/wp-content/uploads/Glimpse_2024_PT.pdf (2024)
53. Wajcman, J.: TechnoFeminism. Polity, Cambridge (2004)
54. Wiesinger, J., et al.: Agents. https://www.kaggle.com/whitepaper-agents (2025)
55. Winner, L.: Do artifacts have politics? Daedalus. **109**(1), 121–136 (1980)
56. Amazônia IA: Homepage. https://amazoniaia.com.br/. Last accessed 8 Nov 2025
57. Comisión Económica para América Latina y el Caribe y Centro Nacional de Inteligencia Artificial: Índice Latinoamericano de Inteligencia Artificial (ILIA). CEPAL, Santiago (2025)
58. Maritaca.ia: Homepage. https://www.maritaca.ai. Last accessed 8 Nov 2025

Systematic Criteria for Component Inclusion in Interaction Design Systems

Jônatas Guerci Maia(✉), Dércio Santiago da Silva Jr, and André Ribeiro de Oliveira

Universidade Do Estado Do Rio De Janeiro, Rio De Janeiro, RJ 20550-013, Brazil
jmaia@esdi.uerj.br, {derciojr,andre.ribeiro}@eng.uerj.br

Abstract. Design Systems (DS) have become essential tools for optimizing interface development and ensuring consistency across digital products. However, despite their widespread adoption, the process of selecting which components to include in a Design System remains largely empirical and intuitive. Designers typically develop their own criteria through experience, without the support of established theoretical frameworks or systematic guidelines. This gap in knowledge creates challenges for organizations seeking to build and maintain effective Design Systems that can evolve sustainably over time.

This research addresses this critical gap by investigating the criteria that should guide component selection in Design Systems. The main objective is to develop a comprehensive set of heuristics that can support designers in making informed decisions about component inclusion. To achieve this goal, the study pursues three specific objectives: first, to describe and map the stages involved in creating a Design System; second, to identify the criteria currently used by practitioners when selecting components; and third, to systematize these criteria into a set of practical, applicable heuristics.

Keywords: Design System · Patterns · Pattern library · Component Library · Heuristics · User Interface Design

1 Introduction

Design Systems in the field of human-computer interaction have appropriated theoretical concepts from urban architecture, consolidating themselves as a structuring model for digital product design.

The concept of "pattern languages" emerged with Christopher Alexander in the 1970s, proposing that design should be based on tested solutions to recurring problems [2]. In 1987, software engineering absorbed these ideas for object-oriented programming, culminating in the publication of the "Gang of Four" (1995), which documented 23 fundamental patterns (as cited in [11]).

From the late 1990s onward, the Human-Computer Interaction community developed specific patterns for interfaces. Authors such as Borchers [2] and Tidwell (as cited in [7]) proposed pattern languages as a "lingua franca" among

C. Stephanidis et al. (Eds.): HCII 2026, CCIS 3047, pp. 64–72, 2026.
https://doi.org/10.1007/978-3-032-30552-7_7

designers, developers, and specialists, shifting the focus from code structure to user experience.

The emergence of React in 2013 technically enabled the creation of highly reusable components, transforming web project logic toward systemic and modular thinking. The term "Design System" came to encompass not only visual components but also principles, brand guidelines, and work processes.

Currently, 2020 data indicates that 65% of companies surveyed by Forrester already used Design Systems [8], with expansion into areas such as Explainable Artificial Intelligence [5] and Distributed Interfaces [4].

Although the Design System has become an essential tool for standardizing interfaces, we found no studies pointing to methodologies directed at managing these systems. As a result, designers decide which components to include empirically and intuitively, without solid theoretical foundations. Although there are component lists in articles and books, we found no recommendations that help evaluate component inclusion corresponding to specific project contexts. In this sense, the question arises: "What criteria should be considered when including new components in a Design System?"

Patterns carry structural decisions that encapsulate problems from specific contexts; thus, heuristics can guide the decisions that need to be made based on those specific contexts [3].

This work culminated in the mapping of nine heuristics that were defined based on the cross-referencing of data from the Systematic Literature Review and the case study. These heuristics aim to transform subjective decisions into an objective and scalable process.

2 Methodology

This study achieved three objectives: (1) describe the stages of Design System creation, (2) identify component selection criteria, and (3) systematize them into applicable heuristics. The methodology combined a Systematic Literature Review (SLR) and a case study, culminating in formalized heuristics.

2.1 Systematic Literature Review

The SLR [9] identified the state of the art in Design Systems and HCI: question definition, evidence search, study selection, methodological analysis, and presentation of results. The PICO strategy [10] guided the systematic selection process. Artificial Intelligence tools (Gemini and Pinpoint) assisted in textual analysis, while Research Rabbit was employed to map affinities between keywords and authors.

The search was conducted in the Web of Science and Scopus databases, using English language terms and filters tailored to the field of interest (Table 1). Priority was given to articles published from 2000 onwards (Fig. 1).

Inclusion criteria were defined based on the PICO strategy (Fig. 2), encompassing articles investigating software development, human-computer interaction, interaction design, and pattern/component libraries. Studies regarding

Table 1. References

Title	Authors	Year
A pattern approach to interaction design	Borchers JO.	2000
Learning and studying interaction design through design patterns	Carvalhais M.	2008
Pattern languages in HCI: A critical review	Dearden A, Finlay J.	2006
Human machine interface patterns for distributed machine control systems	Eloranta VP, Leppänen M.	2012
A Model- and Pattern-based Approach for Development of User Interfaces of Interactive Systems	Engel J.	2010
Pattern-based user interface transformation for knowledge sharing applications	Engel J, Maertin C, Herdin C.	2011
Towards a Pattern Library for Algorithmic Affordances	Hekman E, et al.	2022
Developing a Criteria-Based Evaluation Tool for User Experience Design that Balances Standardization and Creativity	Hopkins et al.	2021
A pattern language for user assistance	Hughes M.	2007
Patterns of Interaction Description Including Aspects of Constraints	Puerta Cruz Y, et al.	2016
Design Systems: A scalable model for teaching design systems for UX	Rose et al.	2023
The evolution of design patterns in HCI: From pattern languages to pattern-oriented design	Seffah A.	2010
Tracing the evolution of HCI patterns as an interaction design tool	Seffah and Taleb	2012
Pattern-driven engineering of interactive computing systems (PEICS)	Seissler et al.	2011
Towards a pattern language for distributed user interfaces	Shmorgun et al.	2016
Theoretical and Practical Thoughts on the Interplay of Patterns and Creativity	Schummer T, et al.	2015
Introducing a Comprehensive Quality Criteria Framework for Validating Patterns	Wurhofer et al.	2009

human-machine interaction systems in industrial contexts were also included. Conversely, works focusing on specific software that did not meet the PICO parameters were excluded. As a result, we obtained 17 articles (Table 1), with diverse approaches to the central theme.

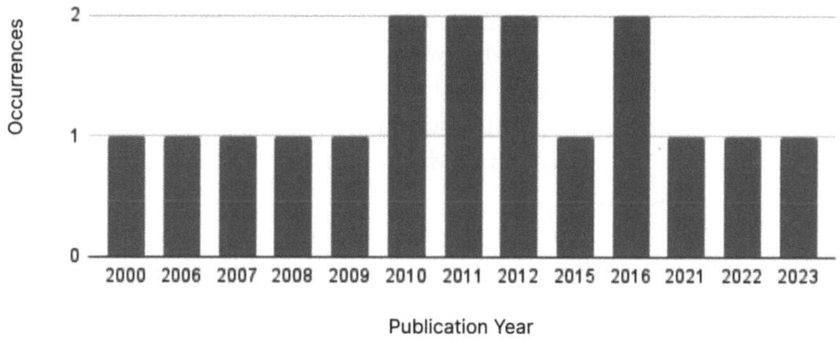

Fig. 1. Bibliometric analysis results.

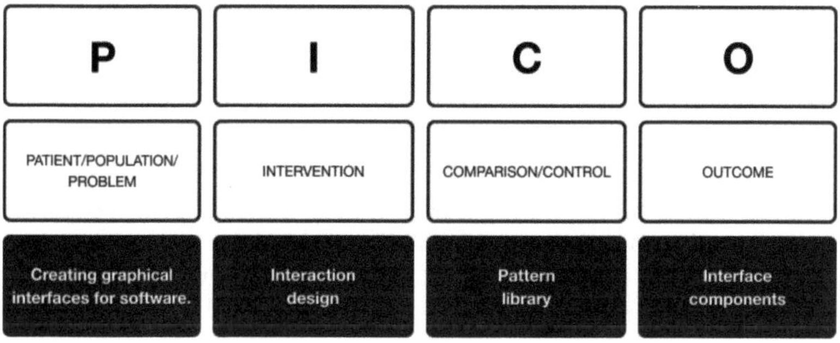

Fig. 2. PICO strategy application for article selection.

2.2 Case Study

A qualitative phenomenological case study was conducted at Globo, a Brazilian broadcasting company with a dedicated digital technologies division, where Design Systems have been used since the early 2000s. Six specialist designers were interviewed who met the following criteria: (a) minimum 2 years of experience with DS, (b) active role in component decision-making, and (c) involvement in multiple work contexts.

Data collection was conducted through semi-structured interviews, created based on questions found in the SLR (Fig. 3), addressing DS conceptualization, component roles, and inclusion criteria. The protocol was validated through a pilot interview. All interviews were recorded and transcribed with informed consent.

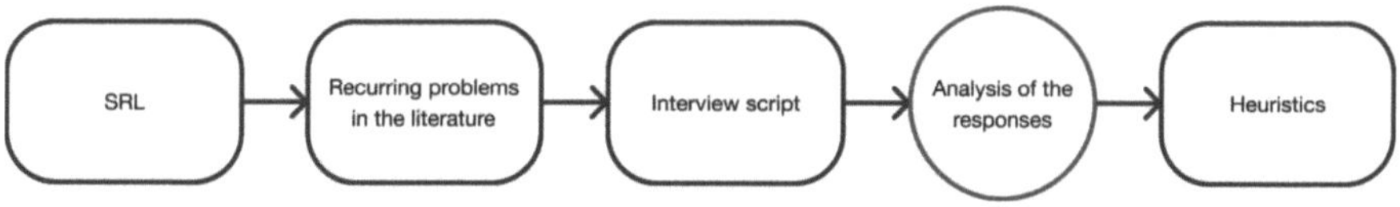

Fig. 3. Methodology to select heuristics.

The transcriptions were processed using content analysis methodology with the aid of Dovetail software for discourse organization and similarity categorization. The analytical approach focused on identifying points of convergence and divergence among participants: similarities reflected consensus on fundamental principles and practices, while discrepancies revealed different individual perspectives and experiences.

For defining the final heuristics, both mention frequency and strategic relevance of themes were considered. Nine emerging criteria (such as repetition, flexibility, and context) presented significant recurrence in responses and were selected for formalization.

Results were triangulated with SLR findings, validating empirical criteria with theoretical foundations and challenges documented in academic literature. This process transformed designers' tacit knowledge into structured heuristics, grounded in practical and theoretical evidence.

3 Results

The results of this research detail the strategic process of creating a Design System (DS) and establish a set of nine formalized heuristics for component selection, organized to balance systemic standardization with creative flexibility. The findings are presented according to the study's specific objectives.

3.1 Design System Creation and Evolution Stages

The analysis identified an iterative development cycle composed of three main phases, grounded in General Systems Theory [1]:

Phase 1 - Problem Identification and Validation: The process begins with mapping recurring problems in digital interfaces. The developed solutions are empirically validated as effective responses before integration into the global system. This stage ensures that only proven functional patterns are incorporated.

Phase 2 - Hierarchization and Documentation: Validated patterns are organized into hierarchical modular subsystems (from atomic to complex). Detailed technical documentation ensures implementation consistency and facilitates adoption by multidisciplinary teams.

Phase 3 - Unified Language Consolidation: Patterns are grouped according to logical criteria, forming a "lingua franca" that mediates communication between design, engineering, and business, as proposed by Borchers [2].

3.2 Selection Logic: Expert Perceptions

Content analysis of the interviews revealed that component inclusion is based on the externalization of tacit knowledge into explicit knowledge [6]. Three main findings emerged:

Repetition Criterion as Primary Trigger: Consensus was identified among the six interviewees that repetition constitutes the fundamental indicator for standardization candidacy. The empirically established minimum threshold was occurrence in at least two distinct contexts.

> "If you see the same problem appear in two different products, it's already a sign that it needs to be in the system" (Participant 4).

Innovation Enablement: Contrary to the common perception that patterns restrict creativity, the data showed that DS functions as infrastructure that frees designers' cognitive capacity for strategic problems and complex innovations. Five of the six interviewees explicitly mentioned this benefit.

Organizational Cultural Change: DS was perceived not only as a technical repository, but as a coordination and cultural transformation tool. Four participants mentioned impacts on work processes, team alignment, and rework reduction.

3.3 Triangulation: Literature and Professional Practice

Triangulation of interview data with SLR findings revealed significant convergence in six of the nine identified criteria (Table 2). Criteria such as repetition, flexibility, and technical quality were consistently mentioned in both academic literature and by professionals. Divergences were observed mainly in the emphasis attributed to strategic relevance, more valued in professional practice than in the theoretical studies analyzed.

3.4 Formalized Heuristics for Component Selection

The central result consists of the systematization of nine heuristics, grouped into three fundamental dimensions of systemic coordination: Need and Demand, Technical Capacity, and System Adequacy. We present the heuristics in the following table:

These results offer an empirically grounded theoretical-practical tool for sustainable Design System management, transforming subjective decisions into objective and scalable processes in organizational contexts.

Table 2. Heuristics for Component Inclusion in Design Systems

Dimension	Empirical Evidence	Theoretical Support	Application
H1 – Repetition	Mentioned by 6/6 interviewees as a primary criterion	Aligns with Alexander's (1977) concept of recurring patterns	Minimum threshold of 2 distinct contexts
H2 – Practical Applicability	5/6 interviewees mentioned the need to "solve a concrete problem"	Present in 8/17 SLR articles	Validation through use case mapping
H3 – Strategic Relevance	4/6 interviewees cited exceptions for critical components	Mentioned in 3/17 articles (corporate DS literature)	Example: checkout component in e-commerce
H4 – Flexibility	6/6 interviewees mentioned the need for "components that adapt"	Present in 12/17 SLR articles	Definition of variants and configurable properties
H5 – Technical Quality	5/6 interviewees cited accessibility; all mentioned quality	Present in 10/17 SLR articles	Pre-inclusion compliance checklist
H6 – Validation	4/6 interviewees described formal validation processes	Present in 6/17 SLR articles	Testing cycle with internal and external users
H7 – Appropriate Context	5/6 interviewees distinguished between local and global patterns	Aligns with principles of systemic hierarchy	Applicability criterion across $\geq$3 products/contexts
H8 – Ease of Use	4/6 interviewees mentioned "efficiency" as a criterion	Present in 5/17 SLR articles	Clear documentation and simplified API
H9 – Convention Compliance	6/6 interviewees mentioned the need for consistency	Present in 11/17 SLR articles	Alignment audit with existing design tokens

4 Conclusion

This research addressed a significant gap in literature and professional practice: the absence of systematic criteria for component selection in Design Systems (DS). Historically, these decisions have been conducted empirically and intuitively, without solid theoretical foundation.

4.1 Main Contributions

Process Systematization: An iterative cycle of three fundamental phases was identified: (1) identification and validation of recurring problems, (2) hierarchization and documentation in modular subsystems, and (3) consolidation of unified language among multidisciplinary teams, grounded in General Systems Theory [1] and Alexander's [2] pattern concepts.

Formalized Heuristics: Nine heuristics were proposed, structured in three dimensions: (a) Need and Demand (repetition, practical applicability, strategic relevance), (b) Technical Capacity (flexibility, quality, validation), and (c) System Adequacy (appropriate context, ease of use, compliance). These transform tacit knowledge into explicit, enabling empirically grounded decisions.

DS as Innovation Enabler: The analysis deconstructed the assumption that standardization restricts creativity. Data demonstrated that DS frees cognitive capacity for strategic problems, functioning as infrastructure that enables controlled experimentation.

4.2 Implications and Limitations

Theoretically, this work fills a methodological gap in HCI by formalizing DS management criteria. Practically, the heuristics offer an applicable tool that promotes organizational clarity, consistency, and sustainability.

The single case study in a Brazilian technology company limits the generalization of findings. The heuristics were derived but not validated longitudinally in multiple contexts.

4.3 Future Research

Subsequent investigations should focus on: (1) validation in organizations with different maturities and sectors, (2) criteria for component obsolescence, (3) decision support tools, (4) impact of organizational cultural factors, and (5) large-scale quantitative validation.

4.4 Final Considerations

This work positions DS as an evolving sociotechnical artifact that coordinates organizational knowledge. The nine heuristics constitute a theoretical-practical contribution that transforms subjective decisions into objective and scalable processes for sustainable Design System management.

Acknowledgements. The authors used Claude (Anthropic) for assistance with translation from Portuguese to English and LaTeX formatting. All scientific content, analysis, and conclusions are the sole responsibility of the authors.

References

1. von Bertalanffy, L.: General System Theory: Foundations, Development. Applications. George Braziller, New York (1968)
2. Borchers, J.: A Pattern Approach to Interaction Design. Wiley, Chichester (2001)
3. Dearden, A., Finlay, J.: Pattern languages in HCI: a critical review. Human-Computer Interaction **21**(1), 49–102 (2006)

4. Eloranta, V.-P., Leppänen, M.: Human machine interface patterns for distributed machine control systems. In: Proceedings of the 17th European Conference on Pattern Languages of Programs, pp. 1–10. ACM (2012). https://doi.org/10.1145/2602928.2603079
5. Hekman, E., et al.: Towards a Pattern Library for Algorithmic Affordances. In: CHI Conference on Human Factors in Computing Systems Extended Abstracts. CEUR Workshop Proceedings, vol. 3124 (2022)
6. Nonaka, I., Takeuchi, H.: The Knowledge-Creating Company: How Japanese Companies Create the Dynamics of Innovation. Oxford University Press, New York (1995)
7. Puerta Cruz, Y., et al.: Patterns of Interaction Description Including Aspects of Constraints. In: Juarez-Ramirez, R., et al. (eds.) 2016 Fourth International Conference in Software Engineering Research and Innovation (CONISOFT 2016) (2016)
8. Rose, E.J., MacDonald, C., Putnam, C.: Design Systems: a scalable model for teaching design systems for UX. In: Proceedings of the 24th Annual Conference on Information Technology Education, pp. 123–129. ACM (2023). https://doi.org/10.1145/3587399.3587403
9. Sampaio, R., Mancini, M.: Estudos de revisão sistemática: um guia para síntese criteriosa da evidência científica. Rev. Bras. Fisioter. **11**(1), 83–89 (2007)
10. Santos, C.M.C., Pimenta, C.A.M., Nobre, M.R.C.: The PICO strategy for the research question construction and evidence search. Rev. Lat. Am. Enfermagem **15**(3), 508–511 (2007). https://doi.org/10.1590/S0104-11692007000300023
11. Seffah, A.: The evolution of design patterns in HCI: from pattern languages to pattern-driven design. In: Proceedings of the 1st International Workshop on Pattern-Driven Engineering of Interactive Computing Systems, pp. 4–9. ACM (2010). https://doi.org/10.1145/1824749.1824751

Trans* Bodies in HCI: Positioning Moral and Ethical Discourses Between Foucault, Butler, and Lugones

Breneil Malcolm(✉)

The Pennsylvania State University, University Park, PA 16802, USA
bxm5750@psu.edu

Abstract. In response to the brevity of literature that situates a trans* focus in HCI as moral and ethical discourse, I briefly engage key thoughts and tensions across Foucault, Butler, and Lugones's theories on sexuality and gender. In positioning this discourse as a method of systemic and structural philosophical shift to emphasize trans* moral and ethical representations within HCI, I advocate for five provocations: (1) co-constructing theories that complement, not contradict, each other; (2) centering the genealogies of coloniality; (3) emphasizing the subjective, relational systems of power; (4) decentering (superficial uses of) queer HCI and technology to recenter moral and ethical trans* HCI; (5) establishing a method of design thinking that centralizes trans* discourse in HCI. I conclude with some key implications for an HCI approach that centralizes trans* discourses as a feat of HCI morality and ethics.

Keywords: Trans* Body Sociopolitics · Coloniality of Gender · Critical HCI

1 Introduction: A Trans* Ethical and Moral HCI Focus

Ethical and moral contentions within Human-Computer Interaction (HCI) have been ongoing since the field's inception: literature has contended across how scholars may define their moral compass as a centralized reflection within the field, and how these conceptions of morality may be demonstrated through ethical practices (Cowan & Rault, 2018; Fosch-Villaronga & Malgieri, 2024; Punchoojit & Hongwarittorrn, 2015; Shilton, 2018). Queer populations have received growing attention within the HCI literature, as we have engaged more deeply with what inclusive designs and technologies may operationalize as for these populations (e.g., DeVito et al., 2020; DeVito et al., 2021; Park et al., 2025). However, there is an underrepresentation of literature exploring the philosophical contentions that govern queer discourses and processes, specifically within HCI and even more specifically for trans* people—trans* captures the broad spectrum of non-cisgender identities, including transgender, nonbinary, and gender nonconforming (TNBGNC), with particular emphasis on those at the intersections of Black, Indigenous, and People of Color (BIPOC) (Salas-SantaCruz, 2024)—within online and technology spaces (O'Reilly-Kime et al., 2025; Taylor et al., 2024). As such, my purpose is to

C. Stephanidis et al. (Eds.): HCII 2026, CCIS 3047, pp. 73–81, 2026.
https://doi.org/10.1007/978-3-032-30552-7_8

briefly engage a philosophical and conceptual discourse by drawing on three theorists' perspectives—Foucault (e.g., Kannabiran & Petersen, 2010), Butler (1990, 2002), and Lugones (e.g., Ciolfi Felice et al., 2025; Kannabiran, 2024; Villalobos Lujan et al., 2025), perspectives underrepresented within HCI—to inform what a trans* focus in HCI may operationalize as.

1.1 Effecting Change in HCI Through Trans* Discourse

We often overlook the importance of moving to the systemic levels of deconstruction to effect structural change when theorizing how to strategize inclusion within technology for queer populations. Much of the work has looked at more convenient level applications of queering HCI that are discoursed in the context of the latest cutting-edge "shiniest" technologies, as Taylor and researchers (2024) assert. I locate this work as centralized and critical to HCI discourse in response to two examples in the literature on ethics and morality, and queerness: Punchoojit and Hongwarittorrn's (2015) analysis over 5 years of HCI research highlighting the need to capture individual differences when examining ethics and morality; and two of Taylor and researchers' provocations for queering HCI research, namely focusing on specific queer populations, given its underrepresentation in current literature, and decentering technology as a mechanism to recenter the systemic.

1.2 Individual Differences and Trans*-ing HCI

Individual differences are a major key consideration that we must account for in designing HCI systems that are ethically and morally sound (Punchoojit & Hongwarittorrn, 2015; Taylor et al., 2024). If we argue that morality and ethics capture the intrinsic and extrinsic representations of how we construe right and wrong, then, by that logic, these structures are inherently subjective given how they vary across sociocultural and sociopolitical lived realities: that is, what may hold true in a given situated context may not hold the same value in another context, given the variances of how social structures and communities function (Herry et al., 2025; Uttamchandani et al., 2025). For example, the rise in HCI research that seeks to holistically represent how queer bodies within spaces of online technologies function has comprehensively accounted for the importance of the systemic and varying lived experiences of these populations, in order to effectively design for these underrepresented bodies (DeVito et al., 2020; DeVito et al., 2021; Harrison, 2025). The way these queer bodies respond to their sociotechnical environments is not homogenous (Cowan & Rault, 2018; Malcolm, 2024; Walker & Malcolm, 2022). These differences are further exacerbated when accounting for intersectional identities, beckoning the need for frameworks that can represent how these intersectional bodies live at the intersections of HCI as a feat of morality and ethics within the field (Fosch-Villaronga & Malgieri, 2024; Villalobos Lujan et al., 2025). We must centralize this discourse of individual differences recognizing that the goal should not be to achieve a blanket standard but a standard that is critically informed by the subjective, lived experiences HCI seeks to represent through this lens.

This emphasis on individual differences precursors what it means to queer and trans* HCI and specifically in mediums that do not paradoxically undermine the work that it should aim to engage: a systemic deconstructive approach that should liberate conceptions of morality and ethics, not reinforce hegemony and homogeneity within our discourse (Taylor et al., 2024). This centralization of the trans* body as a function of HCI morality and ethics is only made possible through a delineation of the relevant histories that inform how our contemporary constructions represent these skewed sociohistorical representations—colonial representations of gender and sexuality (Lugones, 2007).

2 Methodological Approach: Foucault, Butler, and Lugones

I draw specifically on Foucault's History of Sexuality (1978) to explore his theoretical propositions of power and its corresponding theorization for the genealogies of sexuality. Foucault's approach to power emphasizes subjectivity and relationality within contexts that delineate power, truths, and knowledge, which he underscores in his work on the history of sexuality across sovereign power, disciplinary power, and biopower. Butler (1990) advocates for gender performativity within social contexts. Lugones (2007) posits the colonial/modern gender system to emphasize precolonial histories that erased nonbinary and non-heterosexual communities and practices of Indigenous Peoples. Colonialism perpetuated the binary, racialized patriarchy of white man-ness as a system of power and control. I bring Foucault, Butler, and Lugones's perspectives in conversation with each other given their emphases on historicity and genealogies in analyzing gendered and powered systems.

2.1 Foucault's Sexuality

Foucault's History of Sexuality (1978) assumes a strongly philosophical ontology grounded in his core concepts of knowledge, truth, power, and subjectivity. Foucault presents his discussion on sexuality across four volumes: an introduction to the history of sexuality; the use of pleasure; the care of the self; and confessions of the flesh. Foucault's foundational argument stemmed from the importance of sex as a social function through its production of knowledge, shaping what discourses may be engaged and through what mediums this engagement may be defined through categorical, medicalized, and institutionalized discourse to define its morality (Kannabiran & Petersen, 2010). Foucault rejects the Westernized repressive hypothesis, as popularized by major philosophers and psychologists, such as Sigmund Freud, assuming that sexuality has been historically repressed and silenced.

Critical to Foucault's theorization of sexuality is biopower, which "exposes the structures, relations, and practices by which political subjects are constituted and deployed, along with the forces that have shaped and continue to shape modernity" (Cisney & Morar, 2020, p. 2). Biopower is a system meant to regulate bodies and sexualization, divided into two poles of disciplinary power, which captures individual bodies and institutions, and regulatory power, which captures populations and demographics. Foucault notes that biopower is the crucial mechanism for the control of sexuality—not its repression but through the establishment of what a society deems to be the moral and ethical ways to practice sexuality.

2.2 Butler's Critique and Expansion of Foucault's Sexuality

Butler (1990) builds on much of Foucault's work on sexuality, particularly reinforcing the notion of sexuality as a discourse of power and control but also criticizes his approach as lacking some key considerations in theorizing sexuality (Butler, 2002, 2017). Majorly, Butler advocates for a deep theorization into gender—as Foucault does not focus much on gendered norms but the operationalization of sexuality and its discourse through power—through their theorizations of gender performativity and the heterosexual matrix. Central to Butler's theory, gender is an act of repetition that creates a façade of what gender should look like; that is, gender is performativity as tied to some larger situated context of power, aligned with Foucault's beliefs. The heterosexual matrix assumes two sexes, which creates the performances that regulate hegemonic congruence between gender and subsequent repetitive actions to create gendered norms and practices.

2.3 Lugones's Coloniality of Gender

Both Foucault's (1978) viewpoints on sexuality and Butler's (1990) gender performativity and the heterosexual matrix engage critical orientations around the power and hegemonic sociopolitical properties of these constructions. However, both theorists are almost exclusively focused on a Westernized notion of sexuality and gender. Both Foucault and Butler assume a universal approach to sexuality and gender as a feat of European modernity. Lugones (2007) offers a perspective that centralizes the Global South, including perspectives and lived realities of women of color, Indigenous Peoples, and other minoritized and underrepresented populations to reject the notion of a universality of gender. According to Lugones's coloniality of gender, gender has never been a universal construct although painted through this lens as a colonial agenda to privilege whiteness and man-ness. Gender has been practiced differently across sociocultural and transnational contexts, as evidenced through precolonial societies and Indigeneity. The universality of gender is a colonial imposition, at the intersection of race and gender.

Lugones (2007) developed much of her theorizations on the coloniality of gender building on Quijano's (2000) coloniality of power, which asserts that the strife between coloniality and modernity is hinged on the contentions of a capitalist system that pits participants against each other, competing to control the most resources. Lugones criticized Quijano's under-theorization of gender within this capitalist system, asserting the need for a much more nuanced theorization of gender and its colonial histories as represented within today's systems.

2.4 Bridging Foucault, Butler, and Lugones as Colonial Historicity and Genealogy

It becomes evident, then, that a method that commits to a trans* representation as moral and ethical discourse in HCI revolves with its historicity and genealogy. Each theorist makes important contributions that must be comprehensively accounted for in curating an approach that centers trans* discourse: Foucault's (1978) biopolitics and the subjectivity and relational processes that situate sexuality; Butler's (1990) gender performativity and the heterosexual matrix that dictates the bounds and norms of gender and sexuality; and Lugones's (2007) coloniality of gender that rejects the Westernized notion of a universal gender, centralizing underrepresented voices and bodies. Each perspective accounts for the variances that must be accounted for through a logic that grounds individual differences toward a trans*-ing of HCI as moral and ethical discourse.

3 Findings: Five Provocations for Trans* HCI Morality and Ethics

In positioning this discourse as a method of systemic and structural philosophical shift to emphasize trans* moral and ethical representations within HCI, I advocate for five provocations: (1) co-constructing theories that complement, not contradict, each other; (2) centering the genealogies of coloniality; (3) emphasizing the subjective, relational systems of power; (4) decentering (superficial uses of) queer HCI and technology to recenter moral and ethical trans* HCI; (5) establishing a method of design thinking that centralizes trans* discourse in HCI. Throughout and across these provocations, I engage what the intersections across Foucault (1978), Butler (1990), and Lugones (2007) operationalize as when considering how to trans* HCI as moral and ethical discourse.

3.1 Co-Constructing Theories That Complement Each Other

Often, and especially within academic discourse, there is an emphasis on criticism and rejecting prior ways of thinking and being when new knowledge becomes available. This is critical to the continuation of knowledge and critical thinking; however, this too often becomes toxic and a push for a right vs. wrong, which can ultimately be attributed to the broader state of the academy that follows a capitalist systemic function. Competition and who is better than who are praised and reinforced. Yet, in orchestrating a method of trans* morality and ethics in HCI, such approaches are not instrumental (Park et al., 2025).

Instead of focusing on a right or wrong, we need to move toward instrumentality of perspectives. Each of these three perspectives (Butler, 1990; Foucault, 1978; Lugones, 2007) I present all have utility in shaping how we may emphasize trans* livingness because trans* lives are rooted in the realities presented across the perspectives. This is not to undo the value of any perspective or variety of lived experiences; instead, this reinforces the value of these experiences and the salience of our individual differences. What is clear about the trans* experience is its highly varied lived experiences, and frameworks that account for said variances are found in a pluralistic approach to discourse.

3.2 Centering Genealogies of Coloniality

The genealogies of coloniality remain rooted in today's systems, which are further represented within sociotechnical systems and how power is distributed within technology and HCI (Alvarado Garcia et al., 2021). As such, an intentional centering and prioritization of colonial discourse is critical to addressing the gap within an HCI trans* moral and ethical focus, toward deconstructing the systems that continue to perpetuate these inequities (Lugones, 2007). Coloniality is part of our world's history. It was used as a mechanism of power and control to dictate a system that serves whiteness and manness. Addressing these gaps and colonial realities that remain engrained in our systems is foundational to a trans* focus in HCI.

3.3 Subjective, Relational Systems of Power

Following Foucault's (1978) assertions, the systems of power operate through a pull between power and resistance at the subjective and relational levels. Butler (1990) further echoes this subjective and relational underscoring of gendered norms and practices, noting that resistance is only realized through the failure of the gender performativity and as bounded through the heterosexual matrix. Lugones (2007) notes the subjective lived experiences of women of color, Indigenous Peoples, and others of the third gender at the intersections of race and gender that have dictated their subjugations to the colonial oppressive system. Each theorist emphasizes the subjective and relational system of power that governs how gender and sexuality are construed. Consequently, a framework that centralizes these subjective and relational systems of power is warranted to systemically address and advocate for a trans* moral and ethical focus in HCI (Light, 2011).

3.4 Decentering Queer Superficiality to Recenter Trans* Morals and Ethics

Taylor and researchers (2024) highlight the superficiality and convenient focus of queerness in HCI: it is a point of discourse when it can be materially beneficial to those who attempt to engage with these lives. Discourses and initiatives that seek to engage queerness, and specifically transness, must aim to do so through mediums that are authentic and beneficial to the community of trans* bodies, not just the researchers who are trying to get their next publication and recognition for engaging with an underrepresented group. As Taylor and team note, "this strategic use of these groups by HCI researchers plays a crucial role in checking power. We encourage HCI scholars to consider how their technical expertise can serve forms of community accountability, where the tools we build are a means to an end rather than an end in and of itself" (p. 15).

3.5 Design Thinking for Trans* Discourse in HCI

Finally, this discourse serves as a method that can support design thinking toward supporting a trans* moral and ethical focus in HCI. Design thinking is a method that emphasizes iterative processes across empathize, define, ideate, prototype, and test. HCI processes follow understanding users, analysis, design, and implementation. Park and Mckilligan (2018) note the instrumentality of combining HCI and design thinking principles toward creating a stronger, more informed process and product that can comprehensively support the diverse needs of users, which Moeggenberg and researchers (2019) note can be a potent avenue for the work of social justice in HCI. The incorporation of design thinking acts as a moral and ethical focus for trans* bodies by specifically delineating the unique needs of this population to inform designs that are attuned to their lived experiences.

4 Contributions and Implications for HCI: Theorizing Trans* Morality and Ethics

This work creates avenues for expanding our philosophical, theoretical, and methodological repertoire within HCI to explore issues of morality and ethics. I aimed to bring together a novel co-construction of theory, given the absence of work that engages such a theoretical structure, toward imagining what a colonially and genealogically informed notion of morality and ethics may look like in the context of HCI and specifically for trans* populations within these settings. This work further moves to emphasize the systemic by exploring a relational and subjective analytical framework of power, which opposes the norm of critical and systemic practices within the literature.

This work additionally creates a platform to engage in more nuanced approaches for HCI and interdisciplinary discourses for scholars who are interested in centering trans* discourses within HCI and technology. Finally, this discourse engages across the intersections of HCI through ethics; accessibility and universal design: cultural differences and HCI, and gender and diversity; wellbeing; and social and organizational democracy.

Acknowledgments. This work received no funding support. I thank the reviewers for their feedback on further strengthening this final product.

Disclosure of Interests. The author has no competing interests to declare that are relevant to the content of this article.

References

Alvarado Garcia, A., et al.: Decolonial pathways: our manifesto for a decolonizing agenda in HCI research and design. In: Extended Abstracts of the 2021 CHI Conference on Human Factors in Computing Systems, pp. 1–9. Association for Computing Machinery, New York (2021)

Butler, J.: Foucault and the paradox of bodily inscriptions. In: Fitzpatrick, P. (ed.) Foucault and Law, pp. 227–234. Routledge, New York (2017)

Butler, J.: Gender Trouble: Feminism and the Subversion of Identity. Routledge, New York (1990)

Butler, J.: What is critique? An essay on Foucault's virtue. The Political, 220 (2002)

Cisney, V.W., Morar, N. (eds.): Biopower: Foucault and Beyond. University of Chicago Press, Chicago (2020)

Cowan, T.L., Rault, J.: Onlining queer acts: digital research ethics and caring for risky archives. Women Perform.: J. Fem. Theory. **28**(2), 121–142 (2018)

DeVito, M.A., et al.: Queer in HCI: Strengthening the community of LGBTQIA+ researchers and research. In: Kitamura, Y., Quigley, A., Isbister, K., Igarashi, T. (eds.) Extended Abstracts of the 2021 CHI Conference on Human Factors in Computing Systems, pp. 1–3 (2021)

DeVito, M.A., et al.: Queer in HCI: supporting LGBTQIA+ researchers and research across domains. In: Bernhaupt, R., Mueller, F.F. (eds.) Extended Abstracts of the 2020 CHI Conference on Human Factors in Computing Systems, pp. 1–4 (2020)

Fosch-Villaronga, E., Malgieri, G.: Queering the ethics of AI. In: Gunkel, D.J. (ed.) Handbook on the Ethics of Artificial Intelligence, pp. 301–315. Edward Elgar Publishing, Northampton (2024)

Foucault, M.: "What Is Critique" and "The Culture of Self". University of Chicago Press, Chicago (2024)

Foucault, M.: The History of Sexuality. Random House Inc., New York (1978)

Harrison, D.: Why we should care about inclusivity in SportsHCI. In: Proceedings of the First Annual Conference on Human-Computer Interaction and Sports, pp. 1–12 (2025)

Herry, A., Greer, D., Malcolm, B., Elizabeth, S.: "Yes, we exist!": lived experiences from a Caribbean transgender & gender nonconforming group. SAGE Open. **15**(1), 1–13 (2025)

Kannabiran, G., Petersen, M.G.: Politics at the interface: a Foucauldian power analysis. In: Hvannberg, E.P., Lárusdóttir, M.K., Blandford, A., Gulliksen, J. (eds.) Proceedings of the 6th Nordic Conference on Human-Computer Interaction: Extending Boundaries, pp. 695–698. Association for Computing Machinery, New York (2010)

Kannabiran, G.: Dirty interactions. Interactions. **31**(3), 19–21 (2024)

Light, A.: HCI as heterodoxy: technologies of identity and the queering of interaction with computers. Interact. Comput. **23**(5), 430–438 (2011)

Lugones, M.: Heterosexualism and the colonial modern gender system. Hypatia. **22**(1), 186–219 (2007)

Malcolm, B.: Connected learning: a dual reflexive pedagogical identity. In: Proceedings of the 18th International Conference of the Learning Sciences-ICLS 2024, pp. 2443–2444. International Society of the Learning Sciences, USA (2024)

Moeggenberg, Z.C., Walton, R.: How queer theory can inform design thinking pedagogy. In: Proceedings of the 37th ACM International Conference on the Design of Communication, pp. 1–9. Association for Computing Machinery, New York (2019)

O'Reilly-Kime, M., et al.: Finding our joy: queer perspectives on HCI research. In: Yamashita, N., Evers, V., Yatani, K., Ding, X. (eds.) Proceedings of the Extended Abstracts of the CHI Conference on Human Factors in Computing Systems, pp. 1–10 (2025)

Park, S., DeVine, T.A., Toombs, A.L.: Stuck in translation: reflexive practice in queer HCI research from non-western perspectives. In: Yamashita, N., Evers, V., Yatani, K., Ding, X. (eds.) Proceedings of the Extended Abstracts of the CHI Conference on Human Factors in Computing Systems, pp. 1–9 (2025)

Park, H., & McKilligan, S.: A systematic literature review for human-computer interaction and design thinking process integration. In: International Conference of Design, User Experience, and Usability, pp. 725–740. Springer, Cham (2018)

Punchoojit, L., Hongwarittorn, N.: Research ethics in human-computer interaction: a review of ethical concerns in the past five years. In: 2015 2nd National Foundation for Science and Technology Development Conference on Information and Computer Science (NICS), pp. 180–185. IEEE, Piscataway (2015)

Quijano, A.: Coloniality of power and eurocentrism in Latin America. Int. Sociol. **15**(2), 215–232 (2000)

Salas-SantaCruz, O.: What is decolonial trans* feminism and what can it do for queer/trans BIPOC education research? Reimagining knowledge and identity through the convergence of decolonial and trans* feminism. J. Queer Trans Stud. Educ. **1**(1), 4 (2024)

Shilton, K.: Values and ethics in human-computer interaction. Found. Trends Hum.-Comput. Interact. **12**(2), 107–171 (2018)

Taylor, J., Simpson, E., Tran, A.T., Brubaker, J.R., Fox, S.E., Zhu, H.: Cruising queer HCI on the DL: a literature review of LGBTQ+ people in HCI. In: Mueller, F.F., Kyburz, P., Williamson, J.R., Sas, C., Wilson, M.L., Dugas, P.T., Shklovski, I. (eds.) Proceedings of the 2024 CHI Conference on Human Factors in Computing Systems, pp. 1–21 (2024)

Uttamchandani, S., et al.: Queer and trans learning: placemaking, non/dominant imaginaries, and educational dignity towards resistance. In: Proceedings of the 19th International Conference of the Learning Sciences-ICLS 2025, pp. 2336–2344. International Society of the Learning Sciences (2025)

Villalobos Lujan, T., et al.: Interaction design as a form of decolonial care. In: Andolina, S., Bryan-Kinns, N., Alaoui, S.F. (eds.) Proceedings of the 2025 Conference on Creativity and Cognition, pp. 33–38. Association for Computing Machinery, New York (2025)

Walker, D., Malcolm, B.: Synthesis of literature on effective educator practices in the online setting: perspectives from a Caribbean higher education context through university pedagogy. J. Res. Initiatives. **6**(3), 10 (2022)

Charting Pathways to Success in Fourth Wave HCI: Place-Based Methods for Technology Design from Abundant Intelligences

Robert N. Marinov[1(✉)], Orus Mateo Castaño-Suárez[2], Ceyda Yolgörmez[1], Jason Edward Lewis[1], and Sara L. Diamond[2]

[1] Concordia University, Montreal, QC, Canada
robert.marinov@mail.concordia.ca
[2] OCAD University, Toronto, ON, Canada

Abstract. This article presents the overall research design of *Abundant Intelligences*, a research program working to imagine and build artificial intelligence systems through and with local Indigenous communities and their knowledge systems. We situate the program's "Pod-based" design as a way to operationalize the principles of the "fourth wave" of HCI.

Keywords: fourth wave HCI · Indigenous Knowledge Systems · relational accountability · place-based research · Pod-based design · Indigenous Data Sovereignty · research-creation · artificial intelligence

This article presents the "Pod-based" research design of *Abundant Intelligences*, a research program with an Indigenous-led, Indigenous-majority, and transdisciplinary team working to imagine and build artificial intelligence systems through and with local Indigenous communities and knowledge systems. We situate this work within the ongoing movement towards a "fourth wave" of HCI. This research design operationalizes major calls in the fourth wave HCI literature and serves as a replicable format for such critical research-creation goals.

In this article, we distinguish between *research design* at the program level and *research methodology* at the more concrete project level, arguing that the program's territorially-situated "Pod-based" research design serves as a promising format for innovating truly Indigenous-led and culturally-appropriate HCI design methodologies. We present our research by (1) situating our contribution within the relevant literatures; (2) outlining the *Abundant Intelligences* research design; and (3) discussing how it operationalizes four key calls for action in fourth wave HCI.

1 Indigenous HCI Design: Situating Our Contribution

Indigenous questioning and experimentation on digital technology futures has grown since the 1990s and made important contributions to HCI design practice

C. Stephanidis et al. (Eds.): HCII 2026, CCIS 3047, pp. 82–92, 2026.
https://doi.org/10.1007/978-3-032-30552-7_9

[13]. *Abundant Intelligences* (elaborated on in Sect. 2) arose from within this wide-ranging legacy of Indigenous computation arts, design, and techno-scientific methodology.

Indigenous Knowledge Systems (IKS) can bring critical–and necessary–depth to research methodologies [22]. Distinctions between Indigenous onto-epistemologies and their Western counterparts move beyond "the cultural" and constitute a difference in *materialist commitments.* The Western scientific paradigm has historically operated from an "epistemology of control" [10, p. 320], which positions non-human entities as inert resources available for extraction and exploitation [14, p. 9]. In contrast, many Indigenous onto-epistemologies operate from a non-dualist, animate, relational materialism. Dr. Leroy Little Bear articulates this, stating: "In the Indigenous world, everything is animate and has spirit. 'All my relations' refers to relationships with everything in creation." [17, p. 8], as cited in [14, p. 3].

IKS provide structurally distinct epistemic architectures with direct implications for how AI systems are designed, evaluated, and governed. Conceiving of AI, and its materials, as kinship relations subordinates computational systems to what TallBear calls "being in good relation" [25]. To remove the concept of AI from its materiality–from the mines, stones, and the land from which computer hardware emerges–is to sever this relational connection.

With such epistemic foundations, IKS have contributed to a growing body of research on artificial intelligence, including for multi-agent systems [18]; Natural Language Processing [11]; land management [21]; and much more [20]. Nonetheless, IKS remain conceptually isolated from most disciplinary HCI scholarship, representing a critical omission within design paradigms.

1.1 Towards a Fourth Wave in HCI

Beginning in the 1990s, the HCI community increasingly problematized the assumed cultural universalism underpinning mainstream practices [28], leading to growing calls to develop methodologies that engage communities "in their own terms" [7] and to render HCI design more locally situated and accountable [1]. These calls are indicative of what's been termed the "third wave" of HCI; one which attends to "the situated nature of meaning and meaning creation" [9].

More recently, a growing set of calls to "decolonize" and otherwise de-centre HCI design from Western dominance have gained traction. Many of these are situated within the sub-field of HCI for Development (HCI4D) or in peripheral strands of inquiry such as "post-colonial computing", "decolonial computing", and Afro-centric or ArabHCI [3,29]. This scholarship has been grouped loosely into what some call the "fourth wave" of HCI [4]: a movement to reframe and reform the discipline through considerations of ontological justice and centring concerns for cultural/community relevance throughout the design pipeline [1].

1.2 Four Markers of the Fourth Wave

Far from merely aspirational, over the past two decades a plurality of initiatives around the world have employed "community-collaborative approaches (CCA)" to HCI [26], including Participatory Design methods developed and tested with and for Indigenous communities. While a systematic review is beyond our scope here, this growing literature has made several important calls for action towards reforming the discipline of HCI. We have synthesized these into four major themes: (1) relational accountability; (2) Indigenous leadership; (3) de-centring Western methods and epistemologies; and (4) capacity-building and guardianship. These emerge partly from the literature and partly from our own purposive framing of how we understand and aim to advance these calls for action. In Sect. 3, we present *Abundant Intelligences*' work directly in relation to these four themes.

Table 1. Fourth Wave HCI Calls for Action

Main Themes	Key Focus/Problem Areas
Relational Accountability	• Designing "with, rather than for" communities • Developing reciprocal relationships and shared commitments • Working from within relational epistemologies and values
Indigenous Leadership	• Repositioning participation dynamics to empower Indigenous leadership • Community involvement at all stages • Centring marginalized voices
De-centring Western Epistemologies & Methods	• The need for ontological justice in design • Levelling the scientific playing field • Developing culturally appropriate methodologies
Capacity-Building & Guardianship	• Training, uptake, and capacity-building • Local sustainability (i.e., relevance) of the outcomes • Subverting unequal power relations (i.e., Indigenous Data Sovereignty and other considerations)

Concerns for what we term *relational accountability* have been growing [26] since early calls to develop "with, rather than for" communities [28, p. 382]. Relational accountability is enacted, in part, by "developing relationships, demonstrating commitments, and overcoming personal and institutional barriers" [12,

p. 1348]. This includes attention to questions of positionality, reciprocity, and locally-appropriate modalities of participation and knowledge sharing [3,8,29].

Aspirations for *Indigenous leadership* are less pronounced in the HCI literature than for "participation", broadly construed. However, researchers note the need to engage Indigenous communities throughout the design, development, and deployment processes, in part by centring marginalized voices [8]. While existing calls often stop short at "participation", we posit Indigenous *leadership* as a more fitting aspiration.

De-centring Western epistemologies and methods has been a growing focus in HCI as researchers question the "presumed universalism which tends to underlie our computing practice" [4, p. 487]. It is frequently noted that "by privileging a Western science paradigm, common HCI methodologies, including their abstractions and models, perpetuate a locally inappropriate approach" [29, p. 246]. HCI practice must not treat IKS as "niche" but rather embrace the "uncomfortable interactions" [8] between different knowledge systems and develop shared "conversation codes" [1] for research to advance reciprocally and in good faith.

Finally, *capacity-building and guardianship* are also less pronounced in the HCI literature, although important calls have been advanced. More than just "training", attention must be given to "what constitutes useful and usable systems" from within local cultural contexts [1, p. 201]. To be sure, research must ensure that communities maintain guardianship over their cultural materials and develop and retain their data and infrastructural sovereignty [27].

Fourth wave HCI is clearly making important impacts. Nonetheless, many publications remain fairly abstract and aspirational: a set of forward-looking calls, more so than a set of comprehensive methodologies and research designs for operationalizing those calls or bridging theory and practice [4,8]. In response, we present *Abundant Intelligences'* research design as a replicable, Indigenous-led pathway forward for successfully bridging fourth wave HCI theory and practice.

2 *Abundant Intelligences*: Empowering Indigenous communities through a novel research design

Abundant Intelligences is governed by a multi-layered and federated approach to research-creation. Administered out of Concordia University's Indigenous Futures Research Centre, the program decentralizes primary research activities into a "Pod-based" structure, while still ensuring rich forms of shared governance, project steering, mutual responsibility, and relational accountability across Pods and the wider program. Here we present this structure as a way to develop alternative HCI methodologies applicable throughout the entire design pipeline. For further detail on this program, see Lewis et al. [15].

2.1 A Pod-Based Research Design

The program's transdisciplinary team of research and design experts are coalesced into locally-rooted and land-based research clusters called 'Pods', which collaborate with people native to their respective territories in order to bring novel perspectives to AI. There are six Pods in the program, spread across the territories of what are known as Canada, the US, and New Zealand (see abundant-intelligences.net). Each Pod is self-governing and anchored in an Indigenous-led research and media laboratory, ensuring that research is sustained and supported by an institutional space and resources that are themselves adapted to local norms and protocols. Nonetheless, many research activities do occur beyond the laboratories, in various community locales and groupings.

Pods bring Indigenous Knowledge holders, cultural practitioners, language keepers, educational institutions, and community vitalization organizations together with scientists, engineers, artists, social scientists, and humanists to co-steer research and creation activities. The Pods act, then, as key milieux for the transdisciplinary knowledge integration activities essential to the success of our work. They provide a generative space of encounter for meeting, collaborating, and ideating with communities; for training and increasing these communities' capacities in computational technologies; and for building and testing prototypes for novel AI systems.

Pods are self-organizing entities–which is to say, Pod coordinators, community liaisons, and other locally-rooted academic leadership purposively engage with community members and organizations on their own terms and timelines that fit with local norms, rather than university-institutional norms. This helps ensure that Pods act in the best interest of the communities they are integrated with. Community partners and participants are actively involved in conceiving, setting the parameters of, and accruing the skills and materials needed to direct the design of sovereign AI systems that meet their own situated expectations and needs.

As a core element of the *Abundant Intelligences* research design, the Pods are fundamentally serving as *incubators* for the development of place-based, culturally-appropriate methodologies for advancing various stages of the HCI design pipeline [4]. While the activities of individual Pods are currently at a mid-stage of the program, they are already proving to be proficient innovators of locally-rooted AI methodologies (see Sect. 3.3).

This large and ambitious research design undoubtedly requires a certain institutional nimbleness and allyship with strategic actors/researchers. Nonetheless, we hold that it is precisely this type of innovative positioning, at the intersections of institutional-community relations, that is fundamental to enabling academic research to work towards decolonization, Indigenous empowerment, and the spirit of the fourth wave HCI movement. The next section outlines how the Pod structure operationalizes the four calls for action in Table 1.

3 From Research Design to HCI Methodologies: Operationalizing Fourth Wave HCI

As a general framework for research design, the Pod structure can be replicated and adapted to different research programs and their respective resources, as well as to different communities and their local norms and needs, all while facilitating the meaningful operationalization of the fourth wave HCI movement into applied research.

3.1 Relational Accountability

The HCI literature has long debated the nuances, limitations, and biases involved in undertaking HCI design from "out there" versus "in here". By ensuring that community members, with their own kinship relations and responsibilities, are directly embedded in the core research team and program governance, *Abundant Intelligences'* research design not only removes hurdles surrounding positionalities and a need to "go out and find" participant communities for research, but also encourages relational accountability by design.

Such a model makes a crucial difference. As noted by Migueltzinta Solís, Research Consultant for the Niitsitapi Pod, "There's a sense of a larger cohort or community that's being brought into the Pod that is intergenerational and not limited to an academic environment," thus ensuring research follows a model that's not "experimental" but rather "known and familiar to everyone involved. [...] It comes as a big relief because so many students are dealing with code switching and balancing University culture with home cultures" [23]. Pods thus help support a collaborative research dynamic of solidarity, allyship, and co-learning, rather than an outsider-insider dynamic with potentially (neo-)colonial undertones.

Being rooted in local communities also enables Pod members to share and learn together in place-based ways through ceremonies, rituals, and outings across different cultural sites of significance. This all enables accessible, familiar, and culturally-appropriate forms of engagement, participation, and relationship-building amongst the research-community team, thus facilitating community buy-in, meaningful participation, and relational accountabilities.

3.2 Indigenous Leadership

The HCI literature has highlighted the importance of building "with, and not for" local communities. In our view, this is not strong enough. Rather, the aims of fourth wave HCI should be to *centre,* not just consult, communities in the research design and process. Community buy-in, in our work, is not something vaguely "important", but a crucial pillar of responsible scientific practice–a precaution born of a longstanding skepticism of academia and its dark histories of non-reciprocal extraction of Indigenous Knowledges and data [22].

Departing from user-centred design, Participatory Design, and adjacent community-centred approaches whose engagement modalities frequently remain episodic, extractive, or performatively consultative, we advance the Pod-based structure as a research design that enables sustained community *incubation* of HCI design potentials through relational infrastructures. In *Abundant Intelligences,* all research activities are filtered through the Pods and their local governance structures. Pods employ community liaisons at the governance level, and community members on the core research team, while also ensuring that elders, knowledge holders, community partners, and other participants contribute in regularly-occurring, meaningful ways throughout phases of research. In other words, Pods help ensure that community participation does not equate to extractive data collection, but instead to meaningful *community-led* design processes. Together, these provide the modalities for Indigenous *leadership* in HCI research, not simply participation or consultation.

3.3 De-centring Western Epistemologies and Methods

HCI design requires an abundance of intelligences in order to promote community relevance and ontological justice. Designing artificial intelligence systems does, of course, require the uptake of Western knowledges. However, rooting research within community-led Pods promotes a sustained set of discussions and situated methods for interweaving both local Indigenous and Western knowledge systems in ways that enhance one another, helping participants to work through the difficult knowledge translations and needs of developing shared "conversation codes" between them [1].

As such, Pods offer a generative format for articulating HCI design methodologies grounded in Indigenous protocols and knowledges, all while de-centring the Western epistemic defaults. The concrete form of these emerging methodologies exceeds the scope of this article and is, in any case, best articulated by their developers in and with community. What we can affirm here is that the Pod structure has proven highly generative of locally-rooted, culturally-situated Indigenous research-creation methodologies.

These examples indicate the specificity of local applications of IKS and HCI methodologies:

In Aotearoa New Zealand, the Hiringa Te Mahara Pod, housed in the Āpōpō Indigenous CreativeTech Hub at Indigenous Design and Innovation Aotearoa, is applying Kaupapa Māori and Tikanga Māori principles to the conceptualization, design, and evaluation of AI systems, including–among other things–in relation to the development of Māori language-learning apps, the governance of Māori data sovereignty infrastructures, the application of AI within neuroscientific research on Huntington's disease, and more (hiringatemahara.nz).

In the Ka Hawai'i Pae 'Āina Pod, housed at the University of Hawai'i's Create(x) Lab, local knowledges centred on the importance of 'Āina (land) are driving several revitalization projects to counter centuries of colonial erasure. To offer one example, the Abundant Soils project investigates the intersection between 'Ōiwi knowledge systems, Western soil science, and artificial intelligence with the aim of creating more equitable data governance policies for soil sciences and the incorporation of AI therein. The project articulates Indigenous Hawaiians' "multi-faceted relationship to soil" and the material and cultural harms arising from colonial land-use and agricultural practices [19].

In the Wiháŋble S'a Pod, housed at Bard College, Oglála Lakȟóta geometries, cultural knowledges, and philosophy of life are underpinning artistic and neuroscientific research-creation with AI systems, including an "AI-augmented brain-computer interface installation that explores personal and collective dreamscapes through generative artificial intelligence, real-time electroencephalography (EEG) neurofeedback, and Indigenous symbolic systems" [5].

In the Niitsitapi Pod at Iniskim (University of Lethbridge), students, researchers, and elders are advancing an innovative "flux methodology" based in Blackfoot metaphysics and onto-epistemologies. This is applied to various HCI imaginaries and designs, including speculative notions of an "energy-to-energy model" for language learning, presenting a more epistemically-appropriate alternative to speech-to-text models, which flatten Niitsipowahssin language and its (metaphysical) meanings [16].

In the Haudenosaunee Pod, based in Western University's Onkwehonwe Research Environment, relational epistemologies and frameworks, such as the Seventh Generation Principle of ensuring renewable resource use, are shaping approaches to environmental sensing, language and cultural revitalization, and the design and evaluation of AI and its uses [2].

In the T'Karonto Pod, housed at OCAD University (Toronto), the Dish with One Spoon agreement between the Haudenosaunee and Anishinaabe peoples, which supports the sharing of vital resources and keeping those resources intact, is being drawn on as a guide to what is "required of AI, both the creators and the algorithms." This is applied to the investigation of small language models as "safe containers for Indigenous knowledge", VR and AR-based environments for language learning and cultural revitalization, AI integrated methods of urban planning, computational topology and visuospatial methods for mapping knowledge across the network, and more [6,24].

Pod-based researchers and participants are currently advancing some 42 discrete research projects, while an additional seven are advancing through cross-Pod and community partner collaborations within the program. Eight of these are generating locally-rooted AI methodologies; 32 are developing computational systems centred on community needs; four are supporting Indigenous Data Sovereignty infrastructure; and five are producing artistic and knowledge outputs to inform later design.

3.4 Capacity-Building and Guardianship

Concerns with community capacity-building and control (or as we prefer, "guardianship") over data and computational resources do arise in the HCI literature, albeit with less emphasis than is merited. While *Abundant Intelligences* is helping train dozens of Indigenous students and non-Indigenous allies to undertake innovative AI research, capacity-building must entail more than just "teaching" communities to "use" or "adapt to" technologies. Rather, it also means ensuring the relevance of HCI design: that systems are pertinent and value-generating for communities, as defined on their own terms.

A large focus within *Abundant Intelligences* has therefore been on Indigenous Data Sovereignty frameworks for the community control, protection, and care for data and computational infrastructures. With their deep community embeddings, Pods facilitate an approach to research that prioritizes Indigenous relationships/kinships to, and guardianship over, the processes, inputs, and outputs of HCI design, collectively.

4 Conclusion

In conclusion, it should be reiterated that this large and ambitious research design undoubtedly requires a certain institutional nimbleness and allyship with strategic actors/researchers, but that such an approach is fundamental to working towards decolonization, Indigenous empowerment, and the spirit of the fourth wave HCI movement. As our research advances, Pods and the wider program are focused increasingly on forward-looking approaches to AI benchmarking, evaluation, and policy/regulatory contexts, where emphasis on the need for context sensitivity is growing: i.e., how to iterate locally-meaningful measures of success or failure, or to robustly evaluate the scientific merit of AI systems that are rooted in Indigenous Knowledges.

While the breadth of considerations in fourth wave HCI and their implications for Western, Indigenous, and integrative sciences may be daunting, it's crucial to work through them in locally-rooted ways anchored in Indigenous leadership, in order to make a truly meaningful impact on the discipline. We hold that the Pod-based research design provides a compelling structure for thinking through these difficult questions and generating community-oriented alternatives to dominant practices.

Acknowledgments. This research is sponsored by *Abundant Intelligences*, funded by New Frontiers in Research Fund - Transformation (NFRFT-2022-00241) and Social Sciences and Humanities Council Partnership Grant (SSHRC PG #895-2022-0059)

Disclosure of Interests. The authors have no competing interests to declare that are relevant to the content of this article.

References

1. Abdelnour-Nocera, J., Clemmensen, T., Kurosu, M.: Reframing HCI through local and indigenous perspectives. Int. J. Human-Comput. Interaction **29**(4), 201–204 (2013). https://doi.org/10.1080/10447318.2013.765759
2. Abundant Intelligences: 2RO Media Festival 2025 (2025). https://abundant-intelligences.net/events/2ro-media-festival-2025
3. Arueyingho, O., Lawrence, D.O., Webb, H.: Navigating Afrocentric Human-Computer Interaction Research: A Scoping Review and Proposition of Afro-Postmodernism for Decolonial Praxis. In: Extended Abstracts of the CHI Conference on Human Factors in Computing Systems, pp. 1–14. ACM, Honolulu HI USA (2024). https://doi.org/10.1145/3613905.3644072
4. Barcham, M.: Decolonizing Computing and the Quest for Ontological Justice - Putting Fourth-Wave HCI/IxD Into Practice. In: Proceedings of the 35th Australian Computer-Human Interaction Conference, pp. 486–492. ACM, Wellington New Zealand (2023). https://doi.org/10.1145/3638380.3638430

5. Bellemare-Pepin, A., Thölke, P., Jerbi, K., Kite, S.: Oneiris: An AI-augmented Brain-Computer Interface for Exploring Personal and Collective Dreamscapes. In: Proceedings of the Conference on Animation and Interactive Art, pp. 89–98. ACM, Linz Austria (2025). https://doi.org/10.1145/3749893.3749963
6. Diamond, S.: Five Minutes With T'Karonto Pod Co-Lead, Sara Diamond (2025). https://abundant-intelligences.net/blogs/five-minutes-with-tkaronto-pod-co-lead-sara-diamond/. Interviewed by Sabrina Smith
7. Dourish, P., Mainwaring, S.D.: Ubicomp's colonial impulse. In: Proceedings of the 2012 ACM Conference on Ubiquitous Computing, pp. 133–142. ACM, Pittsburgh Pennsylvania (2012). https://doi.org/10.1145/2370216.2370238
8. Farao, J., Pillai, A.G., Mthoko, H., Samuel, M.M., Elmimouni, H., Lazem, S.: Weaving Indigeneity and Culture into the Fabric of HCI Futures. In: Proceedings of the Extended Abstracts of the CHI Conference on Human Factors in Computing Systems, pp. 1–6. ACM, Yokohama Japan (2025). https://doi.org/10.1145/3706599.3706737
9. Harrison, S., Tatar, D., Sengers, P.: The Three Paradigms of HCI. In: Alt. Chi. Session at the SIGCHI Conference on Human Factors in Computing Systems, pp. 1–18. San Jose, California, USA (2007)
10. Hester, L., Cheney, J.: Truth and native American epistemology. Soc. Epistemol. **15**(4), 319–334 (2001). https://doi.org/10.1080/02691720110093333
11. Jones, P.L., Mahelona, K., Duncan, S., Leoni, G.: Kia tangata whenua: artificial intelligence that grows from the land and people. Ethical Space: Int. J. Commun. Ethics **2023**(2/3) (2023). https://ethicalspace.pubpub.org/pub/g3f4k33k
12. Le Dantec, C.A., Fox, S.: Strangers at the Gate: Gaining Access, Building Rapport, and Co-Constructing Community-Based Research. In: Proceedings of the 18th ACM Conference on Computer Supported Cooperative Work & Social Computing, pp. 1348–1358. ACM, Vancouver BC Canada (2015). https://doi.org/10.1145/2675133.2675147
13. Lewis, J.E.: The Future Imaginary. In: Chattopadhyay, B., Dillon, G., Lavender, I., Taylor, T.J. (eds.) Routledge Handbook of CoFuturisms, pp. 11–22. Routledge, New York, NY (2023)
14. Lewis, J.E., Arista, N., Pechawis, A., Kite, S.: Making Kin with the Machines. J. Design Sci. (2018). https://doi.org/10.21428/bfafd97b
15. Lewis, J.E., Whaanga, H., Yolgörmez, C.: Abundant intelligences: placing AI within Indigenous knowledge frameworks. AI Soc. **40**(4), 2141–2157 (2025). https://doi.org/10.1007/s00146-024-02099-4
16. Little Bear, L., First Rider, A., Clark, C., et al.: Soundscape & The Flux: Notes from Niitsitapi Pod. tba: J. Art, Media Visual Culture **7**(1) (2025). https://doi.org/10.5206/tba.v7i1.23155
17. Littlebear, L.: Naturalizing Indigenous Knowledge: Synthesis Paper. Technical report, Aboriginal Learning Knowledge Centre, Canadian Council on Learning, Saskatoon, Saskatchewan and Calgary, Alberta (2009). http://neatoeco.com/iwise3/wp-content/uploads/2015/08/NaturalizingIndigenousKnowledge_LeroyLittlebear.pdf
18. Malenfant, D., Richards, B.A.: The challenge of hidden gifts in multi-agent reinforcement learning. http://arxiv.org/abs/2505.20579 (2025). https://doi.org/10.48550/arXiv.2505.20579, preprint
19. Moniz, M.: Five Minutes with Abundant Intelligences' Postdoctoral Researcher, Melemaikalani Moniz (2026). https://abundant-intelligences.net/blogs/five-minutes-with-abundant-intelligences-postdoctoral-researcher-melemaikalani-moniz. Interviewed by Sabrina Smith

20. Perera, P., Cumbo, B., Bidwell, N.J., et al.: Towards Reciprocity: Mediating Human-Nature Relations Through HCI. In: Proceedings of the 37th Australian Conference on Human-Computer Interaction, pp. 876–884. OzCHI '2025, Association for Computing Machinery, New York, NY, USA (2025). https://doi.org/10.1145/3764687.3769939
21. Robinson, C.J., Macdonald, J.M., Perry, J., et al.: Coproduction mechanisms to weave Indigenous knowledge, artificial intelligence, and technical data to enable Indigenous-led adaptive decision making. Ecol. Soc. **27**(4) (2022). https://doi.org/10.5751/ES-13747-270436
22. Smith, L.T.: Decolonizing Methodologies: Research and Indigenous Peoples. London, second edition edn, Zed (2012)
23. Solís, M.: Five Minutes With Arts, Community, and Research Consultant, Miguel (2025). https://abundant-intelligences.net/blogs/five-minutes-with-arts-community-and-research-consultant-miguel/. Interviewed by Sabrina Smith
24. Castaño Suárez, O.M.: Five Minutes With Toronto Pod Research Coordinator Orus Mateo Castaño-Suárez (2026). https://abundant-intelligences.net/blogs/five-minutes-with-toronto-pod-research-coordinator-orus-mateo-castano-suarez/. Interviewed by Hazel Dreslinski
25. TallBear, K.: Caretaking Relations, Not American Dreaming. Kalfou **6**(1) (2019). https://doi.org/10.15367/kf.v6i1.228
26. Tang, J., Ghoshal, S.: Research and/as relation: documenting experiences of community-collaborative researchers in HCI. Proc. ACM Human-Comput. Interaction **9**(7), 1–30 (2025). https://doi.org/10.1145/3757651
27. The First Nations Information Governance Centre (FNIGC): Ownership, Control, Access and Possession (OCAP^{TM}): The Path to First Nations Information Governance. Technical report, The First Nations Information Governance Centre, Ottawa, Ontario (2014). https://fnigc.ca/wp-content/uploads/2020/09/5776c4ee9387f966e6771aa93a04f389_ocap_path_to_fn_information_governance_en_final.pdf, ISBN 978-0-9879882-8-7
28. Turk, A., Trees, K.: Appropriate computer-mediated communication: an Australian indigenous information system case study. AI Soc. **13**(4), 377–388 (1999). https://doi.org/10.1007/BF01205984
29. Winschiers-Theophilus, H., Bidwell, N.J.: Toward an Afro-Centric Indigenous HCI Paradigm. Int. J. Human-Comput. Interaction **29**(4), 243–255 (2013). https://doi.org/10.1080/10447318.2013.765763

Social Context in HAI: Towards a Theoretical Framework Based on Multi-Perspectival Imaginaries

Anna Lena Menne(✉) and Christian Schulz

Paderborn University, Warburger Str. 100, 33098 Paderborn, Germany
{anna.lena.menne,christian.schulz}@upb.de

Abstract. Despite decades of awareness, asymmetries in conceptual resources, data, and governance between users and developers persist. Meanwhile, socially situated 'end-users' experience harms, such as hidden labor, reinforced stereotypes, and increased unpredictability, as machine learning advances. However, accurately modeling social context does not constitute design justice. This paper reinterprets Giuseppe Mantovani's model of social context in human-computer interaction (HCI) to address the relational emergence and political situatedness of social context in human-AI interaction (HAI). Drawing on the concept of a multi-perspectival algorithmic imaginary, we (1) conceptualize context as nested and entangled relations, (2) identify actors, including users, developers, models, and interfaces, and (3) foreground the organization of relations of power. Recognizing that models are performative rather than predictive, we argue that the sociopolitical situatedness of context must be acknowledged alongside its limits. To challenge design authority, we propose that HCI and HAI strategically foster *intra-actional negotiability*, enabling users to challenge, reinterpret, or modify their relationship with technology through critical (design) practices.

Keywords: Social Context · Situatedness · Imaginaries

1 Introduction

From amusing or irritating to seriously harmful, computer systems often do not work as intended. A socially and politically situated user meets a machine built to follow a predetermined, systematic protocol shaped by 'conceptual models' [1, 2]. These conceptual models simplify users' diverse, dynamic mental models[1] into private, static representations. They become, in effect, 'models of models of users' [4]. The result is that users' actual needs, desires, and capabilities are largely ignored, as has been noted critically in the field of computer science [5]. This disconnect creates hidden labor for users, including

[1] Mental models are often used as a proxy for users' understanding of technology. In computer science and HCI, they still largely rest on the foundations of Craik [3] and Norman [2], which enforce a subject-object split and privilege the designers' perspective. See also [4].

C. Stephanidis et al. (Eds.): HCII 2026, CCIS 3047, pp. 93–106, 2026.
https://doi.org/10.1007/978-3-032-30552-7_10

ongoing troubleshooting and repairs [6]. It also goes unnoticed as users silently compensate for technological shortcomings. When developers assume systems are infallible and dismiss user difficulties, the consequences range from wasted time to a diversion of attention from critical tasks, such as patient care [7]. Moreover, as users repeatedly follow 'unhelpful' pathways, these actions can structurally reinforce conceptual models, creating a self-fulfilling prophecy. Such outcomes directly oppose the goals of computer-supported cooperative work (CSCW) and human-computer-interaction (HCI) to "create computing that supports the betterment of humankind" [8, p. 4].

We are not the first, and we will probably not be the last, to raise concerns about the harms caused by the design asymmetry between so-called 'end-users' and developers. Critiques from nearly 50 years ago linked dominant paradigms in computer science and artificial intelligence (AI), such as rationalism or cognitivism, to structural imbalances in decision-making and in technology design. While cognitivism reduces situated action to plans, although it exceeds formal description [9], the rise of 'technoscience' marginalized or invisibilized any social context that cannot be captured by machines [10]. Hence, the desire to manage situations through technology and planning is unlikely to vanish anytime soon. Meanwhile, more recent books such as *Data Feminism* [11] and *Design Justice* [12] advocate for broader change by providing a shared vocabulary and principles for computer scientists to reference and put into practice. This call for change was foreshadowed in Bødker's [13] waves of HCI, shifting from model-driven cognitive science to participatory and collaborative work practices, then to an emphasis on situated knowledge amid ubiquitous computing. Each 'wave' expanded the theoretical and methodological tools of HCI, but they did not lead to significant changes in power dynamics. While social context in HCI often serves as a reminder to ground interaction in specific use circumstances, D'Ignazio and Klein [11] encourage developers and designers to confront political realities of power, such as whose model is considered and who bears the costs of failures. Nevertheless, despite the growing influence of data feminism across disciplines [14, 15], a genuine shift in power—who controls resources, data, roadmaps, or governance—has yet to materialize [16].

From this perspective, Amershi et al.'s [17] widely cited Guidelines for human-AI Interaction (HAI) are well-intentioned responses to the growing unpredictability of machine learning technologies but ultimately reaffirm the notion that behavior can be anticipated by restoring predictive accuracy, even as large language models (LLMs) and diffusion models exhibit probabilistic, context-sensitive, and evolving behavior. Accuracy in describing situational context is not the same as design justice,[2] although techno-scientific institutions often reward it. Instead, we view the hype surrounding generative systems and the unpredictability introduced by what is increasingly termed 'AI' as an opportunity to move beyond traditional usability expectations.[3] Drawing on posthumanist and relational theories, Frauenberger [19] advocates for a fourth wave of HCI that responds to growing user-AI entanglement, which extends beyond user-centric design

[2] Costanza-Chock [12] highlights design justice as a framework to challenge traditional design by centering those usually excluded, using collaboration and creativity to address community challenges, and making design a tool for liberation rather than serving designers' interests.

[3] Unlike traditional algorithms, generative models are trained on large datasets to detect statistical patterns and generate seemingly novel outputs, e.g., text, images, code, audio, or video.

to the mutual shaping of human and other-than-human entities. Designing 'meaningful relations' rather than 'user experiences' is valuable, but caution is necessary to avoid replacing knowledge hierarchies with an all-encompassing entanglement view. Indeed, Ashby et al.'s [20] call for fourth-wave HCI emphasizes mainstreaming 'political activism' while building on earlier waves. We contend that this demands not only that we unsettle dualisms [21] but also that we reconsider whether computers and their designers can—or should—anticipate social situations. The tension between accuracy-driven computer science and justice-oriented feminism is structural but not inevitable [22]: socio-technical systems can be redesigned to accommodate rather than erase the unpredictability of human-AI interaction.

This paper sketches an initial theoretical framework to address both the relational emergence and political situatedness of social context in HAI. The first part applies a media genealogical perspective [23] to Giuseppe Mantovani's [24] comprehensive model of social context in HCI. Mantovani's model represents one of the earliest serious attempts to incorporate social context into HCI. While the model promotes greater user inclusion and emphasizes situated action, it fails to develop a sociopolitical understanding of situatedness and thus does not sufficiently challenge developers' design authority. Furthermore, the model does not account for the uncertainties and dynamism of context and use, especially given recent advancements in machine learning. Therefore, the second part of the paper revises Mantovani's model through a science and technology studies (STS) and media studies notion of a multi-perspectival algorithmic imaginary [25]. This framework results in three recommendations for future modeling of social context applicable to both HCI and HAI: (1) shifting from hierarchical levels to relational connections; (2) recognizing actors explicitly, without essentializing them; and (3) accounting for power dynamics. Finally, the paper argues that technological design should move away from attempts to control situations through traditional mental models. Instead, we propose 'intra-actional negotiability,' advocating controlled ambiguity that treats users as capable of interpreting and shaping use and outcomes rather than as subjects of paternalistic technological guidance.

2 Social Context in HCI Revisited

Over the course of an influential debate in the journal *Cognitive Science* on the relationship between rule-based and situated approaches in HCI [26], which addressed top-down and bottom-up perspectives, psychologist Giuseppe Mantovani proposed a framework in 1996 for implementing social context in HCI [24]. This framework explicitly integrates both approaches [24, p. 243] and is likely the first detailed attempt to do so comprehensively.

The model includes two horizontal and three vertical axes that outline the relationships and interactions among three levels—*artifacts*, *situations*, and *social context*—and their respective connections to actors' mental models [24, p. 257].

Following Suchman [18], we view 'AI' and 'algorithm' as contested and enacted. Thus, distinguishing generative and rule-based systems is not central to our analysis. Both have long produced volatile user experiences, even as generative systems introduce new uncertainties.

Level 1 is the *social context*, or the 'cultural system' [27], in which social norms and (personal) experiences of the actors are represented that shape the relation between structure and action. So basically, this level addresses the relationship between society and the individual. Social context influences level 2, which concerns the level of *situations*. According to Mantovani, situations are reinterpreted based on individuals' respective opportunities, interests, and goals, as well as on the situation at hand. And finally, level 3 involves *artifacts* as 'embodied objects' [24, p. 252] that represent the relation between tool and user alongside their corresponding tasks or goals (of tool and user), thereby enabling a local interaction with the environment. Mantovani [24, p. 242] terms this the 'task-artifact cycle.'

Mantovani references early Scandinavian participatory design research [28] and explicitly emphasizes the active role of users who, during actual use, alter the technological scripts [29] implemented by designers in the software. Level 2 builds directly on discussions of situated action [9, 30, 31] and can be considered a precursor to situational concepts that have gained prominence in recent years within HCI, especially during the so-called third wave [32, 33]. Mantovani situates this concept at the meso level, noting that situated actions always occur within a social context shaped by norms and users' personal experiences (level 1). In contrast, the task-artifact cycle at level 3 essentially represents an actor-network [34] avant la lettre in the interaction between actor and environment. The focus here, then, is on the micro-level of users' specific interactions with technical systems. However, Mantovani explicitly emphasizes that concentrating solely on these socio-technical interactions is insufficient and, with reference to the then relatively new participatory design research in HCI [35], argues for a stronger involvement of end-users in the development of technical systems [24, p. 252]. This emphasis returns the discussion to level 1 of his model and the inescapable dimension of social context. Mantovani [24, p. 247] writes: "Context as a cultural object cannot simply be reduced to interpersonal relations, understood as the (possibly physical) environment in which the exchange of information occurs. Instead, it is the prerequisite for communication: Social actors exchange meanings—which implies the existence of shared cultural references—not simply bits of information."

Technical objects are, of course, to be included within the 'interpersonal relations' here (addressed by Mantovani at the micro level in level 3). This is a remarkable quote because it not only shows that Mantovani's concept of mental models is much broader than previous approaches to conceptual models in HCI research [2, 36, 37] but is also inextricably linked to social contexts. In contrast to these approaches, his model proceeds simultaneously top-down and bottom-up, explicitly localizing the social both inside and outside of actors: "It is misleading to think that cultural conceptions must be located either outside the person or inside the person" [24, p. 264].

And this is where the second vertical level of his model becomes relevant, which explicitly addresses users' or subjects' mental models in relation to the three horizontal levels of social context, situatedness, and artefacts. In this way, Mantovani avoids a strict distinction between inside and outside, or subject and object, an approach that was uncommon in HCI user modeling at the time. So here, too, the interpretation of situations is influenced by the respective social norms and experiences ('negotiation'/level 1), world models, and specific mental models related to interaction with technical artifacts.

These influences operate bidirectionally, both top-down and bottom-up. An advantage of Mantovani's mental model concept is that users appear to be central for the first time compared to other mental model approaches [2]. However, despite the detailed conceptualization of horizontal and vertical levels and based on reflections on the difficulty of real-world implementation ('riding the tiger' [38]), the model still seems to prioritize developers' perspectives over those of users.

The persistence of developer-user asymmetry is evident in arguments favoring the top-down perspective, which aims to extend prevailing bottom-up approaches of participatory design and situated action by incorporating social context post hoc [24, p. 265]. The issue lies not so much in the top-down perspective itself since systems ultimately require developer implementation, but in the schematic and rigid separation of situations (level 2) from social contexts. This approach treats situatedness primarily as a technical problem to be solved. Although (interpretations of) situations (level 2) are influenced by social contexts (level 1), the latter is explicitly not understood from a sociopolitical perspective. Instead, emphasis is placed on the assumed powerlessness of developers in the face of normative processes such as categorization, defined in an almost naturalized manner as "load-bearing structures of social structures" [24, p. 262]. This asymmetry is also reflected in the language, where the 'we' of the developer perspective contrasts sharply with the 'them' of the users [24, p. 265]. Notably, there is a lack of concrete proposals to strengthen the user perspective and its diverse social contexts, including specific sociopolitical situations. Although the concept of mental models is highly detailed, it remains schematic and rigid, and, above all, it naturalizes social power relations. Mantovani offers no concrete suggestions but remains at an abstract level, thus failing to fulfill the promise of integrating top-down and bottom-up approaches simultaneously. Furthermore, his plea to strengthen users' points of view is postulated from a very privileged (developer) perspective. It must also be noted that the examples Mantovani cites to describe the social context level are problematic from a gender-theoretical perspective. He relies on stereotypical descriptions of women ('knitting and reading'[4]) that appear conservative and reproduce gender stereotypes, indicating that his model should not be adopted uncritically.

In sum, although Mantovani calls for greater user inclusion through mental models, centers the user perspective for the first time, and emphasizes the importance of situatedness [24, p. 252], his account ultimately fails to disrupt design authority. In contrast to approaches that treat 'situatedness' as political [40, 41], Mantovani presents it as an exclusively technical problem to be solved through a schematic and strict separation between social context and situations. Consequently, the different (social) positions of users and developers, including their backgrounds, capabilities, and authority to define problems and solutions, are never meaningfully considered. Moreover, the account is dated regarding generative AI systems. Given that outputs are driven by evolving data and continuous prompting, like recent approaches in social explainable AI (sXAI) [42, 43], context is co-constructed in feedback loops rather than fixed in advance [44].

[4] For a perspective that explicitly challenges such stereotypes in HCI, see [39].

3 Social Context in HAI

3.1 The Multi-Perspectival Algorithmic Imaginary

The concept of a *multi-perspectival algorithmic imaginary* integrates the perspectives of users and developers as they converge at the interface [4, 25]. In this regard, it offers an alternative to the traditionally asymmetric mental models in computer science and HCI, promoting relational and co-constructive user modeling. Bucher's [46, p. 113] 'algorithmic imaginary,' "ways of thinking about what algorithms are, what they should be, how they function, and what these imaginations, in turn, make possible," has been highly influential in media and communication studies to explore how users interpret algorithmic processes.[5] A user scrolling through their social media feed may be uncertain why some posts appear while others are hidden, inferring rules that govern their experience.

The algorithmic imaginary primarily addresses the user's standpoint, which is essential given the frequent omission of users from traditional conceptual models. However, the relationship among users' imaginaries, algorithmic processes, and developers' intentions is largely unexamined. Developers may involve users in A/B testing, influencing the interface's operational logic and subsequent user perception. Hence, the 'design imaginaries' of developers converge with users' algorithmic imaginaries at the interface, which functions less as a mediating artifact and more as a threshold emerging from their active engagement [47].

According to Hookway [48], the interface both connects and defines distinct entities, such as users and developers, by facilitating interaction and regulating the extent to which these entities can act or influence one another through its design. Crucially, the interface constitutes 'a zone of contestation,' where agents interact, struggle, and negotiate power, agency, and subjectivity [48, p. 16]. Therefore, both design and algorithmic imaginaries constitute concrete components of 'AI' infrastructure, shaping one another's behavior through backend processes and creating a continuous interplay.

3.2 From Levels to Relations

The concept of the imaginary facilitates conceptual scaling of social context in HAI by bridging from a micro (user-interface-developer) to a macro (infrastructural and institutional) perspective. This approach parallels Mantovani's [24] model, which seeks to integrate context, situation, and interaction across the three levels.

According to Verran [49], imaginaries are collectively shared images and narratives that facilitate understanding of what exists and how it is known. She asserts, "The imaginary refuses a priori separation of the symbolic and the material, although it recognizes that such category separation might be achieved" [p. 37]. Therefore, imaginaries are performative, structuring the material through what is thinkable and knowable within a given society. Castoriadis [50] argues that the imaginary stabilizes within institutions that set the horizon for conduct. However, this stabilization remains incomplete, as the imaginary, or creative impulses, may also disrupt and remake the given order. This ongoing process unfolds across central significations as well as their peripheral sedimentations. Hence, the imaginary mediates between stabilized and liquefied material-symbolic

[5] Similar discussions have occurred in HCI through the concept of 'folk theories' [45].

orders, forming a theoretical hinge that connects micro-interactions at the interface to broader social structures that shape the distribution of authority, visibility, and resources. In other words, folding what Mantovani [24] referred to as 'interpersonal relations' (level 3) and the 'cultural system' (level 1) into the situation (level 2). Thus, these levels cannot be analyzed or implemented without considering their interrelations.

Move from Levels to Relations: Instead of modeling social context solely at the macro level, we conceptualize contexts through the imaginary, as nested, entangled relations in which each level is folded into and reproduced by the others (see Fig. 1).

3.3 Making Actors Explicit

Barad [51] describes material-symbolic order as ongoing relational events, termed *intra-actions*, in which entities such as 'subjects', 'objects', or 'AI' and their properties are temporary stabilizations enacted by specific material-discursive arrangements, or 'agential cuts.' This applies to both human and other-than-human entities, indicating that users, developers, and models are not fixed, external entities to the interface or usage context but represent identity roles formed through relations with particular systems, interfaces, data practices, work routines, and rules. Users, developers, and models co-constitute one another: models enable certain types of users and developers by defining permissible actions, attention, and relevant skills, while users and developers shape models through design, use, interpretation, resistance, and workarounds. Agency is, thus, "a matter of making iterative changes to particular practices through the dynamics of intra-activity" [51, p. 214]. LLMs, for example, not only respond to prompts, but also produce a kind of user—one who writes prompts in particular ways, learns to manipulate the model, and whose identity becomes legible as a data profile. Models also produce developers who are accountable to metrics, designs in terms of A/B tests, and may interpret inputs as signals for optimization. Consequently, references to user, model, and developer within a multi-perspectival framework denote their roles within specific arrangements, contexts, and historical situations rather than fixed, individual actors. For developers, this may include the team responsible for creating the application in use, as well as the institutional context or company policies. The same applies to users, interfaces, and both rule-based algorithmic and generative models.

Models do not simply appear or disappear in situated performances. Rather, their abstractions, that is, the various forms they assume in specific contexts of use, require concrete material complements to produce effects [52]. A recommendation algorithm exerts influence not merely by existing as a statistical architecture, but becomes consequential only through its relation to datasets, interfaces, users, and institutional settings. Similarly, although LLMs or diffusion models may generate language or images from within an autonomous technical-symbolic system, meaning emerges through interpretation, uptake, and use situated within historical, cultural, and other relational contexts of power [53, 54]. As Suchman [55] argues, humans and machines engage with situations differently. Humans continuously adjust their actions by attending to context, tacit cues, and ambiguity, whereas models operate on formalized, machine-readable representations, establishing a fundamental asymmetry in situational awareness. Therefore, while the symmetry principle is valuable in challenging the assumption that only humans matter, rigid adherence can obscure, if not invisibilize, crucial differences because ontological situatedness does not equate to political situatedness.

Make Actors Explicit: Mantovani's [24] model abstracts agency by obscuring the intra-action among users, developers, interfaces, and models. These entities acquire specific meaning only within their arrangement in a specific social context that connects intra-action (micro), situation (meso), and institutional context (macro). Thus, modelling social context in HAI requires emphasizing the actors who are both stabilized and stabilizing within the material-symbolic arrangement at the interface, where agency is negotiated. This is illustrated by a triangular shape, with the interface as a liminal zone that defines and extends the arrangement (see Fig. 1).

3.4 Accounting for Power

Matzner [41, p. 42] argues that Barad's relational ontology alone cannot adequately address political issues such as authority and visibility, because "ethics and politics do not derive from ontology but pertain to the ontology itself." In other words, historically dominant definitions of problems, harm, good design, and the legitimacy of computer systems are embedded within HAI design, shaping what becomes visible, sayable, real, and relational in the first place. Hence, actors' positions in a multi-perspectival imaginary are co-produced through intra-action, but not on equal terms. In this imaginary, developers, models, and interfaces establish conditions of use, while 'end-users' are subjected to them, experiencing exposure and constraints that tend to increase their vulnerability to harms like classification, surveillance, and exclusion. More powerful positions in these relations, such as those of developers, may even arise from repressing or ignoring their dependence on others, such as users' hidden labor [6]. However, user vulnerability also varies according to which colonial, racial, or gendered histories shape the data categories or default user. Therefore, describing the intra-action among user, developer, and model at the interface alone does not sufficiently address the inequitable distribution of authority, visibility, and resources. The key analytical approach to modeling social context in HAI involves showing how relationality is organized so that certain relations are ignored, hidden, or externalized onto others, while others are granted access to defining the organization of these relations, structuring the imaginary.

Account for Power: Analyses and designs for social context in HAI must recognize that, although users, developers, and models intra-act to distribute agency across their triangular arrangement at the interface, this arrangement is structured by asymmetric cuts. The user's position requires particular attention, as highlighted by the varying thicknesses of the connecting arrows (see Fig. 1). This is necessarily abstract, as the organization of relations changes dynamically from one intra-action to the next.

Matzner [41] contrasts Barad's ontological situatedness following Haraway, proposing 'radical situatedness' to understand the organization of relationality. Haraway [40] defines situatedness as inherently political, emphasizing that all knowledge originates from specific and embodied perspectives. She rejects a universal notion of objectivity, advocating instead for explicit recognition of the origin and limits of knowledge. Thus, acquiring 'better' data from multiple angles or in real time does not enable a complete

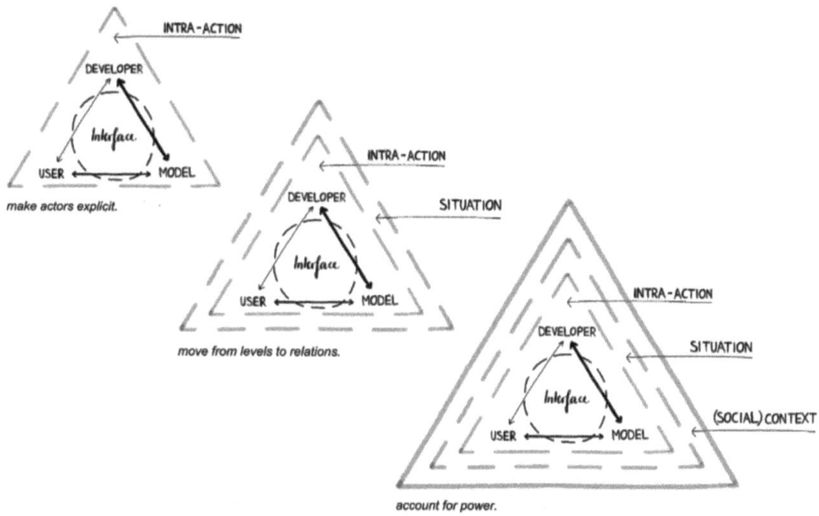

Fig. 1. Proposed framework for Social Context in Human-AI-Interaction

and accurate description or prediction. Situations may become partially intelligible as they unfold, but the idea of complete knowledge contradicts their situatedness. Consequently, Mantovani's [24] column on 'actors' mental models' has been removed from the remodeling in Fig. 1. This does not imply that conceptual or mental models should be abandoned entirely. Rather, they must be recognized for their performativity. Mental models and plans contribute to producing a particular imaginary and, as such, a particular material-symbolic order. By exposing, disrupting, or estranging their historical, material, and linguistic construction, it becomes possible to reveal how relations are organized. Radical situatedness, as outlined by Matzner [41, p. 47], involves ongoing critical practice such as historical deconstruction, breakdown, or failure, "that make it possible to encounter the constitution of a situation *within the situation* – and as such, they are always also encounters of partiality, of situatedness itself." Although critical practices, congruent with critical technical practice [56], do not produce a definitive map of reality, they enable the diagnosis of limits and partiality and reveal ontologically invisible relations. In this regard, the multi-perspectival imaginary and the framework presented in this paper (see Fig. 1) are epistemic tools that not only embrace radical situatedness but also provide a foundation for redesigning the implementation of social context in HCI and HAI, moving beyond abstract concepts to (critical) practice.

4 Designing for Intra-Actional Negotiability

A detailed account of how to implement our framework in practice is beyond the scope of this paper. However, we would like to propose a general direction. Addressing design asymmetry in HCI and HAI requires nurturing *intra-actional negotiability*, which at this preliminary stage may be defined as the genuine negotiation of agency among users, developers, models, and interfaces through critical practice. Genuine negotiation extends beyond rearranging recognized actors to include the negotiation of invisible relations. Importantly, this approach is not merely a call for increased user participation or for documenting exclusion, marginalization, or harm, which can itself cause damage [57]. Instead, design must enable contestation of the system's purpose, measures of harm, criteria for acceptable participation, and the option to refuse participation entirely, aligning with calls for more decentralized and community-driven digitalization [58]. This does not imply abandoning technology but demands a radically situated consideration of the performative nature of foundational concepts and models, emphasizing the mutual shaping of technological systems, imaginaries, and material-discursive orders, as well as who is recognized in these discussions. Without such measures, negotiability risks becoming superficial, even in recent co-construction efforts such as generative UI/UX design [59], where the system remains open only to its own terms.

Designing for intra-actional negotiability need not proceed de novo. On the contrary, existing approaches, such as agonistic or 'infrastructuring' design [16], offer meaningful foundations for elaborating this concept alongside methods of co-construction [42]. For example, Gaver et al. [60, p. 240] emphasize the value of ambiguity in design—not arbitrary ambiguity, but a deliberate resource that enables users to question situational limits and to interpret and integrate systems into their lives, while allowing developers to transcend technological limits: "ambiguity provides a frame of reference that allows the use of inaccurate sensors, inexact mappings, and low-resolution displays because it encourages users to supplement them with their own interpretations and beliefs." Encouraging users to supplement inaccuracies with their own interpretations is significant because situatedness in imaginaries is continuous and collective rather than individual. This suggests that promoting intra-actional negotiability can facilitate the redistribution of agency by enabling the gradual shaping of practices from intra-actions situated in use to those in institutional contexts, linking various intra-actions. From this perspective, although embracing uncertainty and unpredictability may initially appear radical in computer science and related disciplines, it fundamentally signifies design justice: recognizing users as experts of their own lived experiences.

5 Conclusion

Computer systems often fail when users interact with machines governed by rigid protocols and conceptual models. These systems can cause harm by imposing hidden labor and reinforcing stereotypes. Despite decades of recognition of these issues, design asymmetries persist between users and developers regarding control over resources, data, roadmaps, and governance. Concurrently, recent advances in machine learning have increased unpredictability and errors, prompting efforts to restore technological accuracy through renewed guidelines, conceptual models, or plans. However, accurately describing social context does not equate to design justice, which aims to make design a tool for liberation by centering those typically excluded rather than serving designers' interests. Although generative systems increase uncertainty, 'end-user' interactions have historically been volatile even with traditional rule-based algorithms, as users have often been passive recipients. As such, we have taken the current interest in 'AI' as an opportunity to reconsider how social context is typically modeled in HCI.

The paper sketched an initial framework that reinterprets Giuseppe Mantovani's [24] model of social context in HCI, addressing both the relational emergence and political situatedness of social context in HAI. Although advanced for its time, Mantovani's model ultimately prioritizes traditional design authority over the user, is grounded in a primarily technological understanding of situatedness, and does not account for recent advances in machine learning, in which context is increasingly unpredictable. Employing the concept of a multi-perspectival algorithmic imaginary, context is conceptualized as nested and entangled across intra-actional (micro), situational (meso), and institutional (macro) contexts, shifting the hierarchical focus from levels to relations. Modeling social context in HAI requires making actors explicit—users, developers, interfaces, and models—as both stabilizing and stabilized within a material-symbolic arrangement in which agency is negotiated. It is also critical to account for power by showing how relationality is organized so that some relations are marginalized or externalized onto others, with particular attention to users' varying vulnerabilities.

The framework reveals that conceptual models are less predictive than performative and emphasizes the impossibility of accurately anticipating social context or use. Instead, the sociopolitical situatedness of context must be acknowledged, making it essential to highlight the limits and partiality of situations. As such, a future direction for HAI might be to strategically foster ambiguity in design, as this could nurture what we term 'intra-actional negotiability,' encouraging users to supplement, appropriate, and question technologies for themselves, possibly enabling a genuine challenge to design authority and for building computing systems that foster 'the betterment of humankind'.

Acknowledgments. This work is associated with the collaborative research center "Constructing Explainability" (DFG TRR 318/1 2021 – 438445824) and funded by Paderborn University.

Disclosure of Interests. The authors have no competing interests to declare that are relevant to the content of this article.

References

1. Irby, C., Bergsteinsson, L., Moran, T., Newman, W., Tesler, L.: A methodology for user interface design. Office Products Division, Xerox Corporation (1977)
2. Norman, D.A.: Some observations on mental models. In: Gentner, D., Stevens, A.L. (eds.) Mental Models, pp. 7–14. Lawrence Erlbaum Associates, Hillsdale (1983)
3. Craik, K.J.W.: The Nature of Explanation. Cambridge University Press, Cambridge (1943)
4. Schulz, C.: From mental models to algorithmic imaginaries to co-constructive mental models. Navig. Z. Medien- Kulturwiss. **23**(2), 66–76 (2023). https://doi.org/10.25969/mediarep/21634
5. Volkamer, M., Renaud, K.: Mental models—general introduction and review of their application to human-centred security. In: Hutchison, D., Kanade, T., Kittler, J., Kleinberg, J.M., Mattern, F., Mitchell, J.C., et al. (eds.) Number Theory and Cryptography, pp. 255–280. Springer, Berlin (2013). https://doi.org/10.1007/978-3-642-42001-6_18
6. Fox, S.E., Shorey, S., Kang, E.Y., Montiel Valle, D., Rodriguez, E.: Patchwork: the hidden, human labor of AI integration within essential work. Proc. ACM Hum.-Comput. Interact. **7**(CSCW1), 1–20 (2023). https://doi.org/10.1145/3579514

7. Ruckenstein, M.: The darker qualities of repair. Sci. Technol. Stud. **38**(4), 97–113 (2025). https://doi.org/10.23987/sts.149448
8. Hornbæk, K., Kristensson, P.O., Oulasvirta, A.: Introduction to Human-Computer Interaction. Oxford University Press, Oxford (2025)
9. Suchman, L.: Plans and Situated Actions: The Problem of Human-Machine Communication, 1st edn. Cambridge University Press, Cambridge (1987)
10. Haraway, D.: Modest_Witness@Second_Millennium.FemaleMan_Meets_OncoMouse: Feminism and Technoscience. Routledge, New York (1997)
11. D'Ignazio, C., Klein, L.F.: Data Feminism. The MIT Press, Cambridge (2020)
12. Costanza-Chock, S.: Design Justice: Community-Led Practices to Build the Worlds We Need. The MIT Press, Cambridge (2020)
13. Bødker, S.: Third-wave HCI, 10 years later—participation and sharing. Interactions. **22**(5), 24–31 (2015). https://doi.org/10.1145/2804405
14. Lee, V.R., Pimentel, D.R., Bhargava, R., D'Ignazio, C.: Taking data feminism to school: a synthesis and review of pre-collegiate data science education projects. Brit. J. Educ. Technol. **53**(5), 1096–1113 (2022). https://doi.org/10.1111/bjet.13251
15. Gómez, O.A., Bourgeois, J., Kortuem, G.: Sensitive data donation: a feminist reframing of data practices for intimate research contexts. In: Vallgårda, A., Jönsson, L., Fritsch, J., Alaoui, S.F., Le Dantec, C.A. (eds.) DIS '24: Designing Interactive Systems Conference, pp. 2420–2434. Association for Computing Machinery, New York (2024). https://doi.org/10.1145/3643834.3661524
16. Raihan, J.: The colonial legacy of the human in human-computer interaction: implications for critical design approaches. In: AAR 2025: The Sixth Decennial Aarhus Conference: Computing X Crisis, pp. 140–152. Association for Computing Machinery, New York (2025). https://doi.org/10.1145/3744169.3744184
17. Amershi, S., Weld, D., Vorvoreanu, M., Fourney, A., Nushi, B., Collisson, P., et al.: Guidelines for human-AI interaction. In: Brewster, S., Fitzpatrick, G., Cox, A., Kostakos, V. (eds.) CHI '19: CHI Conference on Human Factors in Computing Systems, pp. 1–13. Association for Computing Machinery, New York (2019). https://doi.org/10.1145/3290605.3300233
18. Suchman, L.: The uncontroversial 'thingness' of AI. Big Data Soc. **10** (2023). https://doi.org/10.1177/20539517231206794
19. Frauenberger, C.: Entanglement HCI the next wave? ACM Trans. Comput.-Hum. Interact. **27**(1), 1–27 (2019). https://doi.org/10.1145/3364998
20. Ashby, S., Hanna, J., Matos, S., Nash, C., Faria, A.: Fourth-wave HCI meets the 21st century manifesto. In: Fischer, J.E., Martindale, S., Porcheron, M., Reeves, S., Spence, J. (eds.) HTTF 2019: Halfway to the Future, pp. 1–11. Association for Computing Machinery, New York (2019). https://doi.org/10.1145/3363384.3363467
21. Dahlin, E.: Think differently we must! An AI manifesto for the future. AI & Soc. **39**, 1423–1426 (2024). https://doi.org/10.1007/s00146-022-01620-x
22. Tacheva, Z.: Taking a critical look at the critical turn in data science: from "data feminism" to transnational feminist data science. Big Data Soc. **10**(2) (2022). https://doi.org/10.1177/20539517221112901
23. Monea, A., Packer, J.: Media genealogy: technological and historical engagements of power - introduction. Int. J. Commun. **10**, 41–59 (2016)
24. Mantovani, G.: Social context in HCl: a new framework for mental models, cooperation, and communication. Cogn. Sci. **20**, 237–269 (1996). https://doi.org/10.1207/s15516709cog2002_3
25. Schulz, C.: A new algorithmic imaginary. Media Culture Soc. **45**(3), 646–655 (2023). https://doi.org/10.1177/01634437221136014
26. Norman, D.A.: Cognition in the head and in the world: an introduction to the special issue on situated action. Cogn. Sci. **17**, 1–6 (1993). https://doi.org/10.1207/s15516709cog1701_1

27. Geertz, C.: The Interpretation of Cultures. Basic Books, New York (1973)
28. Bannon, L.J., Bødker, S.: Beyond the interface: encountering artifacts in use. In: Carroll, J.M. (ed.) Designing Interaction: Psychology at the Human-Computer Interface. Cambridge University Press, Cambridge (1991)
29. Akrich, M.: The de-scription of technical objects. In: Bijker, W.L. (ed.) Shaping Technology/Building Society: Studies in Sociotechnical Change, pp. 205–224. The MIT Press, Cambridge (1992)
30. Agre, P.E.: The symbolic worldview: reply to Vera and Simon. Cogn. Sci. **17**, 61–69 (1993). https://doi.org/https://doi.org/10.1207/s15516709cog1701_4
31. Suchman, L.: Response to Vera and Simon's situated action: a symbolic interpretation. Cogn. Sci. **17**, 71–75 (1993). https://doi.org/10.1207/s15516709cog1701_5
32. Duarte, E.F., Baranauskas, M.C.C.: Revisiting the three HCI waves. In: IHC '16: XV Brazilian Symposium on Human Factors in Computing Systems, pp. 1–4. Association for Computing Machinery, New York (2016). https://doi.org/10.1145/3033701.3033740
33. Bødker, S.: When second wave HCI meets third wave challenges. In: Mørch, A., Morgan, K., Bratteteig, T., Ghosh, G., Svanaes, D. (eds.) NORDICHI06: The 4th Nordic Conference on Human-Computer Interaction, pp. 1–8. Association for Computing Machinery, New York (2006). https://doi.org/10.1145/1182475.1182476
34. Latour, B.: Reassembling the Social: An Introduction to Actor-Network-Theory. Oxford University Press, Oxford (2005)
35. Asaro, P.M.: Transforming society by transforming technology: the science and politics of participatory design. Account. Manag. Inf. Technol. **10**, 257–290 (2000). https://doi.org/10.1016/S0959-8022(00)00004-7
36. Johnson-Laird, P.N.: Mental Models: Towards a Cognitive Science of Language, Inference, and Consciousness. Harvard University Press, Cambridge (1983)
37. Gentner, D., Stevens, A.L. (eds.): Mental Models. Lawrence Erlbaum Associates, Hillsdale (1983)
38. Schmidt, K.: Riding a tiger, or computer supported cooperative work. In: Bannon, L. (ed.) Proceedings of the Second European Conference on Computer-Supported Cooperative Work: ECSCW '91, pp. 1–16. Kluwer, Dordrecht (1991)
39. Treusch, P.: Robotic Knitting. transcript Verlag, Bielefeld (2020)
40. Haraway, D.: Situated knowledges: the science question in feminism and the privilege of partial perspective. Fem. Stud. **14**(3), 575–599 (1988). https://doi.org/10.2307/3178066
41. Matzner, T.: Algorithms: Technology, Culture, Politics. Taylor & Francis Group, Milton (2024)
42. Rohlfing, K.J., Främling, K., Lim, B., Alpsancar, S., Thommes, K.: Social Explainable AI. Springer, Singapore (2026)
43. Rohlfing, K.J., Cimiano, P., Scharlau, I., Matzner, T., Buhl, H.M., Buschmeier, H., et al.: Explanation as a social practice: toward a conceptual framework for the social design of AI systems. IEEE Trans. Cogn. Dev. Syst. **13**(3), 717–728 (2021). https://doi.org/10.1109/TCDS.2020.3044366
44. Cai, S., et al.: Agentic feedback loop modeling improves recommendation and user simulation. In: Ferro, N., Maistro, M., Pasi, G., Alonso, O., Trotman, A., Verberne, S. (eds.) SIGIR '25: The 48th International ACM SIGIR Conference on Research and Development in Information Retrieval, pp. 2235–2244. Association for Computing Machinery, New York (2025). https://doi.org/10.1145/3726302.3729893
45. DeVito, M.A., Birnholtz, J., Hancock, J.T., French, M., Liu, S.: How people form folk theories of social media feeds and what it means for how we study self-presentation. In: Mandryk, R., Hancock, M., Perry, M., Cox, A. (eds.) CHI '18: CHI Conference on Human Factors in Computing Systems, pp. 1–12. Association for Computing Machinery, New York (2018). https://doi.org/10.1145/3173574.3173694

46. Bucher, T.: If ... Then: Algorithmic Power and Politics. Oxford University Press, New York (2018)
47. Schulz, C., Matzner, T.: Feed the interface: social-media-feeds als Schwellen. Navig. Z. Medien- Kulturwiss. **20**, 147–164 (2020). https://doi.org/10.25969/mediarep/14954
48. Hookway, B.: Interface. The MIT Press, Cambridge (2014)
49. Verran, H.: Science and an African Logic. University of Chicago Press, Chicago (2001)
50. Castoriadis, C.: The Imaginary Institution of Society. Polity Press, Cambridge (1997)
51. Barad, K.: Meeting the Universe Halfway: Quantum Physics and the Entanglement of Matter and Meaning, 2nd edn. Duke University Press, Durham (2007)
52. Matzner, T.: Algorithms as complementary abstractions. New Media Soc. **26**, 1799–1815 (2024). https://doi.org/10.1177/14614448221078604
53. Klein, L., Martin, M., Brock, A., Antoniak, M., Walsh, M., Johnson, J.M., et al.: Provocations from the humanities for generative AI research. arXiv preprint arXiv:2502.19190 (2025). https://doi.org/10.48550/arXiv.2502.19190
54. Weatherby, L.: Two autonomies of the symbolic order: data and language in neural nets. In: Bajohr, H. (ed.) Thinking with AI: Machine Learning the Humanities, pp. 33–57. Open Humanities Press, London (2025)
55. Suchman, L.: Human-Machine Reconfigurations: Plans and Situated Actions, 2nd edn. Cambridge University Press, Cambridge (2007)
56. Agre, P.E.: Toward critical technical practice: lessons learned in trying to reform AI. In: Bowker, G., Leigh Star, S., Gasser, L., Turner, W. (eds.) Social Science, Technical Systems, and Cooperative Work, 1st edn. Psychology Press (1998)
57. Tuck, E.: Suspending damage: a letter to communities. Harv. Educ. Rev. **79**(3), 409–428. https://doi.org/10.17763/haer.79.3.n0016675661t3n15
58. Ricaurte, P.: The digitalization imperative. Dialogues Digit. Soc. **1**(1), 12–17 (2025). https://doi.org/10.1177/29768640241262263
59. Kumar, T., Tu, X., Zallio, M.: How generative AI is reshaping UI/UX design workflows: a systematic review. In: Human factors in design, engineering, and computing, vol. 199, pp. 2438–2452. AHFE International (2025). https://doi.org/10.54941/ahfe1007056
60. Gaver, W.W., Beaver, J., Benford, S.: Ambiguity as a resource for design. In: Cockton, G., Korhonen, P. (eds.) CHI03: Human Factors in Computing Systems, pp. 233–240. Association for Computing Machinery, New York (2003). https://doi.org/10.1145/642611.642653

A Reproducible Workflow for Diachronic Web Content Analysis

Rahel Püst[1(✉)], Hanno Menting[2], Alexander Riedmüller-Rezzani[2], Anne Fritzen[2], and Michael A. Herzog[1]

[1] Hochschule Magdeburg-Stendal, Breitscheidstr. 2, 39114 Magdeburg, Germany
stefan.puest@h2.de

[2] Hochschule für Musik FRANZ LISZT Weimar, Platz der Demokratie 2/3, 99423 Weimar, Germany

Abstract. Web archives enable diachronic analysis of online communication. Still, heterogeneous page structures, uneven snapshot coverage, and unstable archival quality make it difficult to perform reproducible, auditable large-scale analysis.

This paper presents a reproducible and auditable workflow for diachronic web content analysis that supports thematic tracking in archived institutional web corpora under real archival conditions.

The workflow is implemented as a Python-based pipeline for data collection, preparation, and analysis. It is structured into three macro-stages and seven operational stages, with explicitly defined input and output artifacts. Archived URLs are retrieved via the Wayback Machine CDX API; HTML content is downloaded; visible text is extracted and deduplicated; and candidate 1–3-grams are generated. A multistep linguistic filtering process removes unsuitable keyword candidates. Seed phrases are defined based on domain knowledge, and Sentence-BERT embeddings are used to identify semantically related keyword candidates. Final keyword selection is based on similarity thresholds and manual validation. Year-normalized keyword frequencies are then computed to identify diachronic trends.

The workflow was applied to German music school websites from 2014 to 2024 to trace changes in digitalization-related discourse. The results indicate a strong increase in digitalization-related communication during the pandemic years, with infrastructure-related topics outweighing pedagogical ones.

The contribution of the paper lies not in proposing a novel individual method, but in integrating established techniques into a transparent and inspectable end-to-end procedure. In this way, the workflow supports long-term thematic analysis beyond simple keyword counts while making corpus construction, processing decisions, and archive-related constraints more explicit and auditable.

Keywords: Diachronic Web Analysis · Web Archives · Semantic Keyword Discovery · Web Content Mining

C. Stephanidis et al. (Eds.): HCII 2026, CCIS 3047, pp. 107–117, 2026.
https://doi.org/10.1007/978-3-032-30552-7_11

1 Introduction

Institutional websites serve as interfaces between organizations and the public. They shape how services, values, and strategic orientations are communicated. At the same time, they document socio-technical change, as evolving technologies, policies, and discourses are reflected in public-facing language and content structures. Web archives therefore offer a basis for diachronic analysis, but substantial methodological challenges remain.

Archived web data is often heterogeneous in structure, redundant due to repeated menus and boilerplate, and incomplete due to missing or uneven snapshot coverage [1]. These conditions complicate not only data collection and analysis, but also the reproducibility of research based on archived web materials. In this context, reproducibility depends not only on code, models, or parameter settings, but also on transparent documentation of corpus construction and processing decisions [6]. Such documentation should make explicit which institutions were included, which archived versions were available or missing, how URLs were resolved, which preprocessing and filtering steps were applied, and which intermediate artifacts were retained for inspection.

Although established analysis techniques are available, constructing a reproducible end-to-end workflow remains challenging [8]. Existing work often addresses individual parts of this problem, such as archive access, scraping, or keyword retrieval, but not the full pipeline from target definition and snapshot selection to text preparation, semantic candidate selection, and diachronic analysis in an auditable form.

This paper presents a reproducible workflow for diachronic web content analysis, operationalizing explicit stages with clearly defined inputs and outputs. The workflow integrates archive retrieval via the Wayback Machine CDX API [1], large-scale HTML acquisition, visible-text extraction and deduplication, linguistic filtering, semantic keyword discovery using embeddings [12], and diachronic metrics generation.

2 Novelty and Contributions

The techniques combined in the workflow are well established in prior work [8,9]. The novelty of this paper lies not in proposing a new isolated method, but in integrating established methods into a reproducible and auditable workflow for archived institutional web corpora under real archival conditions. This paper makes four contributions:

First, we provide a modular end-to-end workflow for diachronic web content analysis. Rather than treating collection, cleaning, and institution- and year-specific aggregation and comparison as informal preprocessing, we specify each stage, from target list definition to diachronic analysis. Individual stages can be rerun, replaced, or extended without breaking the overall pipeline.

Second, we treat reproducibility and auditability as a primary design goal. Key decisions such as similarity thresholds and filtering criteria are encoded as explicit parameters, and each stage produces auditable artifacts. Reproducibility is operationalized not only through code availability but through preserved intermediate outputs such as target registers, CDX query results, download logs, filtering outputs, similarity scores, and documented manual validation decisions. Where possible, steps are deterministic[1], allowing other researchers to rerun the workflow, inspect intermediate outputs, and trace how results depend on parameter choices.

Third, we support fuzzy thematic tracking over time by combining corpus-derived n-gram generation, multi-stage linguistic filtering, and embedding-based semantic similarity. This enables diachronic analysis in which terminology changes over time or across institutions, reducing reliance on rigid, manually curated keyword lists.

Finally, we demonstrate the workflow at a realistic scale on an archived dataset of German music school websites, showing that reproducible and auditable diachronic analysis remains feasible even under uneven archival coverage and changing terminology.

3 Related Work

Existing research relevant to this paper spans several domains but typically addresses only specific aspects of the methodological challenge, rather than presenting a reproducible, end-to-end workflow for diachronic analysis of archived institutional websites.

[15] discuss notebook-based and API-supported access to web archives, while [11] emphasize sociotechnical constraints in using national web archives. [4] further highlight epistemological limitations in large-scale analyses of archived web data. [6] argues for a broader understanding of reproducibility in which corpus construction, methodological choices, and interpretive decisions are treated as interdependent rather than cleanly separable. This perspective is particularly relevant for archived web research, where the available sources, their specific points in time, and the researchers' documented selection and processing decisions all influence the basis of the analysis. These contributions enhance understanding of archival research conditions but focus on access, infrastructure, and methodological reflection rather than on a modular workflow.

Another relevant area of research addresses workflow design through diachronic data collection from websites. [5] introduce a reusable four-step scraping workflow for historical organizational website data using the Wayback Machine. This work shows that structured, large-scale data acquisition is feasible. However, the focus remains on web scraping and dataset building rather than on integrating steps such as linguistic filtering, semantic keyword discovery, or long-term thematic analysis across diverse archived corpora.

[1] In the archive retrieval and snapshot acquisition phase described in Sect. 4.2, minor differences between repeated runs may occur due to network-related factors such as request failures, retries, or temporary archive availability. These deviations are made transparent through query logs and can therefore be inspected retrospectively.

A further research area addresses computational keyword expansion and researcher-guided semantic retrieval. [2] evaluate keyword expansion pipelines for social movement data, while [16] propose a multi-step, researcher-driven approach to computational keyword selection in digital media retrieval. These studies show that seed-based and semantically informed keyword selection can be systematically operationalized. However, these methods do not target archived institutional web corpora, which have unstable snapshot coverage, repeated boilerplate content, and inconsistent comparability across years.

Research on institutional website analysis has established that websites are meaningful representations of organizational self-presentation. [3] and [7] illustrate the value of website-based analysis in institutional contexts. [14] states that websites can be understood as communicative documents that are publicly accessible, oriented toward specific audiences, and frequently used for organizational self-presentation and information provision. However, [4] note that most research has focused on interpretive or comparative analysis of current websites, while computational methods for reproducible diachronic thematic analysis across web archives are still developing.

Taken together, prior work addresses important but largely separated parts of the problem. What remains insufficiently developed is a methodological framework that makes the dependencies between corpus construction, archive selection, preprocessing, candidate selection, and real-world archive constraints transparent and reproducible. This gap is particularly important for diachronic analysis, where unstable coverage, repeated boilerplate, and changing terminology can shape results at multiple stages of the pipeline. The present work addresses this gap through an auditable end-to-end workflow for archived institutional web corpora.

4 Workflow Overview

The workflow is structured into three macro-stages:

1. Data Collection (dataset definition and snapshot acquisition),
2. Data Preparation (visible-text extraction, linguistic filtering, and keyword identification), and
3. Data Analysis (diachronic analysis and reporting).

Together, these macro-stages comprise seven operational stages. Each stage has clearly defined inputs and outputs, produces auditable artifacts, and can be rerun independently, given the same recorded inputs and configurations (Fig. 1).

4.1 Dataset Definition and Target List Construction

First, we compile a list of target institutions using current and, where available, historical sources. The primary output is a canonical target register stored as one CSV file per year. It assigns a stable institution identifier and records the

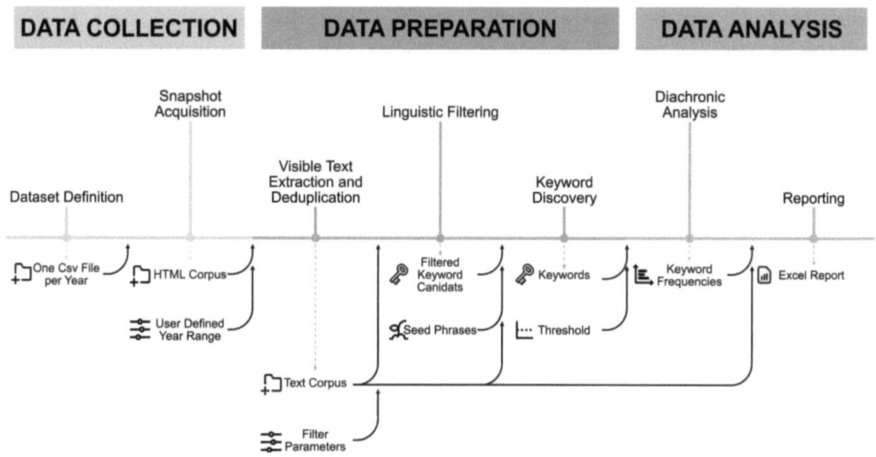

Fig. 1. Overview of the reproducible workflow for diachronic web content analysis, structured into three macro-stages and seven operational stages.

metadata required for subsequent analysis steps, including institution name, region, and base URL. Depending on the institutional context, existing online institutional registers may be used. If such resources are unavailable, the list must be constructed through manual research.

4.2 Archive Retrieval and Snapshot Acquisition

The target register, provided as year-specific CSV files and a defined year range, serves as input to a Python based web crawler. The crawler queries the Wayback Machine CDX API for archived content under each base URL, identifies valid snapshots, and downloads and stores the archived HTML resources in a deterministic directory structure organized by institution and year. If multiple snapshots of a page are available for a given year, the earliest valid snapshot is retained to ensure a consistent temporal reference point across institutions and years. To support reproducibility beyond code availability alone, the workflow preserves all CDX query results, resolved snapshot identifiers, and download logs, including requests, responses, errors, and retries, alongside the raw HTML corpus. This makes retrieval decisions reconstructable and allows both provenance tracking and retrospective inspection of archive coverage, resolution outcomes, and failed download attempts.

4.3 Visible Text Extraction and Deduplication

From the downloaded HTML corpus, we extract the visible text to obtain an analysis-ready representation independent of markup and layout. The extracted text is aggregated into plain-text (.txt) files by year and institution, yielding one text file per institution-year combination. Within these files, each extracted visible-text element is stored on a separate line. To reduce inflation from repeated boilerplate, such as navigation menus or footer elements replicated across many pages, deduplication is performed within each institution-year text corpus on these line-separated text elements so that identical elements appear only once. The resulting outputs are year- and institution-specific plain-text corpora that provide a basis for subsequent linguistic and semantic analysis.

4.4 Linguistic Filtering

For thematic tracking under conditions of terminological variation, we first generate candidate keywords as n-grams from the text corpora. These n-grams are then subjected to a multi-stage linguistic filtering procedure designed to reduce noise while retaining potentially meaningful domain-related expressions. Specifically,

1. inflected forms are lemmatized,
2. stopwords are removed,
3. candidate n-grams are filtered against a reference language corpus, and
4. part-of-speech-based filtering is applied to exclude syntactic patterns that are unlikely to serve as relevant keywords.

The result of this filtering procedure is a plain-text file containing a list of plausible keyword candidates.

4.5 Keyword Identification via Semantic Similarity

The keyword candidates retained after linguistic filtering are subsequently embedded in a semantic vector space using Sentence-BERT, as described by [12]. In parallel, the thematic domain is operationalized through a set of manually defined seed phrases, developed with reference to the research domain and guided by domain-specific expert knowledge. Following [13], semantic similarity between keyword candidates and these seed phrases is computed using cosine similarity, allowing the identification of semantically related expressions beyond exact lexical matches. Candidate selection is controlled by a configurable similarity threshold retained in the workflow configuration, ensuring that selection decisions remain reproducible and reviewable.

Because semantic similarity alone does not guarantee contextual relevance, the automatically selected candidates undergo a final manual validation step. Manual validation follows explicit inclusion and exclusion criteria focused on domain relevance, institutional context, and ambiguity reduction. Candidates are retained only if they refer to concepts relevant to the thematic domain within the institutional communicative context under investigation and are excluded if they are semantically related in general language but contextually irrelevant for the specific research setting.[2] The output of this stage is a validated keyword set with associated similarity scores.

4.6 Diachronic Analysis

Finally, we apply the validated keyword sets to the text corpora to compute yearly keyword frequencies and a set of comparative aggregate indicators. At the corpus level, these include total keyword counts, total word counts, relative frequencies, percentage changes relative to the baseline year, a normalized keyword density index, keyword growth deviation, keyword diversity measured by Shannon entropy, the average number of keyword mentions per institution, and the correlation between text length and keyword mentions across institutions.

4.7 Reporting

Results are exported in a structured Excel-based format that supports further analysis and inspection.

5 Use Case: German Music School Websites (2014–2024)

The workflow was applied to archived websites of German public music schools over an eleven-year period. Table 1 summarizes the main characteristics of the acquired dataset.

Table 1. Dataset facts for the music school use case.

Category	Value
Observation period	2014–2024
Source population	928 public music schools listed in the relevant association register as of 2024
Identifiable institutional websites per year	858–868, depending on the year
Archived institutional websites (all years)	6,097
Minimum number of snapshots in a year	467 (2014)
Maximum number of snapshots in a year	685 (2024)
HTML corpus size	32.95 GB
Number of HTML files	543,190
Extracted plain-text corpus size	199.1 MB
Analytical focus	Digitalization-related discourse on German music school websites

[2] In the present use case, this meant retaining keyword candidates related to digitalization in the context of music school communication while excluding semantically similar but domain-irrelevant expressions.

The use case serves to illustrate the workflow under typical archival conditions rather than to benchmark a novel retrieval model. To examine digitalization-related discourse, seed phrases covering digitalization, online learning, digitally enriched face-to-face teaching, and technological infrastructure were used to identify semantically related keywords in the corpus.

The resulting frequency patterns suggest that digitalization-related keywords remained at a comparatively low and stable level until 2019, increased markedly in 2020 and 2021, and then appear to stabilize again from 2022 onward at a level below the pandemic peak but still substantially higher than before 2020. This pattern likely reflects changing institutional demands during the coronavirus pandemic. Across the observation period, keywords related to infrastructure and digital tools were substantially more prominent than those addressing pedagogical or strategic dimensions of digitalization.

As an initial plausibility check for the diachronic analysis, the workflow was also applied to additional reference topics with clearly datable external events, including COVID-19 and the war in Ukraine. For these topics, the resulting keyword frequencies showed plausible increases in temporal alignment with the respective events.

6 Discussion

A key strength of the workflow lies in its end-to-end practicality under archival constraints. Rather than assuming clean and stable source material, it is designed for typical conditions of archived web data, including incomplete snapshot coverage, unstable or changing URLs, and the technical challenges of large-scale retrieval. In this respect, the workflow contributes not only a sequence of processing steps, but a reproducible way of dealing with the specific uncertainties of web archive research.

At the same time, the workflow addresses terminological variation over time by combining n-gram extraction with embedding-based semantic similarity. This makes it possible to identify thematically related expressions even when vocabulary shifts across years or institutions, thereby supporting diachronic analysis beyond exact keyword matching. Reproducibility is further strengthened through explicit decision points: similarity thresholds, filtering criteria, and manual validation steps are formalized as documented parameters and intermediate artifacts rather than remaining implicit researcher judgments.

Methodologically, the workflow bridges large-scale corpus processing and more interpretive forms of analysis. It is not intended to replace qualitative interpretation, but it can make such interpretation more feasible at scale by structuring large archived corpora, reducing noise, and identifying thematically relevant material for closer examination. In this way, the workflow can serve not only as an instrument for thematic tracking, but also as a transparent preparatory layer for subsequent qualitative analysis.

7 Limitations

Despite its practical and reproducible design, the workflow has important limitations that must be considered when interpreting results.

First, the workflow depends on the availability and quality of archived web data. Snapshot completeness and representativeness are determined by the Wayback Machine's holdings rather than by the researchers. Not all institutions are available for every year; archived versions are not always complete, and URL changes or missing captures can affect comparability across time. The workflow makes these dependencies transparent through explicit corpus construction, documented retrieval steps, and preserved intermediate artifacts, but it cannot eliminate archive-related bias on its own.

Second, the method focuses exclusively on visible text extracted from HTML. Other forms of institutional communication, such as PDFs, newsletters, social media content, or audiovisual materials are not included. The resulting analysis therefore captures only part of institutional communication, limiting both generalizability and interpretive scope.

Third, several processing decisions may influence the resulting keyword sets and diachronic patterns. Linguistic filtering steps, such as lemmatization, stopword removal, reference language corpus–based filtering, and part-of-speech constraints, help reduce noise but may also remove potentially relevant expressions. Likewise, embedding-based semantic selection depends on model choice and similarity thresholds. Although these decisions are explicitly parameterized and documented, their methodological effects have not yet been systematically validated for the workflow as a whole.

Fourth, manual validation remains a bottleneck. While semantic filtering substantially reduces the number of candidate expressions, final validation is still necessary to ensure thematic precision. This introduces an element of subjectivity, although it can be mitigated through clearly defined inclusion and exclusion criteria and more standardized validation procedures.

Finally, the interpretive reach of the resulting metrics remains limited. Keyword frequencies can capture the volume and distribution of thematic references over time, but not communicative stance, contextual meaning, or the depth with which a topic is addressed. The workflow therefore supports transparent and scalable thematic tracking, but it does not replace contextual interpretation. It can, however, provide an empirical basis for it.

8 Conclusion and Future Work

This paper presented a reproducible workflow for diachronic web content analysis that integrates archive retrieval, validation, visible-text extraction, n-gram- and embedding-based keyword discovery, and diachronic reporting. Its contribution lies not in proposing a novel individual method, but in combining established techniques into a practical, auditable end-to-end system for large, heterogeneous archived institutional web corpora.

The demonstration on German music school websites from 2014 to 2024 showed that the workflow is feasible at a realistic scale and can reveal long-term thematic developments despite changing terminology and uneven archival coverage. In this case, it highlighted plausibly interpretable trends, including a sharp rise in digitalization-related discourse during the pandemic years and the continued dominance of infrastructure-related topics over pedagogical ones. The modular design of the workflow has already proven useful beyond the present use case: [10] build on the dataset described here to conduct a qualitative content analysis of how music schools communicate about digitalization. This suggests that individual components and outputs of the workflow can be reused for different analytical purposes within the same research domain.

Subsequent research should prioritize comprehensive methodological validation, which is currently lacking for the workflow as a whole, even though initial plausibility checks using benchmark topics such as COVID-19 and the war in Ukraine yielded temporally plausible patterns. Specifically, future studies should formalize manual validation procedures by establishing annotation guidelines and reliability metrics, and systematically investigate how individual processing decisions shape keyword selection and diachronic trends.

Beyond methodological validation, future work should also examine more systematically how the workflow can support subsequent qualitative analysis by enabling the targeted selection and interpretation of relevant archived materials from large diachronic corpora. At the same time, methodological validation should include sensitivity analyses for preprocessing, filtering, embedding models, tokenization parameters, similarity thresholds, and deduplication methods. While the modularity of the workflow has already been demonstrated within the music school context, its transferability to other institutional domains and languages remains to be established. Future work should therefore assess the workflow across a broader range of institutional domains and languages and extend data extraction to include formats such as PDFs while maintaining provenance.

Acknowledgments. The authors gratefully acknowledge the Internet Archive for providing access to archived web materials through the Wayback Machine. We also thank members of the ODU Web Science and Digital Libraries Research Group for valuable discussions on web archives and methodological challenges in web archive analysis. This work was funded by the Federal Ministry of Education, Research and Technology (BMFTR) through the MusiGeNuM project, grant number 01JKT2410B.

Disclosure of Interests. The authors have no competing interests to declare that are relevant to the content of this article.

References

1. Alam, S., Nelson, M.L., Van de Sompel, H., Balakireva, L.L., Shankar, H., Rosenthal, D.S.H.: Web archive profiling through CDX summarization. In: Kapidakis, S., Mazurek, C., Werla, M. (eds.) Research and Advanced Technology for Digital Libraries, pp. 3–14. Springer International Publishing, Cham (2015)
2. Bozarth, L., Budak, C.: Keyword expansion techniques for mining social movement data on social media. EPJ Data Sci. **11**(1) (2022). https://doi.org/10.1140/epjds/s13688-022-00343-9
3. Bulgrin, E., Weber, S.M.: Websites as institutional imaginary positionings. Zeitschrift für Weiterbildungsforschung **46**(3), 575–592 (2023). https://doi.org/10.1007/s40955-023-00266-6
4. Donig, S., Eckl, M., Gassner, S., Rehbein, M.: Web archive analytics: blind spots and silences in distant readings of the archived web. Digit. Scholarship Humanities **38**(3), 1033–1048 (2023). https://doi.org/10.1093/llc/fqad014
5. Haans, R.F., Mertens, M.J.: The internet never forgets: a four-step scraping tutorial, codebase, and database for longitudinal organizational website data. Organ. Res. Methods **29**(1), 113–141 (2024). https://doi.org/10.1177/10944281241284941
6. Joyeux-Prunel, B.: Digital humanities in the era of digital reproducibility: towards a fairest and post-computational framework. Int. J. Digit. Humanities **6**(1), 23–43 (2024). https://doi.org/10.1007/s42803-023-00079-6
7. Lažetić, P.: Studying similarities and differences in higher education organisations based on their websites – comparative methodological approaches and research potential. Int. J. Soc. Res. Methodol. **23**(1), 75–90 (2019). https://doi.org/10.1080/13645579.2019.1672286
8. Liu, B.: Web Data Mining: Exploring Hyperlinks, Contents, and Usage Data. Springer Berlin Heidelberg (2011). https://doi.org/10.1007/978-3-642-19460-3
9. Manning, C.D., Raghavan, P., Schütze, H.: Introduction to Information Retrieval. Cambridge University Press, Cambridge (2008)
10. Menting, H., Fritzen, A., Riedmüller-Rezzani, A., Püst, R., Herzog, M.A.: Wie musikschulen über digitalisierung sprechen: eine qualitative inhaltsanalyse von musikschulwebseiten. In: AMPF Jahresband 2025 (2026). In press
11. Ogden, J., Maemura, E.: Go fish: Conceptualising the challenges of engaging national web archives for digital research. Int. J. Digit. Humanities, 43–63 (2021). https://doi.org/10.1007/s42803-021-00032-5
12. Reimers, N., Gurevych, I.: Sentence-BERT: Sentence embeddings using Siamese bert-networks. CoRR **abs/1908.10084** (2019). http://arxiv.org/abs/1908.10084
13. Schakel, A.M.J., Wilson, B.J.: Measuring word significance using distributed representations of words (2015). https://arxiv.org/abs/1508.02297
14. Schünzel, A., Traue, B.: Websites. In: Baur, N., Blasius, J. (eds.) Handbuch Methoden der empirischen Sozialforschung, pp. 1001–1013. Springer Fachmedien Wiesbaden (2019). https://doi.org/10.1007/978-3-658-21308-4_71
15. Talboom, L., Bell, M.: Keeping it under lock and keywords: exploring new ways to open up the web archives with notebooks. Archival Sci. **22**(3), 393–415 (2022). https://doi.org/10.1007/s10502-022-09391-6
16. Zhang, Y., Chen, F., Suk, J., Yue, Z.: WordPPR: a researcher-driven computational keyword selection method for text data retrieval from digital media. Commun. Methods Meas. **18**(4), 332–348 (2023). https://doi.org/10.1080/19312458.2023.2278177

Seeing the Same UX Artifacts Differently: Professional Vision in UCASD Teams

Luka Rukonić(✉), Pierre Fastrez, and Suzanne Kieffer

Université catholique de Louvain, Institute for Language and Communication, Louvain-la-Neuve, Belgium
{luka.rukonic,pierre.fastrez,suzanne.kieffer}@uclouvain.be

Abstract. User-centered agile software development (UCASD) approach requires practitioners from agile software development (ASD) and user-centered design (UCD) disciplines to communicate and collaborate to develop useful and usable systems. This collaboration is mediated by the creation and use of various user experience (UX) artifacts. However, the ASD and UCD practitioners interpret and process information through socially distinct professional lenses. Drawing on Goodwin's theory of professional vision (PV), this study investigates how multidisciplinary UCASD practitioners identify relevant information in four UX artifacts. Using eye-tracking we examined the eye movements of UCASD practitioners while looking at four UX artifacts: persona, storyboard, user journey map, and wireframe. Then, we compared the scanpath similarity using the MultiMatch algorithm and AOI strings and described the differences in the professional vision of ASD and UCD practitioners. The results revealed that while both groups exhibit high scanpath similarity, their viewing duration was significantly different. In addition, ASD practitioners had more consistent viewing patterns, while UCD practitioners had more individual approaches.

Keywords: user experience · professional vision · artifact-mediated communication · scanpath similarity

1 Introduction

User-centered agile software development (UCASD) is an integrated, multidisciplinary approach that combines the iterative and flexible nature of agile software development (ASD), with the exploratory and inclusive principles and practices of user-centered design (UCD) [2]. In this context, communication and collaboration between ASD and UCD practitioners are essential success factors for developing useful and usable software. Artifact-mediated communication is a core UCASD principle stating that tangible and up-to-date artifacts should be used to document product and design concepts and be available to all stakeholders [2]. UX artifacts such as personas, user journey maps, wireframes, and storyboards document knowledge about users, user needs, and design solutions addressing their problems.

C. Stephanidis et al. (Eds.): HCII 2026, CCIS 3047, pp. 118–127, 2026.
https://doi.org/10.1007/978-3-032-30552-7_12

However, UCASD practitioners face challenges when working together due to differing worldviews [12–14]. ASD practitioners (i.e., software developers, product owners), and UCD practitioners (i.e., UX researchers, UX designers) in UCASD teams must integrate their specialized knowledge domains. Yet, differences in thinking, vocabulary, and priorities inevitably arise, such as conflating of customers with users, or prioritizing technical over user requirements. These differences are shaped by practitioners' professional vision (PV), socially distinct and profession-specific ways of noticing and interpreting information [8]. In PV theory, selective attention and knowledge-based reasoning are the two intertwined cognitive processes practitioners use to focus their attention on significant events or information. Selective attention refers to recognizing relevant information and suppressing the rest, while knowledge-based reasoning refers to interpreting selected information by applying existing professional knowledge [9]. Thus, PV dictates what is noticed, thereby defining communication and structuring team collaboration.

To date, prior research has mainly focused on empirical descriptions and the situated use of UX artifacts [5,6], with limited attention to the cognitive aspects of communication in UCASD. Furthermore, while PV has been extensively researched in domains such as education [1,4,9] and medicine [7] to study the visual expertise of teachers and radiologists, eye movement research of UCASD practitioners has not yet been reported. To bridge this gap, we collected eye movement data to study the PV of UCASD practitioners and describe their visual trajectories when analyzing the information in UX artifacts. Process-based methods such as eye-tracking (ET) provide a robust means to study the attention and noticing processes and is, therefore, suitable for studying the PV of UCASD practitioners [1,10]. This study sheds light on the mechanisms of artifact-mediated communication, paving the way to improving the collaboration between ASD and UCD teams.

2 Research Method

We conducted this study with 13 UCASD practitioners (9 ASD, 4 UCD), aged between 27 and 50 (M=38, SD=8.69). All participants provided written consent for the collection and processing of their personal data in compliance with the European General Data Protection Regulation (GDPR). While the group sizes were unequal, this distribution reflects the typical composition of UCASD teams, where technical roles often outnumber design roles. The ASD practitioners included software developers, product owners, and scrum masters, while UCD roles involved UX researchers, UX designers, and UX managers. Using ET as a process-based method, we examined how the noticing process of UCASD practitioners' PV guides their attention toward specific AOIs of the four UX artifacts. Specifically, by analyzing AOI strings we identified which elements of UX artifacts were coded as significant through sustained visual attention (AOI revisits), while by analyzing scanpath similarity using the MultiMatch algorithm we identified whether ASD and UCD practitioners adopted different visual trajectories when looking at UX artifacts.

2.1 UX Artifacts and Apparatus

We recorded gaze data using a FOVIO FX3 screen-based eye tracker, while the UX artifacts were displayed on a 27-inch screen at a resolution of 1920×1080 pixels. The participants viewed four UX artifacts in a randomized order: persona, storyboard, user journey map, and wireframe (Table 1). The view time was limited to three minutes per UX artifact, and the participants could stop earlier if they wanted to.

2.2 Scanpath Analysis and Similarity Metrics

Scanpaths show gaze trajectories or sequences of eye movements over the stimuli. They are typically represented using area-of-interest (AOI) strings or spatial (x, y) coordinates of eye fixations to show the location and order in which the participants looked at the stimuli. AOI string is a sequence of characters representing fixation-based AOI hits in the order of occurrence [11]. Scanpath similarity can, therefore, be computed using algorithms that rely on AOIs, such as Levenshtein distance algorithm, or on spatial coordinates, such as MultiMatch algorithm [3]. In this study, we used both AOI strings and spatial coordinates to analyze the scanpaths of ASD and UCD practitioners. First, we defined the AOIs in all four UX artifacts, each AOI representing major structural and semantic elements (e.g., ICT Profile (J) in Personas; Call to Action (D) in Wireframes). Each AOI was assigned a unique alphabetical identifier. Then, we constructed scanpaths of their visual trajectories, represented using AOI strings. We used raw fixation data for each participant and UX artifact as input to the MultiMatch algorithm for scanpath similarity analysis.

We produced AOI strings for each participant and each UX artifact from the ET data to analyze scanpath length and identify the most-visited AOIs. To write AOI strings, we first listed all AOI fixations and then compressed consecutive fixations belonging to the same AOI to a single fixation representing the AOI the participant looked at before exiting that AOI and entering another one. This process is known as spatial downsampling [11], as AOI strings focus on the order of fixations, not their spatial locations (e.g., ABBBCABCCA => ABCABCA). We chose to produce compressed AOI strings to simplify the strings and reduce their lengths. We kept the repeated non-consecutive visits to an AOI and excluded fixations outside AOI boundaries. Because we were interested in investigating how different practitioners notice different elements in UX artifacts, the AOI strings were useful for this purpose, as they enable us to compare the AOI strings between participant groups and UX artifacts when looking for similarities and differences in their visual exploration strategies.

We used the multidimensional MultiMatch algorithm to calculate the similarity between the scanpaths of ASD and UCD practitioners [3]. Unlike traditional string-edit methods, such as Levenshtein's distance [11], that rely on predefined Areas of Interest (AOIs), MultiMatch represents scanpaths as sequences of vectors and compares them across five distinct geometric dimensions: vectors (shape), direction (angle), length (amplitude), position (spatial), and duration

Table 1. Specification of UX artifacts: purpose, listed Areas of Interest (AOIs), and visual definitions.

Artifact	Purpose & AOI List	Visual AOI Definition
Persona	To communicate a collection of attributes for a user profile. **AOIs:** (A) Name, (B) Photo, (C) Demographics, (D) Personality, (E) Habits, (F) Needs, (G) Tasks, (H) Goals, (I) Frustrations, (J) ICT Profile	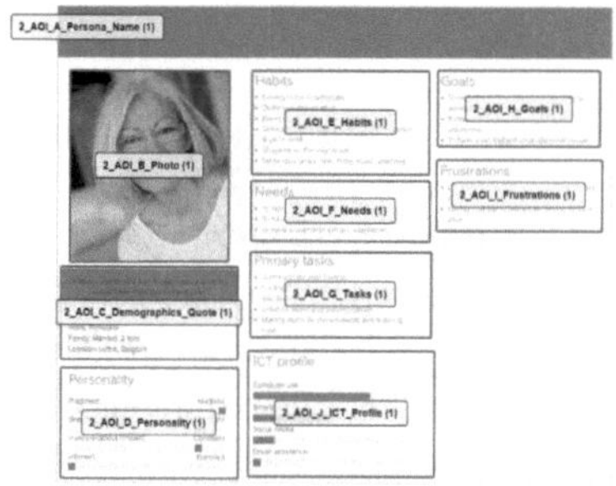
Storyboard	To graphically display a narrative about how the user will interact with a product. **AOIs:** Scene image & Text description (A, B, C, D, E, F, G, H, I, J, K, L)	
User Journey Map	To tell the narrative of the connection between an organization and a user. **AOIs:** (A) Phases, (B) User goals, (C) Images, (D) Actions, (E) Thinking, (F) Emotion Chart, (G) Vertical Row Labels	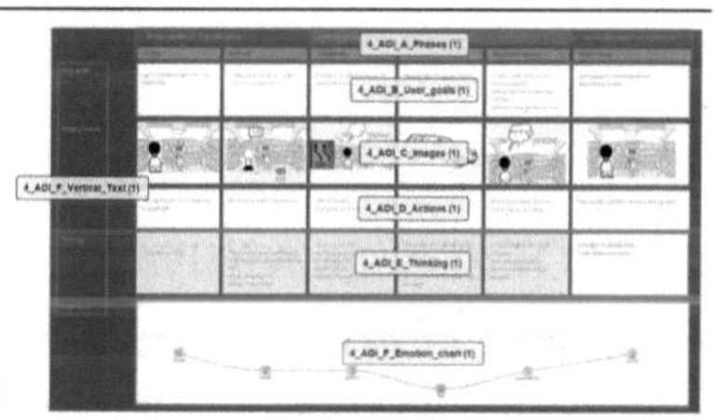
Wireframe	To define the layout, information architecture, and interaction flow. **AOIs:** (A) Horiz. Nav, (B) Vert. Nav, (C) Data Input, (D) Call to Action	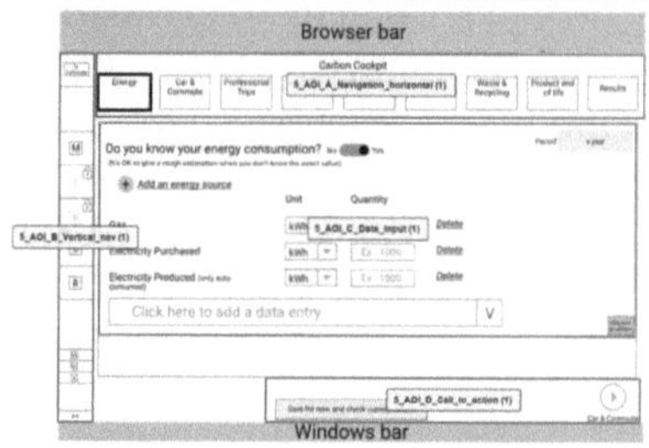

(temporal), as shown in Table 2. Before comparison, the algorithm performs a simplification process (grouping) to account for micro-saccades and fixations that occur in close proximity, ensuring that slight variations in sampling rate or eye movements do not artificially deflate similarity scores. Each dimension results in a score from 0 (completely dissimilar) to 1 (identical).

We conducted two types of analysis: (1) within-group comparisons, measuring the internal visual consensus within the ASD and UCD groups respectively, and (2) between-group comparisons, measuring the visual alignment between ASD and UCD practitioners.

Table 2. Five MultiMatch dimensions definitions used for scanpath comparison [3].

Dimension	Description
Vector (Shape)	The vector difference between aligned saccade pairs; a measure of similarity in scanpath shape
Length	The difference in length between the endpoints of saccade vectors; a measure of similarity in saccadic amplitude
Direction	The angular distance between saccade vectors; a measure of similarity in shape when saccadic amplitudes are different
Position	The difference in position between aligned fixations; a common measure of scanpath similarity in terms of Euclidean distance
Duration	The difference in fixation durations between aligned fixations; a measure of similarity in processing time

3 Results

3.1 AOI Strings Analysis

Scanpath Length. Across all artifacts (Table 3), the ASD practitioners had significantly longer scanpath strings (M = 20.00) compared to UCD practitioners (M = 11.19). This suggests that ASD practitioners employ a more exhaustive visual coding process. They are noticing and processing more individual elements (AOIs) before reaching a conclusion, whereas UCD practitioners may sample the artifact more selectively. The gap is most pronounced in Wireframes (ASD: 13.11 vs. UCD: 6.00) and Personas (ASD: 14.00 vs. UCD: 6.50). In the Wireframe, ASD practitioners (developers/POs) are likely scanning for technical logic and data inputs, leading to more transitions. UCD practitioners, familiar with the structure and purpose of a wireframe, likely look at fewer points to understand the layout. The User Journey Map produced the longest scanpaths for both groups. This suggests that the Journey Map is the most "visually demanding" artifact. However, the ASD group's average of 30.22 transitions suggests an incredibly detailed "sequential highlighting" process compared to the UCD group's 18.75.

Table 3. AOI Behavioral Analysis: scanpath length and AOI revisits.

Artifact	Group	Length	Entry	Top Revisited	Never/Least Visited
Persona	ASD	14.00	B	B, E	Least: A
	UCD	6.50	B	B, G	Never: A
	Combined	11.69	B	B, E	Never: A
Storyboard	ASD	22.67	A	B, E	Least: L
	UCD	13.50	A	B, A	Least: D, H
	Combined	19.85	A	B, E	Least: L
User Journey Map	ASD	30.22	D	B, C	Least: G
	UCD	18.75	A	B, C	Least: G
	Combined	26.69	A	B, C	Least: G
Wireframe	ASD	13.11	C	C, A	Least: B
	UCD	6.00	C	C, A	Least: B, D
	Combined	10.92	C	C, A	Least: B, D

AOI Revisits. The analysis of AOI transitions (Table 3) reveals significant differences in the visual effort and search strategies employed by the ASD and UCD groups. For the Persona, while both groups used the Photo (B) as the primary entry point, the ASD group frequently moved between the Photo (B) and Habits (E), while the UCD group focused on the Photo (B) and Tasks (G). Notably, the Name (A) was the least or never visited AOI for both cohorts, suggesting that the textual identity was secondary to the visual and behavioral attributes.

In the Storyboard, both groups entered at Scene 1 (A). The ASD group frequently revisited Scene 2 (B) and Scene 5 (E). The UCD group showed a more localized pattern, revisiting Scene 1 (A) and Scene 2 (B). The ASD group rarely reached the final Scene 12 (L), indicating a high concentration of visual attention on the earlier stages of the narrative.

The most significant divergence occurred in the User Journey Map. The UCD group followed a structural approach, entering at Phases (A) to orient themselves within the timeline. In contrast, the ASD group utilized a functional approach, entering at Actions (D), the descriptions of what the user is doing with the system. This aligns with the ASD group's focus on functionality over narrative structure. Interestingly, both groups revisited the Images (C) and User Goals (B) frequently, but largely ignored the Vertical Row Labels (G).

The Wireframe was the only artifact where eye movements converged almost entirely. Both groups entered at the Data Input (C) and focused their revisits on Data Input (C) and Horizontal Navigation (A). This indicates the interest in understanding the user interface from the information architecture and task execution perspectives, given that the wireframe represent a design solution for a system. Vertical Navigation (B) and Call to Action (D) were the least visited areas for both groups.

3.2 Scanpath Similarity: MultiMatch Analysis

Table 4 shows the scanpath similarity results of the MultiMatch algorithm. Similarity scores were calculated for all possible unique pairs within each group (Within-ASD, $n = 36$; Within-UCD, $n = 6$) and between groups (Between-Groups, $n = 36$). Reported values represent the mean (M) and standard deviation (SD) of these pair-wise similarity coefficients. Across all four UX artifacts, the practitioners exhibited high similarity regarding the gaze trajectory. Vector similarity scores were consistently the highest across the dataset ($M > 0.90$ for all conditions), suggesting that the fundamental shape and sequence of saccadic movements are nearly identical regardless of professional background. This spatial alignment is further supported by the Length (amplitude) dimension, which remained stable ($M \approx 0.92$), indicating that the gaze shifts during visual trajectories were dictated more by the artifact's layout than by the practitioner's professional vision.

While Position similarity remained high ($0.73 < M < 0.81$), the Direction dimension showed greatest spatial variances between practitioner groups ($0.593 < M < 0.768$). In particular, Persona stands out as the Direction values for the UCD group ($M = 0.593, SD = 0.218$) indicate independent viewing strategies, rather than more systematic ones as in the ASD group ($M = 0.683, SD = 0.083$). High Position scores and varying Direction scores suggest that while both groups look at the same elements (i.e., same AOIs), the visual trajectories (i.e., order of looking at AOIs) are much more individual in the UCD group, compared to the ASD group.

Notably, the Duration dimension exhibited the biggest differences, especially for the Persona and User Journey Map, indicating that the two groups spent different amounts of time processing information during fixations. For the Persona, the Within-ASD group demonstrated higher temporal consistency ($M = 0.404$) compared to the Within-UCD group ($M = 0.314$). Similarly, for the User Journey Map, the Within-ASD group ($M = 0.435$) was higher than the within-UCD ($M = 0.364$), indicating more consistent dwell times of ASD practitioners. These results suggest that ASD practitioners may employ a more standardized, systematic way when extracting information from narrative-heavy artifacts. In contrast, the Wireframe and Storyboard yielded more aligned temporal results between the groups, suggesting that more structured or visually guided layouts facilitate a more unified cognitive processing. Interestingly, the Wireframe had the highest Duration similarity (0.474) among all four UX artifacts, indicating its suitability for multidisciplinary collaboration.

Table 4. MultiMatch Similarity Dimensions (M and SD) across UX Artifacts. Higher values indicate greater scanpath similarity (0.0 to 1.0). Cells highlighted in blue represent significant findings, and cells highlighted in red represent large differences between ASD and UCD groups.

Artifact	Comparison	Vector	Direction	Length	Position	Duration
Persona	Between	0.923 (0.028)	0.646 (0.106)	0.932 (0.019)	0.770 (0.081)	0.373 (0.126)
	Within-ASD	0.930 (0.023)	0.683 (0.083)	0.926 (0.025)	0.772 (0.075)	0.404 (0.091)
	Within-UCD	0.916 (0.022)	0.593 (0.218)	0.923 (0.011)	0.736 (0.058)	0.314 (0.106)
Storyboard	Between	0.926 (0.018)	0.722 (0.078)	0.918 (0.029)	0.749 (0.056)	0.407 (0.099)
	Within-ASD	0.928 (0.015)	0.723 (0.076)	0.924 (0.022)	0.732 (0.042)	0.427 (0.078)
	Within-UCD	0.917 (0.019)	0.768 (0.083)	0.927 (0.022)	0.803 (0.049)	0.402 (0.075)
User Journey Map	Between	0.932 (0.015)	0.705 (0.071)	0.927 (0.018)	0.779 (0.042)	0.395 (0.088)
	Within-ASD	0.939 (0.010)	0.720 (0.060)	0.930 (0.017)	0.792 (0.033)	0.435 (0.076)
	Within-UCD	0.912 (0.022)	0.757 (0.040)	0.898 (0.043)	0.774 (0.036)	0.364 (0.092)
Wireframe	Between	0.906 (0.016)	0.695 (0.094)	0.897 (0.023)	0.794 (0.032)	0.474 (0.095)
	Within-ASD	0.915 (0.013)	0.741 (0.078)	0.910 (0.021)	0.768 (0.037)	0.499 (0.077)
	Within-UCD	0.893 (0.029)	0.766 (0.107)	0.889 (0.006)	0.811 (0.065)	0.461 (0.051)

4 Discussion

To our knowledge, this is the first investigation of visual expertise of UCASD practitioners. The results indicate that the visual expertise of ASD practitioners is characterized by long information processing and a search for technical or task-oriented information. In contrast, UCD practitioners spent less time looking at the UX artifacts, suggesting that their expertise helps them focus their attention to the most important information by applying selective information processing.

UCD practitioners exhibited individualistic eye movements when looking at UX artifacts, as demonstrated by their within-group scanpath similarity scores across all UX artifacts (Table 4). Notably, this highlights the diversity of the UCD discipline, encompassing both the pragmatic and hedonic aspects, but also a diversity of practitioners' profiles. ASD practitioners exhibited higher scanpath similarity, given their in-depth scanning of the UX artifacts' content searching for useful information. This finding indicates a possible lack of familiarity with the UX artifacts or their content. For successful collaboration in UCASD, team members should be familiar with the artifacts used in both ASD and UCD disciplines. Wireframe is a good example of both groups having the same way of looking at a UX artifact, allowing the practitioners to use it collaboratively, while its practical use might still differ.

These findings must be situated within the broader socio-technical context of UCASD. The development of PV is not an isolated cognitive act. Rather, it is shaped by the interplay between organizational culture, workflows, and the material characteristics of UX artifacts, as well as familiarity with UX artifacts.

5 Limitations and Future Research

Several limitations regarding artifact standardization and practitioner background must be acknowledged. Because UX artifacts lack universal layouts, the specific stimuli used in eye-tracking inevitably influence observed visual trajectories. Furthermore, as PV develops over time through domain knowledge, the distinct educational backgrounds and years of experience of participants determine the results. While controlling for these multifaceted contextual factors remains difficult in experimental settings, this study prioritized the authentic backgrounds of active practitioners. These constraints suggest findings reflect the specific PV of the sampled practitioners. Future research should expand these findings through larger sample sizes across multiple teams to capture the variance in PV across different organizational contexts. Furthermore, combining ET with qualitative data, collected using think-aloud protocols or observational methods, is essential for understanding both noticing and reasoning processes of PV. To support theory-building, future studies should investigate how UCASD practitioners apply specific coding schemes, highlighting, and articulation practices to UX artifacts. Analyzing these articulations could clarify the cognitive foundations of artifact-mediated communication.

6 Conclusion

This study provides the first insights into the visual expertise of UCASD practitioners. MultiMatch analysis revealed significant between-group differences: ASD practitioners prioritize prolonged, task-oriented searching, whereas UCD practitioners apply selective information processing. Furthermore, within-group similarity scores show that UCD practitioners exhibit highly individualistic scanpaths, reflecting the discipline's diverse profiles and dual focus on pragmatic and hedonic aspects. Conversely, ASD practitioners show higher within-group consistency when scanning for technical details. The shared visual approach to wireframes confirms their role as effective collaborative UX artifacts. Further research on professional vision in UCASD should deepen our understanding of collaborative practices in multidisciplinary software development contexts, and potentially reduce the friction between disparate practitioner groups.

Acknowledgments. This study was supported by the Wal4XR project financed by the Service Public de Wallonie (SPW) under grant no. 2310144.

Disclosure of Interests. The authors have no competing interests to declare that are relevant to the content of this article.

Data Availability. All data used in this study is available at: https://doi.org/10.5281/zenodo.18955456

References

1. Biermann, A., Brünken, R., Lewalter, D., Grub, A.S.: Assessment of noticing of classroom disruptions: a multi-methods approach. Front. Educ. **8**(October), 1–12 (2023). https://doi.org/10.3389/feduc.2023.1266826
2. Brhel, M., Meth, H., Maedche, A., Werder, K.: Exploring principles of user-centered agile software development. Inf. Softw. Technol. **61**, 163–181 (2015). https://doi.org/10.1016/j.infsof.2015.01.004
3. Dewhurst, R., Nyström, M., Jarodzka, H., Foulsham, T., Johansson, R., Holmqvist, K.: It depends on how you look at it: Scanpath comparison in multiple dimensions with MultiMatch, a vector-based approach. Behav. Res. Methods **44**(4), 1079–1100 (2012). https://doi.org/10.3758/s13428-012-0212-2
4. Duvivier, V., Derobertmasure, A., Demeuse, M.: Eye tracking in a teaching context: comparative study of the professional vision of university supervisor trainers and pre-service teachers in initial training for secondary education in French-speaking Belgium. Front. Educ. **9** (2024). https://doi.org/10.3389/feduc.2024.1326752
5. Garcia, A., Silva da Silva, T., Selbach Silveira, M.: Artifacts for agile user-centered design: a systematic mapping. In: Proceedings of the 50th Hawaii International Conference on System Sciences, pp. 5859–5868 (2017). http://hdl.handle.net/10125/41870
6. Garcia, A., da Silva, T.S., Silveira, M.S.: Artifact-facilitated communication in agile user-centered design. In: Kruchten, P., Fraser, S., Coallier, F. (eds.) XP 2019. LNBIP, vol. 355, pp. 102–118. Springer, Cham (2019). https://doi.org/10.1007/978-3-030-19034-7_7
7. Gegenfurtner, A., Lehtinen, E., Säljö, R.: Expertise differences in the comprehension of visualizations: a meta-analysis of eye-tracking research in professional domains. Educ. Psychol. Rev. **23**(4), 523–552 (2011). https://doi.org/10.1007/s10648-011-9174-7
8. Goodwin, C.: Professional vision. Am. Anthropol. **96**(3), 606–633 (1994). https://doi.org/10.1525/aa.1994.96.3.02a00100
9. Grub, A.S., Biermann, A., Lewalter, D., Brünken, R.: Professional vision and the compensatory effect of a minimal instructional intervention: a quasi-experimental eye-tracking study with novice and expert teachers. Front. Educ. **7**(May), 1–17 (2022). https://doi.org/10.3389/feduc.2022.890690
10. Guan, Z., Lee, S., Cuddihy, E., Ramey, J.: The validity of the stimulated retrospective think-aloud method as measured by eye tracking. In: Proceedings of the SIGCHI Conference on Human Factors in Computing Systems, CHI 2006, pp. 1253–1262. Association for Computing Machinery, New York, NY, USA (2006). https://doi.org/10.1145/1124772.1124961
11. Holmqvist, K., Nyström, M., Andersson, R., Dewhurst, R., Halszka, J., van de Weijer, J.: Eye Tracking: A Comprehensive Guide to Methods and Measures. Oxford University Press, United Kingdom (2011)
12. Kashfi, P., Feldt, R., Nilsson, A.: Integrating UX principles and practices into software development organizations: a case study of influencing events. J. Syst. Softw. **154**, 37–58 (2019)
13. Pillay, N., Wing, J.: Agile UX: integrating good UX development practices in Agile. In: 2019 Conference on Information Communications Technology and Society, ICTAS 2019, pp. 1–6 (2019). https://doi.org/10.1109/ICTAS.2019.8703607
14. Rose, E.J., Tenenberg, J.: UX as disruption: managing team conflict as a productive resource. Int. J. Sociotechnol. Knowl. Dev. (IJSKD) **7**(3), 1–19 (2015). https://doi.org/10.4018/ijskd.2015070101

A Semantic Model of Information and Communication Technology Components (ICTC)

Blanche Schoch[1,2](✉) and Thomas Schlegel[2]

[1] University of Education Karlsruhe, 76133 Karlsruhe, Germany
blanche.schoch@hs-furtwangen.de
[2] Institute for Intelligent Interactive and Ubiquitous Systems, Furtwangen University, 78120 Furtwangen, Germany

Abstract. Digital teaching and learning environments in higher education rely on numerous information and communication technology components (ICTC), whose interplay often remains opaque to instructors and students. This paper presents a semantic model that formally describes these components, their properties, and their functional relationships. Building on ontology-engineering methods and HCI theory, the model integrates technical, organizational, and interaction-related elements into a machine-readable structure. Using a hybrid lecture as a prototypical scenario, the model visualizes interaction chains, formalizes dependencies, and provides a foundation for context-sensitive support systems. A conceptual and scenario-based evaluation shows that the model can harmonize heterogeneous IT landscapes, improve system transparency, and reduce cognitive load. Limitations and future work include OWL implementation, empirical validation, and adaptive assistance systems.

Keywords: Semantic Modeling · Information and Communication Technology Components · Higher Education Technology

1 Introduction

Digital transformation has significantly reshaped academic education. Teaching, learning, research, and administration increasingly depend on information and communication technology components (ICTC) [1, 2]. Despite their central role, universities often operate heterogeneous, historically grown system landscapes [3, 4].

Numerous studies show that universities worldwide are expanding their digital infrastructures, yet they often operate with heterogeneous, historically evolved system landscapes [1, 5]. Different departments use divergent terminology, and technical and organizational elements are often considered separately, even though they are closely intertwined in practice [3, 6]. This fragmentation not only complicates technical integration but also hinders interdisciplinary communication between faculty, IT departments, and administrative units.

C. Stephanidis et al. (Eds.): HCII 2026, CCIS 3047, pp. 128–138, 2026.
https://doi.org/10.1007/978-3-032-30552-7_13

A semantic model can remedy this by providing a common language, a consistent understanding of terms, and an interoperable structure. Ontologies have proven to be a suitable means of formally describing complex domains and mapping relationships between entities [7, 8]. This article develops such a model for ICTC in higher education. It is based on the ontology engineering methods of Noy and McGuinness [9] and integrates established vocabularies such as FOAF [10], DCMI [11], AIISO [12], SIOC [13], SKOS [14], and PROV-O [15].

From the perspective of Human-Computer Interaction (HCI), however, the selection and combination of ICTC represents not only a technical problem but, above all, an interaction-related one. Faculty and students navigate complex, often opaque system landscapes in which interaction paths, operational logic, and technical dependencies are not clearly discernible. A lack of system transparency leads to increased cognitive load, inefficient workflows, and suboptimal user experiences [16, 17]. A semantic model can address these challenges by making interaction structures visible, supporting mental models, and forming the basis for adaptive, context-sensitive interfaces [4, 18]. In doing so, this paper addresses central HCI issues such as usability, explainability, interaction quality, and system transparency.

The goal of this paper is to develop a prototypical semantic model for ICTC in higher education. The model is intended to be both theoretically sound and practically applicable. It addresses the question of how ICTC can be defined, categorized, and described in terms of their functional relationships. A use case demonstrates the application of the model and shows how it can contribute to improving interaction quality in hybrid teaching-learning scenarios.

2 Background on ICTC

The development of a semantic model for ICTC requires a solid theoretical foundation that considers technical, organizational, and interaction-related aspects. This chapter introduces the central concepts relevant to modeling the domain. It covers the conceptual classification of ICTC, requirements for their formal description, and theoretical perspectives from HCI that illustrate why a semantic model is necessary not only from a technical standpoint but also in terms of interaction.

2.1 Definition of Terms

ICTC encompass hardware, software, networks, data objects, security mechanisms, and organizational roles that support information processing in higher education [19, 20]. Literature distinguishes between technical and socio-technical components [21, 22], both of which must be integrated into a semantic model to reflect real university systems. Since higher education IT is embedded in organizational structures, a semantic model must capture both technological and procedural aspects to represent the domain adequately.

2.2 Requirements for Modeling

A semantic model must provide clear terminology [23], hierarchical structure [24], and the ability to represent functional relationships [25]. Interoperability with standards such as ITIL [26] or ISO/IEC 27001 [27, 28] and adaptability to institutional specifics [29] are essential. Ontologies support these requirements by enabling machine-readable, structured representations [30]. They enable machine-readable descriptions and thus support automation, analysis, and integration into complex IT landscapes.

2.3 Interaction-Theoretical Approaches to Embedding

HCI theories highlight why ICTC modeling must include interaction aspects. Affordances often remain hidden in complex platforms [16], distributed cognition emphasizes the role of artifacts in cognitive processes [17], and situated action shows that ICTC suitability depends on context [31] emphasizes that actions are context dependent. The selection of suitable ICTC thus depends on situational factors such as room type, group size, or teaching format. The semantic model operationalizes this context dependency. Context-aware computing [18] provides a foundation for integrating situational factors into the model.

These theoretical perspectives illustrate that ICTC are not merely technical artifacts, but integral parts of complex interaction systems. A semantic model must therefore consider both technical and interaction-related dimensions.

3 Case Study

The practical relevance of the semantic model can be particularly well illustrated using a realistic application scenario. Hybrid teaching formats have become established in higher education and place high demands on the coordination and interaction of numerous ICTC. The case study of a hybrid lecture therefore serves as an exemplary scenario to highlight the complexity of the systems involved and to demonstrate the model's potential for analysis, planning, and decision support.

3.1 Hybrid Lecture as an Exemplary Application Scenario

Hybrid lectures involve simultaneous on-site and online participation, requiring coordinated use of LMS, media technology, conferencing tools, networks, and assessment systems. Teaching spans preparation, delivery, interaction, and follow-up, each involving different ICTC. This scenario illustrates the heterogeneity of ICTC and the need for structured representations to support planning and decision-making.

3.2 Interaction-Based Analysis of the Application Scenario

Hybrid teaching reveals typical HCI challenges: fragmented system landscapes, inconsistent interaction paths, hidden dependencies, and limited system explainability. These factors increase cognitive load and complicate troubleshooting. The semantic model addresses these issues by visualizing interaction chains and clarifying dependencies, supporting accurate mental models and more efficient workflows.

4 Development of the Semantic Model

The development of the semantic model follows the established ontology engineering methods of Noy and McGuinness [9] and is guided by the principles of Linked Data architecture [28]. The goal is the formal description of ICTC as well as their functional relationships in the context of academic teaching, learning, and research processes. The model is intended to be both theoretically sound and practically applicable, providing a foundation for interoperability, system transparency, and context-sensitive interaction support.

Modeling takes place in several steps: determining the scope of the domain, reusing existing ontologies, identifying relevant concepts, defining classes and properties, and instantiation based on a prototypical application scenario. The following sections describe these steps in detail.

4.1 Determining the Scope of the Domain and the Objectives

Relevant ICTC were identified through literature review, system analysis, and expert interviews. Categories include media technology, LMS, conferencing tools, network services, data objects, and organizational roles. These terms form the basis for the class hierarchy and semantic relations.

4.2 Reuse of Existing Ontologies

The reuse of established ontologies is a central principle of ontology engineering, as it ensures interoperability, standard compliance, and connectivity to existing semantic ecosystems. For the present model, ontologies were identified that provide relevant concepts and structures and can be integrated into the domain of higher education IT.

FOAF is used to describe individuals, organizations, and social relationships and enables the modeling of roles such as instructors, students, or IT support. DCMI provides standardized metadata for learning materials and digital resources. AIISO maps academic organizational structures and supports the modeling of institutional contexts. SIOC enables the description of communication platforms and interactions, while SKOS provides taxonomic structures that can be used for the classification of ICTC. Finally, PROV-O supports the modeling of data provenance, processes, and versioning.

The integration of these ontologies ensures that the model remains compatible with existing standards and can be embedded in heterogeneous university systems.

4.3 Identification and Systematization of Relevant Terms

Identifying relevant terms forms the basis for developing a consistent ontology. Drawing on the literature, existing higher education systems, and domain-specific requirements, key categories were identified that reflect the diversity of ICTC. These include hardware components such as smartboards, document cameras, or server clusters; software components such as learning management systems, video conferencing tools, or research software; data objects such as lecture recordings, digital teaching materials, or research data; network and communication technologies such as eduroam, VPN, or VoIP systems; as well as organizational roles and processes that structure the operation and use of these systems.

These terms form the terminological basis for the subsequent modeling and are formalized in the following sections.

4.4 Structure of the Class Hierarchy

Based on the identified terms, a class hierarchy was developed that forms the structural foundation of the semantic model. The hierarchy follows established principles of ontology development and distinguishes between superclasses such as *HardwareComponent*, *SoftwareComponent*, *DataObject*, *NetworkComponent*, *OrganizationalRole*, *Process*, *SecurityComponent*, *LearningActivity*, and *ResearchActivity*.

These superclasses are further differentiated by specific subclasses to reflect the functional diversity of the ICTC. For example, the *HardwareComponent* class includes subclasses such as *EndDevice*, *Server*, or *MediaTechnology*, while *SoftwareComponent* is subdivided into *LearningManagementSystem*, *VideoConferencingTool*, or *AssessmentPlatform*. The class structure thus forms the taxonomic foundation of the model.

4.5 Semantic Properties and Relations

In addition to the taxonomic structure, the semantic description of ICTC requires the definition of properties that formally express the relationships between entities. These properties can be distinguished into object and data type properties.

Object properties such as *usesHardware*, *generatesData*, *transmits*, *managedBy*, *supportsActivity*, *authenticatedBy*, or *participatesIn* describe functional relationships between components, roles, and processes. Data type properties such as *hasVersion*, *hasFormat*, *hasAccessLevel*, or *hasBandwidth* capture specific characteristics of individual instances.

These properties enable the formal representation of complex interaction chains and technical dependencies.

4.6 Instantiation of the Model Based on an Application Scenario

To demonstrate practical applicability, the model was instantiated using the "Hybrid Lecture" use case. In this process, specific systems, roles, and data objects were modeled as instances of the previously defined classes. Examples include *Moodle* as an instance of the *LearningManagementSystem* class, *Zoom* as a *VideoConferencingTool*, *Smartboard_01* as *MediaTechnology*, *LectureRecording_2026_01* as *LectureRecording*, or *eduroam* as *WIFI*.

These instances demonstrate how the model can represent real university systems and form the basis for analyses, visualizations, and automated recommendations.

4.7 Formal Constraints to Ensure Model Consistency

To ensure the formal consistency of the model, various constraints have been defined. These include cardinality constraints (e.g., every *LectureRecording* must have at least one generatesData relationship with a *LectureCaptureSystem*), value ranges (e.g., allowed formats for *hasFormat*), domain and range definitions, as well as disjointness constraints that ensure that classes such as *HardwareComponent* and *SoftwareComponent* do not overlap.

These constraints ensure the logical consistency of the model and prevent semantic ambiguities.

4.8 Semantic Relations Between ICTC

The functional relationships between ICTC are described by semantic relations that formally express interactions, dependencies, and responsibilities. Examples include Zoom *usesHardware Smartboard_01*, *Opencast generatesData LectureRecording_2026_01*, or *Lecturer_Mueller participatesIn HybridTeaching_Week3*.

These relations illustrate how technical, organizational, and interaction-related elements are linked in hybrid teaching-learning scenarios and form the basis for further analysis.

5 Evaluation of the Semantic Model

The evaluation of the semantic model aims to examine its theoretical foundation, practical applicability, and compatibility with existing university systems. Since the implementation of the model is not yet complete, the evaluation is based both on a prototypical application scenario and on a conceptual analysis of established criteria from ontology and HCI research. The evaluation demonstrates the extent to which the model is suitable for mapping complex ICTC, visualizing interaction processes, and forming the basis for adaptive, context-sensitive systems.

5.1 Application Scenario

The first form of evaluation is based on the application of the model in the use case of the hybrid lecture. Modeling the scenario demonstrated that the model is capable of consistently capturing technical, organizational, and interaction-related components and formally representing their relationships. Instructors who followed the prototypical modeling process reported that the representation of dependencies between hardware, software, networks, and roles led to a better understanding of the technical prerequisites and interaction chains.

In particular, the explicit modeling of roles, processes, and data flows was perceived as helpful, as it clarifies which components are necessary for specific activities and how they interact with one another. The modeling made it easier for instructors to formulate technical requirements more clearly and to identify potential bottlenecks in the teaching-learning process.

5.2 Theoretical-Conceptual Evaluation

The model demonstrates completeness, consistency, and interoperability through the integration of established ontologies. Its relevance for HCI lies in supporting transparency, usability, and reduced cognitive load. The structure aligns with distributed cognition, situated action, and context-aware computing, ensuring theoretical validity.

5.3 Limitations

Despite the positive results, the model has several limitations that must be addressed in future work. First, the evaluation has so far been based primarily on a prototypical application scenario and a conceptual analysis. Broader empirical validation in various higher education contexts is still pending.

Second, security components have so far been modeled only at an abstract level. A more detailed integration of data protection and security ontologies is necessary to address the growing requirements for IT security and compliance.

Third, the model has not yet been integrated into existing campus management systems. However, such integration is crucial to fully exploit the model's potential for automated analyses, context-sensitive recommendations, and adaptive interaction support.

6 Results and Implications of the Model

The model provides a structured representation of ICTC, improving transparency and supporting decision-making. It enhances communication between technical and non-technical stakeholders and forms a basis for user-centered design. By modeling interaction chains and contextual factors, it supports adaptive, context-sensitive interfaces. Semantic models unfold their full potential when integrated into user-friendly tools that translate semantic structures into actionable guidance.

7 Limitations of the Model

Despite the positive results, the developed semantic model has several limitations that must be considered when interpreting the results and planning future work. These limitations arise both from the model's current stage of development and from structural peculiarities of higher education IT landscapes.

First, the model has so far been developed and evaluated primarily in the context of German-speaking universities. Although many of the modeled components are widely used internationally, institutional differences, varying IT governance structures, and differing regulatory frameworks may limit its transferability. Systematic international validation is therefore still pending.

Second, the OWL implementation of the model is still under development. The evaluation to date is based on conceptual analyses and prototypical modeling, but not on a fully implemented ontology that has been integrated into production systems. Only through full implementation can aspects such as inference capability, performance, and interoperability be empirically tested.

Third, large-scale empirical validation is currently lacking. Feedback to date has primarily come from expert discussions and the exemplary application in the hybrid lecture use case. A broader evaluation involving faculty, IT specialists, and students from various universities is necessary to comprehensively assess the model's practicality and comprehensibility.

Finally, the availability of context-related data varies considerably between universities. Many of the context-sensitive functions envisaged in the model – such as adaptive recommendations or automated interaction support – require a consistent and machine-readable database, which is not always available in practice. This structural limitation may restrict the model's potential applications and necessitates institutional adaptations.

Overall, these limitations show that the model provides a solid foundation but must be further developed and empirically validated to realize its full potential in various higher education contexts.

8 Prospects for Future Work

The results of the modeling work show that the semantic model developed provides a solid foundation for the systematic description of ICTC in higher education. At the same time, numerous avenues open for further research and development work that can expand the model's potential and enhance its practical effectiveness.

A key next step is the full OWL implementation of the model. Only through a formally complete ontology can inference mechanisms be utilized, automatic consistency checks performed, and complex dependencies analyzed algorithmically. Such an implementation would also lay the groundwork for integration into existing higher education systems and enable the development of semantically enriched assistance functions.

Furthermore, broad empirical validation is necessary. While previous evaluations provide valuable insights, systematic studies involving faculty, students, IT specialists, and administrative units at various universities are required. Such studies could clarify how understandable and useful the semantic structures are in practice, which forms of visualization are particularly suitable, and what requirements different user groups place on such a model.

Another promising line of research concerns the integration of context-sensitive mechanisms. The model already provides a formal basis for describing contextual factors; future work could build on this to develop adaptive systems that recommend contextually appropriate technologies to instructors, check technical prerequisites, or detect interaction problems early on. This would require close integration of ontology engineering, HCI, and learning analytics.

In addition, the model opens up potential for the automated analysis and optimization of digital teaching and learning processes. By combining semantic structures with usage data, patterns could be identified that indicate inefficient interaction pathways, technical bottlenecks, or suboptimal system configurations. Such analyses could support universities in further developing their digital infrastructures in a targeted manner.

Finally, there is the possibility of extending the model to other domains, such as research processes, exam management, or administrative workflows. The model's underlying structure is flexible enough to accommodate such extensions and thus serve as a comprehensive reference model for higher education IT in the long term.

Overall, it is evident that the developed model not only provides a theoretical foundation for describing ICTC but also opens up diverse perspectives for research, development, and practical application. Further work on these points can significantly contribute to making digital university systems more transparent, interoperable, and user-friendly.

9 Conclusion

The present semantic model offers a structured approach to describing ICTC in higher education. By integrating technical, organizational, and interaction-related elements, it creates a unified semantic foundation that makes the complexity of digital higher education systems visible and facilitates their analysis. The modeling demonstrates that ontologies are a suitable means of harmonizing heterogeneous IT landscapes, making interaction processes transparent, and laying the groundwork for adaptive, context-sensitive support systems.

Its application in the hybrid lecture use case demonstrates that the model is not only theoretically sound but also practically applicable. It enables the systematic mapping of relevant components, the representation of functional dependencies, and the analysis of key interaction chains. At the same time, the evaluation shows that the model can contribute to improving communication between technical and non-technical actors by providing a shared conceptual framework and supporting mental models.

Nevertheless, the model remains a first step. The complete OWL implementation, empirical validation in various higher education contexts, and the integration of context-sensitive mechanisms are central tasks for future work. In the long term, the model can serve as a foundation for intelligent assistance systems that support instructors and students in digital teaching and learning environments, reduce technical complexity, and improve the quality of interaction.

Overall, this work demonstrates that semantic modeling is a promising approach for shaping the digital transformation of higher education not only technically but also in terms of interaction. The model provides a robust foundation for research, development, and practical application and opens diverse perspectives for the further development of digital higher education systems.

Acknowledgments. The information was collected as part of the doctoral thesis "Information Technology Components in Knowledge Transfer" within the framework of the "Knowledge Media" doctoral program and is funded by the LGFG scholarship (Graduate funding from the state of Baden-Württemberg). The authors would like to thank everyone who contributed to the development of the ontology. We would also like to thank you in advance for any additional comments and suggestions you may submit via email.

Disclosure of Interests. The authors have no competing interests to declare that are relevant to the content of this article.

References

1. Redecker, C.: European framework for the digital competence of educators: DigCompEdu. Joint Research Centre (JRC) Science for Policy report. 95 (2017). https://doi.org/10.2760/159770
2. Bates, A.W. (Tony): Teaching in a digital age: guidelines for designing teaching and learning for a digital age. BCcampus (2015)
3. Ellis, R.A., Goodyear, P.: The Education Ecology of Universities: Integrating Learning, Strategy and the Academy, pp. 1–252. Routledge, London (2019). https://doi.org/10.4324/9781351135863
4. Selwyn, N.: Education and Technology: Key Issues and Debates, p. 216. Bloomsbury, London (2017)
5. Langer-Crame, M., Newman, T., Beetham, H., Killen, C., Knight, S.: Digital experience insights survey 2019: findings from students in UK further and higher education Section 3 (2019)
6. Orlikowski, W.J.: Sociomaterial practices: exploring technology at work. Organ. Stud. **28**, 1435–1448 (2007). https://doi.org/10.1177/0170840607081138
7. Gruber, T.R.: A translation approach to portable ontology specifications. Appeared Knowl. Acquis. **5**, 199–220 (1993)
8. Antoniou, G., van Harmelen, F.: A semantic web primer second edition. Knowl. Eng. Rev. **24**, 415–415 (2008)
9. Noy, N.F., Mcguinness, D.L.: Ontology development 101: a guide to creating your first ontology (2001)
10. FOAF Vocabulary Specification. https://xmlns.com/foaf/spec/. Last accessed 1 Mar 2026
11. DCMI: DCMI metadata terms. https://www.dublincore.org/specifications/dublin-core/dcmi-terms/. Last accessed 1 Mar 2026
12. Academic Institution Internal Structure Ontology (AIISO). https://vocab.org/aiiso/. Last accessed 1 Mar 2026
13. SIOC Core Ontology Specification. http://rdfs.org/sioc/spec/. Last accessed 1 Mar 2026
14. SKOS Simple Knowledge Organization System Namespace Document - HTML Variant, 18 August 2009 Recommendation Edition. https://www.w3.org/2009/08/skos-reference/skos.html. Last accessed 1 Mar 2026
15. The PROV Namespace. https://www.w3.org/ns/prov#. Last accessed 1 Mar 2026
16. Norman, D.A.: The Design of Everyday Things. Basic Books, New York (2014)
17. Hutchins, E.: Cognition in the Wild. The MIT Press, Cambridge (1995). https://doi.org/10.7551/mitpress/1881.001.0001
18. Dey, A.K.: Understanding and using context. Pers. Ubiquit. Comput. **5**, 4–7 (2001). https://doi.org/10.1007/s007790170019
19. Laudon, K.C., Laudon, J.P.: Management Information Systems: Managing the Digital Firm, p. 587. Pearson, Harlow (2022)
20. Zawacki-Richter, O., Marín, V.I., Bond, M., Gouverneur, F.: Systematic review of research on artificial intelligence applications in higher education—where are the educators? Int. J. Educ. Technol. High. Educ. **16**, 39 (2019). https://doi.org/10.1186/s41239-019-0171-0
21. Bostrom, R.P., Heinen, J.S.: MIS problems and failures: a socio- technical perspective. MIS Q. **1**, 17–32 (1977). https://doi.org/10.2307/248710
22. Alter, S.: Work system theory: overview of core concepts, extensions, and challenges for the future. J. Assoc. Inf. Syst. **14**, 72–121 (2013). https://doi.org/10.17705/1jais.00323
23. Guarino, N.: Formal ontology in information systems. In: Proceedings of the First International Conference (FOIS'98), June 6–8, Trento, Italy, p. 337 (1998)

24. Gómez-Pérez, A., Fernández-López, M., Corcho, O.: Ontological Engineering—With Examples from the Areas of Knowledge Management, E-Commerce and the Semantic Web, 1st edn. Springer, London (2004). https://doi.org/10.1007/b97353
25. Uschold, M., Gruninger, M.: Ontologies: principles, methods and applications. Knowl. Eng. Rev. **11**, 93–136 (1996). https://doi.org/10.1017/s0269888900007797
26. ITIL® Foundation: ITIL 4 edition (2019)
27. ISO/IEC 27001:2022 - Information security management systems. https://www.iso.org/standard/27001. Last accessed 18 Mar 2026
28. Shadbolt, N., Hall, W., Berners-Lee, T.: The semantic web revisited. IEEE Intell. Syst. **21**, 96–101 (2006). https://doi.org/10.1109/MIS.2006.62
29. Weller, M.: 25 Years of Ed Tech. Athabasca University Press, Athabasca (2020). https://doi.org/10.15215/aupress/9781771993050.01
30. Staab, S., Studer, R.: Handbook on Ontologies. Springer, Berlin (2009). https://doi.org/10.1007/978-3-540-92673-3
31. Suchman, L.: Plans and Situated Actions, p. 224. Cambridge University Press, Cambridge (1987)

Articulating More-than-Human Agency in Playful Interaction Design through Design Fiction

Yutong Sun(✉)

School of Architecture, Design and Planning, The University of Sydney, Sydney, Australia
ysun0714@uni.sydney.edu.au

Abstract. This paper examines how design fiction can be used to articulate more-than-human agency in playful interaction design. In Animal–Computer Interaction (ACI), animal agency is often difficult to interpret beyond human-centred assumptions and behaviour-based evaluations of interaction. More-than-human design (MTHD) offers a useful analytical lens, yet questions remain about how its commitments can be translated into concrete design practice. Building on this, the study draws on MTHD and uses play—operationalised through gameplay—as an interaction domain for examining animal agency. Methodologically, the paper employs design fiction and world-building to develop three speculative worlds in which domestic cats are framed as potential players within game-like systems. Comparing these worlds makes it possible to examine how different configurations of play shape participation, control, and responsibility in human–animal–technology relations.

The findings indicate that agency in multispecies play does not reside in any single actor, but emerges through changing relations among cats, caregivers, technologies, and regulatory arrangements. Across the speculative scenarios, responsibility for participation and welfare is distributed across multiple actors and system logics rather than resting solely with the caregiver, while the scope of play remains shaped by predefined rules and boundaries rather than open-ended collaboration. On this basis, The paper demonstrates the methodological value of design fiction by using contrasting speculative worlds to make different assumptions about agency, responsibility, and control visible, comparable, and open to critical reflection. It thus offers a design-oriented account of how more-than-human agency can be articulated in ACI, MTHD, and playful interaction design.

Keywords: Design Fiction · Animal–Computer Interaction · More-than-Human Design · Speculative Design · Playful Interaction · Multispecies Play

C. Stephanidis et al. (Eds.): HCII 2026, CCIS 3047, pp. 139–149, 2026.
https://doi.org/10.1007/978-3-032-30552-7_14

1 Introduction

Across much of the world, demographic transitions are reshaping the structure and meaning of family life. Declining fertility rates and smaller household structures, driven by economic and cultural factors, are altering long-standing arrangements of kinship and companionship [9]. In these contexts, companion animals are increasingly repositioned within family life [10, 14, 27, 32]. These shifts have been accompanied by growing public and commercial interest in pet-oriented care practices, reflected in increasing attention to pet wellbeing, lifestyle products, and expectations that digital and interactive technologies may play a role in animals' everyday lives [2, 29].

As animals have become increasingly entangled with digital and interactive technologies across domestic and environmental contexts, Animal–Computer Interaction (ACI) has emerged within Human–Computer Interaction (HCI) to address animal–technology relations and their ethical implications [20]. Building on user-centred and participatory traditions of HCI together with ethology and animal welfare science, ACI has developed a range of approaches for studying multispecies interaction [17]. However, these approaches can still struggle to account for animal agency beyond human-centred models of interaction [17, 18, 25]. In this study, animal agency is understood as animals' capacity to participate in, influence, or withdraw from interaction within socio-technical systems.

In this research project, play—operationalised through gameplay—is treated as an interaction domain for examining animal agency. Gameplay foregrounds voluntary engagement and shifts in participation, without presupposing language or fixed outcomes [19, 21].

Theoretically, the study draws on more-than-human design (MTHD) as an analytical lens for examining animal agency beyond human-centred models of interaction. However, questions remain about how more-than-human design commitments can be translated into concrete design processes and interactional settings [12, 24].

Methodologically, the broader research project adopts a Research through Design (RtD) framework and proceeds in two phases: Phase 1 combines speculative inquiry with subsequent interviews and thematic analysis, while Phase 2 extends the inquiry through prototype-mediated interactions. This paper focuses on the speculative component of Phase 1, which uses design fiction and world-building to explore how animal agency might be framed within human-designed systems. Through speculative worlds and artefacts, this component makes assumptions about agency, participation, and responsibility available for examination, while creating space to consider how more-than-human design concerns might be engaged in practice [6, 22, 25]. Domestic cats are selected as the focal species due to the existing body of research on feline play behaviours [7] and their relevance within digitally mediated domestic play contexts [26, 31], making them a useful context for exploring playful multispecies interaction.

2 Related Work

2.1 Animal–Computer Interaction (ACI) and Animal Agency

Within ACI, animals have been conceptualised in multiple ways, including as users of interactive systems and participants in multispecies interaction [16,19]. However, their involvement is still frequently interpreted through behavioural and physiological response, reflecting the field's early engagement with HCI usability and user-experience frameworks [16,17]. Methodological studies in ACI highlight challenges such as novelty effects and habituation, while also noting the difficulty of interpreting animal engagement as evidence of preference. As a result, animal agency can be difficult to distinguish from novelty, compliance, or other situated forms of response. [18]. Scholars have also highlighted asymmetries in multispecies interaction and the risk of anthropocentric projection when interpreting animal behaviour [16,25]. More recent work further suggests that agency may be shaped not only through interaction design, but also through broader data-driven and infrastructural systems [23]. These challenges indicate the need for alternative ways of conceptualising animal agency beyond human-centred models of interaction.

2.2 More-than-Human Design (MTHD) and Design Practice

More-than-human design (MTHD) extends design inquiry beyond human users by foregrounding relational, ecological, and multispecies concerns [13]. Recent work spans conceptual, methodological, and practice-based strands. At the conceptual level, scholars explore frameworks for decentring the human and reconfiguring justice beyond anthropocentrism [5], yet these concepts are often difficult to operationalise in concrete design settings [11,12]. At the methodological level, researchers explore how nonhuman actors might be represented or engaged in design processes, while confronting ongoing challenges of interpretation and mediation [28]. At the practice level, situated design interventions demonstrate how more-than-human perspectives can be enacted within complex socio-technical and ecological contexts [1,24,30]. Some researchers argue that more-than-human concepts require clearer practical methods to guide design work [12]. Others suggest that uncertainty, negotiation, and instability are not problems to resolve, but central characteristics of more-than-human design [24].

2.3 Design Fiction as an Inquiry Strategy

Design fiction was first articulated by Sterling (2009) and Bleecker (2009), and has since been adopted within HCI as a design-oriented approach for rendering sociotechnical assumptions visible and open to critique [3,22]. Prior work shows that design fiction can take multiple forms, including speculative scenarios, narrative constructions, and collections of interrelated artefacts that together constitute imagined contexts [6]. While design fiction has been applied across diverse domains, its conceptual openness has raised questions about how its critical intent and methodological role should be defined and assessed [4].

2.4 Playful Interaction as a Research Context

Play and gameplay have been widely used within HCI as interactional contexts for studying engagement, experience, and participation beyond task-oriented efficiency [21]. By providing rule-based, yet open-ended structures, gameplay creates bounded settings in which shifts in engagement, adaptation, and breakdown can be observed over time. This framing has also been extended to research involving nonhuman participants, where disengagement, resistance, or partial participation may reveal how animals relate to designed systems, rather than being interpreted simply as failures [19]. Scholars have noted that play is not a neutral framing, as game systems embed assumptions about what counts as meaningful participation and thereby shape how agency is recognised within interaction [8,19].

3 Method/Approach

This paper examines the speculative component of Phase 1, in which design fiction was employed through a world-building approach to explore how animal agency may be framed within human–animal–technology relations. The speculative worlds and artefacts were examined comparatively and interpretively, focusing on how each scenario positioned the animal, human caregiver, and technological system, and how agency, participation, and responsibility were distributed across these relations.

4 Study Description

Through a world-building approach, this study introduces a layered, parallel speculative world structure. As illustrated in Fig. 1, the study begins with a macro-level what-if proposition that establishes an overarching fictional condition and frames the speculative space. Within this shared frame, three parallel speculative worlds are developed, each structured around its own what-if scenario and oriented toward a particular configuration of agency, responsibility, or participation in play.

Each world—including the macro world—is organised through a set of speculative artefacts that take multiple representational forms, including platform interfaces, policy notices, promotional media, and situated play scenarios. As shown in Fig. 2, these artefacts are distributed across macro-, meso-, and micro-levels. At the macro level, artefacts express overarching system logics; at the meso level, they specify the social, institutional, and technical arrangements through which multispecies interaction is organised; and at the micro level, they depict situated moments of play, interaction, or response. In World 3, for example, the Instagram reel was treated as a meso-level artefact because it foregrounded the mediated interface and interactional arrangement of human–cat co-play, rather than a single situated moment of play.

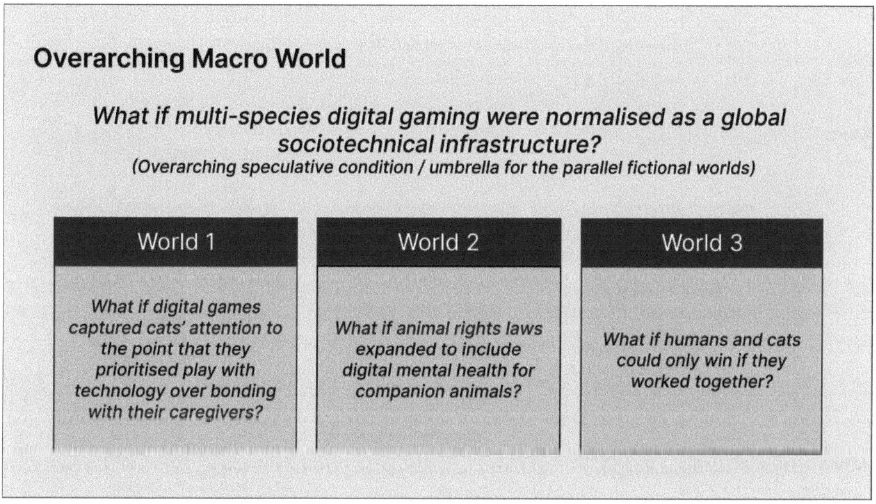

Fig. 1. Overview of the layered speculative world structure. The macro world establishes the overarching fictional context, while three parallel speculative worlds explore different what-if scenarios related to agency, responsibility, and participation in play.

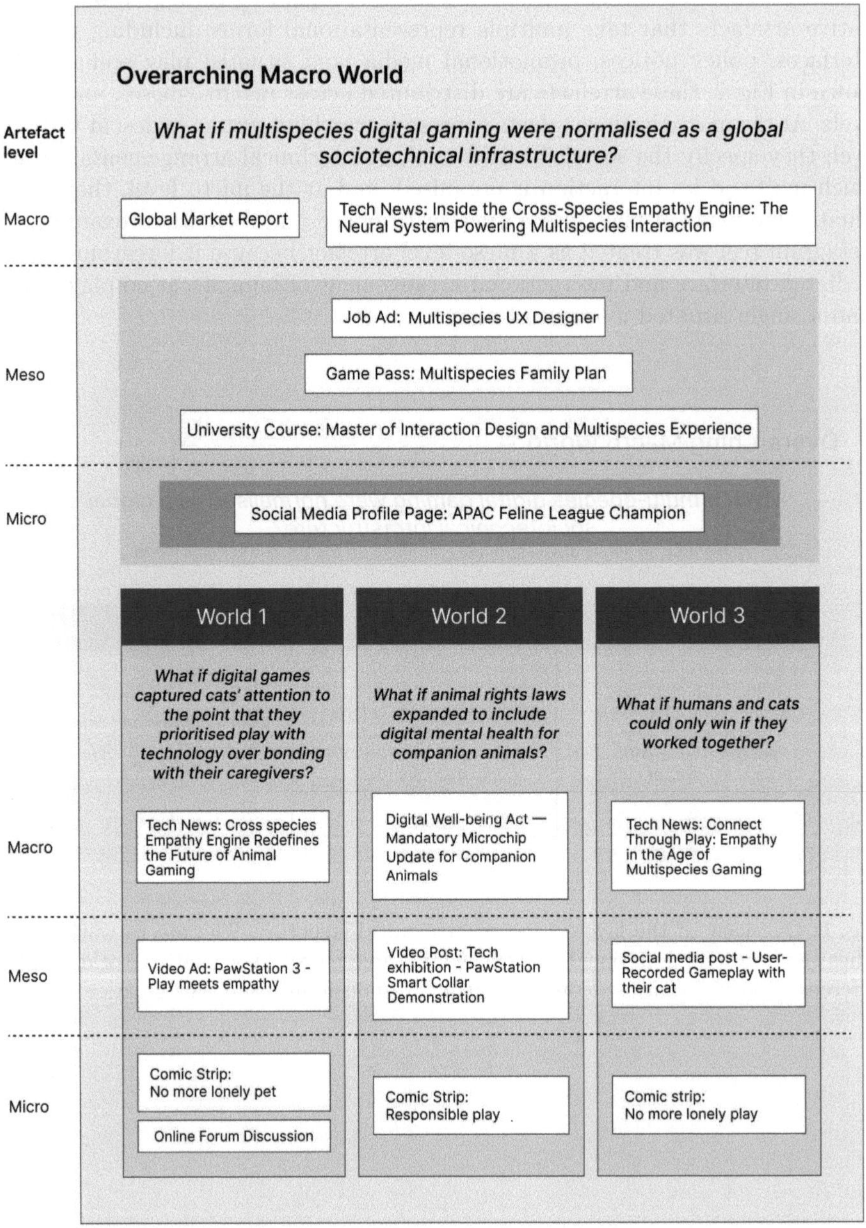

Fig. 2. Artefact-level organisation of the speculative worlds. Across the macro world and the three parallel worlds, artefacts in multiple representational forms were distributed across macro-, meso-, and micro-levels. These levels broadly correspond to wider system conditions, interactional arrangements, and situated moments of play, interaction, and response.

5 Findings and Reflections

The three parallel worlds each foreground a different tension in multispecies play. World 1 imagines a system in which digital play competes with caregiver bonding. World 2 situates play within a digital rights framework, foregrounding tensions between participation, welfare, and regulation. World 3 frames play as a technologically mediated but relationally interdependent activity, highlighting tensions between autonomous participation and co-play.

Comparing the three worlds made clear that the key issue was not simply whether animals could participate, but how participation was structured, governed, and sustained through interfaces, infrastructures, and system rules. Three findings emerged from this comparison.

5.1 Finding 1: Agency is Relationally and Dynamically Configured

Across the speculative worlds, agency is framed not as a fixed property of any single actor, but as something that emerges through shifting relations among the cat, caregiver, technologies, and regulatory structures. As these relations change across the worlds, so too do the ways agency is expressed and the effects it has on play. Figure 3 helps visualise the relative influence of these actors in shaping play in each world. These findings suggest that more-than-human agency is relational and configurational rather than fixed, stable, or self-contained.

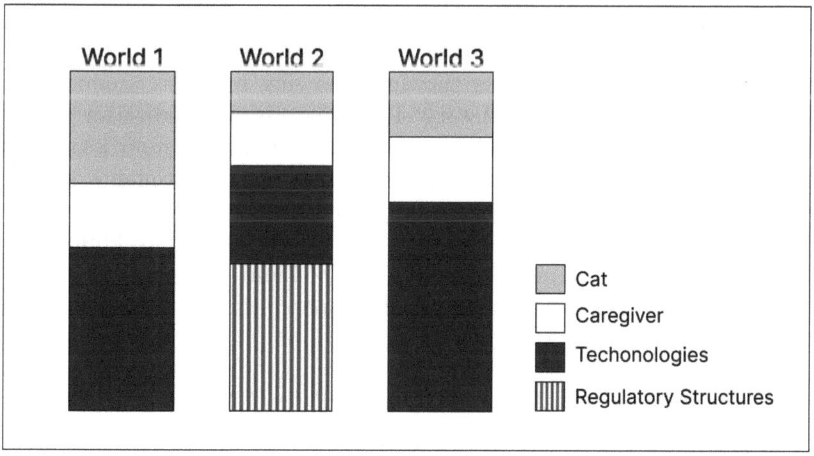

Fig. 3. Shifting relational configurations of play across the three speculative worlds. Interpretive diagram showing how the relative roles of cat, caregiver, technologies, and regulatory structures change across the worlds. The proportions are conceptual rather than quantitative, and are intended to summarise comparative differences across the speculative configurations.

5.2 Finding 2: Responsibility is Redistributed into System Logics

A second recurring pattern concerns the redistribution of responsibility for governing play. This pattern is most explicit in World 2, where participation is organised through a digital rights framework that regulates welfare, permissions, and acceptable forms of interaction. Across the speculative worlds more broadly, responsibility for participation, regulation, and the evaluation of play is distributed across caregivers, designers, interfaces, preconfigured rules, and institutional logics, rather than residing solely in situated caregiving judgment. As a result, accountability becomes more difficult to locate when adverse consequences arise.

5.3 Finding 3: Play is Negotiated within System-Defined Boundaries

A third recurring pattern shows that play is framed less as an open-ended or co-creative activity and more as a process of negotiation within system-defined boundaries. Animals are able to influence the unfolding of interaction through response, persistence, withdrawal, or partial participation, yet this influence remains conditioned by preconfigured rules, regulatory structures, or interface designs. In World 3, for example, play can only continue when both human and cat provide input, making cooperative play possible only within a predefined interactional structure. Although the degree of openness varies across the worlds, play is consistently organised as a managed process rather than an unconstrained form of interaction.

Overall, the findings show that agency in multispecies play is not located in the animal alone, but emerges through changing relations among the cat, caregiver, technologies, and regulatory structures. Responsibility for participation and welfare is distributed across multiple actors and system logics, rather than resting solely with the caregiver. Play is also shaped by predefined rules and boundaries, rather than unfolding as a fully open-ended activity. In this way, the study shows the value of design fiction for articulating more-than-human agency in playful interaction design is making different configurations of play visible and comparable, while surfacing tensions around care, control, and participation for critical reflection.

Acknowledgments. The author would like to thank Dr. Rodrigo Hernández Ramírez for his feedback on this work.

Disclosure of Interests. The author has no competing interests to declare that are relevant to the content of this article.

References

1. Akmal, H.A., Coulton, P.: More-than-human game design: playing in the internet of things. Acta Ludologica **4**(1), 72–92 (2021)
2. American Pet Products Association: Pet Industry Market Size, Trends and Statistics (2026). https://americanpetproducts.org/industry-trends-and-stats. Accessed 12 Jan 2026
3. Baumer, E.P.S., Blythe, M., Tanenbaum, T.J.: Evaluating design fiction: the right tool for the job. In: Proceedings of the 2020 ACM Designing Interactive Systems Conference, pp. 1901–1913 (2020). https://doi.org/10.1145/3357236.3395464
4. Cardenas Cordova, D., Kelly, N., Rezayan, L.: A systematic literature review of the speculative design process and a proposed framework for speculative design. Des. Sci. **11**, e38 (2025). https://doi.org/10.1017/dsj.2025.10030
5. Coskun, A., et al.: More-than-human concepts, methodologies, and practices in HCI. In: CHI Conference on Human Factors in Computing Systems Extended Abstracts, pp. 1–5 (2022). https://doi.org/10.1145/3491101.3516503
6. Coulton, P., Lindley, J., Sturdee, M.: Design fiction as world building. In: Proceedings of the ACM Conference on Designing Interactive Systems (DIS '17) (2017). workshop paper
7. Delgado, M., Hecht, J.: A review of the development and functions of cat play, with future research considerations. Appl. Anim. Behav. Sci. **214**, 1–17 (2019). https://doi.org/10.1016/j.applanim.2019.03.004
8. Driessen, C., Alfrink, K., Copier, M., Lagerweij, H., van Peer, I.: What could playing with pigs do to us? Game design as multispecies philosophy. Antennae: J. Nat. Visual Cult. **30**, 79–102 (2014)
9. Esteve, A., et al.: A global perspective on household size and composition, 1970–2020. Genus **80**(1), 2 (2024). https://doi.org/10.1186/s41118-024-00211-6
10. Fernandes, J., Sousa, L., Sá-Couto, P., Tavares, J.: Companion animals: Associations with social isolation, loneliness, and satisfaction with life in Portuguese community-dwelling older adults. Anthrozoös **37**(2), 361–377 (2023). https://doi.org/10.1080/08927936.2023.2287313
11. Fieuw, W., Foth, M., Caldwell, G.: Towards a more-than-human approach to smart and sustainable urban development: designing for multispecies justice. Sustainability **14**(2), 948 (2022). https://doi.org/10.3390/su14020948
12. Genç, Ç., Bertran, F.A., Gabrielaitis, L., Ahmed, E., Spors, V.: Designing our way through abstractions: calling for more practice-based more-than-human design research. In: Proceedings of the Halfway to the Future Symposium, pp. 1–10 (2024). https://doi.org/10.1145/3686169.3686195
13. Giaccardi, E., Redström, J., Nicenboim, I.: The making(s) of more-than-human design: introduction to the special issue on more-than-human design and HCI. Hum.-Comput. Interact. **40**(1–4), 1–16 (2025). https://doi.org/10.1080/07370024.2024.2353357
14. Gillet, L., Kubinyi, E.: Redefining parenting and family - the child-like role of dogs in western societies. Eur. Psychol. **30**(2), 96–115 (2025). https://doi.org/10.1027/1016-9040/a000552
15. Gray, S., et al.: Gorilla game lab: eExploring modularity, tangibility and playful engagement in cognitive enrichment design. In: Proceedings of the Fifth International Conference on Animal-Computer Interaction, pp. 1–13 (2018). https://doi.org/10.1145/3295598.3295604

16. Hirskyj-Douglas, I., Lucero, A.: On the internet, nobody knows you're a dog... unless you're another dog. In: Proceedings of the 2019 CHI Conference on Human Factors in Computing Systems, pp. 1–12 (2019). https://doi.org/10.1145/3290605.3300347
17. Hirskyj-Douglas, I., Pons, P., Read, J.C., Jaen, J.: Seven years after the manifesto: literature review and research directions for technologies in ACI. Multimodal Technol. Interact. **2**(2), 30 (2018). https://doi.org/10.3390/mti2020030
18. Hirskyj-Douglas, I., Webber, S.: Reflecting on methods in animal computer interaction: novelty effect and habituation. In: Eighth International Conference on Animal-Computer Interaction, pp. 1–11 (2021). https://doi.org/10.1145/3493842.3493893
19. Jørgensen, I.K.H., Wirman, H.: Multispecies methods, technologies for play. Digit. Creativity **27**(1), 37–51 (2016). https://doi.org/10.1080/14626268.2016.1144617
20. Mancini, C.: Animal-computer interaction: a manifesto. Interactions **18**(4), 69–73 (2011). https://doi.org/10.1145/1978822.1978836
21. Mandryk, R.L., Mirza-Babaei, P., Denisova, A., Freeman, G., Johnson, D.: Games and play SIG: connecting games research to the broader HCI context. In: Extended Abstracts of the CHI Conference on Human Factors in Computing Systems, pp. 1–6 (2024). https://doi.org/10.1145/3613905.3643986
22. Muller, M., et al.: Understanding the past, present, and future of design fictions. In: Extended Abstracts of the 2020 CHI Conference on Human Factors in Computing Systems, pp. 1–8 (2020). https://doi.org/10.1145/3334480.3375168
23. Neethirajan, S.: Agency in livestock farming–a perspective on human-animal-computer interactions. Hum.-Centric Intell. Syst. **5**(3), 291–307 (2025). https://doi.org/10.1007/s44230-025-00108-3
24. Nicenboim, I., Lindley, J., Redström, J.: More-than-human design and AI: exploring the space between theory and practice. In: DRS2024: Boston (2024). https://doi.org/10.21606/drs.2024.948. Accessed 23 June 2024
25. North, S.: Hey, where's my hay?: Design fictions in horse-computer interaction. In: Proceedings of the Fourth International Conference on Animal-Computer Interaction, pp. 1–5 (2017). https://doi.org/10.1145/3152130.3152149
26. Noz, F., An, J.: Cat cat revolution: an interspecies gaming experience. In: Proceedings of the SIGCHI Conference on Human Factors in Computing Systems, pp. 2661–2664 (2011). https://doi.org/10.1145/1978942.1979331
27. Peterson, H., Engwall, K.: "why would you want a baby when you could have a dog?" Voluntarily childless women's "peternal" feelings, longing and ambivalence. Soc. Sci. **8**(4), 126 (2019). https://doi.org/10.3390/socsci8040126
28. Romani, A., Casnati, F., Ianniello, A.: Codesign with more-than-humans: toward a meta co-design tool for human-non-human collaborations. Eur. J. Fut. Res. **10**(1), 17 (2022). https://doi.org/10.1186/s40309-022-00205-7
29. Samsung Electronics Co.: Three in Five Europeans Agree Pet-Friendly Products Are as Important as Child-Friendly (2022). https://news.samsung.com/uk/three-in-five-europeans-agree-pet-friendly-products-are-as-important-as-child-friendly. samsung Newsroom UK. Accessed 12 Jan 2026
30. Stead, M., Coulton, P., Pilling, F., Gradinar, A., Pilling, M., Forrester, I.: More-than-human-data interaction: bridging novel design research approaches to materialise and foreground data sustainability. In: Proceedings of the 25th International Academic Mindtrek Conference, pp. 62–74 (2022). https://doi.org/10.1145/3569219.3569344

31. Trindade, R., Sousa, M., Hart, C., Vieira, N., Rodrigues, R., França, J.: Purrfect crime: exploring animal computer interaction through a digital game for humans and cats. In: Proceedings of the 33rd Annual ACM Conference Extended Abstracts on Human Factors in Computing Systems, pp. 93–96 (2015). https://doi.org/10.1145/2702613.2728660
32. Volsche, S.: Pet parenting in the united states: investigating an evolutionary puzzle. Evol. Psychol. **19**(3), 14747049211038296 (2021). https://doi.org/10.1177/14747049211038297

Feature Complexity in Super Apps: How Feature Heterogeneity and Interrelatedness Shape Cognitive Load, Usability, and Continuance

Ran Zheng(✉) and Hyung Koo Lee

HEC Montréal, Montréal, Canada
{ran.zheng,hyung-koo.lee}@hec.ca

Abstract. Super apps combine multiple services within a single platform, but moving from one service to another can impose substantial cognitive effort when the system does not preserve task context. Research on super apps has focused primarily on adoption and platform growth, leaving cross-service transitions underexamined. This paper proposes a research model that explains such transitions through two design-relevant constructs: feature heterogeneity, or how dissimilar consecutive services are, and feature interrelatedness, or how well the interface connects them. Grounded in the literature of cognitive load theory and cognitive offloading, the paper proposes four hypotheses linking feature heterogeneity and feature interrelatedness to cognitive load, usability, and continuance intention. A 2 $\times$ 2 factorial design is employed for the proposed experiment, in which feature heterogeneity and feature interrelatedness are manipulated as between-subjects factors. Feature heterogeneity is operationalized by pairing service tasks that are relatively similar or different in nature, whereas feature interrelatedness is manipulated using data carryover, contextual prompting, and interface filtering in a web-based prototype super app. The paper concludes by outlining the planned study and discussing its expected theoretical and practical contributions.

Keywords: Super Apps · Feature Heterogeneity · Interrelatedness · Cognitive Offloading · Cognitive Load · Usability · Continuance Intention

1 Introduction

Super apps are digital platforms that integrate multiple services within one interface, allowing users to complete activities such as messaging, payments, ride-hailing, or food ordering without leaving the application [17, 21]. Grab and WeChat are prominent examples of this model. Many such ecosystems expand through app-within-app or mini-program arrangements that let services share identity, payment, and data infrastructures while remaining distinct interaction modules [17, 21]. Although the super-app ecosystem originated in East and Southeast Asia, Western platforms, including PayPal, Uber, and Revolut, have begun pursuing similar consolidation strategies [8, 22], reflecting broader industry interest in multi-service bundling. Recent work suggests that Western diffusion remains institutionally and strategically unsettled, especially as super

C. Stephanidis et al. (Eds.): HCII 2026, CCIS 3047, pp. 150–161, 2026.
https://doi.org/10.1007/978-3-032-30552-7_15

apps enter mobility and other highly regulated service domains [22]. Their appeal lies in convenience and service consolidation, but consolidation does not guarantee a coherent user experience. A ride-hailing module and a food-delivery module may coexist in the same application while still relying on different task structures, information needs, and decision processes. When a user finishes a ride and then orders food to the drop-off location, the system may preserve that context and guide the transition, or it may require the user to reconstruct the next task from the beginning. Such friction can increase effort, slow task completion, and weaken the perceived usability of the platform.

The literature on super apps has mainly focused on adoption, platform trust, platformization, and growth strategy [8, 9, 21, 22], what draws people in, how firms expand, and how ecosystems consolidate rather than what happens once users are inside the app. Users transition between different services when using a super app, however, such cross-service transitions have received little attention in the literature. This gap matters because platforms such as Grab and Gojek continue to add services on the assumption that a larger portfolio creates more user value, yet there is little evidence about whether poorly supported transitions between those services erode the expected gains.

We address this gap by considering feature heterogeneity (i.e., how different two services are) and feature interrelatedness (i.e., how well the interface connects them) from Fürst et al. [6]. These constructs move the discussion of super-app complexity away from raw feature counts and toward the similarity and quality of connection between services. In other words, they make it possible to explain not only whether services differ, but also whether the interface helps users bridge those differences. Drawing on the perspectives of Cognitive Load Theory [18], task switching [13, 16], and cognitive offloading [15], we investigate how feature heterogeneity and interrelatedness influence users' cognitive load, which in turn influences usability perceptions and continuance intentions. To test our research model, we propose a controlled 2×2 experiment with interactive web mockups in which users perform single cross-service episode. Throughout, service refers to a discrete functional module, and cross-service episode refers to the transition from completing one service task to beginning another.

2 Relevant Literature and Hypotheses Development

2.1 Relevant Literature on Super Apps

Super-app research has been centered primarily around adoption intentions, platform trust, privacy risk, platformization, and regulatory diffusion [8, 9, 17, 21, 22]. While important, these studies treat the app as a black box. More recent conceptual work has clarified how super apps expand through conglomeration strategies and how they may become infrastructure for multimodal mobility and adjacent services [21, 22]. They explain why firms pursue integration, but fail to consider what happens during super app use after integration: how users navigate between services, the problems arising from poorly supported cross-service transitions, and the design choices that impact usability. Table 1 summarizes the key studies investigating super apps. Existing super-app studies have mainly addressed platform-level adoption, growth strategies, and regulatory trends. However, little is known about cross-service use and how it influences super app usability. The present study addresses this gap by investigating feature complexity suggested by

Fürst et al. [6] as an important factor influencing usability and continuance, and the role of cognitive load in explaining these relationships. The research model for this study is presented in Fig. 1.

Table 1. Summary of Related Studies on Super Apps and Feature Complexity

Study	Method	Context	Key Findings
Steinberg [17]	Case study	LINE in East Asia	LINE became a super app by layering services and mini-program functionality onto a messaging platform, showing how platformization can concentrate multiple services within one interface.
van der Vlist et al. [21]	Analytical	Global digital economy	Super-appification reflects conglomeration strategies in which platforms absorb adjacent services and infrastructures into broader ecosystems.
Hasselwander and Weiss [9]	Survey	Super-app adoption intention	Adoption intentions are shaped by UTAUT2-related drivers and perceived risk, emphasizing entry into the ecosystem rather than behavior during use.
Hasselwander [8]	Lit. review	Platform growth strategies	Super apps grow through bundling, ecosystem orchestration, and adjacent-service expansion, but the review does not address user cognition during cross-service use.
Weiss and Hasselwander [22]	Conceptual	Mobility and multi-service ecosystems	Super apps may coordinate multimodal mobility and adjacent services, but institutional and regulatory constraints shape how these ecosystems evolve.

(*continued*)

Table 1. *(continued)*

Study	Method	Context	Key Findings
Fürst et al. [6]	Experiment	Consumer product adoption	Feature heterogeneity and feature interrelatedness jointly shape perceived complexity and adoption outcomes, suggesting that feature relations matter in addition to feature counts.
Thompson et al. [19]	Experiment	Consumer products	Adding features can initially increase perceived capability but later reduce perceived ease of use and satisfaction when the product becomes harder to process.

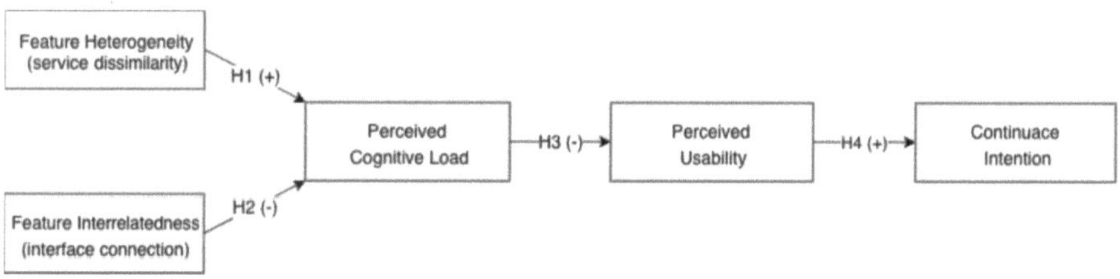

Fig. 1. Conceptual model for the proposed study.

2.2 Feature Complexity: Heterogeneity and Interrelatedness

Fürst et al. [6] argue that complexity depends not only on the number of features in a product, but also on how those features relate to one another. They distinguish between feature heterogeneity, or the degree to which features differ, and feature interrelatedness, or the extent to which features share inputs, outputs, or structural connections. This distinction is especially relevant for super apps because users do not experience service portfolios as abstract bundles; they experience them as sequences of concrete tasks that may or may not connect smoothly. This relational view also complements feature-fatigue research, which shows that adding capability can reduce downstream user evaluations when the resulting system becomes harder to process and use [19].

In super apps, feature heterogeneity is the conceptual distance between services: ride-hailing and courier delivery share spatial logic and address fields, whereas ride-hailing and restaurant browsing involve fundamentally different interaction patterns. On the other hand, feature interrelatedness captures whether the interface acknowledges any link between those services, for example, by carrying over the ride's drop-off address into the food module. These are design choices, and they can be implemented well or poorly regardless of how different the underlying services happen to be.

2.3 Feature Heterogeneity and Cognitive Load

Cognitive Load Theory distinguishes among intrinsic, extraneous, and germane load [18]. As the present study focuses on task execution rather than learning, the most relevant dimensions are intrinsic load and, especially, extraneous load. When interacting with interfaces, extraneous load arises when users must spend mental effort on avoidable coordination work rather than on the focal task itself. Poor interface design increases this burden by requiring users to reconstruct the context that the system could have preserved [11].

Task-switching research further shows that switching costs increase when the outgoing and incoming tasks rely on different rules, cues, and response mappings [13, 16]. In super apps, moving from ride-hailing service to courier delivery service requires users to continue working with a similar location-based task structure. Moving from ride-hailing to restaurant reservation, by contrast, requires users to shift toward a different task structure centered on search, comparison, and item selection. As the similarity between two different services decreases, the transition involves more mental reconfiguration, thereby leading users to experience greater cognitive load. Research on interruption and resumption in mobile contexts supports this argument, showing that resumption becomes more difficult when fewer contextual cues are preserved [4, 23].

Hypothesis 1: Higher feature heterogeneity between services increases perceived cognitive load.

2.4 Feature Interrelatedness and Cognitive Load

Cognitive offloading refers to the delegation of mental work to the external environment [15]. In the context super-apps, feature interrelatedness can be viewed as a system-level form of cognitive offloading: the interface reduces the need for users to remember, infer, or reconstruct information when transitioning across services. When the system carries forward relevant context, prompts the next likely action, or narrows the option space, it reduces the mental coordination required of the user.

Chalmers and Galani [3] describe this principle as seamful design: rather than concealing the boundary between modules, the interface gives users a structure for crossing it. In a cross-service episode, this means the system takes responsibility for preserving task-relevant information during transition, an address, a location-based filter, a contextual prompt, so that the user can start the next task with relevant contextual information. Kirsh [12] suggests that modifying the external environment to reduce cognitive demands is often more efficient than performing the equivalent mental work internally. When feature interrelatedness is high, the system should reduce avoidable coordination effort and therefore lower perceived cognitive load.

Hypothesis 2: Perceived cognitive load is lower when cross-service transitions are supported by feature interrelatedness than when they are not.

2.5 Cognitive Load, Usability, and Continuance

Perceived cognitive load matters because it shapes how users evaluate the overall interaction experience. Prior research on usability and human-computer interaction suggest that interface-imposed cognitive load negatively influences usability judgements [2, 11]. In the context of super apps, when a cross-service transition requires excessive mental effort, users are more likely to perceive the system as confusing, inefficient, or difficult to use.

Hypothesis 3: Higher cognitive load decreases perceived usability.

Usability is one of the key determinants of users' intentions to continue using a system [1, 20]. Fürst et al. [5] suggest that users evaluate not only individual functions but also how smoothly system components work together over time. In the context of super apps, this implies that usability depends not only on the quality of individual services but also on how smoothly users can switch between them. Accordingly, if a super app is perceived as easy to use and effective across consecutive tasks, users should be more willing to continue using the super app.

Hypothesis 4: Higher perceived usability increases continuance intention.

3 Methodology

3.1 Experimental Design and Scenario

The proposed study employs a 2×2 factorial design, in which feature heterogeneity (low vs. high) and feature interrelatedness (absent vs. present) are manipulated as between-subjects factors. Participants will be randomly assigned to one of the four conditions (C1 – C4). The unit of analysis is a single cross-service episode where the user completes two service tasks in sequence. The scenario is implemented through a fictional super-app prototype called "Voya X," designed to control for the visual style (e.g., typography, palette, grid, and screen count) while manipulating only the service pairing and feature interrelatedness. The super app includes three service tasks: (1) a ride service task, in which the user books a ride and arrives at the destination the user, (2) a courier service task, in which the user sends a package, and (3) an eats service task, in which the user browses restaurants, selects items, and confirms an order.

3.2 Manipulations

Four interactive super app mockups corresponding to the four experimental conditions (shown in Table 2) were developed. In all conditions, the user first completes the ride service task and arrives at the destination. Then, the user completes an additional task in Voya X that differs according to the feature heterogeneity manipulation. In the low heterogeneity conditions (C1 and C2), the user continues with the courier service task whose task structure remains relatively similar to that of the ride service task. In the high heterogeneity conditions (C3 and C4), the user instead proceeds with the eats service task, for which the transition requires a more substantial change in task structure.

Table 2. Experimental Conditions and Manipulations

Condition	Feature Heterogeneity	Feature Interrelatedness (Three-Layer Operationalization)
C1	Low: Ride → Courier	**Low:** no data carryover; no contextual prompt; no proximity filtering
C2	Low: Ride → Courier	**High:** address auto-fill; "Send Now 'banner; pre-filtered nearby options
C3	High: Ride → Eats	**Low:** manual re-entry; generic navigation; default citywide list
C4	High: Ride → Eats	**High:** address auto-fill; "Hungry?" banner; nearby restaurants filtered

The feature interrelatedness manipulation comprises three layers that are either all present (C2 and C4) or all absent (C1 and C3), depending on the condition. In the data layer, the ride destination address is automatically transferred to the next service task in the present condition but must be manually re-entered in the absent condition. In the intent layer, a contextual banner (e.g., "Send Now" or "Eat") appears on the final screen of the ride service task and offers a one-tap call to action in the present condition, whereas generic icons are shown in the absent condition. In the interface layer, options are pre-filtered by proximity (e.g., nearby couriers or restaurants) in the present condition, whereas users see a default unfiltered list in the absent condition.

3.3 Participants and Procedure

The participants will be recruited through Prolific. The target population consists of users who are familiar with mobile service applications and who are able to complete a short web-based interaction scenario in English. Data collection will take place online through participants' web browsers. Figure 2 summarizes the experimental procedure.

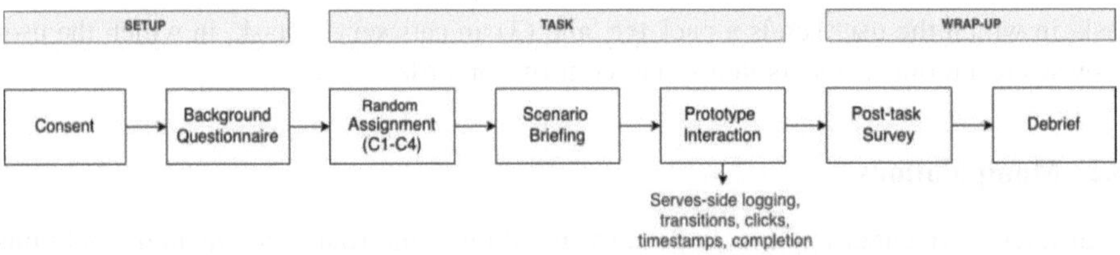

Fig. 2. Planned study procedure. Participants first provide consent and complete a background questionnaire, then receive one of four experimental conditions, complete the prototype task, and answer the post-task survey. Server-side logs capture behavioral data during the interaction stage.

Participants will first review the consent form and provide consent, after which they will complete a brief background questionnaire covering demographics, prior familiarity with super apps, and general switching habits. They will then be randomly assigned to one of the four experimental conditions and complete the assigned cross-service scenario in the Voya X prototype. Finally, they will complete a post-task questionnaire containing measures of cognitive load, perceived usability, continuance intention, as well as the manipulation check questions. Throughout the prototype session, server-side logs will capture screen transitions, initial interactions, selection events, and task-completion timestamps.

3.4 Measures

The planned study relies on self-reported measures for the constructs in the research model, complemented by supplementary behavioral measures captured through server-side logs.

Primary Self-Report Measures. Cognitive load will be measured with three items adapted from the Raw Task Load Index (Raw TLX) [7]. The Raw TLX is a multi-dimensional workload assessment instrument originally comprising six subscales: mental demand, physical demand, temporal demand, effort, performance, and frustration [14]. Since the present task involves a brief digital interaction with minimal physical or time-pressure demands, only three subscales are retained: mental demand, effort, and frustration. Each item is reworded to reference the cross-service transition context (e.g., "How much mental activity was required in total to complete both tasks?").

Perceived usability will be measured using two items adapted from the System Usability Scale (SUS) [2]. The SUS is a ten-item instrument that is widely used as a rapid measure of perceived usability in HCI research. For the purposes of this study, two items capturing ease of use and task efficiency were selected and adapted to fit the consecutive-task scenario.

Continuance intention will be measured using two items adapted from Bhattacherjee's [1] expectation-confirmation model of IS continuance, focusing on willingness to reuse the system and willingness to recommend it for similar tasks. The measures for cognitive load will be rated using semantic differential scales, whereas all other measures will be rated using 7-point Likert scales.

Manipulation Checks. The manipulation checks for feature interrelatedness will examine whether participants perceived contextual prompting and data carryover across services. For feature heterogeneity, the manipulation checks will assess the perceptions of similarity between the two services and between the actions involved with them. All manipulation check items will be rated using 7-point Likert scales. The measurement items and manipulation checks are presented in Table 3.

Supplementary Behavioral Measures. Server-side logs will capture behavioral indicators including navigation lag time (in milliseconds) between completing a trip and entering a second service, task duration, banner uptake in high interrelatedness conditions, and completion status. These measures are intended to complement the self-report data and to help verify that the manipulations operate as designed.

Table 3. Measurement Items and Manipulation Checks

Construct	Item
Cognitive Load [7]	How much mental activity was required to complete both service tasks? How hard did you have to work mentally to complete the two service tasks? How stressed or annoyed did you feel during the two service tasks?
Usability [2]	I found this super app easy to use for these consecutive service tasks. I felt I could efficiently complete my goal using this super app.
Continuance Intention [1]	I would use this super app again for similar service tasks. I would recommend this super app to a friend for similar service tasks.
Interrelatedness Checks	The super app prompted me with the next service at the right. The super app automatically carried my data into the next service.
Heterogeneity Checks	The second service felt different from the ride service. The two service tasks required different kinds of actions.

3.5 Data Analysis

The planned analysis will proceed in three stages. First, the manipulation checks will be assessed to ensure that the feature heterogeneity and interrelatedness manipulations are successful. Second, the effects of feature heterogeneity and feature interrelatedness on perceived cognitive load will be tested using a two-way ANOVA. Third, the sequential mediation pathway from the experimental conditions to continuance intention through perceived cognitive load and perceived usability will be tested using Hayes' PROCESS macro (Model 6) with bootstrapped confidence intervals [10]. Behavioral logs will be used as supplementary evidence for task flow validation, manipulation fidelity, and descriptive comparisons of transition behavior.

4 Expected Contributions

This study is expected to contribute to the literature on super apps in two ways. First, it shifts research attention from platform-level adoption and growth strategies toward the design of cross-service transitions and their implications on usability. By focusing on a single episode in which a user transitions from one service to another, the proposed study will provide insights into how the user experience of a super app depends not only on the design of individual services but also on how effectively the platform supports transitions between them.

Second, the study offers a theoretically grounded and operationally concrete account of feature interrelatedness. The proposed three-layer manipulation translates the abstract idea of connected features into specific interface mechanisms that can be designed and empirically tested: data carryover, contextual prompting, and interface filtering. In doing so, it provides a clearer basis for examining how design choices may reduce cognitive effort in using super apps, thereby improving usability and continuance.

The study also provides practical implications for platform teams. The findings from the study can guide designers in improving multi-service experiences: not by merely expanding the range of services, but by making transitions between services easier for users to understand and complete. This is particularly relevant for emerging Western super-app initiatives in mobility and fintech, where service breadth alone is unlikely to sustain continued use if cross-service seams remain cognitively costly [22].

5 Limitations and Future Work

Like any study, this research is not without its limitations. First, the proposed study prioritizes causal clarity over full ecological realism. A controlled experiment helps isolate the effects of heterogeneity and interrelatedness but may omit real-world factors such as personalization, prior history, and habitual usage patterns. In addition, the design focuses on only two service pairings, and the extent to which the findings generalize to other combinations of super-app services remains to be established.

Future research could extend the study by considering additional service pairings, as well as using complementary methods. Field studies or longitudinal studies could examine how transition friction accumulates over repeated use and in more naturalistic settings. It would also be useful to compare host-platform, mini-program, and more tightly integrated native-module architectures to determine whether feature interrelatedness mechanisms operate similarly across different super-app configurations.

6 Conclusion

Adding services to a platform does not, by itself, produce a coherent ecosystem. The quality of cross-service transitions, whether they are deliberately designed or left as afterthoughts, matters at least as much as the breadth of the service portfolio. This paper proposes a research model grounded in research on feature complexity, cognitive load theory, and cognitive offloading to investigate cross-service transitions. The three-layer operationalization of feature interrelatedness (Data–Intent–Interface) provides an adjustable design lever that can reduce much of the context reconstruction that users would otherwise need to perform themselves.

The study is expected to contribute to the super app literature by shedding light on how service differences and interface support shape cognitive load, usability, and continuance intention. The findings of the study may also provide empirical support for the argument that complexity in super apps arises less from the number of features than from the seams between services. To improve usability, designers may therefore need to focus more on preserving context across services so that users can transition between them with minimal cognitive effort.

References

1. Bhattacherjee, A.: Understanding information systems continuance: an expectation-confirmation model. MIS Q. **25**(3), 351–370 (2001). https://doi.org/10.2307/3250921
2. Brooke, J.: SUS: a "quick and dirty" usability scale. In: Jordan, P.W., Thomas, B., Weerdmeester, B.A., McClelland, I.L. (eds.) Usability Evaluation in Industry, pp. 189–194. Taylor & Francis (1996)
3. Chalmers, M., Galani, A.: Seamful interweaving: heterogeneity in the theory and design of interactive systems. In: Proceedings of the 2004 Conference on Designing Interactive Systems (DIS '04), pp. 243–252. ACM (2004). https://doi.org/10.1145/1013115.1013149
4. Czerwinski, M., Horvitz, E., Wilhite, S.: A diary study of task switching and interruptions. In: Proceedings of the SIGCHI Conference on Human Factors in Computing Systems (CHI '04), pp. 175–182 (2004). https://doi.org/10.1145/985692.985715
5. Fürst, A., Friedrich, R., Prigge, J.K., Moosbrugger, E.: Monetization of internet-of-things systems: how interoperability and safeguarding drive customer acquisition, retention, and expansion. Int. J. Res. Mark. (2025). https://doi.org/10.1016/j.ijresmar.2025.11.002
6. Fürst, A., Pecornik, N., Hoyer, W.D.: How product complexity affects consumer adoption of new products: the role of feature heterogeneity and interrelatedness. J. Acad. Mark. Sci. **52**(2), 329–348 (2024). https://doi.org/10.1007/s11747-023-00933-7
7. Hart, S.G., Staveland, L.E.: Development of NASA-TLX (task load index): results of empirical and theoretical research. In: Hancock, P.A., Meshkati, N. (eds.) Human Mental Workload, pp. 139–183. North-Holland (1988). https://doi.org/10.1016/S0166-4115(08)62386-9
8. Hasselwander, M.: Digital platforms' growth strategies and the rise of super apps. Heliyon. **10**(5), e25856 (2024). https://doi.org/10.1016/j.heliyon.2024.e25856
9. Hasselwander, M., Weiss, D.: Super app adoption intention based on UTAUT2 with perceived risk. In: Proceedings of the 57th Hawaii International Conference on System Sciences, pp. 4010–4019, Honolulu (2024). https://doi.org/10.2139/ssrn.4784554
10. Hayes, A.F.: Introduction to Mediation, Moderation, and Conditional Process Analysis: a Regression-Based Approach, 3rd edn. The Guilford Press, New York (2022)
11. Hollender, N., Hofmann, C., Deneke, M., Schmitz, B.: Integrating cognitive load theory and concepts of human–computer interaction. Comput. Hum. Behav. **26**(6), 1278–1288 (2010). https://doi.org/10.1016/j.chb.2010.05.031
12. Kirsh, D.: Adapting the environment instead of oneself. Adapt. Behav. **4**(3–4), 415–452 (1996). https://doi.org/10.1177/105971239600400307
13. Monsell, S.: Task switching. Trends Cogn. Sci. **7**(3), 134–140 (2003). https://doi.org/10.1016/S1364-6613(03)00028-7
14. Paas, F., Tuovinen, J.E., Tabbers, H., Van Gerven, P.W.M.: Cognitive load measurement as a means to advance cognitive load theory. Educ. Psychol. **38**(1), 63–71 (2003). https://doi.org/10.1207/S15326985EP3801_8
15. Risko, E.F., Gilbert, S.J.: Cognitive offloading. Trends Cogn. Sci. **20**(9), 676–688 (2016). https://doi.org/10.1016/j.tics.2016.07.002
16. Rubinstein, J.S., Meyer, D.E., Evans, J.E.: Executive control of cognitive processes in task switching. J. Exp. Psychol. Hum. Percept. Perform. **27**(4), 763–797 (2001). https://doi.org/10.1037/0096-1523.27.4.763
17. Steinberg, M.: Line as super app: platformization in east Asia. Soc. Media Soc. **6**(2), 1–10 (2020). https://doi.org/10.1177/2056305120933285
18. Sweller, J.: Cognitive load during problem solving: effects on learning. Cogn. Sci. **12**(2), 257–285 (1988). https://doi.org/10.1207/s15516709cog1202_4
19. Thompson, D.V., Hamilton, R.W., Rust, R.T.: Feature fatigue: when product capabilities become too much of a good thing. J. Mark. Res. **42**(4), 431–442 (2005). https://doi.org/10.1509/jmkr.2005.42.4.431

20. Venkatesh, V., Morris, M.G., Davis, G.B., Davis, F.D.: User acceptance of information technology: toward a unified view. MIS Q. **27**(3), 425–478 (2003). https://doi.org/10.2307/30036540
21. van der Vlist, F.N., Helmond, A., Dieter, M., Weltevrede, E.: Super-appification: conglomeration in the global digital economy. New Media Soc. **27**(6), 3314–3337 (2025). https://doi.org/10.1177/14614448231223419
22. Weiss, D., Hasselwander, M.: Super apps and the mobility transition. Environ. Innov. Soc. Trans. **55**, 100955 (2025). https://doi.org/10.1016/j.eist.2024.100955
23. Zhang, C., Wei, D.P., Ji, Y., Chen, D., Li, X.Y., Gong, X.D.: The influence of interface attributes and interaction elements on user performance and cognitive load in task interruption scenarios. Int. J. Ind. Ergon. **108**, 103761 (2025). https://doi.org/10.1016/j.ergon.2025.103761

[illegible]

Visual Perception and User Interface Design

Making Prototypes Talk: Communication and Programming Strategies in Design Students' Interactive Prototyping

Andrea Alessandrini(✉)

University of Urbino, Urbino 61029, Italy
andrea.alessandrini@uniurb.it

Abstract. This study investigates troubleshooting in physical computing prototypes within design education contexts. We examine how students address breakdowns arising from the integration of hardware and software, including sensors, microcontrollers, and digital services. Through empirical observations and interviews, we show how reasoning emerges through iteration, material feedback, and collaboration. We highlight challenges related to communication infrastructures and programming strategies. The findings contribute to understanding the cognitive processes involved and offer implications for designing more effective maker learning environments and instructional supports for debugging in complex interactive systems, fostering problem-solving skills and advanced computational thinking among students engaged in design practices.

Keywords: Design · Education · Interactivity · Communication · Practices · Programming · Prototyping Tools

1 Introduction

Interactive prototyping in Human–Computer Interaction (HCI) and design education increasingly involves heterogeneous systems that integrate sensors, microcontrollers, mobile devices, and software services [1–3]. Within this context, maker education and physical computing have become key approaches for introducing computational concepts through hands-on, constructionist learning. Physical computing connects abstract computational ideas with tangible outcomes by linking code to sensors, actuators, and physical materials. This connection supports iterative cycles of experimentation, testing, and refinement typical of design-based learning. Prototyping kits and modular electronics allow learners to construct circuits and program interactive behaviours, supporting exploration through material interaction. Maker-oriented environments offer valuable educational opportunities, as tools are becoming more sophisticated while remaining accessible to novices [4, 5]. However, integrating hardware and software introduces additional complexity. Breakdowns may arise from software errors, wiring mistakes, circuit instability, or mismatches between code and hardware behaviour. Such issues are common in physical computing, making troubleshooting a routine part of the process. Debugging is particularly challenging because learners must reason across tightly coupled hardware and software components [6, 7].

C. Stephanidis et al. (Eds.): HCII 2026, CCIS 3047, pp. 165–170, 2026.
https://doi.org/10.1007/978-3-032-30552-7_16

Studies of collaborative debugging highlight how learners interpret system behaviour through social interaction, material feedback, and iterative hypothesis testing [8–11]. While novices often experience frustration and uncertainty, collaboration and prior experience can mitigate these challenges. Despite this, gaps remain in understanding how learners engage with complex systems that combine multiple technologies [12]. Similarly, research on sensor use in education highlights the challenges novices face when selecting and integrating hardware components into working systems [13–15]. While troubleshooting is recognised as central to maker-based learning, limited research has examined how students reason about communication infrastructures and programming strategies during debugging. This paper addresses this gap by investigating troubleshooting practices in interactive physical computing prototypes. It analyses how learners reason across hardware and software during system breakdowns and provides empirical insights into how design students navigate communication and programming challenges in interactive prototyping.

2 Method

The study took place within the Design Department, involving a cohort of students from both Product Design (PD) and Interaction Design (IxD) programs. Over the course of two semesters, students were tasked with developing unique design outcomes based on self-selected project briefs. The learning environment was a studio-style classroom where each student maintained an individual workspace while participating in a shared, collaborative atmosphere. Of the 57 students invited to participate in the research, 19 provided informed consent for an in-depth study. This participant group comprised 11 men and eight women, with ages ranging from 23 to 27 years. The students utilised a diverse array of specialised technologies to realise their projects, with the most prevalent tools being the Processing programming language, Arduino microcontrollers, and various sensors and actuators. The raw data consists of prototype analyses, researcher field notes, and video-recorded semi-structured interviews. As noted in our previous work [16, 17], these sessions captured the technical procedures and decision-making processes involved in the students' design work. While the initial study provided a descriptive overview of student progress, the current analysis employs a more rigorous thematic coding approach aimed at generating higher-level theoretical insights. We systematically re-examined all data related to equipment, technology, and procedural workflows. Our analytical process transitioned from initial descriptive coding to a more abstract, interpretive level, eventually reaching thematic saturation. This iterative re-coding allows for a deeper exploration of prototype communication, providing a new perspective on the existing dataset.

3 Results

The results show that the communication architecture of the interactive artefact prototypes developed during university teaching activities involved several key components, including communication libraries, communication protocols, data processing mechanisms, and network communication features. Communication libraries enabled the interaction between different hardware and software components of the prototypes. In some cases, ad hoc serial communication protocols were developed to identify and interpret users' input actions. Another relevant aspect concerned the processing of communication data to manage and interpret information exchanged between system components. Additionally, some prototypes required network communication via Wi-Fi, although this was sometimes constrained by the university's network security policies. Finally, the identification and management of input data sources within networked communication environments emerged as a critical aspect of prototype development.

For brevity, we focus here on the characteristics and strategies related to the use of communication libraries. For example, a student project involving the design of a tangible programming environment based on physical language blocks for young children illustrates the complexity of communication in interactive prototypes. The system used a computer, a webcam, TUIO [18], and reacTIVision [19] to track and interpret physical interactions. As participant A33 explains: "*Basically, it's this library for connecting with ... I can't remember the name, it's a library for Processing. The library for Processing allows me to get the information I have been tracking ... so that library lets me interact with reacTIVision here in the program*" (see Fig. 1).

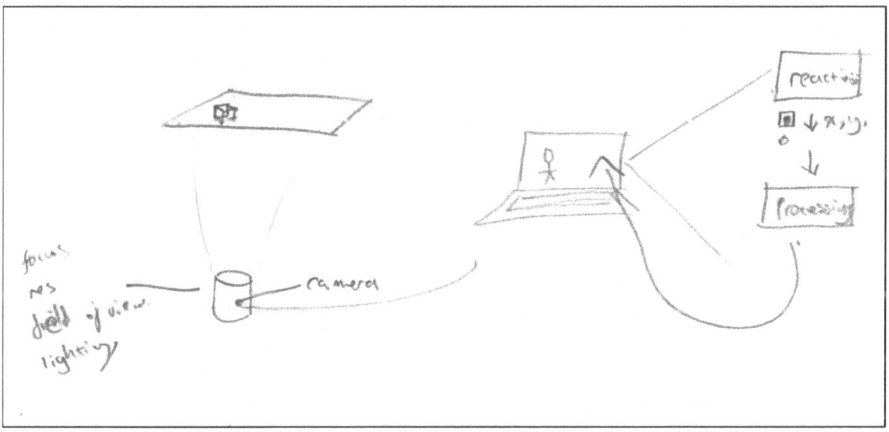

Fig. 1. Schematic of the interactive system, composed of a camera and a computer running Processing and reactiVsion to track objects on a surface (A33).

This example highlights how communication with external libraries and software frameworks constitutes a crucial aspect of programming tangible interactive systems. Understanding, planning, implementing, and debugging these communication mechanisms is therefore a fundamental skill for interaction design students when developing tangible prototypes of interactive artefacts and systems.

4 Discussion

The findings highlight how communication infrastructures become a central locus of complexity when design students develop interactive physical computing prototypes. While prior work on maker education emphasises troubleshooting across hardware and software components, the present analysis shows that students must also reason about communication layers that connect heterogeneous elements of a system. In the examined projects, communication libraries, protocols, and data processing routines acted as mediating structures through which sensors, microcontrollers, and software environments exchanged information. These results extend existing studies on debugging in physical computing contexts, which often focus on circuit construction or programming errors [20, 21]. Our findings suggest that learners must additionally understand how external libraries and frameworks structure communication between components. For example, the case involving reacTIVision and Processing illustrates how students depend on specialised libraries to translate sensor data into programmatic events. This introduces a layer of abstraction that can both enable rapid development and complicate troubleshooting when communication fails.

The results also resonate with research on collaborative debugging and material feedback in maker environments. Students frequently interpret system behaviour through iterative experimentation, testing hypotheses about how data flows between components. However, the presence of multiple communication channels—serial connections, libraries, and networked services—requires learners to develop strategies for identifying where breakdowns occur. From an educational perspective, these findings suggest that teaching interactive prototyping should address not only electronics and programming but also communication architectures and data flow reasoning. Supporting students in conceptualising these infrastructures may help them better diagnose and resolve breakdowns in complex interactive systems [13, 22].

5 Conclusion

There are increasing efforts to better understand and support communication and troubleshooting in interactive prototyping, although significant challenges remain before these systems become fully transparent and manageable. Advancing these capabilities will enable design students to gain greater control over complex technologies, integrating them effectively into everyday creative and learning practices within contemporary design education contexts and future practice.

Acknowledgements. We would like to thank all the design students and instructors who participated in our field study research.

Disclosure of Interests. The author has no competing interests to declare that are relevant to the content of this article.

References

1. Alessandrini, A., Rizzo, A., Rubegni, E.: Drama prototyping for the design of urban interactive systems for children. In: Proceedings of the 8th International Conference on Interaction Design and Children, pp. 198–201. Association for Computing Machinery, New York (2009). https://doi.org/10.1145/1551788.1551827

2. Alessandrini, A.: End-user construction mechanisms for the internet of things. In: Proceedings of the 27th International BCS Human Computer Interaction Conference, pp. 1–6. British Computer Society, London (2013)
3. Rubegni, E., Brunk, J., Caporali, M., Gronvall, E., Alessandrini, A., Rizzo, A.: Wi-Wave: urban furniture for browsing internet contents in public spaces. In: Proceedings of the 15th European Conference on Cognitive ergonomics: The Ergonomics of Cool Interaction, p. 10. ACM (2008). https://doi.org/10.1145/1473018.1473032
4. Martin, L.: The promise of the maker movement for education. J. Pre-Coll. Eng. Educ. Res. **5** (2015). https://doi.org/10.7771/2157-9288.1099
5. Alessandrini, A.: How design students construct electronic circuit designs for tiny interactive prototypes: a study in an undergraduate course. In: Presented at the C and C 2025—Proceedings of the 2025 Conference on Creativity and Cognition (2025). https://doi.org/10.1145/3698061.3734400
6. Booth, T., Stumpf, S., Bird, J., Jones, S.: Crossed wires: investigating the problems of end-user developers in a physical computing task. In: Proceedings of the 2016 CHI Conference on Human Factors in Computing Systems, pp. 3485–3497. Association for Computing Machinery, New York (2016). https://doi.org/10.1145/2858036.2858533
7. Alessandrini, A.: Advanced electronic connections challenges for design students engaged with constructing prototypes of interactive artefacts. In: Presented at the C and C 2025—Proceedings of the 2025 Conference on Creativity and Cognition (2025). https://doi.org/10.1145/3698061.3734396
8. Jayathirtha, G., Fields, D., Kafai, Y.: Pair debugging of electronic textiles projects: analyzing think-aloud protocols for high school students' strategies and practices while problem solving. In: 14th International Conference of the Learning Sciences: The Interdisciplinarity of the Learning Sciences, ICLS 2020—Conference Proceedings (2020)
9. Fields, D.A., Searle, K.A., Kafai, Y.B.: Deconstruction kits for learning: students' collaborative debugging of electronic textile designs. In: Proceedings of the 6th Annual Conference on Creativity and Fabrication in Education, pp. 82–85 (2016)
10. Alessandrini, A.: Components and events identification challenges and practices in interactive prototypes construction: a field study in a design course. In: Stephanidis, C., Antona, M., Ntoa, S., Salvendy, G. (eds.) HCI International 2023—Late Breaking Posters, pp. 3–7. Springer, Cham (2024). https://doi.org/10.1007/978-3-031-49212-9_1
11. Alessandrini, A.: A study of electronic circuit design in tiny interactive prototypes in an undergraduate course. In: Stephanidis, C., Antona, M., Ntoa, S., Salvendy, G. (eds.) HCI International 2025 Posters, pp. 333–337. Springer, Cham (2025). https://doi.org/10.1007/978-3-031-94153-5_32
12. Jayathirtha, G., Kafai, Y.B.: Interactive stitch sampler: a synthesis of a decade of research on using electronic textiles to answer the who, where, how, and what for K--12 computer science education. ACM Trans. Comput. Educ. **20**, 1–29 (2020)
13. Karvinen, K.: Choosing novice friendly sensors. Int. J. Electr. Eng. Educ. **56**, 251–264 (2019)
14. Alessandrini, A.: Selection of technologies during design learning activities in an undergraduate course. In: Proceedings of the 16th Conference on Creativity & Cognition, pp. 561–565. Association for Computing Machinery, New York (2024). https://doi.org/10.1145/3635636.3664251
15. Alessandrini, A.: How design students select maker technologies in their undergraduate projects. In: Proceedings of the European Conference on Cognitive Ergonomics 2024, pp. 1–4 (2024). https://doi.org/10.1145/3673805.3673838
16. Alessandrini, A.: How an undergraduate group of design students solved wiring errors during the prototyping of an interactive artifact. In: Proceedings of the 33rd European Conference on Cognitive Ergonomics (2022). https://doi.org/10.1145/3552327.3552345

17. Alessandrini, A.: A study on prototyping in a design course. In: Presented at the (eds) Human-Computer Interaction – INTERACT 2023 Lecture Notes in Computer Science (2023). https://doi.org/10.1007/978-3-031-42293-5_41
18. TUIO Homepage. http://www.tuio.org
19. reacTIVision Homepage. http://reactivision.sourceforge.net
20. Alessandrini, A.: Strategies, practices, and challenges in interactive prototypes construction: a field study in a design course. In: Proceedings of the European Conference on Cognitive Ergonomics 2023, pp. 1–4 (2023). https://doi.org/10.1145/3605655.3605661
21. DesPortes, K., DiSalvo, B.: Trials and tribulations of novices working with the Arduino. In: Proceedings of the 2019 ACM Conference on International Computing Education Research, pp. 219–227. Association for Computing Machinery, New York (2019). https://doi.org/10.1145/3291279.3339427
22. Tuhkala, A., Isomäki, H., Hartikainen, M., Cristea, A., Alessandrini, A.: Design of a learning space management system for open and adaptable school facilities. In: Costagliola, G., Zvacek, S., Uhomoibhi, J., Escudeiro, P., B.M., M.L. (eds.) Commun. Comput. Info. Sci., pp. 22–43. Springer (2018). https://doi.org/10.1007/978-3-319-94640-5_2

Visual Design of Pedagogical Agents in 360-Degree Panoramic Shopping Interfaces Impacts on Consumer Shopping Experience

Kun Chen and Weimin Zhai(✉)

School of Design and Innovation of Shenzhen Technology University, Shenzhen 518118, China
zhaiweimin@sztu.edu.cn

Abstract. The 360° panoramic shopping interface offers immersive experiences but imposes higher cognitive and operational demands on users, particularly on mobile devices. Instructional agents may mitigate these challenges, yet their effectiveness in e-commerce contexts remains underexplored. This study investigates how the visual design of instructional agents—real-human, cartoon character, or none—affects consumers' shopping experience in mobile 360° panoramic interfaces. A single-factor between-participants experiment was conducted with 27 participants randomly assigned to three conditions. Participants completed product search tasks using interactive prototypes, followed by subjective evaluations of satisfaction, interest, purchase willingness, and preference. These findings indicate that incongruent human-like representations may detract from user experience, possibly due to uncanny valley effects or increased cognitive load. Cartoon character agents provide guidance without compromising experience, representing a safer design choice. This study extends instructional agent research to immersive e-commerce and offers practical implications for interface designers.

Keywords: Visual Design of Instructional Agents · 360° Panoramic Shopping Interface · Consumer Shopping Experience · Technology Acceptance Model (TAM) · Cognitive Load Theory (CLT)

1 Introduction

With the rapid development of mobile Internet, online shopping has become one of the important consumption methods in consumers' daily lives. Compared with traditional APP-based shopping, the 360° panoramic shopping interface provides consumers with a shopping experience closer to offline scenarios through rotatable and immersive browsing. This shopping method can enhance consumers' overall perception of goods and the sense of environmental atmosphere to a certain extent, thereby improving the sense of reality and participation in the shopping process [13]. Studies have shown[1] that compared with traditional 2D images, 360° panoramic display can significantly improve users' shopping interest, participation and positive emotions, and may have a positive impact on purchase intention. By providing more comprehensive visual information, 360° panoramic shopping helps users construct more accurate mental representations, thereby reducing perceived risk [15].

C. Stephanidis et al. (Eds.): HCII 2026, CCIS 3047, pp. 171–181, 2026.
https://doi.org/10.1007/978-3-032-30552-7_17

However, while the 360° panoramic shopping interface brings an immersive experience, it also places higher requirements on users' information acquisition and interface operation. For example, in the 360° panoramic interface, information may be scattered in three-dimensional space in the form of "virtual annotations" or "hotspots", and users must operate independently to rotate the perspective and search to discover and obtain this information. This requires users not only to browse information independently, but also to actively explore the shopping scene, which undoubtedly increases the complexity of information acquisition [15]. At the operational level, users need to learn new interaction methods: such as dragging and sliding to rotate the perspective, as well as zooming and clicking hotspots. Compared with traditional clicking and scrolling, these operations have higher accuracy and learning costs, especially when used for the first time.

In addition, due to the characteristics of the 360° panoramic shopping interface, such as variable perspective, unfixed information distribution, and less intuitive interaction paths than traditional web pages, users may face problems such as unfamiliar operation, difficulty in target positioning, and increased cognitive load when they first come into contact with it. Especially on mobile devices, limited by screen size and interaction methods, users are more likely to experience operational confusion during browsing, thereby affecting their use efficiency and overall shopping experience [12]. To improve such problems, the guidance design in the interface has gradually attracted attention.

As a personalized guiding element, instructional agents usually appear in the form of virtual characters or avatars. They are designed to interact with learners to simulate the roles of mentors, peers or coaches, thereby guiding, motivating and supporting the learning process [11]. In fields such as digital learning, virtual environments and human-computer interaction, instructional agents have been proven to have a certain impact on users' attention allocation, emotional experience and task completion. For example: instructional agents have a significant positive impact on retention tests, transfer tests and other learning outcomes [3]; in VR environments, instructional agent prompts can reduce the time for object search, and this prompt method does not affect learning outcomes [5], etc. However, in online shopping, especially in 360° panoramic shopping scenarios, whether instructional agents can also effectively improve user experience still needs further discussion.

This study explores the impact of the type of virtual instructional agents in 360° panoramic shopping interfaces on users' experience, so as to improve the usability of instructional agents. Based on relevant research on instructional agents, this study attempts to evaluate the types of virtual instructional agents and compare users' task performance and subjective evaluations when operating instructional agent prompts on mobile devices. The main purposes of this study include: to compare the differences in consumers' subjective evaluations among different visual types of instructional agents (real-human instructional agents, cartoon character instructional agents, and no instructional agents).

2 Literature Review

This chapter aims to sort out and analyze the core concepts and theoretical foundations of this study. First, it explores the characteristics of 360° panoramic shopping interfaces and their application in immersive shopping scenarios, explaining the potential experience advantages and operational challenges brought by such interfaces; then, it explains the relevant connotations of the Technology Acceptance Model and Cognitive Load Theory, as the theoretical basis for this study to analyze the impact of instructional agent visual design on consumers' shopping experience.

2.1 360° Panoramic Shopping Interface

The 360° panoramic shopping interface can integrate products, space and interactive behaviors into the same interface. Consumers can not only read product information, but also independently search for the location of products and feel the effect of products in their respective spaces. This display method can not only enhance consumers' participation in the shopping process, but also improve consumers' perception and understanding of products [8]. However, while the 360° panoramic shopping interface brings an immersive experience, it also increases some complexity in use: in the 360° panoramic shopping interface, information is not arranged in order, but changes with the rotation of the perspective, so users need to constantly change the perspective to search and integrate information. This form of operation will increase the operation time and understanding burden of beginners [10]. Especially in the mobile device environment, limited by screen size, touch methods and perspective switching mechanisms, consumers are more likely to experience a sense of disorientation, operational uncertainty, and even affect the overall task completion efficiency and subjective experience [10].

Therefore, how to improve user experience through effective interface prompts and guidance design has become a worthy issue to explore. For this study, instructional agents, as a personalized guiding element, can be used as a way to detect whether this pain point can be improved—by setting different instructional agent objects and text prompt dialog boxes under the 360° panoramic shopping interface to assist participants in completing operational tasks.

2.2 Technology Acceptance Model and Cognitive Load Theory

Since this study explores the impact of different instructional agent visual designs on consumers' shopping experience. In the 360° panoramic shopping experience, consumers are not only involved in the acceptance of new interaction methods, but also involved in the psychological burden during the operation process. Therefore, the Technology Acceptance Model (TAM) and Cognitive Load Theory (CLT) are taken as the main theoretical foundations.

TAM is mainly used to explain users' acceptance and willingness to use new technologies, new systems or new interfaces. The model holds that users' acceptance of a system is usually affected by their perception of whether the system is "easy to use" and "helpful in completing tasks" [4]. The theory provides a basis for studying whether consumers are willing to accept such interfaces and whether they think they have good operability and value.

CLT emphasizes that people have limited cognitive resources when processing tasks. If the interface information is too complex, the operation path is not clear, or it is necessary to process too many visual and functional clues at the same time, it may increase the psychological burden of users during task execution, thereby affecting learning, understanding and operational performance [14]. This theory can help explain why different instructional agent designs may lead to different shopping experience results.

2.3 Summary

From the above literature, it can be seen that compared with traditional graphic pages, the 360° panoramic shopping interface has a stronger sense of space, immersion and interactivity; however, its need for constant perspective conversion and non-linear information distribution will increase the operation difficulty and cognitive burden. It can be seen that adding an appropriate guidance mechanism in the interface to help users understand the operation method and successfully complete tasks is an important research to improve user experience. Under the TAM and CLT theories, we can understand users' acceptance of the 360° panoramic shopping interface and whether the interface processing will cause users to have information processing pressure and affect users' operation experience. Therefore, this study compares the differences in consumers' subjective evaluations under three conditions (real-human instructional agents, cartoon character instructional agents, and no instructional agents) with the mobile 360° panoramic shopping interface as the experimental background.

3 Research Methods

This study investigates the impact of the visual design of instructional agents on participants' operational performance and subjective evaluations when operating the 360° panoramic virtual shopping interface on mobile devices. The study adopts a single-factor three-level between-participants experimental design, and the independent variables of the experiment are real-human instructional agents, cartoon character instructional agents and no instructional agents. The dependent variables of the experiment are the participants' subjective evaluation.

3.1 Participants

A total of 27 participants were recruited via convenience sampling. All completed the experiment individually in a quiet, face-to-face setting. The sample comprised 16 males (59%) and 11 females (41%). Age distribution: 21 participants (78%) aged 18–28, 4 (15%) aged 29–39, and 2 (7%) aged 40–50. Regarding mobile shopping experience, 15 participants (56%) had over 3 years of experience, while the remainder had varying durations. In the past month, mobile shopping frequency was less than 4 times for 8 participants (30%), 5–10 times for 12 (44%), and higher frequencies for the rest. For 360° panoramic image experience, 3 participants (11%) had never heard of it, 12 (44%)

were aware but had not used it, 9 (33%) used it occasionally, and 2 (7%) used it frequently. All participants had normal or corrected-to-normal vision and were proficient in using mobile applications. Participants were randomly assigned to three experimental groups, with each session lasting approximately 10 min. Informed consent was obtained prior to participation.

3.2 Experimental Design and Prototype Design

The software production process of the experimental operating system is as follows: first, search for 2:1 high-resolution images suitable for 360° panorama on various furniture websites as experimental materials. As shown in Fig. 1.

Fig. 1. 360° panoramic rendering of the virtual furniture interior scene in the experiment.

Then, the virtual exhibition hall rendering was loaded into the VR Panorama Cloud Platform of the "Wasai" application for prototype production, and the parameters required for the experiment were set, and finally output as an interactive prototype that can run on mobile devices. The content displayed in the exhibition hall is the display of furniture in the family living room. To better observe each piece of furniture, a translucent search icon will be placed on the main part of each piece of furniture. Clicking the icon can enter the detailed product information interface, including the product name, price and introduction. During the operation, the participants change the viewing angle by sliding the mobile phone screen. Due to the special presentation effect of the 360° panoramic image, all furniture information will show different perspective ratios as the user's perspective changes. When the participants enter the 360° virtual shopping interface, the instructional agent and the auxiliary text dialog box will appear at the bottom of the mobile phone interface. This prompt area is fixed at the bottom of the interface and does not change with the perspective, which is used to prompt the participants how to use the interface. The carrier of the experiment is the participants' own mobile phones. After the shopping interface is produced through the Wasai website, an exclusive scene QR code will be generated. The participants can experience the shopping interface by scanning the QR code with the WeChat APP on their own mobile phones. This experiment designed a total of 3 mobile application prototypes, where the independent variable of the experiment is the type of instructional agent, including three conditions: real-human instructional agents, cartoon character instructional agents and no instructional agents. As shown in Fig. 2.

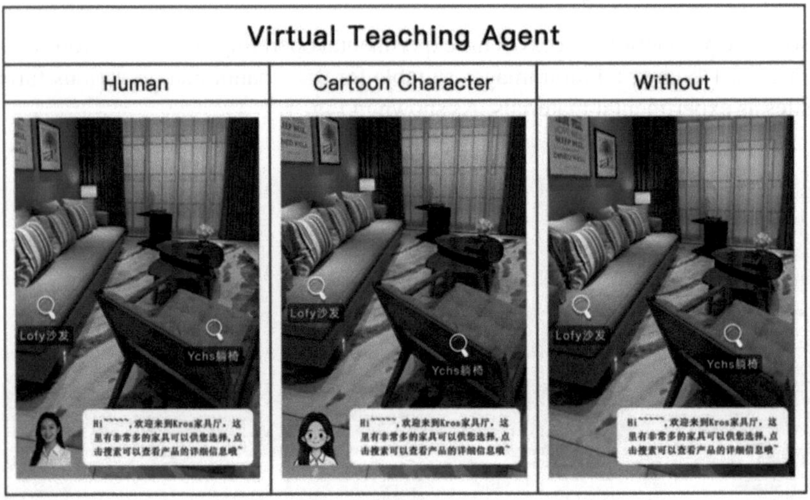

Fig. 2. Prototype Design of Virtual Instructional Agent for the Experiment.

The three groups of experimental prototypes are consistent in scene content, commodity information, interaction methods and text description content, and only differ in the presentation form of instructional agents, to ensure that the experimental results are mainly caused by independent variables.

3.3 Experimental Procedure

This study was conducted by face-to-face individual testing. Before the experiment, the researcher first explained the research purpose, experimental procedure and operation precautions to the participants, and conducted the experiment after obtaining their consent. Then, the participants first filled out a basic information questionnaire to collect demographic data, mobile shopping experience and 360° panoramic image use experience. The relevant process is shown in Fig. 3.

After filling out the basic information, the participants were randomly assigned to one of the three experiments: the real-human instructional agent group, the cartoon character instructional agent group and the no-instructional agent group. The three groups of experimental prototypes were consistent in scene content, product information, interaction methods and text prompt content, and only differed in the presentation form of instructional agents.

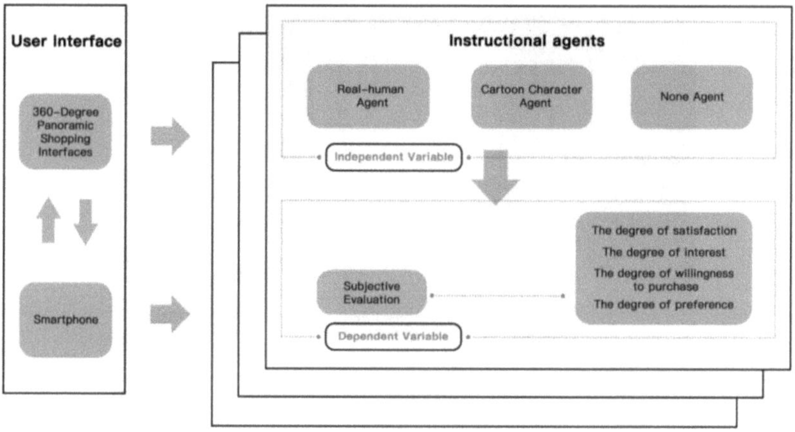

Fig. 3. Experimental Flowchart.

At the start of the formal experiment, the participants used their own mobile phones to scan the QR code to enter the corresponding 360° panoramic shopping interface, and became familiar with the basic operation methods under the unified explanation of the researcher. Then, the participants completed the designated product search and information browsing tasks according to the instructions.

After completing the task, the participants filled out a subjective evaluation questionnaire to understand their feelings about the interface's satisfaction, interest, willingness to purchase, and preference. After filling out the questionnaire, a short interview was conducted to supplement the participants' views on the visual design of instructional agents and the overall shopping experience. The entire experimental process was completed in about 10 min. As shown in Fig. 4.

Fig. 4. Experimental Procedure.

4 Experimental Results

The experiment results were analyzed based on a between-participants one-way ANOVA (shown in Table 1). By using the SPSS software, the participants' subjective evaluations (including satisfaction, interest, willingness to purchase, and preference) were analyzed.

Table 1. The one-way ANOVA results of participants' subjective evaluations.

	Sources	SS	df	MS	F	P	η^2
The degree of satisfaction	different visual types of instructional agents	12.07	2	6.04	4.83	0.017*	0.29
The degree of interest	different visual types of instructional agents	17.56	2	8.78	4.96	0.016*	0.29
The degree of willingness to purchase	different visual types of instructional agents	18.96	2	9.48	6.36	0.006*	0.35
The degree of preference	different visual types of instructional agents	12.07	2	6.04	4.08	0.030*	0.25

* Significant difference at $\alpha = 0.05$ level (*$p < 0.05$)

The results of the one-way ANOVA on participants' subjective evaluations are presented in Table 1. A significant difference was found in satisfaction ($F = 4.83$, $p = 0.017 < 0.05$). Post hoc comparisons revealed that the Without instructional agent condition and the human instructional agent condition differed significantly ($p = 0.029 < 0.05$). Additionally, a significant difference was also observed between the cartoon character instructional agent and human instructional agent conditions ($p = 0.007 < 0.05$). However, no significant difference was found between the without instructional agent and cartoon character instructional agent conditions ($p = 0.533 > 0.05$). These results indicate that satisfaction with the human instructional agent (M = 4.89, SD = 1.36) was significantly lower than that with the without instructional agent (M = 6.11, SD = 1.17) or the cartoon character instructional agent (M = 6.44, SD = 0.73).

A significant difference was found in the degree of interest ($F = 4.96$, $p = 0.016 < 0.05$). Post hoc comparisons revealed that the Without instructional agent condition and the human instructional agent condition differed significantly ($p = 0.003 < 0.05$). Additionally, a significant difference was also observed between the cartoon character instructional agent and human instructional agent conditions ($p = 0.006 < 0.05$). However, no significant difference was found between the without instructional agent and cartoon character instructional agent conditions ($p = 0.485 > 0.05$). These results indicate that satisfaction with the human instructional agent (M = 4.56, SD = 1.81) was significantly lower than that with the without instructional agent (M = 6.00, SD = 1.22) or the cartoon character instructional agent (M = 6.44, SD = 0.73).

A significant difference was found in the degree of willingness to purchase ($F = 6.36$, $p = 0.006 < 0.05$). Post hoc comparisons revealed that the Without instructional agent condition and the human instructional agent condition differed significantly ($p = 0.005 < 0.05$). Additionally, a significant difference was also observed between the cartoon character instructional agent and human instructional agent conditions ($p = 0.005 < 0.05$). However, no significant difference was found between the without instructional agent and cartoon character instructional agent conditions ($p = 1.000 > 0.05$). These results indicate that satisfaction with the human instructional agent (M = 4.33, SD = 1.41) was significantly lower than that with the without instructional agent (M = 6.11, SD = 1.17) or the cartoon character instructional agent (M = 6.11, SD = 1.05).

A significant difference was found in the degree of preference ($F = 4.08$, $p = 0.030 < 0.05$). Post hoc comparisons revealed that the Without instructional agent condition and the human instructional agent condition differed significantly ($p = 0.044 < 0.05$). Additionally, a significant difference was also observed between the cartoon character instructional agent and human instructional agent conditions ($p = 0.012 < 0.05$). However, no significant difference was found between the without instructional agent and cartoon character instructional agent conditions ($p = 0.567 > 0.05$). These results indicate that satisfaction with the human instructional agent (M = 4.78, SD = 1.48) was significantly lower than that with the without instructional agent (M = 6.00, SD = 1.22) or the cartoon character instructional agent (M = 6.33, SD = 0.87).

5 Discussion

This study examined how different instructional agent visuals (real-human, cartoon character, none) affect consumers' subjective shopping experience in a mobile 360° panoramic interface. Results showed significant differences across satisfaction, interest, willingness to purchase, and preference, highlighting the importance of agent visual design in immersive e-commerce environments. Notably, the real-human agent received consistently lower ratings than both the cartoon and no-agent conditions—a finding that contradicts assumptions that human-like agents enhance user experience. This may reflect the uncanny valley effect [14], where near-realistic representations provoke discomfort, particularly when visually misaligned with a stylized virtual environment. No significant differences emerged between the cartoon agent and no-agent conditions across any measure, suggesting that cartoon agents neither significantly enhance nor impair user experience. Their stylized appearance likely aligns well with the artificial nature of the interface, supporting the idea that visual congruence with the virtual environment may outweigh realism [15]. The poor performance of the real-human agent suggests that incongruent agent design can actively harm user experience. Drawing on the Technology Acceptance Model and Cognitive Load Theory, such agents may reduce perceived ease of use and introduce extraneous cognitive load, diverting attention from the shopping task. Theoretically, these findings extend instructional agent research from educational to immersive e-commerce contexts, showing that agent design can influence affective and conative outcomes like satisfaction and purchase intention. Practically, they suggest that cartoon agents are a safe choice, while realistic human agents should be used cautiously in virtual shopping environments.

Limitations include the small sample size ($N = 27$) and brief task duration. Future research should explore longer-term effects, task and product variability, and incorporate objective measures such as eye-tracking or task completion time.

6 Conclusion

This study investigated how instructional agent visual design impacts consumer experience in mobile 360° shopping. A between-participants experiment comparing real-human, cartoon, and no-agent conditions revealed three key findings: (1) Visual design significantly affects subjective evaluations (satisfaction, interest, purchase intent), indicating agents serve aesthetic and emotional roles beyond guidance. (2) Real-human agents rated significantly lower than both cartoon and no-agent conditions, likely due to environmental incongruence or the uncanny valley effect. (3) Cartoon agents performed similarly to the no-agent condition, suggesting they provide guidance without cognitive burden or negative affect when visually congruent. These findings highlight the need to align agent design with immersive contexts. For practitioners, cartoon agents are a safer choice, whereas human-like agents require cautious implementation.

References

1. Agost, M.J., Vergara, M., Bayarri-Porcar, V.: Perceiving design features in new interaction environments: comparing rendered images, 360 rotation, AR, immersive and non-immersive VR, and real product interaction. Appl. Sci. **14**(11), 4470 (2024)
2. Broeck, M.V.D., Kawsar, F., Schöning, J.: It's all around you: exploring 360 video viewing experiences on mobile devices. In: Proceedings of the 25th ACM International Conference on Multimedia, pp. 762–768 (2017)

3. Castro-Alonso, J.C., Wong, R.M., Adesope, O.O., Paas, F.: Effectiveness of multimedia pedagogical agents predicted by diverse theories: a meta-analysis. Educ. Psychol. Rev. **33**(3), 989–1015 (2021)
4. Davis, F.D.: Perceived usefulness, perceived ease of use, and user acceptance of information technology. MIS Q. **13**(3), 319–340 (1989)
5. Decker, D., Merkt, M.: Look at me! Can an instructional agent facilitate orientation and support learning in VR? Educ. Technol. Res. Dev. **73**, 1–31 (2025)
6. Diekhof, E.K., Kastner, S., Deinert, D., Foerster, M., Steinicke, F.: The uncanny valley effect and immune activation in virtual reality. Sci. Rep. **15**(1), 30473 (2025)
7. Gladstone, J.R., Schroeder, N.L., Heidig, S., Zhang, S., Palaguachi, C., Pitera, M.: Do pedagogical agents enhance student motivation? Unraveling the evidence through meta-analysis. Educ. Psychol. Rev. **37**(3), 72 (2025)
8. Jin, B., Kim, G., Moore, M., Rothenberg, L.: Consumer store experience through virtual reality: its effect on emotional states and perceived store attractiveness. Fash. Text. **8**(1), 19 (2021)
9. Joshi, S., Rambola, R.K., Churi, P.: Evaluating artificial intelligence in education for next generation. J. Phys.: Conf. Ser. **1714**(1), 012039 (2021)
10. Lu, X., Hsiao, K.L.: Effects of diffusion of innovations, spatial presence, and flow on virtual reality shopping. Front. Psychol. **13**, 941248 (2022)
11. Martha, A.S.D., Santoso, H.B.: The design and impact of the instructional agent: a systematic literature review. J. Educ. Online. **16**(1), n1 (2019)
12. Prakash, Y., Nayak, A.K., Sunkara, M., Jayarathna, S., Lee, H.N., Ashok, V.: All in one place: ensuring usable access to online shopping items for blind users. Proc. ACM Hum.-Comput. Interact. **8**(EICS), 1–25 (2024)
13. Shinde, Y., Lee, K., Kiper, B., Simpson, M., Hasanzadeh, S.: A systematic literature review on 360° panoramic applications in Architecture, Engineering, and Construction (AEC) industry. J. Inf. Technol. Constr. **28**, 405–437 (2023)
14. Sweller, J.: Cognitive load during problem solving: effects on learning. Cogn. Sci. **12**(2), 257–285 (1988)
15. Zhai, W., Lin, Z., Xu, B.: Exploring the effects of virtual annotation background display mode and transparency through a 360-degree panorama approach to online shopping. Asia Pac. J. Mark. Logist. **36**(5), 1045–1068 (2024)

Do Passkey Explanations Discourage Adoption?

Zainab Husain[1(✉)], Eric Spero[2], and Robert Biddle[1,2]

[1] Carleton University, Ottawa, Canada
zainabhusain3@cmail.carleton.ca, robert.biddle@carleton.ca
[2] University of Auckland, Auckland, New Zealand
eric.spero@auckland.ac.nz

Abstract. Despite their advantages over traditional passwords, passkeys have experienced slow adoption among users. To better understand this issue, we examined public-facing materials designed to explain passkeys to general users. We found that these materials tend to emphasize the underlying mechanisms of passkeys, such as public key cryptography, rather than user-relevant functionality.

We conducted a study in which participants read one of two explanatory texts: one reflecting current approaches to explaining passkeys, and the other a proposed user-focused alternative. Our findings show a significant difference in participants' comprehension and mental models of passkeys, suggesting a pathway toward improving adoption through clearer, user-centered communication.

Keywords: Passkeys · Phishing · Authentication · Cybersecurity

1 Introduction

Although passwords have been the cornerstone of digital security for decades, they remain highly vulnerable to well-known threats. Within the first 3 months of 2024, just short of one million phishing attacks were recorded. In addition, the rise of AI threatens to increase both the number and sophistication of these attacks.[1]

Due to the clear shortcomings of passwords, passkeys were created as a standards-based way to safely sign into accounts. The private component of the key is stored securely and is never shared with services, allowing it to be resistant to many cyber threats, such as phishing. Users use PINs or biometrics on local devices to access the private key, which is how they are authenticated.

Despite clear advantages over passwords, passkeys are experiencing slow adoption among users. To understand this, we investigated websites as well as other material that aim to explain passkeys to users in order to observe a connection (or lack thereof) between user understanding and adoption of passkeys. Our

[1] https://nordvpn.com/blog/phishing-statistics/.

C. Stephanidis et al. (Eds.): HCII 2026, CCIS 3047, pp. 182–192, 2026.
https://doi.org/10.1007/978-3-032-30552-7_18

findings indicate that the material tends to emphasize explaining the core mechanisms of passkeys—such as public key cryptography—rather than the functions which are relevant to users.

We conducted a study to examine users' attitudes and understanding of passkeys among individuals with limited prior exposure. Participants were presented with one of two text explanations: one reflecting information currently provided by large technology companies, and another taking a more user-centred approach that considers the audience's ability to understand key technical concepts.

2 Background

Phishing is a common cybercrime where attackers attempt to trick users into revealing sensitive information, such as login credentials. A common technique is to send messages persuading users to log in to an imitation of a legitimate website, thus revealing their credentials to the attacker.

Passkeys are resistant to credential phishing for several reasons. First, passkeys are bound to the domain where they were registered, meaning they cannot be used on fraudulent websites. As a result, users cannot unknowingly authenticate on phishing sites or disclose credentials. Second, passkeys require access to a trusted device to authorize authentication. The private key is stored on the user's device and may be made available across trusted devices via password managers or cloud syncing, but can only be used after the device is unlocked. Finally, passkeys allow users to authenticate without sharing reusable secrets. Unlike passwords, which are transmitted to the website, passkeys do not expose information that can be captured and reused by attackers.

Passkeys are based on public-key cryptography. During registration, a key pair is generated and scoped to the service: the public key is stored by the website, while the private key remains on the user's device, typically within secure hardware such as a Trusted Platform Module (TPM) or secure enclave. The private key cannot be read or exported. During login, the website sends a challenge to the user's device, which must be approved by the user. The private key signs this challenge, and the resulting signature is verified using the stored public key. This process authenticates the user by proving possession of the private key, without transmitting sensitive information that could be reused in an attack.

Past research has explored several aspects of passkeys, with particular attention given to technical usability and deployability. A recurring theme among the existing literature is the focus on technical barriers of adoption, while user-facing communication and comprehension remained largely unexplored.

A prior literature review in 2025 by Matzen et al. [4] focuses on the existing research on passkeys and end-users. The analysis consists of technical challenges and user-centric perspectives of the technology with the goal of improving user adoption of passkeys. As a strategy to improve user adoption, the paper correctly identifies the requirement of greater user education through public-facing material to improve user perception of passkeys. While it makes valid claims on methods to improve users' awareness of the technology, Matzen et al. does not provide any content analysis or review on existing public material in order to explain the current attempts at explanations. The paper places less emphasis on the communication of the technology compared to UX design and implementation barriers.

In 2024, a literature review by Blessing et al. [1] reviews the security, privacy, usability and recoverability aspects of end-to-end-encrypted authentication schemes. They put a strong focus on challenges caused by device loss and account recovery. They do not address user understanding or perception of passkeys, instead focusing largely on technical usability concerns.

In 2025, Buttner et al. [2] provided a comparative analysis of the security, deployability and usability of synced passkeys and device bound passkeys. While this study highlights the benefits of passkeys over traditional password based systems, and focuses on technical usability, the paper does not discuss the understanding of passkeys beyond the context of deployability.

Other studies, such as Holtgrave et al. in 2025 [3] focus on acceptance and usability of various authentication methods within enterprise settings, which is irrelevant to our scope.

Collectively, these studies offer valuable insights on technical usability, deployability and enterprise adoption, but there is a clear lack of research on how passkeys are explained by public facing material. Each of the related studies provide insights on technical usability or enterprise adoption, but it reveals a critical gap in current research: the insufficient attention placed on how passkeys are presented and explained by public facing material. This is an important aspect of research on passkey adoption as user understanding of the technology is reliant on the information shared through such communication channels. While this gap has been identified by Matzen et al. it is an area that has yet to be explored.

3 Method

In order to create two distinct text stimuli for our survey study, we identified 10 publicly available sources for qualitative analysis. These sources were selected based on their prominence in Google search results for queries that users might plausibly enter to learn about passkeys, such as "passkey", "how do passkeys work", and "what is a passkey". The selected sources include Apple Support, Dashlane, FIDO Alliance, Google Account Help, Google Safety, LastPass, Mastercard, Microsoft Security, Microsoft Support, and 1Password.

We performed a qualitative analysis of these web pages. This process began with a preliminary round of open coding, in which segments of text were labelled and noted. Through this process, we identified recurring patterns across the texts, including the use of technical terminology, detailed technical explanations, metaphorical analogies, and undefined terms or concepts. We then conducted axial coding to examine relationships between these features, identifying the co-occurrence of dense technical jargon, unexplained concepts, and a lack of focus on user-relevant functionality. Finally, we performed selective coding to synthesize these findings into a central theme: that public-facing explanations of passkeys tend to prioritize technical accuracy at the expense of user-centered clarity.

Building on this analysis, we constructed two short text segments. The *Baseline Text* was designed to reflect the characteristics of existing public explanations, incorporating similar terminology, content, and levels of technical detail. In contrast, the *Proposed Text* was designed to address the shortcomings identified during our analysis, emphasizing user-relevant functionality and prioritizing clarity over technical detail. The two texts are presented below.

Baseline Text:

Passkeys are a simpler and more secure replacement for passwords since they are phishing resistant and don't require anything to memorize or type in. Instead, you can sign-in to your accounts using biometrics or a PIN.

For the passkey to work, two cryptographic keys are generated: a public key, and a private key. The public key is stored on the website and is openly accessible, and the private key is kept hidden on your device. The private key never leaves your device, and there are no shared secrets. Your device and the authenticator communicate to authenticate your log-in without revealing the private key, making the passkey secure, and highly phishing-resistant.

Passkeys are created based on a set of open standards, and many platform vendors offer secure syncing features so that you can use your passkeys from any device.

Proposed Text:

Passkeys replace passwords as a new, secure login method. One reason for this is that attackers can trick users into entering passwords into illegitimate websites where they can be copied and reused to access your accounts, finances, and to impersonate you (a form of 'phishing'). Conversely, passkeys aren't shared or entered on websites. They are securely stored in password managers, built into all major platforms.

During account registration, your password manager saves the website's address and creates a passkey: a complicated string of characters secured within your manager. A mathematically linked key is sent to the website. To log in, you unlock your password manager (using biometrics or a PIN). This checks that the website is the one you registered with, and your passkey matches the website's key.

Your passkey is never sent to websites, so it cannot be phished, and you only need to unlock your device to securely log in.

This study was approved by our university's research ethics board. Participants provided informed consent prior to participation.

Participants were recruited via Prolific. In total, 183 participants completed the study (Baseline: n = 91, Proposed: n = 92). Participants were screened for low prior exposure to passkeys, and individuals with cybersecurity expertise or highly technical backgrounds were excluded. Participants were recruited from the United States, and we aimed to approximate the national distribution of educational attainment.

The sample included 97 women, 81 men, and 4 non-binary participants (mean age = 43.4 years). Educational attainment included 2 participants with less than high school education, 79 with a high school diploma, 25 with trade or vocational training, 62 with a bachelor's degree, 12 with a master's degree, and 2 with a PhD.

Participants were randomly assigned to one of two conditions and shown either the Baseline Text or the Proposed Text. After reading the assigned text, participants completed a set of post-intervention questions using 7-point Likert scales. These items assessed (i) participants' conceptual understanding and mental models of passkeys and passwords, including common misconceptions (e.g., whether passkeys are shared with websites or can be phished), and (ii) their attitudes toward passkeys, including perceived security, usability, and willingness to adopt them.

4 Results

4.1 Descriptive Statistics

Table 1 summarizes participants' post-intervention responses to items on passkey adoption, password security, and passkey understanding for the Baseline Text and Proposed Text conditions.

Passkey Understanding. Participants in both groups demonstrated a basic understanding of passkeys. They agreed that passkeys are phishing-resistant (Med = 6) and can be used in place of passwords across websites and applications (Med = 6).

However, clear differences emerge in participants' conceptual understanding. Participants in the Baseline group more frequently endorsed misconceptions about how passkeys function. They expressed neutrality regarding whether passkeys are shared with websites' servers (Med = 4), whereas participants in the Proposed group disagreed with this statement (Med = 2). Similarly, the Baseline group reported higher agreement that passkeys are sent to websites during login (Med = 6 vs. Med = 5).

Differences also appear in usability and interaction expectations. Participants in the Proposed group more strongly agreed that passkeys can be used via a password manager (Med = 6 vs. Med = 4). The Baseline group showed greater uncertainty about whether passkeys could be used on fraudulent websites, whereas the Proposed group expressed clearer disagreement (Med = 2).

Table 1. Post-intervention survey responses for the Baseline Text (A) and Proposed Text (B) conditions. Values show the median (med), mean (M), and standard deviation (SD) for each Likert-scale item. Responses are reported as raw values; reverse-worded items have not been reverse-scored. Responses were measured on a 7-point Likert scale (1 = strongly disagree, 7 = strongly agree).

Question	A_{med}	A_M	A_{SD}	B_{med}	B_M	B_{SD}
Password Understanding						
Passwords are shared with websites' servers when you register and login	5	4.65	1.72	6	5.05	1.63
People can be tricked into entering a password on a fake version of a website	7	6.37	1.01	7	6.41	0.87
Passkey Understanding						
A passkey is a complicated sequence of characters	4	4.23	1.79	6	5.91	1.44
No one could guess your passkeys to enter your accounts	5	4.88	1.74	6	5.15	1.63
Passkeys are phishing-resistant	6	5.62	1.32	6	5.65	1.22
Passkeys can be used instead of passwords on apps and websites	6	6.13	0.78	6	6.29	0.78
The website has a 'key' corresponding to your passkey	5	5.07	1.58	6	5.48	1.61
You only need to unlock your password manager to use your passkey	4	3.95	1.64	6	5.70	1.36
Passkeys are shared with websites' servers when you register and login	4	3.58	1.75	2	3.04	2.07
Passkeys must be learned/memorised	2	2.85	1.86	2	2.46	1.74
People can be tricked into entering passkeys on fake version of a legitimate website	3	3.23	1.72	2	2.70	1.71
When you login, the passkey is sent to the website to verify your identity	5	5.07	1.50	6	5.15	1.97
You can accidentally use a passkey on a website you have not registered with	2	2.63	1.36	2	2.36	1.62
Passkey Adoption						
Passkeys provide valuable security improvements over passwords	6	5.97	0.90	6	6.11	0.94
I am in favour of using passkeys instead of passwords on all websites and platforms	5	4.00	1.47	5	5.21	1.54
Passkeys are complicated to use during logins	2	2.75	1.50	2	2.87	1.69
I would not trust passkeys to keep my accounts secure	2	2.74	1.29	2	2.45	1.49
I'm not interested in using a different sign-in method instead of passwords	3	3.12	1.72	2	2.86	1.78

Overall, responses in the Proposed condition are more consistent with a correct conceptual model of passkeys, indicating a more accurate understanding of how they function.

Passkey Adoption. Participants in both groups expressed positive attitudes towards passkeys. Participants generally agreed that passkeys provide security improvements (Med = 6) and were supportive of their adoption, while disagreeing with statements expressing distrust and difficulty of use (Med = 2).

Differences between conditions were limited. Participants in the Proposed group expressed slightly stronger disagreement with disinterest in adopting alternative sign-in methods (Med = 2 vs. Med = 3), suggesting marginally greater openness to adoption.

4.2 Inferential Statistics

To assess differences between conditions, we computed aggregate scores for passkey adoption and authentication security understanding by averaging responses across the relevant items (after reverse-coding where appropriate), such that higher scores indicate greater adoption and more accurate understanding. The understanding construct reflects participants' conceptual knowledge of passkey functionality, whereas adoption reflects self-reported attitudes and intentions to use passkeys. The understanding score was derived from items in the *Password Understanding* and *Passkey Understanding* sections of Table 1, while the adoption score was derived from items in the *Passkey Adoption* section.

We tested for differences between conditions using a one-sided Wilcoxon rank-sum test, expecting higher scores in the Proposed condition. The distributions of both aggregate scores are shown in Fig. 1.

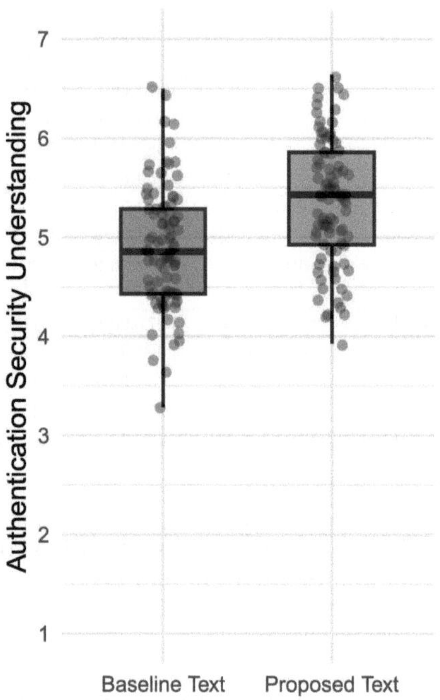

(a) Authentication security understanding

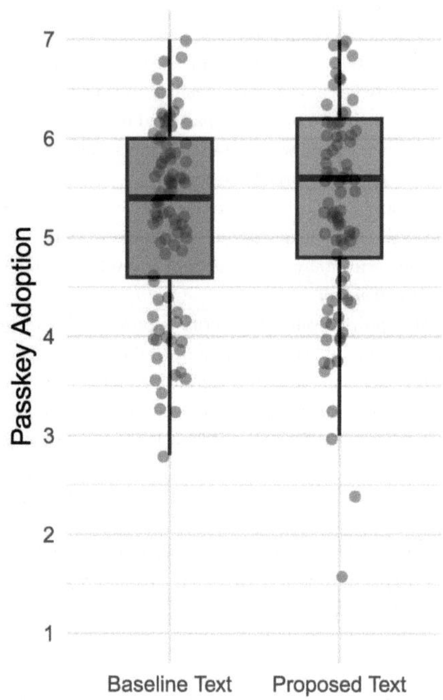

(b) Passkey adoption

Fig. 1. Comparison of Baseline Text and Proposed Text conditions on authentication security understanding and willingness to adopt passkeys.

The Proposed condition showed higher understanding scores (Med = 5.43, M = 5.36, SD = 0.62) than the Baseline condition (Med = 4.86, M = 4.89, SD = 0.61), and this difference was statistically significant (W = 5838, $p < .001$).

The Proposed condition showed slightly higher adoption scores (Med = 5.6, M = 5.43, SD = 1.15) than the Baseline condition (Med = 5.4, M = 5.27, SD = 0.99), although this difference was not statistically significant (W = 4524, p = .14).

4.3 Qualitative Responses

Participants' open-ended responses provide additional insight into how users understood and reasoned about passkeys after reading the texts.

Across both conditions, participants' comments about passkey understanding reflected a mixture of learning and residual confusion. In the Baseline condition, several responses indicated that participants still lacked a clear mental model of how passkeys work, with comments such as "I have not received enough information about passkeys to make an informed decision about them," "I felt like I'm more confused now about what they are," and "I'm still confused how a passkey generates a new password and how it really knows that it's 'me'." At the same time, some Baseline participants reported improved understanding (e.g., "I actually didn't have much clue about passkeys so this was very informative and interesting" and "I feel like I understand passkeys a lot better now"). Proposed responses showed a similar pattern. Some participants indicated that the text improved their understanding (e.g., "Thank you for teaching me how these work" and "now that I know a little more information, I'd be willing to try it"), while others remained uncertain, stating for example, "I'm still confused about how to use passkey," "I think I need a longer explanation with some examples," and "Although you explained passkeys, I'm still uncertain of how to use them." These comments suggest that neither text fully resolved users' uncertainty, with participants in both conditions expressing a mixture of learning and residual confusion.

A prominent theme across responses was a desire for more practical, experience-oriented explanations. Many participants indicated that abstract descriptions were insufficient, instead requesting concrete examples, demonstrations, or opportunities for hands-on use. For instance, participants suggested that "an informative video about passkeys would be useful," that "an educational example could alleviate these hesitations," and that they would better understand passkeys if they could "experience it first hand." These responses suggest that users are not only seeking conceptual explanations, but also procedural and experiential understanding of how passkeys function in practice.

Concerns about device dependence and account recovery were also widespread. Participants frequently asked what would happen if a device was lost, stolen, or unavailable (e.g., "What happens then when the device is stolen or otherwise compromised?"), and noted that "if something happens to your device, it can make it very difficult for you to gain access to your own accounts again." Closely related concerns involved cross-device usability, with participants reporting difficulties logging in from other devices or uncertainty about how passkeys function across platforms.

Participants also exhibited confusion about how passkeys relate to other authentication mechanisms. Some responses suggested that participants conflated passkeys with familiar concepts such as passwords, biometric login, or authentication apps. For example, participants questioned whether passkeys were "similar to authenticator apps like Google authenticator" or stated "I'm not sure if a pass key is different from using a fingerprint," indicating gaps in their mental models.

A further barrier to adoption related to concerns about biometric authentication. Some participants expressed discomfort with the use of biometric data, perceiving it as more invasive or vulnerable than passwords (e.g., "I have a difficult time trusting the security of passkeys since it uses my biometric data, which I find more invasive than a password"), while others were hesitant to rely on biometrics at all (e.g., "I generally do not like ... giving out my biometric information so I am hesitant to go away from passwords"). These responses suggest that uncertainty about how biometric data is stored and protected may contribute to scepticism toward passkeys.

Finally, while participants often acknowledged the security advantages of passkeys, a general scepticism toward security technologies remained evident. Some participants emphasised that "everything can be hacked," indicating persistent distrust even in the presence of improved authentication mechanisms.

Altogether, these responses suggest that while participants engaged with the explanations, key challenges remain in supporting users' understanding of how passkeys work in practice. In particular, the need for concrete examples, procedural guidance, and clarity around recovery and failure scenarios appears central to improving user comprehension and adoption.

5 Discussion

Our findings suggest that improving the way passkeys are explained can significantly enhance users' conceptual understanding of the technology. Participants exposed to the Proposed Text exhibited higher understanding scores than those in the Baseline condition. However, this improvement did not translate into a statistically significant increase in adoption intentions. This suggests that while clearer, user-focused explanations are effective in shaping mental models, adoption decisions are influenced by additional factors beyond understanding alone.

The observed differences in understanding between conditions reflect broader limitations in current approaches to communicating passkeys. Public-facing materials often emphasize technical properties, such as phishing resistance, without clearly explaining the underlying threats or their implications for users. More generally, these materials tend to rely on technical jargon, present concepts in an unclear sequence, and place insufficient emphasis on user-relevant functionality. These characteristics likely contribute to the weaker understanding observed in the Baseline condition.

At the same time, improved understanding alone appears insufficient to drive adoption. Qualitative responses indicate that concerns about device dependence, account recovery, and cross-device usability persist even when users demonstrate a clearer conceptual understanding of how passkeys function. These concerns reflect uncertainties about how passkeys behave in real-world scenarios, suggesting that understanding the underlying mechanism does not necessarily translate into confidence in their practical use. These concerns represent practical barriers that are not addressed through explanation alone, and may help explain why improvements in understanding did not translate into increased adoption intentions. These concerns directly align with the absence of a significant adoption effect, suggesting that practical uncertainties—rather than conceptual misunderstandings—may play an important role in limiting adoption.

A further contributing factor may be the nature of the measures used. Adoption was assessed using self-reported Likert-scale items, which may be influenced by response biases such as social desirability or acquiescence. Participants may express generally positive attitudes toward security-enhancing technologies regardless of their level of understanding. In contrast, the understanding measures required participants to evaluate specific statements about passkey functionality, which more directly reflects conceptual knowledge. This distinction may help explain why differences between conditions were more clearly observed in understanding than in adoption.

These concerns suggest that effective explanations of passkeys should go beyond describing their underlying mechanisms, and also address how the technology behaves in practical scenarios. In particular, explanations of recovery, device loss, and cross-device usage may help users develop confidence in adopting passkeys.

A limitation of this study is the potential alignment between the Proposed Text and the understanding measures. Some survey items reflect concepts and terminology emphasized in the explanatory text, which may have contributed to improved performance through familiarity with phrasing rather than deeper conceptual understanding. While the qualitative responses suggest that participants in the Proposed condition developed more coherent mental models, future work should employ measures that are less directly aligned with the explanatory content.

6 Conclusions

This work examined how passkeys are communicated in public-facing materials and how these explanations influence user understanding and adoption. Our findings suggest that explanations which prioritise user-relevant functionality over technical detail significantly improve users' conceptual understanding of passkeys. However, this improvement did not translate into a corresponding increase in adoption intentions.

These results suggest that while improving explanatory clarity is necessary, it is not sufficient to drive adoption. Users' decisions appear to be shaped not only by their understanding of how passkeys work, but also by practical concerns related to usability, recovery, and cross-device access.

Overall, this work highlights the importance of designing explanations that support both conceptual understanding and practical confidence. Improving how security technologies are communicated represents a promising direction for supporting their broader adoption.

Acknowledgement. This study was funded by the Natural Sciences and Engineering Research Council of Canada (NSERC) RGPIN-2022-04887.

Disclosure of Interests. The authors have no competing interests to declare that are relevant to the content of this article.

References

1. Blessing, J., Hugenroth, D., Anderson, R.J., Beresford, A.R.: SoK: web authentication in the age of end-to-end encryption. In: Proceedings on Privacy Enhancing Technologies (PETS), pp. 560–589 (2025)
2. Büttner, A., Gruschka, N.: Device-bound vs. synced credentials: a comparative evaluation of passkey authentication. In: Proceedings of the 11th International Conference on Information Systems Security and Privacy (ICISSP 2025) – Volume 2, pp. 651–659 (2025)
3. Holtgrave, J.U., Klivan, S., Marky, K., Fahl, S.: A Qualitative study of adoption barriers and challenges for Passwordless authentication in German public administrations. In: CHI '25: Proceedings of the 2025 CHI Conference on Human Factors in Computing Systems (2025)
4. Matzen, A., et al.: Challenges and potential improvements for passkey adoption—a literature review with a user-centric perspective. Appl. Sci. **15** (2025)

MoE-Precip: Adaptive Mixture-of-Experts Fusion and an Interactive Web-Based Visual Analytics Interface for Multimodal Precipitation Forecasting

Quinn Krommenhoek[1], Kofi Osei[2], Sai Deepthi Yeddula[3], Dongji Feng[1(✉)], and Chen Jiang[4(✉)]

[1] School of Computing and Design, California State University Monterey Bay, Seaside, CA 93955, USA
dfeng@csumb.edu
[2] Gustavus Adolphus College, St. Peter, MN 56082, USA
[3] School of Engineering and Computer Science, Oakland University, Rochester, MI 48309, USA
[4] Samuel Ginn College of Engineering, Auburn University, Auburn, AL 36849, USA
jiangc2013@gmail.com

Abstract. Accurate precipitation forecasting is essential for agriculture, disaster response, and climate adaptation, yet it remains challenging because the information needed for prediction is inherently multimodal. Radar, satellite imagery, and surface gauges provide complementary observations, but they differ substantially in spatial and temporal resolution and exhibit distinct domain characteristics. For example, atmospheric variables are similarly heterogeneous: u/v wind captures momentum, whereas temperature and humidity encode the thermodynamic state of the atmosphere. Nevertheless, many existing methods [1,2] collapse these diverse inputs into a single shared representation, an approach that can be brittle and may generalize poorly across weather regimes and sensing conditions. At the same time, the growing complexity of multimodal forecasting models makes their behavior more difficult to interpret, thereby limiting users' ability to understand why a prediction succeeds or fails across regions, timesteps, and weather regimes.

To address this limitation, we present MoE-Precip, a visual analytics system that bridges complex multimodal precipitation modeling and practical decision-making. The system is built around an adaptive Mixture-of-Experts (MoE) architecture [3], in which expert subnetworks are organized by Earth-system components and sensing modalities, such as momentum and thermodynamics [4]. This structure enables specialized modeling of recurring spatio-temporal regimes, including convective bursts and rainband evolution. A dynamic router further learns context-dependent expert weights, allowing heterogeneous signals to be fused adaptively rather than compressed into a single shared representation.

To support interpretation and analysis, MoE-Precip provides a web-based interface through which users can scrub through time, select input

C. Stephanidis et al. (Eds.): HCII 2026, CCIS 3047, pp. 193–202, 2026.
https://doi.org/10.1007/978-3-032-30552-7_19

modalities and features, and examine synchronized Observed–Predicted–Error views. These linked views allow users to rapidly identify forecast successes and failures, detect grid-level and regional biases, and diagnose breakdowns associated with specific weather regimes. The interface also summarizes error patterns across space, time, and regimes, helping users calibrate trust in the model and gain insight into its performance characteristics.

We tested MoE-Precip on a curated multimodal dataset (https://www.noaa.gov) that captures real-world conditions during Hurricane Ian (2022) and its impacts in South Florida [5].

Keywords: Visual Analytics · Multimodal Learning · Remote Sensing · Human-Computer Interaction

1 Introduction

Accurate precipitation forecasting is essential for informing agriculture and disaster management. Modern weather forecasting systems increasingly rely on integrating diverse, multi-source observational data, such as radar reflectivity, satellite imagery, and atmospheric measurements. The multi-source data provides invaluable insights into evolving weather patterns and opens new avenues for real-time monitoring and management. The trade-off in modeling with multi-source data is the data's highly heterogeneous nature. For example, data from multiple sources can be highly diverse, with varying spatial and temporal resolutions and physical features. This is the main reason that integrating multi-source data into commonly used deep learning architectures may be less successful than using single-source data.

Although recent advances in machine learning have improved weather prediction capabilities [1,2], many models remain limited in their ability to efficiently process heterogeneous multimodal data inputs. In particular, variations in data format, temporal alignment, and regional relevance complicate joint learning across modalities. The standard architecture in the most commonly used modeling methodologies often treats all inputs uniformly, neglecting the fact that different data sources may contribute differently depending on the spatial or temporal context.

To address this limitation, we propose a visual analytics system that supports the exploration and analysis of climate-related variables while forecasting precipitation rates, providing a useful reference for severe weather monitoring and assessment. The system is centered on an adaptive Mixture-of-Experts (MoE) model for precipitation forecasting, in which each expert specializes in a specific data modality or spatiotemporal pattern. Then, a dynamic router routes input to the most relevant experts according to the current context. This modular architecture achieves a balance between specialization and scalability, improving both predictive accuracy and interpretability under complex climate conditions. The system also features a browser-based visualization Interface that allows users to interactively inspect climate variables used in the prediction model. Through transparent views of weather patterns across space and time, the platform facilitates a deeper understanding of model behavior and supports more effective analysis of severe weather events.

2 System Design

2.1 MoE-Climate Dataset

This section introduces the *MoE-Climate* dataset used in this project, and it supports a variety of climate-related modeling tasks. The raw data used to construct the MoE-Climate dataset were collected by the National Oceanic and Atmospheric Administration (NOAA) using multiple remote-sensing platforms and in-situ devices. These sources vary in both spatial and temporal resolution and collectively cover the entire continental United States. For this study, we extracted and processed a regional subset centered on South Florida to capture the atmospheric dynamics of a specific extreme weather event: Hurricane Ian.

As shown in Table 1, this dataset includes high-resolution gridded climate observations for the South Florida region during the landfall of Hurricane Ian in 2022 [5]. The temporal span extends from 00:00 on September 23 to 23:00 on October 1, with an hourly temporal resolution. The data is spatially organized into a 100 × 100 grid, where each grid cell corresponds to a 3 km × 3 km area, allowing fine-grained monitoring of localized weather patterns.

Each point in the grid includes a comprehensive set of atmospheric variables sampled at 50 vertical pressure levels. These variables include precipitation rate, total accumulated precipitation, cloud cover, and 18 additional climate-related features. As detailed in Table 1, the dataset also provides metadata, including grid id, latitude, longitude, global grid dimensions (1799 × 1059), and grid spacing. Each observation is timestamped, allowing for dynamic temporal analysis throughout the entire hurricane period.

Table 1. A snapshot of the climate data used in the study that contained both spatial and temporal inputs. The dataset included grid metadata and time-series measurements, including precipitation rate, total precipitation, cloud cover, and 16 additional meteorological features.

GridID	Longitude	Latitude	Grid Points	Grid Spacing	Vertical Level
1	122.71	21.13	1799 × 1059	3 km	50
Time Stamp	2022/09/23 00:00	2022/09/23 01:00	2022/09/23 02:00	...	2022/10/02 00:00
Precipitation rate (mm/hour)	0.0	0.72	0.94	...	0
Total Precipitation (mm)	0.01	1.88	4.3	...	31.61
...	...	...	...	...	...
Cloud cover	50%	70%	100%	...	20%

2.2 Knowledge-Guided Feature Grouping

To support the design of our modular MoE model, we partitioned the full set of climate variables into subsets according to their shared physical properties. This knowledge-guided grouping is determined by domain-specific classifications provided by the National Oceanic and Atmospheric Administration (NOAA) [4]. As shown in Table 2, the variables are organized into six physically meaningful categories: Momentum, Temperature, Moisture, Mass, Cloud, and Radiation.

2.3 System Architecture

As shown in Fig. 1, the MoE-Precip system consists of two main components: a multimodal precipitation prediction model and an interactive Visualization and Analytics Interface. The overall design connects predictive modeling with human-centered visual analysis.

The prediction model integrates heterogeneous weather data from multiple sources. These multimodal inputs are first fed into a shared latent space, which aligns information from different data sources into a unified representation. This shared feature space supports joint learning across modalities while preserving complementary weather information.

Based on this representation, the model employs an MoE architecture with specialized experts for data collected from different sources. Each expert is designed to focus on a physically meaningful subset of variables. An adaptive gating network then dynamically weights the contributions of these experts according to the current weather context, and the fused expert outputs are used to produce the final precipitation prediction.

The Visualization and Analytics Interface complements the model by allowing users to explore both input variables and forecast results. The interface supports visual inspection of weather conditions such as cloud cover, moisture, and temperature, as well as comparisons of observed and predicted precipitation and the prediction error. This side-by-side design helps users identify spatial patterns, assess forecast quality. The technical details of the interface are presented in Sect. 3.

3 Visualization Interface System

3.1 System Overview

Climate data, with their high density and multi-dimensionality, are inherently difficult to interpret directly. Our goal is to enable seamless transitions across different data representations, allowing us to better interpret our model's predictions by visualizing how data points are distributed across space and time. To achieve this goal, a Web-Based Application was developed as a thin layer of abstraction to reduce cognitive load when working with a broad, heterogeneous dataset. When observed in real-time, it is important that the subtle nuances in the changing data can be assessed with precision. Data is read directly from

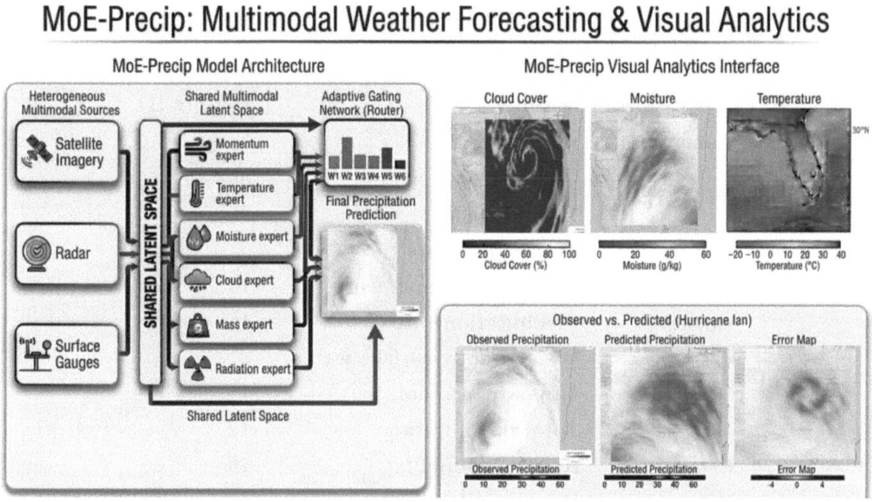

Fig. 1. Overview of the MoE-Precip framework, including the multimodal forecasting architecture and the visual analytics interface, this figure is shown for illustrative purposes.

the file and indexed by date and time. Each point is then mapped to its corresponding 3 km × 3 km point and time index. This approach has been optimized to minimize overhead and update quickly so that the broad geographical range can be easily observed over time. The data set provided consists of 10,000 grid points every hour over 9 days, which is hardly legible to the human eye in its traditional format.

3.2 Technical Framework

Our web application was made using HTML5, CSS3, and standard JavaScript up to date with ES2025 standards. For portability, the application is implemented as a static web application that requires only an HTTP file server for deployment. The rendering is powered by Leaflet.js[1] a well-established open-source library. The map layouts consist of an OpenStreetMap[2] for street view, ArcgIsOnline[3] for Satellite, and OpenTopoMap[4] for topography. JavaScript has become a staple in the industry, leading to most major web browsers supporting it. The SpiderMonkey(FireFox) and V8(Google) engines have trade offs, but have both made JavaScript run more efficiently in the browser with the use of WebAssembly. The emphasis of minimizing dependencies eliminates the problem of out of date frameworks. The universal use of JavaScript leads to frameworks

[1] https://leafletjs.com/.
[2] https://openstreetmap.us/.
[3] https://www.arcgis.com/index.html.
[4] https://opentopomap.org/.

Table 2. Feature group mapping. Specific features are referred to as their corresponding Feature ID in the released source code.

Feature Group	Features	Feature ID
Momentum	Wind speed	5
	U component of wind	8
	V component of wind	9
Temperature	2 m temperature	6
	Dew point temperature	10
Moisture	Precipitation rate	1
	Plant canopy surface water	3
	Moisture availability	11
	Total precipitation	12
	Relative humidity	16
Mass	Pressure:CloudBase	7
	Pressure:CloudTop	15
Cloud	Cloud cover	2
	Low cloud cover	13
	Medium cloud cover	14
Radiation	SBT collected by GOES 11 C3	18
	SBT collected by GOES 11 C4	19
	SBT collected by GOES 12 C3	4
	SBT collected by GOES 12 C4	17

SBT stands for Surface Brightness Temperature, a satellite-derived radiation variable included under the Radiation group; GOES stands for Geostationary Operational Environmental Satellite; C stands for channel.

for streamlined processes such as React. However, recent history has shown that applications dependent on this infrastructure can pose security threats[5]. The application runs on a server hosted by California State University, Monterey Bay.Our code can be found in GitHub

3.3 Visualization Design

The six categories described in Table 2 vary in the units that represent them and in their respective numerical range. The method of representing this was simply to apply a rainbow scale [6,7] which represents lower or weaker numbers as more blue and becomes more red as the value increases. Due to the varying input ranges, when looking at the visualization for anything other than temperature, the subtle variations are less discernible. After presenting and discussing

[5] https://react.dev/blog/2025/12/03/critical-security-vulnerability-in-react-server-components.

this with HCI experts, it was found that specialized color mapping provides an accurate representation of the data.

For instance, in Fig. 2d, we can observe patterns common to temperature, such as a cold front denoted by the large blue area. In contrast, for cloud coverage you can determine where heavy cloud formations form. Using a blue-scale for precipitation and related fields substantially improved interpretability, while fields with an easily identifiable range, such as cloud cover, are well represented as Fig. 2a.

4 Implementation

When loaded, the visualization creates a color range to represent possible values. Each color is determined by its position within the range of values. This is intended to present the information in a more familiar manner, making comprehension more intuitive. Contemporary forecasting systems use the rainbow scale as it easily expresses extreme differences in the data, but for forecasts not representing temperature it is more intuitive to have a scale that represents rain rather than general meteorological intensity. To better understand how variables change over time, an option is available to automatically scrub through the time index.

4.1 Prediction Analysis

The multi-dimensional nature of the data requires human inquiry and reasoning. The application offers a "Prediction View," shown in Fig. 3, that renders predicted values alongside the actual values. The prediction view updates simultaneously with the actual view, showing the values side by side. The legend remains the same for both predicted and actual values to ensure consistent color differences. The predicted view is consistent with the bounds and coloring of the actual map. Hovering over a grid cell on any map simultaneously displays the corresponding values. In addition, we implemented an Error Map View to explicitly visualize the difference between predicted and actual values. Together, these views retain the main characteristics and constraints of the original map design, promoting an honest and effective comparison (Fig. 4).

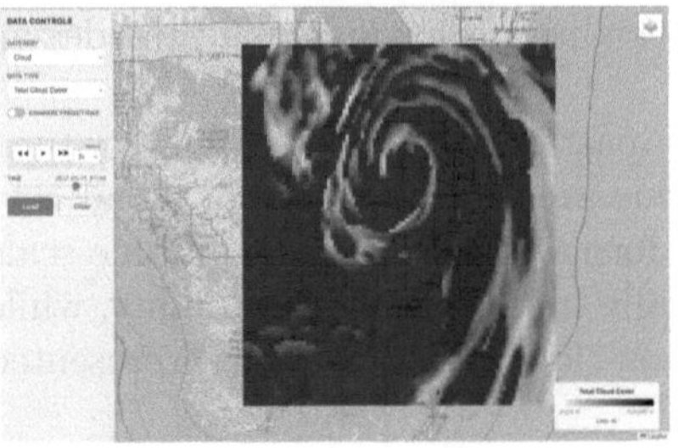

(a) Total Cloud Cover

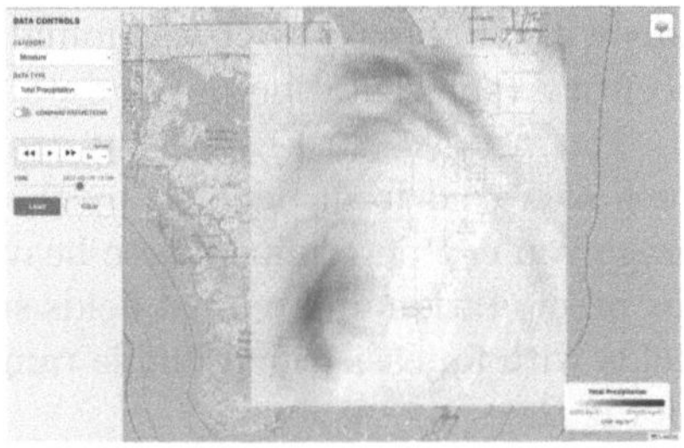

(b) Total Precipitation

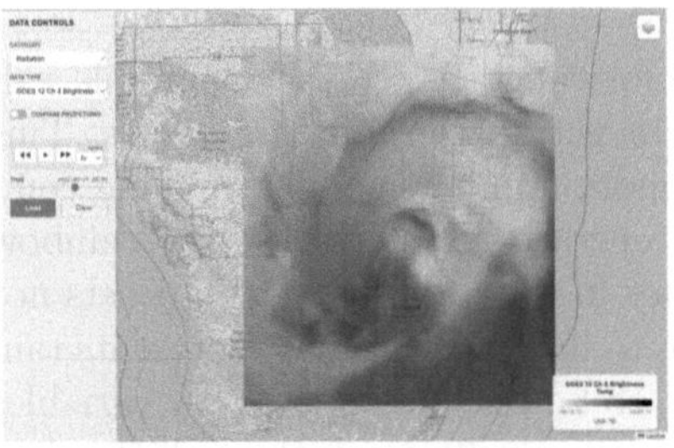

(c) GOES-12 Channel 4 Brightness Temperature

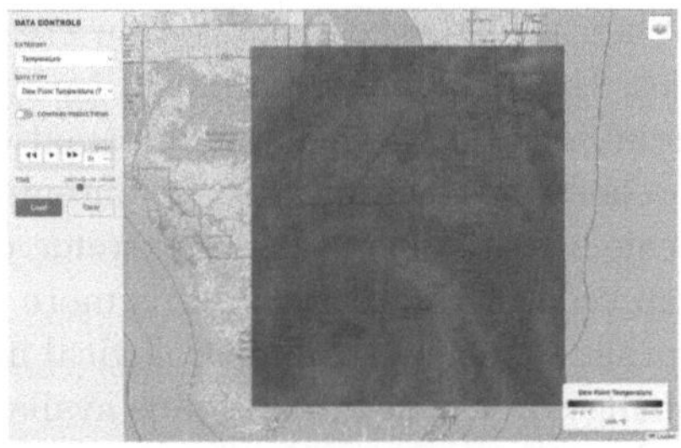

(d) Dew Point Temperature

Fig. 2. Interactive Visualizations of the dataset over South Florida. (a) displays widespread cloud presence. (b) displays total precipitation, illustrating localized rainfall patterns with areas of higher accumulation. (c) depicts GOES-12 Channel 4 brightness temperature, where colder values indicate higher cloud tops associated with convective activity. (d) shows spatial distribution of dew point temperature, highlighting consistently high moisture levels across the region.

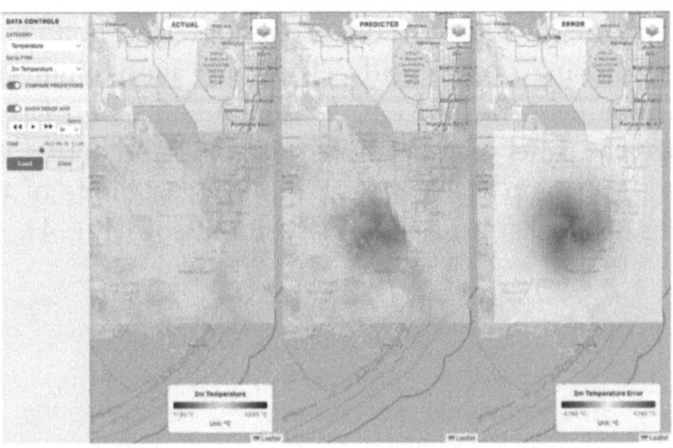

Fig. 3. Interactive visualization of 2 m air temperature over South Florida at 21:00 on September 26, 2022, showing the actual temperature observations (left), model-predicted temperature (center), and the corresponding prediction error map (right). The interface supports side-by-side comparison of observed and predicted spatial temperature patterns.

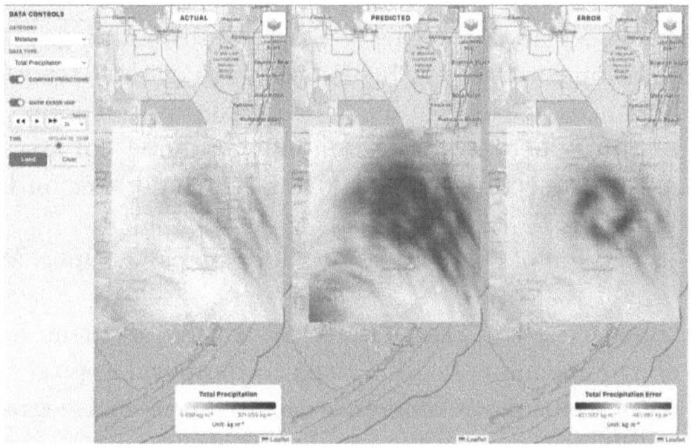

Fig. 4. Interactive visualization of total precipitation over South Florida at 13:00 on September 28, 2022, showing the actual observations (left), model-predicted precipitation (center), and the corresponding prediction error map (right). The interface allows side-by-side comparison of spatial precipitation patterns and highlights areas of overestimation and underestimation.

5 Conclusion and Future Work

This application reduces cognitive load by allowing users to view complex meteorological data across space and time. Because geoscientific prediction involves large volumes of heterogeneous variables that evolve continuously, understanding model behavior requires more than examining isolated values from the dataset. Through the design of coordinated views, consistent color mapping, and side-by-side comparisons of observed, predicted, and error maps, the interface helps users to identify where and when forecasts succeed or fail. This interactive application can also be extended to other spatiotemporal tasks [8,9], including traffic prediction, crop yield prediction, and wildfire detection. In future work, we plan to broaden the scope of the interface to support a wider range of applications and more informed decision-making.

Acknowledgements. We thank California State University (Monterey Bay), School of Computing and Design, for their continuous support.

References

1. Salman, A.G., Kanigoro, B., Heryadi, Y.: Weather forecasting using deep learning techniques. In: 2015 International Conference on Advanced Computer Science and Information Systems (ICACSIS), pp. 281–285. IEEE (2015)
2. Ham, Y.-G., Kim, J.-H., Luo, J.-J.: Deep learning for multi-year ENSO forecasts. Nature **573**(7775), 568–572 (2019)
3. Masoudnia, S., Ebrahimpour, R.: Mixture of experts: a literature survey. Artif. Intell. Rev. **42**, 275–293 (2014)
4. NOAA National Centers for Environmental Information (NCEI). Data access (2024). Accessed 12 June 2025

5. Jiang, C., Wang, W., Pan, N., Ku, W-S.: A multimodal geo dataset for high-resolution precipitation forecasting. In: Proceedings of the 31st ACM International Conference on Advances in Geographic Information Systems, pp. 1–4 (2023)
6. Liu, Y., Heer, J.: Somewhere over the rainbow: an empirical assessment of quantitative colormaps. In: Proceedings of the 2018 CHI Conference on Human Factors in Computing Systems, pp. 1–12 (2018)
7. Brittney, B., et al.: Usage of color scales on radar maps. J. Oper. Meteor **2**, 169–179 (2014)
8. Yeddula, S.D., Jiang, C., Hui, B., Ku, W-S.: Traffic accident hotspot prediction using temporal convolutional networks: a spatio-temporal approach. In: Proceedings of the 31st ACM International Conference on Advances in Geographic Information Systems, pp. 1–4 (2023)
9. Jiang, C., Yeddula, S.D., Ku, W.-S.: A convolutional neural network model for accurate short-term leaf area index prediction. Model. Earth Syst. Environ. **10**(5), 6397–6412 (2024)

Calibrated Recommendations with Dynamic User Preferences

Kun Lin[1(✉)], Masoud Mansoury[2], Farzad Eskandanian[1], Milad Sabouri[1], and Bamshad Mobasher[1]

[1] DePaul University, Chicago, IL 60604, USA
{klin13,feskanda,msabouri}@depaul.edu, mobasher@cs.depaul.edu
[2] Delft University of Technology, Delft, The Netherlands
m.mansoury@tudelft.nl

Abstract. Calibration in recommender system is a beyond-accuracy performance criterion ensuring user's varied preferences to be presented in the recommendations with the corresponding portions. With standard approach, the corresponding portions are based on the preference distribution in user's full history. This approach is with a hidden assumption that user's preference is static. However, user's preference is dynamic, varying across short- and long-term, and also across different contexts. Blindly calibrating a recommendation based on full profile may inherit stale user interests. In this work, we segment user profile representing user's dynamic preference, and explore pre- and post-processing to incorporate dynamic user preference to generate calibrated recommendations. With datasets from three domains and analysis at both whole population and specific user group level, we present the impact of including dynamic preference to calibration under the impact of different types of users and domains.

Keywords: Recommender systems · calibration · preference dynamics

1 Introduction

Recommender systems are expected to provide recommendations that represent a user's preference. Yet, due to the recommender algorithms being designed to optimize towards higher accuracy, the generated recommendations can easily amplify a user's preference [11], or amplify some hidden bias like popularity bias [2], which also results the recommendations not aligning to a user's preference as shown in their previous behavior. This types of bias amplification can lead to long-term negative impacts, like "rabbit hole" [14,21] effect or filter bubbles [13]. To address the issue and ensure the recommendations appropriately representing a user's preference, one beyond-accuracy concept, *Calibration*, was introduced from machine learning to recommender system [18]. Calibration measures the distribution-aware agreement of the preferences between the recommendations and the user profiles. Take a book recommender as the example,

C. Stephanidis et al. (Eds.): HCII 2026, CCIS 3047, pp. 203–214, 2026.
https://doi.org/10.1007/978-3-032-30552-7_20

the generated recommendation is considered calibrated if a user with 70% interest in Fantasy book genre and 30% in History books, receives similar genre ratios in that recommendation. Given that, the metric calibration can evaluate how algorithms change the distribution from input training data to output recommendations.

However, given the context of recommender systems, the a user's preference can be dynamic which may vary across short-term versus long-term, or across different contexts like gym or work space. A user who was into Fantasy books may grow out of that genre over years and develop more interest in History books. In the context of a user's dynamic preference, calibration only considering the full user profile may include stale preference or out-of-context preferences. This kind of "calibrated" recommendations diverge from the a user's current preferences. Most previous work in calibrated recommendations [6,18] mainly refer to the full user profile as the target preference distribution for calibration.

In this work, we explored this type of misalignment based on the short-term and long-term dynamic across multiple domains. To incorporate the preference dynamic into calibration, we explored pre- and post-processing approaches. Conventionally, the recommendations are optimized towards calibration via re-ranking based on the full user profile preference distribution. To explore the calibration based on dynamic preferences with the post-processing approach, we used full-profile user preference distribution as the baseline, and meanwhile, explored varied user preferences based on recency-based segmented user profiles. The goal of this preliminary work is to understand the impacts of different approaches blending preference dynamic to calibration.

2 Calibration

The base formulation of calibration concept has three important parts and researches are active in these directions, the target user preference [6,21], the recommendation distribution [7], and the divergence metric evaluating the distribution differences between them [17]. Our work focus on redefining the target user preference to adapt to the dynamics in recommender systems. One related research also discussed impact of the user preference evolution on calibration [21]. Other than using preference existing in the profile, they calibrated the base recommendations based on the predicted the a user's preference. Our approach is to segment the existing profile for better calibration. Meanwhile, another active calibration research direction is about how to achieve calibration. Post-processing approaches are common but may be with different optimization strategies [3,16,18], like maximum marginal relevance (MMR) [4]. Recently, pre-processing approach is also being actively researched. [9] proposed a fine-tuning approach for calibration.

The calibration formulation in this work is based on target preference distribution ($p(c|u)$) and recommended preference distribution ($q(c|u)$) for a user u over item categories c. We used Kullback-Leibler divergence (KL-divergence) [8] to evaluate the distribution difference between target $p(c|u)$ and recommended

$q(c|u)$ distributions as shown in Eq. 2. For post-processing, we just applied the MMR as the optimization, which is the initial calibration approach used in Steck's work [18]. In the formulation of MMR, parameter λ is used determine the trade-off between accuracy and calibration. We experimented multiple λ values but the results presented in this paper is based on $\lambda = 0.8$ because calibration is the priority focus of this research and we assign higher weight to it.

$$p(c|u) = \frac{\sum_{i \in I_u} p(c|i)}{|I_u|} \qquad q(c|u) = \frac{\sum_{i \in R_u} p(c|i)}{|R_u|} \tag{1}$$

$$MC_{KL}(p||q) = KL(p||\tilde{q}) = \sum_{c \in C} p(c|u) \log \frac{p(c|u)}{\tilde{q}(c|u)}, \tag{2}$$

3 Experimental Setup

3.1 Dynamic Preference Simulation

Our simulation process is shown in Fig. 1, which mainly based on the segmented user profiles which are created via extended time windows from most recent interactions to further history. Based on the domain characteristics, the time window size varies, where more dynamic domains like short-video are with shorter extending time window. We suppose these segments present users' dynamic preferences from short-term to long-term. Given the segments, we explored two approaches blending these dynamic to calibration, either via pre-processing or the post-processing.

For both approaches, we applied Bayesian Personalized Ranking (BPR) [15] as the base recommender model, and split the corresponding dataset randomly into 80% training, 10% validation, and 10% test sets. All the models are tuned towards higher NDCG@10 in validation set. Considering the sparsity differences, the hyperparameter range for tuning was different across datasets. For KuaiRec and GoodReads, we used embedding size between 64 to 128, while for the more sparser dataset Yelp, the embedding size range was between 128 to 1024. The learning rate was consistent ranging from 0.0001 to 0.01. For evaluation, besides of calibration, we included the accuracy with NDCG@10 and the diversity with Intra List Distance (ILD) [22]. The evaluation methodology is different for pre-process and post-process with more details in Sect. 4. So, most of the pre- and post-processing results are not directly comparable expect ILD, which is evaluated only on the recommendation list and fully independent from training and test sets.

Pre-process. For pre-processing calibration, the goal is to focus on the right part of user profile to train the model and generate recommendations showing a user's dynamic preferences. We used the segmented profile as an independent dataset to generate recommendations. It means that the segmented profile was split for modeling and evaluation. The modeling process is as mentioned above. The accuracy evaluation was based on the test set in the given segment, and the calibration is also measured upon the preference distribution from the training and validation set in the given segment.

Post-process. For post-processing calibration, we used a user's full profile to generate base recommendations, and re-ranked the top 50 items in base recommendations using MMR [4] to calibrate the top 10 recommendations to the preferences in different profile segments, including the full profile. The post-processing calibration based on the full profile is the standard calibration proposed in [18] and is regarded as the comparison baseline. The accuracy evaluation was via the comparison of the re-ranked recommendations and the test set of the full dataset, and calibration is with two approaches, based on full profile and based on the segment used for re-ranking.

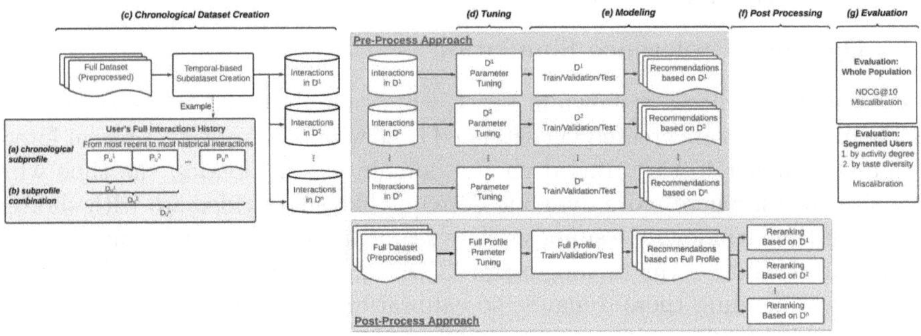

Fig. 1. Experiment workflow for dynamic calibration

3.2 User Groups

User behavior and preference patterns varied in the same domain. These characteristics are shown to be related to calibration. Lin [12] showed the user preference entropy is the most important user characteristics predicting calibration degree. As entropy evaluates how even a distribution is, preference entropy is to evaluate a user's preference intensity across item categories. A more even distribution is with higher entropy and vice versa. Another characteristic is from the work [16] proposing a personalized calibration. They used user activity as the indicator about a user's confidence towards calibration. In this work, we used percentile approach grouping users based on their profile entropy and user activity degree. Our investigation focus on the whole population and also on these specific user groups.

3.3 Datasets

Our work included three datasets from distinct domains, short-videos (KuaiRec), books (GoodReads), and restaurants (Yelp). Users in different domains may be with distinct preference dynamic patterns. For example, users are more likely with quicker preference evolvement for watching short-videos than for reading books. To ensure users are with temporal dynamic user preferences, we preprocessed GoodReads and Yelp datasets ensuring that users are with both short-term and long-term preferences available. Statistic details of the datasets are shown in Table 1

Table 1. Statistics of the Preprocessed Datasets.

Dataset	User	Item	Category (#)	Interaction	Sparsity	Window
KuaiRec	1,411	3,327	content tag (31)	1,799,403	61.6%	1 day
GoodReads	865	1,662	book genre (7)	104,325	92.7%	0.5 year
Yelp	2,389	37,915	category (179)	200,141	99.8%	1 year

KuaiRec dataset [5] is collected on a short-video platform, Kuaishou[1]. We employed the fully-observed version of the published dataset, where users reviewed all the videos and left feedback. We referred to watch_ratio as the user's preference signal, and defined the its mean (0.9) as the user interest threshold. Interactions with no less than 90% watch ratio are positive representing a user's preference and labeled as "1", while others are "0".

GoodReads dataset [19,20] gathered user-book interactions on booking review website[2]. To reduce the sparsity and focus on users with short- and long-term preferences, three steps filtering were applied. First, users with 20 to 50 annual interactions from year 2010 to 2017 were filtered in, and books with no less than 1000 user interactions were included. Then, we filtered users again to include users with more than 4 annual interactions post the item filtering.

Yelp dataset [1] is from business review platform[3] with user leaving ratings and reviews towards visited businesses. Each business is with listed business categories following Yelp's guideline[4]. For businesses, we only focused on the restaurants, which were defined as business including categories "restaurants" or "food". We used the listed subcategories in the guideline as the categories presenting a user's preference distribution for calibration. Business with at least one qualified subcategories were preserved. For users, we filtered in users with at least 3 interactions per year from the year 2017 to 2019.

---

[1] https://www.kuaishou.com/cn.

[2] https://www.goodreads.com/.

[3] http://www.yelp.com/.

[4] https://business.yelp.com/resources/articles/yelp-category-list/?domain=local-business.

4 Results

4.1 Pre-processing Calibration

Pre-process calibration incorporate the preference diversity at the pre-processing stages by segmenting profiles for recommender modeling and recommendation creation. Each profile segment can be taken as an independent dataset that is to be split into training and test sets, to be trained to generate recommendations, and to be evaluated. All the results showing in Fig. 2 and Fig. 3 are evaluations based on the segmented profile based on the time window size.

Whole Population. The most calibrated training window size varied across domains. For KuaiRec, the miscalibration is lowest at Window 5 (5 days), every early comparing to the full profile; for GoodReads, the lowest miscalibration is at Window 7 (3.5 years), in the middle of full profile; and for Yelp, it is Window 5 (5 years), the last time window. These three domains are with different characteristics like preference evolving speed and interaction frequency. As Yelp is the sparsest dataset and users are with fewest interactions comparing to other domains, it needs longer time window to learn the user preference and train the model. That's why the NDCG@10 and calibration both increase with longer profile window. For GoodReads, though the lowest miscalibration window is in the middle of the full profile, the miscalibration difference from that window to longer window size is not much. Meanwhile, the accuracy is with some fluctuation but overall it keeps the increasing trend. For book reading, a user's preference over genres does not change as much as the other two domains. When the preference is stable, the longer profile windows provide more data with similar distribution and the model can be trained more accurate. That's probably the reason for our observation in GoodReads.

For KuaiRec, the NDCG keeps the increasing trend regardless of the miscalibration value. This pattern varied from the pattern in previous work [10], where the optimal calibration were with the highest NDCG@10. The experiment settings from these two work are not exactly the same. In the previous work, we repeated the modeling six times with different random seeds, and the results were based on the average of the six times. Some variations and bias can be averaged out in the previous work. In this current work, we only picked one random seed and run the experiment. The differences mainly exists in the shorter window size. When the window size is small, the dataset is small and recommendation quality is not stable. Another evidence for this is that the diversity (ILD) was very high at Window 1 and then decreased and further increased. With small dataset, the high intra list diversity may be due to the model providing random recommendations because of lack of training data. Further dataset characteristics analysis will be conducted to better understand the difference here.

Another interesting observation is the ILD with GoodReads, which decreases with longer window. We assumed the diversity is to increase with longer training window. The early stage high ILD may be the same reason as above that there were not enough data training model, which generate some random recommendations increasing the diversity. But it further goes down even with higher

NDCG. One possible explanation is that users have more focused reading preference and the lower ILD is the reflection of a user's preference. This is another hypothesis that need further investigation.

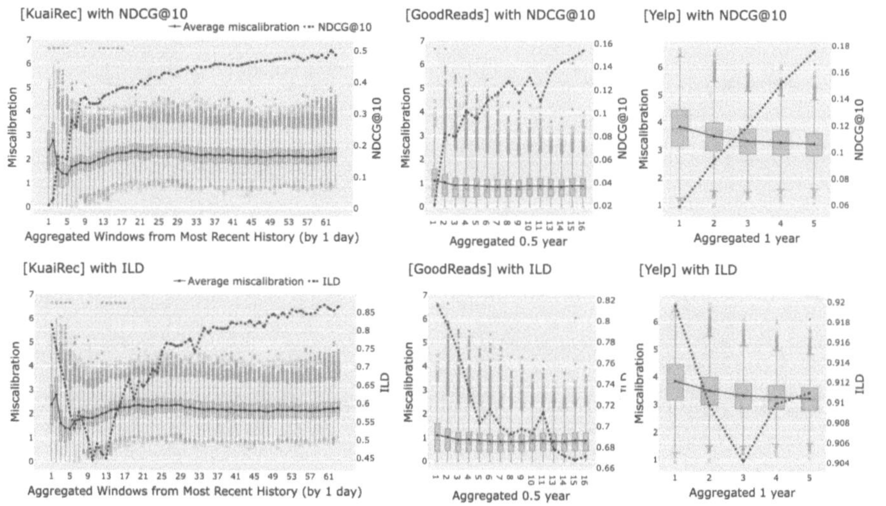

Fig. 2. Preprocess Approach: Miscalibration and other recommender system properties over time

Grouped Population. For users with higher activity degrees, they received different degree miscalibration across domains. In KuaiRec, this group exhibits more miscalibration, while in GoodReads and Yelp, they received with more calibration. KuaiRec is a short-video platform where user preferences evolve faster, and active users may be with more diversified and actively preference evolvement. GoodReads and Yelp are with sparser data and less user preference evolvement speed. For active users on these platforms, more data can significantly benefit the modeling of their preference.

For users with more focused preference (with lower entropy), they mostly received the least miscalibrated recommendations, especially with longer time windows for training. Besides of Yelp whose least miscalibration is based on all aggregated windows, KuaiRec and GoodReads are the ones with optimal miscalibration window smaller than the full profile. For both domains, users with lower entropy are with longer profile windows to generate more calibrated recommendations.

4.2 Post-processing Calibration

For post-processing calibration, our goal is to investigate the differences of calibrated recommendations being reranked based on dynamic preferences and the

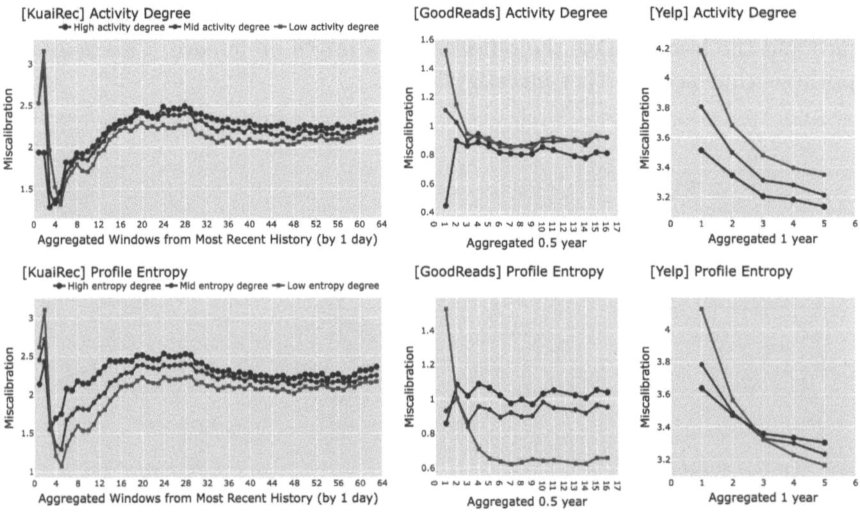

Fig. 3. Preprocess Approach: Miscalibration over time by user segments

full profile preferences. The calibrated recommendation based on full profile is the standard calibration approach [18]. It is represented by the last aggregated windows in the Fig. 4 and Fig. 5, where the biggest aggregated window is the full available profile of a given user. Given we assume the extending aggregated profile windows represent a user's dynamic preferences, other results in Fig. 4 and Fig. 5 are the calibrated recommendations based on dynamic preferences.

To validly compare the two types post-processed calibrated recommendations based on different types of preferences, the base recommendation is the same one that was trained with full dataset, and all the evaluation are based on the full profile. The NDCG@10 is calculated by comparing to the test set of the full profile, and the miscalibration is using full profile's training and validation set as target preference. The ILD is independently based on recommendation list. So, all the results in this section, can be compared. The only changing factor in this set of experiment is what preference was used as target calibration preference to post process the base recommendation.

Whole Population. For the whole population based comparison, results are shown in Fig. 4. As the miscalibration results are based on the full profile preference, the longer the aggregated window is, the target distribution is closer to the full profile preference distribution. That's why we observed that the miscalibration decreases with extending aggregated profile windows. Only exception happens with KuaiRec, where the miscalibration based on window 1 is lower than window 2 and 3. This may be due to some users did not have any interaction records in the window 1. In this case, due to no target preferences available for post-processing, we just kept the original base recommendation that were trained with full profile. These base recommendations align better to the full profile preference than the re-ranked recommendations based on very short-term preferences.

KuaiRec shows very different accuracy (NDCG@10) pattern from GoodReads and Yelp. For GoodReads and Yelp, NDCG increases to a point and then decreases, which happens at Window 14 (7 years) for GoodReads and at Window 4 (4 years) for Yelp. For KuaiRec, NDCG is highest at Window 1 and decreases afterwards, but the NDCG by Window 4 (4 days) outperforms calibrated recommendation based on longer preference window.

The diversity (ILD) increases with extended window size and stays stable at some point, which is around Window 25 (25 days) for KuaiRec, around Window 6 (3 years) for GoodReads, and Window 3 (3 years) for Yelp. For the ILD decrease with window size smaller than Window 5 (5 days) in KuaiRec, it may be also due to not all the base recommendations were calibrated due to a portion of users without any interactions in the first few windows, which is the same reason as the observation in miscalibration of these windows.

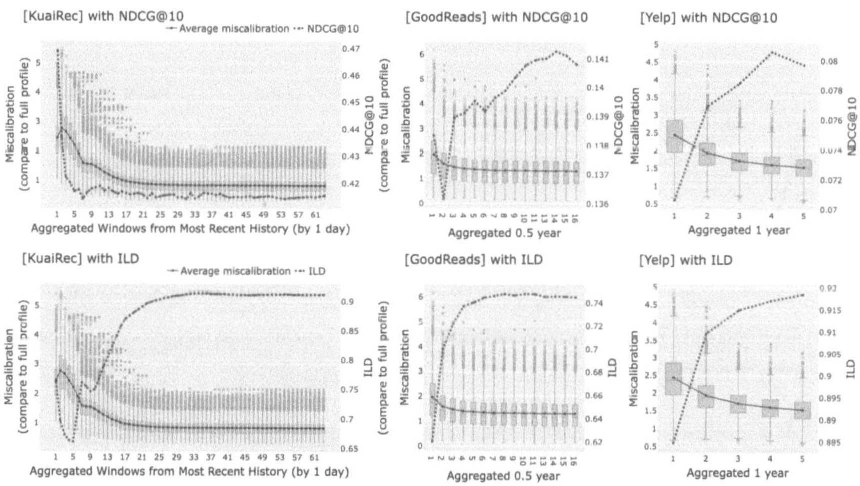

Fig. 4. Postprocess Approach: Miscalibration and other recommender system properties over time

Grouped Population. For the grouped population results shown in Fig. 5, it overall follows the same miscalibration trends as whole population. For KuaiRec, it shows least differences across the groups. Only for the low activity group, it shows slightly higher miscalibration when the preference window size is smaller than Window 10 (10 days), while the miscalibration decreases with the window extending. At Window 17 (17 days), the miscalibration from the low activity group is lower than other groups with same preference window. Similar pattern is observed in GoodReads and Yelp. For GoodReads, it's Window 3 (1.5 years) and for Yelp, the flipping point is Window 4 (4 years). Before the point, miscalibration is higher with this group and lower afterwards. This is due to users with low activity degree needs more time to build enough preference and also this group of users can benefit most from the calibration post-processing. However, comparing to the three domains, KuaiRec is least sensitive to this factor, which may be due to two reasons – 1) users are with much higher interaction frequency, and 2) a user's preference on short videos evolving much faster than others.

One unique pattern with GoodReads on entropy based grouping is that the mid-entropy (green line) and low-entropy group (blue line) are with lowest miscalibration much earlier before the full profile (last aggregated window). For mid-entropy, that point is Window 8 (4 years), and for low-entropy group, it is Window 7 (3.5 years). The grouping is based on a user's full profile characteristics. Before developing to a more evenly distributed preference (lower entropy), these users experienced new preference creation and development stages. When they are with more uneven distribution (higher entropy), the preference may be more helpful for postprocessing to calibrated recommendations. It may indicate the users interest developing process may be another factor to be considered in future work.

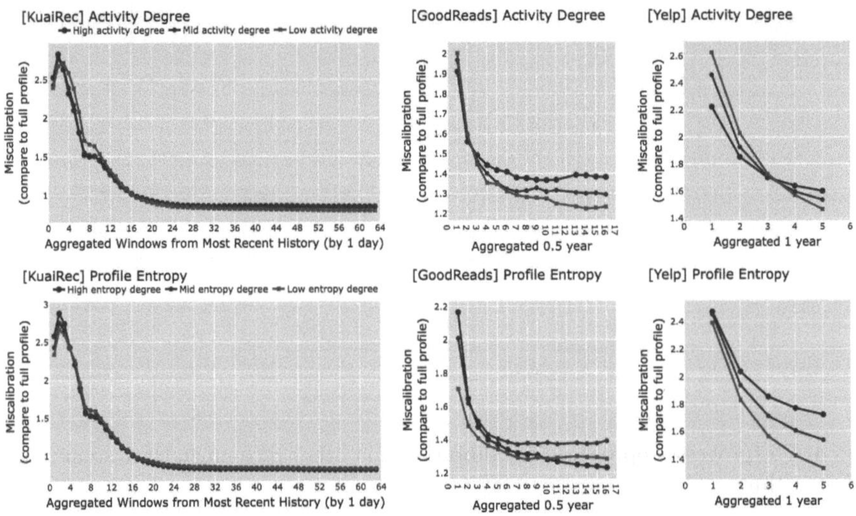

Fig. 5. Postprocess Approach: Miscalibration over time by user segments

5 Discussion

Our experiments explored incorporating dynamic preferences to calibration via pre- and post-processing approaches. For pre-process, the optimal least miscalibration window selection is domain sensitive. Preference stability and dataset sparsity are the two key factors influencing the optimal decision, where shorter windows suit fast-evolving and more dense domains like short video (KuaiRec) while longer windows are for more preference stable and sparse domain like book (GoodReads) and restaurants (Yelp). For post-process, the base model is already trained on full profile so the sparsity is not a critical factor in this approach. However, the preference evolving speed is an important factor where the accuracy of short video domain decrease with extending target preference window for calibration re-ranking, while GoodReads and Yelp are generally with higher accuracy with extending calibration window. The classic trade-off relationship between accuracy and calibration may be due to misrepresentation of the current user preferences, especially for fast preference evolving domains. User groups analysis shows user groups get influenced more via pre-process approach more than post-process for fast preference evolving domain (KuaiRec). For less preference dynamic domains or more sparse domains, the optimal window selection for both pre- or post-calibration approach are related to the two user characteristics. The interesting further research direction is to personalize the optimal window size to ensure that the dynamic preference-based calibration. Here are also some limitations in this paper to be addressed in future, like the reliance on manual user profile segmentation as preference dynamic proxies, and some observations that are required further investigation for a thorough understanding.

References

1. Yelp open dataset. https://business.yelp.com/data/resources/open-dataset/. Accessed 16 May 2023
2. Abdollahpouri, H., Mansoury, M., Burke, R., Mobasher, B.: The connection between popularity bias, calibration, and fairness in recommendation. In: Proceedings of the 14th ACM Conference on Recommender Systems, pp. 726–731 (2020)
3. Abdollahpouri, H., et al.: Calibrated recommendations as a minimum-cost flow problem. In: Proceedings of the Sixteenth ACM International Conference on Web Search and Data Mining, pp. 571–579 (2023)
4. Carbonell, J., Goldstein, J.: The use of MMR, diversity-based reranking for reordering documents and producing summaries. In: Proceedings of the 21st Annual International ACM SIGIR Conference on Research and Development in Information Retrieval, pp. 335–336 (1998)
5. Gao, C., et al.: Kuairec: a fully-observed dataset and insights for evaluating recommender systems. In: Proceedings of the 31st ACM International Conference on Information & Knowledge Management. CIKM 2022, pp. 540–550 (2022). https://doi.org/10.1145/3511808.3557220
6. Kaya, M., Bridge, D.: A comparison of calibrated and intent-aware recommendations. In: Proceedings of the 13th ACM Conference on Recommender Systems, pp. 151–159 (2019)
7. Kleinberg, J., Ryu, E., Tardos, É.: Calibrated recommendations for users with decaying attention. arXiv preprint arXiv:2302.03239 (2023)
8. Kullback, S.: Information theory and statistics. Courier Corporation (1997)

9. Lesota, O., Bajko, A., Walder, M., Wenzel, M., Tommasel, A., Schedl, M.: Fine-tuning for inference-efficient calibrated recommendations. In: Proceedings of the Nineteenth ACM Conference on Recommender Systems, pp. 1187–1192 (2025)
10. Lin, K., Mansoury, M., Eskandanian, F., Sabouri, M., Mobasher, B.: Beyond static calibration: the impact of user preference dynamics on calibrated recommendation. In: Adjunct Proceedings of the 32nd ACM Conference on User Modeling, Adaptation and Personalization, pp. 86–91 (2024)
11. Lin, K., Sonboli, N., Mobasher, B., Burke, R.: Crank up the volume: preference bias amplification in collaborative recommendation. arXiv preprint arXiv:1909.06362 (2019)
12. Lin, K., Sonboli, N., Mobasher, B., Burke, R.: Calibration in collaborative filtering recommender systems: a user-centered analysis. In: Proceedings of the 31st ACM Conference on Hypertext and Social Media, pp. 197–206 (2020)
13. Nguyen, T.T., Hui, P.M., Harper, F.M., Terveen, L., Konstan, J.A.: Exploring the filter bubble: the effect of using recommender systems on content diversity. In: Proceedings of the 23rd International Conference on World Wide Web, pp. 677–686 (2014)
14. O'Callaghan, D., Greene, D., Conway, M., Carthy, J., Cunningham, P.: Down the (white) rabbit hole: the extreme right and online recommender systems. Soc. Sci. Comput. Rev. **33**(4), 459–478 (2015)
15. Rendle, S., Freudenthaler, C., Gantner, Z., Schmidt-Thieme, L.: BPR: Bayesian personalized ranking from implicit feedback. arXiv preprint arXiv:1205.2618 (2012)
16. Seymen, S., Abdollahpouri, H., Malthouse, E.C.: A constrained optimization approach for calibrated recommendations. In: Proceedings of the 15th ACM Conference on Recommender Systems, pp. 607–612 (2021)
17. da Silva, D.C., Durão, F.A.: Introducing a framework and a decision protocol to calibrated recommender systems: Dc da silva, fa durão. Appl. Intell. **53**(19), 22044–22072 (2023)
18. Steck, H.: Calibrated recommendations. In: Proceedings of the 12th ACM Conference on Recommender Systems, pp. 154–162 (2018)
19. Wan, M., McAuley, J.: Item recommendation on monotonic behavior chains. In: Proceedings of the 12th ACM Conference on Recommender Systems, pp. 86–94 (2018)
20. Wan, M., Misra, R., Nakashole, N., McAuley, J.: Fine-grained spoiler detection from large-scale review corpora. arXiv preprint arXiv:1905.13416 (2019)
21. Zhao, X., Zhu, Z., Caverlee, J.: Rabbit holes and taste distortion: distribution-aware recommendation with evolving interests. In: Proceedings of the Web Conference 2021, pp. 888–899 (2021)
22. Ziegler, C.N., McNee, S.M., Konstan, J.A., Lausen, G.: Improving recommendation lists through topic diversification. In: Proceedings of the 14th International Conference on World Wide Web, pp. 22–32 (2005)

Evaluation of the Effect of Color Characteristics in Spatial Images on Moving Experiences

Shukuka Ninomiya(✉), Erika Furuguti, Narumon Jadram, and Midori Sugaya

College of Engineering, Shibaura Institute of Technology, 3-7-5, Toyosu, Koto-ku, Tokyo 135-8548, Japan
al20113@shibaura-it.ac.jp

Abstract. In spatial design, it is important not only to satisfy the functional requirements appropriate for users' purposes but also to evoke moving experiences. This is because the elicitation of moving experiences has been reported to have positive effects on users' psychological states, such as reducing stress and improving subjective well-being. Among the various elements that constitute space, color plays a particularly important role. Color is known to be processed rapidly and intuitively among visual information and is strongly associated with emotional responses. Therefore, clarifying the relationship between color characteristics and emotional experiences can provide fundamental knowledge for intentionally designing moving experiences. In this study, we investigated the influence of color characteristics in spatial images on moving experiences. Specifically, multiple spatial images with different color characteristics were presented to participants, and the degree to which moving experiences were evoked was measured through subjective questionnaire evaluations. The results revealed a negative correlation between the colorfulness of spatial images and moving experience scores. These findings suggest that when the variation of colors in a space becomes excessive, visual load may increase and the elicitation of moving experiences may be suppressed.

Keywords: First Keyword · Second Keyword · Third Keyword

1 Introduction

In spatial design, designers are required to create spaces that satisfy the functional requirements appropriate for the users' purposes. Among various objectives of spatial design, it is particularly important to design spaces that evoke moving experiences [1]. This is because moving experiences refer to strong emotional experiences in which emotions such as joy, surprise, and awe are intertwined [2], and it has been reported that evoking such experiences can contribute to reducing users' stress and enhancing their sense of happiness [3].

On the other hand, spatial design consists of various elements, including color, materials, and form. Among these elements that compose a space, color has been widely studied because it is processed quickly and intuitively as visual information and plays

C. Stephanidis et al. (Eds.): HCII 2026, CCIS 3047, pp. 215–225, 2026.
https://doi.org/10.1007/978-3-032-30552-7_21

an important role in evoking specific emotions [4, 5]. For example, red and orange are known to evoke emotions such as excitement, whereas blue and green evoke feelings of calmness and tranquility [4].

Yildirim et al. investigated the effects of three types of living room color schemes—warm colors, cool colors, and achromatic colors—on mood and preference [5]. As an evaluation method for mood and preference, they used a questionnaire based on the Semantic Differential (SD) method [6]. The SD method measures individuals' impressions of a target using pairs of opposing adjectives. The results showed that warm colors tended to elicit stronger responses for impressions such as "high arousal," "exciting," and "stimulating," whereas cool colors tended to evoke impressions such as "relaxing," "spacious," and "calm." In addition, achromatic colors were shown to evoke negative emotions. As described above, many studies have evaluated the emotions and impressions evoked by the color characteristics of space.

However, the influence of color characteristics in spatial design on moving experiences has not been sufficiently clarified. Therefore, the relationship between color characteristics and emotional experiences remains unclear. As a result, it is currently difficult for designers to intentionally design spaces that evoke moving experiences.

Many studies have proposed methods for quantifying the color characteristics of images [7, 8]. Hasler et al. proposed three methods (M1, M2, and M3) for quantifying the colorfulness of natural images [7]. In their study, the colorfulness of images was objectively evaluated using statistical measures of each color component in the CIELAB color space. In addition, RMS contrast, which is an index that evaluates the overall visual clarity of an image, has been widely used as a method for assessing contrast, one of the color characteristics of images [8].

Thus, many studies, including that of Hasler et al., have quantified the color characteristics of images. However, to the best of our knowledge, the influence of these color characteristics on the moving experiences evoked by spatial images has not been sufficiently discussed.

2 Purpose/Proposal

The purpose of this study is to clarify the influence of color characteristics in spatial design on moving experiences. To achieve this purpose, this study designs and conducts an experiment to evaluate moving experiences evoked by spatial images. Based on the experimental results, the relationship between the color characteristics of spatial images and moving experiences is statistically analyzed.

Specifically, the color characteristics of spatial images are first quantified as objective numerical features. Next, an experiment is designed using these quantified spatial images. In the experiment, spatial images are presented to participants, and the degree of moving experience evoked by each image is evaluated. The evaluation results are collected as moving experience scores. A statistical significance test is then conducted between the moving experience scores and the color characteristics of the spatial images in order to verify the hypothesis.

To evaluate the color characteristics of spatial images, multiple image features are used. The first feature is the colorfulness index proposed by Hasler et al. The second feature is RMS contrast. These features are described in Sects. 2.1 and 2.2, respectively. In addition, moving experiences evoked by spatial images are evaluated using a seven-point subjective rating scale (1–7), where values closer to 7 indicate stronger moving experiences. The obtained scores are defined as moving experience scores, and their relationships with colorfulness and RMS contrast are analyzed. The details of the method are described in the following sections.

2.1 Colorfulness Index

In spatial design, color characteristics are one of the elements that influence users' emotions [4]. Among these characteristics, the diversity and vividness of colors have been shown to affect emotional evaluations [7]. Since moving experiences involve strong emotional arousal, it is possible that the diversity of colors, namely colorfulness, is related to moving experiences. Therefore, in this study, a colorfulness index was adopted as one of the color characteristics of spatial images.

Hasler and Süsstrunk proposed a method for measuring the colorfulness of natural images [7]. In their study, an experiment was conducted in which 84 images were evaluated in terms of colorfulness using a seven-point scale. The colorfulness of each image was rated using seven categories: not colorful, slightly colorful, moderately colorful, averagely colorful, quite colorful, very colorful, and extremely colorful. Based on the experimental results, colorfulness indices that showed a high correlation with subjective evaluations were derived.

To measure the colorfulness of images, Hasler and Süsstrunk used the CIELAB color space and examined the indices shown in Table 1. The CIELAB color space was proposed by the International Commission on Illumination (CIE) and is a perceptually uniform color space designed based on human visual perception [8]. In this color space, a color is represented by three components: L* representing lightness, a* representing the red–green axis, and b* representing the blue–yellow axis [8]. Using the a* and b* components in the CIELAB color space, Hasler and Süsstrunk examined several combinations of statistical measures, including the standard deviation and mean values of color differences, as well as their linear combinations and weighted sums (Table 1). As a result, the following two indices showed particularly high correlations with subjective evaluations:

1. $M(1) = \sigma_{ab} + 0.37 \times \mu_{ab}$ (Correlation: 93.7%)
2. $M(2) = \sigma_{ab} + 0.94 \times \mu_{C}$ (Correlation: 94.0%)

   In addition, Hasler and Süsstrunk proposed another index, M(3), based on an opponent color space, which achieved a correlation of 95.3% with subjective colorfulness evaluations [7]. Unlike M(1) and M(2), M(3) does not require conversion to the CIELAB color space and can be calculated directly from RGB data, making it suitable for real-time processing. The calculation method of M(3) is shown below:
3. $M(3) = \sigma_{rgyb} + 0.3 \times \mu_{rgyb}$

   - $\sigma_{rgyb} = \sqrt{(\sigma_{rg}^2 + \sigma_{yb}^2)}$
   - $\mu_{rgyb} = \sqrt{(\mu_{rg}^2 + \mu_{yb}^2)}$
   - σ_{rg}, σ_{yb}:standard deviations of rg and yb
   - μ_{rg}, μ_{yb}:mean values of rg and yb

- rg = R - G
- yb = (R + G)/2 - B

Table 1. Indices examined in the previous study.

Index	Symbol	Definition
Standard deviation of red–green axis	σ_a	Standard deviation of the a* axis (red–green) in CIELAB
Standard deviation of blue–yellow axis	σ_b	Standard deviation of the b* axis (blue–yellow) in CIELAB
Spread of color distribution	σ_{ab}	$\sqrt{\sigma_a^2 + \sigma_b^2}$
Distance of color centroid	μ_{ab}	Distance between the centroid of the color distribution and neutral gray
Standard deviation of chroma	σ_C	Standard deviation of chroma (color intensity)
Mean chroma	μ_C	Mean value of chroma

Table 2 summarizes the formulas and characteristics of M(1), M(2), and M(3).

Table 2. Formulas and characteristics of colorfulness indices.

Method	Formula	Correlation	Characteristics
M (1)	$\sigma_{ab} + 0.37 \times \mu_{ab}$	93.7%	Intuitive but slightly lower correlation
M (2)	$\sigma_{ab} + 0.94 \times \mu_C$	94.0%	Considers two-dimensional colorfulness and is computationally simple
M (3)	$\sigma_{rgyb} + 0.3 \times \mu_{rgyb}$	95.3%	Highest correlation and low computational cost

In this study, the colorfulness of all spatial images presented as stimuli was calculated using the formulas of M(1), M(2), and M(3). Figure 1 shows an example of a spatial image with a high colorfulness value (M3), while Fig. 2 shows an example of a spatial image with a low colorfulness value (M3).

2.2 Contrast Index

Among the color characteristics of images, contrast was selected as another feature that may be related to moving experiences. Contrast is a visual characteristic that represents the difference between the bright and dark regions of an image and is known as one of the statistical properties of visual stimuli [9]. Differences in contrast have been reported to be associated with users' emotional responses [10]. Since image contrast influences

Fig. 1. Example of a spatial image with a high colorfulness value (M3).

Fig. 2. Example of a spatial image with a low colorfulness value (M3).

emotional responses, this study adopted contrast as one of the color characteristics of spatial images.

Among various contrast indices, Root Mean Square (RMS) contrast is a widely used measure for quantifying image contrast because it considers the overall luminance variation of an image and can be applied to complex visual stimuli [9]. Therefore, in this study, RMS contrast was used to quantify the magnitude of luminance variation in spatial images [9]. The RMS contrast is calculated as shown in Eq. (1). A higher value indicates a larger variation in brightness and thus a higher contrast.

$$C_{RMS} = \sqrt{\frac{1}{N}\sum_{i=1}^{N}\left(I_i - \overline{I}\right)^2} \tag{1}$$

$$0 \leq C_{RMS} \leq 127.5$$

I_i represents the luminance value of pixel i,
$\overline{I}$ represents the mean luminance value of the image, and
N represents the total number of pixels in the image.

The RMS contrast of each spatial image was calculated. Figure 3 shows an example of a spatial image with a high RMS contrast value, while Fig. 4 shows an example of a spatial image with a low RMS contrast value.

Fig. 3. Example of a spatial image with a high RMS contrast value.

Fig. 4. Example of a spatial image with a low RMS contrast value.

3 Evaluation Experiment of Moving Experiences

This study aims to clarify the relationship between the color characteristics of spatial images and moving experiences. To achieve this objective, an evaluation experiment was conducted. In the experiment, spatial images with different color characteristics, described in Sects. 2.1 and 2.2, were presented to participants, and subjective evaluations were obtained through a questionnaire to determine whether moving experiences were evoked. The spatial images consisted of five sets of 20 images each, for a total of 100 images. In each experimental session, one set of 20 spatial images was used. The experiment was conducted with 10 participants for each set.

In the experiment, spatial images were presented on a 32-in. monitor, and the monitor was adjusted so that the participants' line of sight was perpendicular to the screen. The distance between the participant and the monitor was approximately 30 cm. The experiment was conducted in a private room. The room temperature was maintained at 22 °C, and partitions were placed on three sides of the desk on which the monitor was installed. An overview of the experimental setup is shown in Fig. 5.

3.1 Experimental Procedure

The experimental procedure is described as follows.

1. Participants sat in front of the display and rested with their eyes open for 40 s (80 s only for the first trial).
2. A spatial image was presented for 40 s, and participants were asked to observe it.
3. Participants answered a questionnaire.

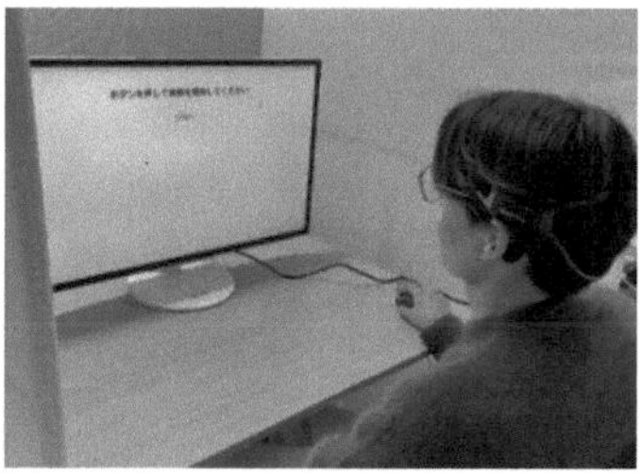

Fig. 5. Experimental scene.

4. Steps (1)–(3) were repeated for 20 spatial images.

To prevent order effects, the spatial images were presented in a random order.

In the questionnaire, participants evaluated whether the spatial image evoked moving experiences using a seven-point scale (1–7). The results of the questionnaire were averaged across all participants to obtain the moving experience score for each spatial image. A score closer to 7 indicates that the image strongly evoked moving experiences, whereas a score closer to 1 indicates that it did not evoke moving experiences.

4 Results

Statistical analyses were conducted to examine the relationship between the moving experience scores obtained in the experiment and the color characteristics of the images, including colorfulness (M1, M2, M3) and RMS contrast. Specifically, significance tests and correlation analyses were performed.

4.1 Results of the Significance Test

For the colorfulness indices of the spatial images (M1–M3) and the RMS contrast index, the moving experience scores obtained from the subjective questionnaire were used to classify the images into three categories: non-moving (scores ≤ 3), moving (scores ≥ 5), and neutral (score $= 4$). Based on this classification, significance tests were conducted to examine differences between the moving and non-moving spatial image groups. When the data satisfied the assumption of normality, an independent-samples t-test was applied. When normality was not satisfied, the Mann–Whitney U test was used.

Among the four indices examined, only the M3 colorfulness index showed a significant difference between the moving and non-moving groups ($t(29) = -2.285$, $p = 0.045$), as shown in (Fig. 6). The detailed results of the significance tests for all indices are summarized in Table 3.

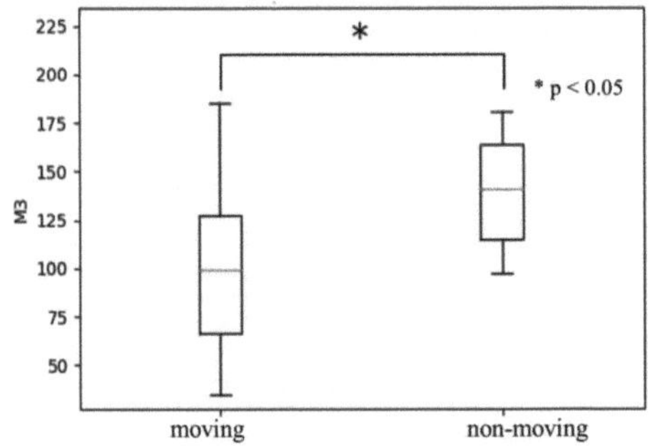

Fig. 6. Results of the significance test of M3 between "moving" and "non-moving" groups.

Table 3. Results of the significance tests between "the moving" and "non-moving" groups.

Index	Test Method	Test Statistic	df	p-value	Significance
M1	Mann-Whitney U test	99	NAN	1	Not significant
M2	Mann-Whitney U test	105	NAN	0.811	Not significant
M3	t-test	−2.285	29	0.045	Significant
RMS Contrast	t-test	−0.695	29	0.535	Not significant

4.2 Results of the Correlation Analysis

Correlation analysis was conducted to examine the relationship between each index and the moving experience score. When normality was satisfied, the Pearson correlation coefficient was used, and when normality was not satisfied, the Spearman correlation coefficient was applied.

Among the four indices—colorfulness (M1–M3) and contrast—only M3 showed a negative correlation with the moving experience score ($r = -0.30$, $p = 0.002$), as shown in Fig. 7. As illustrated in Fig. 7, spatial images with higher colorfulness tend to show lower moving experience scores.

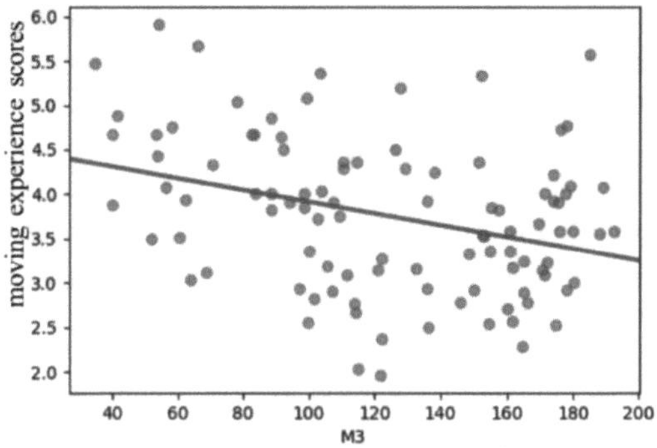

Fig. 7. Scatter plot with regression line between the M3 index and moving experience scores.

No significant correlation was found between RMS contrast and the moving experience score. This result indicates that there is no significant relationship between contrast and moving experiences in spatial images. The detailed results of the correlation analyses are summarized in Table 4.

Table 4. Results of the correlation analysis between each index and the moving experience score.

Index	Correlation Method	Correlation Coefficient (r)	p-value	Result
M1	Spearman correlation	0.0016	0.988	No correlation
M2	Spearman correlation	−0.0267	0.792	No correlation
M3	Spearman correlation	−0.3041	0.002	Significant correlation
RMS Contrast	Pearson correlation	0.0601	0.552	No correlation

From these results, it is suggested that spatial images with higher colorfulness may be less likely to evoke moving experiences.

5 Discussion

This study examined the effects of colorfulness and contrast in spatial images on moving experiences using subjective evaluations. The results of the statistical analyses showed that the colorfulness index M3 exhibited a significant difference between the moving and non-moving groups ($p = 0.045$). Furthermore, a significant negative correlation was found between the M3 colorfulness index and the moving experience score ($r = -0.30$, $p = 0.002$). These results indicate that images with higher colorfulness tend to produce lower moving experience scores, suggesting that moving experiences may become weaker as colorfulness increases. One possible explanation is that excessive variation in colors may increase visual load or disperse visual attention, thereby suppressing moving experiences [11].

In contrast, RMS contrast did not show a significant relationship with moving experiences. RMS contrast is a metric based on the standard deviation of luminance values and quantifies the variability of brightness within an image. However, it primarily captures local luminance variations within the image [9]. Therefore, it may not sufficiently reflect the overall impression of a space, such as spatial coherence or atmosphere. Previous studies have reported that impressions and aesthetic evaluations of images are influenced not only by low-level visual features but also by higher-level features, such as spatial structure and semantic elements [12].

This study has several limitations. First, the colorfulness indices (M1–M3) were originally proposed and validated for natural images. Therefore, they may not be fully suitable for spatial images that include artificial compositions or designed environments [7]. The inconsistency observed in some of the results may partly be due to the appropriateness of the selected indices. Second, moving experiences were measured using a seven-point subjective rating scale and binary classification, which may not fully capture the different types of moving experiences, such as surprise, joy, or relaxation. Future studies should adopt more detailed emotion classifications to examine the components of moving experiences from multiple perspectives.

6 Conclusion and Future Work

This study aimed to clarify the influence of color characteristics in spatial images on moving experiences. An experimental evaluation was conducted using spatial images with different color characteristics, and the relationship between these characteristics and moving experiences was analyzed through subjective evaluations by participants. The results revealed a negative correlation between the colorfulness index and moving experience scores. These findings suggest that excessive variation in colors within a spatial image may increase visual load and make it more difficult to evoke moving experiences.

For future work, it is necessary to reconsider appropriate indices for measuring colorfulness and contrast in spatial images. In addition, further research should explore other color-related features beyond colorfulness and contrast and investigate their relationships with moving experiences.

Acknowledgments. This study was made possible through the generous support of NOMURA Co., Ltd., who provided the design space images used in the experiment. We would also like to express our sincere gratitude to Mr. Tadanori Eto, Mr. Kazuhiro Suzuki, Dr. Masataka Myonaka, Mr. Tomohito Oyanagi, and the rest of the team for their invaluable advice and assistance throughout the course of this research.

References

1. Yanai, H., Yasumoto, Y., Matsuoka, Y.: Analyzing influence of picture size on deep emotion. In: Proceedings of the 65th Annual Conference of the Japanese Society for the Science of Design, pp. 196–197 (2018)

2. Yasuda, S., et al.: A review of psychological research on Kando as an inclusive concept of moving experiences. Front. Psychol. **13**, 974220 (2022)
3. Tokaji, A.: Mechanisms for evoking emotional responses of "Kandoh (the state of being emotionally moved)". Cogn. Stud. **8**(4), 360–368 (2001)
4. Enwin, A.D., Ikiriko, T.D., Jonathan-Ihua, G.O.: The role of colours in interior design of liveable spaces. Eurasian J. Theor. Appl. Sci. **1**(4), 242–262 (2023)
5. Yildirim, K., Hidayetoglu, M.L., Capanoglu, A.: Effects of interior colors on mood and preference: comparisons of two living rooms. Percept. Mot. Skills. **112**(2), 509–524 (2011)
6. Osgood, C.E., Suci, G.H., Tannenbaum, P.H.: The Measurement of Meaning. University of Illinois Press, Chicago (1957)
7. Hasler, D., Suesstrunk, S.E.: Measuring colorfulness in natural images. In: Human Vision and Electronic Imaging VIII, pp. 87–95. SPIE (2003)
8. CIE: Colorimetry, 3rd Edition, CIE Publication 15:2004
9. Peli, E.: Contrast in complex images. J. Opt. Soc. Am. A. **7**(10), 2032–2040 (1990)
10. Lu, Z., et al.: Distinct effects of contrast and color on subjective rating of fearfulness. Front. Psychol. **6**, 1521 (2015)
11. Madan, C.R., et al.: Visual complexity and affect: ratings reflect more than meets the eye. Front. Psychol. **8**, 2368 (2018)
12. Oliva, A., Torralba, A.: Modeling the shape of the scene: a holistic representation of the spatial envelope. Int. J. Comput. Vis. **42**(3), 145–175 (2001)

UI Screen Summarization from Smartphone Screenshots Using Visual and Structural Information

Ryotaro Nomoto[1] and Yoshihisa Shinozawa[2(✉)]

[1] Graduate School of Science and Technology, Keio University, Yokohama, Japan
[2] Faculty of Science and Technology, Keio University, Yokohama, Japan
shino@ae.keio.ac.jp

Abstract. Automated UI summarization is crucial for enhancing accessibility and facilitating design search. However, existing models such as Screen2Words and Versatile UI Transformer (VUT) often underutilize critical semantic text, component dimensions, and application-level context. We propose an enhanced framework that augments the VUT baseline with three human-centered features: (1) word-level semantic representations to preserve granular textual information, (2) component size features to reflect visual salience, and (3) application descriptions for contextual grounding. These features are jointly processed through a Transformer-based architecture to achieve a holistic understanding of UI screens. Evaluations on the Screen2words dataset demonstrate that our approach consistently outperforms the original VUT model. Our results underscore the importance of integrating semantic, structural, and contextual information, bridging the gap between complex visual layouts and human-centric natural language descriptions.

Keywords: UI summarization · Multimodal Learning · Transformer

1 Introduction

In modern society, mobile devices such as smartphones and tablets have become an indispensable infrastructure in our daily lives. Users enjoy a wide range of services, including finance, transportation, entertainment, and communication, through a diverse array of applications (apps). The foundation of these applications is the User Interface (UI) screen, which serves as the point of contact with the user. On a UI screen, executable actions and presented information are visually organized, allowing users to instantaneously interpret the intent and perform operations.

In recent years, "UI Understanding," the field of research aimed at enabling computers to comprehend these UI screens, has been actively pursued. Among the various tasks in this field, "UI Summarization"—which involves describing the entire content of a screen using short natural language—has attracted significant attention as a multimodal challenge at the intersection of computer vision, natural language processing, and structural analysis.

C. Stephanidis et al. (Eds.): HCII 2026, CCIS 3047, pp. 226–236, 2026.
https://doi.org/10.1007/978-3-032-30552-7_22

The necessity for automated UI summarization technology is strongly recognized from two primary perspectives. The first is the improvement of accessibility. When individuals with visual impairments operate mobile devices, they generally rely on screen readers. Prominent examples include "VoiceOver" [1] for iOS and "TalkBack" [2] for Android. However, these systems depend on sequential processing—reading aloud the text at the specific location touched by the user—which creates a limitation in immediately grasping the overall layout or the primary purpose of the screen (e.g., "This is a money transfer amount entry screen"). Previous research [3] has reported this limitation, suggesting that providing a high-level summary of the entire UI screen would drastically improve convenience for visually impaired users.

Second, automated summarization enables more efficient language-based UI search and management. When exploring new design concepts, UI designers frequently refer to design-sharing platforms such as UpLabs [4] and Dribbble [5]. However, current search mechanisms on these platforms are largely limited to simple keyword-based systems. By automatically assigning detailed summaries to each screen, it becomes possible to perform semantic searches, which is expected to significantly enhance the productivity of design workflows.

With the advancement of image processing and natural language processing technologies based on neural networks, UI summarization has evolved as an application of automated image captioning. The early Neural Image Caption (NIC) [6] model adopted an Encoder-Decoder architecture using a CNN as the encoder and an RNN as the decoder; however, it faced constraints due to the difficulty of parallel processing in RNNs. Subsequently, the Transformer [7], introduced in 2017, surpassed these previous methods in both computational efficiency and accuracy, becoming the current mainstream architecture.

In the field of UI understanding, research progressed from Widget Captioning [8], which generates descriptions for individual UI components, to the proposal of Screen2Words [9] for entire screen summarization. More recently, the Versatile UI Transformer (VUT) [10] was introduced, capable of multi-task learning across various UI-related tasks, and has demonstrated improved summarization accuracy. Nevertheless, these existing methods still struggle to fully integrate essential information such as the geometric "size information" of UI components, UI-specific "detailed textual features," or the "domain knowledge" of the overall application.

In this study, we use the existing VUT model as a baseline and propose improvements to capture the structural and contextual features of UI screens more precisely. Specifically, we focus on the following three key aspects:

1. **Detailed Word-level Feature Extraction**: We extract features that preserve lexical semantics from the textual information contained within the view hierarchy.
2. **Introduction of Component Size Features**: We integrate geometric features regarding the "size" of each element to reflect visual importance within the model.
3. **Advanced Integration of App Descriptions**: We utilize pre-trained models to vectorize application meta-information, leveraging it as a global context.

In this paper, through evaluation experiments using the Screen2Words dataset, we demonstrate that our proposed method achieves superior accuracy over the baseline VUT and verify its effectiveness from quantitative perspectives.

2 Related Work

2.1 Widget Captioning

Widget Captioning [8], which generates natural language descriptions for individual elements (widgets) within a UI screen, is a fundamental technology in UI understanding. This approach employs an Encoder-Decoder architecture that integrates visual information derived from screenshots with structural information from the view hierarchy. The model architecture primarily consists of three components: an Image Encoder, a Structural Encoder, and a Transformer Decoder.

1. Structural Feature Extraction (Structural Encoder):
   For all elements on the UI screen, the model retrieves several attributes: type (indicating the role of the component), click (indicating clickability), bounds (representing spatial coordinates), and dom (denoting the position within the hierarchical structure). These attributes are transformed into vectors via embedding layers and fed into the Structural Encoder. This encoder utilizes the Transformer [8] architecture to compute self-attention between all components, enabling the extraction of features that account for the spatial and functional relationships among elements within the screen.
2. Visual Feature Extraction (Image Encoder):
   The model applies bounding box information from the view hierarchy to the screenshot to crop individual component regions. These cropped images are resized to a predefined scale and processed by a CNN-based (Convolutional Neural Network) Image Encoder, which extracts the visual features unique to each component.
3. Feature Integration and Generation (Decoder):
   For each component, the structural features from the Structural Encoder and the visual features from the Image Encoder are concatenated to form an integrated feature representation. Finally, this sequence of feature sets, corresponding to the number of components, is fed into a Transformer Decoder to autoregressively generate a natural language description that explains the function of the target widget.

2.2 Screen2Words

This research [9] proposes a task designed to comprehensively understand multimodal UI data and describe its essence in natural language.

1. Task and Dataset Overview:
   The goal of this task is to generate a concise natural language description (approximately 5–10 words) from a screenshot of an Android application. The dataset comprises 22,417 Android UI screens and approximately 100,000 human-annotated summaries. While the task shares similarities with image captioning and text summarization, its unique characteristic lies in the requirement to understand the specific multimodal structural data inherent to UIs.
2. Feature Extraction and Preprocessing:
   The Screen2Words model utilizes five variables derived from the view hierarchy (type, clickability, dom, pos, and screen text) along with the application description (App description) as input features.

3. Model Architecture:
   An encoder-decoder model combining Transformer and ResNet [11] architectures is employed for automated screen summarization.

   - View Hierarchy Feature Extraction: The aforementioned five variables are concatenated for each component and projected back to the original dimensionality through a fully connected (FC) layer. A sequence of (number of components +1) vectors—consisting of these component-wise vectors plus the application description vector prepended at the beginning—is fed into a Transformer Encoder to obtain structural features.
   - Visual Feature Extraction: For grayscale screenshots, individual components are cropped based on bounding box information from the view hierarchy and resized to 64x64 pixels. These are processed through a ResNet to extract component-specific visual features. To maintain consistency, features are also extracted from the entire screenshot, resulting in a total of (number of components +1) visual feature vectors.
   - Feature Integration and Summarization Generation: The extracted view hierarchy features and visual features are concatenated for each component, with their dimensionality adjusted via an FC layer. These integrated features are then fed into the Multi-Head Attention layer of the Transformer Decoder (serving as Key and Value) to autoregressively generate the final summary.

2.3 VUT (Versatile UI Transformer)

Li et al. [10] proposed the Versatile UI Transformer (VUT), which accepts multimodal inputs—including images, structures, and language—to perform five different UI-related tasks within a single unified model. It has been reported that by jointly training on multiple tasks, VUT achieves accuracy that either surpasses or matches baseline models trained on individual tasks. To perform screen summarization, VUT consists of the following four primary network modules.

1. Image Embedder:
   The Image Embedder takes the screenshot as input and outputs visual features. The architecture employs a ResNet-50 as its backbone. The final fully connected (FC) layer and the preceding average pooling layer are removed, and the resulting output is compressed via an FC layer before being fed into the Image-Structure Transformer.
2. Structure Embedder:
   The Structure Embedder processes information from the view hierarchy to output structural features. It utilizes five types of information: type, clickable, text, screen pos, and dom pos. Among these, type, clickable, and text are processed in the same manner as in Screen2Words. In contrast, screen pos and dom pos are transformed into vectors using Learnable Fourier Features [12].
3. Image-Structure Transformer:
   This module consists of a stack of six Transformer Encoder layers, where image features and view hierarchy features are input in parallel. For positional encoding, the structural features use the aforementioned pos information, while the image features utilize a 2D extended fixed positional encoding similar to that used in Detection

Transformer [13]. These encodings are added at the beginning of each layer within the encoder.

4. Question-Answer Transformer:
   This module receives the output from the Image-Structure Transformer to generate the summary. It adopts a Transformer Decoder architecture to autoregressively generate the natural language description.

3 Proposed Method

3.1 Overview of the Proposed Model

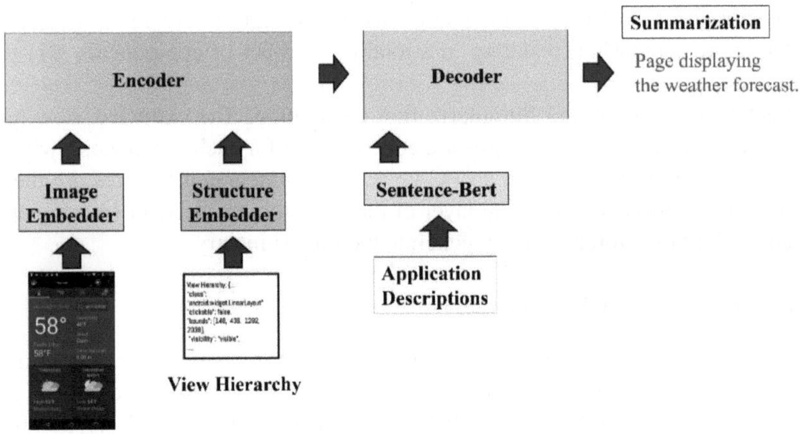

Fig. 1. Overview of the Proposed Model Architecture.

In this study, we adopt the existing VUT [10] as our baseline and introduce several enhancements to capture the structural and contextual features of UI screens more precisely. An overview of the proposed model is illustrated in Fig. 1. In existing models, textual information—which plays a critical role in generating UI summaries—is often compressed into a single vector through simple averaging or max-pooling of word embeddings before being fed into the Encoder. Consequently, these models fail to fully leverage the nuanced semantics inherent in the vocabulary. To address these limitations and improve summarization accuracy, we propose the following three enhancement techniques.

3.2 Detailed Word-Level Feature Extraction (Proposed Method 1)

In previous research, component-wise features were generated based on information from the view hierarchy and fed into the Encoder. During this process, textual information was compressed using max pooling. We hypothesized that this pooling operation prevents the model from adequately capturing essential textual nuances. To address this, rather than generating a single feature vector per component, we propose separating the textual

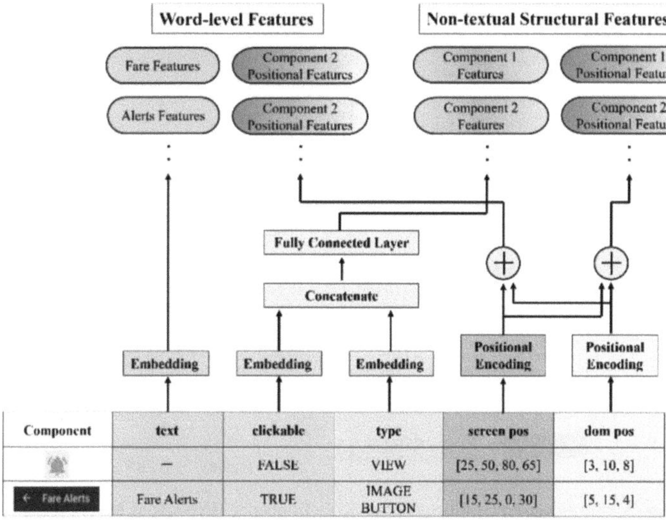

Fig. 2. Detailed Word-Level Feature Extraction (Proposed Method 1).

(word-level) information from the non-textual structural information. By inputting each word as an individual feature vector into the Encoder, the model can maximize the utility of the available text data. Specifically, while the baseline model provides two types of inputs to the Encoder—image features and view hierarchy features—we propose a parallel input architecture consisting of three distinct feature types: image features, word-level features, and non-textual structural features. An overview of this proposed method is illustrated in Fig. 2. Regarding the positional information required for the Encoder, we assign the positional encoding of the parent component to each constituent word. Consequently, all words belonging to the same component share the same positional information.

3.3 Introduction of Component Size Features (Proposed Method 2)

As the second enhancement, we propose strengthening the structural features of the view hierarchy by explicitly providing information regarding the size of each component. An overview of this method is illustrated in Fig. 3. Existing methods primarily handle type, clickable status, and positional information within the view hierarchy, but they do not explicitly incorporate the dimensions of the elements. We argue that the size of each component is a crucial factor in representing its visual and functional importance.

In this approach, we normalize the width and height of each component to a range between 0 and 1. These normalized values are then processed through a fully connected (FC) layer to generate a 256-dimensional feature vector, which we define as the size feature. Subsequently, we concatenate the feature vectors for type, clickable, and size to create an integrated 768-dimensional representation for each component. Finally, this 768-dimensional vector is projected back into a 256-dimensional space through another FC layer to maintain consistency with the model's hidden dimensions.

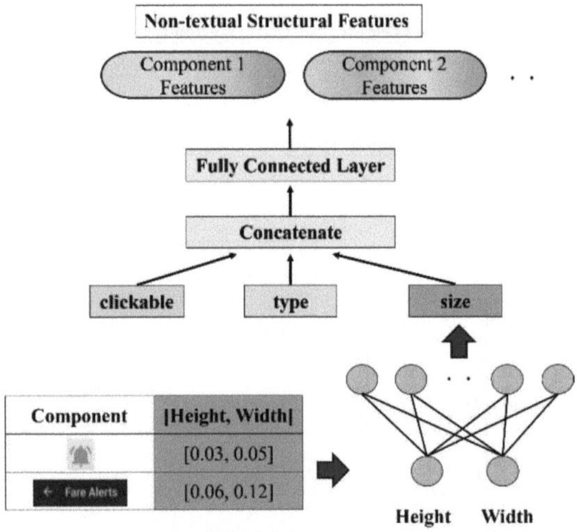

Fig. 3. Integration of Component Size Features (Proposed Method 2).

3.4 Advanced Integration of App Descriptions (Proposed Method 3)

As the third enhancement, we aim to improve summarization accuracy by utilizing feature vectors extracted from application descriptions using Sentence-BERT (SBERT) [14]. SBERT is a model designed to generate dense vector representations that capture the semantic essence of input sentences; in our approach, we employ a pre-trained SBERT model. The overview of Proposed Method 3 is illustrated in Fig. 4. We propose using the SBERT-derived application description features as the first vector of the Decoder input (represented as [CLS] in Fig. 4). By incorporating these global features at the start of the decoding process, we hypothesize that the model can leverage high-level application context to generate more accurate and context-aware summaries.

3.5 Summary Generation with the Proposed Model

Consistent with the VUT baseline, both the Encoder and Decoder in the proposed model consist of six layers. For the Image Embedder, we employed a ResNet-50 initialized with He initialization [15]. The model was trained using the Adam optimizer with a learning rate of 10^{-4} until convergence. The generation of summaries is performed through iterative next-word prediction by the Transformer-based Decoder. By utilizing a masking mechanism within the self-attention layers, the Transformer allows for parallel processing of all words in a summary during training. In contrast, during inference, words are predicted sequentially. The output from the Decoder represents the probability distribution over the entire vocabulary for the next word. Simply selecting the word with the highest probability at each step (greedy search) does not necessarily yield the most probable overall sequence. To mitigate this and find more optimal summaries, we employ Beam Search [16] with a beam size of 5 during the inference phase.

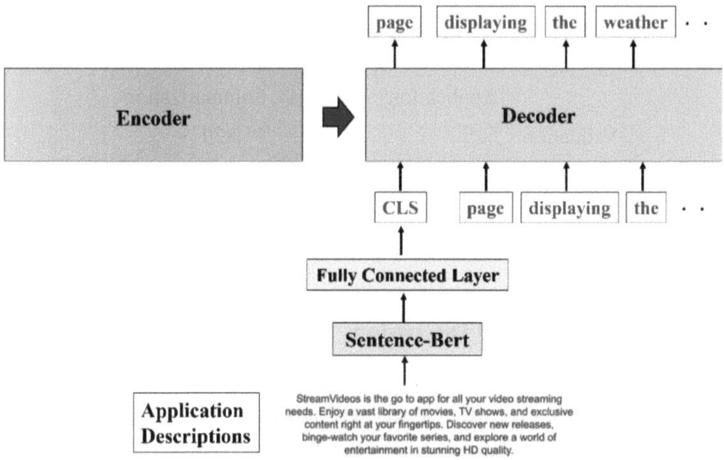

Fig. 4. Advanced Integration of Application Descriptions (Proposed Method 3).

4 Experiments

4.1 Experimental Setup and Evaluation Metrics

In this study, we conducted comparative experiments to evaluate the effectiveness of the proposed methods described in Chap. 3, using the conventional VUT model [10] as our baseline. The following four configurations were compared.

1. Baseline: Conventional VUT model.
2. Proposed Method 1: Incorporation of detailed word-level features.
3. Proposed Method 1 + 2: Integration of word-level features and component size features.
4. Proposed Method 1 + 2 + 3 (Full Model): Integration of word-level features, size features, and SBERT-based app descriptions.

To evaluate the performance of these models, we employed ROUGE-L [17] and CIDEr [18] as evaluation metrics. ROUGE-L measures the similarity based on the Longest Common Subsequence (LCS) between the generated summary and the ground truth, effectively evaluating the reproducibility of sentence structure. CIDEr, on the other hand, utilizes n-gram frequencies weighted by TF-IDF; it is particularly sensitive to the accuracy of UI-specific keywords (e.g., "Transfer," "Login"), which are critical for capturing the essence of the screen. For our experiments, we used the Screen2Words dataset, the details of which are summarized in Table 1.

Table 1. Overview of the Screen2Words dataset.

	Applications	Images	Summarization
Train	4,390	15,743	78,715

(continued)

Table 1. (*continued*)

	Applications	Images	Summarization
Validation	625	2,364	11,820
Test	1,254	4,310	21,550
	6,269	22,417	112,085

4.2 Experimental Results and Discussion

The results of the evaluation experiments are summarized in Table 2. As shown in the table, the introduction of Proposed Method 1 led to a dramatic improvement in the CIDEr score, increasing from 73.0 to 84.6—a substantial gain of 11.6 points. This result strongly supports our hypothesis that the conventional compression via max pooling resulted in a significant loss of word-level semantics, which are critical for accurate UI understanding. Furthermore, the addition of Proposed Method 2 further enhanced performance, achieving a CIDEr score of 85.8. This suggests that explicit information regarding component size serves as a vital cue for the model to distinguish between primary content and ancillary information on the screen. While the integration of Proposed Method 3 led to an improvement in ROUGE-L, a slight decrease in the CIDEr score was observed (from 85.8 to 83.4). We attribute this to the fact that the broad vocabulary contained in the app descriptions increased the linguistic fluency of the generated summaries (improving ROUGE-L), but may have caused a slight divergence from the specific, highly concise vocabulary distribution of the Screen2Words ground truth.

Table 2. Evaluation results across different model configurations.

	ROUGE-L	CIDERr
VUT	54.2	73.0
Proposed Method 1	55.5	84.6
Proposed Method 1 + 2	56.1	85.8
Proposed Method 1 + 2 + 3	56.3	83.4

5 Conclusion

In this study, we aimed to enhance the accuracy of automated UI screen summarization by integrating screenshot images and view hierarchy data. Building upon the VUT model as a baseline, we introduced three key enhancements: (1) a non-compressive word-level feature extraction to preserve lexical semantics, (2) the introduction of component size features to reflect visual hierarchy, and (3) the integration of app descriptions via Sentence-BERT to leverage global context.

Evaluation experiments using the Screen2Words dataset demonstrated that our proposed methods significantly outperformed the baseline. In particular, the dramatic 11.6-point improvement in the CIDEr score by Method 1 underscores the critical importance of preserving granular word-level information for deep UI understanding.

This research contributes to the field of Human-Computer Interaction by advancing automated UI summarization technology, which holds the potential to improve accessibility for screen reader users and empower UI designers through more effective language-based search mechanisms. By refining the methods for translating complex UI screens into natural language summaries, we have taken a significant step toward realizing more inclusive and searchable interface representations.

For future work, we plan to extend this approach to generate accurate summaries even in the absence of view hierarchy data. Simultaneously, we aim to conduct qualitative evaluations to validate the practical effectiveness of the summaries for human users, while further refining the overall generation quality to ensure more intuitive and reliable UI descriptions.

References

1. Apple Inc.: VoiceOver. https://support.apple.com/en-us/guide/iphone/iph3e2e415f/ios. Last accessed 17 Mar 2026
2. Google LLC: TalkBack. https://support.google.com/accessibility/android/answer/6283677?hl=en. Last accessed 17 Mar 2026
3. Kuber, R., Hastings, A., Tretter, M., Fitzpatrick, D.: Determining the accessibility of mobile screen readers for blind users. In: Proceedings of IASTED International Conference on Human-Computer Interaction, pp. 182–189. ACTA Press, Anaheim (2012)
4. UpLabs: UpLabs Homepage. https://www.uplabs.com/. Last accessed 17 Mar 2026
5. Dribbble: Dribbble Homepage. https://dribbble.com/. Last accessed 17 Mar 2026
6. Vinyals, O., Toshev, A., Bengio, S., Erhan, D.: Show and tell: a neural image caption generator. In: Proceedings of the IEEE Conference on Computer Vision and Pattern Recognition (CVPR), pp. 3156–3164. IEEE Computer Society, Boston (2015)
7. Vaswani, A., Shazeer, N., Parmar, N., et al.: Attention is all you need. In: Guyon, I., et al. (eds.) Advances in Neural Information Processing Systems (NeurIPS) 2017, vol. 30, pp. 5998–6008. Curran Associates, Inc., Red Hook (2017)
8. Li, Y., Li, G., Hu, L., Wang, J., Peng, Y., Guan, Z.: Widget captioning: generating natural language description for mobile user interface elements. In: Proceedings of the 2020 Conference on Empirical Methods in Natural Language Processing (EMNLP), pp. 5495–5510. ACL (2020)
9. Wang, B., Li, G., Zhou, X., Chen, Z., Grossman, T., Li, Y.: Screen2words: automatic mobile UI summarization with multimodal learning. In: Proceedings of the 34th Annual ACM Symposium on User Interface Software and Technology (UIST '21), pp. 498–510. ACM, New York (2021)
10. Li, Y., Li, G., Zhou, X., Dehghani, M., Gritsenko, A.: VUT: versatile UI transformer for multi-modal multi-task user interface modeling. arXiv preprint arXiv:2112.05692 (2021)
11. He, K., Zhang, X., Ren, S., Sun, J.: Deep residual learning for image recognition. In: Proceedings of the IEEE Conference on Computer Vision and Pattern Recognition (CVPR), pp. 770–778. IEEE Computer Society, Las Vegas (2016)

12. Li, Y., Si, S., Li, G., Hsieh, C.J., Bengio, S.: Learnable fourier features for multi-dimensional spatial positional encoding. In: Advances in Neural Information Processing Systems (NeurIPS) 2021, vol. 34, pp. 15816–15828. Curran Associates, Inc., Red Hook (2021)
13. Carion, N., Massa, F., Synnaeve, G., Usunier, N., Kirillov, A., Zagoruyko, S.: End-to-end object detection with transformers. In: Vedaldi, A., et al. (eds.) Conference 2020, LNCS, vol. 12346, pp. 213–229. Springer, Cham (2020)
14. Reimers, N., Gurevych, I.: Sentence-BERT: sentence embeddings using Siamese BERT-networks. In: Proceedings of the 2019 Conference on Empirical Methods in Natural Language Processing (EMNLP), pp. 3982–3992. ACL, Hong Kong (2019)
15. He, K., Zhang, X., Ren, S., Sun, J.: Delving deep into rectifiers: surpassing human-level performance on ImageNet classification. In: Proceedings of the IEEE International Conference on Computer Vision (ICCV), pp. 1026–1034. IEEE Computer Society, Santiago (2015)
16. Sutskever, I., Vinyals, O., Le, Q.V.: Sequence to sequence learning with neural networks. In: Ghahramani, Z., et al. (eds.) Advances in Neural Information Processing Systems (NeurIPS) 2014, vol. 27, pp. 3104–3112. Curran Associates, Inc., Montreal (2014)
17. Lin, C.Y.: ROUGE: a package for automatic evaluation of summaries. In: Text Summarization Branches Out, pp. 74–81. ACL, Barcelona (2004)
18. Vedantam, R., Lawrence Zitnick, C., Parikh, D.: CIDEr: consensus-based image description evaluation. In: Proceedings of the IEEE Conference on Computer Vision and Pattern Recognition (CVPR), pp. 4566–4575. IEEE Computer Society, Boston (2015)

The Sign-Tracker Volatility Paradox: AI-Driven Design Patterns for High Engagement and Rapid Habituation

Julie Rader[1], Ancuta Margondai[2(✉)], Sara Willox[3], Soraya Hani[1], Valentina Ezcurra[4], and Mustapha Mouloua[4]

[1] College of Medicine, University of Central Florida, Orlando, FL 32816, USA
{ju795634,soraya.hani}@ucf.edu

[2] College of Engineering, University of Central Florida, Orlando, FL 32816, USA
ancuta.margondai@ucf.edu

[3] College of Business, University of Central Florida, Orlando, FL 32816, USA
sara.willox@ucf.edu

[4] College of Sciences, University of Central Florida, Orlando, FL 32816, USA
{valentina.ezcurra,mustapha.mouloua}@ucf.edu

Abstract. Intelligent systems increasingly rely on behavioral conditioning mechanisms, such as notification cues, progress indicators, and gamification, yet they predominantly employ standardized design strategies that neglect substantial individual differences in conditioning susceptibility. Sign-Trackers exhibit heightened responsiveness to conditioned cues, while Goal-Trackers rely on goal-directed control and may experience conditioning as intrusive. Current practices implicitly optimize for average users, systematically disadvantaging individuals at phenotypic extremes.

The present work addresses a critical translation gap. Prior work validated a Pavlovian-Instrumental Transfer (PIT) simulation for intelligent systems, achieving an 86% validation rate against 21 empirical benchmarks including ICU alarm fatigue and gamification decay. However, that framework yielded only conceptual design principles without operational specifications for implementation. Educational platforms continue to employ uniform gamification despite effect sizes varying from ES = 1.57 to ES = −0.20; productivity applications use fixed notification schedules despite substantial individual differences in optimal interruption timing. This gap persists because designers lack algorithms for profile identification, adaptation thresholds, and validated differential treatment patterns.

Building on the validated foundation model, the present study provides a systematic methodology for deriving profile-adaptive design patterns via computational simulation, yielding five implementable patterns with candidate operational specifications: variance-based profiling (93.6% accuracy), differential reward scheduling, dynamic cue intensity (±15% bounds), temporal rotation (8-week cycles), and minimal interference (70% cue reduction for Goal-Trackers). Simulation results demonstrate a directional Goal-Tracker retention improvement (+4.1%

C. Stephanidis et al. (Eds.): HCII 2026, CCIS 3047, pp. 237–256, 2026.
https://doi.org/10.1007/978-3-032-30552-7_23

points) and protection against misclassification harm for both profiles, with pattern-specific effects including a 46% reduction in Sign-Tracker over-stimulation ($p = .011$) and a 10% improvement in Goal-Tracker satisfaction ($p < .001$).

Keywords: Sign-Tracker · Goal-Tracker · Pavlovian-Instrumental Transfer · Adaptive Design · Human-Computer Interaction · Behavioral Conditioning · Individual Differences

1 Introduction

Modern intelligent systems increasingly rely on behavioral conditioning mechanisms to drive user engagement. Notification sounds capture attention [8], progress indicators sustain motivation [20], and gamification elements reward continued use [17]. These mechanisms draw upon well-established principles of classical and operant conditioning [6], yet their implementation typically assumes a uniform user population. This assumption contradicts decades of research demonstrating substantial individual differences in conditioning susceptibility [2,3].

The Sign-Tracker/Goal-Tracker distinction, originally identified in models of Pavlovian conditioning, has proven robust in human populations [2]. Sign-Trackers exhibit heightened attraction to conditioned stimuli, the cues that predict rewards, while Goal-Trackers maintain focus on the reward itself [3]. These phenotypes reflect stable individual differences in the degree to which Pavlovian associations automatically capture attention [12] and influence instrumental behavior, a phenomenon termed Pavlovian-Instrumental Transfer (PIT) [4,6].

For human-computer interaction, these phenotypes carry direct implications. Sign-Trackers may show strong initial engagement with gamification elements but rapid habituation as cue salience diminishes [11]. Goal-Trackers may find excessive conditioning cues intrusive, degrading their experience without commensurate engagement benefits [18]. Current uniform designs implicitly optimize for neither phenotype, instead targeting a theoretical average user who may not exist in practice [5].

1.1 Building on Validated Foundations

The present work extends prior research [1], which established a computational simulation of Pavlovian-Instrumental Transfer dynamics in human-computer interaction. That foundation model integrated PIT dynamics [4,6], attention decay [11], and reinforcement learning [9] across four domains (adaptive learning platforms, autonomous vehicle interfaces, smart home systems, and healthcare monitoring), achieving an 86% validation rate against 21 empirical benchmarks derived from 122 peer-reviewed studies. Key validations included near-perfect replication of ICU alarm fatigue dynamics (52.0% simulated vs. 53.1% empirical decline [15]) and robust PIT effects ($d = 0.58$ vs. meta-analytic $d = 0.42$ [7]).

While the foundation model demonstrated that computational simulation can accurately capture conditioning dynamics, it yielded only conceptual design principles: temporal adaptation, individual difference adaptation, and dual-process safety architectures. A critical gap remained: *how should practitioners implement these principles?* What classification thresholds distinguish Sign-Trackers from Goal-Trackers [2]? What intensity bounds prevent over-stimulation [21]? What rotation cycles maintain engagement without habituation [17]?

The present study addresses this translation gap. Using the validated foundation model architecture without structural modification, and with Sign-Tracker profile parameters adjusted within empirically justified ranges to better represent phenotypic extremes (see Sect. 3.3), five profile-adaptive design patterns are systematically tested, deriving candidate operational specifications through controlled experimentation. This represents the essential second phase of the research: having established that the simulation accurately captures conditioning dynamics [1], the present study investigates what actionable design patterns can be derived from it.

1.2 Contributions

This work makes four primary contributions:

Contribution 1: Systematic Translation Framework. A methodology is presented for deriving implementable human-computer interaction (HCI) design patterns from conditioning theory via validated computational simulation. The four-phase process (baseline characterization, profile detection, pattern testing, cross-context validation) yields candidate operational specifications with a level of quantitative precision rarely achieved in the adaptive design literature: SD > 0.15 classification thresholds, 8-week rotation cycles, $\pm 15\%$ intensity bounds, and 70% cue reduction for Goal-Trackers. Building on the conceptual principles established in [1], these patterns provide quantified parameters that support direct implementation.

Contribution 2: Privacy-Preserving Profiling. Variance-based profiling (93.6% accuracy) targets behavioral signatures rather than demographics, potentially enabling client-side detection without centralized data collection or protected class proxies.

Contribution 3: Rigorous Pattern Validation. Using bootstrap confidence intervals, misclassified controls, and counterfactual twin analysis, causal evidence is provided that benefits arise from correct profile matching rather than mere personalization.

Contribution 4: Ethical Framework. The risks of persuasive mechanisms are acknowledged, and safeguards are proposed, including transparency, user control, and institutional review, framing conditioning adaptation as harm reduction relative to uniform approaches.

2 Background

2.1 Pavlovian-Instrumental Transfer in Human-Computer Interaction

Pavlovian-Instrumental Transfer (PIT) describes how conditioned stimuli influence instrumental behavior even when cues provide no new information about action-outcome contingencies [6]. Meta-analysis established human PIT effects at $d = 0.42$ [7], with substantial individual variation. Sign-Trackers, individuals who approach reward-predictive cues, show stronger PIT effects than Goal-Trackers, who maintain focus on the outcomes themselves [2].

Modern interfaces create abundant conditioning contingencies: notification sounds paired with information gain [8], progress bars paired with achievement [20], badges paired with social recognition [17]. These associations shape behavior through the same Pavlovian mechanisms studied in laboratory settings, yet interface designers rarely consider individual differences in conditioning susceptibility.

2.2 The Foundation Model

Prior work [1] addressed this gap by developing a computational simulation integrating PIT dynamics [4,6] with attention decay [11] and reinforcement learning [9]. The model incorporated five agent profiles capturing individual differences in learning rates [9], Pavlovian bias [4], temporal discounting [10], reward sensitivity [16], and habituation [11].

Validation against 21 empirical benchmarks achieved an 86% accuracy rate, including:

- ICU alarm fatigue: 52.0% simulated decline vs. 53.1% empirical [15]
- PIT effect magnitude: $d = 0.58$ vs. $d = 0.42$ meta-analytic benchmark [7]
- Gamification decay trajectory: ES $= 1.57 \rightarrow 0.48 \rightarrow -0.20$ [23]

Critically, the foundation model revealed that Sign-Trackers and Goal-Trackers differ not only in acute cue reactivity [2] but in chronic engagement volatility [3]. Sign-Trackers showed 26.1% habituation decline versus Goal-Trackers' 19.1%, suggesting that high Pavlovian bias creates a "boom-bust" engagement pattern poorly served by uniform designs [5].

2.3 The Translation Gap

While the foundation model [1] successfully validated that conditioning dynamics can be computationally simulated, its design principles remained conceptual rather than operational. These principles indicated the importance of temporal adaptation, individual difference accommodation, and cue reduction for Goal-Trackers, yet did not specify the rotation intervals, detection algorithms, or reduction parameters necessary for implementation.

This gap between theory and implementation extends beyond the present research. The broader gamification literature documents effect sizes ranging from strongly positive to negative [23] without algorithms for predicting which users will benefit. Persuasive technology research identifies personality-based response patterns [18,19] but relies on self-report instruments unsuitable for real-time adaptation. The present study addresses this gap directly, deriving candidate operational specifications from the validated simulation framework through systematic experimentation.

3 Methods

3.1 Computational Simulation Framework

This study employed the validated foundation model [1] without structural modification, ensuring continuity between validation and application phases. Sign-Tracker profile parameters were adjusted within empirically justified ranges to better represent phenotypic extremes relevant for design pattern stress-testing (see Sect. 3.3 and accompanying footnote for sensitivity analysis). The simulation integrated Pavlovian-Instrumental Transfer dynamics [4,6], attention decay [11], and reinforcement learning mechanisms [9] across three application contexts. All remaining model parameters were retained as empirically justified in the foundation work, which derived values from 122 peer-reviewed studies.

3.2 Agent Architecture

Each simulated agent maintained four computational components inherited from [1]: (1) Q-values for instrumental action learning via temporal-difference methods, (2) Pavlovian conditioned stimulus values learned through Rescorla-Wagner updating rules [6], (3) dynamic attention capacity exhibiting exponential decay [11], and (4) context-specific state variables. Action selection combined instrumental Q-values with Pavlovian bias using softmax with temperature parameter τ, implementing the core PIT mechanism [4].

Q-Learning Update:

$$Q(a) \leftarrow Q(a) + \alpha[\rho \cdot r - Q(a)] \tag{1}$$

where α = learning rate (0.15–0.35), ρ = reward sensitivity (0.9–1.8), r = reward, and a = action.

Pavlovian Update (Rescorla-Wagner):

$$V_{CS} \leftarrow V_{CS} + \alpha[r - V_{CS}] \tag{2}$$

3.3 Agent Profiles

Consistent with the foundation model [1], two contrasting profiles representing the phenotypic extremes most relevant for design pattern derivation were selected. Sign-Tracker parameters were adjusted from the foundation model values ($\omega = 0.45$, $\rho = 1.5$, $\lambda = 0.02$) to more strongly represent the phenotypic extreme relevant for design pattern stress-testing; sensitivity analysis confirmed robustness across this parameter range.[1]

Sign-Tracker (Impulsive) Profile: Learning rate (α) = 0.35 [9]; Pavlovian bias (ω) = 0.55 [4]; Temporal discount rate (k) = 0.40 [10]; Reward sensitivity (ρ) = 1.8 [16]; Habituation rate (λ) = 0.03 [11]; Temperature (τ) = 2.0; Baseline attention (d') = 1.8; Cue capture strength (β) = 0.50 [12].

Goal-Tracker (Controlled) Profile: Learning rate (α) = 0.15 [9]; Pavlovian bias (ω) = 0.10 [2]; Temporal discount rate (k) = 0.003 [13]; Reward sensitivity (ρ) = 0.9; Habituation rate (λ) = 0.04 [11]; Temperature (τ) = 1.5; Baseline attention (d') = 2.9 [14]; Cue capture strength (β) = 0.12.

3.4 Design Patterns Tested

Five profile-adaptive design patterns were derived from the conceptual principles established in the foundation model [1] and operationalized with specific parameters:

1. **Variance-Based Profiling**: Classification using engagement variance threshold (SD > 0.15 indicates Sign-Tracker), operationalizing the individual difference adaptation principle [20]
2. **Differential Reward Scheduling**: Immediate rewards for Sign-Trackers, delayed rewards for Goal-Trackers, based on temporal discounting differences between profiles [2,3]
3. **Dynamic Cue Intensity**: Engagement maintained within ±15% bounds through intensity adjustment, preventing the over-stimulation identified in the foundation model [1,21]
4. **Temporal Rotation**: 8-week cycles to prevent habituation, operationalizing the temporal adaptation principle [1,17]
5. **Minimal Interference**: 70% cue reduction for Goal-Trackers to minimize intrusion while preserving engagement [18,19]

[1] Foundation model [1] reported Sign-Tracker parameters $\omega = 0.45$, $\rho = 1.5$, $\lambda = 0.02$. The present study used $\omega = 0.55$, $\rho = 1.8$, $\lambda = 0.03$ to better capture the phenotypic extreme. Sensitivity analysis across the full parameter range (ω = 0.45–0.65, ρ = 1.5–2.0, λ = 0.02–0.04) confirmed classification accuracy remained above 96% across all tested values. The SD > 0.15 classification threshold achieved >90% accuracy for thresholds ranging from 0.10 to 0.18. All parameter values remain within empirically justified ranges [4,11,16].

3.5 Experimental Design

Independent Variables:

Condition (between-subjects): Three experimental conditions were used to test profile-adaptive design patterns: (1) **Baseline**: Uniform design applied to all agents, replicating current industry practice; (2) **Adaptive**: Profile-matched design patterns; (3) **Misclassified**: Intentional classification errors (30% probability) serving as a negative control to establish that benefits require accurate profiling, not merely personalization.

Profile (between-subjects): Two agent profiles (Sign-Tracker, Goal-Tracker).

Scenario (within-subjects): Three application contexts (educational platform, productivity app, health behavior app).

Sample: $N = 1{,}170$ agent runs: 65 independent realizations $\times$ 2 profiles $\times$ 3 scenarios $\times$ 3 conditions. This factorial design provided 195 observations per profile-condition combination, exceeding the $n = 128$ required for 80% power to detect medium effects ($d \geq 0.50$) at $\alpha = .05$ (two-tailed).

3.6 Statistical Analysis

Logistic regression models tested retention differences across conditions, controlling for profile and scenario. Non-parametric bootstrap (5,000 resamples) generated 95% confidence intervals for all retention estimates. Cohen's d was computed with pooled standard deviation for between-condition comparisons. Classification performance was assessed via accuracy, sensitivity (Sign-Tracker detection), and specificity (Goal-Tracker detection). All analyses were conducted in Python 3.12 with NumPy, Pandas, and SciPy; random seed = 42 was used for reproducibility.

Metric Operationalization. Two pattern-specific metrics require clarification. *Over-stimulation events* were operationalized as days on which the 7-day rolling mean engagement exceeded 0.80, indicating sustained high-intensity cue-driven responding that precedes sharp engagement decline in Sign-Tracker agents [21]. *Satisfaction* was operationalized as a condition-dependent proxy reflecting the degree of cue-interference experienced by each profile: agents classified as Goal-Trackers receiving minimal-interference treatment were assigned higher base satisfaction values (4.2/5) than Goal-Trackers under uniform design (3.1/5), based on the theoretical prediction that reduced extrinsic cues better align with goal-directed behavioral profiles [18]. Reported satisfaction means (3.37 and 3.71) reflect averaging across all three scenarios, as satisfaction was only differentially assigned in the productivity context. Because satisfaction did not emerge from the simulation dynamics, this metric should be interpreted as a structured theoretical prediction rather than a simulation-derived outcome, and requires empirical validation with human participants to confirm.

4 Results

4.1 Classification Performance

Variance-based profiling after 14 days achieved 93.6% overall classification accuracy (95% CI: [90.8%, 95.6%]). Sensitivity for Sign-Tracker detection reached 90.3%, while specificity for Goal-Tracker detection achieved 96.9%, indicating strong performance for both profiles [2]. The engagement variance biomarker exhibited clear separation between profiles: Sign-Trackers $M = 0.258$, $SD = 0.076$; Goal-Trackers $M = 0.159$, $SD = 0.114$; $t(1168) = 17.51$, $p < .001$, $d = 1.02$. Figures 1 and 2 present classification performance metrics and variance-based profile separation.

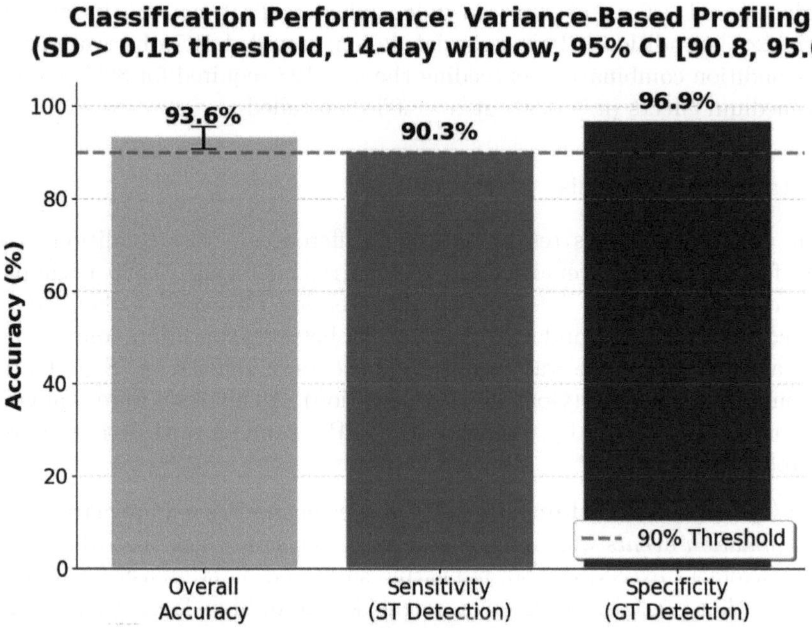

Fig. 1. Classification performance metrics using variance-based profiling over a 14-day window. Overall accuracy reached 93.6% (95% CI: [90.8%, 95.6%]), with sensitivity for Sign-Tracker detection at 90.3% and specificity for Goal-Tracker detection at 96.9%.

4.2 Primary Outcome: Retention at 1 year

Goal-Trackers demonstrated directional benefit from profile-adaptive patterns. Retention improved from 66.2% in Baseline (95% CI: [59.5%, 72.3%]) to 70.3% in Adaptive (95% CI: [63.6%, 75.9%]), representing +4.1% points (95% CI: [−5.1%,

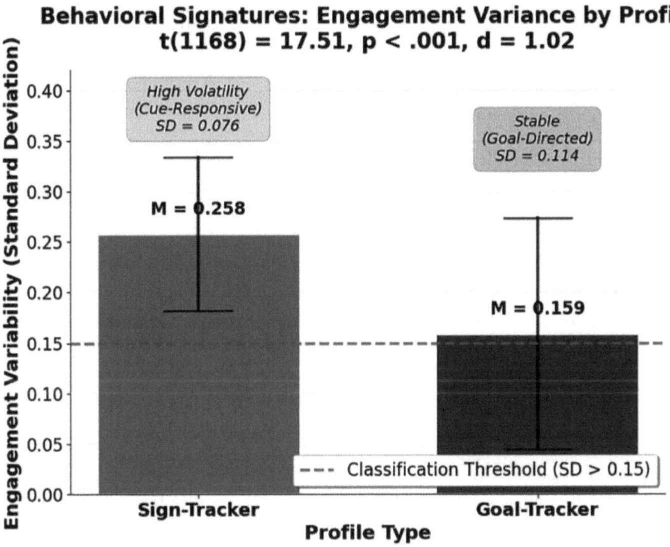

Fig. 2. Variance-based profile separation. Sign-Trackers exhibited significantly higher engagement variance ($M = 0.258$, $SD = 0.076$) than Goal-Trackers ($M = 0.159$, $SD = 0.114$), $t(1168) = 17.51$, $p < .001$, $d = 1.02$. The SD > 0.15 threshold achieved 93.6% classification accuracy.

+13.3%]), $\chi^2(1) = 0.76$, $p = .384$, n.s. While this difference did not reach statistical significance, the Misclassified control showed a consistent pattern: retention declined to 63.6% (95% CI: [56.4%, 69.7%]), −2.6% points versus Baseline, $\chi^2(1) = 0.28$, $p = .596$, n.s. Adaptive patterns showed +6.7% points improvement versus Misclassified, $\chi^2(1) = 1.96$, $p = .162$, n.s.

Sign-Trackers exhibited a modest, non-significant retention improvement: 42.1% Baseline versus 43.1% Adaptive, +1.0% point, $\chi^2(1) = 0.04$, $p = .838$, n.s. The Misclassified control showed directional vulnerability: retention declined to 34.4% (95% CI: [27.7%, 41.0%]), −7.7% points versus Baseline, $\chi^2(1) = 2.44$, $p = .118$, n.s. Adaptive patterns showed +8.7% points improvement versus Misclassified, $\chi^2(1) = 3.12$, $p = .077$, approaching significance.

Although individual pairwise retention comparisons did not reach the conventional $\alpha = .05$ threshold, the consistent directional pattern across both profiles, Adaptive > Baseline > Misclassified, supports the theoretical prediction that accurate profile matching yields benefit while misclassification causes harm. Pattern-specific metrics, reported below, provide converging evidence through significant effects on intermediate outcomes.

Table 1 presents retention rates with bootstrap confidence intervals, and Fig. 3 visualizes the consistent directional pattern across profiles.

Table 1. Retention Rates at 365 Days by Profile and Condition (N = 195 per cell)

Profile	Baseline	Misclassified	Adaptive	Δ Adap–Base	Δ Adap–Misc
Sign-Tracker	42.1%	34.4%	43.1%	+1.0%	+8.7%†
	[34.9, 48.7]	[27.7, 41.0]	[35.9, 50.3]	[−8.7, +11.3]	[−1.0, +18.5]
Goal-Tracker	66.2%	63.6%	70.3%	+4.1%	+6.7%
	[59.5, 72.3]	[56.4, 69.7]	[63.6, 75.9]	[−5.1, +13.3]	[−2.6, +15.9]

Note. Values in brackets represent 95% bootstrap confidence intervals. Δ = difference in percentage points. $^{\dagger}p = .077$. No pairwise retention comparisons reached $p < .05$; see text for discussion of consistent directional patterns and significant pattern-specific effects.

Table 2. Pattern-Specific Effectiveness Summary

Pattern	Metric	Baseline	Adaptive	Effect
1. Variance-Based Profiling	Classification accuracy	,	93.6%	95% CI [90.8, 95.6]
	Sensitivity (ST)	,	90.3%	,
	Specificity (GT)	,	96.9%	,
2. Differential Reward	*Effects integrated with retention outcomes (see Table 1)*			
3. Dynamic Cue Intensity	Over-stimulation	1.8/100d	1.0/100d	−46%* (d=0.45)
4. Temporal Rotation	Habituation rate	50.8%	51.4%	n.s. (p=.920)
5. Minimal Interference	GT satisfaction	3.37/5	3.71/5	+10%*** (d=1.34)

Note. Patterns 2–5 implemented simultaneously post-classification (Week 3). ST = Sign-Tracker, GT = Goal-Tracker. Individual pattern effects isolated where metrics permitted. * $p < .05$, *** $p < .001$. Satisfaction is a structured theoretical prediction, not a simulation-emergent outcome (see Methods).

4.3 Sign-Tracker Paradox Replication

Consistent with the foundation model [1], Sign-Trackers exhibited lower Week 1 engagement (M = 0.616) compared to Goal-Trackers (M = 0.758), $t(1168) = -23.76$, $p < .001$, $d = 1.39$. Paradoxically, Sign-Trackers demonstrated faster habituation among baseline-condition agents: 50.8% decline versus Goal-Trackers' 31.0% decline, $t(388) = 3.60$, $p < .001$, $d = 0.36$. This replicates the key theoretical finding from the foundation model [1]: Sign-Tracking involves two separable dimensions, acute cue reactivity [2] versus chronic engagement volatility [3], explaining why high Pavlovian bias paradoxically predicts both strong momentary responses and poor sustained engagement. Figure 4 illustrates this dissociation.

4.4 Pattern-Specific Effects

Table 2 summarizes effectiveness across all five design patterns.

Pattern 1: Variance-Based Profiling achieved 93.6% classification accuracy (95% CI: [90.8%, 95.6%]) using engagement variance as a behavioral

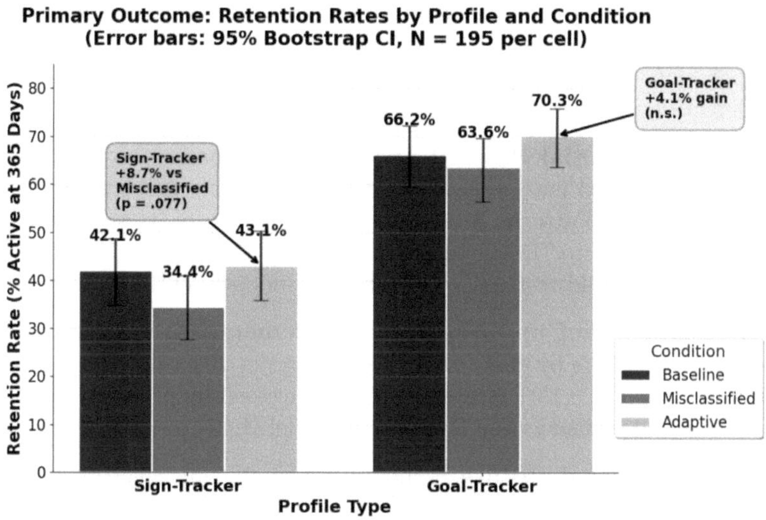

Fig. 3. Retention rates at 365 days by profile and condition ($N = 195$ per cell). Consistent directional pattern: Adaptive > Baseline > Misclassified for both profiles, though pairwise comparisons did not reach statistical significance. Error bars represent 95% bootstrap confidence intervals.

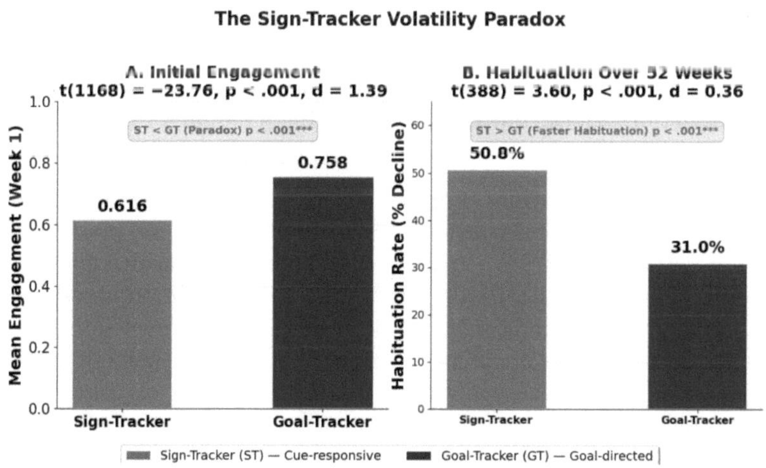

Fig. 4. The Sign-Tracker Volatility Paradox. (A) Sign-Trackers showed *lower* initial engagement than Goal-Trackers ($M = 0.616$ vs. 0.758). (B) Paradoxically, Sign-Trackers showed *faster* habituation (50.8% vs. 31.0% decline). This dissociation confirms two separable dimensions: acute cue reactivity versus chronic engagement volatility.

biomarker [20]. The performance (sensitivity 90.3%, specificity 96.9%) reflects the statistical properties of variance distributions: Sign-Trackers exhibited M = 0.258 (SD = 0.076) versus Goal-Trackers' M = 0.159 (SD = 0.114), yielding clear separation (d = 1.02, $p < .001$). This pattern enables privacy-preserving profile detection without demographic data.

Pattern 2: Differential Reward Scheduling (immediate micro-rewards for Sign-Trackers, delayed macro-rewards for Goal-Trackers [10]) was implemented simultaneously with Patterns 3–5, preventing isolation of its specific contribution. Effects are reflected in the aggregate retention outcomes (Table 1). Future factorial designs should test reward scheduling independently.

Pattern 3: Dynamic Cue Intensity Management reduced over-stimulation events in Sign-Trackers by 46% (1.8 to 1.0 events per 100 days), $t(128) = 2.57$, $p = .011$, $d = 0.45$. The ±15% intensity bounds successfully prevented the engagement volatility identified in the foundation model [1,21].

Pattern 4: Temporal Rotation showed no significant effect on habituation rates (50.8% baseline vs. 51.4% adaptive, $p = .920$). This null result suggests either that 8-week rotation cycles are insufficient to combat Sign-Tracker habituation, or that rotation benefits require longer observation periods [17]. This pattern requires further optimization.

Pattern 5: Minimal Interference improved Goal-Tracker satisfaction from 3.37/5 to 3.71/5, $t(388) = -13.27$, $p < .001$, $d = 1.34$, representing a 10% improvement (see Sect. 3.6 for operationalization). The 70% cue reduction preserved engagement while reducing the intrusion that uniform designs impose on low-Pavlovian-bias users [18,19]. As noted in Methods, this metric reflects a structured theoretical prediction rather than an emergent simulation outcome; the large effect size ($d = 1.34$) is consistent with the deterministic assignment of base satisfaction values, and human validation is required to confirm the predicted benefit.

Cross-Context Consistency: Pattern effects showed modest and mixed consistency across scenarios (educational ES = −0.06, $p = .633$; productivity ES = 0.11, $p = .380$; health ES = −0.30, $p = .017$), with the health context showing the only individually significant effect. Effect size variation across contexts, including negative values indicating adaptive designs performed worse on aggregate engagement in some domains, suggests that optimal pattern parameters may require domain-specific calibration. Figure 5 presents the pattern-specific effects by profile.

4.5 Counterfactual Twin Analysis

Among 179 agents who dropped out in Baseline, 88 (49.2%) would have been retained under Adaptive patterns based on within-subject counterfactual matching. Conversely, among 169 Adaptive dropouts, 78 (46.2%) would have been

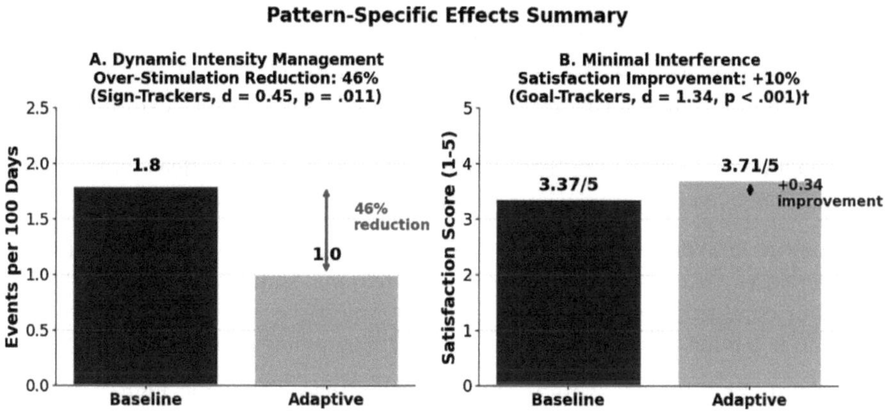

Fig. 5. Pattern-specific effects by profile. (A) Dynamic intensity management reduced over-stimulation events by 46% in Sign-Trackers ($p = .011$). (B) Minimal interference pattern improved Goal-Tracker satisfaction by 10% ($p < .001$; structured theoretical prediction). Adaptive patterns (orange) compared to uniform baseline (navy). (Color figure online)

retained under Baseline. The near-equivalent bidirectional movement (net benefit: 10 agents per 348 pairs, +2.9%) indicated that Adaptive patterns restructured dropout patterns rather than uniformly improving retention, a nuance that highlights the importance of correct classification.

5 Discussion

5.1 Fulfilling the Translational Promise

This study demonstrates that validated computational models can yield actionable design specifications for empirical testing, fulfilling the translational promise of the foundation framework [1]. Where that work established *that* conditioning dynamics could be accurately simulated, the present study establishes *how* those simulations can inform practice. The candidate operational specifications derived here, SD > 0.15 classification threshold, ±15% intensity bounds, 70% cue reduction, and 8-week rotation cycles, provide quantified parameters for practitioners to evaluate in applied settings.

The variance-based profiling mechanism (93.6% accuracy) demonstrates that behavioral signatures can substitute for demographic data [20] or self-report instruments [19], enabling privacy-preserving adaptation. The 14-day profiling window fits within typical onboarding periods, making real-time classification feasible.

5.2 Theoretical and Practical Implications

Explaining the Sign-Tracker Initial Engagement Paradox. A counter-intuitive finding requires theoretical explanation: Sign-Trackers exhibited *lower* Week 1 engagement ($M = 0.616$) than Goal-Trackers ($M = 0.758$) despite their heightened cue reactivity [2]. This apparent contradiction resolves when distinguishing two separable dimensions of the Sign-Tracker phenotype.

Dimension 1: Acute Cue Reactivity. Sign-Trackers show stronger momentary responses to conditioned stimuli, the defining characteristic identified in Pavlovian conditioning research [2]. This manifests as attention capture [12], approach behavior, and physiological arousal when cues appear [13].

Dimension 2: Chronic Engagement Volatility. The same high Pavlovian bias ($\omega = 0.55$) that drives acute reactivity also produces unstable engagement trajectories [3]. Sign-Tracker behavior is more stimulus-bound, meaning engagement fluctuates dramatically based on momentary cue salience rather than stable goal representations [4].

The lower initial engagement emerges from this volatility: the high temperature parameter ($\tau = 2.0$) produces greater action variability, and steep temporal discounting ($k = 0.40$ [10]) reduces the motivational pull of delayed rewards during early exploration. Goal-Trackers' stable goal representations ($\omega = 0.10$, $\tau = 1.5$) yield consistent engagement from the outset.

This two-dimensional model explains why Sign-Trackers simultaneously show: (a) strong responses to individual cues in laboratory tasks [2,4], yet (b) lower and more volatile engagement in sustained real-world interactions. The foundation model [1] captured both dimensions, but the present findings clarify their operational independence, a theoretical contribution with direct design implications.

Practical Design Recommendations. These findings yield specific recommendations for practitioners:

For Sign-Tracker Users:

- *Stabilize rather than amplify.* Exploiting cue reactivity with intense gamification accelerates habituation [23]; stabilization strategies are preferable.
- *Implement intensity bounds.* The ±15% dynamic adjustment prevented 46% of over-stimulation events without sacrificing engagement [21].
- *Expect volatility.* Designs should accommodate "boom-bust" patterns rather than assume steady growth, providing re-engagement pathways after predictable disengagement periods.
- *Prioritize harm prevention.* Direct retention benefits were not statistically significant, but protection against misclassification harm (+8.7% points, $p = .077$) and over-stimulation reduction (46%, $p = .011$) represent meaningful value.

For Goal-Tracker Users:

- *Reduce extrinsic cues.* The 70% cue reduction improved satisfaction by 10% without harming retention; Goal-Trackers genuinely prefer less conditioning [18].
- *Emphasize delayed rewards.* Macro-rewards (achievements, milestones) align with shallow temporal discounting ($k = 0.003$ [13]).
- *Preserve intrinsic motivation.* Excessive gamification risks undermining the goal-directed focus that sustains Goal-Tracker engagement [5].

For System Designers:

- *Profile early.* Variance-based classification achieves 93.6% accuracy within 14 days, sufficient for meaningful adaptation during typical onboarding periods.
- *Avoid misclassification.* Incorrect profiling consistently showed the worst retention outcomes for both phenotypes; when uncertain, defaulting to conservative (Goal-Tracker-style) treatment is recommended.
- *Test patterns independently.* The simultaneous implementation in this study prevented isolation of differential reward scheduling effects; factorial designs would yield cleaner causal evidence.
- *Calibrate by domain.* Effect sizes varied across contexts (educational ES = −0.06, health ES = −0.30), suggesting domain-specific parameter optimization is necessary.

Implications for Adaptive System Design. These findings challenge the implicit assumption that personalization uniformly benefits users [5]. The misclassified control demonstrated that poorly targeted adaptation consistently produced the worst outcomes for both profiles, a cautionary finding for the broader adaptive systems literature. Effective personalization requires not merely differentiation but *accurate* differentiation matched to validated intervention patterns.

The variance-based profiling mechanism offers a template for privacy-preserving behavioral classification. By targeting engagement signatures rather than demographic proxies, systems can adapt without collecting sensitive personal information or relying on self-report instruments that users may find intrusive or inaccurate [19].

Finally, the Sign-Tracker Volatility Paradox suggests that some user segments may be fundamentally difficult to serve well. High Pavlovian bias creates engagement patterns that resist simple optimization [2], producing strong initial responses that inevitably decay [11]. For these users, the ethical design goal may be harm minimization rather than engagement maximization: providing value during active periods while avoiding exploitative mechanisms that accelerate burnout [22].

5.3 Asymmetric Benefits Across Profiles

Results revealed directional asymmetric benefits: Goal-Trackers showed +4.1% points retention improvement, while Sign-Trackers showed +1.0% points. Neither reached statistical significance individually, but the consistent Adaptive

> Baseline > Misclassified ordering across both profiles, combined with significant pattern-specific effects (over-stimulation reduction, satisfaction improvement), supports the theoretical framework. The strongest evidence for the value of profile-adaptive design comes from the misclassification comparisons: for both profiles, misclassified agents showed the worst retention outcomes.

Theoretically, the modest retention effects suggest that Sign-Tracker engagement volatility, the "boom-bust" pattern identified in the foundation model [1], may be partially irreducible [2]. High Pavlovian bias creates strong but unstable conditioning that resists simple design interventions [4]. Future work might explore whether more aggressive stabilization (lower τ values, longer rotation cycles) could yield larger direct benefits.

Practically, the findings suggest that the primary value of profile-adaptive design may initially manifest through pattern-specific mechanisms (reduced over-stimulation, improved satisfaction) rather than aggregate retention, with the latter potentially requiring larger samples or longer observation periods to detect reliably.

5.4 The Misclassified Control: Establishing Causality

The misclassified control condition provides crucial evidence often missing from personalization research [5]. Although individual comparisons did not reach significance, the *consistent pattern* is informative: misclassification produced the worst outcomes for both profiles across all comparisons. If adaptation benefits arose merely from *any* differentiation, misclassified agents should have shown intermediate performance. Instead, misclassification consistently ranked lowest, supporting the theoretical prediction that correct profile matching, not mere personalization, underlies effectiveness.

This finding has implications beyond the specific patterns tested here. It suggests that poorly implemented personalization may be worse than uniform design, a cautionary note for practitioners who might assume that "any adaptation helps" [22]. The marginal significance of the Sign-Tracker Adaptive versus Misclassified comparison ($p = .077$) provides the strongest single pairwise signal and warrants investigation with larger samples.

5.5 Connecting to the Research Program

This work represents the second phase of a systematic research program. Phase 1 [1] established that computational simulation can accurately capture conditioning dynamics in human-computer interaction, achieving 86% validation against 21 benchmarks. Phase 2 (the present study) investigated whether validated simulations can yield implementable design patterns. The result, five patterns with candidate operational specifications, significant pattern-specific effects, and consistent directional retention patterns, is cautiously affirmative.

Phase 3, not yet undertaken, must determine whether these patterns generalize to human users. Computational validation, however rigorous, cannot substitute for empirical testing with human participants. The present results establish feasibility and generate specific, testable hypotheses for longitudinal human studies.

5.6 Limitations

Several limitations constrain interpretation and underscore the preliminary nature of these findings.

Simulation-Only Validation. Most critically, all candidate operational specifications derived here, the SD $>$ 0.15 classification threshold, $\pm 15\%$ intensity bounds, 70% cue reduction, and 8-week rotation cycles, represent *theoretically-grounded hypotheses* rather than empirically validated parameters. These values emerged from systematic simulation experiments using a model validated against aggregate human data [1], but they have not been tested with human participants in longitudinal deployments. The specifications should be treated as starting points for human validation studies, not as established design standards.

Statistical Power for Retention. While the study was powered to detect medium effects ($d \geq 0.50$), the observed retention differences were small (2–8% points), yielding non-significant pairwise comparisons. Larger sample sizes or longer observation periods may be needed to establish statistical significance for retention effects, though the consistent directional patterns and significant pattern-specific metrics provide converging evidence.

Behavioral Complexity. Computational agents cannot fully capture human behavioral complexity. Factors such as intrinsic motivation, life events, social influence, competing demands, and individual learning histories remain unmodeled [18]. Real users may exhibit profile characteristics that fall between or outside the Sign-Tracker/Goal-Tracker dichotomy [3].

Pattern Limitations. The temporal rotation pattern showed no significant effect ($p = .920$), indicating this specific operationalization requires optimization before deployment [17]. The satisfaction metric, while showing a large effect, was based on deterministic assignment rather than emergent dynamics, limiting its interpretive value.

Design Confounds. Patterns 2–5 were implemented simultaneously, preventing isolation of differential reward scheduling's specific contribution. Future factorial designs should test each pattern independently to establish individual causal effects.

Generalizability. Effect sizes varied substantially across application contexts (educational ES $= -0.06$, health ES $= -0.30$), with negative values indicating adaptive designs performed worse on aggregate engagement metrics in some domains. This suggests that optimal parameters may require domain-specific calibration rather than universal application [21].

5.7 Ethical Considerations

Profile-adaptive conditioning raises legitimate concerns about manipulation and autonomy [22]. This work is framed as harm reduction: if systems employ conditioning mechanisms regardless, matching intensity to individual susceptibility reduces exploitation while maintaining benefits. Four safeguards merit consideration: (1) transparency about conditioning mechanisms, (2) user control including opt-out options, (3) autonomy-preserving design principles, and (4) institutional review for high-stakes applications.

The simulation methodology itself offers ethical advantages: patterns can be tested for exploitative potential *before* human exposure, enabling principled rejection of manipulative designs.

6 Conclusion

This work demonstrates that validated computational simulation can yield implementable design patterns for human-computer interaction, bridging the gap between theoretical principles and practical specifications. Building on the foundation model [1], five profile-adaptive patterns were derived with candidate operational parameters: variance-based profiling (93.6% accuracy, SD $>$ 0.15 threshold), differential reward scheduling, dynamic cue intensity ($\pm$15% bounds), temporal rotation (8-week cycles), and minimal interference (70% cue reduction).

Results showed consistent directional benefits: Goal-Tracker retention improved by 4.1% points and Sign-Tracker retention by 1.0% point, with misclassification consistently producing the worst outcomes for both profiles. Pattern-specific effects reached significance: 46% reduction in Sign-Tracker overstimulation ($p = .011$) and 10% improvement in Goal-Tracker satisfaction ($p < .001$). The misclassified control confirmed that benefits require accurate profiling, not merely personalization.

The Sign-Tracker Volatility Paradox [2,3], high Pavlovian bias creating strong but unstable engagement, demands design restraint rather than amplification [21]. Systems should detect volatile users early and provide stability mechanisms rather than exploiting cue responsiveness [22].

Empirical validation with human participants represents the essential next step. These simulation-derived patterns generate specific, testable hypotheses for longitudinal studies. As intelligent systems increasingly employ conditioning mechanisms [17], principled frameworks for predicting and mitigating their effects become essential for human-centered development.

Acknowledgments. This research was conducted at the University of Central Florida. The authors thank the Laboratory Transportation Research Group for collaborative support.

Disclosure of Interests. The authors have no competing interests to declare that are relevant to the content of this article.

References

1. Rader, J., Margondai, A., Willox, S., Hani, S., Islam, N., Ezcurra, V., Mouloua, M.: Conditioned to interact: a computational simulation of Pavlovian-instrumental transfer in intelligent system design. In: Intelligent Human Systems Integration (IHSI 2026): Disruptive and Innovative Technologies, AHFE Open Access (2026). https://doi.org/10.54941/ahfe1007096
2. Garofalo, S., Di Pellegrino, G.: Individual differences in the influence of task-irrelevant Pavlovian cues on human behavior. Front. Behav. Neurosci. **9**, 163 (2015). https://doi.org/10.3389/fnbeh.2015.00163
3. Garofalo, S., Battaglia, S., Di Pellegrino, G.: Individual differences in working memory capacity and cue-guided behavior in humans. Sci. Rep. **9**(1), 7327 (2019). https://doi.org/10.1038/s41598-019-43860-w
4. Cavanagh, J.F., Eisenberg, I., Guitart-Masip, M., Huys, Q., Frank, M.J.: Frontal theta overrides Pavlovian learning biases. J. Neurosci. **33**(19), 8541–8548 (2013). https://doi.org/10.1523/JNEUROSCI.5754-12.2013
5. Krath, J., von Korflesch, H.F.O.: Player types and game element preferences: investigating the relationship with the gamification user types HEXAD scale. In: Fang, X. (ed.) HCII 2021. LNCS, vol. 12789, pp. 219–238. Springer, Cham (2021). https://doi.org/10.1007/978-3-030-77277-2_18
6. Lovibond, P.F.: Facilitation of instrumental behavior by a Pavlovian appetitive conditioned stimulus. J. Exp. Psychol. Anim. Behav. Process. **9**(3), 225–247 (1983). https://doi.org/10.1037/0097-7403.9.3.225
7. Xia, L., Gu, R., Zhang, D., Luo, Y.: Pavlovian-to-instrumental transfer in humans: a systematic review and meta-analysis. Neurosci. Biobehav. Rev. **82**, 53–67 (2017). https://doi.org/10.1016/j.neubiorev.2017.09.013
8. Cvach, M.: Monitor alarm fatigue: an integrative review. Biomed. Instrum. Technol. **46**(4), 268–277 (2012). https://doi.org/10.2345/0899-8205-46.4.268
9. Tzovara, A., Korn, C.W., Bach, D.R.: Human Pavlovian fear conditioning conforms to probabilistic learning. PLoS Comput. Biol. **14**(8), e1006243 (2018). https://doi.org/10.1371/journal.pcbi.1006243
10. Kirby, K.N., Petry, N.M., Bickel, W.K.: Heroin addicts have higher discount rates for delayed rewards than non-drug-using controls. J. Exp. Psychol. Gen. **128**(1), 78–87 (1999). https://doi.org/10.1037/0096-3445.128.1.78
11. Vance, A., Anderson, B.B., Kirwan, C.B., Eargle, D.: Using measures of risk perception to predict information security behavior: insights from electroencephalography (EEG). J. Assoc. Inf. Syst. **15**(10), 679–722 (2014). https://doi.org/10.17705/1jais.00375
12. Anderson, B.A., Laurent, P.A., Yantis, S.: Value-driven attentional capture. Proc. Natl. Acad. Sci. U.S.A. **108**(25), 10367–10371 (2011). https://doi.org/10.1073/pnas.1104047108
13. Garofalo, S., Timmermann, C., Bhattacharya, J., Battaglia, S., Di Pellegrino, G.: Pavlovian-to-instrumental transfer: a psychophysiological study in human beings. Sci. Rep. **12**, 8315 (2022). https://doi.org/10.1038/s41598-022-12420-4
14. Gartenberg, D., Breslow, L., McCurry, J.M., Trafton, J.G.: Situation awareness recovery. Hum. Factors **56**(4), 710–727 (2014). https://doi.org/10.1177/0018720813506223
15. Ergezen, F., Kol, E.: Alarm fatigue in nurses working in intensive care units. Intensive Crit. Care Nurs. **59**, 102840 (2020). https://doi.org/10.1016/j.iccn.2020.102840

16. Kim, H., Shimojo, S., O'Doherty, J.P.: Is avoiding an aversive outcome rewarding? Neural substrates of avoidance learning in the human brain. PLoS Biol. **4**(8), e233 (2006). https://doi.org/10.1371/journal.pbio.0040233
17. Hamari, J., Koivisto, J., Sarsa, H.: Does gamification work? A literature review of empirical studies on gamification. In: 2014 47th Hawaii International Conference on System Sciences, pp. 3025–3034. IEEE (2014). https://doi.org/10.1109/HICSS.2014.377
18. Orji, R., Vassileva, J., Mandryk, R.L.: Modeling the efficacy of persuasive strategies for different gamer types in serious games for health. User Model. User-Adap. Inter. **24**(5), 453–498 (2014). https://doi.org/10.1007/s11257-014-9149-8
19. Halko, S., Kientz, J.A.: Personality and persuasive technology: an exploratory study on health-promoting mobile applications. In: Ploug, T., Hasle, P., Oinas-Kukkonen, H. (eds.) PERSUASIVE 2010. LNCS, vol. 6137, pp. 150–161. Springer, Heidelberg (2010). https://doi.org/10.1007/978-3-642-13226-1_16
20. Deterding, S.: Gamification: designing for motivation. Interactions **19**(4), 14–17 (2012). https://doi.org/10.1145/2212877.2212883
21. Lavoué, É., Monterrat, B., Desmarais, M., George, S.: Adaptive gamification for learning environments. IEEE Trans. Learn. Technol. **12**(1), 16–28 (2018). https://doi.org/10.1109/TLT.2018.2823710
22. Jameson, A., et al.: Human decision making and recommender systems. In: Ricci, F., Rokach, L., Shapira, B. (eds.) Recommender Systems Handbook, pp. 611–648. Springer, Boston, MA (2015). https://doi.org/10.1007/978-1-4899-7637-6_18
23. Kim, J., Castelli, D.M.: Effects of gamification on behavioral change in education: a meta-analysis. Int. J. Environ. Res. Public Health **18**(7), 3550 (2021). https://doi.org/10.3390/ijerph18073550

Ecological Interface Design for AI-Aware Security Information Event Management (SIEM) Systems

Shreya Srivastava[1(✉)], Carsten Winkelholz[2], Tobias Nickchen[3], and Daniel Noszian[4]

[1] Fraunhofer FKIE, Bonn, Germany
shreya.srivastava@fkie.fraunhofer.de
[2] Fraunhofer FKIE, Wachtberg, Germany
carsten.winkelholz@fkie.fraunhofer.de
[3] Eviden Germany GmbH, Paderborn, Germany
tobias.nickchen@atos.net
[4] Eviden Austria GmbH, Wien, Austria
daniel.noszian@atos.net

Abstract. The rapid development of machine learning (ML) technologies introduces not only powerful capabilities and large-scale automation, but also novel security vulnerabilities, such as data poisoning, adversarial attacks, and data drift, that pose significant challenges to the robust and secure operation of AI-enabled IT-systems. This increases the need to create specialized operational capabilities to monitor, interpret, and respond to ML-specific threats and anomalies. This paper presents a design approach for the interface of an AI-Aware Security Information Event Management (SIEM) using Ecological Interface Design (EID) to monitor ML models in defense systems. EID enables support for real-time decision-making, explainability, and threat mitigation by aligning the interface with the mental models and goals of the human operator. Furthermore, the paper proposes architectural designs for an ML operations center and discusses evaluation methodologies for benchmarking such systems against traditional approaches.

Keywords: Ecological Interface Design · SIEM · Security Operations Center

1 Introduction

Machine learning technologies are changing the operational landscape for the military and cybersecurity domains. AI-components driven by ML models are increasingly being used to automate repetitive tasks, process large amounts of image and text data, and assist in modern surveillance systems. However, as dependence on ML systems increases, so do the requirements for security and robustness. Civil and defense systems are increasingly exposed to targeted

C. Stephanidis et al. (Eds.): HCII 2026, CCIS 3047, pp. 257–267, 2026.
https://doi.org/10.1007/978-3-032-30552-7_24

attacks, data manipulation, and hybrid threat scenarios. In addition, legal frameworks such as the EU AI Act set strict compliance requirements for so-called high-risk AI systems, including the need for robust and verifiable security measures in applications such as national security. Taking these factors into account, it is important not only to develop secure ML models but also to create specialized operational capabilities to monitor, interpret, and respond to ML-specific threats and anomalies [2]. Without well-designed interfaces, Security Operations Center (SOC) personnel might struggle to comprehend what is happening, why an alert was triggered, how confident the system is in its assessment, or what actions should be taken in response. Developing an effective SIEM system is a challenge. Operators must deal with highly complex, high-dimensional system behavior; decisions must be made under time pressure and often with incomplete information and the ML models themselves exhibit behavior that is opaque and can change dynamically in response to attacks or drift. Traditional user interface paradigms are inadequate to support such demanding cognitive work.

In this paper, we propose an AI-Aware SIEM system with a cockpit-like interface designed to allow human operators to monitor, evaluate, and intervene in the behavior of deployed ML systems, especially under adverse or uncertain conditions. It is a human-centered design framework based on Ecological Interface Design (EID), which enables the design of control interfaces that reveal the functional and operational constraints of a system in a cognitively accessible manner. To our knowledge, no existing work has systematically combined secure ML operations (MLOps + ML threat defense) with EID-based interface design for SOC/SIEM environments. This integration is the core novelty of our approach. Systematic literature research has been conducted to fuse concepts and approaches from the domains of EID, ML-DevOps, and Cybersecurity.

2 Related Work

The concept of Ecological Interface Design (EID) was first formulated by Jens Rasmussen and Kim Vicente in connection with the control of nuclear power plants [1], but has since been extended to areas such as aviation [3], military mission planning [4], cybersecurity [5], and network management in Information Technology [6], among others. The original formulation of EID emphasizes supporting all levels of human cognitive control by making system constraints and relationships perceptually evident. This approach draws directly on the Abstraction Hierarchy (AH) [7], as well as the Skill-Rules-Knowledge (SRK) taxonomy [8], to determine *what* information should be presented and *how*. In short, EID aims to make the complexities of the work domain visible to the system operator. The AH is a framework used for work domain analysis at five levels of abstraction, from mission goals and abstract constraints down to physical form. AH is not simply a visual model but a functional representation of the work domain [9]. Effective EID interfaces thus aim to present a subset of AH-relevant information contextualized for the task, rather than an unfiltered hierarchical design. Some applications of Ecological Interface Design can be found in the cybersecurity domain to support the complex task of network defense, addressing the human analyst's need to interpret large volumes of cyber data [5]. Recent work has proposed Integrated Ecological Interface Design (iEID) to support means-end reasoning in real SOC workflows. The approach aims to address challenges such as severity assignment in security incidents, incorporating functional models that map decision-making elements into interface design [10].

Security Operations Centers (SOCs) integrate people, processes, and technologies to identify, detect, and mitigate threats in networks and critical infrastructure, typically relying on a mixture of automated detection tools and human interpretation via dashboards [11]. Research on SOC visualization highlights the need for advanced data presentation approaches that can support analysts' situational awareness and decision-making under high pressure [12]. Systematic reviews on Cyber Situational Awareness (CSA) visualizations show that the majority of existing visualization techniques focus on perceptual-level (i.e., basic threat awareness) rather than supporting higher levels of comprehension and projection, revealing gaps in how dashboards present both threat impact and response planning data to different stakeholder groups [13]. Practical work also explores how SIEM data and structured threat frameworks (e.g., MITRE ATT&CK) can be integrated into interactive dashboards to enhance coverage understanding, detection gaps, and situational analysis in SOC environments [14].

3 Methodological Concepts

3.1 Abstraction Hierarchy

The abstraction hierarchy is a framework for representing a workspace in a way relevant to interface design. It describes the system architecture as a multi-layered model with several levels of abstraction, which together represent both the goal of the system and the way in which it achieves this goal. There are two dimensions of abstraction that operate simultaneously: means-end abstraction and part-whole abstraction [20]. The means-end dimension captures the relationships between ends, functions, and physical elements by linking higher-level goals (why) with lower-level mechanisms (how). Each level defines both the means for the next higher level and the goals to be achieved with the means of the next level. The part-whole abstractions decompose or aggregate elements at each level of the means-end abstraction. Rather than displaying arbitrary data points, EID-based interfaces take into account the relationships defined within the hierarchy, either visually or through interaction, making both higher-level goals and lower-level system states perceptible to the user. This enables operators not only to detect deviations, but also to explore and understand their causes and effects [21]. The means-end relationships, which are often represented by the "why-what-how" connections between levels, thus serve as the backbone for supporting cognitive flexibility and situational awareness in complex systems.

The functional purpose of the AI-Aware SIEM is to ensure the secure and robust operation of ML models in defense systems, detect and mitigate cyber attacks or failures in ML pipelines, and maintain trust in the operation and continuity of the mission. The abstract functions serve to maintain the robustness of the model against unwanted inputs, disturbances, etc., ensure accurate and trustworthy predictions in different contexts, minimize anomaly detection and response time, and maximize the explainability of ML results. The general functions are the subtasks that are performed to fulfill the abstract functions. These include monitoring the performance of the ML models in real time, classifying threat types based on rules and information, generating countermeasures and impact assessments, and performing root cause analysis of errors using visual analytics. The physical functions define the underlying mechanisms, algorithms, services, or tools required to implement the general functions of the system. In the context of AI-Aware SOC, these are data quality checks, visualization modules (cockpit), log collection and correlation engine, threat taxonomy classifier, and integrated response orchestration. Lastly, the physical forms are the components that make up the system. These can also be regarded as the specific elements that are presented to the operator at the interface level, such as assets deployed, specific network components, and logs, etc. By structuring information according to the Abstraction Hierarchy, the AI-Aware SIEM cockpit can display higher-level mission objectives linked to subordinate model and sensor behavior, ensuring that both strategic and operational perspectives remain connected. In combination with the decision ladder, this framework systematically supports the operator's thought process, from the perception of anomalies to diagnosis and target selection to the implementation and evaluation of corrective measures. Figure 1 depicts the hierarchy and relation among the levels.

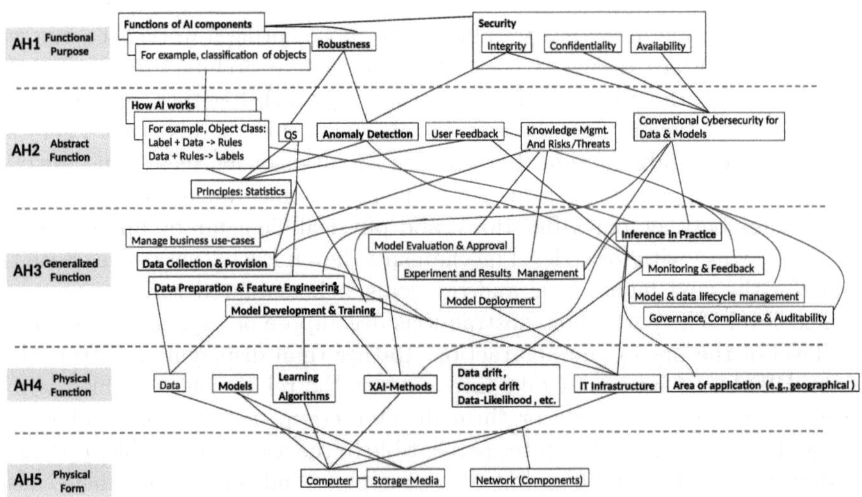

Fig. 1. Abstraction Hierarchy of IT-system with AI components including MLOps perspective.

3.2 Skill-Rule-Knowledge Taxonomy

The Skill-Rule-Knowledge (SRK) framework describes how operators shift between three qualitatively different modes of cognitive engagement depending on how familiar and well-structured a situation is, and critically, how information needs to be presented differently at each level to support effective action. At the **skill-based** level, behavior is automatic and perception-driven. An experienced SOC analyst does not consciously read every metric on their dashboard, they *notice* that something looks wrong before they can articulate what. A cluster of red nodes in the asset-risk graph, or a KPI counter that has jumped overnight are perceived as deviations from an expected visual pattern before any deliberate interpretation occurs. Rasmussen [16] describes this information as *signals*, continuously tracked, responded to through practiced sensorimotor routines, with minimal attentional load. At the **rule-based** level, the analyst has moved from noticing to recognizing. The information becomes a *sign*, indicating a type of known situation that calls for a known response. For instance, when a metric trend line shows detection rate declining across consecutive evaluations, they apply the associated procedure: flag the alert, escalate to SOC, and initiate retraining. The rule may live in a playbook or an SOP, but in experienced operators it has been internalized to the point where recognition and response feel nearly automatic. At the **knowledge-based** level, the information must function as *symbols* because the situation does not match anything previously encountered. The behavior is enabled by graph-based modeling and exploratory analytics, which fuel deeper reasoning and adaptive problem solving. By structuring security data (alerts, assets, incidents, models, risks, etc.) as a graph with rich interconnections, analysts can traverse attack paths, infer causal relationships, and explore scenarios that do not conform to predefined patterns.

By aligning visual analytics with the SRK taxonomy, the AI-aware SIEM dashboard can better allocate cognitive load across human and automated processes

4 Implications in Cockpit Design

The proposed dashboard architecture addresses a fundamental challenge in Security Operations Center (SOC) environments that integrate machine learning operations (MLOps): the need to support heterogeneous cognitive demands within a single operational interface. SOC analysts do not operate at a fixed level of abstraction. During routine monitoring they perform rapid, pattern-driven assessments; during active incident response they engage in structured rule-following; during novel or ambiguous threat scenarios they reason causally from first principles. A dashboard that serves only one of these modes fails the operator in the moments that matter most. The foundation of the dashboard is a graph-based data model that represents the operational environment according to the levels of the abstraction hierarchy whose node types are derived from a formal data model spanning the MLOps and cybersecurity SOC domains. Node types include Models, Datasets, Assets, Incidents, Alerts, Indicators, Risks,

Threats, Runs, and Pipelines. Each node carries typed properties and participates in directional, typed relationships with temporal metadata.

4.1 Situation Overview

The graph structure of the data serves as the semantic substrate from which interactive dashboard views are derived. The information shown on the dashboard is also organized according to different abstraction levels, such that the overall system status is seen first to understand what is happening, and on drilling down, an operator can investigate why it happened and how it can be analyzed. Figure 2 shows how the individual levels are distributed across dedicated dashboards that are linked via shared filters.

At the top is the Functional Purpose level, represented by the status overview of operational risk map and Key Performance Indicators (KPIs), which convey the system's overall operational integrity. These visualizations enable operators to immediately recognize operational readiness and overall system reliability. This level supports Endsley's Level 3 situational awareness [24] and shows how the current system state impacts mission objectives. At the next level, abstract functions define what good performance means, regardless of how it is achieved. In the dashboard, this is reflected in abstract metrics such as the model confidence score, relative detection rates, the degree of explainability, and false alarm rates.

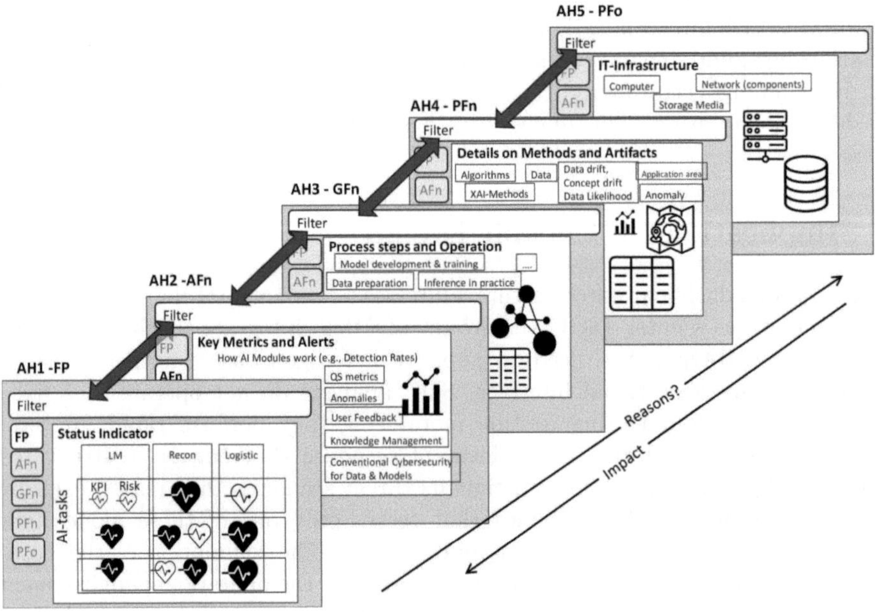

Fig. 2. Dashboards for situation awareness based on abstraction hierarchy.

Below that, the level of generalized functions captures how the system conceptually achieves its goals. In this case, we consider the complete development lifecycle of the AI modules. This layer contributes most to understanding the system. Concept graph shows where threats, risks, and alerts are located, thereby enabling causal inferences about the causes of anomalies.

The level of physical functions translates these conceptual activities into observable system mechanisms. Here, the detailed diagnostic dashboard provides, for example, interactive visualizations of specific feature drift charts and anomaly indicators. These elements make the underlying calculations and processes visible, enabling operators to understand not only what happened, but also why. Finally, the physical form encompasses the tangible artifacts, such as the technical infrastructure as well as the data used for training (including metadata). Detailed information on all artifacts can be accessed via tables. The seamless integration between these levels ensures that users can move up the hierarchy at any time to understand the purpose, or down to investigate the cause, which supports the important EID principle of linking means and ends.

4.2 Visualizations to Support Skill-Rule-Knowledge Behavior

The SRK framework distinguishes three qualitatively different modes of human cognitive behavior in complex socio-technical systems. The dashboard satisfies behaviors through a layered visualization architecture organized around the scenario life cycle, from steady-state monitoring through degradation detection, cross-domain escalation, impact radius assessment, incident formalization, and post-incident audit. Figure 3 illustrates the features and layout of the dashboard.

Skill-based behavior is supported by visualizations that encode system state as pre-attentive perceptual attributes such as color, spatial position, and motion, that can be assessed without deliberate reading. The primary instrument is the concept graph at the top level, which is zoom-able and features embedded per-node visualizations with colored status indicators reflecting the current health or state of each component. Edges between nodes can be highlighted to reveal dependencies and relationships across the system, providing an intuitive means of tracing how issues propagate through the architecture. The dashboard further supports cross-filtering across multiple views, including detailed graph visualizations enabling comparative analysis of two or more models or assets. This allows operators to identify shared characteristics, overlapping failure patterns, and common root causes, supporting more effective and targeted diagnosis of system-wide issues. At the top level, a Domain-by-AI-tasks risk matrix provides a complementary overview, where each cell displays the performance of the models deployed and the risks associated with it. Rule-based behavior is supported through structured rule application and triage filters. Known alert handling procedures and detection logic are surfaced in the interface via consistent filtering, labeling, and procedural workflows [10], according to MITRE ATT&CK techniques. This not only improves situational clarity, but also ensures that analysts can reliably apply standard operating procedures and maintain consistency in decision-making when handling common or expected events. Knowledge-based behavior is supported by visualizations that make the causal structure of the situation explicit and traversable, enabling the analyst to construct or verify a mental model of an unfamiliar failure scenario. The data graph that presents the full path of affected nodes, correlated nodes, and causation nodes. Supporting the knowledge-based layer are the spider diagram per affected asset type showing capability coverage before and after model degradation, enabling the analyst to reason about the operational consequences of a technical failure, and a subgraph showing the affected model, the assets associated with it, and also the entities which are common to multiple affected models/assets to analyze causal relationships.

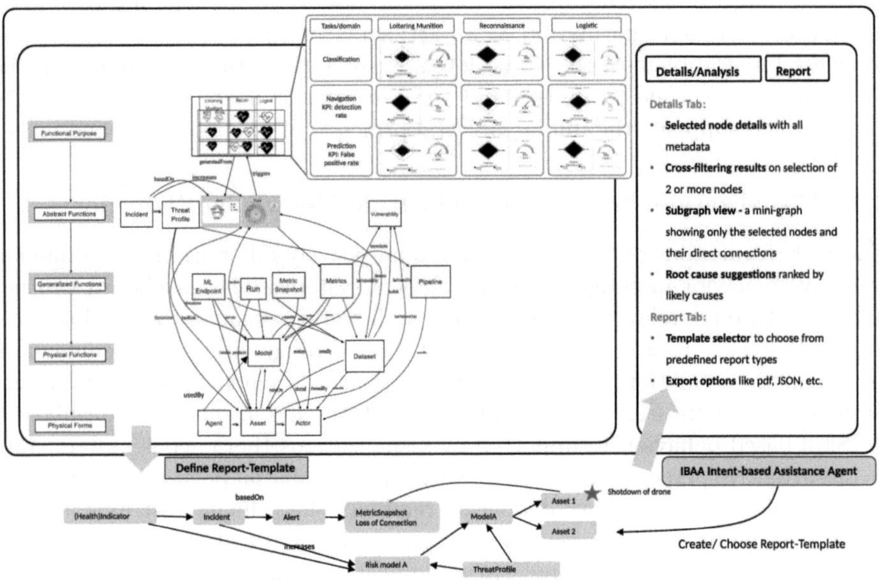

Fig. 3. Interactive dashboard layout showing navigation and details.

To illustrate the reporting workflow, consider a concrete operational scenario in which a loitering munition asset (here, a drone) loses connection unexpectedly, indicated by the"Loss of Connection" metric snapshot, which is flagged as a critical incident and propagated upward through the health indicator chain, triggering an alert linked to the affected asset and its associated model. This incident trace, spanning from the low-level health indicator through the alert, metric snapshot, model, and ultimately the compromised asset, forms the basis of a structured incident report. Such a scenario represents one instantiation of a broader library of report templates, which may also include threat assessment reports or vulnerability exposure reports tailored to different operational needs. Rather than requiring the operator to manually navigate this chain and assemble a report, the IBAA (Intent-Based Assistance Agent) can ask the operator to just choose the template and then it will populate it with the traced entities, risk scores, and timeline of events. The operator may also instruct the IBAA to create a custom template for novel incident types not yet covered by the existing library, making the reporting mechanism both reactive to known failure patterns and extensible to emerging operational scenarios.

5 Evaluation of EID-Based Dashboards and Interfaces

5.1 Goals of Evaluation

Evaluating interfaces such as the SOC requires demonstrating that the design improves overall operator's performance in monitoring, diagnosing, and responding to anomalous conditions. The system should also reduce cognitive load, allowing operators to allocate mental resources more efficiently during both routine and critical tasks. Moreover, the design should also aim to enhance operator trust and auditability, meaning that users feel confident in the system's outputs and can trace and justify decisions based on the displayed information. Finally, the interface design should also support correct SRK mode transition, ensuring that the operators can engage in appropriate cognitive strategy, whenever and wherever it is needed.

A number of studies have adopted empirical evaluations to compare EID designs against traditional or baseline interfaces [17]. One notable example applied EID principles to network management displays and evaluated the resulting interface against an industry standard tool in detection and diagnosis tasks [6]. Although the traditional tool offered slightly faster detection, the EID interface faster and more accurate diagnosis, and was qualitatively preferred by professional operators, indicating enhanced comprehension and problem-solving support in complex tasks. In the domain of industrial power plants, studies have shown that operators show broader performance benefits when using an ecological interface. It has been shown to improve situational awareness, particularly in the monitoring and detection phase, revealing that it can enhance early recognition of system anomalies in complex tasks [18,19]. An empirical evaluation of an ecological interface for military command and control showed that ecological displays were easier to learn and apply and improved usability [22].

5.2 Design of Evaluation

To evaluate the current system specifically, a mixed methods evaluation strategy is appropriate, combining both quantitative performance metrics and qualitative cognitive measures. Standard approaches include the Situation Awareness Global Assessment Technique (SAGAT) [23], and usability instruments such as the System Usability Scale (SUS) or Questionnaire for User Interaction Satisfaction (QUIS) to capture subjective ease-of-use and cognitive support. In SAGAT, freeze probes are inserted at three moments in a pre-constructed operational scenario. At each freeze, participants respond to queries drawn directly from the simulation at that moment in time to determine their knowledge of the situation, which are later on evaluated against the data from simulation computers. This multi-faceted evaluation not only aligns with demonstration practices in HCI and SOC dashboard research but also reflects the EID literature's emphasis on situation awareness and cognitive workload as key outcome variables. Overall, EID-based dashboards have been shown to support more accurate diagnostic decision making both experimentally and through professional user feedback, deeper system understanding, and reduced cognitive strain in complex monitoring tasks compared with traditional designs.

References

1. Vicente, K.J., Rasmussen, J.: Ecological interface design: theoretical foundations. IEEE Trans. Syst. Man Cybern. **22**(4), 589–606 (1992). https://doi.org/10.1109/21.156574
2. Zhang, X., Jaskolka, J.: Conceptualizing the secure machine learning operations (SecMLOps) paradigm. In: IEEE 22nd International Conference on Software Quality, Reliability and Security (QRS), Guangzhou, China, 2022, pp. 127–138 (2022). https://doi.org/10.1109/QRS57517.2022.00023
3. Paassen, V., Marinus, M., Ellerbroek, J., Comans, J., Borst, C., Mulder, M.: Ecological interface design for aircraft guidance and conflict avoidance. In: ASME 2012 11th Biennial Conference on Engineering Systems Design and Analysis, ESDA 2012. 2, pp. 889–896 (2012). https://doi.org/10.1115/ESDA2012-82977
4. Lintern, G., Miller, D., Baker, K.: Work centered design of a Usaf mission planning system. In Proceedings of the Human Factors and Ergonomics Society Annual Meeting, vol. 46, pp. 531–535 (2002). https://doi.org/10.1177/154193120204600366
5. Bennett, K.B., Bryant, A., Sushereba, C.: Ecological interface design for computer network defense. Hum. Factors **60**(5), 610–625 (2018). https://doi.org/10.1177/0018720818769233
6. Burns, C.M., Kuo, J., Ng, S.: Ecological interface design: a new approach for visualizing network management. Comput. Netw. **43**(3), 369–388 (2003). https://doi.org/10.1016/S1389-1286(03)00287-1. ISSN 1389-1286
7. Rasmussen, J.: The role of hierarchical knowledge representation in decision making and system management. IEEE Trans. Syst. Man. Cybern. **SMC-15**(2), 234–243 (1985). https://doi.org/10.1109/TSMC.1985.6313353
8. Rasmussen, J.: Skills, rules, and knowledge; signals, signs, and symbols, and other distinctions in human performance models. IEEE Trans. Syst. Man. Cybern. **SMC-13**(3), 257–266 (1983). https://doi.org/10.1109/TSMC.1983.6313160
9. Borst, C., Bijsterbosch, V.A., van Paassen, M.M., Mulder, M.: Ecological interface design: supporting fault diagnosis of automated advice in a supervisory air traffic control task. Cogn. Technol. Work **19**(4), 545–560 (2017). https://doi.org/10.1007/s10111-017-0438-y
10. Negi, R., Pranaikumar, A., Singh, A., Kant, V.: Supporting Means-Ends Reasoning In Cybersecurity-critical Case Management Using Integrated Ecological Interface Design Process. INCOSE HSI 2024
11. Vielberth, M., Böhm, F., Fichtinger, I., Pernul, G.: Security operations center: a systematic study and open challenges. IEEE Access **8**, 227756–227779 (2020). https://doi.org/10.1109/ACCESS.2020.3045514

12. Axon, L., AlAhmadi, B.A., Nurse, J.R.C., Goldsmith, M., Creese, S.: Data presentation in security operations centres: exploring the potential for sonification to enhance existing practice. J. Cybersecur. **6**(1), tyaa004 (2020). https://doi.org/10.1093/cybsec/tyaa004
13. Liuyue, J., Asangi, J., Mehwish, N., Marthie, G., Mansooreh, Z., Babar, M.A.: Systematic literature review on cyber situational awareness visualizations. IEEE Access, **10**, 1–1 (2022). https://doi.org/10.1109/ACCESS.2022.3178195
14. Diaz, S.L., Pastrana, S., Nadeem, A.: Critical path prioritization dashboard for alert-driven attack graphs. arXiv (2023). https://doi.org/10.48550/arXiv.2310.13079
15. Lin, C., Shiang, W., Chuang, C., Liou, J.: Applying the skill-rule-knowledge framework to understanding operators' behaviors and workload in advanced main control rooms. Nuclear Eng. Des. 270, 176–184 (2014). https://doi.org/10.1016/j.nucengdes.2013.12.051. ISSN 0029-5493
16. Rasmussen, J.: Skills, rules, and knowledge; signals, signs, and symbols, and other distinctions in human performance models. IEEE Trans. Syst., Man, Cybern. **SMC-13**(3), 257–266 (1983). https://doi.org/10.1109/TSMC.1983.6313160
17. Vicente, K.J.: Ecological interface design: progress and challenges. Hum. Factors: J. Hum. Factors Ergon. Soc. **44**(1), 62–78 (2002). https://doi.org/10.1518/0018720024494829
18. Burns, C.M., et al.: Evaluation of ecological interface design for nuclear process control: situation awareness effects. Hum. Factors: J. Hum. Factors Ergon. Soc. **50**(4), 663–679 (2008). https://doi.org/10.1518/001872008X312305
19. Jamieson, G.A.: Ecological interface design for petrochemical process control: an empirical assessment. IEEE Trans. Syst. Man Cybern. Part A Syst. Hum. **37**(6), 906–920 (2007). https://doi.org/10.1109/TSMCA.2007.897583
20. Lind, M.: Making sense of the abstraction hierarchy in the power plant domain. Cogn.Tech. Work **5**, 67–81 (2003). https://doi.org/10.1007/s10111-002-0109-4
21. Lau, N., et al.: Ecological interface design in the nuclear domain: an application to the secondary subsystems of a boiling water reactor plant simulator. IEEE Trans. Nucl. Sci. **55**(6), 3579–3596 (2008). https://doi.org/10.1109/TNS.2008.2005979
22. Hall, D.S., Shattuck, L., Bennett, K.: Evaluation of an ecological interface design for military command and control. J. Cogn. Eng. Decis. Making **6**, 165–193 (2012). https://doi.org/10.1177/1555343412440696
23. Endsley, M.R.: Situation awareness global assessment technique (SAGAT). In: Proceedings of the IEEE 1988 National Aerospace and Electronics Conference, Dayton, OH, USA, vol. 3, pp. 789–795 (1988). https://doi.org/10.1109/NAECON.1988.195097
24. Endsley, M.R.: Toward a theory of situation awareness in dynamic systems. Hum. Factors J. **37**(1), 32–64 (1995). https://doi.org/10.1518/001872095779049543

Gender by Design: Visual Communication in Digital Health Platforms for Women's Health

Luciana Terceiro[1(✉)], Maria Hägglund[1,2], and Anna Kharko[1,3]

[1] Participatory eHealth and Health Data Research Group, Department of Women's and Children's Health, Uppsala University, Uppsala, Sweden
luciana.terceiro@uu.se

[2] Uppsala University Hospital, Uppsala, Sweden

[3] Centre for Primary Care and Health Services Research, University of Manchester, Manchester, UK

Abstract. Digital Health Platforms (DHPs) have expanded rapidly, offering new possibilities for healthcare access, monitoring, education, and treatment across diverse contexts. Despite their potential, DHPs risk reinforcing existing health inequities due to unequal access to technology, limited digital or health literacy, and poor consideration of users' social contexts. Several health frameworks, including the World Health Organisation, emphasise that digital health (DH) must be ethical, safe, inclusive, and aligned with the social determinants of health. Within this landscape, women's healthcare remains markedly under-researched, receiving a disproportionately small share of DH investment, contributing to persistent gaps in care quality and raising concerns about bias in women-focused DHPs. This study examined how graphic user interface design in women-focused DHPs functions as a mechanism of mediation and control, reinforcing norms and stereotypes and shaping subjectivities. The study adopts an abductive approach, applying critical discourse analysis and feminist and queer theories to a corpus of women-focused DHPs identified through a survey of peer-reviewed research databases. The study analyses how dominant aesthetics, often characterised by pink colours, infantilised illustrations, and care-oriented imagery, reinforce normative femininity, gender stereotypes, and power hierarchies. By integrating critical discourse analysis and feminist and queer theoretical lenses, the study examines how visual interfaces reveal intersectional gaps in representation and proposes alternative approaches that expand inclusivity and diversity within DH.

Keywords: eHealth · Digital Health · Digital Health Platforms · Women's Health · Mobile Applications · Critical Feminist Theory · GUI · Femtech

1 Introduction

Digital Health Platforms (DHPs) have expanded rapidly in recent years, offering new possibilities for healthcare. DHPs serve a broad range of purposes, from health education and informational support to medication adherence, chronic disease monitoring, and a variety of treatments across diverse populations and contexts [31]. These platforms take

C. Stephanidis et al. (Eds.): HCII 2026, CCIS 3047, pp. 268–281, 2026.
https://doi.org/10.1007/978-3-032-30552-7_25

the form of websites, mobile applications, and increasingly, other interfaces such as for smartwatches and extended reality devices. Although figures vary across sources, estimates suggest that between 100,000 and 350,000 health-related mobile applications are available in Apple and Google app stores alone [2]. DHPs can extend healthcare reach beyond geographical constraints, accommodate users with limited mobility or rigid schedules, and support greater individual autonomy in health management.

Despite their potential, DHPs can introduce or intensify social inequalities. Key challenges include unequal access to devices and Internet connectivity, inadequate adaptation to varying levels of digital and health literacy, and insufficient understanding of the social contexts of intended users. Without careful attention, DHP development risks widening the digital divide [19, 20, 39], rendering access to care even more uneven for already marginalised populations. Addressing these risks requires that DHP development be grounded in social determinants of health [24], considering structural, environmental, social, individual, and biological factors that can affect health outcomes. The World Health Organisation underscores this imperative, asserting that digital health services must be integrated into healthcare systems in an ethical, safe, reliable, and equitable manner, guided by principles of transparency, accessibility, privacy, and confidentiality [42].

Within the broader DHP landscape, platforms addressing women's health constitute a notable and underserved category. Although women represent approximately half of the global population, digital health investment in women's health accounts for just 8.5% of the total investment [15]. Research investment in women's health also falls short of demonstrated need, signalling a persistently undervalued area [35]. The consequences are material: conditions such as endometriosis and pregnancy complications remain chronically under-researched and frequently undiagnosed [12], contributing to a health gap in which women spend approximately 25% of their lives in worse health than men [12].

The limitations of women's digital health go beyond economic investment. Technology is not a neutral artefact: from its conception and development, it carries specific worldviews, assumptions, and embedded values. The field of Information Technology exhibits a pronounced gender imbalance, with women accounting for approximately 26.7% of the workforce [5]. The result is a technology that does not fully reflect women's needs and values. In digital health, women remain marginalised from decisions across research, design, development, and investment processes. Patients or users may not immediately perceive these structural exclusions; however, this systematic exclusion is materialised through the visual interfaces that mediate access to the digital solutions and shape interaction. Graphical user interfaces (GUIs) do not merely display information; they also construct subject positions, signal who belongs, and communicate assumptions about who the intended user is. As Davis argues, interfaces provide affordances that shape what actions and identities are made possible [7]; the GUI thus functions as a kind of "gatekeeper" [40], signalling who has access, in what capacity, and on whose terms. Colour, iconography, photographic representation, and illustration style collectively constitute a visual discourse that defines who counts as a health subject and whose experiences are centred within health technology. From a Critical Discourse Analysis (CDA) perspective, these choices may reflect and reinforce power relations embedded in design practice; from feminist and queer perspectives, they raise urgent questions about which bodies are made visible, which are rendered absent, and what ideological work that visibility, or invisibility, performs.

Drawing on feminist and queer theories, this research analyses the visual language of DHPs aimed at women, examining how GUI design functions as a mechanism of mediation and control. The study seeks to answer the following research questions:

RQ1. How do DHPs for women construct their visual communication narratives?
RQ2. What are the implications of these choices for the representation and inclusion of diverse women's health individuals?

2 Theoretical and Analytical Frameworks

This study is situated at the intersection of CDA and feminist and queer theoretical traditions. Together, these perspectives provide the conceptual foundation for examining how GUI in women's DHPs function not just as aesthetic configurations, but as sites where meanings about gender, health, and subjectivity are constructed and normalised.

Design is not a neutral practice. As Ehrnberger et al. argue, design shapes and reinforces social divisions, reproducing the gender structures that organise societies [10, 11]. Graphic elements such as typography, colour, and iconography carry culturally embedded gender codes that influence how digital artefacts are interpreted and by whom they are perceived as intended [28]. Technologies do not simply reflect existing social norms; they also participate in their reproduction, embedding dominant ideologies and contributing to what has been described as matrices of domination within technological systems [22]. This study therefore interrogates how visual interfaces represent women, and what articulations of femininity, embodiment, and health they produce and normalise [32].

To examine how DHPs construct their visual communication narratives (RQ1), CDA provides the overarching theoretical approach for understanding visual interfaces as discursive practices and as forms of social action that construct meaning and position subjects [13]. Applied to digital interfaces, CDA treats visual elements, such as colour palettes, illustrations, photographs, and iconography, as semiotic resources that communicate assumptions about who the user is, what health means, and which bodies belong within the space of care [16, 21]. Familiar and easily recognisable interface conventions can reduce cognitive effort and facilitate navigation [23], yet precisely because of their familiarity, they tend to naturalise the stereotypes and worldviews embedded within them [25]. CDA provides the framework to identify and analyse these visual components and to situate them within the broader social norms and stereotypes that shape and sustain them.

To address the implications of these choices for the representation of diverse women (RQ2), feminist theory extends CDA by foregrounding how gender operates within design practices and technological systems. An intersectional feminist approach recognises that representations of gender cannot be analysed in isolation but must be understood in relation to race, class, age, ability, and sexual and gender identity. This perspective interrogates whose bodies are positioned as normative health subjects and whose experiences remain marginalised, simplified, or invisible within digital health environments. This approach is complemented by queer theory, which draws critical attention not only to what is present in a visual field, but to what is structurally absent. The concept of 'queering' design, as proposed by Portinari [30], offers a means of disrupting these normative patterns: it provokes design to interrogate its own role, transforming it from an agent that reproduces normativity into one that opens new possibilities of existence and representation [30]. To queer DHP design is thus to question which bodies have access, on whose terms, and at what cost to those whose identities and experiences are excluded or distorted [22].

3 Methodology

3.1 Research Paradigm

The investigation is grounded in a feminist research paradigm and guided by the precepts of standpoint theory. Standpoint theory argues that mainstream natural and social sciences, despite claims of objectivity and neutrality, are often shaped by androcentric perspectives, a dominant masculine framework for producing and validating knowledge [4]. The feminist paradigm challenges this assumption by emphasising that knowledge should be rooted in lived experience. It further asserts that the systematically different experiences of women constitute a distinct and legitimate epistemic standpoint from which research can be generated and evaluated [17]. Adopting this paradigm, the present study analyses DHPs aimed at women through a feminist lens, enabling a critical examination of who is represented in this domain and which intersectional factors are at play. The research strategy is abductive, enabling an iterative movement between theoretical frameworks and empirical data [4].

3.2 Data Collection Method

The study analysed DHPs drawn from a corpus of peer-reviewed clinical research on women's health. Sixty-nine studies were selected from an initial pool of 10,457 records identified across seven databases, PubMed, IEEE Xplore, CINAHL, Scopus, Web of Science, APA PsycINFO, and ACM Digital Library, as part of a broader systematic literature review on DHPs conducted previously by the authors [38]. That review was not originally focused on women's health. The present study applied an additional selection layer to identify studies relevant to gender and design. Inclusion criteria required that studies: 1) focused on women's health conditions; 2) involved DHPs in the form of mobile applications or websites; 3) were designed to deliver a health intervention for a current health condition or health-related behaviour; and 3) included visual material, such as screenshots or interface images. Studies had to be published in English in peer-reviewed journals between 2018 and 2024. The dataset with included studies is publicly available at Zenodo [37]. No sensitive or personal data were collected, and the study presented no ethical concerns requiring formal review.

3.3 Analytical Method

In this study, CDA is operationalised through a systematic examination of the visual and semiotic elements that structure the user interface. The analysis treats these interface elements as discursive resources that contribute to shaping particular understandings of gender, health, and the intended user. Following corpus selection, the visual interfaces of each DHP were analysed using the visual materials published within or as supplementary material to the selected articles. The analysis focused on four visual dimensions: colour palette, iconography, photographic representation, and illustration representation. The analytical procedure followed an iterative process. First, interface elements were documented and categorised across the selected platforms. The visual material was organised on Figma software. Patterns were then identified and compared to detect recurring motifs, stylistic conventions, and representational strategies (see Fig. 1).

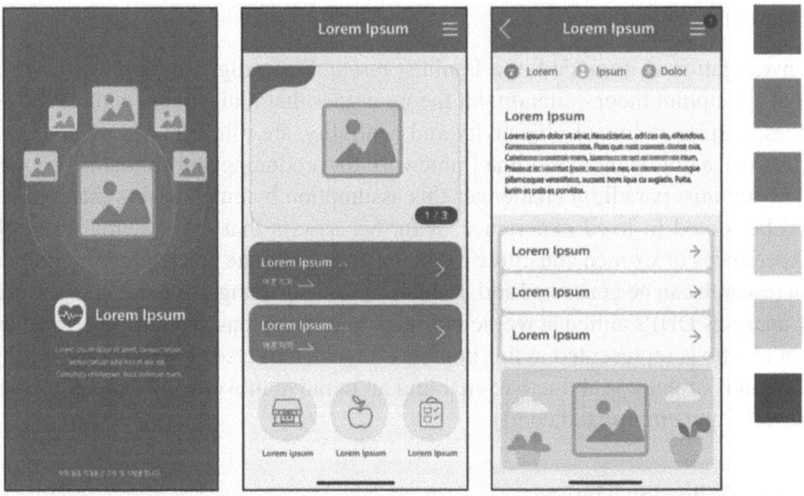

Fig. 1. A schematic representation of how the colour palettes were created. Available screenshots were organised on Figma software, and interface colours were collected as swatches. The first swatches represent the dominant colours.

To address RQ1, the observations were subsequently interpreted through CDA, allowing the analysis to connect platform's design choices to broader cultural discourses surrounding femininity, health, and embodiment. To address RQ2, each visual dimension was examined in relation to how it frames the platform visually and how it signals assumptions about users' identities, bodies, and health practices. Through feminist and queer lens, attention was paid not only to what is visually present within the interface but also to what is absent or marginalised. Patterns of visibility and omission were interpreted as discursive effects that shape which bodies, identities, and experiences are recognised as legitimate users of digital health technologies.

3.4 Positionality and Reflexivity

The first author acknowledges her role as an active participant in the research process and reflects on how her own subject position informs observation, interpretation, and analysis [29]. She identifies as a cisgender Latin woman with a professional background in design and a research focus on gender and technology since 2016. Occupying primarily an insider position, as a designer, a researcher in the field of DHPs, and a potential user of these technologies, this positionality is treated as a methodological resource rather than a limitation [9]. The insider perspective enables the author to engage with the analysis through lived experience, aligning with the feminist theoretical frameworks that guide this study.

4 Results

A total of 69 DHPs were included in this analysis. The resulting corpus spans a range of conditions and contexts, including breast cancer, pregnancy, prenatal and postnatal care, contraception, osteoporosis, postpartum depression, and cardiovascular health. Platforms addressing pregnancy and maternal health constituted the largest category, followed by breast cancer–related applications (see Table 1).

Table 1. Studies by health topics.

Health topic	Number of studies	Conditions
Pregnancy / Maternal Health	30 (43.5%)	Gestational diabetes management, prenatal and antenatal care support, pregnancy monitoring, labour support, pelvic floor muscle, maternal mental wellbeing during pregnancy
Breast Cancer	22 (31.9%)	Breast cancer rehabilitation programs, symptom monitoring during treatment, survivorship support tools, exercise and lifestyle interventions, patient-reported outcome monitoring
Sexual & Reproductive Health	4 (5.8%)	Contraception and reproductive education, sexual health information, period tracker
Polycystic Ovary Syndrome (PCOS)	2 (2.9%)	Self-management support
Mental Health	2 (2.9%)	Psychological wellbeing support, stress and mood monitoring tools
Other Health Topics	9 (13%)	General women's health support, lifestyle and health promotion tools, chronic disease management interventions

The studies were conducted across 29 different countries (see Table 2).

Visual material was first coded descriptively across four dimensions: colour palette, photographs, illustrations, and iconography. Through iterative coding, recurring visual

Table 2. Studies by continent.

Continent	Number of studies	Countries
Asia	26 (37.7%)	South Korea, Taiwan, Iran, China, Bangladesh, India, Malaysia, Saudi Arabia, Vietnam, Indonesia, Pakistan, China
Europe	18 (26.1%)	Netherlands, Spain, Denmark, Germany, Italy, Sweden, Norway, Serbia, Switzerland.
North America	16 (23.2%)	USA, Canada, Mexico
Oceania	4 (5.8%)	Australia
South America	4 (5.8%)	Brazil, Chile
Africa	1 (1.4%)	Ethiopia

patterns emerged, including dominant colour groupings, illustration and iconography conventions, and patterns in the representation of human bodies. These patterns are reported below across each dimension.

The most notable pattern across the dataset is the dominance of gender-coded colour palettes. Of the 69 platforms analysed, 38 (55. 1%) employed a palette in which pink or purple was the dominant colour, a proportion that substantially exceeds any other colour group (see Fig. 2).

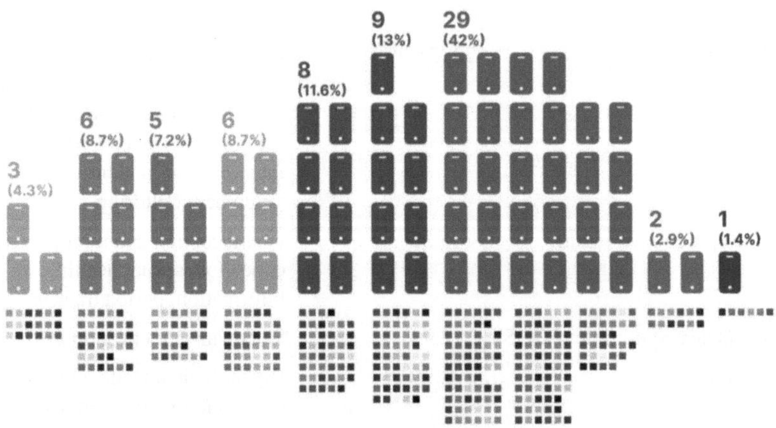

Fig. 2. Distribution of platforms according to their predominant colours.

The remaining 31 platforms used palettes in which yellow, green, blue, turquoise, salmon, red, or grey predominated, with each category appearing in 1.4%–11.6% of platforms (see Table 3). The concentration of pink and purple tones across a majority of women-focused DHPs points to a consistent, deliberate visual convention of gender coding.

Table 3. Palette distribution according to dominant colour.

Dominant colour	Count ($N = 69$)
Pink	29 (42%)
Purple	9 (13%)
Blue	8 (11.6%)
Turquoise	6 (8.7%)
Salmon	6 (8.7%)
Green	5 (7.2%)
Yellow	3 (4.3%)
Red	2 (2.9%)
Grey	1 (1.4%)

Regarding imagery, 39 of the 69 platforms presented photographs or illustrative images of people. The racial and ethnic composition of human representation was markedly uneven. Among the 39 platforms, 25 (64.1%) depicted white women exclusively. Black, Asian, Muslim, Latin, and Indian women appeared in a combined total of 12 platforms (see Table 4).

Table 4. Racial and ethnic representation in images presented in the platforms.

Representation	Count ($N = 39$)
White women	30 (76.9%)
Black women	5 (12.8%)
Muslim women	2 (5.1%)
Asian women	2 (5.1%)
Latin women	2 (5.1%)
Indian women	1 (2.6%)

Percentages do not sum to 100% due to some studies include more than one representation.

The representation of older women was limited: only 2 platforms included images of them. No platform portrayed individuals with visible disabilities. Men were depicted in only one illustration and one icon, representing a father figure, which suggests a heteronormative family structure. There was no depiction of other family structures.

Iconographic content was prevalent across all analysed platforms: 66 of the 69 DHPs displayed icons in their visual interface. Icons were primarily oriented toward functional purposes and organised into two main categories. The first concerns platform structure and navigation, such as icons for profile, settings, content areas, reminders, activities, and messaging (see Fig. 3A). The second concerns health monitoring resources: icons for tracking weight, blood pressure, glucose levels, steps taken, caloric intake, sleep quality, medication schedules, and mood (Fig. 3B). Together, these two categories construct health as a domain of individual self-management and quantifiable performance. Icons representing gender symbols were identified in only a few studies: six platforms displayed gendered icons featuring elements associated with female representation, such as dresses and long hair (Fig. 3C).

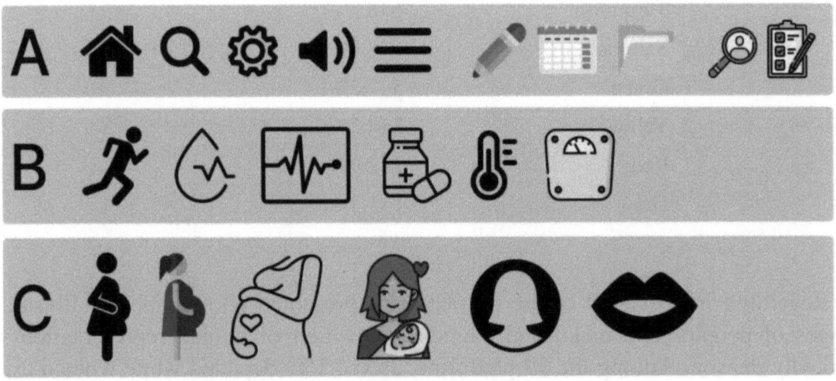

Fig. 3. Illustrative sample of icon types and styles.

5 Discussion

Combining CDA alongside feminist and queer perspectives, this study examines how the visual design of women-focused DHPs constructs narratives of women's health and shapes which bodies and identities are recognised as legitimate users of digital health technologies.

Women-focused DHPs display a remarkably consistent visual grammar characterised by pink-dominant colour palettes, cartoon-like or "cute" aesthetics illustration styles, and imagery that places women primarily in reproductive and caregiving roles. Across the analysed GUI, a coherent visual discourse emerges in which the implied DHPs users are typically represented as or suggested to be white, cisgender, heterosexual, conventionally feminine, able-bodied, and young to middle-aged. CDA, combined with feminist and queer perspectives, reveals how these visual elements collectively stabilise assumptions about to whom women's digital health technologies are designed and whose bodies are rendered peripheral or invisible.

Colour plays a prominent role in shaping these meanings. The widespread use of pink, purple, salmon, and pastel tones reflect what feminist scholarship has described as the "pinkification" of women's health [14, 18, 36]. This visual regime has migrated from breast cancer awareness campaigns into a near-universal signifier for female healthcare. Such colour schemes communicate meaning before textual content is consumed, signalling both the intended audience and the kind of femininity associated with the platform. While this visual shorthand may enhance recognisability and usability, it simultaneously reinforces a narrow and binary conception of womanhood. In doing so, it excludes individuals who do not identify within this framework, including transgender men, nonbinary people, and other gender-diverse individuals who share many of the same health concerns but remain visually absent from these spaces [3, 27, 33].

Patterns of representation in photographic imagery further reinforce these exclusions. Across the dataset, whiteness frequently appears as the unmarked norm, presented as universal, while other racial identities remain marginal or absent [26]. This dynamic is particularly significant in platforms addressing conditions that disproportionately affect communities of colour, such as maternal health or gestational diabetes [8, 34]. When such platforms consistently depict white women, they reproduce structural inequities in whose health experiences are considered visible and central within design decisions. This absence shapes the perceived relevance and accessibility of these platforms for the populations they are intended to serve. For instance, although 26 studies (37.7%) were conducted in Asia, Asian, Indian, or Muslim women were identifiable in only 5 studies (12.8%). Illustrative conventions compound these dynamics.

The recurring use of stylised, "cute," or cartoon-like female avatars, often positioned as guides or educators, reflects a broader cultural expectation that women perform warmth and emotional accessibility even in contexts associated with expertise. These aesthetic choices soften authority through feminised visual language. At the same time, the representation of pregnancy and maternity through exclusively cisgender-feminine imagery reinforces cisnormative assumptions about reproduction. Transgender and nonbinary individuals who experience pregnancy are thereby rendered structurally invisible within platforms that directly address their health needs. The prevalence of pregnancy- and maternity-focused platforms within the sample may partially explain the predominant image representation. However, contemporary understandings of pregnancy have expanded beyond narrow depictions of young, cisgender women. Older pregnant individuals, transgender men, and nonbinary people are increasingly recognised within reproductive healthcare contexts [6, 33]. The continued dependence on conventional maternal imagery, therefore, reproduces a limited representation. Moreover, the relative absence of partners, family members, or broader care networks reinforces the idea that reproductive health and caregiving are primarily individual responsibilities carried by women [1]. In doing so, these visual narratives contribute to normalising the gendered distribution of care and the expectation that women manage reproductive health largely on their own.

Icon systems and tracking features further shape how health is conceptualised within these platforms. Despite appearing as functional elements, many icons emphasise self-monitoring metrics, such as weight, steps, calories, mood, or glucose levels, aligning with what has been described as a "quantified self" framework. Within this logic, health becomes a matter of individual measurement and personal responsibility [14].

Taken together, these design choices reveal that the creators of these platforms are not only deciding what to include but also determining what remains structurally absent, as pointed out by Yang [41]. The recurring invisibility of transgender and nonbinary people, racial diversity, older and disabled bodies, and non-heteronormative family structures reflects the continued organisation of digital health technologies around a narrow normative user. These absences have material implications, shaping who feels addressed by these platforms and whose health experiences remain marginalised within digital health design.

5.1 Limitations

Several limitations of this study warrant acknowledgement. The corpus was derived from a systematic review not originally designed to focus on women's health, which may have introduced selection gaps in the range of conditions and contexts represented. Additionally, visual analysis was constrained to the interface material published alongside each article, typically a limited number of screenshots, rather than access to complete platforms. This limitation restricts the comprehensiveness of visual analysis and may mean that patterns identified here do not fully capture the range of design choices in any given platform. Future research would benefit from direct access to complete platform interfaces and from purposively constructed corpora that account for a broader range of health conditions, geographic contexts, and target populations.

6 Conclusion

This study reveals a coherent and largely consistent visual discourse across women-focused DHPs, one that constructs the normative health subject through pink-dominant colour palettes, cisgender-feminine illustration conventions, and white-centred representation. These patterns are not incidental design choices but reflect and reproduce structural assumptions about whose bodies, identities, and health experiences count within digital health infrastructure. The visual interface, as this analysis demonstrates, is not a neutral medium: it is an active gatekeeper that shapes access, belonging, and the conditions of health-related self-understanding.

Addressing these patterns requires more than adding surface-level diversity. It demands a structural reimagining of design practice: interfaces that refuse to reproduce gender binaries, that incorporate representational diversity as a default rather than an exception, and that actively interrogate the norms structuring visual communication in health technology. Practically, this means diversifying the representation of health subjects across race, ethnicity, gender identity, age, body type, and ability; challenging the equivalence of women's health with reproductive and maternal identity; critically examining the ideological implications of colour conventions; and engaging transgender, nonbinary, and LGBTQ+ communities in participatory design processes.

The development of DHPs represents a significant opportunity to embed health equity, feminist values, and queer inclusivity into widely deployed healthcare infrastructure. Realising this potential requires moving beyond representation as an aesthetic add-on toward a foundational rethinking of who counts as a health subject, whose knowledge is authoritative, and what health ultimately means in its full social, political, and embodied complexity.

Disclosure of Interests. The authors have no competing interests to declare that are relevant to the content of this article.

References

1. Al-Mutawtah, M., et al.: Women's experiences of social support during pregnancy: a qualitative systematic review. BMC Pregnancy Childbirth. **23**(1), 782 (2023). https://doi.org/10.1186/s12884-023-06089-0
2. Aungst, T., et al.: The good, the bad, and the poorly designed: the mobile app stores are not a user-friendly experience for health and medical purposes. Digit. Health. **8**, 205520762210900 (2022). https://doi.org/10.1177/20552076221090038
3. Bauer, G.R., et al.: "I don't think this is theoretical; this is our lives": how erasure impacts health care for transgender people. J. Assoc. Nurses AIDS Care. **20**(5), 348–361 (2009). https://doi.org/10.1016/j.jana.2009.07.004
4. Blaikie, N.: Approaches to Social Enquiry: Advancing Knowledge. Polity, Cambridge (2007)
5. Chang, J.: Decoding the gender gap: unseen forces of inequity in IT. Gend. Work Organ. **33** (2025). https://doi.org/10.1111/gwao.70042
6. Chemim, A.K., et al.: Experiencing pregnancy at an advanced maternal age in a private hospital. Rev. Rene. **23**, e70958 (2022). https://doi.org/10.15253/2175-6783.20222370958
7. Davis, J.L.: How Artifacts Afford: The Power and Politics of Everyday Things. The MIT Press, Cambridge (2020)
8. Dickens, L.T.: Disparities in diabetes in pregnancy and the role of social determinants of health. Curr. Diab. Rep. **25**(1), 33 (2025). https://doi.org/10.1007/s11892-025-01587-1
9. Dwyer, S.C., Buckle, J.L.: The space between: on being an insider-outsider in qualitative research. Int J Qual Methods. **8**(1), 54–63 (2009). https://doi.org/10.1177/160940690900800105
10. Ehrnberger, K., et al.: Becoming the energy aware clock: revisiting the design process through a feminist gaze. In: Presented at the Nordes 2013: Experiments in Design Research (2013). https://doi.org/10.21606/nordes.2013.027
11. Ehrnberger, K., et al.: Visualising gender norms in design: meet the mega hurricane mixer and the drill Dolphia. Int. J. Des. **6**(3), 85–98 (2012)
12. Ellingrud, K., et al.: Closing the Women's Health Gap: A $1 Trillion Opportunity to Improve Lives and Economics. World Economic Forum (2024)
13. Fairclough, N.: Critical Discourse Analysis: The Critical Study of Language. Longman, London (1995)
14. Gibson, A.F., et al.: "If you grow them, know them": discursive constructions of the pink ribbon culture of breast cancer in the Australian context. Fem. Psychol. **24**(4), 521–541 (2014). https://doi.org/10.1177/0959353514548100
15. Growth, G.: Femtech's rise and roadblocks: digital health funding. Growth and Gaps. https://www.galengrowth.com/femtechs-rise-and-roadblocks-digital-health-funding-growth-and-gaps/. Last accessed 6 Dec 2025
16. Han, C.: How to do critical discourse analysis: a multimodal introduction. Aust. J. Linguist. **35**(4), 415–418 (2015). https://doi.org/10.1080/07268602.2015.1033673
17. Harding, S.G., Hintikka, M.B.: Discovering Reality: Feminist Perspectives on Epistemology, Metaphysics, Methodology, and Philosophy of Science. Springer, Dordrecht (1983). https://doi.org/10.1007/0-306-48017-4
18. Hughes, K., Wyatt, D.: The rise and sprawl of breast cancer pink: an analysis. Vis. Stud. **30**(3), 280–294 (2015). https://doi.org/10.1080/1472586X.2015.1017351
19. Jenkins, C.L., et al.: Digital health intervention design and deployment for engaging demographic groups likely to be affected by the digital divide: protocol for a systematic scoping review. JMIR Res. Protoc. **11**(3), e32538 (2022). https://doi.org/10.2196/32538
20. Krukowski, R.A., et al.: Digital health interventions for all? Examining inclusivity across all stages of the digital health intervention research process. Trials. **25**(1), 98 (2024). https://doi.org/10.1186/s13063-024-07937-w

21. Magalhães, I.: Critical discourse analysis and the semiotic construction of gender identities. DELTA. **21**(spe), 179–205 (2005). https://doi.org/10.1590/S0102-44502005000300011
22. de O. Martins, L.P.: Privilege and oppression: towards a feminist speculative design. In: Presented at the Design's Big Debates—DRS International Conference 2014 June 16 (2014)
23. Mazumder, F.K., Das, U.K.: Usability guidelines for usable user interface. Int. J. Res. Eng. Technol. **3**(9), 79–82 (2014)
24. Mechael, P.N.: State of gender in digital health: where we are and what needs to happen to maximize benefits for all. Womens Health Nurs. **31**(2), 81–87 (2025). https://doi.org/10.4069/whn.2025.06.25
25. Metaxa-Kakavouli, D., et al.: Gender-inclusive design: sense of belonging and bias in web interfaces. In: Proceedings of the 2018 CHI Conference on Human Factors in Computing Systems, pp. 1–6. ACM, Montreal (2018). https://doi.org/10.1145/3173574.3174188
26. Muñoz, J.E.: Disidentifications: Queers of Color and the Performance of Politics. University of Minnesota Press, Minneapolis (1999)
27. Norris, M., Borneskog, C.: The cisnormative blindspot explained: healthcare experiences of trans men and non-binary persons and the accessibility to inclusive sexual & reproductive healthcare, an integrative review. Sex. Reprod. Healthc. **32**, 100733 (2022). https://doi.org/10.1016/j.srhc.2022.100733
28. Oliveira, G.A.F., Lima, S.: Análise semântica de capas tipográficas de livros feministas: discussões sobre performatividade de gênero. Rev. Bras. Des. Inf. **18**(2), 1–26 (2021)
29. Olmos-Vega, F.M., et al.: A practical guide to reflexivity in qualitative research: AMEE Guide No. 149. Med. Teach. **45**(3), 241–251 (2023). https://doi.org/10.1080/0142159X.2022.2057287
30. Portinari, D.: Queerizar o Design. Arcos Des. **10**(1) (2017). https://doi.org/10.12957/arcosdesign.2017.30937
31. Rosa, C., et al.: Using digital technologies in clinical trials: current and future applications. Contemp. Clin. Trials. **100**, 106219 (2021). https://doi.org/10.1016/j.cct.2020.106219
32. Sanchez, A.: Hombre, varones y sociedades de la diferencia (sobre la posibilidad de penetrar a la masculinidad). In: XI Jornadas de Sociología. Facultad de Ciencias Sociales, Buenos Aires (2015)
33. Sbragia, J.D., Vottero, B.: Experiences of transgender men in seeking gynecological and reproductive health care: a qualitative systematic review. JBI Evid. Synthesis. **18**(9), 1870–1931 (2020). https://doi.org/10.11124/JBISRIR-D-19-00347
34. Shen, J.J., et al.: Disparities in adverse maternal outcomes among five race and ethnicity groups. J. Womens Health. **31** (2022). https://doi.org/10.1089/jwh.2021.0495
35. Smith, K.: Women's health research lacks funding—these charts show how. https://www.nature.com/immersive/d41586-023-01475-2/index.html. Last accessed 6 Dec 2025
36. Sulik, G.A.: Pink Ribbon Blues: How Breast Cancer Culture Undermines Women's Health. Oxford University Press, Oxford (2010)
37. Terceiro, L.: Dataset - HCII26 poster "Gender by design: visual communication in digital health platforms for women's health". https://zenodo.org/doi/10.5281/zenodo.19069469 (2026). https://doi.org/10.5281/ZENODO.19069469
38. Terceiro, L., et al.: Research participants' engagement and retention in digital health interventions research: protocol for mixed methods systematic review. JMIR Res. Protoc. **14**, e65099 (2025). https://doi.org/10.2196/65099
39. Veinot, T.C., et al.: Good intentions are not enough: how informatics interventions can worsen inequality. J. Am. Med. Inform. Assoc. **25**(8), 1080–1088 (2018). https://doi.org/10.1093/jamia/ocy052
40. Voinea, D.V.: Reconceptualizing gatekeeping in the age of artificial intelligence: a theoretical exploration of artificial intelligence-driven news curation and automated journalism. Journalism Media. **6**(2), 68 (2025). https://doi.org/10.3390/journalmedia6020068

41. Yang, Y.: Gender uptake: theorizing the semiotics of (un)doing gender. Sociol. Theory. **43**(4), 360–384 (2025). https://doi.org/10.1177/07352751251368897
42. World Health Organization: Global Strategy on Digital Health 2020–2025. WHO, Geneva (2021)

Dark Mode vs. Light Mode: Effects on Mobile Focus, Readability, and Task Performance

Christopher Vargas(✉)

Independent Researcher, Los Angeles Metropolitan Area, USA
Chrismvarg@gmail.com

Abstract. Dark mode has become a widely adopted feature across mobile operating systems and applications, often promoted as reducing eye strain and improving visual comfort. Despite its popularity, empirical evidence regarding its effects on usability and task performance remains mixed. This poster extended abstract presents a pilot study examining how dark mode versus light mode affects focus, readability, and task performance on mobile devices. Using a within subjects design, 28 adult smartphone users completed reading, information search, and structured data entry tasks in both interface modes. Exploratory findings suggest that light mode supported faster reading performance, higher perceived readability, and lower cognitive workload, while dark mode was associated with greater visual comfort and lower reported eye strain. These findings indicate a tradeoff between efficiency and comfort, suggesting that interface mode selection should depend on task context, environment, and user preference.

Keywords: Dark Mode · Light Mode · Mobile Interfaces · Usability · Readability · Cognitive Load

1 Introduction

Visual themes have become a core component of modern interface customization. Among these themes, dark mode has emerged as one of the most requested and widely implemented features across smartphones, tablets, and desktop systems. Many users report preferring dark mode because it appears visually cleaner, more modern, and less fatiguing during prolonged use. In response, major platforms such as iOS and Android now provide system wide dark mode settings.

At the same time, light mode remains the default presentation style for many productivity tools, reading applications, and information dense interfaces. Traditional positive polarity displays (dark text on light backgrounds) have historically been associated with strong readability and efficient visual scanning. As a result, interface designers face an increasingly common question: should systems prioritize user comfort through dark mode or optimize performance through light mode?

Although online discussion strongly favors dark mode in many communities, research findings remain mixed. Some studies suggest positive polarity supports faster reading and improved comprehension, while others indicate darker displays may reduce

C. Stephanidis et al. (Eds.): HCII 2026, CCIS 3047, pp. 282–286, 2026.
https://doi.org/10.1007/978-3-032-30552-7_26

glare and discomfort in low light environments. However, many prior studies rely on static text samples rather than realistic interactive smartphone tasks.

The present study investigates whether dark mode and light mode differentially affect user focus, readability, and task performance during common mobile interactions. Understanding these tradeoffs may help designers make more evidence based decisions when implementing theme options

2 Related Work

Prior human computer interaction research has shown that display polarity can influence visual perception and reading efficiency. Positive polarity interfaces often provide stronger contrast sensitivity under standard lighting conditions, which may improve reading speed and text recognition. Negative polarity displays may reduce perceived luminance intensity and be experienced as more comfortable in dim environments.

Recent work has also emphasized the importance of subjective experience in interface evaluation. A design that performs well objectively may still be rejected if users perceive it as unpleasant or visually tiring. Likewise, users may prefer aesthetically appealing interfaces even when performance outcomes are weaker.

This distinction is especially relevant for dark mode. Many users strongly prefer dark mode, yet preference alone does not necessarily indicate better usability outcomes. Therefore, both objective metrics (speed, accuracy) and subjective metrics (comfort, workload, preference) should be considered together.

3 Method

3.1 Participants

Twenty eight adult smartphone users (ages 18–45) participated. All reported normal or corrected to normal vision and regular smartphone use.

3.2 Design

A within subjects experimental design was used. All participants completed tasks in both dark mode and light mode conditions. Condition order was counterbalanced to reduce learning and fatigue effects.

3.3 Apparatus

A smartphone prototype was created with identical layout, spacing, typography, and interaction components across conditions. Only text/background color polarity changed between modes. Screen brightness was fixed across sessions.

3.4 Tasks

Participants completed three task categories:

1. Reading comprehension tasks involving short passages and multiple choice questions.
2. Information search tasks requiring location of specific details in a structured interface.
3. Structured data entry tasks requiring form completion.

3.5 Measures

Objective measures included task completion time and task accuracy. Subjective measures included NASA-TLX workload ratings and 7 point Likert ratings for readability, comfort, and eye strain.

4 Results

Exploratory findings suggested that reading tasks were completed faster in light mode than dark mode. Reading accuracy was also slightly higher in light mode. Differences for information search and data entry tasks were comparatively small.

Participants reported lower perceived workload in light mode than dark mode. This suggests that higher readability may reduce mental effort during reading intensive tasks.

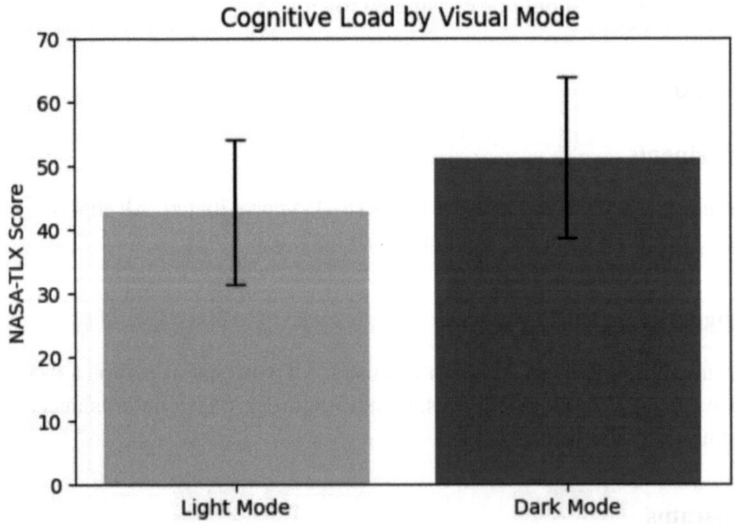

Fig. 1. Mean NASA-TLX cognitive load scores by visual mode. Error bars represent standard deviation.

As shown in Fig. 1, dark mode produced higher average workload scores than light mode. While both conditions remained within moderate ranges, the difference suggests interface theme may influence perceived mental demand during task completion.

5 Subjective Experience and Discussion

Participants rated light mode as more readable overall, while dark mode was rated as more visually comfortable. Dark mode was also associated with slightly lower reported eye strain. Most participants indicated a preference for dark mode for general use (Fig. 2).

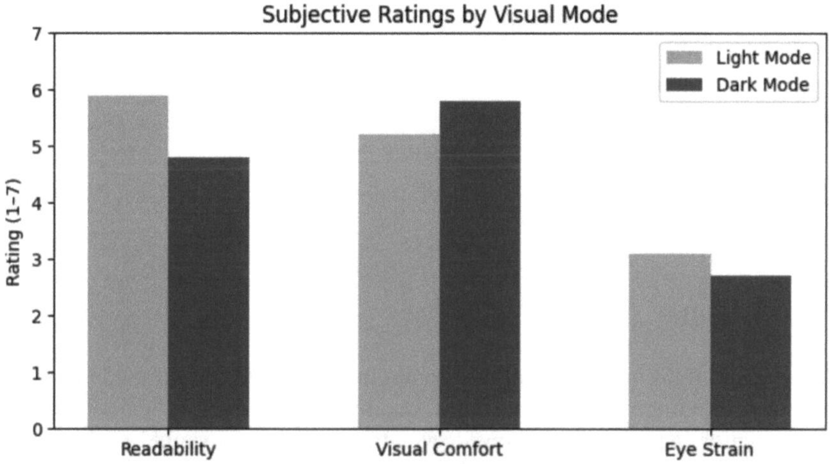

Fig. 2. Subjective ratings for readability, visual comfort, and eye strain across light and dark mode conditions.

These findings reinforce the distinction between performance oriented outcomes and preference oriented outcomes. Users may prefer dark mode because it feels more comfortable, even when objective performance is stronger in light mode.

One explanation is that light backgrounds may better support text clarity and rapid scanning, particularly for reading tasks. Conversely, dark backgrounds may reduce brightness intensity and create a more relaxed viewing experience during longer sessions or in dim environments.

6 Design Implications

The findings suggest several implications for mobile interface design:

1. Use light mode for reading heavy workflows where efficiency and comprehension are priorities.
2. Offer dark mode for extended use sessions or nighttime contexts.
3. Provide user controlled switching between modes.
4. Maintain strong contrast ratios and accessible typography in both themes.
5. Consider adaptive themes based on ambient lighting or usage context.

Rather than treating one mode as universally superior, systems should support flexible personalization.

7 Limitations and Future Work

This pilot study used a modest sample size and controlled environment. Real world smartphone use includes interruptions, movement, varying brightness, and diverse task contexts that may affect outcomes differently.

Future research should include:

- Larger and more diverse participant samples
- Longitudinal real world usage studies
- Age related comparisons
- OLED vs. LCD device comparisons
- Physiological measures such as eye tracking or pupillometry

These directions would provide a richer understanding of how visual themes affect behavior over time.

8 Conclusion

Dark mode and light mode each offer meaningful advantages. Light mode may better support faster reading, stronger readability, and lower workload, while dark mode may improve comfort and reduce perceived eye strain. Designers should evaluate theme decisions based on task demands, environmental context, and user preference rather than relying solely on trends or anecdotal claims.

This work contributes to ongoing HCI discussions regarding personalization, accessibility, and evidence based interface design.

References

1. Apple: Human Interface Guidelines: Dark Mode
2. Google: Material Design: Dark Theme
3. Buchner, A., Baumgartner, N.: Text-background polarity and performance
4. Piepenbrock, C., et al.: Display polarity and readability research
5. Sweller, J.: Cognitive load theory
6. Wickens, C. D.: Attention and workload in human factors

From Live-Action to Virtual Production: A New Workflow for Filmmaking

Weilong Wu(✉) and Haoyu Li

School of Film Television & Communication, Xiamen University of Technology, Xiamen, China
wu_academic@163.com

Abstract. **Objectives:** This article examines the integration of virtual production technology into film and television production, highlighting its role in the industry's digital transformation. Unlike traditional green-screen methods, which often isolate actors from their final environment, virtual production creates an immersive experience by combining LED virtual studios, motion capture, and real-time rendering engines. This allows actors to perform within visually coherent scenes, enhancing the authenticity and continuity of their performances. The "what you see is what you get" paradigm shifts portions of post-production work into the shooting stage, streamlining workflows and unlocking new creative possibilities.

In action filmmaking, virtual production's value is particularly evident. It enables the safe simulation of high-risk sequences—such as chases and explosions—within a controlled studio environment, reducing safety hazards and physical constraints. Real-time rendering technologies generate striking, immersive effects, while virtual camera systems offer directors unprecedented flexibility to adjust shots and capture dynamic tension in real time.

Ultimately, virtual production does not seek to replace on-location shooting entirely. Instead, it reconfigures production logic through digital mediation, fostering a new, industrialized paradigm of virtual-physical synergy. This transition expands the creative and technical horizons of action cinema, signaling a broader shift towards a more efficient and flexible future for the entire industry.

Keywords: Virtual Production · Action Cinema · Production Logic

1 Introduction

Today, the rapid evolution of digital technology and its deep integration with the film and television industry are driving a shift from traditional on-location shooting to digital virtual production. As the core driver, virtual production—based on real-time rendering, LED stages, motion capture, and camera tracking—integrates pre-production, filming, and post-production into a unified digital system, breaking the limits of space, time, and visual imagination. According to the Global Film and Television Production Technology Development Report (2025), the virtual production market is expected to grow at a CAGR of 27.6% (2020–2025), with over 60% of sci-fi, fantasy, and action films adopting it by

W. Wu and H. Li—These authors contributed equally to this study.

C. Stephanidis et al. (Eds.): HCII 2026, CCIS 3047, pp. 287–297, 2026.
https://doi.org/10.1007/978-3-032-30552-7_27

2025 [1]. Films such as Avatar: The Way of Water, Avatar: Fire and Ashes, and The Wandering Earth 2 demonstrate its value in improving efficiency and expanding visual expression [2].

Traditional on-location shooting, once dominant, relies on real environments to achieve realism but faces growing limitations, including environmental constraints, high costs for complex scenes, and technical challenges. Its linear workflow—pre-production, shooting, post-production—leads to long cycles, high communication costs, and potential mismatches between creative intent and final visuals. It can also create barriers in cross-cultural communication. In contrast, virtual production enables flexible digital scene construction and cultural adaptation, offering richer possibilities for global dissemination.

Current research mainly focuses on technical aspects and case studies, lacking systematic analysis of integration mechanisms, production logic, and impacts on creative thinking and cultural expression. In the Chinese context, insufficient localization further widens the gap between technology and creative needs [3].

This study examines the integration logic of virtual production, analyzing its framework, integration models, and application across production stages. It explores how the technology reshapes workflows, creativity, and industry systems, while identifying challenges such as technological adaptation, talent, and standards. Ultimately, it aims to support digital transformation, enhance cultural expression, and provide theoretical and practical guidance for the Chinese film industry's shift toward a digitally driven, integrated virtual-real production model.

2 Theoretical Foundation

2.1 The Theory of Technical Aesthetics in Film and Television Production

The theory of technical aesthetics in film and television examines the dialectical relationship between technology and artistic expression, emphasizing how technological development drives aesthetic evolution while being guided by artistic needs. The integration of technology and art forms its core logic. In The Work of Art in the Age of Mechanical Reproduction, Walter Benjamin argued that technological advancement reshapes both the production and reception of art, enabling mass dissemination. This provides a foundation for understanding how film and television, as mechanically reproduced art forms, have always been closely tied to technological innovation.

Traditional film and television aesthetics center on on-location shooting and the "imitation of reality," prioritizing realism and immediacy. With digital technology, aesthetics have shifted toward "constructing reality." Virtual production, as a key digital form, moves beyond imitation to create virtual scenes, characters, and effects, enabling precise realization of creative imagination and expanding audiovisual expression beyond physical limits [4].

The "ontology of the image" proposed by André Bazin highlights the camera's ability to record reality. Virtual production extends this from "recording reality" to "constructing reality." Although digitally created, virtual images are still grounded in artistic intention and narrative needs, thus retaining ontological value. Its aesthetic core lies in unifying "technical authenticity" and "artistic authenticity," where real-time rendering and LED technologies enhance realism and immersion while serving narrative expression.

While existing theories—such as Benjamin's and Bazin's—offer a framework for analyzing differences between virtual production and traditional filming, most research focuses on earlier digital techniques like CGI and green-screen compositing. There is still a lack of systematic analysis of virtual production aesthetics, especially under the "virtual-real integration" model. Therefore, this study builds on these theories to examine how virtual production reshapes technical aesthetics and expands artistic expression, providing a theoretical basis for its application.

2.2 Media Convergence Theory

Media convergence theory, proposed by American communication scholar Paul Levinson, emphasizes the integration of different media forms across technology, content, channels, and industry, leading to new media systems. Initially rooted in journalism and communication studies, it has expanded into film, television, and culture, becoming a key framework for analyzing digital-era convergence. In this context, virtual production represents the digital transformation of traditional film and television production through the integration of digital media technologies.

Henry Jenkins further develops this idea through "convergence culture," highlighting "participatory culture," where audiences shift from passive consumers to active participants. This perspective explains how virtual production lowers barriers to creation: digital tools enable broader participation in content production, while immersive visual effects transform viewing from passive observation to active engagement, enhancing audience experience and reshaping cultural consumption [5].

Although existing media convergence research provides important theoretical support, it mainly focuses on communication and distribution, with limited attention to production processes. There is still a lack of systematic analysis of how virtual production restructures workflows and industrial systems. Therefore, this study builds on media convergence theory to examine the integrated application of virtual production across the entire production process, exploring its role in industrial transformation and cultural innovation.

2.3 The Theory of Industrialized Film and Television Production

The theory of industrialized film and television production originates from industrial manufacturing concepts such as standardization, process optimization, and specialization. Its core is to apply industrial management models to film and television production to achieve efficiency, quality improvement, and cost reduction. Its main features include standardized workflows across all stages, specialized technical application, and a large-scale industrial system integrating production, distribution, and marketing.

Traditional production typically relies on on-location shooting and follows a linear process of "set construction—shooting—post-production." Although standardized to some extent, it is constrained by physical space and environmental conditions, limiting efficiency and scalability. Virtual production technology, however, introduces a non-linear system of "digital virtual production–hybrid shooting–end-to-end digital collaboration." Through digital scene construction and real-time rendering, it enables reusable virtual environments, improves efficiency, and reduces costs. At the same time, its digital collaboration platforms enhance communication across all stages, streamlining workflows and lowering production risks [6].

The industrialization of the Chinese-language film and television industry started relatively late and still faces challenges such as weak standardization, limited technical expertise, and insufficient industry coordination, especially compared to Hollywood. Virtual production technology offers new opportunities for upgrading. Its application in films such as The Wandering Earth demonstrates its potential in promoting industrial development. However, current use remains fragmented, lacking a systematic integration model. Existing research mainly focuses on Hollywood and general development paths, with insufficient attention to how virtual production integrates with and drives the upgrading of the Chinese-language industry.

Building on existing theories of industrialization, this study uses concepts such as standardization and specialization to analyze how virtual production restructures workflows and enhances industrialization. It further examines the current state of the Chinese-language film and television industry to explore pathways for localized integration, aiming to reveal how technological convergence drives industrial and digital transformation, and to provide a theoretical framework for future development [7].

3 Research Methods and Data Analysis

3.1 Research Design

This study adopts a mixed-methods approach combining literature review, case analysis, and questionnaire surveys to examine the current status, integration mechanisms, challenges, and optimization strategies of virtual production technology in film and television. This ensures the objectivity, rigor, and practical value of the research.

The literature review, as the foundation of the study, systematically examines domestic and international research on virtual production, film and television aesthetics, media convergence, and industrial production theory. It clarifies the development, core frameworks, and technical principles of virtual production while identifying gaps in existing research. In addition, industry reports and data from global and Chinese-language film and television sectors are analyzed to provide empirical support.

Case analysis serves as the core method. Representative cases include international productions such as The Mandalorian and Avatar: The Way of Water, as well as Chinese-language films like The Wandering Earth 2 and Creation of the Gods I: Kingdom of Storms. By comparing application models, integration paths, and outcomes across different production scales, this study explores the adaptability of virtual production and summarizes key experiences and challenges.

The questionnaire survey functions as a supplementary method, targeting industry professionals (e.g., directors, cinematographers, VFX artists, producers) and film students and scholars. Conducted both online and offline—through industry platforms, social media, companies, and universities—it aims to assess awareness, application, needs, and challenges related to virtual production. The survey is anonymous and voluntary, ensuring ethical compliance and sample reliability.

3.2 Data Collection and Sample Description

For this study, literature and industry data were collected from academic databases such as China National Knowledge Infrastructure, Wanfang Database, and Web of Science, as well as industry platforms including the China Film Association, EntGroup Data, and Maoyan Professional Edition. In total, over 200 academic papers, 30+ industry reports, and more than 100 datasets were collected, providing solid support for theoretical and empirical analysis.

Case selection followed the principles of typicality and representativeness, including six core cases. Internationally, The Mandalorian represents LED virtual production in television, while Avatar: The Way of Water demonstrates full-process integration of technologies such as motion capture and real-time rendering. In Chinese-language cinema, The Wandering Earth 2 showcases digital scene construction in sci-fi production, and Creation of the Gods I: Kingdom of Storms reflects hybrid virtual–live-action production. Additionally, low-to-mid-budget works were included to examine lightweight application models.

A total of 150 questionnaires were distributed, with 132 valid responses (88% response rate). The sample included industry professionals, researchers, and university faculty and students, covering fields such as directing, cinematography, visual effects, and production management, with visual effects representing the largest proportion. The questionnaire consisted of four modules: basic information, awareness of virtual production, application status and needs, and challenges with related suggestions, ensuring a comprehensive understanding of industry practices and demands..

3.3 Data Analysis Methods

This study combines content analysis and statistical analysis of literature and industry data. Through secondary analysis of academic literature, it identifies key arguments, findings, and limitations to construct the theoretical framework. At the same time, statistical analysis of industry data is used to evaluate market size, adoption rates, and development trends of virtual production technology, providing empirical support for industry analysis.

Using a combination of comparative and case study methods, the study conducts cross-case analysis across dimensions such as technical models, integration pathways, production outcomes, cost control, and industry collaboration. This approach reveals differences in the application and adaptability of virtual production across production scales and genres, while also summarizing integration mechanisms with traditional filming and key challenges.

Survey data are analyzed through both quantitative and qualitative methods. Quantitatively, SPSS is used for descriptive statistics, including means, standard deviations, and frequency distributions, to assess industry awareness, application status, and demand. Qualitatively, content analysis of open-ended responses identifies major challenges and optimization strategies, providing practical support for the study's conclusions.

4 Core Framework and Integration Models of Virtual Production Technology

4.1 Core Components of Virtual Production Technology

Virtual production technology is an integrated digital production system combining digital technology, film and television techniques, and artificial intelligence. It consists of three core modules—hardware, software, and production workflows—which operate collaboratively to enable full-process application in film and television production.

Hardware forms the foundation, including LED virtual production systems, motion capture, camera tracking, and supporting equipment. LED systems display real-time virtual scenes, replacing green screens and providing realistic lighting and interaction. Motion capture records actors' movements and expressions to drive virtual characters, while camera tracking synchronizes camera movement with virtual scenes to ensure accurate perspective and a "what-you-see-is-what-you-get" effect. Supporting equipment such as digital cameras, lighting, and audio systems further enhances automation and integration.

The software system acts as the core control center, including real-time rendering engines, 3D modeling tools, digital twin systems, and collaboration platforms. Engines like Unreal Engine and Unity enable real-time rendering of virtual scenes. Modeling tools such as Maya and Blender provide digital assets, while digital twins recreate real environments. Cloud-based collaboration platforms support data sharing and coordination across all production stages.

The production workflow integrates these technologies into a non-linear process of "pre-production digital preparation—mid-production hybrid filming—post-production refinement." Pre-production uses modeling and virtual rehearsals to design scenes and shooting plans; mid-production enables real-time interaction between actors and virtual environments; post-production focuses on minor refinements, as most visual effects are completed during filming, significantly improving efficiency and reducing production time.

4.2 Models of Integration Between Virtual Production and Traditional On-Location Filming

The emergence of virtual production does not replace traditional on-location filming; instead, it integrates with it to form a hybrid model that combines the strengths of both, achieving a "blend of virtual and real." Based on the level of application and integration, this model can be divided into three types: lightweight, moderate, and deep integration, each suited to different production scales and genres.

The lightweight integration model is an entry-level approach characterized by "on-location filming as the primary method, supplemented by virtual production." It applies virtual technology only to specific scenes—such as special effects, virtual props, or small background environments—mainly to solve issues that are difficult or costly to achieve in reality. This model requires minimal equipment, such as small LED screens or simple rendering systems, and is widely used in low- to medium-budget productions due to its low cost and technical threshold.

The moderate integration model emphasizes a balance between virtual and real elements, applying virtual production across multiple key stages and scenes. It typically involves medium-scale LED studios with motion capture and camera tracking systems, enabling virtual set construction and interactive filming. This model is suitable for medium-budget genres and achieves a balance between visual quality and cost by combining virtual environments with on-location shooting.

The deep integration model represents a high-level fusion in which virtual production serves as the core throughout the entire process, from pre-production to post-production, while on-location filming is only supplementary. It requires large-scale LED studios and full technical systems, including real-time rendering and motion capture, resulting in high costs and technical demands. This model is mainly used in high-budget productions such as science fiction and fantasy films, enabling highly immersive and visually complex results, as exemplified by The Wandering Earth 2.

4.3 Core Characteristics and Value of Technological Convergence

The integration of virtual production with traditional on-set filming has broken conventional technical and workflow limitations, forming four core characteristics: digitalization, integration, immersion, and efficiency. These features have reshaped production methods and promoted the digital transformation of the film and television industry.

Digitalization is reflected in the full-process transformation of production, from pre-production modeling and pre-visualization to hybrid filming and post-production refinement. Digital technologies overcome spatial and temporal constraints, allowing virtual scenes to be repeatedly modified and reused, while enabling traceable and adjustable data management, thereby enhancing flexibility.

Integration is demonstrated in the restructuring of production workflows. It breaks the traditional linear separation of stages and enables synchronization across pre-production, filming, and post-production. All stages become interconnected, reducing communication costs and production risks.

Immersion is reflected in both production and viewing experiences. During filming, real-time rendered virtual environments allow actors to perform more naturally compared to green-screen setups. For audiences, highly realistic virtual scenes enhance engagement, especially in genres like science fiction and fantasy.

Efficiency is shown through improved production speed and cost control. The "what-you-see-is-what-you-get" approach reduces post-production revisions and shortens production cycles. Virtual sets replace physical construction, allowing flexible reuse while lowering costs related to set building and on-location shooting.

5 Application Logic and Optimization Strategies for Virtual Production Technology

5.1 Tiered Application Logic for Virtual Production Technology

The application of virtual production technology follows a selective logic based on "genre, scale, and production stage," rather than universal use. Filmmakers choose appropriate integration models and technical approaches according to project needs.

Genre adaptation is the primary principle. High-demand genres such as science fiction, fantasy, and action—requiring complex virtual scenes and effects—are suited to deep integration. Genres like period dramas or light sci-fi, which balance realism and visual effects, fit moderate integration. Realism-focused genres such as drama, art films, and documentaries are better suited to lightweight integration. For example, Planet Earth III adopts limited virtual production only in high-risk scenes, ensuring safety while maintaining realism.

Scale adaptation focuses on aligning technology with budget and production size. Large-scale, high-budget projects can support full virtual production systems and deep integration, while medium-budget productions favor moderate integration to balance cost and quality. Low- to medium-budget projects typically adopt lightweight integration to control costs while meeting basic visual needs.

Stage-specific adaptation ensures precise application across production phases. In pre-production, technologies such as 3D modeling and virtual rehearsals are used for planning; in mid-production, LED virtual production, motion capture, and camera tracking enable real-time interaction; in post-production, digital refinement and optimization are emphasized. Each stage has distinct priorities but functions collaboratively within an integrated system.

5.2 Key Challenges in the Integrated Application of Virtual Production Technologies

Although virtual production has made notable progress in integrating with traditional filming, it still faces key challenges in technology, talent, and creative processes.

From a technical perspective, the main issues are limited localization and the lack of unified standards. Core technologies—such as Unreal Engine and Mo-Sys camera tracking system—are largely imported and designed for Hollywood systems, leading to mismatches with Chinese-language production practices. In addition, the absence of standardized equipment specifications, workflows, and data formats across companies results in poor data sharing and "data silos," reducing efficiency and scalability.

In terms of talent, there is both a shortage of interdisciplinary professionals and an imbalanced structure. Traditional film students often lack technical skills, while technical specialists lack creative and narrative abilities. Although there is a sufficient number of technical personnel, there is a shortage of creative-technical professionals—such as directors and cinematographers—capable of managing virtual-real integration, leading to a gap between technology and storytelling.

On the creative side, challenges stem from outdated mindsets and improper use of technology. Some creators still rely on traditional filming approaches and fail to fully utilize virtual production, while others overemphasize visual effects and treat it as mere spectacle, neglecting narrative and emotional expression. This results in an imbalance where technology outweighs artistic storytelling.

5.3 Optimization Strategies for the Integrated Application of Virtual Production Technologies

In response to the challenges in integrating virtual production technology, this study proposes optimization strategies across three dimensions—technology, talent, and creative production—to promote coordinated development.

On the technical front, the focus is on localization and standardization. This includes strengthening collaboration between domestic technology companies and film production teams to adapt imported technologies to Chinese-language production needs, while increasing R&D of independent core technologies to reduce reliance on foreign systems. At the same time, organizations such as China Film Association should lead the establishment of unified standards for equipment, workflows, and data formats, enabling data sharing and efficient collaboration across the industry.

In terms of talent, the goal is to cultivate multidisciplinary professionals and build industry exchange platforms. Higher education should integrate film studies with fields like digital technology and AI, offering courses in virtual production and 3D modeling, while strengthening university–industry collaboration to enhance practical skills. Additionally, industry platforms such as training programs and workshops should be developed to promote communication between creative and technical professionals.

On the creative front, emphasis is placed on transforming creative thinking and reinforcing the principle that technology serves storytelling. Through training and case studies, creators can better understand and apply virtual production, avoiding overreliance on visual effects. At the same time, innovation should combine virtual-real integration with local cultural elements, ensuring that virtual production enhances narrative expression and supports the global dissemination of Chinese-language film and television culture.

6 Conclusion

This study systematically examines the integration of virtual production with traditional filmmaking through theoretical analysis, case studies, and surveys. It analyzes the core framework, integration models, application logic, and key challenges of virtual production, proposing targeted optimization strategies. The main conclusions are as follows:

First, the integration of virtual production and on-location shooting is complementary rather than substitutive. It can be categorized into three models—lightweight, moderate, and deep—depending on application depth. These models suit different genres and scales of production. The integration is characterized by digitalization, integration, immersion, and efficiency, enhancing not only production efficiency and visual effects but also creative thinking, industry upgrading, and cross-cultural communication.

Second, the application of virtual production follows a tiered logic based on subject matter, scale, and production stage. Selecting the appropriate technical approach ensures that technology serves the creative process and storytelling, avoiding excessive or inappropriate use.

Third, current challenges include insufficient localization, a lack of multidisciplinary talent, weak industrial collaboration, and outdated creative mindsets. These hinder the localized application and industrial advancement of virtual production in Chinese-language filmmaking. Addressing these requires coordinated efforts across technology, talent, and creativity.

Fourth, the localized integration of virtual production presents a key opportunity for digital and industrial transformation in Chinese-language film and television. It enhances visual expression and cross-cultural communication. Through localized adaptation, talent cultivation, and creative innovation, the industry can shift from a technology-driven to a creativity-driven, technology-enabled model, achieving high-quality development.

7 Discussion and Analysis

While this study-maintained rigor in design and execution, several limitations should be acknowledged. First, the case study selection, while covering various genres and production scales, was predominantly focused on science fiction, fantasy, and action productions, with limited inclusion of drama, art films, and documentaries. This restricts the ability to fully capture the application logic of virtual production across all film and television genres. Second, although the questionnaire sample demonstrated a degree of professionalism, its size was relatively small and geographically concentrated in first-tier production cities such as Beijing, Shanghai, and Zhejiang. The underrepresentation of second- and third-tier regions may limit the generalizability of the findings to the national industry.

These limitations point to directions for future research. Subsequent studies should broaden the scope of case analyses to include a wider variety of production types and expand the sample size and geographic reach of surveys to enhance representativeness. Additionally, ongoing attention should be paid to emerging developments and practical applications of virtual production, ensuring that research data and case studies remain current. Finally, a more comprehensive analytical framework—integrating technological, industrial, creative, and policy dimensions—should be developed to further explore the integrated application logic and optimization pathways of virtual production technology.

As a product of digital-technology convergence, virtual production is undergoing rapid evolution. Future advancements will expand both the depth and breadth of its integration into filmmaking, driven by technological trends and industry demands.

Technologically, AI will integrate deeply with virtual production, enhancing automation in scene modeling, character generation, shot design, and capture, thereby boosting efficiency. AI-driven virtual avatars will mature, performing more naturally alongside live actors and potentially becoming central to productions. Meanwhile, metaverse integration will enable immersive, remote, cross-regional collaboration, overcoming physical constraints.

In creation and dissemination, virtual production will expand visual expression and lower entry barriers, allowing broader creative participation. It will also facilitate cross-cultural communication by digitally reconstructing local cultural elements—enabling content with distinctive characteristics to transcend cultural barriers and reach international audiences.

In summary, virtual production has reshaped production processes and creative approaches, driving digital transformation and cultural dissemination. As technology advances, it will become the mainstream production model. The Chinese-language film industry must seize this opportunity to promote localized integration, fostering coordinated development across technology, talent, industry, and creativity to achieve digital and industrial upgrading in the digital age.

Acknowledgments. This work was funded by Xiamen Municipal Science and Technology Program Project-Industry-Academia-Research Collaboration Project (Funding Number: 2024CXY0405).

References

1. Ma, J.: Research on the application of virtual shooting technology in radio and television. Video Eng. **49**(11), 202-204 (2025). https://doi.org/10.16280/j.videoe.2025.11.057
2. Li, Z.: Virtual shooting expands the boundaries of film and television production. People's Daily Overseas Edition, p. 8 (2025). https://doi.org/10.28656/n.cnki.nrmrh.2025.000090
3. Liu, M.Y., Wang, X.X.: Analysis of film simulation based on virtual shooting technology. Contemp. Anim. (4), 96–100 (2024). https://d.0j7.cn/1MUcX7k
4. Guo, P.P., Xu, Q.: Development of domestic XR virtual shooting technology: Current situation, challenges and future trends. Film Stud. (7), 162–164 (2024). https://d.0j7.cn/frCPv4Z
5. Wu, J.M.: Analysis of virtual reality panoramic shooting technology based on Unity3D. Electron. Technol. **53**(6), 366–367 (2024). https://d.0j7.cn/IhOv17g
6. Cheng, F.F.: Current status and value analysis of virtual shooting technology applied in film production. Film Stud. (1), 32–34 (2023). https://d.0j7.cn/mdRGP
7. Xie, X.L., Xu, G.J., Li, X.X., et al.: Research on integrated application of XR and AIGC technologies in film and television creation: A case study of the micro-drama Floating Life Like a Dream. Western Radio & TV, **46**(17), 93–96 (2025). https://d.0j7.cn/VcJugy7

Design Factors Influencing the Detectability of Visual Warning HMIs for Motorcyclists

Yanbin Wu(✉), Ken Kihara, and Yuji Takeda

National Institute of Advanced Industrial Science and Technology (AIST), Higashi 1-1-1, Tsukuba 3059566, Japan
wu.yanbin@aist.go.jp

Abstract. Motorcycle-related accidents remain a persistent road safety issue, partly because motorcycles cannot easily accommodate advanced preventive safety systems and rely heavily on riders' perception and judgment. Visual warning human–machine interfaces (HMIs) may support safe riding, but empirical design guidelines for motorcycle warning displays remain limited. This study investigated how basic visual parameters of an LED-based warning HMI affect riders' detectability and response. Two simulator-based experiments were conducted. In Experiment 1, participants rode repeated daytime scenarios while LED warnings were presented under eight conditions varying in display position, luminance, and illumination pattern. In Experiment 2, the detectability of a flickering warning was examined under a much lower presentation frequency. Reaction time and miss rate were measured, and in Experiment 2 rider sleepiness was additionally considered. Results showed that visual warnings positioned closer to the rider's forward line of sight tended to yield fewer misses than lower or lateral placements. Signal type had a clearer effect: flickering warnings produced the lowest miss rates, outperforming both standard- and high-luminance steady-on (with single onset) warnings. Experiment 2 further confirmed that the benefit of flickering persisted even when warnings were rare. Sleepiness in Experiment 2 was associated with slower responses. These findings suggest that motorcycle warning HMIs should prioritize placement near the rider's natural gaze direction and use temporal modulation, such as flickering, to enhance perceptual salience.

Keywords: Motorcycle Safety · HMI · Rider assistance · Perceptual salience

1 Introduction

Motorcycle safety remains a persistent challenge in road transportation. The World Health Organization reports that powered two- and three-wheelers account for a substantial share of global road crash deaths, while their fleet has expanded rapidly in many regions over the past decade [1]. For riders, safety is shaped not only by physical exposure but also by the demands of the riding task itself, which requires continuous balance control, path tracking, hazard perception, and rapid manual responses. Furthermore, motorcycles can often be underestimated or overlooked by car drivers [2]. Compared with passenger cars, powered two-wheelers also pose additional challenges for

C. Stephanidis et al. (Eds.): HCII 2026, CCIS 3047, pp. 298–307, 2026.
https://doi.org/10.1007/978-3-032-30552-7_28

assistance-system design because their dynamics are strongly influenced by roll motion and the rider's body and control inputs. From a Human Machine Interaction (HMI) perspective, this means that rider support cannot depend only on sensing or automation, it also depends on how safety-relevant information is presented to the rider at the right moment and with minimal disruption to the primary riding task.

Accordingly, research on rider assistance systems has increasingly emphasized the design of rider-facing HMIs. Early work such as the SAFERIDER project noted that, although advanced driver assistance system (ADAS) and in-vehicle-information-system research had generated substantial HMI knowledge, comparable development in the motorcycling domain tended to lag behind [3]. Biral et al. developed a curve warning system and reported that, when the warning HMI was active, riders produced earlier and stronger corrective actions in a riding simulator, and later road-based evaluation showed that riders also responded positively to the system [4]. More recent work explored motorcycle head-up display (HUD) concepts using immersive simulation to investigate effective display position and information amount [5, 6].

With the development of advanced displaying technologies such as HUDs, the trade-off between informativeness and workload has also been examined recently. Gebretsadik and Suzuki compared alert-based and continuous real-time feedback HMIs for motorcycle safety and found that alert-based presentation yielded shorter reaction times, longer minimum time-to-collision, and lower perceived workload than continuous feedback [7]. In parallel, they also pointed out that HMIs requiring high workload can degrade riders' primary riding performance in demanding conditions. Taken together, previous research has mainly focused on warning modality and concept evaluation, while offering fewer concreate design rules for the low-level perceptual properties of visual warnings. Questions such as where a simple visual warning should be placed, how salient it should be, and whether temporal modulation improves detectability remain comparatively underexplored.

This gap is important because visual warning effectiveness is shaped by the characteristics of peripheral perception while riding a motorcycle. Outside the motorcycling domain (i.e., for car drivers), Takahashi showed that a blinking visual cue presented around 26° from the visual center could serve as an effective peripheral warning without being overly annoying and proposed preliminary guidance for vehicle implementation [8]. Biswas et al. showed that peripheral target detection during active driving is not uniform: the functional field of view exhibits task-dependent asymmetries, and detection is inhibited immediately after saccades before recovering during fixation [9]. These findings imply that warning effectiveness depends not only on what information is shown, but also on where it is placed relative to the rider's natural line of sight and how its temporal characteristics attract attention. For motorcycle HMIs, such perceptual considerations are especially important because riders must maintain continuous visual monitoring of the road while simultaneously stabilizing and controlling the vehicle.

A further issue is rider state. Bougard et al. reported that motorcycle handling and emergency braking performance vary with time of day and can be impaired after sleep deprivation; in a later dynamic-simulator study, emergency braking performance again deteriorated under sleep deprivation, increasing the distance required to stop [10]. These findings suggest that the effectiveness of a warning HMI should not be treated as a fixed property of the display alone. Rather, interface effectiveness is likely to interact with rider vigilance and workload, making it important to evaluate warning designs under conditions that reflect realistic variation in rider state.

Against this background, the present study investigates fundamental visual parameters of LED-based warning HMIs for motorcyclists. Rather than comparing broad warning modalities or complete assistance concepts, we focus on basic perceptual design variables that can directly inform HMI implementation: display position, luminance, and illumination pattern. Two riding-simulator experiments were conducted. Experiment 1 examined how these parameters affect reaction time and miss rate during repeated daytime riding scenarios. Furthermore, because safety-critical alerts are likely to occur infrequently in real-world riding, the effect of low warning frequency on visual detectability should also be considered. Repeated warning presentations may increase expectancy, making warnings easier to detect in typical experimental settings than in actual use. Experiment 2 aims to examine this by testing whether the detectability of the optimal visual warning found in Experiment 1 persists when the warning occurs very infrequently. In addition, rider sleepiness is assessed to examine whether rider states moderate warning detectability. By investigating the detectability of a simple visual warning, this study aims to provide actionable design guidance for rider-facing HMIs in safety-critical motorcycle contexts.

2 Methods

2.1 Ethics Statement

This research was approved by the institutional review board at the National Institute of Advanced Industrial Science and Technology (Experiment Plan No. 人2024–1455). All the participants signed an informed consent before proceeding with the experiment.

2.2 Apparatus

Both experiments used the HONDA Rider Trainer riding simulator modeled after an automatic scooter (Honda Motor Co., Ltd.). The riding scene was presented on a 49-inch curved display (LG Electronics, 49GR85DC-B). The distance from the rear edge of the simulator seat to the center of the display was 1420 mm, and the height from the floor to the display center was 1190 mm. The viewing distance from the participant to the center of the display varied slightly depending on riding posture. In Experiment 1, the mean viewing distance was 1128 mm (SD = 58 mm); in Experiment 2, it was 1132 mm (SD = 36 mm).

Participants responded to LED warnings by pressing a button installed near the base of the left handlebar, at a location reachable by the left index finger. Multicolor LEDs (Inolux, IN-P1554FCH) were used as visual warning devices. LEDs were mounted at five possible locations: at the center of the handlebar, 100 mm above the center, 200 mm above the center, and 280 mm to the left or right of the center (see Fig. 1). These placements created different downward gaze angles between the rider's eye point and the LED. In Experiment 1, the mean downward gaze angles relative to horizontal direction for the upper, middle, lower, and lateral LED warnings were 30.6° (SD = 3.1°), 41.1° (SD = 2.9°), 51.8° (SD = 2.1°), and 33.3° (SD = 3.8°), respectively. In Experiment 2, the mean downward gaze angles were 30.1° (SD = 2.7°), 40.5° (SD = 2.6°), 51.2° (SD = 2.3°), and 32.6° (SD = 3.3°), respectively. To control background visibility, the area behind the LEDs was covered with white fabric. The experimental room was illuminated throughout the trials rather than kept dark, so that the warnings were evaluated under a bright indoor environment. Participants did not wear helmets in the experiment.

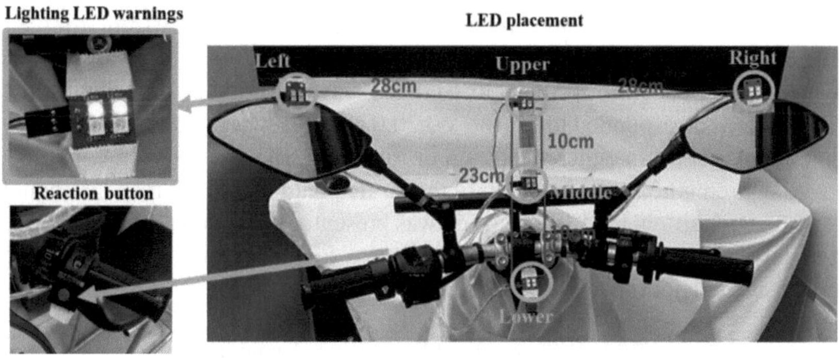

Fig. 1. The riding simulator and the placement of the LED warnings.

2.3 Measures

In both experiments, the primary dependent variables were reaction time and miss rate for LED warning detection. Reaction time was defined as the interval between LED onset and the participant's button press. Based on the overall distribution of responses, trials with reaction times of 3 s or longer were classified as misses. In experiment 2, subjective sleepiness was assessed after each run using the Karolinska Sleepiness Scale (KSS).

3 Experiment 1

Experiment 1 examined how the basic parameters of an LED warning HMI, including display position, luminance, and illumination pattern, affect riders' visual detectability.

3.1 Participants

Sixteen Japanese native speakers (18–59 years old, mean age = 39.6 years) participated. All participants regularly rode motorcycles approximately once per week or more. Recruitment was conducted through a staffing agency, and participants were paid for their participation. Each participant attended four experimental sessions over 4 days, with each session lasting approximately 2 h.

3.2 Design and Conditions

Participants rode a 3-min daytime riding scenario 24 times per day, resulting in a total of 96 runs in the four-day experiment. During each day's 24 runs, the LED warning was presented 8 times in total, once for each experimental condition (see Table 1). Averagely, LED warning was presented once per 9 mins. LED onset was scheduled outside curve segments to avoid biasing reaction time by steering demands.

As shown in Table 1, eight conditions were tested, varying in position, luminance, and illumination pattern. Position was defined as lower (handlebar center), middle (100 mm above center), upper (200 mm above center), or lateral (left or right, 280 mm from center). Luminance was set to either standard or high. In the LED control settings, standard luminance corresponded to RGB = 30:10:0 and was measured as 655 cd/m^2, whereas high luminance corresponded to RGB = 60:20:0 and was measured as 1170 cd/m^2. The illumination pattern was either steady-on or flickering. In the steady-on condition, the LED warning remained illuminated until the participant pressed the response button. In the flickering condition, the LED warning was presented with an on-duration of 125 ms and an equivalent off-duration, corresponding to a frequency of 4 Hz. These temporal parameters were determined in a pilot study.

Table 1. Summary of Experiment Conditions.

Condition No.	Position	Luminance	Illumination pattern
1	Lower	Standard (655 cd/m^2)	Steady-on
2	Middle	Standard (655 cd/m^2)	Steady-on
3	Upper	Standard (655 cd/m^2)	Steady-on
4	Lateral (Left or right)	Standard (655 cd/m^2)	Steady-on
5	Lower	High (1170 cd/m^2)	Steady-on
6	Middle	High (1170 cd/m^2)	Steady-on
7	Lower	Standard (655 cd/m^2)	Flickering (4 Hz)
8	Middle	Standard (655 cd/m^2)	Flickering (4 Hz)

3.3 Procedures

Before the trials, participants were instructed to follow traffic rules, ride at approximately 50 km/h unless traffic signs indicated otherwise and use only the right brake lever. They were also instructed to always keep their left index finger on the response button while riding. Participants were told that one of the LEDs might illuminate during riding and that they should press the response button as quickly as possible while maintaining safe riding.

3.4 Results

Across all responses, 11.1% of warning presentations were classified as misses. When miss trials were excluded, mean reaction times ranged from approximately 0.90 to

1.10 s. While no significant differences in reaction time were observed among conditions, significant differences were found for the miss rates.

To examine the effect of LED position (see Fig. 2a), miss counts under the matched standard-luminance steady-on conditions (Table 1, Condition No.1–4) were compared across the upper, middle, lower, and lateral positions using a Friedman test. The effect of position was not statistically significant, $\chi^2(3) = 4.86$, $p = .182$. Descriptively, however, the upper position yielded the lowest miss rate (7.8%), followed by the middle position (15.6%), whereas the lower and lateral positions both showed higher miss rates (23.4%).

To examine the effects of luminance and illumination pattern (see Fig. 2b), analyses were restricted to the middle and lower positions (Table 1, Condition No.1–2 and 5–8), for which all three signal types were available. A binomial generalized linear mixed-effects model with participant as a random intercept showed no significant main effect of position, $F(1, 380) = 0.33$, $p = .567$, but a significant main effect of signal type, $F(2, 380) = 8.45$, $p < .001$. Descriptively, miss rates were highest for the standard-luminance steady-on condition (middle: 15.6%, lower: 23.4%), lower for the high-luminance steady-on condition (middle: 9.4%, lower: 7.8%), and lowest for the standard-luminance flickering condition (middle: 1.6%, lower: 0.0%). These results indicate that flickering substantially improved detectability, and that this benefit was larger than that obtained by increasing luminance alone.

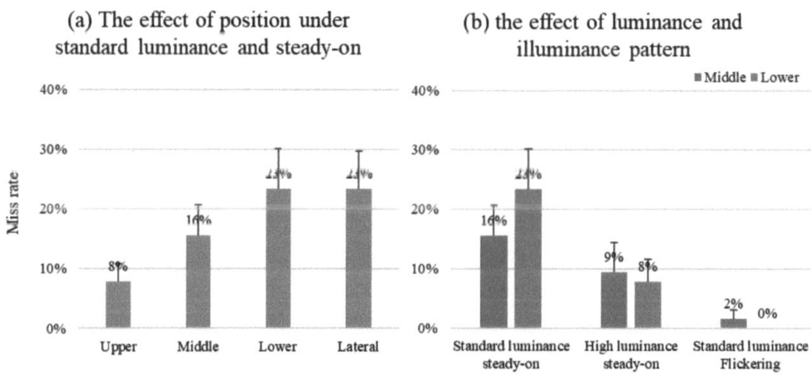

Fig. 2. The result of miss rates showing (a)the effect of position under standard luminance and steady-on conditions, and (b) the effect of luminance and illuminance patterns. Error bar = standard error.

4 Experiment 2

Experiment 2 examined whether the advantage of flickering LED warnings observed in Experiment 1 would remain when warning events occurred very infrequently. This was necessary because the relatively frequent warning presentations in Experiment 1 may have increased participants' expectancy of LED onset and their arousal level may maintain in a high level, possibly leading to a high detection rate of the visual warnings.

4.1 Participants

A different group of 16 Japanese native speakers (18–59 years old, mean age = 40.4 years) participated. All participants regularly rode motorcycles at least once per week. Recruitment was conducted through a staffing agency, and participants were paid for their participation. Each participant completed two 2-h sessions over 2 days. None had participated in Experiment 1. Informed consent was obtained before participation.

4.2 Design and Conditions

Participants rode the same 3-min daytime simulator course for 24 runs per day, resulting in a total of 48 runs in the two-day experiment. Unlike Experiment 1, the LED warning was presented only twice during each day's 24 runs, at random timings. Thus, the warning frequency was approximately once every 36 min on average, much lower than in Experiment 1 where the warning frequency was approximately once every 9 min.

Only one warning condition was tested: the lower-position, standard-luminance, 4-Hz flickering LED, which had shown the lowest miss rate in Experiment 1. Standard luminance was again set to RGB = 30:10:0 (655 cd/m^2). Before the experiment, participants were informed that the LED at the lower position might illuminate during riding. Other instructions and procedures were the same as in Experiment 1.

4.3 Results

No participant failed to respond within 3 s to the visual warning presentation. Thus, the miss rate was 0% in Experiment 2. This finding indicates that a 4-Hz flickering LED remained highly detectable even when warning signals occurred rarely and were therefore less predictable.

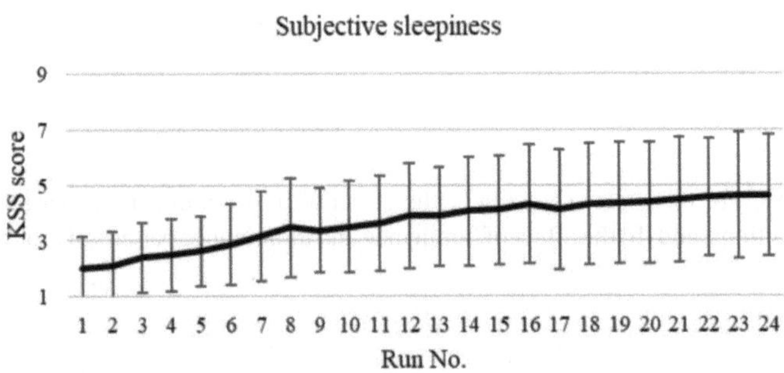

Fig. 3. Changes in KSS score across the 24 runs. Error bar = standard deviation.

Figure 3 shows the result of changes in KSS score. KSS scores gradually increased over repeated runs, rising from approximately 2.0 at the beginning to around 4.5 by the 16th run, after which they stabilized. This pattern indicates that sleepiness increased over time in the simulator task.

Because there were no missed trials, the effect of sleepiness was evaluated using reaction time rather than miss rate. As shown in Fig. 4, reaction times were compared between arousal (KSS ≤ 6) and sleepy (KSS > 6) states. Fifty-five samples were labeled as arousal and 9 sample were labeled as sleepy. A simple unpaired t-test ($p = 0.01$) indicates that reaction times tend to be shorter when participants were in a more alert state (KSS ≤ 6) than when they were sleepy (KSS > 6), suggesting that drowsiness slowed responses even when warnings were successfully detected.

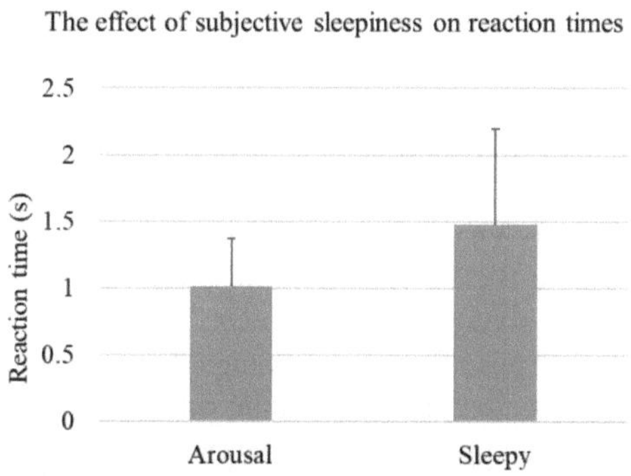

Fig. 4. The effect of subjective sleepiness on reaction times. Error bar = standard deviation.

5 Discussions

Across two simulator experiments, this study examined how basic visual properties of a rider-facing LED warning HMI affect detectability during motorcycle riding. In Experiment 1, the matched four-position comparison showed no statistically significant overall effect of position, but the descriptive pattern was consistent: warnings placed closer to the rider's forward line of sight produced fewer misses than lower or lateral placements. In contrast, signal types had a clear effect. Miss rates were highest for standard-luminance steady-on warnings, lower for high-luminance steady-on warnings, and lowest for standard-luminance flickering warnings. Experiment 2 further showed that the benefit of flickering persisted even when warning events were rare, as no missed detections occurred in the lower-position flickering condition. Moreover, even when sleepiness increased with longer riding duration, it delayed responses by approximately 0.5 s but did not lead to any missed warnings. Together, these findings suggest that temporal modulation may contribute more strongly to detectability than luminance increase alone, while placement relative to the rider's natural gaze direction also appears important. This is broadly consistent with prior motorcycle HMI research, which emphasized the importance of effective warning presentation but has offered fewer concrete perceptual design guidelines [11].

One practical implication concerns visual warning LED placement. Although the position effect was not statistically significant in the matched analysis, the upper position yielded the lowest miss rate, followed by the middle position, while the lower and lateral positions showed more misses. This pattern is theoretically plausible because warnings presented nearer the rider's forward line of sight should require less attentional shift from the roadway. Related work on peripheral visual cues and the functional field of view in driving likewise suggests that detection depends strongly on where a cue appears relative to the visual center and ongoing task demands [8]. For rider-facing visual warnings, the present results support placing simple warning cues as close as feasible to the rider's primary line of sight.

A second implication concerns temporal modulation. Flickering warnings were more detectable than steady-on warnings, even when the steady-on signal had higher luminance. This suggests that increasing salience through time-varying presentation may be more effective than increasing brightness alone. Additionally, flickering also appeared to mitigate the disadvantage of less optimal placement. In the steady-on conditions, warnings presented at the lower position showed relatively high miss rates, suggesting that this location was less favorable for visual detection. However, when the same lower-position warning was presented as a flickering signal, miss rates were substantially reduced, reaching the lowest level observed in the experiment. This suggests that temporal modulation can partially overcome positional disadvantages by increasing perceptual salience, even when the warning is located farther from the rider's natural forward line of sight. That is useful for motorcycle applications, where display size, mounting location, and brightness may be constrained. The result of Experiment 2 further indicated that even under rare-event conditions, the flickering warning remained highly detectable. From a design perspective, these results make flickering a promising strategy for infrequent but safety-critical alerts.

Experiment 2 also suggested that rider state may influence warning response. Although no warnings were missed, reaction times tended to be slower in the sleepy state than in the aroused state. This aligns with prior motorcycle research showing that reduced alertness can impair riding-related responses [10]. Even highly detectable warnings may therefore not yield equally rapid reactions across rider states, which suggests that rider-facing HMIs should be evaluated under non-ideal vigilance conditions as well.

This study has several limitations. First, both experiments were conducted in a simulator, which cannot fully reproduce real riding conditions such as vibration, weather, ambient light variation, and complex traffic. Second, only a limited set of warning parameters was tested. In particular, only one flicker frequency was examined, and the factorial comparison was not fully balanced across all positions. Third, the sleepy-state sample in Experiment 2 was small, so that finding should be interpreted cautiously. Future work should validate these findings in more realistic environments, examine additional warning parameters such as flicker frequency and color, and explore how visual warnings interact with rider state and other modalities such as haptic cues. Overall, the present results suggest that motorcycle warning HMIs should prioritize reliable detection through placement near the rider's natural gaze direction and the use of flickering signals, before adding greater informational complexity.

Acknowledgments. We thank Shingo Ueda, Hiroto Yao, Yoshiki Nagasaki, Takuya Fukami, and Gonta Tanaka for their useful suggestions on this research, and their participation in the pilot study to determine the experiment conditions.

Disclosure of Interests. The authors have no competing interests to declare that are relevant to the content of this article.

References

1. World Health Organization (WHO): Powered two-and three-wheeler safety: a road safety manual for decision-makers and practitioners (2022). https://www.who.int/publications/i/item/9789240060562. Last accessed 16 Mar 2026
2. Wu, Y., Kihara, K., Takeda, Y.: Following car reduces motorcycles' size-arrival effect: a study using online experiments. Appl. Ergon. **114**, 104153 (2024)
3. Diederichs, J.F., Fontana, M., Bencini, G., Nikolaou, S., Montanari, R., Spadoni, A., et al.: New HMI concept for motorcycles—the SAFERIDER approach. In: International Conference on Engineering Psychology and Cognitive Ergonomics, pp. 358–366. Springer, Berlin (2009)
4. Biral, F., Da Lio, M., Lot, R., Sartori, R.: An intelligent curve warning system for powered two wheel vehicles. Eur. Transp. Res. Rev. **2**(3), 147–156 (2010)
5. Ogi, T.: Design and evaluation of HUD for motorcycle using immersive simulator. In: SIGGRAPH Asia Head-Up Displays and Their Applications, p. 5. ACM, New York (2015)
6. Sevarin, A., Will, S., Rößer, J., Mikschofsky, N., Menato, L., Hammer, T., et al.: Assessment of visual and haptic HMI concepts for hazard warning of powered two-wheeler riders. In: Proceedings of the 13th International Motorcycle Conference, Cologne (2020)
7. Gebretsadik, K.H., Suzuki, K.: Riding behavior-based HMIs for motorcycle safety: a comparative study of alert and real-time feedback systems. J. Adv. Mech. Des. Syst. Manuf. **18**(5), JAMDSM0055 (2024)
8. Takahashi, H.: Visual cue in the peripheral vision field for a driving support system. J. Adv. Comput. Intell. Intell. Inform. **21**(3), 543–558 (2017)
9. Biswas, A., Admoni, H.: Characterizing drivers' peripheral vision via the functional field of view for intelligent driving assistance. In: 2023 IEEE Intelligent Vehicles Symposium (IV), pp. 1–8. IEEE (2023)
10. Bougard, C., Espié, S., Larnaudie, B., Moussay, S., Davenne, D.: Effects of time of day and sleep deprivation on motorcycle-driving performance. PLoS One. **7**(6), e39735 (2012)
11. Will, S., et al.: Assessment of human machine interfaces for hazard warning of powered two-wheeler riders. In: Proceedings of the Driving Simulation Conference 2021 Europe VR, pp. 83–89. Driving Simulation Association, Munich (2021)

Designing an Interactive Size Chart to Improve Fit in DIY Garment Making

Sujin Yoo(✉), Mia Lopez, Steve Marschner, and Fatma Baytar

Cornell University, Ithaca, NY 14850, USA
sy797@cornell.edu

Abstract. DIY garment making has seen a resurgence in interest over the past three decades and offers potential benefits for sustainable clothing practices. However, prior research indicates that home sewers frequently experience garment fit challenges, leading to frustration and material waste. As digital tools become more widely adopted, there is a growing need to explore how such technologies can support improved fit outcomes and sewing workflows. This study conducted a needs assessment with 50 female home sewers to identify key challenges and inform design implications. Based on these findings, we developed an interactive size chart integrated with a fit-adjustment tool and evaluated it through an in-person pilot study using usability testing, user experience questionnaires, and interviews. Results suggest that well-designed digital tools embedded within the sewing workflow can significantly improve garment fit outcomes while enhancing efficiency and user satisfaction. Future work will focus on developing a standalone system that supports a wider range of garments and on conducting evaluations with a larger, more diverse participant sample.

Keywords: DIY · Home sewing · Virtual Fit · 3D · Interactive Size Chart

1 Literature Review

1.1 Garment Fit Challenges in Home Sewing

Home sewing has been widely discussed in recent literature for its potential to promote sustainability [1, 2]. Participation in home sewing has also grown over the last three decades [3, 4]. However, home sewers frequently experience fit issues that can lead to material waste and frustration. Prior research shows that many home sewers repeatedly adjust patterns to improve fit, yet remain generally dissatisfied with both the outcomes and the adjustment process [5]. Another recent study confirms that manual pattern alterations do not consistently yield satisfactory results in Do-it-Yourself (DIY) garment-making [6]. To address these challenges, researchers have proposed simplifying pattern adjustment methods, improving education, and integrating digital technologies into the fitting process [5]. While tools such as 3D body scanning and computer-aided design (CAD) systems offer potential improvements, they often remain inaccessible to non-expert users. These limitations highlight the need for more intuitive and accessible

C. Stephanidis et al. (Eds.): HCII 2026, CCIS 3047, pp. 308–314, 2026.
https://doi.org/10.1007/978-3-032-30552-7_29

solutions to support fit customization in DIY garment making. Further research in this area can help make fit adjustments more intuitive for home sewers, enhance their overall sewing experience, and potentially contribute to the sustainability benefits of home sewing.

1.2 Current Solutions for Fit Issues in DIY Garment Making

Prior research shows that while home sewers frequently attempt fit adjustments [5], there is limited understanding of how these adjustments are performed in practice. More accessible and customizable tools have emerged, such as FreeSewing [7], which generates patterns based on user-provided body measurements, and independent pattern makers offering personalized designs through platforms (e.g., Etsy). However, there is little empirical evidence evaluating the effectiveness of these solutions for improving fit outcomes. In contrast, digital tools such as CLO3D provide advanced 3D visualization and pattern-adjustment capabilities, but they often pose barriers for non-expert users due to steep learning curves, the need for spatial reasoning, and exploratory workflows [8].

Despite increasing adoption in industry contexts, research on how home sewers engage with these tools and whether they effectively support fit adjustment remains limited. While Human–Computer Interaction (HCI) research has explored digital fitting in ready-to-wear contexts, such as virtual try-on and apparel customization [9–11], comparatively little work addresses the needs of home sewers. To bridge this gap, this study introduces an interactive 3D size-chart prototype that integrates digital visualization with pattern-adjustment support. Such tools may improve fit accuracy, enhance usability, and enable more efficient use of materials, thereby supporting more sustainable home-sewing practices.

2 Methods

2.1 Participants and IRB

In accordance with IRB Protocol #IRB0149225, approved by Cornell University's Institutional Review Board, this study recruited participants who were female home sewers, aged 18 years or older, residing in the U.S., and who wear U.S. misses/women's sizes 0–20. Recruitment was conducted via digital posters on social media platforms, including Instagram, Facebook, and Reddit sewing communities, in compliance with each platform's guidelines. Eligible participants were provided with a comprehensive informed consent form to ensure they were fully briefed on the study's nature. Given the digital recruitment method, a rigorous post-screening process was implemented to maintain data integrity in alignment with IRB recommendations. This process included manual filtering of responses to remove incomplete, inconsistent, or potentially automated (bot-generated) entries. Additionally, all identifiable data were removed to ensure participant privacy.

2.2 Needs Assessment

The needs assessment was conducted through an online survey administered via Qualtrics. The survey examined common fit-related challenges, garment adjustment practices, attitudes toward digital technologies, and sewing experience among 50 female home sewers. Participants ranged in age from 18 to 64 years, with the majority between 18 and 34 years (n = 36, 72%). The questionnaire included a mix of binary (yes/no), multiple-choice, and 7-point Likert-scale items ranging from strongly disagree (1) to strongly agree (7). Several questions also provided an "Other (please specify)" option, and open-ended responses were collected to capture detailed user experiences and challenges. The goal of this needs assessment was to identify key pain points in garment fit adjustment and to inform the design of an interactive system that supports intuitive, real-time fit exploration for non-expert users.

2.3 Interactive System Design and Implementation

The prototype was implemented using the CLO3D API [12], which provides access to 3D garment simulation and custom avatar generation. In this study, CLO3D was used as a real-time visualization environment to display garment fit, while all interactive controls were handled externally. Participants were not required to have prior experience with CLO3D or garment design software. Interactive functionality was enabled via a Touch Portal [13] interface on a tablet PC, which served as a remote-control system (Fig. 1).

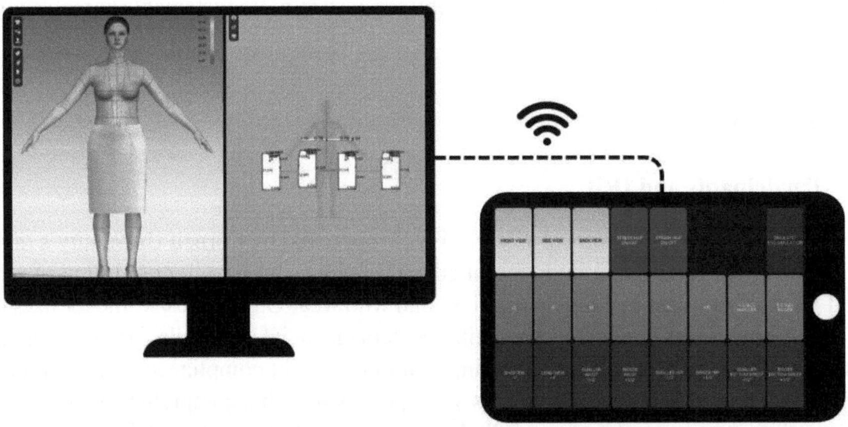

Fig. 1. Prototype setup showing the interactive 3D size chart interface, external controller (Touch Portal on tablet), and CLO3D simulation window.

This interface allowed users to adjust garment parameters through predefined macro buttons, eliminating the need for complex manual manipulation typically required in professional design tools. Users could perform common fit adjustments, such as modifying waist girth, changing skirt length, and switching between size increments through single-tap interactions. These adjustments were based on findings from a formative study, which indicated that non-expert users often struggle with traditional garment editing workflows. The system operated by manipulating key garment vertices within the CLO3D environment via the API. For example, length adjustments were achieved by programmatically modifying vertex positions around the hemline in fixed increments. These operations were mapped to shortcut commands, which were then triggered via the Touch Portal interface, enabling real-time updates to the garment simulation. An example of CLO3D simulations and stress maps across three conditions is shown in Fig. 2. The stress map uses color gradients to represent the magnitude of tension across the garment when fitted onto the avatar. Areas of high stress are typically shown in red, indicating regions where the fabric is stretched tightly and may result in poor fit or discomfort, while lower-stress areas appear in cooler colors (e.g., blue), indicating looseness.

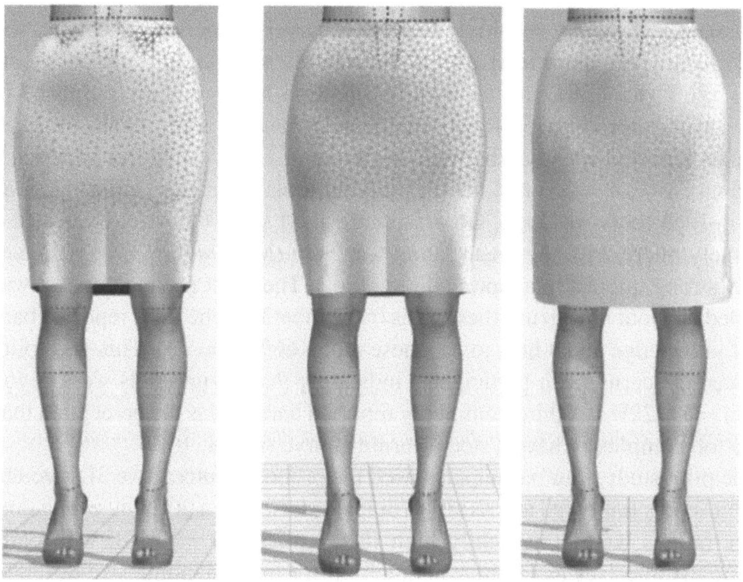

Fig. 2. Example CLO3D stress maps across the three treatment conditions: (a) traditional size chart only condition with the tight fit at the waist, (b) interactive size chart only condition with relatively better fit, and (c) interactive size chart combined with the fit-adjustment tool with the best fit.

2.4 Pilot User Study

A pilot user study was conducted with four participants to evaluate the task performance and usability of the proposed prototype. A standard pencil-skirt pattern with two darts was used as the test garment. Each participant's body measurements were collected to generate a personalized avatar within the system. Participants first selected a skirt size using a traditional paper-based size chart. They then received a brief training session on the interactive system, including basic navigation (e.g., avatar rotation) and the functions of the macro buttons for garment adjustments. Following training, participants used the interactive tool to explore size options, visualize garment fit, and perform simple adjustments (e.g., waist and length modifications) until they were satisfied with the result. To compare approaches, a rubric was developed to evaluate differences between fit outcomes obtained using the traditional size chart and those achieved with the interactive system. Task performance metrics included task success and completion time. Usability was assessed using the USE Questionnaire (Usefulness, Satisfaction, and Ease of Use) [14].

3 Results and Discussion

3.1 Findings

Needs assessment survey results indicate a relatively experienced cohort, with 84% (n = 42) identifying as at least intermediate level. A majority reported encountering fit issues (76%, n = 38), and the same proportion had previously adjusted patterns, consistent with prior work [5]. Regarding time spent on fit adjustments, over half of the participants reported spending between 30 min and 1 h. Despite this experience, most participants (76%, n = 38) had not used digital tools for pattern adjustment, although interest in such tools was high. On a 5-point Likert scale (1 = not interested at all, 5 = extremely interested), the mean rating was 3.96 (Mdn = 4, SD = 1.01), indicating generally strong interest in adopting digital tools. The most reported barrier was a lack of knowledge about how to use these tools (66%, n = 33). The most reported barrier was a lack of knowledge about how to use these tools (66%, n = 33). This was followed by cost-related concerns, with participants indicating that digital tools were beyond their budget (n = 11, 22%). A third commonly reported barrier was the perception that digital tools are too complex or have a steep learning curve (n = 8, 16%).

In the pilot study, four participants used the proposed interactive 3D size-chart prototype. Fit scores improved across all participants based on a 20-point evaluation rubric. Usability ratings were consistently high (M = 6.75, SD = 0.50), with participants describing the interface as intuitive and helpful for understanding size differences and personal fit needs. Participants also reported increased confidence in size selection and greater satisfaction with both fit outcomes and time efficiency. For example, Participant A noted that the "interactive size chart gives me a much clearer sense of size differences and helps me better understand my own needs." In terms of task performance, the mean completion time for selecting a size was 28.62 s (SD = 15.28). To adjust the fit, the mean completion time was 73.70 s (SD = 36.08), representing a significant improvement compared to the average time spent on fit adjustments (at least 30 min) reported in our needs assessment survey.

Using skirt simulations demonstrated how the interactive size chart and fit-adjustment tool could potentially improve the initial fit of garments for home sewers. The preliminary results highlighted how interactive visualization could help users make more confident fit decisions, potentially reducing the physical iterations common in sewing practices and minimizing material waste. The findings contribute to the growing field of digital tools for sustainable design and user-centered garment making, and emphasize the value of integrating apparel expertise with HCI methods. Furthermore, the findings point to new directions for HCI research in home sewing, digital apparel design, and sustainable creative practice.

3.2 Limitations and Future Work

This work had several limitations. The sample size was relatively small, with 50 survey responses and a pilot study involving four participants, which limits the generalizability of the findings. In addition, fit assessment was based on rubric-guided visual evaluation within the CLO3D environment. Although this approach is commonly used, it introduces subjectivity in both interpretation and judgment. Future studies could incorporate more objective measures, such as quantitative stress and strain data or physical garment validation. The evaluated workflow was also specific to a CLO3D and Touch Portal setup, meaning the results reflect this particular implementation rather than a standalone solution. Future work should explore independent or web-based systems to examine how these design concepts translate across different platforms and support a broader range of home-sewing practices.

Acknowledgments. This study was partly supported by the Cornell Center for Social Sciences, the Cornell University Department of Human-Centered Design for thesis support, the Human Ecology Alumni Association through the Alan D. Mathios Research and Service Grant, and the International Textile and Apparel Association through the Oris Glisson Fellowship.

References

1. Cooke, S.: Material encounters: fashion sustainability examined through beginners' experiences of learning to sew clothes at home. Ph.D. dissertation, The Open University (2024). https://www.proquest.com/dissertations-theses/material-encounters-fashion-sustainability/docview/3122639374/se-2
2. Kaipainen, M., Pöllänen, S.: Garment sewing as a leisure craft. Techne Ser. **28**(1), 1–15 (2021). https://erepo.uef.fi/items/5a558b37-e5e2-4fe1-b353-d105600c2221
3. Bain, J.: Darn right I'm a feminist sew what? The politics of contemporary home dressmaking: sewing, slow fashion and feminism. Women's Stud. Int. Forum. **54**, 57–66 (2016). https://doi.org/10.1016/j.wsif.2015.11.001
4. Martindale, A., McKinney, E.: Why do they sew? Women's motivations to sew clothing for themselves. Cloth. Text. Res. J. **38**(1), 32–48 (2020). https://doi.org/10.1177/0887302X19872552
5. LaBat, K., Salusso, C., Rhee, J.: Home sewers' satisfaction with fit of apparel patterns. J. Fash. Mark. Manag. **11**(3), 429–440 (2007). https://doi.org/10.1108/13612020710763155
6. Lansdell, L.E., Stannard, C.R.: Home sewing patterns and perceived success of pattern alterations for fit. In: Making Waves Toward a Sustainable and Equitable Future (2025). https://doi.org/10.31274/itaa.18787
7. FreeSewing: https://freesewing.org/
8. Islam, M.N.-U., Hasan, S.M.M., Akter, M., Chowdhury, M.K.H.: A sustainable approach to clothing design: integration of zero- waste design and 3D virtual prototyping. In: Proceedings of ICTSE 2025 (2025)

9. Islam, T., Miron, A., Liu, X., Li, Y.: Deep learning in virtual try-on: a comprehensive survey. IEEE Access. **12**, 29475–29502 (2024). https://doi.org/10.1109/ACCESS.2024.3368612
10. Morelli, D., Fincato, M., Cornia, M., Landi, F., Cesari, F., Cucchiara, R.: Dress code: high-resolution multi-category virtual try-on. arXiv preprint arXiv:2204.08532 (2022). https://doi.org/10.48550/arXiv.2204.08532
11. Menon, G., Peter, A.P., Jomon, E., Varghese, J., Antony, M.A.: Apparel customization using generative AI. In: Proc. 10th Int. Conf. Advanced Computing and Communication Systems (ICACCS), pp. 1486–1490 (2024). https://doi.org/10.1109/ICACCS60874.2024.10717142
12. CLO Virtual Fashion: CLO3D developer documentation. https://developer.clo3d.com/
13. Touch Portal: Touch Portal—remote macro control deck. https://www.touch-portal.com/
14. Lund, A.M.: Measuring usability with the USE questionnaire. Usability Interface. **8**(2), 3–6 (2001)

UX Evaluation, Metrics, and Research Methods

User Experience Research Methodology for Optimizing the Institutional Enrollment System

Alejandra Alvarez(✉), Harold Castañeda, Carlos Varela, Javier Ramirez, and Christian Lozano

Corporación Universitaria Taller Cinco, 58 North Highway Kilometer 19, Chia, Colombia
alejandra.alvarez@taller5.edu.co

Abstract. Digital transformation has become a central driver of the Fourth Industrial Revolution, reshaping educational systems through the integration of emerging technologies and data-driven decision-making. This study analyzes the institutional digital transformation process implemented by Taller Cinco within the framework of Education 4.0, emphasizing the convergence between human intelligence and artificial intelligence to enhance learning environments and organizational performance. Using an institutional case study approach, the research examines how the institution has developed a hybrid pedagogical and technological ecosystem that integrates synchronous and asynchronous learning platforms, data analytics, and user-centered design methodologies to improve both academic and administrative processes. Particular attention is given to the implementation of digital infrastructures, including learning management systems, cloud-based institutional information systems, and customer relationship management (CRM)-based analytics integrated with digital marketing attribution models. The study also examines the development of SPOT T5, a multidisciplinary initiative designed to optimize user experience and institutional efficiency through behavioral analytics, iterative prototyping, and machine-learning-supported decision-making. Based on these findings, the study proposes the Taller Cinco Intelligent Education Ecosystem Framework, a conceptual model that illustrates how digital infrastructure, data intelligence, hybrid pedagogical environments, and organizational innovation converge to enable data-driven governance and adaptive learning ecosystems. The results suggest that the integration of technological intelligence with human-centered design can strengthen institutional resilience, improve student retention, and support more strategic decision-making processes in higher education. The case of Taller Cinco illustrates how universities can evolve toward intelligent organizations capable of responding dynamically to technological change while fostering creativity, critical thinking, and collaborative innovation within the Education 4.0 paradigm.

Keywords: Digital Transformation · Education 4.0 · Artificial Intelligence · Data-Driven Higher Education · Human-Centered Design

C. Stephanidis et al. (Eds.): HCII 2026, CCIS 3047, pp. 317–324, 2026.
https://doi.org/10.1007/978-3-032-30552-7_30

1 Introduction

Digital transformation, understood as the comprehensive change driven by the application of digital technologies across all spheres of society, currently represents the core of the Fourth Industrial Revolution [1]. This transformation transcends the simple adoption of digital tools; rather, it involves the intelligent integration of emerging technologies such as artificial intelligence (AI), the Internet of Things (IoT), cloud computing, big data analytics, and immersive environments (AR/VR), operating in synergy with human capabilities strengthened through digital literacy and continuous learning. Within this new paradigm, the capacity to generate, process, and apply data in real time becomes a fundamental pillar of competitiveness, agility, and innovation. From this perspective, digital transformation should not be understood merely as a technological upgrade but as a strategic and systemic evolution that requires organizations to continuously adapt to shifting market dynamics, regulatory frameworks, and the increasingly complex expectations of digitally empowered users [2]. Institutions seeking to remain competitive in the 4.0 era must therefore embed technological intelligence within every layer of decision-making and service delivery, enabling more responsive and adaptive organizational models.

Within this context, higher education institutions face a particularly significant challenge: redefining their pedagogical models, governance structures, and technological infrastructures to remain relevant in an increasingly digital knowledge economy [3]. Beyond technological pressures, universities must also respond to rigorous quality assurance systems designed to evaluate institutional performance, academic standards, and governance practices. In Colombia, these challenges are reflected in the national accreditation system led by the Consejo Nacional de Acreditación (CNA), which establishes demanding standards of high quality that institutions must demonstrate through evidence-based management, continuous improvement processes, and transparent academic and administrative practices. Consequently, digital transformation becomes not only a technological imperative but also a strategic enabler for achieving institutional quality objectives. The integration of digital infrastructures, advanced analytics, and institutional information systems enables universities to strengthen traceability, monitoring, and evidence-based decision-making processes required by contemporary accreditation frameworks. In this sense, the development of intelligent data ecosystems becomes essential for supporting governance models aligned with both national and international quality assurance standards [4].

In response to these dynamics, Taller Cinco has adopted a disruptive institutional approach aligned with the principles of Technology 4.0, aiming to enhance human intelligence (HI) through the convergence of artificial intelligence, advanced analytics, and agile educational methodologies. The institution envisions a model in which human and artificial intelligences coevolve, fostering creativity, adaptability, and critical thinking as central drivers of innovation within higher education environments. This vision has guided the progressive development of a hybrid pedagogical and technological ecosystem that integrates both physical and digital environments in order to create a more seamless learning experience. At the core of this transformation lies the integration of user-centered methodologies—particularly UX/UI design—combined with data-driven design principles. Through continuous monitoring of user interaction data, behavioral analytics, and iterative feedback loops, the institution has begun to develop responsive educational systems capable of dynamically adapting to student needs. Such an approach not only enhances the user experience but also converts data into actionable insights that support institutional decision-making and continuous improvement processes [5].

To operationalize this vision, Taller Cinco has implemented a comprehensive strategy for the design and implementation of experiential and experimental learning spaces. These environments function as "living laboratories", where students participate in collaborative creation processes supported by digital technologies such as virtual prototyping, immersive simulation, and cloud-based collaboration platforms. This approach aligns with the institutional didactic principle of "Feeling and thinking to transform," which seeks to form individuals capable of operating effectively in cyber-physical environments where the boundaries between digital and physical realities are increasingly blurred. In operational terms, the institution's transition toward Technology 4.0 began with the adoption of Zoom Education for synchronous virtual learning and Moodle as a learning management system (LMS) supporting asynchronous interaction. These platforms established the technological foundation for a hybrid educational model capable of ensuring learning continuity, flexibility, and personalized educational experiences. During the COVID-19 pandemic, this model demonstrated a significant level of institutional resilience, achieving a student retention rate of 91.86% during the 2020–2 academic period, illustrating the effectiveness of the institution's rapid technological adaptation.

However, the transformation process also revealed important structural limitations in the institution's legacy information infrastructure, which had not undergone substantial modernization for more than 15 years. Administrative processes such as enrollment management, certification, financial operations, and academic tracking were fragmented across multiple systems, limiting operational efficiency and negatively affecting the overall user experience. Recognizing the strategic importance of modern digital infrastructure, Taller Cinco partnered with Innovesting in 2021 to modernize its Institutional Information System (IIS), introducing cloud-based management, integrated online payment systems, and real-time academic monitoring capabilities. Despite these advances, post-implementation evaluations revealed additional operational challenges. The redesigned admissions process continued to rely heavily on physical procedures, generating bottlenecks and frustration among applicants. This situation highlighted a key lesson in digital transformation within the Industry 4.0 paradigm: technological implementation alone is insufficient without a comprehensive redesign of institutional processes centered on human experience and supported by empirical research on user behavior and system usability.

To address these limitations, the institution launched SPOT T5, a multidisciplinary innovation initiative inspired by Industry 4.0 principles such as interconnectivity, cyber-physical integration, and intelligent automation. The initiative applies agile methodologies, UX research techniques, and iterative prototyping processes to design digital solutions aimed at simplifying user interaction and improving administrative efficiency. By capturing data from multiple user touchpoints, the initiative enables predictive analytics capable of anticipating student needs and informing institutional decision-making processes in real time. In parallel with the transformation of academic and administrative processes, the institution also identified the need to redesign its institutional communication and marketing strategies. The digital transformation process revealed important limitations in the existing customer relationship management (CRM) infrastructure, which lacked standardized data structures capable of accurately tracking the admissions funnel and measuring the effectiveness of digital marketing campaigns. As a result, Taller Cinco initiated a comprehensive diagnostic process aimed at restructuring its CRM architecture, integrating campaign attribution mechanisms through standardized UTM parameters and aligning marketing analytics with institutional decision-making processes.

This transformation also led to the redefinition of institutional buyer personas, enabling a deeper understanding of the motivations, digital behaviors, and decision journeys of prospective students across different generational segments. By integrating CRM analytics, campaign tracking, and behavioral data, the institution has begun to develop a data-driven marketing strategy capable of linking branding, communication, and recruitment efforts with measurable performance indicators. This approach allows the institution to monitor user journeys across multiple digital touchpoints and progressively optimize student recruitment strategies through marketing intelligence and predictive analytics. Consequently, digital transformation has begun to expand beyond the educational and administrative domains to encompass institutional branding and marketing governance, positioning data analytics as a key instrument for aligning communication strategies with enrollment growth objectives and long-term institutional sustainability.

Ultimately, the ongoing transformation process at Taller Cinco illustrates how higher education institutions can progressively evolve toward more intelligent organizational models, in which digital ecosystems operate as adaptive systems capable of learning, responding, and continuously improving. By integrating human creativity with technological intelligence, the institution has started to modernize its educational and administrative systems while strengthening its capacity to meet the rigorous standards of quality, governance, and institutional accountability required by contemporary higher education systems. To conceptualize this evolving institutional transformation process, this study proposes the Taller Cinco Intelligent Education Ecosystem Model. At the foundation of the model lies digital infrastructure that enables data capture across academic, administrative, and marketing processes. These data streams feed analytics, ACADEMICsoft and CRM systems that generate actionable insights for institutional decision-making. Building upon this foundation, hybrid pedagogical ecosystems integrate digital and physical learning environments, while organizational innovation initiatives—such as SPOT T5 and emerging data-driven marketing strategies—provide the experimental groundwork that informs the gradual development of a more adaptive and intelligent institutional ecosystem capable of responding to the evolving demands of the Fourth Industrial Revolution.

2 Materials and Methods

This research was conducted under the User Experience Research (UX Research) approach, which focuses on understanding users' needs, motivations, and behaviors during their interaction with digital systems. This approach is grounded in the User-Centered Design (UCD) paradigm, which establishes that technological systems should be designed by considering the cognitive, behavioral, and emotional characteristics of end users [6].

Additionally, the study adopted the Lean UX methodological framework [7], which promotes iterative processes of research and hypothesis validation through the direct observation of user behavior. According to this framework, the objective of the research is not limited to producing analytical documentation, but rather to generate actionable knowledge capable of improving the real user experience within the digital system. From a methodological perspective, the study followed a mixed-methods approach, combining qualitative and quantitative techniques This approach enables the integration of empirical evidence derived both from users' perceptions and from their actual behavior while interacting with the system. The methodological design was structured into three complementary levels of analysis. The integration of these levels enabled the development of a methodological triangulation process, which strengthens the validity of the results by contrasting multiple sources of information. This is presented in Table 1.

Table 1. Methodological design.

Methodological Level	Objective
Primary Research	To understand the direct experience of users
Secondary Research	To analyze trends and reference models of enrollment systems
Usability Evaluation	To identify interaction problems within the system

Source: Own elaboration (2026)

3 Results

The documentary analysis made it possible to understand user behavior in online service acquisition processes. Several studies on e-commerce indicate that a significant proportion of users with internet access regularly conduct digital transactions. This finding is relevant for the present study, as it suggests that applicants possess sufficient digital competencies to complete online enrollment processes, provided that the system offers a clear and efficient user experience. In order to understand students' perceptions of the enrollment system, two focus group sessions were conducted with active students from the institution. Participants were selected considering variables such as age, academic semester, and previous experience with the enrollment system. The results indicated that students expect digital processes that are: simple, intuitive and fully self-managed. Additionally, participants expressed frustration with the complexity of some forms and the lack of guidance during the registration process. To validate the qualitative findings, an online survey was designed and distributed to active students at the institution. The target population consisted of approximately 900 students, from which a representative sample of 210 participants was calculated, considering a 90% confidence level and a 5% margin of error. The results demonstrate that the institution's digital presence and the clarity of the information available online play a decisive role in applicants' enrollment decisions (Table 2).

Table 2. Main survey results.

Finding	Percentage (%)
Students who learned about the institution through the internet	52
Users who compare several options before making a decision	25
Users influenced by testimonials	21
Users who prioritize ease of use	15

Source: Own elaboration (2026)

Later, to evaluate users' real interaction with the system, moderated usability tests were conducted with six external participants. During the tests, users were asked to complete three main tasks: Explore the main page of the institutional portal, consult information about an academic program and Initiate the enrollment process. The results made it possible to identify several frictions in the user experience. The findings in Table 3 were consistent with the usability principles established by Nielsen [8], according to which digital systems should minimize the user's cognitive load and provide clear feedback during interaction.

Table 3. Problems Identified in the Usability Test.

Problem	Level of Criticality
Long forms	High
Confusing iconography	Medium
Lack of guidance in the process	High
Unclear error messages	Critical

Source: Own elaboration (2026)

Later the web analytics analysis made it possible to examine the actual behavior of users within the institutional portal, as well as the bounce rates where a high number was identified on pages related to the admission process (Table 4).

Table 4. Interactions per page.

Page	Homepage	Graphic Design Program	Admissions Page
Number of visits	119,523	87,108	8,236
Bounce rates	56.9%	80.5%	78%

Source: Own elaboration (2026)

These results demonstrate that the institution's digital presence and the clarity of the information available online play a decisive role in applicants' enrollment decisions. The triangulation of qualitative and quantitative techniques made it possible to consistently identify several problems associated with the user experience of the institutional enrollment system. The results of the study reveal three main issues: usability problems, mainly associated with the complexity of the registration process; deficiencies in digital communication, related to the clarity of the information available to applicants; and limitations in the mobile experience, considering that most users access the system from mobile devices. These findings provide a solid empirical basis for designing improvement strategies aimed at simplifying the enrollment process, optimizing the user experience, and increasing the conversion rate of prospective applicants.

4 Conclusions and Discussions

This study analyzed the ongoing digital transformation process at Corporación Universitaria Taller Cinco within the framework of Education 4.0, focusing on the institutional initiatives developed through the SPOT T5 program and the progressive redesign of academic, administrative, and marketing systems. The findings demonstrate that digital transformation in higher education cannot be understood solely as the implementation of technological tools but must be approached as a systemic organizational process involving governance, pedagogical innovation, data analytics, and user-centered design. The results of the UX research conducted on the institutional enrollment system revealed that technological modernization alone does not guarantee an efficient digital experience for users. Despite the implementation of online admission systems, usability tests, focus groups, and web analytics identified several interaction barriers affecting applicants' ability to complete the registration process autonomously. Issues such as complex forms, insufficient system guidance, unclear feedback messages, and high bounce rates within admission-related pages indicate that user experience plays a critical role in the effectiveness of digital institutional systems.

The integration of qualitative and quantitative research techniques—including focus groups, surveys, usability testing, and web analytics—allowed the study to triangulate evidence and identify consistent patterns in user behavior. The findings highlight three central challenges affecting the institutional admission process: usability limitations in the registration interface, insufficient clarity in digital communication strategies, and the need to optimize mobile user experiences given the predominance of smartphone-based access. In response to these findings, the study emphasizes the strategic importance of incorporating UX research methodologies into institutional digital transformation processes. User-centered design approaches enable universities to redesign digital systems based on real user behavior rather than institutional assumptions, ultimately improving system efficiency and reducing operational burdens on administrative and commercial teams [9, 10].

Another key contribution of this research is the identification of the role that data ecosystems play in enabling institutional decision-making. The restructuring of the institutional customer relationship management (CRM) architecture, combined with campaign attribution models and behavioral analytics, represents an important step toward aligning digital marketing strategies with institutional recruitment objectives. Through the integration of CRM analytics, UTM campaign tracking, and buyer persona modeling, Taller Cinco has begun to develop a data-driven approach to student recruitment that connects branding, communication strategies, and enrollment performance indicators. Furthermore, the SPOT T5 initiative demonstrates the potential of multidisciplinary innovation environments to function as experimental laboratories for institutional digital transformation. By integrating agile methodologies, UX research techniques, and iterative prototyping processes, SPOT T5 provides a framework through which technological experimentation can inform broader institutional strategy and governance.

References

1. Schwab, K.: The Fourth Industrial Revolution. World Economic Forum (2016)
2. Kane, G.C., Palmer, D., Phillips, A.N., Kiron, D., Buckley, N: Strategy, not technology, drives digital transformation. MIT Sloan Management Review and Deloitte University Press (2015)
3. Hussin, A.A.: Education 4.0 made simple: ideas for teaching. Int. J. Educ. Lit. Stud. **6**(3), 92–98 (2018). https://doi.org/10.7575/aiac.ijels.v.6n.3p.92
4. Dwivedi, Y.K., et al.: Impact of COVID-19 pandemic on information management research and practice: transforming education, work and life. Int. J. Inf. Manag. **55**, 102211 (2020). https://doi.org/10.1016/j.ijinfomgt.2020.102211
5. Siemens, G., Long, P.: Penetrating the fog: analytics in learning and education. EDUCAUSE Rev. **46**(5), 30–40 (2011)
6. Norman, D.A.: The Design of Everyday Things: Revised and Expanded Edition. Basic Books (2013)
7. Gothelf, J., Seiden, J.: Lean UX: Designing Great Products with Agile Teams, 2nd edn. O'Reilly Media (2016)
8. Nielsen, J.: Usability Engineering. Morgan Kaufmann (1993)
9. Ramírez, J.A., et al.: Development of a mobile application based on the internet of things (IoT) for the creation of closed security circuits in small localities. In: International Conference on Human-Computer Interaction, pp. 130–140. Springer, Cham (2025)
10. Navarro, E., Yepes, I.C., Sierra, J., Garcia-Tirado, J., Ramírez, J.A., Barros, C.: Implementation of artificial intelligence for tax processes: bibliometric analysis from an international view. In: International Conference on Human-Computer Interaction, pp. 329–340. Springer, Cham (2025)

Putting the User First: A User-Centered Approach to AI System Evaluation

Nichole Breeland(✉), Jake A. Whritner, Christine S. P. Yu, Aarit Ahuja, and Rachel L. Kelly

Exponent, Inc., Menlo Park, CA, USA
nbreeland@exponent.com

Abstract. While trust and transparency are commonly studied in generative AI (genAI) research, the field lacks a unified, user-centered framework for organizing variation in how users engage with and evaluate genAI systems. The main goal of the current study was to empirically evaluate if a four-persona (Skeptic, Vigilant, Enthusiast, Learner) framework developed based on previous literature could characterize genAI users. Specifically, we aimed to examine whether these hypothesized personas differed on dimensions of trust and reliance, transparency and explainability, decision-making behaviors, and user competence and self-efficacy. Survey data collected from 500 respondents did not support the originally hypothesized persona types; instead, a Principal Component Analysis (PCA) identified two independent dimensions of AI attitudes—Engagement and Scrutiny—from which a revised four-persona framework (Principled Skeptic, Indifferent Non-User, Critical Adopter, Uncritical Adopter) was derived. Using this framework, personas differed systematically in patterns of genAI use, trust and reliance, transparency and explainability, decision-making behaviors, and perceived competence, highlighting the relevance of engagement and scrutiny for understanding variation in genAI onboarding, training, and user-centered system evaluation.

Keywords: Generative AI · User Experience Research · Trust and Transparency · Personas · User-Centered Design · Human–AI interaction · AI User Attitudes · AI Trust and Reliance · AI Personas · AI Adoption

1 Introduction

1.1 Objective and Significance

As generative artificial intelligence (genAI) systems become increasingly integrated into daily life, understanding the diversity of user experiences, expectations, and concerns may play a key role in successful deployment. Trust and transparency are among aspects of user experience (UX) that are critical to effective genAI use, with studies showing that design reliability and explanation can shift behaviors and decision making [1–3]. However, genAI systems introduce distinct UX challenges due to their nondeterministic qualities. These challenges are compounded by various intrinsic user attributes (e.g., attitudes, beliefs, or needs) that drive AI-related user behavior [4–6].

C. Stephanidis et al. (Eds.): HCII 2026, CCIS 3047, pp. 325–336, 2026.
https://doi.org/10.1007/978-3-032-30552-7_31

Current research on genAI remains fragmented, with most studies examining trust and reliance, transparency and explainability, and decision-making in isolation rather than considering these dimensions together as part of the broader user experience. This has limited the field's ability to develop a holistic understanding of how users perceive and interact with AI systems in practice. Notably, persona-based segmentation of genAI users is largely absent or still in early conceptual stages [7–10], constraining efforts to systematically link user characteristics with patterns of use, trust and reliance, transparency and explainability, decision-making, and competence and self-efficacy. To address this gap, the present study applies a persona-driven framework to empirically examine variation in user behaviors and perceptions across these key dimensions, thus providing a more integrated, user-centered foundation for understanding genAI interaction.

1.2 Persona Definitions

The existing literature demonstrates that patterns and perceptions around AI use vary. The present study aimed to investigate the extent to which these patterns and perceptions mapped to four hypothesized personas (see Table 1 for abbreviated description and OSM for full description) [22].

Table 1. Hypothesized Persona Definitions.

Type	Citations	Description
AI-Adverse Skeptic	[5, 11–16]	Distrustful and risk-averse, avoids genAI use and disengages quickly after errors while prioritizing transparency and safeguards.
Vigilant User	[3, 9, 12, 17]	Actively uses and monitors genAI, calibrating trust and reliance based on performance, context, and transparency cues.
Automation Enthusiast	[2, 7, 12, 18, 19]	Highly positive and adoption-oriented, emphasizing benefits and tending toward over-reliance with reduced critical oversight.
Learner	[6, 10, 15, 20]	Curious and exploratory, engages with genAI to build understanding and competence through hands-on use and feedback.

1.3 Hypotheses

We hypothesized that the proposed genAI user personas would represent distinct user orientations and would differ systematically across key dimensions of trust and reliance, transparency and explainability, decision-making behaviors, and competence and self-efficacy, reflecting different patterns of engagement, oversight, and risk across user types (see Table 2).

Table 2. Hypothesized Pattern of Results by Persona and Domain.

Domain	Persona			
	Skeptic	Vigilant	Enthusiast	Learner
Patterns of use	Personal	Both[3]	Both[3]	Personal
Trust and reliance[1]	Low	Moderate	High	Moderate
Transparency and explainability[1]	Low	Moderate	High	Moderate
Decision-making[2]	Often	Often	Rarely	Sometimes
Competence and self-efficacy[1]	Moderate	High	High	Low

[1]Reflects respondents' perceptions of the construct. [2] Reflects frequency of fact checking. [3]Both personal and work use.

2 Methods

2.1 Participants

The present study includes $N = 500$ participants recruited to achieve a balanced sample across age, gender, and AI experience (i.e., novice, somewhat experienced, experienced, very experienced; non-AI users were not eligible to participate). Recruitment targets for age (18–65+ years) and gender were based on U.S. Census data to ensure demographic representativeness. Participants were recruited and compensated via a third-party market research firm. The sample size was determined to ensure validity of statistical testing and to be representative of the large total population (i.e., any general user of genAI chat platforms) [21]. See OSM for data cleaning procedures and demographic details [22].

2.2 Survey Design

To test the hypothesized genAI user personas and their perspectives on trust and reliance, transparency and explainability, decision-making behaviors, and competence and self-efficacy, this survey leveraged a mixed-methods design and included questions aimed at identifying the four hypothesized personas and evaluating whether persona groups demonstrate systematic differences in perspectives on trust and reliance, transparency and explainability, decision-making behaviors, and competence and self-efficacy (see Table 3 for examples; see OSM for full question set [22]) [10, 23–25].

Table 3. Survey Question Examples by Domain.

Domain	Question Example
Persona Questions (40 questions total, 10 per persona)	
Skeptic	When an AI system makes a mistake, I lose trust in it quickly.

(*continued*)

Table 3. (*continued*)

Domain	Question Example
Vigilant	I seek out information about how AI systems make decisions.
Enthusiast	I rarely question the recommendations provided by AI systems.
Learner	I seek out training or educational resources about AI.
AI User Experience Questions	
Patterns of use	In what context do you use genAI chat platforms?
Trust and reliance	I would trust genAI chat platforms completely.
Transparency and explainability	I understand the limitations of genAI chat platforms.
Decision-making[1]	How often do you fact-check responses for your use of genAI chat platforms.
Competence and self-efficacy	I know how to format prompts to optimize responses.

Note. Question list is non-exhaustive. Respondents answered most questions via a Likert scale or categorical response option choice. All respondents answered the open-ended question: "Please briefly describe any concerns you have about genAI chat platforms that discourage you from using them more" which is described alongside trust and reliance.

3 Results

This section summarizes the primary findings and highlights key differences across the identified user personas. First, we describe the analysis and refinement of the personas, followed by an examination of differences across major dimensions of AI interaction, including genAI use, trust and reliance, transparency and explainability, decision-making, and user competence and self-efficacy. Additional analyses and supporting statistics are reported in the OSM [22].

3.1 Persona Development

We set out to test a theoretically motivated framework proposing four AI user personas: Skeptic, Vigilant, Enthusiast, and Learner. Correlation analyses revealed that only Skeptic attitudes formed a distinct cluster; items intended to capture Vigilant, Enthusiast, and Learner personas overlapped heavily, suggesting that these three types do not represent separate psychological constructs (see Fig. 1).

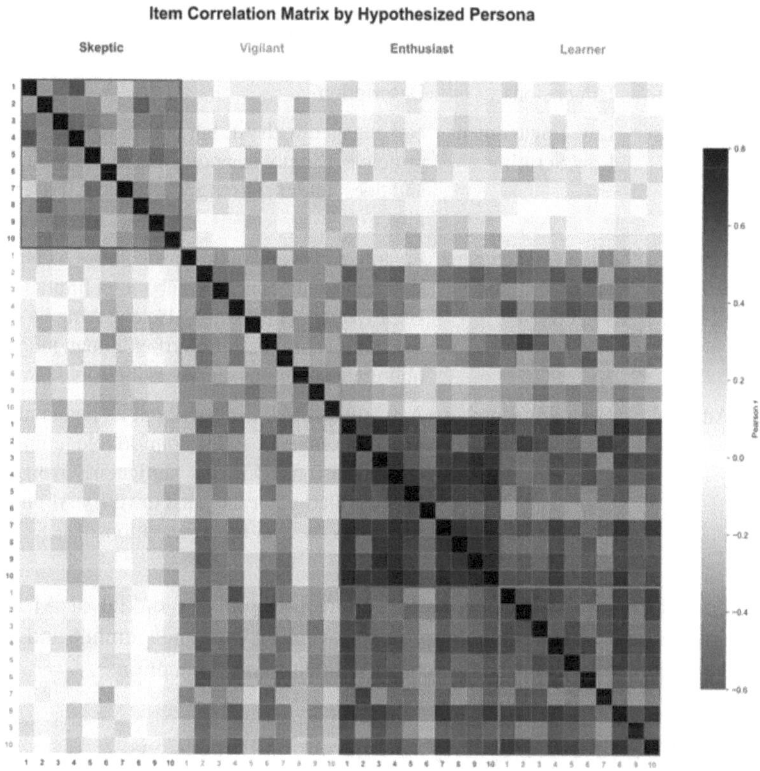

Fig. 1. Correlation matrix showing Skeptic attitudes form a distinct cluster while Vigilant, Enthusiast, and Learner show strong correlation with each other.

To uncover the underlying structure, we conducted a Principal Component Analysis (PCA), which identified two independent dimensions explaining approximately 50% of the total variance. The first, AI Engagement, captured enthusiasm, and active use of AI, while the second, AI Scrutiny, reflected critical evaluation and caution. Importantly, these dimensions are orthogonal: a person can be highly engaged with AI while simultaneously applying critical scrutiny, or disengaged yet not skeptical. Moreover, this 2D space can be divided into four quadrants to create interpretable archetypes that refine the original persona concept (see Table 4; see OSM for additional details [22]).

Table 4. Revised genAI User Personas.

Type	Dimensions	Description
Principled Skeptic	Low Engagement High Scrutiny	Not actively involved with AI and holds substantive concerns about it. Worried about ethics, bias, and the displacement of human judgment. Their disengagement is driven by considered critique rather than indifference.

(continued)

Table 4. (*continued*)

Type	Dimensions	Description
Indifferent Non-User	Low Engagement Low Scrutiny	Not engaged with AI, but not for reasons of principle. Simply has not adopted the technology and does not hold strong views about it in either direction.
Critical Adopter	High Engagement High Scrutiny	Equally active and enthusiastic about AI but simultaneously concerned about its limitations. Uses AI frequently while also checking its outputs, worrying about bias, preferring human judgment in important situations, and wanting robust oversight.
Uncritical Adopter	High Engagement Low Scrutiny	Actively uses AI, excited about its potential, tries new tools eagerly, and is comfortable letting AI make decisions. Does not particularly worry about bias, regulation, or the need to verify AI outputs. Embraces AI with few reservations.

This updated 2D framework provides a more interpretable model of AI attitudes than the hypothesized four-persona approach, revealing that engagement and scrutiny operate independently and jointly shape user behavior and perceptions.

3.2 Persona Differences Across Key AI Interaction Dimensions

Using the revised 2D persona framework, we explored how users differ in their genAI interactions across the key dimensions of patterns of use, trust and reliance, transparency and explainability, decision-making, and user competence and self-efficacy. This approach allows us to examine how the independent dimensions of engagement and scrutiny relate to behaviors and experiences with AI.

Patterns of Use. To characterize use cases, we drew on a taxonomy developed by Chatterji and colleagues, who identified seven broad conversation topics reflecting common user-requested capabilities of ChatGPT: writing, practical guidance, technical help, multimedia, information seeking, self-expression, and other [26]. A Chi-square test of independence revealed a statistically significant association between persona type and genAI use case ($\chi^2(df = 21, N = 1347) = 50.80$, $p < 0.001$). Follow-up assessment of standardized residuals revealed that Indifferent Non-Users ($z = 2.01$, $p < 0.05$) and Principled Skeptics ($z = 2.13$, $p < 0.05$) use genAI for more general information seeking purposes. Principled Skeptics also use genAI for other conversational topics ($z = 2.62$, $p < 0.05$). Critical Adopters are more likely to use genAI for technical help compared to all other personas ($z = 2.40$, $p < 0.05$). Relatedly, genAI usage context depends on persona type ($\chi^2(df = 3, N = 682) = 24.88$, $p < 0.001$). Critical Adopters are more likely to use genAI at work ($z = 2.55$, $p < 0.05$) compared to Principled Skeptics ($z = -2.53$, $p < 0.05$). These findings suggest that persona type is meaningfully associated with technical use of genAI platform capabilities and reliance on those capabilities in work contexts.

Trust And Reliance. To examine persona differences in trust and reliance on genAI chat platforms, we first assessed the internal consistency of the four relevant items using Cronbach's alpha. The scale demonstrated high reliability ($\alpha = 0.93$), supporting the creation of an average trust score across the four items. An ANOVA revealed a statistically significant difference in composite trust score across persona groups ($F(3, 496 = 129.93$, $p < 0.001$, $\eta^2 = 0.44$). Post-hoc comparisons revealed significant differences among all four personas, with Uncritical Adopters ($M = 5.62$, $SD = 0.88$ on a 7-point scale from 1, "*Strongly Disagree*" to 7, "*Strongly Agree.*") reporting the highest trust-and-reliance score, followed by Critical Adopters ($M = 5.21$, $SD = 1.24$), Indifferent Non-Users ($M = 4.03$, $SD = 1.29$), and Principled Skeptic ($M = 2.87$, $SD = 1.23$). These findings suggest that persona type is meaningfully associated with users' trust and reliance on genAI platforms.

Additionally, participants' responses to a question regarding whether they had any concerns about genAI platforms that keep them from using it more were analyzed using qualitative thematic analysis. Interrater reliability was assessed on a 30% subset of responses, yielding substantial agreement (Cohen's $\kappa = 0.84$). Principled Skeptics most frequently mentioned accuracy, quality, and performance (32.2%), privacy and security (21.7%), or impact on work or society (14.8%) whereas Indifferent Non-Users and Critical Adopters reported concerns related to privacy and security (27.4%–30.1%), accuracy, quality, and performance (20.0%–22.1%), or otherwise reported no concerns (18.5%–21.3%). Uncritical Adopters were most likely to report no concerns (31.3%), with concerns related to privacy and security (22.6%), accuracy, quality, and performance (17.4%) emerging as second and third most frequently reported.

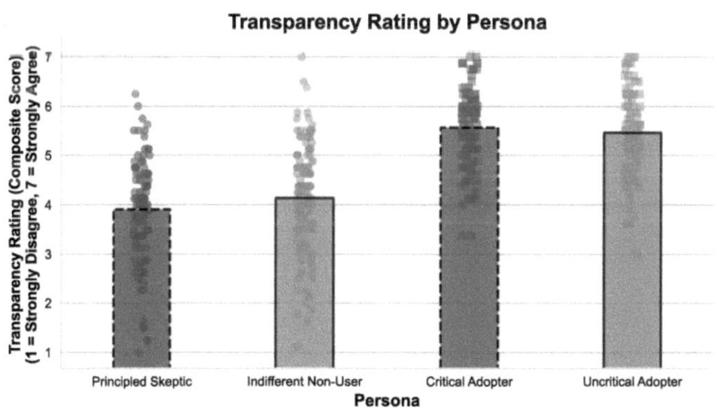

Fig. 2. Persona type is associated with ratings of genAI system transparency. Error bars represent standard error of the mean.

Transparency And Explainability. To examine users' perception of genAI chat platforms transparency and explainability across personas, we first assessed the internal consistency of eight relevant items ($\alpha = 0.89$) and generated an averaged transparency-and-explainability score. An ANOVA showed a statistically significant difference in the composite transparency-and-explainability score across persona groups ($F(3, 496) = 107.75$, $p < 0.001$, $\eta^2 = 0.36$). Post-hoc comparisons showed that both Critical Adopters ($M = 5.56$, $SD = 0.77$) and Uncritical Adopters ($M = 5.46$, $SD = 0.86$)

reported significantly higher understanding of platform capabilities, limitations, and reasoning processes when compared to Indifferent Non-Users ($M = 4.13$, $SD = 1.05$) and Principled Skeptics ($M = 3.90$, $SD = 1.02$), while the Adopters did not differ significantly from one another, and Non-Users did not differ significantly from Skeptics (see Fig. 2). These findings suggest that persona type is associated with users' perceptions of how genAI platforms operate and the transparency of the underlying system. Notably, this persona-level difference in transparency ratings falls along the line of the first principal component of AI Engagement, with the two Adopter personas (who ranked highly on the AI Engagement axis), providing higher ratings than the Non-Users and Skeptics (who ranked low on the AI Engagement axis). Thus, this finding suggests that merely engaging with the technology and adopting it in one's daily life, regardless of inherent skepticism or scrutiny, can lead to a higher degree of perceived system transparency.

Decision Making. We examined how persona type relates to users' decision-making behaviors when interacting with genAI chat platforms by asking respondents how often they fact-check genAI responses across various use cases. An ANOVA revealed a statistically significant difference in fact-checking frequency averaged across use case ($F(3, 496) = 16.41$, $p < 0.001$, $\eta^2 = 0.09$). Post-hoc comparisons indicated that both Critical Adopters ($M = 2.55$, $SD = 0.73$) and Principled Skeptics ($M = 2.53$, $SD = 0.90$) engaged in fact-checking significantly more often than Indifferent Non-Users ($M = 2.00$, $SD = 0.71$) and Uncritical Adopters ($M = 2.18$, $SD = 0.73$), while Critical Adopters and Principled Skeptics did not differ significantly, and Indifferent Non-Users and Uncritical Adopters did not differ significantly (see Fig. 3). These findings suggest that persona type is meaningfully associated with how critically users evaluate genAI outputs. In contrast to the earlier finding on transparency, the persona-level difference in fact-checking frequency falls along the line of the second principal component of AI Scrutiny, indicating that regardless of one's degree of engagement, individuals with high inherent skepticism are more likely to fact-check the outputs of a genAI platform.

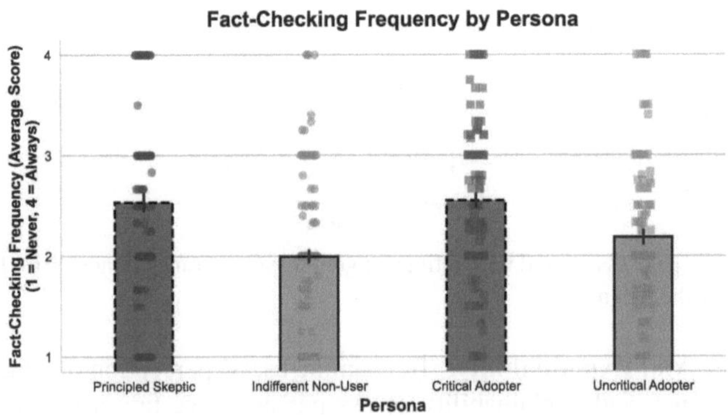

Fig. 3. Persona type is associated with genAI response fact-checking frequency, regardless of use case. Error bars represent standard error of the mean.

User Competence and Self-Efficacy. To examine users' confidence and skill in interacting with genAI chat platforms, the internal consistency of two related items was confirmed using Cronbach's alpha ($\alpha = 0.85$), supporting the creation of a composite user-competence/self-efficacy score by averaging these items. An ANOVA showed a statistically significant difference in self-reported competence and efficacy ($F(3, 496) = 55.75, p < 0.001, \eta^2 = 0.25$). Post-hoc comparisons indicated that Critical Adopters ($M = 5.51, SD = 1.08$) and Uncritical Adopters ($M = 5.40, SD = 1.33$) reported higher competence in formatting and refining prompts than Indifferent Non-Users ($M = 3.98, SD = 1.39$) and Principled Skeptics ($M = 3.86, SD = 1.52$), while the Adopters did not differ significantly from one another, and Non-Users did not differ significantly from Skeptics (see Fig. 4). These results suggest that persona type is meaningfully associated with usage and users' ability and confidence in effectively interacting with genAI platforms. As with transparency and explainability, the persona-level difference in user competence and self-efficacy ratings falls along the line of the first principal component of AI Engagement, with the two Adopter personas providing higher ratings than the Non-Users and Skeptics. Thus, this finding again suggests that engaging with the technology and adopting it in one's daily life, can lead to a higher degree of perceived self-efficacy in using genAI tools, regardless of inherent scrutiny.

Fig. 4. Persona type is meaningfully associated with user competence and self-efficacy ratings. Error bars represent standard error of the mean.

4 Discussion

The present study's user-centered, persona-driven approach to AI system evaluation contributes to the field by demonstrating how trust and reliance, transparency and explainability, decision-making behaviors, and user competence and self-efficacy co-vary as part of a broader pattern of genAI engagement and scrutiny. The goal of the present research was to develop a user-centered framework for understanding variation in genAI use by empirically examining whether theoretically derived personas from prior literature (i.e., Skeptic, Vigilant, Enthusiast, and Learner) captured meaningful differences in users' attitudes, behaviors, and experiences with AI systems. Our analyses revealed that only Skeptic attitudes formed a distinct cluster and that items hypothesized to capture the other three personas (i.e., Vigilant, Enthusiast, and Learner) strongly correlated with each other, suggesting that they did not represent separate psychological constructs. Thus, we updated our persona model to a 2D framework, revealing that engagement and scrutiny operate independently and jointly characterize patterns of user behavior and perceptions. The updated 2D framework provides a more interpretable model of AI attitudes than the original approach and identifies four distinct user personas (i.e., Uncritical Adopters, Critical Adopters, Indifferent Non-Users, and Principled Skeptics) defined by their relative levels of engagement and scrutiny.

Using the revised 2D persona framework, clear patterns emerged across genAI use, trust and reliance, transparency and explainability, decision-making behaviors, and user competence and self-efficacy. The two Adopter personas (i.e., Critical and Uncritical) were characterized by higher overall engagement with genAI, including greater use for work-related and technical tasks, whereas Principled Skeptics and Indifferent Non-Users reported lower engagement and more general, information-seeking use. Correspondingly, Adopters reported higher trust and reliance on genAI platforms than Non-Users and Skeptics. Perceived transparency and explainability, as well as self-reported competence and self-efficacy, were also higher among Adopters than among Non-Users and Skeptics, with little differentiation between Critical and Uncritical Adopters on these dimensions. In contrast, decision-making behaviors showed a different pattern: fact-checking frequency was higher among personas characterized by greater scrutiny (i.e., Critical Adopters and Principled Skeptics) than among Indifferent Non-Users and Uncritical Adopters. These results indicate that persona groups defined by engagement and scrutiny differ systematically in how they use genAI, how much they trust and understand it, how critically they evaluate its outputs, and how competent they perceive themselves to be when interacting with it.

It should be noted that, because genAI systems and their use are rapidly evolving, the patterns observed in this study reflect a snapshot in time and may change as technologies mature and user familiarity increases. Future research using longitudinal designs or complementary behavioral measures could further examine the stability and evolution of engagement and scrutiny across genAI users.

Taken together, the present study advances the literature by offering an integrated, persona-driven framework for evaluating genAI use that addresses the need for more unified examinations using shared metrics to characterize how trust and reliance, transparency and explainability, decision-making behaviors, and user competence and self-efficacy vary across different genAI user types [7, 9, 12]. These findings document systematic differences across user patterns of engagement and scrutiny that are relevant to how transparency mechanisms, controls, and educational resources are experienced, underscoring potential limitations of uniform design assumptions. More broadly, these results illustrate how variation in users' attitudes and behaviors could correspond with differences in how AI systems are experienced across application contexts, including healthcare, education, and consumer products.

Acknowledgments. We would like to thank Dr. Shukri Souri and Dr. John Pye for their continued support.

Disclosure of Interests. The authors have no competing interests to declare that are relevant to the content of this article.

References

1. Chen, V., Liao, Q.V., Vaughan, J.W., Bansal, G.: Understanding the role of human intuition on reliance in human-AI decision-making with explanations. http://arxiv.org/abs/2301.07255 (2023). https://doi.org/10.48550/arXiv.2301.07255.
2. Dunning, R.E., Fischhoff, B., Davis, A.L.: When do humans heed AI agents' advice? When should they? Hum. Factors. **66**, 1914–1927 (2024). https://doi.org/10.1177/00187208231190459
3. Elder, H., Canfield, C., Shank, D.B., Rieger, T., Hines, C.: Knowing when to pass: the effect of AI reliability in risky decision contexts. Hum. Factors. **66**, 348–362 (2024). https://doi.org/10.1177/00187208221100691
4. Ehsan, U., Liao, Q.V., Muller, M., Riedl, M.O., Weisz, J.D.: Expanding Explainability: towards social transparency in AI systems. In: Proceedings of the 2021 CHI Conference on Human Factors in Computing Systems, pp. 1–19. ACM, Yokohama Japan (2021). https://doi.org/10.1145/3411764.3445188
5. Haresamudram, K., Larsson, S., Heintz, F.: Three levels of AI transparency. Computer. **56**, 93–100 (2023). https://doi.org/10.1109/MC.2022.3213181
6. Spallazzo, D., Sciannamè, M., Ceconello, M.: User Experience + Artificial Intelligence: Assessing the Qualities of AI-Infused Systems. Springer Nature Switzerland, Cham (2025). https://doi.org/10.1007/978-3-031-77521-5
7. Bach, T.A., Khan, A., Hallock, H., Beltrão, G., Sousa, S.: A systematic literature review of user trust in AI-enabled systems: an HCI perspective. Int. J. Hum.–Comput. Interact. **40**, 1251–1266 (2024). https://doi.org/10.1080/10447318.2022.2138826
8. Jones-VanMieghem, C., Papandreou, A., Dolan, L.: What kind of AI users are there? Poster presented at Indiana University School of Medicine Education Day, Indianapolis, IN, April 26 (2024). https://hdl.handle.net/1805/40376
9. Lai, V., Chen, C., Smith-Renner, A., Liao, Q.V., Tan, C.: Towards a science of human-AI decision making: an overview of design space in empirical human-subject studies. In: 2023 ACM Conference on Fairness Accountability and Transparency, pp. 1369–1385. ACM, Chicago IL USA (2023). https://doi.org/10.1145/3593013.3594087
10. Liu, J., Karimnazarov, J., White, R.W.: Trapped by expectations: Functional fixedness in LLM-enabled chat search, arXiv:2504.02074 (2025). https://doi.org/10.48550/arXiv.2504.02074
11. Dietvorst, B.J., Simmons, J.P., Massey, C.: Algorithm aversion: people erroneously avoid algorithms after seeing them err. J. Exp. Psychol. Gen. (2015). https://doi.org/10.1037/xge0000033
12. Zerilli, J., Bhatt, U., Weller, A.: How transparency modulates trust in artificial intelligence. Patterns. **3**(4), 100455 (2022). https://doi.org/10.1016/j.patter.2022.100455
13. Andrada, G., Clowes, R.W., Smart, P.R.: Varieties of transparency: exploring agency within AI systems. AI & Soc. (2022). https://doi.org/10.1007/s00146-021-01326-6
14. Larsson, S., Heintz, F.: Transparency in artificial intelligence. Internet Pol. Rev. **9**(2) (2020). https://doi.org/10.14763/2020.2.1469
15. Liao, Q.V., Wortman Vaughan, J.: AI transparency in the age of LLMs: a human-centered research roadmap. Harvard Data Sci. Rev., Special Issue 5. (2024). https://doi.org/10.1162/99608f92.8036d03b

16. Balasubramaniam, N., Kauppinen, M., Hiekkanen, K., Kujala, S.: Transparency and explainability of AI systems: ethical guidelines in practice. In: Gervasi, V., Vogelsang, A. (eds.) Requirements Engineering: Foundation for Software Quality. REFSQ 2022. LNCS, vol. 13216. Springer, Cham (2022). https://doi.org/10.1007/978-3-030-98464-9_1
17. Lee, J.D., See, K.A.: Trust in automation: designing for appropriate reliance. Hum. Factors. **46**(1), 50–80 (2004)
18. Parasuraman, R., Riley, V.: Humans and automation: Use, misuse, disuse, abuse. Hum. Factors. **39**(2), 230–253 (1997). https://doi.org/10.1518/001872097778543886
19. Parasuraman, R., Manzey, D.H.: Complacency and bias in human use of automation: an attentional integration. Hum. Factors. **52**(3), 381–410 (2010). https://doi.org/10.1177/0018720810376055
20. Gröner, F., Chiou, E.K.: Investigating the impact of user interface designs on expectations about large language models' capabilities. Proc. Hum. Factors Ergon. Soc. Annu. Meet. **68**(1), 155–161 (2024). https://doi.org/10.1177/10711813241260399
21. Krejcie, R.V., Morgan, D.W.: Determining sample size for research activities. Educ. Psychol. Meas. **30**(3), 607–610 (1970). https://doi.org/10.1177/001316447003000308
22. Open Science Framework (OSF): Project repository. https://osf.io/a26kb/overview?view_only=ad0bc513afa24d49b2566c958020e238
23. Höddinghaus, M., Sondern, D., Hertel, G.: The automation of leadership functions: would people trust decision algorithms? Comput. Hum. Behav. **116**, 106635 (2021). https://doi.org/10.1016/j.chb.2020.106635
24. Zhao, R., Benbasat, I., Cavusoglu, H.: Do users always want to know more? Investigating the relationship between system transparency and users' trust in advice-giving systems. In: Proceeding of the European Conference on Information Systems (ECIS) (2019)
25. Yu, L., Li, Y.: Artificial intelligence decision-making transparency and employees' trust: the parallel multiple mediating effect of effectiveness and discomfort. Behav. Sci. **12**(5), 127 (2022). https://doi.org/10.3390/bs12050127
26. Chatterji, A. et al.: How people use ChatGPT. In: NBER Working Paper w34255 (2025). https://doi.org/10.3386/w34255

Improving Usability and Workflow Efficiency in Finite Element Analysis (FEA) Software: A Heuristic Evaluation and Prototype Exploration

Seth Y. Christensen(✉) and Ethan T. Hawkes

Brigham Young University, Provo, UT 84602, USA
seth.christensen@byu.edu

Abstract. Finite Element Analysis (FEA) software is fundamental in modern engineering, enabling virtual stress testing of infrastructure and equipment. However, existing FEA tools often impose rigid workflows and interaction patterns that increase user cognitive load and create steep learning curves.

This work explores improved workflow and interaction patterns through a UX-focused critique of current FEA systems. We conducted a heuristic evaluation of five established FEA products and three adjacent 3D modeling tools, analyzing traditional usability principles alongside information architecture, progressive disclosure, and accessibility considerations. Each software was evaluated across 13 heuristic categories using a 5-point severity scale.

Three recurring themes emerged: (1) inconsistent UI and information architecture across tools and menus, leading to fragmented workflows; (2) weak information affordance, such as heavy abbreviations and unlabeled features that impede recognition; and (3) limited progressive disclosure, with poorly grouped settings and visual clutter that overwhelm users. These issues contribute to workflow inefficiency by reducing contextual guidance and increasing cognitive overhead.

We translated findings into low-fidelity wireframes that addressed identified challenges. Early user feedback from five participants with intermediate to advanced CAD/FEA experience during usability interviews revealed strong reliance on prior mental models, discoverability challenges, and ambiguity arising from combining 2D and 3D tooling, while also demonstrating general success in workflow progression and a positive reception of novel features such as versioning branches.

This paper presents the heuristic evaluation methodology, synthesized findings, and initial expert insights, offering actionable opportunities to reduce friction in FEA workflows and guide future interface design improvements.

Keywords: Finite Element Analysis (FEA) · Usability · Heuristic Evaluation · Workflow Design · Information Architecture · Progressive Disclosure · CAD Software

C. Stephanidis et al. (Eds.): HCII 2026, CCIS 3047, pp. 337–347, 2026.
https://doi.org/10.1007/978-3-032-30552-7_32

1 Introduction

Finite Element Analysis (FEA) software represents a critical category of engineering tools that enable virtual stress testing, structural analysis, and performance prediction across diverse domains, including aerospace, automotive, civil engineering, and biomedical applications. Despite their technical sophistication and widespread adoption, these systems often impose significant usability barriers that impede both novice adoption and expert efficiency. Users must navigate complex workflows spanning geometry preparation, mesh generation, boundary condition specification, solver configuration, and results interpretation—each stage presenting unique interaction challenges and cognitive demands.

1.1 Motivation

The usability challenges in FEA software manifest across multiple dimensions. First, inconsistent information architecture across tools and workflow stages creates fragmented user experiences, forcing practitioners to rebuild mental models as they transition between preprocessing, solving, and post-processing environments. Second, weak information affordance (characterized by heavy use of abbreviations, unlabeled icons, and implicit functionality) impedes feature discoverability and increases reliance on recall rather than recognition. Third, limited progressive disclosure results in dense interfaces that present all functionality simultaneously, overwhelming users with visual clutter and poorly grouped settings.

These usability barriers have tangible consequences. Novice users face steep learning curves that delay productive work and may discourage adoption of simulation-driven design practices. Expert users experience workflow inefficiencies that accumulate across repeated analysis cycles, reducing productivity and increasing cognitive load. Furthermore, poor usability can contribute to errors in model setup or results interpretation, with potential implications for engineering decision-making.

Despite the critical importance of usability in engineering software, FEA tools have received limited attention in the HCI research community. While substantial work exists on usability in general-purpose CAD systems, the unique challenges of FEA workflows (e.g., integrating geometric modeling, numerical simulation, and scientific visualization) remain underexplored.

1.2 Research Questions and Contributions

This work addresses three primary research questions: RQ1: What are the primary usability challenges in current FEA software, as identified through systematic heuristic evaluation? RQ2: How do these challenges manifest across different workflow stages, and what patterns emerge across tools? RQ3: Can alternative interface designs informed by usability heuristics and progressive disclosure strategies address identified challenges?

This paper contributes: (1) systematic heuristic evaluation of five major FEA platforms and three 3D modeling tools across 13 evaluation categories, (2) synthesis of findings through affinity diagram analysis identifying four primary categories of usability issues, (3) comprehensive tool inventory audit organized by workflow stage, (4) low-fidelity wireframe prototypes demonstrating alternative interface designs, and (5) empirical findings from usability testing with five expert users.

2 Literature Review

Finite Element Analysis (FEA) software enables virtual stress testing and structural analysis across diverse engineering domains. This review examines usability challenges in FEA and related engineering software, cognitive load in complex interfaces, and design strategies for improving workflow efficiency.

2.1 Usability in Engineering Software

Engineering software presents unique usability challenges distinct from general-purpose applications. Dinkel et al. [3] demonstrated that user-centered GUI redesign of an FE program, employing requirement analysis and ribbon menu structure, substantially improved usability and supported wider adoption. Li et al. [6] developed a CAE-specific perceived usability assessment instrument, arguing that standard metrics lack domain specificity to capture the challenges of engineering software. Their diagnostic study revealed that generic instruments fail to address CAE-specific information architecture issues.

Lindemann et al. [8] presented Forcepad, a 2D finite-element tool using a "painting with stiffness pixels" metaphor to flatten the learning curve. This demonstrates that domain-specific interaction metaphors can substantially reduce cognitive load in early-stage workflows. Zapf et al. [16] proposed a framework linking simulation theory with practice through context-sensitive help, workflow schemes, and modular handbooks, emphasizing that situationally adapted technologies improve user-program interaction.

2.2 Cognitive Load and Workflow Design

Cognitive Load Theory [15] provides a framework for understanding how interface design impacts user performance through intrinsic complexity, extraneous load from poor design, and germane load from learning. Baig and Kavakli [1] provided empirical evidence from EEG studies that the input modality significantly affects cognitive load during 3D modeling. Suˇznjevi'c et al. [14] demonstrated, through longitudinal analysis, that the iterative methodology improved usability and reduced workload across heterogeneous platforms, with implications for cross-tool FEA workflows.

Lee et al. [5] proposed refined UI principles specific to complex 3D parametric tools, arguing that Nielsen's generic heuristics [9] are insufficient alone for parametric engineering tools. They advocate domain-specific principles that address complexity, representation affordances, and task-aligned tool organization. Li et al. [7] synthesized CAD/CAM usability evaluation methods, emphasizing that insufficient attention to information architecture necessitates domainspecific evaluation heuristics.

2.3 Design Strategies

Norman's [12] concept of affordance is particularly relevant to FEA software, where users must understand complex relationships between geometric entities, material properties, and analysis results. Camba [2] demonstrated that annotated parametric CAD models reduced alteration time and errors through improved information affordance. Gonz'alez [4] and Pietrzak et al. [13] introduced bidirectional programming approaches linking code and 3D views, demonstrating that such features streamline design and reduce errors by improving visibility between representations.

Progressive disclosure (i.e., revealing information gradually to avoid overwhelming users) is addressed by several studies. Dinkel et al. [3] implemented progressive disclosure through ribbon organization and staged access, demonstrating that layered interfaces reduce surface complexity while maintaining advanced functionality. Lindemann et al. [8] embodied progressive disclosure through simplified feature sets for conceptual design contexts.

2.4 Research Gaps

Despite substantial research on engineering software usability, significant gaps remain in FEA-specific user experience research. Most studies focus on CAD and general CAE tools, with limited attention to complete FEA workflows encompassing preprocessing, solving, and post-processing. Insufficient research addresses information architecture for hierarchical relationships between geometric entities, mesh elements, material properties, and analysis results. The systematic application of progressive disclosure principles in FEA contexts and the understanding of expert versus novice needs remain underexplored, motivating the current study.

3 Methodology

This study employed a multi-method approach combining heuristic evaluation, affinity diagram synthesis, tool inventory audit, wireframe development, and usability testing to systematically identify usability challenges and validate design solutions.

3.1 Heuristic Evaluation

Five FEA platforms (ANSYS, MSC Patran, Simcenter 3D, Altair HyperWorks, Abaqus) and three 3D modeling tools (Houdini, Spline, Blender) were evaluated. For each platform, 2–4 h of instructional and workflow demonstration videos were analyzed, with detailed observations recorded for specific usability issues, interface patterns, and interaction challenges.

Each interface was evaluated across 13 criteria derived from Nielsen's heuristics [9] and domain-specific principles [5]: Visibility of System Status, Match Between System and Real World, User Control and Freedom, Consistency and Standards, Error Prevention, Recognition Rather Than Recall, Flexibility and Efficiency of Use, Help Users Recognize/Diagnose/Recover from Errors, Help and Documentation, Information

Architecture, Progressive Disclosure, WCAG Accessibility Standards, and CAD/FEA Workflow Integration (FEA only).

Each category was scored on a five-point scale: 5 (Optimal: no issues, direct task completion), 4 (Cosmetic/Minor: minor issues, no impediment), 3 (Moderate: indirect completion, some confusion), 2 (Major: frequent errors, workarounds needed), 1 (Critical: repeated unsuccessful completion). Scores were aggregated to produce overall usability scores (FEA: 65 points; non-FEA: 60 points).

3.2 Affinity Diagram and Tool Inventory

Insights from the heuristic evaluation were organized into an affinity diagram through multi-step grouping, establishing four primary categories: Affordances and Signifiers, Inconsistent Information Architecture, Visual Hierarchy and Progressive Disclosure, and Workflow Inefficiency. Each category was further divided into 3–5 subcategories.

A tool inventory audit identified common functions across the five FEA platforms, organized by workflow stage (Geometry, Boundary Conditions, Mesh, Solution/Solve). Each tool was assigned a standardized name and definition, providing a consolidated view of shared functionality to inform wireframe development.

3.3 Wireframe Development and Usability Testing

Low-fidelity wireframes addressed three design objectives: improving UI consistency and information architecture, strengthening tool affordances and signifiers, and implementing progressive disclosure. The tool inventory ensured industry-standard functionality while redesigning grouping and architecture to reduce cognitive load.

Five participants with intermediate to advanced CAD/FEA experience (university students and faculty using SolidWorks, ANSYS, Rhino, and LS-DYNA) completed tasks that represent common FEA steps: locating tools, navigating workflow stages, and progressing through simulation preparation. Think-aloud protocol captured navigation patterns, confusion points, mental model reliance, label interpretation, and task completion success.

4 Results

4.1 Heuristic Evaluation Findings

The heuristic evaluation revealed substantial variation in usability across platforms. Table 1 presents overall scores. Altair HyperWorks achieved the highest FEA score (51/70, mean 3.92/5), while Abaqus and MSC Patran scored lowest (31/70 each, mean 2.38/5). Among non-FEA tools, Blender achieved the highest mean (4.18/5 across 11 heuristics).

Table 2 shows average scores by heuristic category. Help and Documentation (4.25/5) and WCAG Accessibility (4.12/5) scored highest, indicating adequate documentation and a baseline level of accessibility. Recognition Rather Than Recall (2.25/5) and Information Architecture (2.38/5) scored lowest, suggesting systems struggle with discoverability, menu organization, and interface state visibility.

Table 1. Platform-level usability scores.

Rank	Tool	Heuristics	Total Mean
1	Altair HyperWorks	13	51/70 3.92/5
2	Blender	11	46/70 4.18/5
3	Spline	11	43/70 3.91/5
3	ANSYS	13	43/70 3.31/5
5	Houdini	12	33/70 2.75/5
5	Simcenter 3D	13	33/70 2.54/5
7	Abaqus	13	31/70 2.38/5
7	MSC Patran	13	31/70 2.38/5

Qualitative themes included: (1) discoverability and labeling issues (missing labels, abbreviations, small icons), (2) information architecture problems (dense pop-ups, nested menus, fragmented tool placement), (3) weak state visibility and selection feedback, and (4) workflow inconsistency across stages.

Table 2. Average scores by heuristic category.

Heuristic	Tools	Mean
Help and Documentation	8	4.25/5
WCAG Accessibility Standards	8	4.12/5
Match Between System and Real World	8	3.75/5
User Control and Freedom	8	3.50/5
Visibility of System Status	8	3.38/5
Help Users Recognize/Diagnose Errors	6	3.33/5
CAD/FEA Workflow Integration	5	2.80/5
Error Prevention	8	2.75/5
Consistency and Standards	8	2.75/5
Progressive Disclosure	8	2.75/5
Flexibility and Efficiency of Use	8	2.75/5
Information Architecture	8	2.38/5
Recognition Rather Than Recall	8	2.25/5

4.2 Affinity Diagram Synthesis

Analysis organized 127 observations into four primary categories: (1) Affordances and Signifiers (32 observations): unclear labels, weak visual differentiation, insufficient state feedback; (2) Inconsistent Information Architecture (38 observations): fragmented tool placement, inconsistent grouping, poor hierarchy, unclear workflow transitions; (3) Visual Hierarchy and Progressive Disclosure (29 observations): dense interfaces, poor visual prioritization, lack of contextual presentation; (4) Workflow Inefficiency (28 observations): excessive clicks, lack of automation, poor stage integration, redundant data entry.

4.3 Usability Testing Findings

Ten primary patterns emerged from five testing sessions:

1. Strong reliance on prior mental models (5/5): All participants mapped expected workflows from SolidWorks, ANSYS, Rhino, LS-DYNA onto the prototype, expecting traditional sketch-to-extrusion pipelines.
2. Ambiguity from combining 2D and 3D tooling (4/5): Users noted these represent different modeling stages, typically separated in other systems.
3. Discoverability challenges (4/5): Trial-and-error behavior when locating features, scanning multiple interface areas before committing to actions.
4. Inconsistent labeling (3–4/5): Ambiguity in labels (e.g., "Edit" vs. "Quick Edit," "Cleanup") required interpretation.
5. Cognitive load from visual density (3/5): Moments of overload with dense or repetitive elements, particularly in project setup.
6. Geometry editing challenges (4/5): Uncertainty with cleanup workflows; preference for direct manipulation over abstract tools.
7. Consistent viewport navigation expectations (5/5): Universal expectation for mouse-based controls (scroll-to-zoom, click-and-drag pan).
8. General workflow progression success (5/5): All participants progressed through major stages; separation was understood and appreciated.
9. Limited understanding of "Main Branch" feature (4/5): Initial misinterpretation, but positive reception after explanation.
10. Need for adaptive interfaces (1/5): One advanced participant highlighted differentiated experiences for novice versus expert users.

Results highlight tension between leveraging familiar paradigms and introducing innovations. Challenges emerged from misalignment with mental models, ambiguous labeling, weak discoverability, and insufficient onboarding for novel features.

5 Discussion

The findings highlight a fundamental tension in FEA software design: balancing workflow innovation with users' deeply ingrained mental models from existing CAD and FEA systems. While the prototype introduced promising concepts, usability challenges emerged when innovations diverged from established conventions without sufficient guidance.

5.1 Alignment with Usability Heuristics

The observed issues directly map to Nielsen's heuristics [9]. Participants' attempts to map the interface to familiar CAD workflows indicate partial violation of the *match between the system and the real world*. Users' exploratory navigation and reliance on trial-and-error demonstrate failures in *recognition rather than recall*—the lowest-scoring heuristic (mean = 2.25/5) in our evaluation. Universal expectations for mouse-based viewport controls reinforce the importance of *consistency and standards*. Cognitive overload from dense interfaces suggests opportunities for improved *aesthetic and minimalist design* through progressive disclosure.

5.2 Cognitive Load and Mental Models

Findings align with Cognitive Load Theory [15]. Participants demonstrated high extraneous cognitive load when interpreting ambiguous labels, navigating poorly differentiated elements, and resolving uncertainty about action locations. This burden slowed interaction without contributing to task completion. Users relied heavily on mental model transfer from tools like SolidWorks and ANSYS, reducing intrinsic load when the system aligned with expectations but increasing effort when it did not. Combining 2D and 3D tools disrupted expected modeling sequences, forcing users to reconcile conflicting paradigms. This echoes Baig and Kavakli's [1] observation that interface choices significantly affect cognitive workload.

Effective FEA design should: (1) minimize extraneous load through clear hierarchy and labeling, (2) leverage existing mental models where possible, and (3) introduce new paradigms gradually with appropriate scaffolding.

5.3 Information Architecture and Discoverability

Difficulty locating features indicates challenges with information architecture and affordance design. Users relied on hierarchical scanning, trial-and-error, and naming assumptions, suggesting the system lacks strong signifiers. Integrating multiple tool types (sketching and 3D modeling) weakened information architecture by obscuring conceptual boundaries. Participants' suggestions to separate these tools reinforce the importance of clear conceptual grouping, aligning with Lee et al.'s [5] argument for domain-specific principles addressing task-aligned tool organization.

The heuristic evaluation supports this interpretation, with Information Architecture scoring lowest (mean = 2.38/5). Dense pop-up windows, nested menus, and fragmented tool placement repeatedly increased navigation burden across evaluated platforms.

5.4 Novel Features and Onboarding

The "Main Branch" versioning feature represents a key innovation, but initial comprehension was consistently low. This highlights a common UX challenge: novel features require explicit onboarding and strong affordances to be discoverable. Once explained, participants recognized its value for iterative workflows. Introducing advanced concepts should be accompanied by: (1) clear labeling and visual cues, (2) contextual explanations or tooltips, and (3) progressive disclosure of functionality, aligning with Dinkel et al.'s [3] findings on staged access reducing surface complexity.

5.5 Design Implications

These findings suggest six implications for FEA interface design:

- **Leverage existing mental models:** Align core workflows with established CAD/FEA conventions to reduce friction and learning curves.
- **Prioritize clear information architecture:** Group related tools and separate distinct conceptual stages to improve discoverability.
- **Reduce cognitive load:** Use visual differentiation, progressive disclosure, and concise labeling to support faster comprehension.
- **Support discoverability:** Ensure users can easily identify where actions should occur without trial-and-error.
- **Introduce novel features with guidance:** Pair innovative functionality with onboarding mechanisms.
- **Design for diverse expertise:** Provide flexible interaction models accommodating varying experience levels, as suggested by Zapf et al.'s [16] situationally adapted technologies.

These recommendations are grounded in established HCI principles and supported by empirical evidence from both heuristic evaluation and usability testing.

6 Limitations

Several limitations should be considered when interpreting these findings. First, the heuristic evaluation at this stage of the study was conducted by a single evaluator, which may introduce subjectivity. Nielsen and Molich [11] recommend using multiple evaluators (typically 3–5) to increase problem identification and reduce bias. Second, the evaluation was conducted through video analysis rather than direct hands-on interaction, potentially emphasizing commonly visited interface areas over edge cases and less frequent features.

Third, the wireframes were intentionally low-fidelity, focusing on layout and information architecture rather than detailed visual or interaction design. Some usability challenges may reflect prototype limitations rather than underlying interface concepts. Higher-fidelity prototypes with interactive elements and realistic visual design would provide greater validation reliability across the entire interactive experience.

Fourth, usability testing with five participants from academic settings (undergraduate students, graduate students, and faculty) limits generalizability. While appropriate for formative testing [10], larger and more diverse samples, including industry practitioners and novice users, would strengthen findings. Finally, the evaluation focused on five major commercial FEA platforms and three 3D modeling tools, excluding open-source tools, specialized applications, and emerging cloud-based platforms. Software interfaces also evolve through updates, potentially affecting temporal validity of specific findings, though broader patterns and design principles remain relevant.

7 Conclusion and Future Work

This study investigated usability challenges in FEA software through systematic heuristic evaluation, affinity diagram synthesis, and usability testing of alternative interface designs. The findings reveal consistent patterns across major commercial platforms, with particular weaknesses in recognition rather than recall (mean = 2.25/5), information architecture (mean = 2.38/5), and progressive disclosure (mean = 2.75/5).

Three primary themes emerged: (1) inconsistent UI and information architecture across tools and workflow stages, (2) weak information affordance characterized by unclear labeling and insufficient visual differentiation, and (3) limited progressive disclosure resulting in dense interfaces. These challenges contribute to increased cognitive load, reduced workflow efficiency, and steep learning curves.

Usability testing demonstrated that users rely heavily on mental models from existing CAD/FEA systems, and that deviations from established conventions require explicit guidance and strong affordances. While participants navigated the proposed workflow structure, they encountered challenges with discoverability, ambiguous labeling, and interpretation of novel features.

Future work should develop higher-fidelity interactive prototypes evaluated through extensive testing with diverse participant samples. Longitudinal studies comparing traditional and redesigned interfaces would provide evidence of practical impact on productivity. Further refinement of domain-specific heuristics through collaboration with practitioners would strengthen assessment frameworks. Research should also investigate adaptive interfaces for diverse expertise levels, integration of AI-assisted workflows, and cross-platform workflow integration to improve information continuity across heterogeneous tool ecosystems.

By grounding design decisions in established usability principles, leveraging users' existing mental models, and carefully introducing innovations with appropriate guidance, future FEA interfaces can reduce friction, improve efficiency, and support a broader range of users in engineering analysis and simulation-driven design.

References

1. Baig, M.Z., Kavakli, M.: Analyzing novice and expert users' cognitive load in using a multimodal interface system. In: Proceedings of the International Conference on Human-Computer Interaction. Springer, Cham (2018)
2. Camba, J.D.: Annotation mechanisms to manage design knowledge in complex parametric models and their effects on alteration and reusability. J. Comput. Inf. Sci. Eng. **15**, 1–10 (2015)
3. Dinkel, C., et al.: User-oriented optimization of the GUI of a finite element programme to enhance the usability of simulation tools. In: Proceedings of the International Conference on Engineering Design (2018)
4. González, J.: Facilitating programming-based 3D computer-aided design using bidirectional programming. In: Proceedings of the ACM Conference on Human Factors in Computing Systems (CHI) (2024)
5. Lee, G., et al.: Usability principles and best practices for the user interface design of complex 3D architectural design and engineering tools. Autom. Constr. **26**, 1–22 (2010)
6. Li, G., et al.: Perceived usability of computer-aided engineering software. J. Eng. Des. **34**(5), 345–367 (2023)

7. Li, Y., Hedlind, M., Kjellberg, T.: Usability evaluation of CAD/CAM: state of the art. Procedia CIRP. **36**, 205–210 (2015)
8. Lindemann, J., et al.: Finite-element software for conceptual design. Adv. Eng. Softw. **41**(9), 1089–1096 (2010)
9. Nielsen, J.: Usability Engineering. Morgan Kaufmann, San Francisco, CA (1994)
10. Nielsen, J.: Why You Only Need to Test with 5 Users. Nielsen Norman Group (2000) https://www.nngroup.com/articles/why-you-only-need-to-test-with-5-users/
11. Nielsen, J., Molich, R.: Heuristic evaluation of user interfaces. In: Proceedings of the SIGCHI Conference on Human Factors in Computing Systems, pp. 249–256 (1990)
12. Norman, D.A.: The Psychology of Everyday Things. Basic Books, New York, NY (1988)
13. Pietrzak, T., Girouard, A., Casiez, G.: Introducing bidirectional programming in constructive solid geometry-based CAD. In: Proceedings of the ACM Conference on Human Factors in Computing Systems (CHI) (2024)
14. Sužnjević, M., et al.: Longitudinal usability and UX analysis of a multiplatform house design pipeline: insights from extended use across web, VR, and mobile AR. Int. J. Hum.-Comput. Interact. **41**(1), 1–18 (2025)
15. Sweller, J.: Cognitive load during problem solving: effects on learning. Cogn. Sci. **12**(2), 257–285 (1988)
16. Zapf, J., Alber-Laukant, B., Rieg, F.: Usability compliant supportive technologies in simulation-driven engineering. In: Proceedings of the International Conference on Engineering Design (2011)

Constraint-Guided SUS Inference from Natural Language Feedback

Leticia Cianconi[1], Luciana Terceiro[2], and Jefferson O. Silva[1,3(✉)]

[1] Pontifical Catholic University of São Paulo (PUC-SP), São Paulo, Brazil
jefferson.oliveira@prof.inteli.edu.br
[2] Department of Women and Children's Health, Uppsala University, Uppsala, Sweden
luciana.terceiro@uu.se
[3] Institute of Technology and Leadership (INTELI), São Paulo, Brazil

Abstract. The System Usability Scale (SUS) remains widely adopted due to its psychometric grounding, low administration cost, and well-established normative benchmarks [7,17]. However, conventional survey-based administration faces practical limitations at scale, including self-selection bias, respondent fatigue, and operational costs that grow with user base size [6,8]. Naturally occurring user feedback—app reviews, support tickets, discussion forums—contains linguistically encoded signals of usability perception that machine learning models can extract at scale [1,4]. Yet existing approaches treat the task as sentiment classification or thematic categorization, operating independently of formal psychometric instruments.

This independence introduces an underexplored validity risk: unconstrained neural models may generate predictions that violate the structural properties of SUS—item polarity, inter-item consistency, and score range boundaries—while remaining statistically plausible. Evidence from adjacent domains confirms that statistical performance and psychometric coherence can diverge substantially [15,16].

We propose a neuro-symbolic framework that addresses this risk directly. Neural components interpret natural language feedback; symbolic layers encode the structural constraints of SUS as explicit, enforceable rules within the inference process [5]. Rather than replacing SUS, the approach preserves its psychometric foundations while enabling large-scale usability assessment from naturally occurring feedback.

Keywords: User experience · Usability · Neuro-Symbolic Artificial Intelligence · SUS · Psychometric evaluations

1 Introduction

When millions of users interact with a digital system every day, understanding their experience becomes both essential and paradoxical. The very scale that

C. Stephanidis et al. (Eds.): HCII 2026, CCIS 3047, pp. 348–357, 2026.
https://doi.org/10.1007/978-3-032-30552-7_33

produces abundant traces of user behavior also makes traditional psychometric evaluation difficult to sustain. The System Usability Scale (SUS) remains one of the most widely used instruments for usability assessment due to its strong psychometric foundations, low administration cost, and well-established normative benchmarks [7,17]. However, administering SUS surveys across large or continuously evolving user populations faces practical limitations, including self-selection bias, respondent fatigue, and operational costs that grow rapidly with scale [6,8]. As a result, organizations often face a trade-off between maintaining rigorous usability measurement and relying on more scalable, but less structured, forms of feedback.

To address this limitation, researchers have explored machine learning methods that infer usability signals from naturally occurring sources such as app reviews, support tickets, and discussion forums [1,2,13]. These studies show that perceptions of usability, learning difficulty, and user confidence can be detected in large collections of unstructured text. However, many existing approaches treat the task as sentiment analysis or thematic classification, operating independently of formal usability instruments. As a consequence, their predictions may appear statistically reasonable while violating the structural assumptions that give psychometric tools like SUS their interpretability, such as item polarity, internal consistency relationships, and valid score ranges.

This tension raises a central question: *how can usability inference be automated at scale while preserving the psychometric structure that makes established instruments meaningful and comparable?*

In this paper, we propose a neuro-symbolic approach to this problem. Neural models are used to interpret natural language feedback, while symbolic constraints encode the structural properties of SUS directly in the inference process. This combination is designed to enable large-scale usability estimation without discarding the theoretical assumptions embedded in the original instrument [5]. Rather than replacing SUS or approximating it loosely, the proposed framework encodes its psychometric structure as explicit constraints that guide model outputs. Evidence from related domains suggests that unconstrained neural models can generate predictions that violate instrument assumptions when applied to structured assessments [15,16]. Without explicit constraints, automated usability inference is likely to face similar issues.

This paper makes three contributions. First, we identify an underexplored methodological risk in automated usability analysis: predictions that are statistically plausible but psychometrically invalid. Second, we formalize the structural constraints of SUS as symbolic rules that can be integrated into a neural inference pipeline. Third, we present a neuro-symbolic architecture that preserves instrument validity while enabling scalable usability assessment.

2 Background

2.1 Psychometric Structure of SUS

Brooke developed the SUS as a 10-item Likert scale for rapid subjective usability assessments [7]. Originally described as a "quick and dirty" usability scale, subsequent empirical work has demonstrated that SUS is a robust, standardized questionnaire applicable across a wide range of technologies and interface types. Following validation studies report strong reliability, with Cronbach's alpha typically ranging between 0.85 and 0.91 [3,10,11].

Three structural properties underpin its psychometric strength. The first item is the polarity relationships. SUS items purposefully alternate between positively and negatively worded statements. Brooke designed this structure to reduce acquiescence bias by requiring respondents to engage attentively with each item rather than adopting a uniform response pattern [7]. The odd-numbered items (1, 3, 5, 7, 9) are positively framed, and the scoring subtracts 1 from the raw response. Even-numbered items (2, 4, 6, 8, 10) are negatively framed, and scoring subtracts the raw response from 5 before aggregation. The polarity structure ensures that individual item contributions remain directionally consistent in the final score [14]. The second item is the consistency rules. Psychometric analyses of large SUS datasets consistently identify a dominant underlying factor representing perceived usability [10]. Correlations among item pairs are statistically significant, indicating that the ten items collectively reflect a coherent construct. The third item is the score range and boundaries. SUS scores are computed by summing polarity-adjusted item contributions and multiplying by 2.5, producing a bounded value in the interval between 0 and 100 [3]. Although expressed on a 0–100 scale, the result is not a percentage but a normalized usability index that enables comparison across systems. Established interpretive benchmarks place scores below 50 as unacceptable, scores near 68 as average, and scores above 85 as indicative of excellent usability [3]. These benchmarks provide the normative context that gives SUS measurements their comparative meaning across studies.

2.2 Neural Approaches to UX Evaluation

Research on neural approaches and automated UX evaluation has converged on three broad directions: inference from behavioural interaction logs, adaptive interfaces driven by physiological signals, and large language model (LLM)–based automation of evaluation processes.

Yang et al. show that deep neural networks can infer UX quality from minimal interaction data, such as click coordinates and time spent, using a convolutional–recurrent architecture that distinguishes successful from unsuccessful task completions [18]. The approach treats neural models as scoring mechanisms for interface redesign, enabling data-driven iteration without the need for repeated user recruitment. However, the authors observe that behavioural signals alone are insufficient for capturing higher-level UX dimensions such as learnability, indicating that interaction logs encode only a partial signal of the overall experience.

Gaspar-Figueiredo proposes a more dynamic perspective, framing interface adaptation as a reinforcement learning problem [9]. In this model, the interface evolves through a Markov Decision Process in which the agent selects modifications based on reward signals derived from task performance, user preferences, and physiological indicators such as EEG, eye tracking, and galvanic skin response. Physiological data are treated as real-time proxies for UX quality, enabling continuous adaptation during interaction rather than retrospective evaluation.

At the system level, recent reviews in the literature highlight the rapid expansion of AI-supported UX workflows. Liu surveys 55 studies between 2014 and 2024, identifying applications of machine learning and generative AI in sentiment analysis, user simulation, automated heuristic evaluation, and session summarization [12].

From a machine learning perspective, automated UX evaluation is typically framed as a prediction problem, where models infer usability signals from large-scale behavioral or textual data. For instance, sentiment analysis of app store reviews can estimate usability dimensions such as effectiveness and satisfaction, while hybrid deep learning models classify feedback according to usability-related attributes [1,2].

Despite their promise, these approaches share several limitations. Models trained on interaction data often reduce experience to discrete behavioral events, overlooking holistic usability constructs. Many systems also operate as opaque black boxes, raising concerns about interpretability. Most critically, current neural approaches rarely enforce the structural constraints of established usability instruments. As a result, automated predictions may appear statistically plausible while violating the psychometric relationships that make instruments such as SUS interpretable and comparable across studies.

3 The Risk of Unconstrained Inference

Automated inference of psychometric constructs from unstructured text introduces a class of validity threats that current approaches typically overlook: models may produce outputs that are statistically plausible yet structurally inconsistent with the instrument they aim to represent. This risk has been documented in adjacent domains where machine learning has been applied to structured psychological instruments.

Speer et al. [15] show that AI-derived scores in organizational assessment frequently violate assumptions required for valid psychometric interpretation—including inter-item consistency and parallelism conditions necessary for reliability estimation—while still achieving high predictive accuracy. Tay et al. [16] reach a similar conclusion in personality assessment: models trained to maximize convergence with self-report instruments tend to inherit measurement assumptions without enforcing them, producing scores that may appear convergently valid while lacking discriminant validity and interpretable consistency across items. The recurring pattern across both studies is the same: statistical performance and psychometric coherence can diverge substantially.

For SUS inference, this risk takes a specific structural form. SUS encodes a deliberate psychometric architecture: its ten items alternate in polarity, with positive and negative statements systematically interleaved and scored in opposite directions, and certain item pairs are theoretically expected to produce consistent signals. An unconstrained neural model has no inherent mechanism to respect these properties. It may assign high values to items that should be low given other responses, invert polarity relationships, or generate score patterns that fall outside interpretable ranges. Outputs may correlate with aggregate SUS scores while remaining individually uninterpretable and collectively incoherent—precisely the failure mode documented by Speer et al. [15] and Tay et al. [16].

The implication is not that neural language models are unsuitable for usability inference, but that predictive adequacy does not automatically translate into measurement validity. Preserving the psychometric meaning of SUS at scale requires treating its structural constraints not as implicit assumptions but as explicit, enforceable properties of the inference architecture.

4 Neuro-Symbolic SUS Inference

The proposed framework combines two complementary components: a neural layer that interprets natural language feedback and a symbolic layer that enforces the structural constraints of SUS on the resulting inferences. Rather than treating these components as a post-processing pipeline, we treat them as integrated stages of the same inference process. The symbolic layer therefore operates as a structural validator within the pipeline, not as an optional post-processing step. Figure 1 shows the overall architecture of the proposed system.

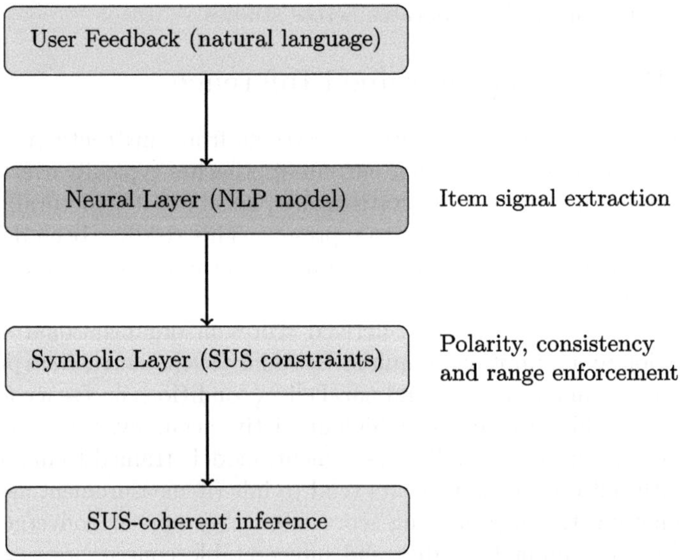

Fig. 1. Proposed neuro-symbolic architecture for SUS inference. The neural layer extracts usability signals from unstructured text; the symbolic layer validates the structural constraints of SUS before producing the final score.

The neural component takes unstructured user feedback as input and produces a preliminary mapping of linguistic signals to SUS item candidates. A transformer-based language model fine-tuned for sentiment or usability signals can serve this role [5]. The output of this layer is a vector of ten raw item estimates $\hat{r} = (\hat{r}_1, \ldots, \hat{r}_{10})$, where each $\hat{r}_i \in \mathbb{R}$ represents the model's unconstrained inference for item i prior to psychometric validation.

4.1 Symbolic Layer: Formalizing SUS Constraints

The symbolic layer encodes the structural properties of SUS as explicit, enforceable rules applied to $\hat{r}$ before the final score is computed. Four constraint classes are defined:

C1—Item scale bounds. Each item must be scored on a 1–5 Likert scale:

```
for each item i in {1, ..., 10}:
    assert 1 <= r_i <= 5
    if r_i < 1: r_i = 1
    if r_i > 5: r_i = 5
```

C2—Polarity alignment. Odd-numbered items (1, 3, 5, 7, 9) are positively worded; even-numbered items (2, 4, 6, 8, 10) are negatively worded. Scoring must reflect this structure:

```
positive_items = {1, 3, 5, 7, 9}
negative_items = {2, 4, 6, 8, 10}

contribution(i) =
    if i in positive_items: r_i - 1
    if i in negative_items: 5 - r_i
```

C3—Score range. The final SUS score must fall within the valid normalized range:

```
SUS_score = 2.5 * sum(contribution(i) for i in 1..10)
assert 0 <= SUS_score <= 100
```

C4—Inter-item consistency. Psychometric instruments often contain items that assess related constructs and are therefore expected to produce consistent signals. When two such items yield contributions that diverge beyond a tolerance threshold τ, the inference is flagged for review. The relevant pairs must be identified from the theoretical structure of the target instrument - the pairs used here serve only to illustrate the mechanism:

```
# illustrative only
consistency_pairs = [(1,3), (2,4), (5,7), (3,6), (7,9)]

for each (i, j) in consistency_pairs:
    if |contribution(i) - contribution(j)| > tau:
        flag_inconsistency(i, j)
```

When inconsistencies are flagged under C4, the symbolic layer surfaces them for practitioner review. The resolution policy—whether automatic filtering, score adjustment, or manual inspection—is left to the practitioner. The appropriate value of τ is a design parameter to be calibrated empirically in future work; its optimal setting will depend on the domain, the neural model, and the acceptable rate of false detections.

4.2 Illustrative Example

To illustrate the framework, consider the following review retrieved from a public mobile application store:

> *"Love the app overall, it's pretty intuitive once you get the hang of it. But honestly it felt clunky at first and I needed to ask for help more than I expected. Not sure I'd feel confident using all the features without a tutorial."*

A neural model processing this text might produce the following raw item estimates. Values are illustrative and constructed for demonstration purposes.

Item	Wording (abbreviated)	Polarity	$\hat{r}_i$
1	Would use frequently	positive	4
2	Unnecessarily complex	negative	3
3	Easy to use	positive	4
4	Need technical support	negative	2
5	Well integrated	positive	4
6	Too much inconsistency	negative	4
7	Most people learn quickly	positive	3
8	Cumbersome to use	negative	2
9	Felt confident	positive	2
10	Need to learn a lot first	negative	3

The symbolic layer identifies two flagged inconsistencies under C4. First, the pair (3, 6): item 3 signals ease of use (positive, $\hat{r}_3 = 4$) while item 6 signals high inconsistency (negative, $\hat{r}_6 = 4$), yielding contribution(6) $= 5 - 4 = 1$. This signal contradicts the ease-of-use inference. Second, the pair (7, 9) reveals tension between the inference that most people learn quickly ($\hat{r}_7 = 3$) and the low confidence signal ($\hat{r}_9 = 2$). The raw estimates yield a SUS score of 57.5, placing the system in the "poor" usability range under standard benchmarks. This score, however, rests on unresolved inconsistencies: a practitioner who reviews and resolves them may arrive at a materially different result. Depending on how the flagged tensions are interpreted, the adjusted score could cross into a higher usability range, a difference with direct consequences for product decisions.

5 Discussion

Several implications follow from the position presented here.

Psychometric Constraints as Design Requirements. A broader implication of this work is methodological. As discussed in Sect. 3, the validity losses observed when neural models are applied to structured instruments appear to be structural rather than incidental. Neural models typically optimize for predictive accuracy, not instrument fidelity. Treating psychometric constraints as explicit design requirements—rather than post-hoc evaluation criteria—makes the problem addressable by design. The neuro-symbolic approach provides one principled instantiation of this idea, but the underlying argument extends to any domain in which structured instruments are used as the basis for automated inference.

Limitations and Open Questions. The framework presented here is conceptual, and several questions require empirical investigation before deployment. First, the consistency threshold τ in C4 must be calibrated using real inference data; its optimal value will depend on the neural model, the feedback domain, and the acceptable rate of false detections. Second, the resolution policy for flagged inconsistencies—whether automatic filtering, score adjustment, or manual inspection—involves a trade-off between automation and interpretability that cannot be resolved purely on theoretical grounds. Third, the neural layer is treated here as a black box. In practice, model architecture and fine-tuning strategy will strongly influence the frequency and nature of flagged inconsistencies, making model selection an integral part of the framework rather than an independent choice.

Connections to Adjacent Communities. This work sits at the intersection of three research communities that rarely interact directly: HCI and usability evaluation, neuro-symbolic AI, and psychometrics. Advances in one area do not always reach the others in a timely manner. The present paper argues that the validity concerns documented in organizational AI assessment [15] and personality measurement [16] are directly relevant to HCI, and that the neuro-symbolic toolbox [5] offers concrete mechanisms to address them. Bridging these communities represents a productive research opportunity.

6 Conclusion

Scaling usability evaluation without sacrificing psychometric rigor is fundamentally a problem of measurement validity. Current approaches to automated usability inference typically operate independently of the structural properties of established instruments, creating validity losses that undermine the interpretability and comparability of results. Evidence from adjacent domains confirms that this problem arises systematically from the mismatch between neural optimization objectives and the fidelity requirements of psychometric instruments [15,16].

The neuro-symbolic framework introduced here addresses this mismatch directly. By encoding the structural constraints of SUS—item polarity, inter-item consistency, and score range boundaries—as explicit rules within the inference process, the approach enables large-scale usability assessment from naturally occurring feedback while preserving the psychometric foundations that give SUS scores their meaning and comparability.

Empirical validation is the necessary next step. Future work should focus on calibrating the consistency threshold τ, evaluating resolution policies against ground-truth SUS data, and examining the sensitivity of the framework to different neural model architectures. The longer-term goal is a validated system capable of continuous, psychometrically grounded usability monitoring at the scale demanded by modern interactive systems.

Disclosure of Interests. The authors have no competing interests to declare that are relevant to the content of this article.

References

1. Alabduljabbar, R.: User-centric AI: evaluating the usability of generative ai applications through user reviews on app stores. PeerJ Comput. Sci. **10**, e2421 (2024)
2. Alowidi, N., Alnanih, R., Alsaleh, N.: Hybrid deep learning approach for automating app review classification: advancing usability metrics classification with an aspect-based sentiment analysis framework. Comput. Mater. Continua **82**(1), 949–976 (2025)
3. Bangor, A., Kortum, P.T., Miller, J.T.: An empirical evaluation of the system usability scale. Int. J. Hum.-Comput. Interact. **24**(6), 574–594 (2008). https://doi.org/10.1080/10447310802205776
4. Baumgartner, J., Ruettgers, N., Hasler, A., Sonderegger, A., Sauer, J.: Questionnaire experience and the hybrid system usability scale: using a novel concept to evaluate a new instrument. Int. J. Hum. Comput. Stud. **147**, 102575 (2021)
5. Belle, V., Fisher, M., Russo, A., Komendantskaya, E., Nottle, A.: Neuro-symbolic AI + agent systems: a first reflection on trends, opportunities and challenges. In: Amigoni, F., Sinha, A. (eds.) Autonomous Agents and Multiagent Systems Best and Visionary Papers, pp. 180–200. Springer, Cham (2024). https://doi.org/10.1007/978-3-031-56255-6_10
6. Boyd, M.R., Bond, R., Vertesi, A., Dogan, H., Magee, J.: How people judge the usability of a desktop graphic user interface at different time points: is there evidence for memory decay, recall bias or temporal bias? Interact. Comput. **31**(2), 221–230 (2019)
7. Brooke, J.: SUS - a quick and dirty usability scale. In: Jordan, P., Thomas, B., Weerdmeester, B. (eds.) Usability Evaluation in Industry, pp. 189–194. Taylor & Francis, London (1996)
8. Drew, M.R., Falcone, B., Baccus, W.L.: What does the system usability scale (SUS) measure? In: Marcus, A., Wang, W. (eds.) DUXU 2018. LNCS, vol. 10918, pp. 356–366. Springer, Cham (2018). https://doi.org/10.1007/978-3-319-91797-9_25
9. Gaspar-Figueiredo, D.: Learning from interaction: user interface adaptation using reinforcement learning (2023). https://doi.org/10.48550/arXiv.2312.07216

10. Lewis, J.R., Brown, J., Mayes, D.K.: Psychometric evaluation of the EMO and the SUS in the context of a large-sample unmoderated usability study. Int. J. Hum.-Comput. Interact. **31**(8), 545–553 (2015). https://doi.org/10.1080/10447318.2015.1064665
11. Lewis, J.R., Sauro, J.: The factor structure of the system usability scale. In: Kurosu, M. (ed.) HCD 2009. LNCS, vol. 5619, pp. 94–103. Springer, Heidelberg (2009). https://doi.org/10.1007/978-3-642-02806-9_12
12. Liu, J.: AI in automated and remote UX evaluation: a systematic review (2014–2024). Adv. Hum.-Comput. Interact. **2025** (2025). https://doi.org/10.1155/ahci/7442179
13. Oztekin, A., Delen, D., Turkyilmaz, A., Zaim, S.: A machine learning-based usability evaluation method for e-learning systems. Decis. Support Syst. **56**, 63–73 (2013)
14. Peres, S.C., Pham, T., Philips, R.: Validation of the system usability scale (SUS): SUS in the wild. In: Proceedings of the Human Factors and Ergonomics Society 57th Annual Meeting, vol. 57, pp. 192–196 (2013). https://doi.org/10.1177/1541931213571043
15. Speer, A.B., Oswald, F.L., Putka, D.J.: Reliability evidence for AI-based scores in organizational contexts: applying lessons learned from psychometrics. Organ. Res. Methods (2025)
16. Tay, L., Woo, S.E., Hickman, L., Saef, R.M.: Psychometric and validity issues in machine learning approaches to personality assessment: a focus on social media text mining. Eur. J. Pers. **34**(5), 826–844 (2020)
17. Vlachogianni, P., Tselios, N.: Perceived usability evaluation of educational technology using the system usability scale (SUS): a systematic review. J. Res. Technol. Educ. **54**(3), 392–409 (2022)
18. Yang, B., Wei, L., Pu, Z.: Measuring and improving user experience through artificial intelligence-aided design. Front. Psychol. **11** (2020). https://doi.org/10.3389/fpsyg.2020.595374

Beyond Simulation: A Task-and Persona-Adaptive Framework for AI in UX Evaluation

Mengyan Guo, Jianpeng Li, Yao Cheng(✉), Zehui Jin, and Luping Wang

Alibaba Cloud Computing, Hangzhou, China
{guomengyan.gmy,jiangpu.ljp,shushi.cy,jinzehui.jzh}@alibaba-inc.com, dopink@msn.com

Abstract. Utilizing AI agents for User Experience (UX) evaluation is a promising approach to overcome the cost and inconsistency challenges of traditional expert methods, such as the "Evaluator Effect." However, current research often relies on simplistic, macroscopic personas, failing to capture the nuanced cognitive differences among experts. This paper addresses this gap by introducing "Twin AIs," personalized agents constructed using a fine-grained, cognitively-grounded model. We conducted a mixed-methods study comparing a group of 16 human experts, their corresponding Twin AIs, and a single General AI in a real-world B2B ease-of-use walkthrough. Our results reveal a crucial "Task Duality": personalization acts as disruptive "noise" in convergent tasks (e.g., quantitative scoring) but as a valuable "signal" in divergent tasks (e.g., problem discovery). Furthermore, we identify a "Diversity Gap," where the AI group achieves superior evaluation breadth but lacks the genuine internal diversity of a human group. These findings lead us to propose a paradigm shift from "simulation" to "augmentation." We contribute the "Task x Persona" Dual Duality framework, a practical guide for strategically deploying AI agents in UX evaluation.

Keywords: AI Personas · User Experience Evaluation · Evaluator Effect

1 Introduction

In the realm of B2B products, where agile development methodologies prevail, rapid, efficient, and insightful User Experience (UX) evaluations are paramount for successful product iteration [29,35]. Expert walkthroughs, as a common method [17,19], offer quick problem discovery but have long faced two major challenges: first, the high temporal and economic costs associated with recruiting and coordinating multiple experts; and second, the "Evaluator Effect," where

M. Guo and J. Li—These authors contributed equally to this work.

C. Stephanidis et al. (Eds.): HCII 2026, CCIS 3047, pp. 358–372, 2026.
https://doi.org/10.1007/978-3-032-30552-7_34

different experts, due to their diverse backgrounds, experiences, and cognitive biases, tend to identify disparate sets of issues, leading to a degree of uncertainty in evaluation outcomes [10,25]. The rise of Large Language Models (LLMs) offers a new paradigm to address these challenges. Building "synthetic agents" through Prompt Engineering to simulate human evaluation has become a popular research avenue [4,7,9,32,37,39,40]. However, existing research on endowing AI with "personality" often focuses on macroscopic roles and environments, with less attention to the nuanced cognitive and decision-making differences among experts. Consequently, the effectiveness and controllability of these methods remain to be validated [2,20,26]. To this end, drawing inspiration from a rich body of theory in psychology and human-computer interaction [5,6,22,27,34,38], this study constructs a fine-grained, structured model to create "Twin AIs." We designed a mixed-methods study on a real-world B2B cloud service management platform to systematically compare the performance of a group of human experts, a group of Twin AIs, and a single General AI. Our aim is to explore the application boundaries, core value, and best practice strategies for AI in UX evaluation. Specifically, this study seeks to answer the following three research questions(RQs):

RQ 1 : Can "Twin AIs" injected with structured personal metadata more accurately simulate the evaluation behaviors of their human counterparts compared to a "General AI"?

RQ 2 : How does an "Twin AI Group" compare to a human expert group and a single General AI in terms of the breadth, perspective, and diversity of their evaluations?

RQ 3 : How do human experts perceive their AI twins and General AI, and what collaborative value do they envision?

2 Related Work

2.1 Automated UX Evaluation for B2B Products

The slow pace of traditional expert evaluation clashes with the rapid rhythm of agile B2B development, creating a significant efficiency bottleneck [10,19,31]. To address this challenge, automated evaluation based on multimodal Large Language Models (LLMs) has emerged. Research has demonstrated that LLMs can comprehend UI and automatically perform tasks such as heuristic evaluation [4,9,32,37,39,40]. While these works confirm the feasibility of using AI for efficient, large-scale evaluation, they mostly position AI as a single, generalized expert tool, overlooking a crucial characteristic of expert evaluation [14].

2.2 From Simulating a Single Expert to the Evaluator Effect

Classic HCI research has long established that a core feature of expert evaluation is the "Evaluator Effect" [10,25]—the phenomenon where different experts, owing to their varied backgrounds and experiences, identify different sets of problems. This diversity is not a flaw but a key to achieving more comprehensive problem coverage. In parallel, another research avenue employs generative AI as a "behavioral simulator." In the area of AI Personalization Injection, existing work often uses role-setting (Prompting) and multi-agent collaboration [2,20,26] to create virtual characters with distinct "personalities." However, these injected personalities are often based on macroscopic demographics or broad behavioral archetypes, rarely delving into the subtle cognitive and decision-making differences among individuals. By bridging these two domains, we identify a critical research gap: despite prior attempts at personalization, few studies have employed fine-grained, cognitively-grounded models to systematically simulate the "Evaluator Effect" itself. Therefore, this study moves beyond viewing AI as a single expert or a simple archetype. We construct an "AI expert group" using a novel structured approach, aiming to empirically test this group's potential and limitations in simulating expert diversity, thereby exploring a new, more comprehensive, and efficient paradigm for AI-powered evaluation.

3 Method

We employed a mixed-methods research design, combining a controlled experiment with semi-structured interviews to gain both quantitative and qualitative in-depth insights.

3.1 Base Model Selection

To ensure that the AI agents in our study were built upon the most capable foundation model, we began by conducting a rigorous base model selection. We adopted a validated methodology from our prior work [14]. This method uses an evaluation framework with 10 dimensions across three modules—Page Recognition, Rule Comprehension, and Output Capability [13,23,24]—to test mainstream multimodal LLMs of the time (e.g., Qwen-3.5, GPT-5.2, Gemini 3-flash) [8,28,30]. To ensure objectivity, we used an "LLM-as-a-judge" mechanism, adding Claude Sonnet 4.6 to form a panel of four large models to evaluate the test results [3]. We then applied a four-step bias correction process: 1) removing model self-evaluations, 2) Z-score standardization [15], 3) consistency-based weight allocation [33], and 4) final weighted score aggregation [16], to mitigate common biases like self-preference in LLM evaluations [36]. Qwen-3.5 achieved the highest overall score in this assessment and was therefore selected as the cognitive core for all AI virtual experts in this study. The evaluation scores are summarized in Table 1.

Table 1. Base Model Evaluation Scores from Different LLM Judges.

Model Under Test	Gemini 3	GPT-5.2	Qwen3.5
Judge: **Gemini 3**	4.97 (Self-eval)	4.48	4.98
Judge: **GPT-5.2**	4.08	4.67 (Self-eval)	4.75
Judge: **Qwen3.5**	4.40	3.50	5.00 (Self-eval)
Judge: **Claude 4.6**	4.83	4.00	4.75

3.2 Participants

We recruited 16 experienced UX experts from the B2B domain. Their work experience ranged from 4 to 15 years ($M = 7.44$, $SD = 2.84$), ensuring both a solid professional foundation and good diversity in seniority within the sample.

3.3 AI Agent Construction

We compared three groups of evaluators:

General AI (GA) : A single, generalized virtual expert based on Qwen-3.5, assigned only a generic "senior UX expert" role with no personalized information.

Human Group (HG) : 16 human experts.

Twin AI Group (TG) : 16 AI twin virtual experts based on Qwen-3.5. Each agent was personalized using a structured 7-dimension model (including role, goals, knowledge, skills, emotional cognition, communication style, and behavioral randomness). The inputs for this model were derived from the metadata of their corresponding human expert (years of experience, job title, academic background, and MBTI personality type [1]). A detailed, side-by-side comparison, illustrating how this metadata translates into the personalized Twin AI prompt versus the generic prompt, is provided in the Appendix A. Our 7-dimension construction method is not ad-hoc but is deeply rooted in classic theories of psychology and HCI. The model deconstructs a virtual persona into three core modules:

The Rational User Profile: This covers the user's role attributes, skills, and knowledge, drawing from Persona Theory [5] and Mental Model Theory [27].

The Affective and Motivational Core:This delineates the user's inner world through goal, emotional cognition, and communication style, with theoretical foundations in the Technology Acceptance Model [6], Cognitive Load Theory [34], and the Big Five Personality Traits [22].

Behavioral Randomness: By incorporating Heuristics and Biases Theory [38], the model can simulate the irrationality and uncertainty present in real-world human decision-making.

Through this multi-dimensional theoretical integration, our AI agents aim to move beyond simple role-playing to achieve a deeper, more fine-grained simulation of human experts.

3.4 Procedure

First, to ensure a shared understanding of the evaluation criteria, we had the 16 human experts briefly review core ease-of-use principles [12]. All participants then provided 10-point ratings for ease-of-use dimensions across three real B2B cloud product pages and documented all ease-of-use issues they found. We then used the same task instructions and evaluation framework for the 16 Twin AIs and the 1 General AI to complete the same evaluation independently. Finally, we conducted semi-structured interviews with three human experts of varying seniority to explore their subjective perceptions of the AI-generated evaluation results.

3.5 Data Analysis

We employed a variety of methods to analyze the data: Mean Absolute Error (MAE) and directional consistency were used to assess rating accuracy [16]; problem coverage and novelty ratio were used to evaluate the breadth and diversity of problem discovery; a paired-samples t-test on the standard deviations of ratings was used to compare group diversity [11]; and thematic analysis was applied to the interview transcripts [21].

4 Results

Our findings reveal that AI plays a complex and dualistic role in UX evaluation.

4.1 RQ1: The Efficacy of Individual Simulation A Contradictory Start

We first examined the effectiveness of personalization injection in simulating the behavior of individual experts (RQ1). The results show that the effect of personalization is highly task-dependent.

Rating Accuracy: General AI Performs Better. In the task of quantitatively rating product ease-of-use, the General AI demonstrated higher accuracy. As detailed in Table 2, the General AI consistently outperformed the Twin AI group in head-to-head comparisons across both Mean Absolute Error (MAE) and directional consistency metrics.

Table 2. Comparison of rating accuracy between the General AI (GA) and the Twin AI (TG) group.

Metric	General AI (GA) Wins	Twin AI (TG) Wins	Ties
Mean Absolute Error (MAE)	**11**	3	2
Directional Consistency	**8**	5	-

Finding 1 In precise rating tasks, the General AI is better at predicting human expert ratings than Twin AIs injected with personalized metadata. This suggests that in convergent tasks demanding precision, personalization injection may introduce unnecessary "noise" that interferes with the AI's core judgment.

Problem Discovery Perspective: Twin AI Is Significantly Better. However, the situation completely reversed when the task shifted to the divergent task of qualitative problem discovery. The Twin AIs' average coverage rate in replicating the issues found by their corresponding human experts (M = 41.40%, SD = 22.18%) was significantly higher than that of the General AI (M = 30.14%, SD = 14.28%). Figure 1 visualizes this performance gap, illustrating the coverage rate for each individual participant.

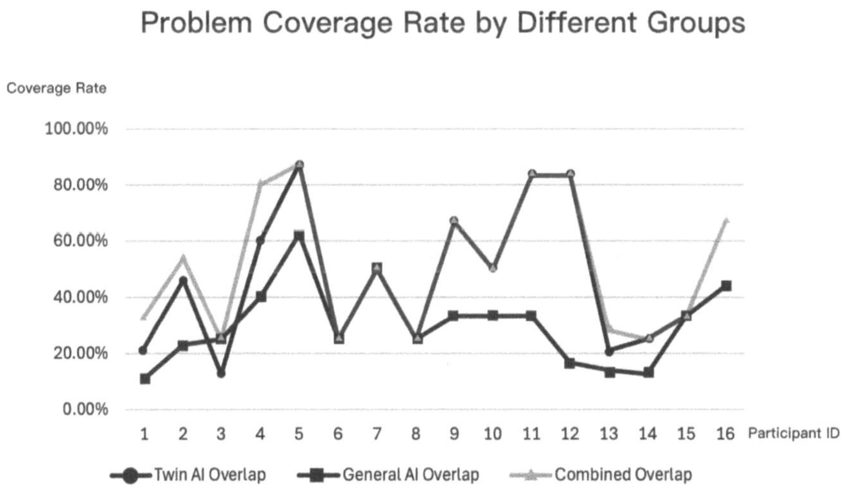

Fig. 1. problem coverage rate with their human counterpart.

Finding 2 In problem discovery tasks, Twin AIs significantly outperform the General AI in reproducing the evaluation perspective of a specific human expert.

This indicates that in divergent tasks encouraging diverse viewpoints, the same personalization injection becomes a valuable "signal," successfully guiding the AI to explore from a perspective closer to its human counterpart.

Summary of RQ1: The effectiveness of personalization injection exhibits a profound duality: it acts as "noise" in accuracy-driven rating tasks but as a "signal" in perspective-driven problem discovery tasks.

4.2 RQ2: Group Behavior Comparison A Separation of Breadth and Diversity

At the group level, we observed another duality in the AI's evaluation capabilities: a separation between its exploratory breadth and its internal diversity.

Evaluation Breadth: The AI Expert Group Surpasses Humans. In terms of problem discovery breadth, the group of 16 Twin AIs performed exceptionally well, identifying 254 issues in total, which condensed to 69 unique issues after deduplication. This surpassed the 16-member human expert group (124 issues, 53 unique) and far exceeded the single General AI (14 issues). Furthermore, the Twin AI group's coverage of human-found issues (54%) was more than three times that of the General AI (16%) (see Table 3 for a summary of these metrics).

Table 3. Comparison of problem discovery breadth and coverage across the three evaluator groups. HG = Human Group, TG = Twin AI Group, GA = General AI.

Metric	HG	TG	GA
Total Issues Found (Raw Count)	124	254	14
Unique Issues Found (Deduplicated)	53	69	14
Coverage of Human-Found Issues	-	54%	16%

Finding 3 The Twin AI Group is a powerful "breadth explorer," with a field of vision that surpasses the human team.

Finding 4 The exploration of the AI expert group is highly relevant to human concerns.

Evaluation Diversity: A Profound "Diversity Gap". Despite its outstanding external breadth, the AI group's internal diversity was lacking. A paired-samples t-test on the standard deviations (SD) of 12 rating items showed that the human expert group's average SD (M = 0.99) was statistically significantly higher than the Twin AI group's (M = 0.60), $t(11) = 5.76$, $p < .001$. In terms of problem discovery, the novelty ratio (unique issues / total issues) for the human group was 0.42, whereas for the Twin AI group, it was only 0.27.

Finding 5 The Twin AI Group exhibits homogenized "computational group-think" and, in its current form, cannot fully simulate the "Evaluator Effect" that arises from genuine human differences in experience and cognition. We term this the "Diversity Gap."

Analysis of Unique Issues: AI's Blind Spots and Human's Habitual Blindness. A qualitative analysis of the issues unique to each group further revealed their capability boundaries. Issues unique to human experts centered on judgments of the overall layout and containment relationships between page elements, reflecting the AI's deficiency in "holistic intuition." Conversely, issues unique to the AI were often those overlooked by human experts due to "habitual blindness," such as ad interference that has long been accepted as a business compromise, or information overload internalized from following design systems (e.g., full-length IDs, timestamps precise to the second). This highlights the AI's unique value as an "objective outsider." Moreover, 13 of the 14 issues (92.86%) found by the General AI were also covered by the Twin AI group, demonstrating that the Twin AI group's capabilities are broadly inclusive of the General AI's. Summary of RQ2: The AI expert group exhibits a "broad yet homogenous" characteristic: it is a powerful breadth explorer but also a consensus-seeker with relatively uniform opinions.

4.3 RQ3: Human Experts' Subjective Perceptions

Interviews with three experts of varying seniority (P1, 4 years; P2, 8 years; P3, 15 years) revealed a core "Inspiration-Tool Paradox."

Pervasive Skepticism About "Exact Simulation". Experts generally did not perceive the AI twin as a "replica" of themselves. On a 7-point scale for the question "Does this report feel like it was written by you?", the mean rating was only 4.67.

The Inspiration-Tool Paradox. When asked to compare the two types of AI, a profound paradox emerged:

Twin AI was Perceived as Generating More Insightful Content. For the question "Is the output valuable for product optimization?", experts rated the Twin AI significantly higher (mean 6.67/7) than the General AI (mean 5.67/7). The junior expert (4 years' experience) showed a stark difference, rating them 7 vs. 4, believing the Twin AI was more inspiring.

General AI was Considered a Better Work Tool. Simultaneously, for "Can it assist/liberate your work?", the General AI won a landslide victory (mean 7.00/7 vs. 5.00/7). All experts agreed that the General AI was the more ideal "assistant" because it was more reliable, predictable, and focused on the ease-of-use metrics themselves. Figure 2 visually summarizes these subjective ratings across all five measured dimensions.

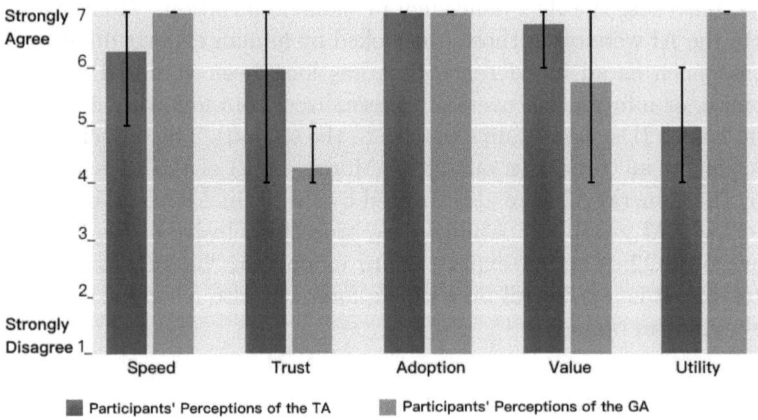

Fig. 2. Experts' Subjective Perceptions.

Summary of RQ3: Experts do not seek an AI that perfectly imitates them. They appreciate the inspirational value of the Twin AI's content but prefer the behavioral patterns of the General AI as a reliable tool. This provides crucial subjective evidence for our subsequent practice framework.

5 Discussion

Our findings point to a conclusion: we should rethink the role of AI in design evaluation, shifting the paradigm from "simulation" to "augmentation."

5.1 Task Duality: Convergent Vs. Divergent Tasks

Synthesizing the findings from RQ1 and RQ2, we can formally propose the core theory of this study: convergent tasks like rating pursue a single optimal solution, in which case personalization injection acts as "noise" that interferes with judgment. In contrast, divergent tasks like problem discovery encourage diverse exploration, where personalization injection becomes a valuable "signal" that guides the AI to broaden its perspective.

5.2 The Illusion of AI Diversity: From "Shallow Prompts" to "Deep Fine-Tuning"

The discovery of the "Diversity Gap" reveals the inherent ceiling of current AI simulation methods based on prompt engineering. The roots of this limitation are twofold: first, the "shallow" descriptive metadata (e.g., job title, MBTI) we use to construct "personality" is insufficient to capture an expert's "deep" experience; second, the way LLMs process information through prompts makes them more like superb "role-players" rather than beings that have truly internalized traits. They enact a generalized portrayal of a "senior designer," not the unique thinking of a specific individual. To truly bridge this gap, future research must move beyond prompt engineering toward model fine-tuning based on real individual or group behavioral data. Only by collecting and training on high-quality, high-depth behavioral data (such as think-aloud protocols or interaction logs) can we hope to create truly high-fidelity synthetic experts.

5.3 From "Simulation" to "Augmentation": Reshaping AI's Role in Design

Our research, particularly the findings from RQ3, clearly shows that pursuing a "perfect imitation" of humans by AI is neither possible nor necessary. Experts place a higher value on AI's collaborative utility as a tool. Therefore, the core role of AI in the design field should shift from "substitutive simulation" to "augmentative collaboration." Its value lies in empowering humans, not becoming them.

5.4 Practical Implications: A "Task X Persona" Dual Duality Framework

Based on the aforementioned paradigm shift, we propose a more operational "Task x Persona" framework to guide the application of AI in different scenarios:

Dimension 1: Simulating "Experts". Enhancing Efficiency (Convergent Tasks): When the goal is rapid, consistent evaluation (e.g., for standardized assessments and quantitative rating), we recommend using a General AI as a standardized tool.

Expanding Horizons (Divergent Tasks): When the goal is to maximize the breadth of problem discovery (e.g., finding interaction and interface flaws), we recommend constructing an AI expert group.

Dimension 2: Simulating "Users". Core Principle: Unlike simulating experts, the primary goal of simulating users is to cover diversity. Therefore, "breadth" is the top priority. Recommended Strategy: In the early stages of product development, the priority should be to build a diverse AI user group to serve as a "hypothesis generator" and "risk scanner." However, practitioners must be acutely aware of the limitations of this "shallow simulation." The long-term goal should be to build a "high-fidelity user model library" based on fine-tuning with real data [2,18].

6 Limitations And Future Work

This study has some limitations. First, while our participant sample size (N=16) is acceptable for mixed-methods research, larger-scale studies are needed to validate our findings. Second, the metadata dimensions used to construct AI personalities were limited; future research could explore richer, "deeper" data inputs. Finally, this study focused only on expert simulation. Future work should empirically test the simulation of users and explore the practical effects of model fine-tuning in enhancing simulation depth.

7 Conclusion

This study empirically reveals the "Task Duality" and "Diversity Gap" in AI-powered UX evaluation, proposing a paradigm shift from "simulation" to "augmentation." The resulting "Task x Persona" Dual Duality framework provides a new theoretical perspective and actionable practical guidelines for the deep integration of AI in the design field. We aim to help researchers and practitioners leverage this powerful technology more strategically.

A Example Prompt Structures and Metadata of Human Expert

Source Metadata	Twin AI Prompt	General AI Prompt
Experience: 15 years Career Path: Creative Designer to UX Designer Major: Computer Science MBTI: INFP-T	**Role:** You are a senior UX designer (Principal Designer) at a leading internet or SaaS company. You have witnessed the evolution from Web 1.0 to the AI era. You are a key liaison between the product and technology teams.	You are a top-tier expert in the field of user interface usability testing.
	Goals: Your work is not just about 'pixel-pushing'; you are driven by a 'quest for meaning.' As an INFP, you pursue the social value and humanistic care behind the product, striving to find the perfect balance between business objectives and user's emotional needs.	
	Knowledge: You work like a 'digital nomad-style artisan,' often wearing noise-canceling headphones while immersed in a dual-monitor setup. Before starting on the computer, you prefer to sketch out ideas on a whiteboard or iPad to clarify the logical flow.	
	Skills: As a 'full-stack' designer with a Computer Science background, you understand the logic of code implementation and can communicate effectively with back-end developers. You possess a strong aesthetic sense and excel at translating abstract business requirements into empathetic user journey maps, which you validate using high-fidelity prototypes.	
	Emotional cognition: You have a gentle demeanor but a sensitive inner world. With a Turbulent ('-T') personality, you are prone to perfectionist anxiety. You feel a deep sense of powerlessness when faced with product decisions that lack empathy and internally resist crude 'boss-like' reviews.	
	Communication style: You embody 'gentle firmness,' preferring to persuade with data analysis over loud arguments. You use tactful yet rigorous communication methods. However, if core UX principles (like accessibility or privacy) are compromised, you show the unyielding resolve of a 15-year veteran.	
	Behavioral randomness: You exhibit certain 'escapist' behaviors, like staring out the window for 10 min when facing a bottleneck. As a UX professional with a CS background, upon encountering counter-intuitive UI, you instinctively frown and mentally refactor its code logic.	

References

1. 16Personalities: Free Personality Test (2024). https://www.16personalities.com/free-personality-test. Accessed on: 26-Oct-2024
2. de Almeida, A., Collins, E., Oran, A.C.: AI in service of software quality: How chatgpt and personas are transforming exploratory testing. In: Proceedings of the XXIII Brazilian Symposium on Software Quality, pp. 179–188. SBQS '2024, Association for Computing Machinery, New York, NY, USA (2024). https://doi.org/10.1145/3701625.3701657
3. Anthropic: Introducing Claude Sonnet 4.6 (2026). https://www.anthropic.com/news/claude-sonnet-4-6. Accessed on: 20-Mar-2026
4. Bisante, A., Datla, V.S.V., Panizzi, E., Trasciatti, G., Zeppieri, S.: Enhancing interface design with AI: an exploratory study on a chatgpt-4-based tool for cognitive walkthrough inspired evaluations. In: Proceedings of the 2024 International Conference on Advanced Visual Interfaces. AVI '2024, Association for Computing Machinery, New York, NY, USA (2024). https://doi.org/10.1145/3656650.3656676
5. Cooper, A.: The Inmates Are Running the Asylum: Why High-Tech Products Drive Us Crazy and How to Restore the Sanity. Sams Publishing (2004)
6. Davis, F.: A Technology Acceptance Model for Empirically Testing New End-User Information Systems: Theory and Results. Massachusetts Institute of Technology, Sloan School of Management, Cambridge, MA (1985). https://books.google.com/books?id=hbx8NwAACAAJ. Doctoral dissertation
7. Dillion, D., Tandon, N., Gu, Y., Gray, K.: Can AI language models replace human participants? Trends Cogn. Sci. **27**(7), 597–600 (2023)
8. Doshi, T.: Gemini 3 Flash: frontier intelligence built for speed (2025). https://blog.google/products-and-platforms/products/gemini/gemini-3-flash/. Accessed on: 20-Mar-2026
9. Duan, P., Warner, J., Li, Y., Hartmann, B.: Generating automatic feedback on UI mockups with large language models. In: Proceedings of the 2024 CHI Conference on Human Factors in Computing Systems. CHI '2024, Association for Computing Machinery, New York, NY, USA (2024). https://doi.org/10.1145/3613904.3642782
10. Dunn, P.G., Hayes, A.: The problems with usability testing. In: Human-Computer Interaction. Design and User Experience: Thematic Area, HCI 2020, Held as Part of the 22nd International Conference, HCII 2020, Copenhagen, Denmark, 19–24 July 2020, Proceedings, Part I, pp. 420–430. Springer-Verlag, Berlin, Heidelberg (2020). https://doi.org/10.1007/978-3-030-49059-1_30
11. Field, A.: Discovering Statistics Using IBM SPSS Statistics, 4th edn. Sage, London (2013)
12. Gao, X., Zhi, S., Wang, X.: Investigating the relationship among ease-of-use, NPS, and customers' sequent spending of cloud computing products. In: Stephanidis, C., Antona, M., Ntoa, S. (eds.) HCI International 2021 - Posters, pp. 417–422. HCII 2021, Springer International Publishing, Cham (2021). https://doi.org/10.1007/978-3-030-78645-8_53
13. Google Cloud: Determine an evaluation method (2026). https://docs.cloud.google.com/vertex-ai/generative-ai/docs/models/determine-eval?hl=en
14. Guo, M., Li, J., Cheng, Y., Jin, Z., Wang, L.: AI UXpert: Comparing the Performance and Perception of AI and Human Experts in B2B Ease of Use Evaluation. In: Extended Abstracts of the 2026 CHI Conference on Human Factors in Computing Systems. CHI EA '2026, Association for Computing Machinery, New York, NY, USA (2026). https://doi.org/10.1145/3772363.3798495. Forthcoming

15. Han, J., Kamber, M., Pei, J.: 3 - data preprocessing. In: Han, J., Kamber, M., Pei, J. (eds.) Data Mining: Concepts and Techniques (Third Edition), pp. 83–124. The Morgan Kaufmann Series in Data Management Systems, Morgan Kaufmann, Boston, third edition edn. (2012). https://doi.org/10.1016/B978-0-12-381479-1.00003-4
16. Hastie, T., Tibshirani, R., Friedman, J.: The Elements of Statistical Learning: Data Mining, Inference, and Prediction. Springer, New York, NY, 2 edn. (2009). https://doi.org/10.1007/978-0-387-84858-7
17. Hollingsed, T., Novick, D.G.: Usability inspection methods after 15 years of research and practice. In: Proceedings of the 25th Annual ACM International Conference on Design of Communication. p. 249–255. SIGDOC '2007, Association for Computing Machinery, New York, NY, USA (2007). https://doi.org/10.1145/1297144.1297200
18. Lei, Y., Wang, T., Lian, J., Hu, Z., Lian, D., Xie, X.: HumanLLM: Towards Personalized Understanding and Simulation of Human Nature. arXiv preprint arXiv:2601.15793 (2026). https://doi.org/10.48550/arXiv.2601.15793
19. Lewis, C., Wharton, C.: Chapter 30 - cognitive walkthroughs. In: Helander, M.G., Landauer, T.K., Prabhu, P.V. (eds.) Handbook of Human-Computer Interaction (Second Edition), pp. 717–732. North-Holland, Amsterdam, second edition edn. (1997). https://doi.org/10.1016/B978-044481862-1.50096-0
20. Liu, Y., Sharma, P., Oswal, M., Xia, H., Huang, Y.: Personaflow: designing LLM-simulated expert perspectives for enhanced research ideation. In: Proceedings of the 2025 ACM Designing Interactive Systems Conference, pp. 506–534. DIS '2025, Association for Computing Machinery, New York, NY, USA (2025). https://doi.org/10.1145/3715336.3735789
21. Lungu, M.: The coding manual for qualitative researchers. American J. Qualitative Res. **6**(1), 232–237 (2022). https://doi.org/10.29333/ajqr/12085. https://ajqr.org/article/the-coding-manual-for-qualitative-researchers-12085
22. McCrae, R.R., Costa, P.T.: An introduction to the five-factor model and its applications. J. Pers. **60**(2), 175–215 (1992)
23. Nielsen, J.: Usability Engineering. Morgan Kaufmann, San Francisco, CA (1993). https://www.nngroup.com/books/usability-engineering/
24. Nielsen, J.: 10 usability heuristics for user interface design (1994). https://www.nngroup.com/articles/ten-usability-heuristics/. Updated on January 30, 2024
25. Nielsen, J., Molich, R.: Heuristic evaluation of user interfaces. In: Proceedings of the SIGCHI Conference on Human Factors in Computing Systems, pp. 249–256. CHI '1990, Association for Computing Machinery, New York, NY, USA (1990). https://doi.org/10.1145/97243.97281
26. Niu, R., et al.: Scenario, role, and persona: a scoping review of design strategies for socially intelligent ai agents. In: Proceedings of the Extended Abstracts of the CHI Conference on Human Factors in Computing Systems. CHI EA '2025, Association for Computing Machinery, New York, NY, USA (2025). https://doi.org/10.1145/3706599.3719762
27. Norman, D.A.: The Design of Everyday Things. MIT Press, Cambridge, MA (2013)
28. OpenAI: Introducing GPT-5.2 (2025). https://openai.com/index/introducing-gpt-5-2/. Accessed on: 20-Mar-2026
29. Qiu, J., Tokuhisa, S.: Dual-track UX: a user experience evaluation method for b2b saas development. In: Proceedings of the Extended Abstracts of the CHI Conference on Human Factors in Computing Systems. CHI EA '2025, Association for Computing Machinery, New York, NY, USA (2025). https://doi.org/10.1145/3706599.3719968

30. QwenTeam: Qwen3.5: (Towards a Native Multimodal Agent) (2026). https://qwen.ai/blog?id=qwen3.5. Accessed on: 20-Mar-2026
31. Rojas, L.F., Quiñones, D., Cubillos, C.: FRAMUX-EV: a framework for evaluating user experience in agile software development. Appl. Sci. **14**(8991) (2024). https://doi.org/10.3390/app14198991
32. Shin, S., Oh, J., Lee, S.: Can LLMs see what i see? A study on five prompt engineering techniques for evaluating UX on a shopping site. In: Proceedings of the Extended Abstracts of the CHI Conference on Human Factors in Computing Systems. CHI EA '2025, Association for Computing Machinery, New York, NY, USA (2025). https://doi.org/10.1145/3706599.3720079
33. Shrout, P.E., Fleiss, J.L.: Intraclass correlations: uses in assessing rater reliability. Psychol. Bull. **86**(2), 420–428 (1979)
34. Sweller, J.: Cognitive load during problem solving: effects on learning. Cogn. Sci. **12**(2), 257–285 (1988)
35. Taraghi, B.: End-to-end quality of experience evaluation for http adaptive streaming. In: Proceedings of the 29th ACM International Conference on Multimedia, pp. 2936–2939. MM '2021, Association for Computing Machinery, New York, NY, USA (2021). https://doi.org/10.1145/3474085.3481025
36. Tarvainen, A., Valpola, H.: Mean teachers are better role models: weight-averaged consistency targets improve semi-supervised deep learning results (2017). https://doi.org/10.48550/arXiv.1703.01780
37. Turbeville, K., et al.: LLM-powered multimodal insight summarization for UX testing. In: Proceedings of the 26th International Conference on Multimodal Interaction, pp. 4–11. ICMI '2024, Association for Computing Machinery, New York, NY, USA (2024). https://doi.org/10.1145/3678957.3685701
38. Tversky, A., Kahneman, D.: Judgment under uncertainty: heuristics and biases. Science **185**(4157), 1124–1131 (1974)
39. Xiang, W., et al.: Simuser: generating usability feedback by simulating various users interacting with mobile applications. In: Proceedings of the 2024 CHI Conference on Human Factors in Computing Systems. CHI '2024, Association for Computing Machinery, New York, NY, USA (2024). https://doi.org/10.1145/3613904.3642481
40. Zhong, M., Chen, R., Chen, X., Fogarty, J., Wobbrock, J.O.: Screenaudit: detecting screen reader accessibility errors in mobile apps using large language models. In: Proceedings of the 2025 CHI Conference on Human Factors in Computing Systems. CHI '2025, Association for Computing Machinery, New York, NY, USA (2025). https://doi.org/10.1145/3706598.3713797

LLMs as Qualitative Analysis Assistants: Comparing Problem Theme Construction with Human Researchers

Hyejoo Heo[1](✉), Youngsoo Shin[2], and Myeong Heum Yeoun[1]

[1] Kookmin University, Seoul, South Korea
qkskskwhsl@kookmin.ac.kr
[2] Pace University, New York City, NY, USA

Abstract. Large language models (LLMs) have recently gained attention as tools for supporting qualitative data analysis. However, limited research has examined how analytical structures generated by LLMs differ from those produced by human researchers in the early problem-definition stage of UX research. This study compares thematic analysis outcomes produced by an LLM and human researchers using the same set of user interview data. Focusing on problem-theme definitions, we analyze differences in the resulting problem structures and evaluate the semantic alignment between the two analyses using Sentence-BERT–based cosine similarity. The results show that the problem themes derived by the two groups exhibit moderate-to-high semantic similarity overall, while relatively lower similarity is observed among the highest-priority core problem themes.

In addition, LLM-generated themes tend to exhibit semantic similarity with multiple human-derived themes rather than forming one-to-one correspondences. This pattern suggests that LLMs organize problem areas in a broader, more integrative manner. These findings indicate that while LLMs can support the exploration of initial problem spaces, human judgment remains essential for contextual understanding and the interpretation of problem structures in UX research. This study highlights the potential of human–AI collaboration in qualitative UX research.

Keywords: Thematic Analysis · Large Language Models · Human–AI Collaboration

1 Introduction

Interview-based qualitative analysis is a key method in UX and HCI research for identifying structural problems in user experience. In particular, the Define stage of the Double Diamond model focuses on organizing problem themes for service improvement by synthesizing experience data collected during exploratory research. This thematic analysis process is labor-intensive, as it requires repeated data review, code generation and refinement, and consensus among researchers.

With the rapid development of large language models (LLMs), their potential as tools to support qualitative data analysis has been widely discussed. Previous studies

C. Stephanidis et al. (Eds.): HCII 2026, CCIS 3047, pp. 373–381, 2026.
https://doi.org/10.1007/978-3-032-30552-7_35

suggest that LLMs can assist multiple stages of qualitative analysis, including code generation, categorization, deductive coding, and theme development. However, much of the existing research primarily focuses on coding accuracy or automation efficiency. Relatively little attention has been paid to how LLMs structure problems during the early problem-definition stage of UX research.

This study addresses this gap by comparing the problem themes identified by human researchers and an LLM (ChatGPT-5.2) using interview data from users of Seoul's public bicycle service, Ttareungyi.

RQ1. To what extent do problem themes derived from the same interview data exhibit semantic alignment between LLM-based analysis and traditional qualitative analysis?
RQ2. What differences exist in the structure and characteristics of problem themes identified by the LLM and by human researchers?

2 Review of Literature

2.1 UX Early Stage and Thematic Analysis

Thematic analysis, as proposed by Braun and Clarke (2006), follows a six-step process: data familiarization, initial code generation, searching for themes, reviewing themes, defining and naming themes, and reporting. In UX research, this method is used not only to identify themes but also to organize them into higher-level problem themes that explain recurring issues in user experience. In the early stages of UX research, the primary goal is to identify recurring experience patterns and underlying problems rather than to develop formal theory. For this reason, inductive thematic analysis is particularly well suited to this stage. However, the process relies heavily on interpretation, and the results may vary depending on the researcher's experience and perspective.

2.2 LLMs in Qualitative Data Analysis

With the rapid development of large language models (LLMs), their application in qualitative research has increased. Because qualitative data analysis involves repeated coding and interpretation, many studies have explored the use of LLMs to reduce analytical workload. For example, Goyanes (2025), Mehta et al. (2025), Yue et al. (2025), Jenner (2025), Rong et al. (2025), and Blondeel et al. (2025) demonstrate that LLMs can assist various stages of qualitative analysis, including initial code generation, code classification, theme development, and deductive coding.

These studies commonly report that LLMs improve efficiency in repetitive tasks such as coding and categorization, while emphasizing that final interpretation and meaning construction still depend on human researchers.

Many of these studies focus on applying predefined codebooks developed by human researchers and evaluating coding accuracy or agreement. In this approach, LLMs are primarily used as automated classification tools. In contrast, comparative research examining the types of analytical outcomes generated by LLMs in the early stages of problem discovery and definition within the Double Diamond process remains limited.

3 Method

This study was designed based on the six phases of thematic analysis proposed by Braun and Clarke (2006). Both the junior researchers and the LLM (ChatGPT-5.2) followed largely the same analytical procedure. The final output, the problem theme definitions, was then compared using semantic alignment matrix analysis.

3.1 Case and Data

Seoul's public bicycle service, Ttareungyi, was selected as the case for this study. Interviews were conducted over six days, from April 21 to April 26, 2025. Two researchers conducted semi-structured interviews with six participants who had used Ttareungyi more than 20 times during the past two years. The total interview transcript consisted of approximately 57,960 characters, which was within the amount that could be processed by the LLM (ChatGPT 5.2) in a single session. Each stage of the analysis is summarized in Table **1**.

Table 1. Thematic Analysis Stages for LLM and UX Researcher.

Stage	Common Analysis Stage	Human Researchers	ChatGPT-5.2
1	Data familiarization	Read the transcripts repeatedly to understand the context	Review the entire transcript and summarize key contexts and overall impressions
2	Initial code generation	Segment meaning units and generate inductive codes (P/C/N)	Split transcripts into meaning units and assign P/C/N tags
3	Searching for themes	Identify tentative themes by grouping similar codes	Identify tentative themes by grouping similar codes
4	Reviewing themes	Integrate overlapping codes and themes to derive the final codebook	Integrate overlapping and similar codes to derive the final codebook
5	Defining and naming themes	Define themes by examining relationships among codes and name them	Construct themes based on code relationships and define their meanings
6	Producing the report	Select representative quotes and produce the problem theme definition	Produce the problem theme definition based on the codebook

3.2 Traditional Thematic Analysis

Three master's-level UX researchers with experience in interview analysis participated as the human analysis group. To minimize the influence of the author's expectations on the analysis process, the author did not participate in the analysis. The participants were provided with analysis guidelines and interview transcripts in advance. They independently conducted coding following the six phases of thematic analysis and later derived the problem theme definitions through collaborative discussion.Although all analysis procedures were conducted in Korean, the results were translated into English for presentation in this paper. The numbers associated with each theme indicate their relative importance (Table 2).

Table 2. problem Theme Definitions by the Researchers.

N	Theme Name	Theme Definition	Representative Quote
1	System Errors in Rental, Return, and Locking Processes	Failures in QR recognition, Bluetooth connection, or GPS errors lead to unsuccessful rentals, returns, or locking actions, often causing delays or user frustration.	"I thought I had returned it, but the next day they contacted me saying it hadn't been processed. They eventually processed the return remotely." "When I lock the bike briefly to stop, it sometimes gets processed as a return even if it's not at the docking station.
2	Malfunctioning Bikes Affect Rental, Return, and Riding	Bike malfunctions lead to discrepancies between the number of bikes shown as available in the app and the bikes that can actually be used, resulting in failed rentals or inconvenience during use.	"Yesterday I tried to rent one because the app said there was one left, but it turned out to be a broken bike."
3	Rental Failures Due to Imbalanced Bike Distribution Across Stations	Users fail to rent bikes when stations lack available bikes due to uneven distribution across docking stations.	"Sometimes the station is full and there's no place to return the bike, so people just leave it next to the station."
4	Inconvenience Due to Limitations of the Public Service System	Operational limitations of the public service system, such as insufficient facilities or inadequate customer support, cause inconvenience during the overall service experience.	"When I try to rent one, there are none available, but when I try to return it later, there are too many bikes and no space." "Even if I return the bike at the nearest station, I still have to walk 700 or 800 m to my destination."

(*continued*)

Table 2. (*continued*)

N	Theme Name	Theme Definition	Representative Quote
5	Inconvenience in Rental and Return Due to Poor Docking Station Management	When bikes are insufficient, excessively concentrated, or poorly organized at stations, the rental or return process becomes delayed or inconvenient.	"If too many bikes are placed in one area, it blocks the pedestrian pathway." "When the station is full, people just leave the bike next to it."
6	Inconvenience Due to Missing or Hard-to-Find Features	Users experience inconvenience when the service lacks certain functions or when they cannot easily find relevant information, such as procedures for accidents or insurance coverage.	"There is insurance for accidents, but it's difficult to find information about it in the app."
7	Negative Perception Caused by Poor Docking Station Management	Poorly organized bikes at stations can obstruct pedestrian paths or create visual clutter, leading to negative perceptions of the service.	"When too many bikes are piled up in one place, it blocks the walkway."
8	Inconvenience Due to Personal Circumstances	Users experience inconvenience due to personal conditions unrelated to the service itself, such as missing notifications, inappropriate clothing, or lack of equipment.	"I often need to check the map while riding, so it would be nice if there were a phone holder installed."
9	Inconvenience Due to External Environmental Factors	External factors such as road conditions, weather, or crowded environments make riding uncomfortable or unsafe.	"Riding in small streets can be really dangerous because cars suddenly appear."

3.3 Thematic Analysis by ChatGPT-5.2

In this study, ChatGPT-5.2 was used as a tool for thematic analysis, and the analysis was conducted by the author. The LLM analysis procedure was designed to follow the same analytical stages used by the junior researchers in order to ensure comparability between the two approaches and maintain consistency in the data processing flow and output structure. The ChatGPT-5.2 analysis was repeated three times using the same interview data and prompt conditions. A similarity evaluation was then conducted to select the final result. Each run was carried out in an independent temporary chat session to prevent any influence from previous conversation contexts or session memory (Table 3).

Table 3. Problem Theme Definitions by the ChatGPT-5.2.

N	Theme Name	Theme Definition	Representative Quote
1	Disruptions in the Core Rental–Return Flow	Errors, failures, or uncertainty during the bike rental or return process interrupt the service flow, causing repeated attempts, delays, and user anxiety.	"Sometimes the rental just doesn't work." "It seems like error management isn't handled very well."
2	Bicycle Quality Variability and Poor Maintenance	Differences in bicycle condition, including malfunctioning parts or insufficient maintenance, lead to inconvenience during use and reduce trust in the service.	"Sometimes the seat keeps sliding down even though I'm not that heavy."
3	Safety Risks During Riding	Road environments such as mixed traffic with cars and pedestrians create safety concerns, leading to user anxiety and avoidance of the service.	"It feels really dangerous, and most users ride on the sidewalk instead of the road."
4	Limited Availability of Bikes and Docking Spaces	A lack of available bikes, docking stations, or return spaces creates uncertainty and prevents users from renting or returning bikes when needed.	"Sometimes when you go to a station, there's nowhere to dock the bike."
5	Insufficient Guidance on Features and Rules	A lack of clear information about functions and rules, such as temporary locking or emergency return, causes confusion about the correct procedures.	"I think it's considered a return, but there wasn't clear guidance about temporary locking near the station or the emergency return service."
6	Environmental Constraints on Usage	Weather conditions such as rain or snow limit the usability of the service and reduce its reliability as a transportation option.	"When it rains or snows, I just don't use it because it feels dangerous."

(continued)

Table 3. (*continued*)

N	Theme Name	Theme Definition	Representative Quote
7	Uncertainty About Post-Incident Support	When accidents or issues occur, unclear information about insurance, support, or response procedures leaves users feeling uncertain and insecure.	"There is insurance provided by the city if an accident happens while riding."

4 Results

To examine the semantic correspondence between the problem themes derived by the LLM (L1–L7) and those identified by human researchers (H1–H9), a semantic alignment matrix analysis was conducted using Sentence-BERT–based cosine similarity. For visual interpretation, similarity scores of 0.6 or higher were highlighted in green, and scores of 0.7 or higher were highlighted in red. The results showed that most theme pairs had similarity scores in the range of 0.40–0.70, indicating a moderate level of semantic relatedness between the themes identified by the two groups. Several theme pairs showed relatively high semantic alignment above 0.70, including L6–H7 (0.758), L7–H6 (0.719), L3–H7 (0.710), L6–H9 (0.712), L5–H5 (0.706), and L5–H6 (0.706). These results suggest that both approaches identified several core problem areas in the interview data in a similar way. However, differences were also observed in the correspondence structure between themes. In particular, relatively lower similarity scores appeared among the highest-priority core problem themes, suggesting that the two groups may have interpreted and structured key problem areas differently. In addition, most LLM-generated themes did not correspond to a single human theme in a one-to-one manner. Instead, they tended to show moderate or higher similarity with multiple human themes. For example, L5 and L6 each showed similarity scores above 0.60 with more than four human themes. These findings indicate that while the LLM and human researchers identified similar problem areas at a general level, differences emerged in how the core problems were structured and organized into themes (Fig. 1).

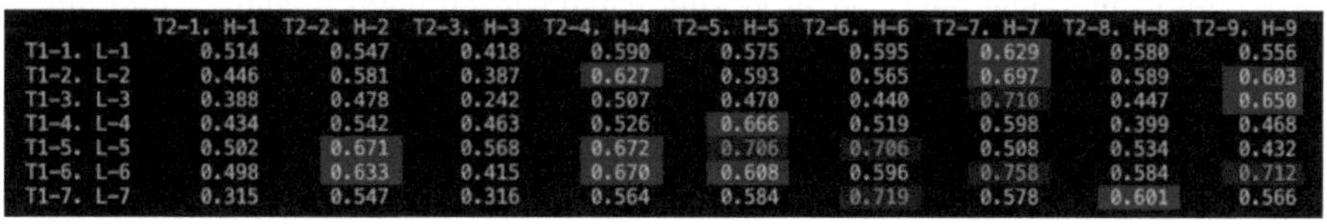

	T2-1. H-1	T2-2. H-2	T2-3. H-3	T2-4. H-4	T2-5. H-5	T2-6. H-6	T2-7. H-7	T2-8. H-8	T2-9. H-9
T1-1. L-1	0.514	0.547	0.418	0.590	0.575	0.595	0.629	0.580	0.556
T1-2. L-2	0.446	0.581	0.387	0.627	0.593	0.565	0.697	0.589	0.603
T1-3. L-3	0.388	0.478	0.242	0.507	0.470	0.440	0.710	0.447	0.650
T1-4. L-4	0.434	0.542	0.463	0.526	0.666	0.519	0.598	0.399	0.468
T1-5. L-5	0.502	0.671	0.568	0.672	0.706	0.706	0.508	0.534	0.432
T1-6. L-6	0.498	0.633	0.415	0.670	0.608	0.596	0.758	0.584	0.712
T1-7. L-7	0.315	0.547	0.316	0.564	0.584	0.719	0.578	0.601	0.566

Fig. 1. Semantic Alignment Matrix Comparison.

5 Conclusion

The semantic alignment analysis in this study showed that the problem themes derived by the LLM and human researchers exhibited moderate or higher levels of semantic similarity overall, with several theme pairs demonstrating particularly high alignment.

These results suggest that the LLM can identify major problem signals present in interview data to a certain extent. However, differences emerged in the structure of theme correspondence. In particular, relatively lower similarity scores were observed among the highest-priority core problem themes, indicating that the two groups may have interpreted and structured key problem areas in different ways. In addition, LLM-generated themes did not typically correspond to a single human theme in a one-to-one manner. Instead, they often showed semantic similarity with multiple human themes simultaneously. This pattern suggests that the LLM tends to organize problems discovered in interview data in a broader and more integrative manner. In contrast, human researchers tended to differentiate problems into more fine-grained interpretive structures by considering contextual factors such as user experience conditions, situations in which problems occur, and usage contexts.

These findings are broadly consistent with observations reported in prior studies on the use of LLMs in qualitative analysis. Previous research has suggested that LLMs can generate codes and themes that are generally aligned with human analysis, while still showing limitations in interpretive depth and contextual integration. For example, Salazar et al. (2025) reported that GPT-4 produced themes that broadly corresponded with human analysis but showed weaker performance in organizing relationships among codes and developing interpretive nuance. Similarly, Rong et al. (2025) emphasized that although LLMs can improve analytical efficiency and identify semantic patterns across texts, final interpretation and contextual judgment still require human validation. These observations align with the findings of the present study, in which the LLM and human researchers identified similar problem areas but differed in how the core problems were interpreted and structured.

These findings highlight that the interpretive role of human researchers remains important in qualitative UX analysis. While LLMs are effective at quickly identifying patterns and suggesting potential categories based on semantic similarity across texts, distinguishing contextual differences in user experience and defining boundaries between problems still requires human judgment. In the UX problem-definition stage, the same phenomenon may be interpreted as different problems depending on the user context or service situation, and such interpretive distinctions cannot be fully captured through semantic similarity analysis alone. Therefore, the results of this study suggest that LLMs should not be viewed as a replacement for qualitative analysis but rather as collaborative tools that support human researchers. LLMs can assist by exploring potential problem areas within interview data and proposing candidate problem themes, while human researchers can refine these outputs by incorporating contextual understanding of user experiences and reconstructing the problem structure. Such a collaborative approach can improve the efficiency of data exploration in UX research while maintaining human-centered interpretive analysis.

In conclusion, this study demonstrates that LLMs can identify problem signals and generate an initial level of problem structure in qualitative UX analysis. At the same time, the interpretation and structuring of core problems still depend heavily on the interpretive judgment of human researchers. These findings suggest that future UX research should consider LLMs not as tools that replace analysis, but as collaborative analytical partners that augment human interpretation.

References

Blondeel, E., Everaert, P., Opdecam, E.: A practical guide to implementing ChatGPT as a secondary coder in qualitative research. Int. J. Account. Inf. Syst. **56**, 100754 (2025)

Braun, V., Clarke, V.: Using thematic analysis in psychology. Qual. Res. Psychol. **3**(2), 77–101 (2006)

Goyanes, M., Lopezosa, C., Jordá, B.: Thematic analysis of interview data with ChatGPT: designing and testing a reliable research protocol for qualitative research. Qual. Quant., 1–20 (2025)

Jenner, S., Raidos, D., Anderson, E., Fleetwood, S., Ainsworth, B., Fox, K., et al.: Using large language models for narrative analysis: a novel application of generative AI. Methods Psychol. **12**, 100183 (2025)

Mehta, S.D., Paul, S., Awiti, E., Young, S., Zulaika, G., Otieno, F.O., et al.: Evaluation of large language models within GenAI in qualitative research. Sci. Rep. **15**(1), 34993 (2025)

Rong, H.H., Davis, J., Rada-Orellana, M.: Benchmarking large language models against qualitative coding and natural language processing in decoding public sentiment on urban upzoning. Urban Inform. **4**(1), 17 (2025)

Salazar, M., Chaw, M., Hellier, Y., Hsia, S., Gruenberg, K.: Comparison of qualitative analyses conducted by artificial-intelligence versus traditional methods. Am. J. Pharm. Educ. **89**, 101882 (2025)

Yue, Y., Liu, D., Lv, Y., Hao, J., Cui, P.: A practical guide and assessment on using ChatGPT to conduct grounded theory: Tutorial. J. Med. Internet Res. **27**, e70122 (2025)

Understanding User Reviews of Digital Wallet Mobile Applications through Topic Modelling

Zheng Han Ho(✉), Chei Sian Lee, and Dion Hoe-Lian Goh

Nanyang Technological University, Wee Kim Wee School of Communication and Information, Singapore, Singapore

w230001@e.ntu.edu.sg, {leeCS,ASHLGoh}@ntu.edu.sg

Abstract. There has been an exponential increase in the use of Digital Wallet Mobile Applications (DWMAs) to make payments in recent years. However, there is a lack of analysis of user reviews of DWMAs and from the analysis results, derive how spending habits could be improved. The aim of the research is to analyze the user reviews of DWMAs, identify topics to explain them, and gain new design insights. We downloaded 35,826 reviews from the Apple App Store and Google Play of three DWMAs from local banks in Singapore and analyzed them using Structural Topic Modeling (STM). Results revealed that the optimal number of topics was 13. Positive reviews were given for DWMAs when their user journeys were smooth and free of technical errors while negative reviews were given when user journeys were plagued by interruptions from the intended task on the DWMA. Linking to the previous work on persuasive interruptions, these interruptions can be harnessed to display pop-up messages that encourage positive financial practices, potentially serving as helpful tools for people to make better spending decisions. The findings of the study serve as an important starting reference for research on DWMA usage in other countries.

Keywords: Digital Wallet Mobile Application · Structural Topic Modeling · User Experience

1 Introduction

Pivotal to providing secure, fast and seamless cashless transactions is the hallmark of a Digital Wallet Mobile Application (DWMA). It stores a person's financial details and digital credentials virtually and allows him or her to make digital payments [1]. Examples of such financial details stored include credit card, debit card and bank account details. In 2020 alone, the number of people using digital banking services was estimated to reach 2.4 billion and this number is expected to reach 3.6 billion in 2026 [2]. This expected large increase in usage of digital banking services can in part be attributed to the popularity of DWMAs. As DWMAs gain popularity, user spending through these platforms also rises, often resulting in overspending [3, 4].

From the existing literature on studying the perceptions of users towards DWMAs, two research gaps have been identified. Firstly, most studies conducted to gather users'

C. Stephanidis et al. (Eds.): HCII 2026, CCIS 3047, pp. 382–389, 2026.
https://doi.org/10.1007/978-3-032-30552-7_36

perceptions of DWMAs have used surveys [5, 6]. This results in general views towards DWMAs with little detail on specific user interfaces and customer journeys which the users particularly like or dislike. Secondly, most existing studies that conduct a topic modelling analysis of online reviews or comments towards DWMAs have done so on data collated from online sources such as social media platforms and forums [7, 8]. While such studies are valuable, these sources cannot ascertain if the reviews and comments were written by those who have actually downloaded the DWMA on their mobile device. Specifically, these posts and reviews may be biased, written to promote or discredit a service [9]. This study aims to address these research gaps through the following objective: To understand the perceptions of users towards specific user interface features or customer journeys of DWMAs.

2 Related Work

Most past studies conducted with regard to gathering and understanding the perceptions of consumers towards DWMAs or digital payments have concentrated on the use of primary data (e.g., surveys) to gather the responses of participants. In these studies [5, 6], the results of the analysis of the surveys agree that the perceived ease of use of the digital wallet has a significant positive effect on both the usage of the digital wallet and the making of digital payments. While these survey studies give researchers a first-hand account of participants' perceptions towards DWMAs, these are generalized perceptions towards the genre of DWMAs and not towards specific DWMAs. Specific views or opinions towards a particular feature in a particular DWMA may be missed and not recorded to be analyzed. Users would usually express their disdain or appreciation for a particular feature in the application through the mobile application store reviews in hopes that it will reach the application creators who will either maintain the well-liked feature or provide a fix for or removal of the disliked feature. Analysis of such reviews will give us insights into the perceptions of users towards specific DWMA features or customer journeys and their spending behaviors as well.

Another shortfall in methodology which is identified from existing studies using topic modelling to analyze DWMA reviews or comments is the medium in which these comments and reviews are collated. Most of these studies tend to gather their reviews and comments from online websites or social media platforms such as Twitter [7, 8]. It is difficult to ascertain if these reviews have been written by a user who has really downloaded this mobile application. Analysis carried out on such reviews will be inaccurate as these reviews could be written by people who may not have even used the DWMA [10]. This will not be an issue for reviews written in the mobile application stores as the user must have already downloaded the application before being able to write a review.

3 Methodology and Results

Analysis for this study was conducted on reviews written for DWMAs of the top three prominent local banks in Singapore and this study was approved by the institutional review board (IRB-2025-323). The interface and design of DWMAs have been found to be one of the main deciding factors in determining user satisfaction and spending behavior [11, 12]. The opinions towards the interface and design of DWMAs are usually written in the application reviews making the analysis of these reviews important. The DWMAs of these banks were selected as they combine for the largest customer base in Singapore providing a diverse set of reviews to be analyzed. Singapore is budding into a vibrant cashless society and there is an increasing number of users conducting digital payments using a DWMA on a day-to-day basis. From paying for food by adults in eateries to students making payment for lunches via a DWMA, the Singapore government has made a consistent effort to ensure that the nation, of all ages, transitions towards a cashless society [13, 14].

Reviews of the three DWMAs were downloaded from the Google Play Store and Apple App Store using a Python script. Reviews written between 2020 to 2024 were analyzed. This time period was selected as it contained the latest perceptions which people had towards these DWMAs and more importantly, it included the COVID-19 pandemic period where people were encouraged to pay via cashless methods to minimize the spread of the virus.

The 35,916 reviews that were extracted were pre-processed. Specifically, reviews written before and after the period from 2020 to 2024 were removed. Duplicated reviews and those not written in English were removed as well. This resulted in 20,700 reviews remaining, and they were further processed to eliminate punctuations, numbers and stop-words, and underwent lemmatization. Application ratings given in each review ranged from one to five stars with one star being the worst and five stars being the best. The ratings for each review were re-labelled as "Lower" for those given a rating between one and three stars while those given a rating between four to five stars were re-labelled as "Higher". After this, the reviews were analyzed using STM with the application ratings given to the DWMA in each review as the covariates.

The results of the STM analysis revealed that the optimal number of topics was thirteen. This was determined based on the residuals measure, held-out likelihood estimation and the semantic coherence values [15, 16]. The thirteen topics were assessed by the authors and then assigned labels to depict what each topic represented.

Table 1 presents the thirteen topics and the ten keywords that are most closely associated with each topic. Topics one, two, seven and ten consisted of positive reviews of the DWMAs with users complimenting the features of the applications being seamless, fast, intuitive and convenient. An example of such reviews is as follows: "convenient, great, awesome and excellent services". These positive qualities allowed the users to complete their intended tasks of paying for transactions and checking account balances smoothly without facing any errors.

Topics three, five, six, eight, nine, eleven, twelve and thirteen consisted of negative reviews with users criticizing the applications of being slow, error-prone, battery draining, and unresponsive. These negative qualities disrupted the intended customer journeys which were related to the authentication process such as logging into the DWMA and updating authentication details. They also disrupted the most essential customer journeys which a DWMA provides - checking account balances and making transactions. This is evident in one such review: "Please do something about it, app keeps crashing, cannot login, even managed to login, cannot do transfer it only Crashed…".

It was noteworthy that topic four was a mix of positive and negative reviews with the users giving an application rating of between three to four. An example of such a review is as follows: "They're not ready for the volume of users…". While the rating was not considered to be low, the reviews still berated the features of the application claiming that they were short of fulfilling the most critical intended functions of a DWMA such as making payments.

Table 1. Analysis results of application reviews using STM.

Topic	Topic Label	Proportion(%)	Keywords	Review Example
1	Highly convenient app	16	Good, convenient, fast, great, excellent, thank, easily, awesome, efficient, love	"Good! Fuss free and convenient!!"
2	Secure, user-friendly app	5	Friendly, secure, like, experience, feature, better, reward, interface, point, risk	"…much easier to browse and redeem rewards directly through the app"
3	Unresponsive app	8	Work, frozen, fix, token, one, doesn't, reinstall, stuck, restart, show	"…screen freeze at front page After so long still have update the app…Smh"
4	Cumbersome app	6	User, slow, function, much, compare, improve, way, feedback, develop, bugging	"…there is no services to locked lost cards or apply debit card online..."
5	Error-prone app	8	Tried, service, error, notification, help, otp, call, terrible, available, receive	"…error message when trying to register an account"
6	Login failure	10	Can't, login, crash, password, forgot, timeout, reset, happen, wrong, key	"app keeps crashing, cannot login, even managed to login, cannot do transfer"
7	Useful transactional app	8	Use, simple, best, cash, reliable, recommend, hawker, online, shop, food	"Rebate using at hawker center and kopishop"
8	Long loading time	8	Time, open, load, problem, hang, long, embarrassing, frustrating, first, close	"Loading time occasionally takes forever"

(continued)

Table 1. (*continued*)

Topic	Topic Label	Proportion(%)	Keywords	Review Example
9	Privacy infringing app	9	Download, ban, antivirus, detect, store, scan, uninstall, star, device, allow	"App installed from the Google play store thinks it's a third party app and does not allow me to proceed"
10	Facilitates monetary transactions	9	Account, transfer, transact, payment, money, card, credit, balance, option, find	"Superfast transactions! Love that we can deduct the amount directly from the bank account without the need to shift money over…."
11	Energy inefficient app	5	Please, issue, bad, latest, batteries, horrible, drain, response, team, check	"Works fine for me but the battery drain is insane…."
12	Impedes payment	6	Worst, update, version, release, new, android, paynow, ever, last, review	"Latest version keeps saying "unable to process this request" when trying to paynow or login"
13	Difficult to update authentication details	4	Code, access, system, useless, finger, upload, unavailable, require, internet, button	"Uninstalling unable to register NEXT button is greyed out"

4 Discussion and Conclusion

The findings of this study show that users tend to enjoy their usage of the DWMAs when the user interface is intuitive and the intended operations of the application functioned as expected without errors being encountered. This is reflected in reviews in topics one, two, seven and ten which complimented on the seamless and efficient features. This allows users to complete their intended customer journeys efficiently, such as making payments via the DWMA in a crowded physical store where there may be time pressure to complete a purchase. This is in line with previous studies which identify that the perceived ease of using a DWMA is positively correlated to the users' spending [17, 18]. Thus, the perceived ease of use of a DWMA and the convenience which it provides to paying can potentially lead to overspending.

On the other hand, if a customer journey tends to encounter interruptions, errors or delays, users may become dissatisfied with the application and abandon usage. This is reflected in reviews in topics three, five, six, eight, eleven, twelve and thirteen which criticized the features of the app for being slow, error-prone and unresponsive. This finding aligns with past work which highlights that inaccessibility, obstacles and barriers encountered when using a DWMA decreases the users' intention to continue using it [12, 19]. This is also supported by the technology continuance theory [20], where operational obstacles and barriers tend to result in poor user satisfaction and attitudes towards the system, thus resulting in system abandonment.

While the findings show that operational constraints tend to lead to discontinuity in DWMA usage, appropriate introductions of such constraints, for example, in the form of pop-ups containing good financial advice, can serve as helpful interruptions to provide opportunities for persuading users to make better financial decisions. This is termed as a persuasive interruption [21, 22]. One purpose for which these pop-ups can help users make better financial decisions is to reduce excessive spending. Put differently, negative user experiences can be used to introduce a break in the users' train of thought in their customer journey of making payments, prompting them to cognitively reflect on their purchases [23]. With such cognitive breaks introduced, users will have an opportunity to reconsider their purchases and potentially help reduce their expenditures.

This study contributes towards highlighting the DWMA characteristics and customer journeys which users find enjoyable and thereby promote sustained usage. This study has also highlighted that operational obstacles faced by users which spark dissatisfaction and thus discontinuity in usage of the DWMA can serve as meaningful opportunities to provide interruptions in user journeys to display persuasive financial advice. This can help to increase financial literacy among users.

This study contributes towards improving the design of the user interfaces and customer journeys of DWMAs to cultivate better spending habits among users by tapping on negative reviews. One way of doing so is to slow down the payment process in the DWMA by introducing nudges in the form of pop-ups to encourage users to reflect on their payments before finalizing them. Finally, recent studies on DWMAs have pointed out that their usage could lead to overspending [24–26]. With the overspending problem via DWMAs becoming more prevalent, it would be helpful to ascertain if in-app persuasive messaging that interrupts the payment journey of a DWMA can lead to more prudent expenditure habits.

The following are the limitations of this study. First, we used only the DWMAs of the major local banks in one country. There are other DWMAs such as those of foreign banks which were not taken into consideration. Future work could include the review of these DWMAs to potentially derive more insights. Secondly, the findings of the study may not be generalizable to other countries with different cultures and social norms as the reviews extracted were limited to those of a single country. However, the study's findings from Singapore could still serve as a good starting reference for DWMA usage in other Asian countries.

Disclosure of Interests.. The authors have no competing interests to declare that are relevant to the content of this article.

References

1. Hassan, M.A., Shukur, Z.: Review of digital wallet requirements. In: 2019 International Conference on Cybersecurity (ICoCSec), pp. 43–48. IEEE (2016). https://doi.org/10.1109/ICoCS
2. Jadil, Y., Rana, N.P., Dwivedi, Y.K.: A meta-analysis of the UTAUT model in the mobile banking literature: the moderating role of sample size and culture. J. Bus. Res. **132**, 354–372 (2021). https://doi.org/10.1016/j.busres.2021.04.052
3. Wei, Q., Xiao, W., Yaqub, R.M.S., Irfan, M., Murad, M., Yaqub, M.Z.: Adoption of digital money (e-wallet) in the post COVID-19 era: the moderating role of low distribution charges and low transit time in impulsive buying: a developing country perspective. Front. Environ. Sci. **10** (2023). https://doi.org/10.3389/fenvs.2022.984316
4. Dev, H. et al.: From cash to cashless: UPI's impact on spending behavior among Indian users. In: Extended Abstracts of the CHI Conference on Human Factors in Computing Systems, pp. 1–10. ACM (2024). https://doi.org/10.1145/3613905/3651050
5. Singh, N., Sinha, N.: How perceived trust mediates merchant's intention to use a mobile wallet technology. J. Retail. Consum. Serv. **52**, 101894 (2020). https://doi.org/10.1016/j.jretconser.2019.101894
6. To, A., Trinh, T.H.M.: Understanding behavioral intention to use mobile wallets in Vietnam: extending the tam model with trust and enjoyment. Cogent Bus. Manag. **8**(1), 1–14 (2021). https://doi.org/10.1080/23311975.2021.1891661
7. Singh, P., Dwivedi, Y.K., Kahlon, K.S., Rana, N.P., Patil, P.P., Sawhney, R.S.: Digital payment adoption in India: insights from twitter analytics. In: Digital Transformation for a Sustainable Society in the 21st Century, vol. 11701, pp. 425–436. Springer (2019). https://doi.org/10.1007/978-3-030-29374-1_35
8. Teng, S., Khong, K.W.: Examining actual consumer usage of E-wallet: a case study of big data analytics. Comput. Hum. Behav. **121**, 106778 (2021). https://doi.org/10.1016/j.chb.2021.106778
9. Han, S., Anderson, C.K.: Customer motivation and response bias in online reviews. Cornell Hosp. Q. **61**(2), 142–153 (2020). https://doi.org/10.1177/1938965520902012
10. Alothali, E., Zaki, N., Mohamed, E.A., Alashwal, H.: Detecting social bots on twitter: a literature review. In: 2018 International Conference on Innovations in Information Technology (IIT), pp. 175–180. IEEE (2018). https://doi.org/10.1109/INNOVATIONS.2018/8605995
11. Lee, Y.Y., Gan, C.L., Liew, T.W., Yan, Z.: The impacts of mobile wallet app characteristics on online impulse buying: a moderated mediation model. Hum. Behav. Emerg. Technol. **1**, 1–15 (2022). https://doi.org/10.1155/2022/2767735
12. Zhou, T.: An empirical examination of users' post-adoption behaviour of mobile services. Behav. Inform. Technol. **30**(2), 241–250 (2011). https://doi.org/10.1080/0144929X.2010.543702
13. Chia, O.: Subsidy window for hawkers to adopt digital payments extended till Dec 2024. The Straits Times. https://www.straitstimes.com/singapore/subsidy-window-for-hawkers-to-adopt-digital-payment-extended-till-dec-2024, last accessed 2026/03/01
14. Ang, A.: Students in S'pore schools embrace switch to e-payments. The Straits Times. https://www.straitstimes.com/singapore/parenting-education/students-in-spore-schools-embrace-switch-to-e-payments-welcome-speed-and-ease-of-transactions, last accessed 2026/03/01
15. Lim, K.K., Lee, C.S.: Review of in-app nudges towards user decision behaviour: a topic modeling approach. In: International Conference on Asian Digital Libraries, pp. 263–269. Springer (2023). https://doi.org/10.1007/978-981-99-8085-7_24
16. Weston, S.J., Shryock, I., Light, R., Fisher, P.A.: Selecting the number and labels of topics in topic modeling: a tutorial. Adv. Methods Pract.. Psychol. Sci. **6**(2) (2023). https://doi.org/10.1177/25152459231160105

17. Aji, H.H., Adawiyah, W.R.: How e-wallets encourage excessive spending behavior among young adult consumers? J. Asia Bus. Stud. **16**(6), 868–884 (2022). https://doi.org/10.1108/JABS-01-2021-0025
18. Rathore, H.S.: Adoption of digital wallet by consumers. BVIMSR's J. Manag. Res. **8**(1), 69 (2016)
19. Abdul-Halim, N.A., Vafaei-Zadeh, A., Hanifah, H., Teoh, A.P., Nawaser, K.: Understanding the determinants of e-wallet continuance usage intention in Malaysia. Qual. Quant. **56**(5), 3413–3439 (2022). https://doi.org/10.1007/s11135-021-01276-7
20. Liao, C., Palvia, P., Chen, J.L.: Information technology adoption behavior life cycle: toward a technology continuance theory (TCT). Int. J. Inf. Manag. **29**(4), 309–320 (2009). https://doi.org/10.1016/j.ijinfomgt.2009.03.004
21. Kupor, D.M., Tormala, Z.L.: Persuasion, interrupted: the effect of momentary interruptions on message processing and persuasion. J. Consum. Res. **42**(2), 300–315 (2015). https://doi.org/10.1093/jcr/ucv018
22. Kupor, D.M., Liu, W., Amir, O.: The effect of an interruption on risk decisions. J. Consum. Res. **44**(6), 1205–1219 (2018). https://doi.org/10.1093/jcr/ucv018
23. Kupor, D.M., Reich, T., Shiv, B.: Can't finish what you started? The effect of climactic interruption on behavior. J. Consum. Psychol. **25**(1), 113–119 (2015). https://doi.org/10.1016/j.jcps.2014.05.006
24. Ahn, S.Y., Nam, Y.: Does mobile payment use lead to overspending? The moderating role of financial knowledge. Comput. Hum. Behav. **134**, 107319 (2022). https://doi.org/10.1016/j.chb.2022.107319
25. Manshad, M.S., Brannon, D.: Haptic-payment: exploring vibration feedback as a means of reducing overspending in mobile payment. J. Bus. Res. **122**, 88–96 (2021). https://doi.org/10.1016/j.jbusres.2020.08.049
26. Park, J., Lee, C., Thomas, M.: Why do cashless payments increase unhealthy consumption? The decision-risk inattention hypothesis. J. Assoc. Consum. Res. **6**(1), 21–32 (2021). https://doi.org/10.1086/710251

Evaluating the Usability of Infotainment System Rotary Controllers for Drivers with Disabilities

Olivia H. Honan(✉), Kailey Hrbek, Brandon D. Dreslin, Shawn Mathura, Brandon Ibarra, Barbara S. Chaparro, and Alex Chaparro

Embry-Riddle Aeronautical University, Daytona Beach, FL 32114, USA
honano@my.erau.edu

Abstract. Modern vehicles have become reliant on multifunction control interfaces for infotainment, navigation, and environmental systems, making the design of physical controls critical to usability, performance, and driver comfort. Multi-function rotary controllers are becoming increasingly common, yet it is unclear how design variations may influence comfort, ease of use, and ergonomic strain for users with disabilities. Supported by the EcoCAR Electric Vehicle Challenge, this study presents results from a qualitative usability study exploring variations of in-vehicle multi-function rotary controller design in terms of user performance and preferences. Four multi-function rotary controller designs were evaluated: the stock controller for the 2023 Cadillac LYRIQ and three controller attachment prototypes developed to improve accessibility for drivers with physical limitations. Participants completed infotainment-related tasks using each controller. Data was collected from seven participants with disabilities from the Embry-Riddle Aeronautical University (ERAU) student population, including individuals with upper-limb mobility impairments. Data for each participant is summarized individually to understand why specific controller attachments are reported to be easier, more comfortable, or less demanding for different types of disabilities. By comparing interactions across controller designs, this study examines the features and adjustable elements (e.g., height, shape, and required force) that align with specific disability-related needs. Findings build on existing accessibility design frameworks and highlight the need for inclusive design approaches that consider individual interaction strategies, suggesting that current in-vehicle controls do not equally support drivers with disabilities and warrant further research on how these controls can better support disability-related interaction needs.

Keywords: Disability-Centered Design · Human–Vehicle Interaction · Adaptive Interfaces

1 Introduction

Modern vehicles increasingly rely on multifunction human–machine interfaces (HMIs) to support safety, comfort, and convenience features, with many original equipment manufacturers consolidating inputs into fewer digital and physical controls, often using

C. Stephanidis et al. (Eds.): HCII 2026, CCIS 3047, pp. 390–401, 2026.
https://doi.org/10.1007/978-3-032-30552-7_37

rotary controllers for menu navigation and interaction [1]. Input modality affects mental workload, efficiency, and task performance [2], with touchscreen, rotary, and voice interfaces exhibiting tradeoffs in glance behavior, task time, and error rates [2–4]. However, the physical demands of automotive input devices—such as repetitive, coordinated movements and fine motor actions (e.g., pushing, pulling, twisting)—remain underexplored, despite posing challenges for older adults and drivers with disabilities who may have reduced strength, dexterity, or range of motion [5].

Repetitive hand movements and non-neutral postures are linked to upper-extremity discomfort and musculoskeletal disorders [6, 7]. Although ergonomic assessment methods are well established in occupational contexts [8, 9], they have seen limited application in evaluating in-vehicle controls [10, 11], leaving the physical effort required for modern vehicle interaction insufficiently characterized.

Supported in part by the EcoCAR Electric Vehicle (EV) Challenge, this study evaluates the physical demands and usability of four multifunction rotary controller designs used to operate the 2023 Cadillac LYRIQ infotainment system [12]. One controller was the stock design, while three were customizable attachment prototypes developed as part of HarmonIQ, a biometric-based, user-centered vehicle customization system created by Embry-Riddle Aeronautical University (ERAU) in collaboration with Bethune-Cookman University to improve accessibility for older adults and drivers with disabilities. This paper compares controller designs through a usability study with disabled drivers, examining why specific attachments feel easier, more comfortable, or more manageable for different users, with the goal of informing future HarmonIQ development and similar accessible HMI systems.

1.1 Background and Related Work

Physical input devices such as rotary controllers, joysticks, and haptic dials are widely used in vehicle interfaces and can provide beneficial tactile feedback that supports eyes-free interaction [13, 14]. However, these devices also pose usability challenges. Dashboards with single-function physical controls can become cluttered, increasing selection errors [3, 13], and physical controls are relatively static compared to adaptive software-based interfaces [3, 15]. Replacing physical controls with touchscreens further increases visually demanding interaction and associated safety concerns [3, 13].

These challenges are amplified for drivers with physical or cognitive disabilities, for whom meeting the perceptual, cognitive, and motor demands of driving can be especially difficult. Disability prevalence has been correlated with higher traffic fatality rates in the U.S., indicating a population-level relationship between impairment distribution and crash vulnerability [16]. Despite this risk, accessibility and adaptive technology legislation remains underdeveloped, leaving designers with few standardized guidelines for inclusive systems [16]. Infotainment and secondary control use can further compound this risk [17], requiring drivers to divert visual attention to locate controls, interpret icons, and verify inputs, thereby increasing visual and cognitive demand [18]. As noted in [19], many adaptive in-vehicle interfaces still assume a "standard" driver profile, underscoring the need for early integration of accessibility into HMI development rather than post-hoc adaptations.

Despite extensive controller research, important gaps remain in understanding multifunction rotary controllers that combine dial, push, and joystick inputs within a single control (Fig. 1). Prior work often examines inputs independently, relies on simplified laboratory setups, and rarely measures wrist posture, muscle effort, or changes in control use over time [14]. As a result, designers lack evidence on how specific properties of these hybrid controls affect performance, comfort, and wrist load during infotainment interaction, particularly for drivers with motor impairments.

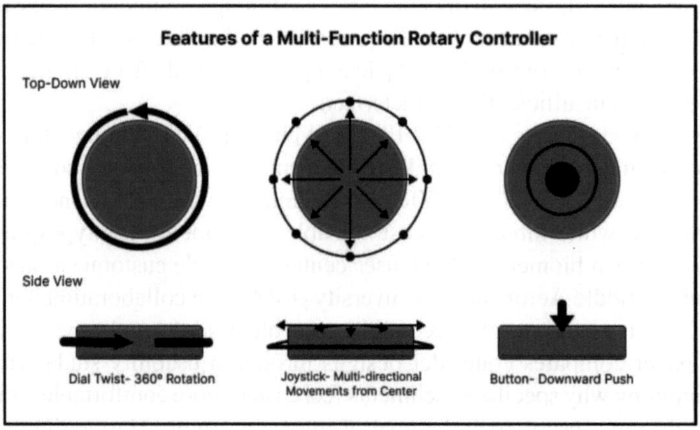

Fig. 1. Multi-Function Rotary Controller Movement Dynamics Diagram.

2 Method

2.1 Study Overview

This research was reviewed and approved by the ERAU Institutional Review Board (IRB No. 26-070).

This study employed a within-subjects design to evaluate the usability and ergonomic characteristics of multifunction rotary controllers intended for in-vehicle interaction. Participants completed a series of infotainment interaction tasks using four different multi-function rotary controllers. The four conditions included the stock 2023 Cadillac LYRIQ controller and three controller attachment design prototypes. Each participant interacted with all controller designs while performing the same set of tasks, allowing direct comparisons of usability, user experience, and ergonomic outcomes across conditions.

2.2 Participants

Seven participants were recruited from ERAU through word of mouth. Participants were at least 18 years of age and provided informed consent before participation. The study targeted ERAU students with disabilities.

Participant ages ranged from 18 to 42 years (M = 23.71, SD = 8.77). Anthropometric measurements were collected in inches and included arm length, forearm length, and hand length. Participant arm length ranged from 23.25 to 31.5 in. (M = 26.68, SD = 2.88). Forearm length ranged from 9.5 to 14.13 in. (M = 10.45, SD = 1.64). Hand length ranged from 2.5 to 8 in. (M = 6.89, SD = 1.96).

2.3 Apparatus

Vehicle Setup. Participants were seated in the driver's seat of a 2023 Cadillac LYRIQ and used the rotary controller to interact with the vehicle's infotainment system. A GoPro Hero 4 recorded participants' hand movements during controller interaction, while a GoPro Hero 7 captured the infotainment display to document task time, errors, and interaction behavior.

Multi-function Rotary Controller Designs. The four controller conditions (Fig. 2) included the built-in stock controller for the 2023 Cadillac LYRIQ (Stock Model A) and three controller attachment prototypes (attachments B, C, and D) developed to explore alternative rotary control designs aimed at improving accessibility and ease of interaction. The designs varied in height, shape, and curvature. All attachment prototypes were mounted on the same textured attachment base and secured over the stock controller during use.

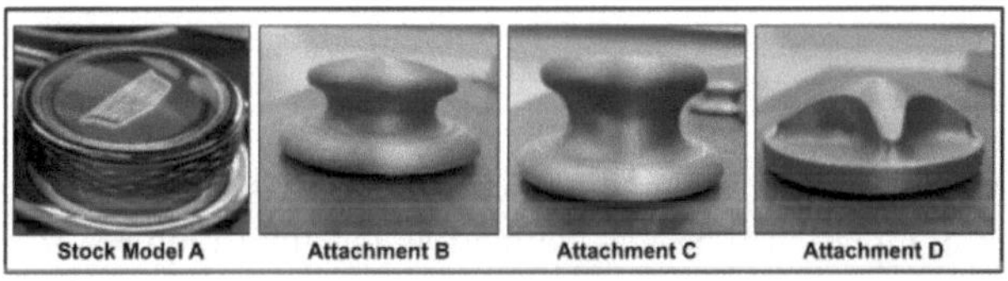

Fig. 2. Rotary Controller for the 2023 Cadillac LYRIQ (Stock Model A); HarmonIQ Controller Attachment Prototype (Attachment B); HarmonIQ Controller Attachment Prototype (Attachment C); HarmonIQ Controller Attachment Prototype (Attachment D).

2.4 Tasks

Participants completed a set of in-vehicle tasks reflecting common infotainment interactions using the vehicle's rotary control interface. Tasks required combinations of rotational input (e.g., dial twists), button presses, and multidirectional control (e.g., joystick movements) to navigate menus, make selections, and adjust settings. All participants completed the same task set under each condition. To minimize directional bias for tasks involving continuous value adjustments (e.g., radio tuning, climate control), task parameters such as starting values and target selections were alternated between conditions (e.g., 65 to 75 on condition 1, then 75 to 65 on condition 2).

A summary of tasks and associated interaction requirements is provided in Table 1. All tasks were performed within the Cadillac LYRIQ infotainment system, with the Maps task using Apple CarPlay and all other tasks using native vehicle interface applications.

Table 1. Description of in-vehicle tasks and associated interaction demands.

Task	Description of Interaction Demands
Maps	Participants were instructed to navigate to Apple CarPlay, open the Maps application, and enter a full address ("300 Madison Dr") into the search bar. This task required **minimal joystick usage** and primarily involved **continuous rotational input** to navigate menus and scroll through letters, along with **button presses to confirm selections.**
Climate	Participants were instructed to locate the climate control interface, activate the air conditioning, and adjust the cabin temperature from 75 °F to 65 °F. Required **joystick usage** for selection navigation, **minimal rotational input** for value adjustment, and **button presses for selection and activation.**
Radio	Participants were instructed to navigate to the audio interface, select the FM radio option, and adjust the station from an initial frequency (e.g., 102.5) to a target frequency (e.g., 93.1). This task involved primarily **rotational input for tuning** and **minimal joystick movements** and **button presses for selection.**
Charging	Participants were instructed to locate the charging interface and set the vehicle's charge limit to 80%. This task primarily involved navigating the menu with **joystick input** and **minimal rotational input** and pressing buttons **to confirm selections.**

2.5 Measures

Performance Metrics. Performance metrics included task completion time, success, and errors. Task completion time was defined as the time required to complete each task, while task success reflected correct completion of the required interaction. Task errors included incorrect menu selections and overshoot or undershoot of target values. All measures were collected through behavioral observation and verified using recorded video footage.

Subjective Metrics. Subjective usability was assessed using rating scales, think-aloud verbalizations during and after the task, and interview questions. Following each task, participants completed two Likert scales measuring perceived ease of use (1 = extremely difficult; 5 = extremely easy) and comfort (1 = extremely uncomfortable; 5 = extremely comfortable). At the end of each condition, participants completed a post-scenario questionnaire adapted from the Hand Activity Level–Threshold Limit Values (HAL-TLV) framework to assess perceived force required for gripping, twisting, and directional pushing, using the following scale: "Nothing at all; Extremely Weak (Just Noticeable); Very Weak; Weak (Light); Moderate; Strong (Heavy); Very Strong; Extremely Strong (Almost Maximum)." Participants then made comparative judgments across controller conditions, regarding ease of use, comfort, and overall preference. Open-ended interviews after each condition and a structured post-test interview captured additional feedback on preferences, challenges, and potential improvements.

2.6 Procedure

Following informed consent, participants completed a demographic questionnaire, and anthropometric measurements were collected using a fabric tape measure for arm, forearm, and hand length, all measured in inches using standardized procedures. Participants were then seated in the driver's seat, adjusted it to a comfortable position, and asked to imagine preparing for a road trip that involved interacting with multiple infotainment features via the rotary controller.

Controller conditions and task sets were partially counterbalanced to minimize order effects. For each condition, participants completed all tasks while verbalizing their thoughts, followed by a survey rating perceived ease of use and comfort. After completing tasks for a given controller, participants rated the perceived force required to grip, twist, and push the controller. After all conditions, participants completed a final survey and a brief post-test interview.

3 Results

3.1 Performance

All participants completed the tasks for each controller successfully, but time-on-task (Table 2) and error rate (Table 3) were highly variable across controller variants and participants. Rather than reflecting how well a given controller design supports performance, these results demonstrate the highly individualized nature of each participant's experience, shaped by their unique accessibility needs.

Table 2. Mean (SD) Time by Task in Seconds.

Controller	Maps	Climate	Radio	Charging
Stock Model A	84.8 (31.9)	35.1 (13.4)	36.7 (16.8)	19.9 (9.7)
Attachment B	68.3 (16.9)	25.9 (10.1)	21 (11.6)	13.6 (4)
Attachment C	72.1 (24.1)	22.9 (4.1)	21.7 (7.6)	10.7 (4.1)
Attachment D	86 (40.3)	37.1 (22.4)	26.3 (10.5)	19.1 (11)

Table 3. Mean (SD) Errors by Task.

Controller	Maps	Climate	Radio	Charging
Stock Model A	6 (5.7)	4.14 (3.3)	2.29 (2.6)	1.14 (1.7)
Attachment B	6.14 (6.8)	4.3 (4.1)	1.4 (1.5)	1.3 (1.9)
Attachment C	6.43 (4.9)	5.14 (4.7)	1.9 (1.9)	.71 (1.5)
Attachment D	7.4 (5.9)	3.3 (2.5)	2.1 (2.8)	1.6 (1.7)

3.2 Overall Preference Across Controllers

No single controller was preferred across all participants; preferences were highly individualized and closely tied to motor capabilities and interaction strategies. Each participant demonstrated a clear most- and least-preferred controller, with designs rated as most comfortable and easiest to use often aligning with overall preference, underscoring the importance of comfort and ease in this design space.

Across participants, controllers B, C, and D were preferred by at least one participant but were just as likely to be most disliked by another. Only one participant disliked the stock controller, and none preferred it. Table 4 summarizes participants' disability types, most and least preferred controllers (see Fig. 2 for reference), and the primary reasons for these selections.

Table 4. Participant Disability Type and Preferences.

Participant- Disability Type	Preferred Controller	Least Preferred Controller
P1-Cognitive/Mental	**Attachment B** – Easiest to use – Most comfortable – Preferred for consistent use – More comfortable on the wrist because it was at the same level as the armrest	**Attachment C** – Most difficult – Most uncomfortable – Greater force is required to grip, twist, and use joystick – Taller than armrest, the grip hurt the fingers and wrist – Difficult to use for extended periods – User's longer nails to pressed into the thumb while gripping
P2-Mobility, Physical	**Attachment C** – Easiest to use – Most comfortable – Preferred for consistent use – Attachment fit finger length most comfortably – Easier to grip	**Attachment D** – Most difficult – Most uncomfortable – Uncomfortable with their finger length – Wants more height between the top and base to create more "grip space"
P3-Cognitive/Mental	**Attachment B** – Easiest to use – Most comfortable – Preferred for consistent use – Allowed for greater hand position variability	**Stock Model A** – Most difficult – Most uncomfortable – Gripping was more difficult – Would like more texture for grip – It would be improved if it were taller – Would require more attention to avoid driving mistakes – More force required to grip and utilize the joystick

(*continued*)

Table 4. (*continued*)

Participant- Disability Type	Preferred Controller	Least Preferred Controller
P4-Mobility, Physical, Visual	**Attachment D** – Easiest to use – Most comfortable – Preferred for consistent use – Required the least force to grip and twist – Felt more control while using this attachment – Easier for them to use when their hands are aching from diabetes – Less likely to obstruct additional adaptive equipment, such as hand controls	**Attachment C** – Most difficult – Most uncomfortable – More force was required to twist this attachment effectively – Too tall for their hand to sit naturally – Creates pressure on the base of the fingers – Too smooth; would be difficult to maneuver – Might obstruct their usage of other in-vehicle adaptive equipment
P5-Mobility, Physical, Auditory	**Attachment C** – Easiest to use – Most comfortable Preferred for consistent use – Required the least force to grip and use the joystick – Could adjust hand position; much more comfortable for their nerve damage	**Attachment D** – Most difficult – Most uncomfortable – Required the most force to grip – Grooves were too shallow and felt awkward and uncomfortable – Twisting interaction felt too fast and difficult to control – Wrist was in an uncomfortable position when using this attachment
P6-Mobility, Physical, Other	**Attachment C** – Easiest to use – Most comfortable – Preferred for consistent use – Attachment felt secure and would not detach during use. – Not too sensitive; made tasks feel easier	**Attachment D** – Most difficult – Liked the texture, but disliked "everything else" – Disliked that this attachment did not feel secure – Twisting motion too sensitive; made menu navigation more difficult

(*continued*)

Table 4. (*continued*)

Participant- Disability Type	Preferred Controller	Least Preferred Controller
P7-Physical	**Attachment D** – Easiest to use – Preferred for consistent use – Grooves allowed them to use the controller without needing to grip – Required the least force for twisting and joystick	**Attachment C** – Most difficult – Most uncomfortable – Required the most force to twist – Rounded top; could not use down pressure to twist the attachment – Wanted a flattened top for easier twisting

3.3 Perceived Ease of Use and Comfort

Perceived ease of use and comfort strongly aligned with overall preference, with participants consistently selecting the controllers they found easiest and most comfortable to also be preferred for consistent use. Participants with mobility-related and physical disabilities generally prioritized low activation force, secure attachment, and controller shape, preferring attachments that required minimal force, remained stable during use, and supported multiple hand positions.

Participants with cognitive or mental disabilities preferred attachments that supported natural hand positions and minimized anticipated attentional demands during driving. Controllers that allowed the fingers to remain fully extended and required little attention to maintain control of were often preferred.

3.4 Disability Specific Interaction Differences

Differences in overall preference emerged based on the nature of the disability. For example, one participant with a nonfunctioning right hand preferred attachment D because its grooved design allowed full use of the controls, whereas attachment C was too smooth to apply sufficient downward pressure for twisting. Participants with mobility or physical disabilities that limit grip or fine-motor control may prefer controllers with higher twisting sensitivity, particularly when interactions rely on downward pressure rather than grip. Hard edges or grooves were similarly preferred, as they could be leveraged without sliding.

Participants whose physical disabilities affected their ability to maintain hand or arm postures preferred high sensitivity joystick and grip interactions and lower twisting sensitivity. These features reduced sustained muscle activation, allowing manipulation while resting on a support. This group prioritized adjustable hand positions that enabled use of the center console or armrest; one participant noted their preferred controller allowed manipulation from the side while using the center console for support, while their least preferred forced the wrist into an uncomfortable position.

Participants with cognitive or mental disabilities showed distinct preference patterns, prioritizing comfort and natural hand positions with the hand fully extended over the controller. While not explicitly stated, limiting pain and discomfort may support focus by reducing attentional demands. One participant noted their least preferred controller would require greater attention to avoid mistakes while driving. Controls that feel seamless and require minimal cognitive effort during multitasking may better support this group.

4 Discussion

The findings indicate that, in terms of rotary controller design for infotainment use, preferences amongst users with disabilities are primarily determined by the degree of alignment between a given controller and the user's unique interaction strategy. Given that there was no single preferred controller across participants, it is likely that ergonomic success in this context is not determined by aggregate comfort or ease for a given design, but by the unique experience of comfort and ease that translates into a given user's preference, based on how well their needs are supported.

4.1 Neutral Design Is Not Accessible Design

Results indicated no strong preference for or dislike of the stock controller. Participant responses highlighted the gap between designing for an "average" user and addressing individual needs. Although the design did not cause direct issues, it failed to support unique interaction strategies and was not preferred by any participants. This challenges the assumption that meeting basic usability needs constitutes accessibility; rather, accessibility requires actively supporting individual users' needs for successful interaction, not merely avoiding problems.

4.2 Implications for Design

These findings suggest that adaptability and customization offer a promising direction for inclusive infotainment design. Rather than pursuing a one-size-fits-all solution, designers can better support drivers with disabilities by enabling users to select resistance, shape, height, and surface texture to match their preferred interaction strategies. As understanding of individual interaction mechanics and design support continues to evolve, this process could eventually be as streamlined as obtaining prescription glasses, with assessment, fitting, and a resulting component that is customized to support specific accessibility needs.

4.3 Limitations and Future Work

This study has several limitations. The small sample size limits generalizability, and participants were drawn exclusively from a university student population, which is not representative of the broader driving population, particularly older adults with disabilities. Tasks were performed in a stationary vehicle and therefore did not capture real-world driving demands, including divided attention and vehicle motion. Additionally, the study did not include ergonomics metrics needed to assess posture or potential long-term strain associated with each controller.

Future work should address these limitations and examine interaction strategies across a wider range of attachment designs, the full infotainment system, and the vehicle as a whole, to better understand how drivers with disabilities can be supported throughout the driving experience, including through simple, cost-effective solutions.

5 Conclusion

This study examined how drivers with disabilities perceive differences in rotary controller design for infotainment control tasks. Findings indicate there is no universal solution; instead, optimal design depends on individual needs and interaction strategies. The results provide guidance for designing accessible, ergonomic interfaces that accommodate varied motor abilities and demonstrate how disability-specific interaction strategies shape user preferences. More broadly, this work highlights the importance of user-centered refinement in vehicle HMI design, particularly for drivers with disabilities who face distinct ergonomic challenges. Future work with larger, more diverse samples and dynamic driving environments will be essential to validate these findings and inform continued prototype development.

Disclosure of Interests. The authors have no competing interests to declare that are relevant to the content of this article.

References

1. Harvey, C., Stanton, N.A., Pickering, C.A., McDonald, M., Zheng, P.: To twist or poke? A method for identifying usability issues with the rotary controller and touch screen for control of in-vehicle information systems. Ergonomics. **54**(7), 609–625 (2011)
2. Harvey, C.: Touch screen vs. rotary controller: how usable are the two major in-vehicle information system technologies? In: Adjunct Proceedings of the Second International Conference on Automotive User Interfaces and Interactive Vehicular Applications AutomotiveUI 2010, p. 1 (2010)
3. DeGuzman, C.A., Demir, B., Ayas, S., Donmez, B.: A review of in-vehicle touchscreen safety and usability. Transp. Res. Interdisc. Perspect. **36**, 101873 (2026)
4. Suh, Y., Ferris, T.K.: On-road evaluation of in-vehicle interface characteristics and their effects on performance of visual detection on the road and manual entry. Hum. Factors. **61**(1), 105–118 (2019)
5. Chaparro, A., Rogers, M., Fernandez, J., Bohan, M., Choi, S.D., Stumpfhauser, L.: Range of motion of the wrist: implications for designing computer input devices for the elderly. Disabil. Rehabil. **22**(13–14), 633–637 (2000)
6. Keir, P.J., Farias Zuniga, A., Mulla, D.M., Somasundram, K.G.: Relationships and mechanisms between occupational risk factors and distal upper extremity disorders. Hum. Factors. **63**(1), 5–31 (2021)

7. Lotter, O., Lieb, T., Breul, V., Molsner, J.: Is repetitive workload a risk factor for upper extremity musculoskeletal disorders in surgical device mechanics? A cross-sectional analysis. Int. J. Environ. Res. Public Health. **17**(4), 1383 (2020)
8. Krishnan, A. et al.: Data-driven ergonomic risk assessment of complex hand-intensive manufacturing processes. Commun. Eng. **4**(1), Article 45 (2025)
9. Sancini, A. et al.: Risk of upper extremity biomechanical overload in automotive facility. Biomed. Environ. Sci. **26**(1), 70–75 (2013)
10. Young, K.L., Koppel, S., Charlton, J.L.: Toward best practice in human-machine interface design for older drivers: a review of current design guidelines. Accid. Anal. Prev. **106**, 460–467 (2017)
11. Lowe, B.D., Dempsey, P.G., Jones, E.M.: Ergonomics assessment methods used by ergonomics professionals. Appl. Ergon. **81**, 102882 (2019)
12. About the EcoCAR EV Challenge. https://avtcseries.org/about-the-ecocar-ev-challenge/, last accessed 2026/03/21
13. Farimani, H.: Investigating the User Experience of Physical and Digital Interfaces in Automotive Design (2020)
14. Tan, Y.H., Ng, P.K., Saptari, A., Jee, K.S.: Ergonomics aspects of knob designs: a literature review. Theor. Issues Ergon. Sci. **16**(1), 86–98 (2015)
15. Dicianno, B.E., Cooper, R.A., Coltellaro, J.: Joystick control for powered mobility: current state of technology and future directions. Phys. Med. Rehabil. Clin. N. Am. **21**(1), 79–86 (2010)
16. Bastola, A., Wang, H., Boroujeni, S.P.H., Brinkley, J., Moshayedi, A.J., Razi, A.: Driving toward inclusion: a systematic review of AI-powered accessibility enhancements for people with disability in autonomous vehicles. IEEE Access. **13**, 61384–61415 (2025)
17. Chen, K.B., Savage, A.B., Chourasia, A.O., Wiegmann, D.A., Sesto, M.E.: Touch screen performance by individuals with and without motor control disabilities. Appl. Ergon. **44**(2), 297–302 (2013)
18. Strayer, D.L., Cooper, J.M., Goethe, R.M., McCarty, M.M., Getty, D.J., Biondi, F.: Assessing the visual and cognitive demands of in-vehicle information systems. Cogn. Res.: Princ. Implic. **4**(1), 18 (2019)
19. Wirtz, L., Sever, E., Eckstein, L.: Adaptive human-machine interfaces and inclusivity in the automotive field: a review. In applied human factors and ergonomic (AHFE) international 2024, accessibility. Assist. Technol. Digit. Environ. **121**, 46–60 (2024)

Usability Study on Fuzzy Search in E-commerce Websites: A Case Study of Taobao

Yicheng Ji, Fengyi Lin, Zhecheng Li, Yu Chen(✉), and Yuqi Liu

Department of Industrial Design, School of Design, South China University of Technology, Guangzhou, China
chenyu1@scut.edu.cn

Abstract. This study examines fuzzy search usability in e-commerce through a user testing study on Taobao. Fifty participants completed both fuzzy and precise search tasks, with behavioral metrics, SUS scores, and semi-structured interviews collected. Findings reveal that fuzzy retrieval took three times longer than precise search, yielding an overall SUS score of 65.8—below the "good" threshold. Three fuzzy input types and three behavioral paths were identified, with key usability breakdowns in semantic understanding, result feedback, and interface adaptability across user groups. Drawing on Norman's Execute–Evaluate model, the study offers design recommendations for improving semantic guidance, filtering mechanisms, and multimodal search support in e-commerce search systems.

Keywords: Fuzzy search · E-commerce platform · Usability study · User testing · Taobao · Mental model · Cognitive load · Search interaction design · Semantic understanding · User experience

1 Research Background and Significance

Search functions are the primary entry point of e-commerce platforms and directly influence shopping efficiency and purchase decisions. While current systems perform well with precise queries, they often struggle with fuzzy search, where users express needs using ambiguous, informal, or incomplete language [1].

Fuzzy search reflects a gap between users' mental models and structured product databases. When systems fail to interpret these inputs effectively, users experience longer task times, repeated query reformulation, and increased cognitive load.

Although prior research has explored query ambiguity and ranking algorithms, fewer studies examine fuzzy search from a usability and cognitive interaction perspective in real commercial platforms.

This study uses Taobao as a case to investigate how fuzzy search usability issues emerge in practice. Guided by Norman's Execute–Evaluate model [2], we analyze breakdowns in user intention execution and result evaluation, aiming to provide design insights for improving semantic guidance and feedback mechanisms in e-commerce search systems.

C. Stephanidis et al. (Eds.): HCII 2026, CCIS 3047, pp. 402–410, 2026.
https://doi.org/10.1007/978-3-032-30552-7_38

2 Research Objectives and Core Focus

The research has three primary objectives:

- To examine behavioral patterns and cognitive strategies during fuzzy search
- To identify usability friction points that affect efficiency and user experience
- To evaluate how current search interface design and feedback mechanisms influence user performance

By comparing fuzzy search tasks with precise search tasks, this study analyzes differences in task time, interaction effort, and perceived cognitive load.

2.1 Research Questions and Core Concepts

This study is guided by the following research questions:

1. What behavioral patterns and cognitive strategies do users exhibit during fuzzy search tasks?
2. What usability issues and interaction barriers reduce efficiency and increase cognitive load?
3. How do existing search interface designs and feedback mechanisms contribute to or mitigate these issues?

Core concepts include:

Fuzzy Search: Ambiguous, informal, or exploratory user queries
Usability: Efficiency, effectiveness, and user satisfaction
Mental Model Alignment: The consistency between user expectations and system feedback

Participants were asked to complete both precise search tasks and fuzzy search tasks under controlled conditions. Behavioral data (task time, number of clicks, query reformulations) and subjective data (perceived difficulty, satisfaction, cognitive load) were collected.

The experimental design focuses on comparing:

- Interaction effort between fuzzy and precise search
- Query reformulation frequency
- User adaptation strategies
- Perceived alignment between user intention and system feedback

3 User Testing Method

3.1 User Testing Method

An in-person user testing study was conducted to observe how participants naturally formulate and refine vague shopping queries on Taobao. The study adopted a within-subjects design in which each participant completed both fuzzy search tasks (using ambiguous, colloquial, or scenario-based language) and a benchmark task (using a precise, well-defined keyword), enabling direct comparison of behavioral and efficiency indicators across conditions. Real-time clickstream data was recorded throughout each session, capturing task completion time, effective click counts, keyword modification frequency, and task completion rate.

3.2 Questionnaire and Interview Method

Immediately following task completion, participants filled in two standardized scales. The SUS Scale (10 items, 0–100 points; =70 = "good" usability) measured overall subjective perception of Taobao's fuzzy retrieval function. A Task-Specific Scale (5-point Likert) assessed satisfaction with semantic understanding accuracy and result relevance for each fuzzy task. These two instruments directly underpin the usability metric results reported in Sect. 5.2.

3.3 Data Analysis Method

Behavioral metrics (task completion time, click counts, error rates) were analyzed using descriptive statistics and inferential tests. Between-group comparisons were conducted where appropriate to examine differences across user groups.

4 Testing Procedure

4.1 Pre-Test Preparation

Participant Recruitment. A total of 50 participants were recruited via purposive sampling, carefully covering three age groups (18–30, 30–45, 45+), an equal split of high/low-frequency users (25 each), and balanced north-south regional backgrounds (26 northern, 24 southern). This sample size was determined to ensure sufficient statistical power ($a = 0.05$, $ß = 0.80$) for reliable group comparison analyses, and its demographic distribution aligned with Taobao's overall user structure as documented in the 2024 Taobao User Behavior Report [4]. The sampling design is consistent with established standards for medium-scale usability research in the field of human-computer interaction (HCI) [3] (Table 1).

Table 1. Demographic Information of a Subset of Participants.

Participant	Age	Region	Usage Frequency
1	20	Guangdong	Once a week
2	21	Hunan	Once a month
3	42	Inner Mongolia	Twice a week
4	47	Sichuan	Once every three months
5	50	*Liaoning*	Once a month
...	...	...	...

Task Design. Three distinct types of experimental tasks were designed to simulate real-world fuzzy retrieval scenarios:

Benchmark Task: Participants were asked to search for well-defined, standardized items (e.g., "18k gold necklace") to establish a baseline of operational performance in obstacle-free search scenarios.
Visually-Driven Fuzzy Retrieval: Target item images (e.g., "ratchet wrench", "rope flower", "dress fitting head cover") were displayed for 5 s, followed by a 3-s flash review to simulate visual memory in fragmented browsing. Participants were required to conduct searches based on descriptions of the items' visual features.
Context-Driven Fuzzy Retrieval: Specific life pain points were presented (e.g., "the switch of the car sundry box is damaged", "the rental house door lock is not safe"), prompting participants to express their needs through functional fuzzy descriptions and search for appropriate solutions (e.g., "car glove box replacement", "door stopper for rental houses").

Each participant completed 9 tasks in total: 1 benchmark task, 4 visually-driven fuzzy retrieval tasks, and 4 context-driven fuzzy retrieval tasks. To eliminate potential order effects, the sequence of the 8 fuzzy retrieval tasks was counterbalanced across all participants.

Observation Metrics. Core usability metrics were defined with clear operational definitions to ensure data objectivity and measurability:

Efficiency: Task completion time (total duration from search initiation to target confirmation) and number of effective clicks (excluding accidental clicks or browsing of irrelevant pages).
Interaction: Keyword modification frequency (number of times participants revise search terms to adjust intentions), associative word usage rate (proportion of tasks where system-recommended associative words are adopted), and filtering tool calls (number of times filtering functions like price or sales volume are used).
Effectiveness: Task completion rate (proportion of tasks where highly relevant commodities are successfully found) and relevance of the top 20 search results (evaluated using a 5-point Likert scale: 1 = completely irrelevant, 5 = fully matched, based on alignment with retrieval intentions).

Questionnaire and Interview.

SUS Scale: A standardized 10-item assessment tool (scoring range 0-100 points), where a score of =70 indicates "good" usability, used to measure participants' overall subjective perception of Taobao's fuzzy retrieval function.
Task-Specific Scale: A 5-point Likert scale designed to evaluate satisfaction with two key dimensions of each fuzzy retrieval task: semantic understanding accuracy and result relevance.
Semi-structured Interviews: Conducted with 15 randomly selected participants (3 from each age group) to explore keyword extraction logic for unknown commodities, cognitive

friction factors (e.g., advertising interference), and expectations for multimodal input methods (e.g., voice and image search).

4.2 Pre-Test and Formal Testing

Pre-Test. A pilot test was conducted with 5 participants who met the sampling criteria to refine the experimental design. Key optimizations included adding functional description prompts (e.g., guiding participants to input "right-angle fixing piece" when unable to name "angle bracket") to reduce keyword expression difficulty.

Formal Testing. The formal test was carried out in a controlled laboratory environment with standardized conditions: all participants used the same smartphone model, Taobao App version, stable network connection, and received consistent verbal instructions to avoid interpretation biases.

During task completion, real-time clickstream data was recorded, and the think-aloud protocol was implemented to capture participants' mental processes and decision-making.

Immediately after all tasks, participants completed the SUS scale and task-specific satisfaction scale, and selected participants participated in 15-min semi-structured interviews.

5 Results and Analysis

5.1 Fuzzy Input Types and Behavioral Paths

Fuzzy Input Type Statistics.

Semantic fuzzy input (68.3%): The most common type, involving non-standard descriptions of functions, scenarios, or styles (e.g., "anti-prying devices suitable for rental houses"), with an average matching degree of 2.1 points (scenario-based descriptions: 2.4 points; stylized descriptions: 1.8 points).
Spelling/expression deviation (23.5%): Includes spelling mistakes, synonym replacement, and colloquial expressions (e.g., "angle bracket" miswritten as "horn horse"), with an average matching degree of 1.9 points (synonym replacement: 2.2 points; spelling mistakes: 1.6 points).
Semantic expansion (8.2%): Keywords supplemented with restrictive conditions to clarify intentions (e.g., "dress fitting head cover that prevents makeup smudging"), with an average matching degree of 2.7 points—the highest relevance among the three types (Fig. 1).

Behavioral Path Analysis.

Three typical behavioral paths emerged from the data:
Efficient convergent (32.0%): Average completion time of 198 s, 92.3% completion rate, and 3.8-point satisfaction score, characterized by accurate initial keywords and active use of auxiliary tools.

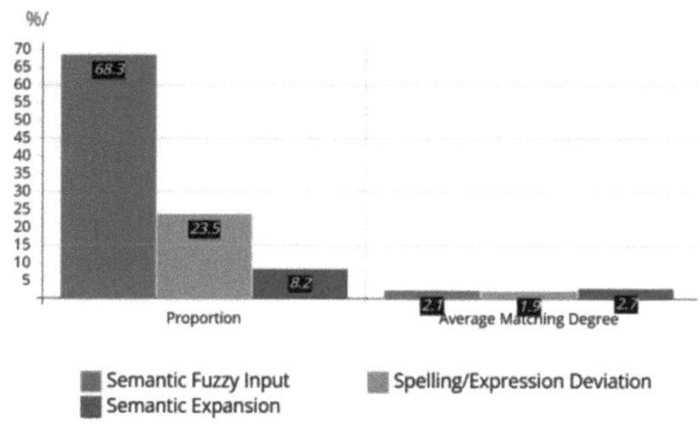

Fig. 1. Proportions are reported as percentages, while average matching degree is measured on a 1-5 scale.

Exploratory corrective (48.0%): The most prevalent path, with an average completion time of 275 s, 76.5% completion rate, and 3.1-point satisfaction score, involving repeated keyword modifications to approach the target.
Divergent abandonment (20.0%): Average completion time of 342 s, 18.7% completion rate, and 2.0-point satisfaction score, marked by unstructured keyword changes and eventual task abandonment.
Key finding: The use of filtering tools and associative words significantly improved path convergence ($?^2 = 12.68$, $p < 0.001$), highlighting the value of system auxiliary functions.

5.2 Usability Metric Analysis

Learnability. High frequency users outperformed low-frequency users, achieving a 23.6% higher completion rate and 31.4% higher tool utilization rate ($t = 4.89$, $p < 0.001$).

44.4% (4 of 9) of middle-aged and elderly users reported operational difficulties, primarily with keyword modification and filter selection; the average scores for SUS learnability-related items were 3.2 and 3.0 points (out of 5).

Search Efficiency. Fuzzy retrieval tasks took three times longer than the benchmark task (256s vs. 85s; $F = 18.32$, $p < 0.001$), with highly ambiguous terms requiring the longest time.

Young users completed tasks significantly faster than middle-aged and elderly users (205 s vs. 326 s; $t = 7.35$, $p < 0.001$) and achieved a higher effective click ratio (68.3% vs. 45.2%; $?^2 = 14.89$, $p < 0.001$).

Error Rate/Fault Tolerance. On average, each fuzzy retrieval task involved 1.2 spelling mistakes, 41.3% invalid clicks, and 1.8 path divergences.

62.3% of spelling mistakes and 45.7% of dialect inputs were unrecognized by the system, resulting in an average matching degree of 1.6 points.

User Satisfaction. The overall SUS score was 65.8 points, categorized as "acceptable" but below the 70-point threshold for "good" usability.

The lowest scores were observed for semantic understanding accuracy (3.1 points) and result relevance (3.0 points), the primary sources of user dissatisfaction.

Significant group differences existed: young users (3.6 points) > family users (3.1 points) > middle-aged and elderly users (2.3 points; $F = 12.47$, $p < 0.001$) (Fig. 2).

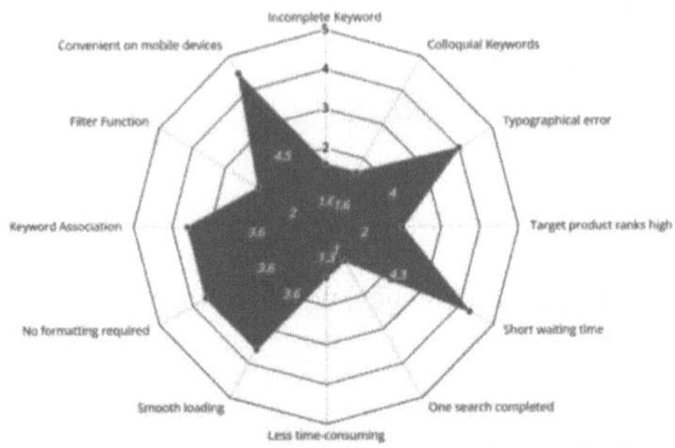

Fig. 2. Radar chart of usability-related dimension scores (1-5) in Taobao fuzzy search tasks. The system scored highest on mobile convenience and short waiting time, and lowest on time consumption and keyword flexibility-related dimensions.

5.3 Interface and Feedback Mechanism Evaluation

Search Suggestions and Association Function. The average relevance score of associative words to fuzzy intentions was 2.8 points (scenario/functional keywords: 3.2 points; stylized keywords: 2.3 points; $t = 5.21$, $p < 0.001$).

Key limitations included delayed updates after keyword modification and a lack of restrictive associative directions (e.g., price ranges for "cost-effective tablets").

Semantic Relevance of Recommended Products. Among the top 20 search results, 28.3% were highly relevant, 45.7% partially relevant, and 26.0% irrelevant.

Paid promotion products occupied the top 2 positions, pushing highly relevant natural results to the 3–10th place and prolonging retrieval paths.

Cognitive Load. 66.0% of participants reported experiencing information overload from mixed content (e.g., ads, recommendation streams) on result pages.

42.0% found filtering conditions overly complex ($?^2 = 19.36$, $p < 0.001$), and 38.0% encountered difficulties with interface navigation (e.g., resetting filters).

5.4 Analysis of Typical User Cases

Efficient vs. Confused Users.

Efficient users (young/high-frequency): Demonstrated clear retrieval strategies, accurate keyword extraction, and proficient use of auxiliary tools to optimize results.
Confused users (middle-aged/elderly/low-frequency): Used vague keywords, rarely utilized system tools, and often misinterpreted recommendation streams as search results, leading to inefficient paths.

Search Strategies.

Function-Oriented (42.0%): Dominated by Family Users, Focusing on "function + category" Keyword Combinations (E.G., "eye-protecting children's study desk") with an Average Matching Degree of 2.4 Points.
Scenario-oriented (36.0%): Preferred by young users, centered on usage scenarios (e.g., "commute large-capacity bag") with an average matching degree of 2.1 points.
Trial-and-error (22.0%): Mainly adopted by middle-aged and elderly users, involving random keyword modifications with an average matching degree of 1.7 points ($?^2 = 23.71$, $p < 0.001$).

6 Conclusions and Improvements

6.1 Summary of Usability Issues

Insufficient Semantic Understanding: Poor mapping of scenario/stylized vocabulary and weak handling of colloquial, dialect, and typo inputs.
Poor Interactive Design Adaptability: Overly complex filters, information overload on result pages, and redundant operational paths for core functions.
Low Feedback Mechanism Effectiveness: Irrelevant associative words, commercial interference in result sorting, and delayed feedback after keyword modification.
Weak Group Adaptability: Inadequate support for middle-aged/elderly users, unresolved cross-regional language differences, and neglected niche group needs.

6.2 Analysis of Cognitive Mechanisms

Intention Expression: Difficulties in extracting standardized vocabulary for fuzzy needs and mismatches between diverse user mental models and unified system logic.

Result Evaluation: High cognitive load in judging result relevance, gaps between standardized system feedback and users' fuzzy cognition, and lack of strategy guidance for poor initial results.

Decision Execution: Cognitive resources occupied by redundant information, operational memory burdens from complex processes, and reduced trust due to commercialized sorting.

6.3 Improvement Recommendations

Search Interface Design Optimization. Simplify filtering functions with a "basic + advanced" hierarchy and provide "one-click filtering" templates for middle-aged and elderly users.

Optimize result page layout by reducing ad frequency, visually distinguishing promotions, and highlighting core commodity information.

Add quick operation entrances for keyword modification history and commonly used filter combinations to shorten operational paths.

Support a switchable "simple mode" with larger fonts and simplified interface elements to accommodate diverse visual needs.

User Experience Enhancement Strategies. Implement personalized associative word recommendations tailored to different user groups (stylized/scenario-based for young users, function-focused for families, colloquial synonyms for middle-aged/elderly users).

Optimize result sorting by introducing a "fuzzy relevance weight" that prioritizes highly relevant natural results over paid promotions.

Provide proactive keyword optimization suggestions and scenario-based keyword templates to assist users in clarifying fuzzy needs.

Add "recommendation reason" labels on result pages to enhance transparency and user trust.

System Usability Improvement Directions. Voice optimization: Strengthen recognition of colloquial and dialect expressions, and add a semantic parsing function to convert oral descriptions into standardized search terms.

Image upgrade: Enhance the "Snap & Search" function to support partial screenshot search and feature description + image combined search.

Acknowledgments. We sincerely thank Professor Liu Yuqi and Professor Chen Yu for their valuable guidance and continuous support throughout this research. We are grateful to all participants for their time and effort in the user testing.

References

1. Luo, X. et al.: AliCoCo: Alibaba E-commerce cognitive concept net. In: SIGMOD '20, LNCS, vol. 12113, pp. 1–15. Springer, Heidelberg (2020)
2. Norman, D.A.: The Design of Everyday Things, 1st edn. Basic Books, New York, NY (1988)
3. Brooke, J.: SUS: a "quick and dirty" usability scale. In: Usability Evaluation in Industry, pp. 189–194. Taylor & Francis (1996)
4. Alibaba Group: Taobao User Behavior Report 2024. Alibaba Research Institute (2024)

User Evaluation of an Interactive Map-based SNS Search System Using LLM-based Personas

Tomonari Kamba(✉)

Toyo University, Information Networking for Innovation and Design,
1-7-11 Akabanedai, Kita-ku, Tokyo 115-8650, Japan
kamba@iniad.org

Abstract. To mitigate filter bubbles, we are developing an interactive map-based SNS search system that presents users with diverse perspectives. As a preliminary evaluation of its effectiveness, this study employs multiple personas generated by a large language model (LLM) as experimental subjects and observes changes in their post selection tendencies when the system is used continuously. Specifically, for a given search keyword, 100 SNS posts were retrieved, and the LLM automatically generated axis labels and coordinate values to construct an interactive map. These were presented to personas whose characteristics were defined through prompts, and each persona sequentially selected and viewed 10 posts that they found interesting. After viewing each post, the personas were instructed to update their internal states if they experienced reactions such as understanding, empathy, or aversion. In addition, some personas were given an extra instruction before the experiment to "observe the entire map broadly."

The experiment was conducted over seven days. The results indicate that this additional instruction had a noticeable effect in the early stages, encouraging broader exploration; however, its influence gradually diminished, and the personas tended to revert to preferences aligned with their original character settings. While evaluations using LLM-based personas may differ from actual human behavior, this approach offers the advantage of easily configuring diverse attributes and personalities. In this study, the personas were implemented using GPT-4o. Future work will compare these results with evaluations by human participants to further examine the validity and limitations of using LLM-based personas for user studies.

Keywords: Filter Bubble · SNS · Interactive Map

1 Introduction

In recent years, social networking services (SNS) have become major platforms through which people collect and disseminate news and opinions. However, there is growing concern about the emergence of so-called filter bubbles and echo chambers, in which users are primarily exposed to information that aligns with their own interests and positions, thereby limiting exposure to diverse perspectives and leading to the polarization of thoughts and attitudes [1, 2]. In particular, recommendation functions and timeline optimization mechanisms are known to reinforce existing preferences and are considered key factors that hinder diverse information exposure [3–5].

C. Stephanidis et al. (Eds.): HCII 2026, CCIS 3047, pp. 411–420, 2026.
https://doi.org/10.1007/978-3-032-30552-7_39

To address this issue, we have developed an interactive map-based SNS search system that extracts multiple perspectives from SNS search results in real time using a large language model (LLM), specifically GPT-4o, and visualizes them on a two-dimensional map, thereby encouraging users to engage in more balanced browsing behavior [6].

In this study, to conduct an efficient proxy evaluation of the system, we introduce multiple virtual "participants" by assigning artificial personas to the same LLM (GPT-4o). We then observe changes in their browsing tendencies as these participants repeatedly use the system, and further discuss how these behaviors differ from those of actual human users.

2 Related Work

2.1 Filter Bubbles and Mitigation Approaches

Filter bubbles and echo chambers are known to increase the risk of ideological polarization and the spread of misinformation, which can ultimately contribute to social division and conflict. While these issues also require political and institutional solutions, a variety of technical approaches for mitigating them have been explored.

For example, prior studies have proposed methods that combine visualization and interaction, such as Opinion Space [7] and DaCENA [8], as well as approaches that promote encounters with unexpected or exploratory information, often referred to as serendipity [9–12]. Our system aims to support the natural expansion of users' perspectives by presenting diverse viewpoints extracted by an LLM from SNS search results in the form of an interactive map.

2.2 UI Evaluation Using LLM-based Personas

In general, user interface evaluations based on real user studies and experiments require substantial cost and time. As an alternative, recent research has explored methods that assign personas to LLMs in order to simulate user responses and behaviors for evaluation purposes. This approach facilitates controlled conditions and repeated experiments, and has been shown to be useful for early-stage evaluations and hypothesis testing [13–15].

In this study, as an initial experiment to investigate how an interactive map-based SNS search system influences browsing behavior, we adopt LLM-based personas as experimental subjects.

3 Overview of the SNS Search System

The interactive map-based SNS search system used for user evaluation in this study was developed and reported by the authors in prior work [6]. An example of the user interface is shown in Fig. 1. At present, the system targets X (formerly Twitter) as the data source.

When a user enters a search keyword (e.g., presidential election), the system automatically extracts multiple axes (perspectives) and the characteristics of their opposing ends (e.g., economic policy, proactive / passive) from the X search results using an LLM. Each post is then scored according to its positioning along these perspectives and

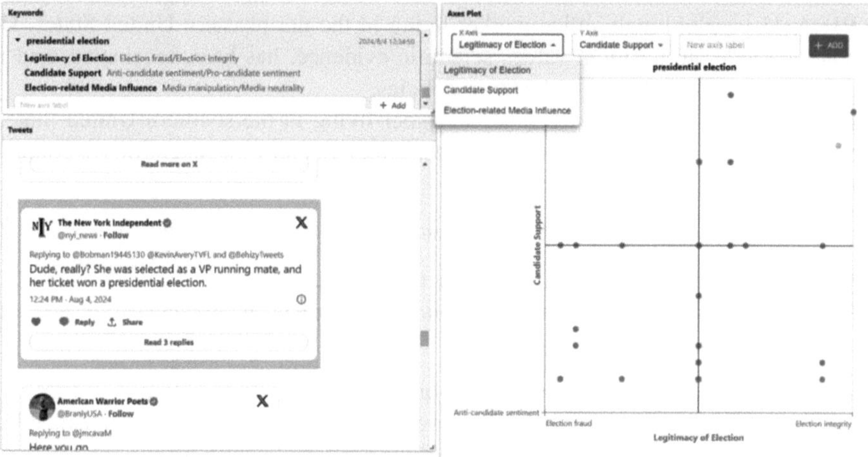

Fig. 1. Example of the system user interface.

is placed as a node on a two-dimensional map composed of any selected pair of axes. Users can switch between different axes and also add new axes using their own words.

Clicking on a node on the map is synchronized with the corresponding post, which is automatically scrolled and displayed on the left side of the screen. In Fig. 1, X posts retrieved using the keyword presidential election are plotted on a map with two axes: Legitimacy of election and Candidate support. Through such visualization and interaction, the system aims to encourage users to browse information while being more aware of diversity and balance in viewpoints.

4 Evaluation Experiment Using LLM-based Personas

4.1 Experimental Setup

To examine changes in participant behavior when using the system, we conducted a preliminary evaluation using personas assigned to an LLM (ChatGPT-4o) instead of human participants. When a search keyword is provided, the system computes the axis labels of the interactive map and the coordinate values of 100 SNS posts retrieved from the search results within approximately 10 s using the LLM. These results are then passed to the personas defined through prompts, and each persona selects 10 posts of interest within a few seconds and displays them on the map. If the persona experiences reactions such as understanding, empathy, or aversion, these are reflected in its internal character settings. This process simulates how human users may adjust their own perspectives after reading posts.

In the experiment, some personas were given an additional instruction before the experiment to "observe the entire map broadly," and their behavior was compared with that of personas who did not receive this instruction.

As the search keyword, we selected vaccination, a topic that tends to generate polarized opinions. We defined two contrasting personas, both modeled as U.S. residents:

- **P1:** A 45-year-old male office worker living in the northeastern United States. He holds a moderate position, values scientific evidence, has been vaccinated, and is cautious about mandatory vaccination policies.
- **P2:** A 35-year-old female freelance designer living in the southern United States. She prioritizes individual freedom, is unvaccinated, and is skeptical of government messaging.

Furthermore, we assigned two experimental conditions to each persona:

- **Control condition:** No additional instruction is given.
- **Nudge condition:** Before the first session, the persona is encouraged to "observe the entire map broadly."

For these two personas under two conditions (2 personas × 2 conditions = 4 patterns), we conducted the experiment once per day over seven consecutive days, from September 25 to October 1, 2025, using the X search results available at each time point.

4.2 Results

Reason for selection: This persona holds a slightly positive view of vaccine effectiveness and a neutral attitude toward scientific authorities, and tends to seek information that confirms existing beliefs. The selected posts largely align with these values, reinforcing prior beliefs while also including a moderate level of novelty, such as personal vaccination experiences.

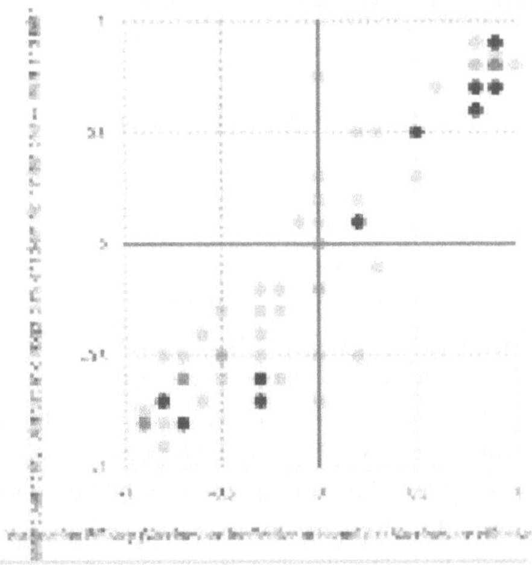

Fig. 2. Example of post selection results by an LLM-based persona (Selected posts are highlighted in blue. The textual explanation shown above is automatically generated by the LLM and explains why these posts were selected, based on the persona's attributes and preferences.).

Figure 2 shows an example of post selection results by a persona. The system also displays textual explanations for the reasons behind each selection. Figure 3 illustrates

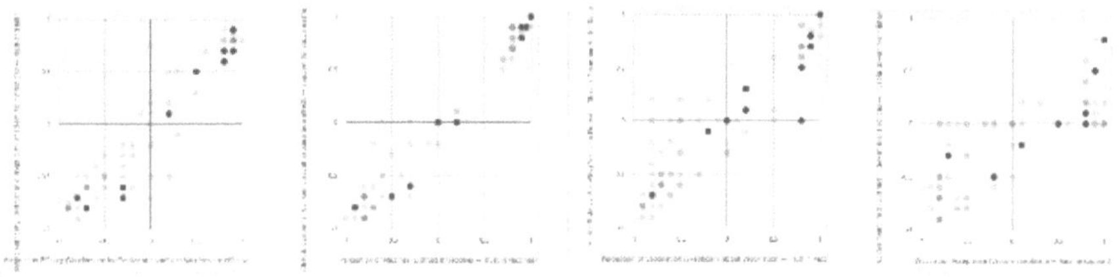

(a) P1-Control

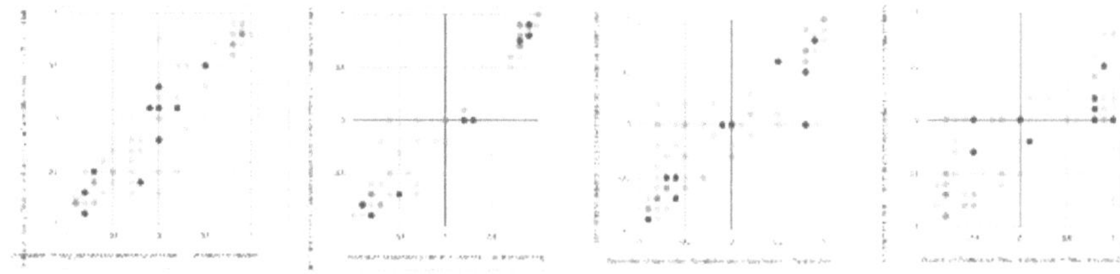

(b) P1-Nudge

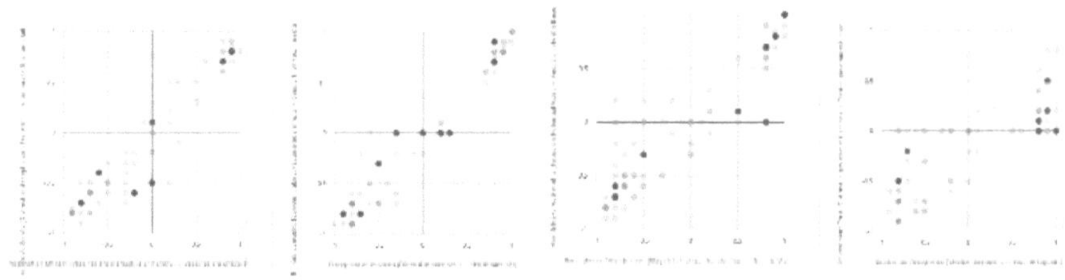

(c) P2-Control

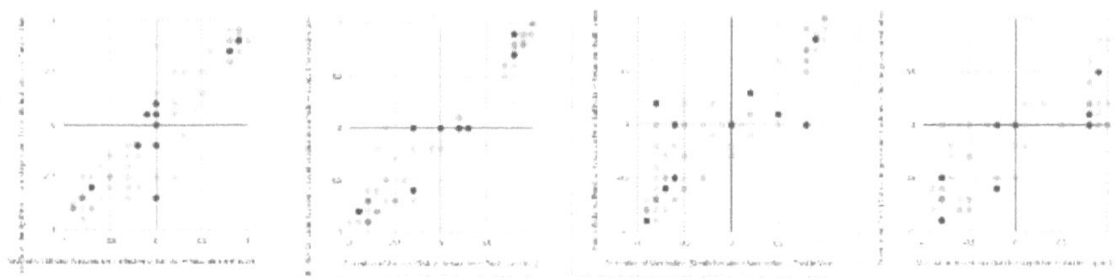

(d) P2-Nudge

Fig. 3. Changes in selected posts on the map by LLM-based personas over time (the first two days and the last two days of the 7-day period).

changes in the positions of selected posts on the map during the experimental period, comparing the first two days and the last two days of the seven-day experiment.

To evaluate these changes, we introduce the following two metrics:

- **Coverage:** The extent to which the selected posts are distributed across all four quadrants of the map. Coverage is computed as the fraction of quadrants that contain at least one selected post (i.e., the number of occupied quadrants divided by four). The minimum value is one quadrant (25%), and the maximum is four quadrants (100%). A higher coverage indicates that the persona is viewing posts from a wider range of quadrants, which are assumed to represent diverse perspectives and opinions, such as affirmative and negative viewpoints.

- **Balance:** The proportion of selected posts that are located within a radius of 0.6 from the center of the map. We use 0.6 as an empirical threshold on the normalized map to distinguish moderate from extreme positions. A higher balance indicates that the persona is viewing more moderate posts rather than focusing only on extreme positions.

Figure 4 shows the transitions of coverage and balance over the seven-day period. Since the daily values are discrete, regression lines are plotted for visualization purposes. The dark black lines represent P1 (the moderate persona), and the gray lines represent P2 (the freedom-oriented persona). Solid lines indicate the Control condition (no additional instruction), and dashed lines indicate the Nudge condition (with the instruction to "observe the entire map broadly").

From these results, several notable patterns can be observed.

5 Differences Between Personas

For P1 (the moderate persona, dark black), both coverage and balance remained stable or showed a slight increasing trend over time. In other words, repeated use of the system led to a gradual convergence toward more balanced post selection.

In contrast, for P2 (the freedom-oriented persona, gray), the persona initially selected relatively diverse and moderate posts, but both coverage and balance decreased over time. This indicates that the selections became increasingly biased, suggesting that the initial exploratory behavior diminished and the persona gradually focused on posts with a specific tendency.

6 Differences Between Control and Nudge Conditions

Under the Nudge condition (dashed lines), both coverage and balance were generally slightly higher than those under the Control condition, and this effect was particularly pronounced for P2. This suggests that even a simple intervention such as encouraging users to "observe the entire map broadly" can promote more diverse information exposure to some extent.

However, this effect did not persist strongly over time. While a clear difference was observed in the early stages, the gap between the two conditions tended to shrink after several days.

7 Discussion

7.1 Changes in Browsing Tendencies

In this study, changes in browsing behavior were examined using two metrics: coverage and balance. Both metrics were defined under the assumption that relatively higher values are preferable. That is, we assume that it is desirable for users to view posts from

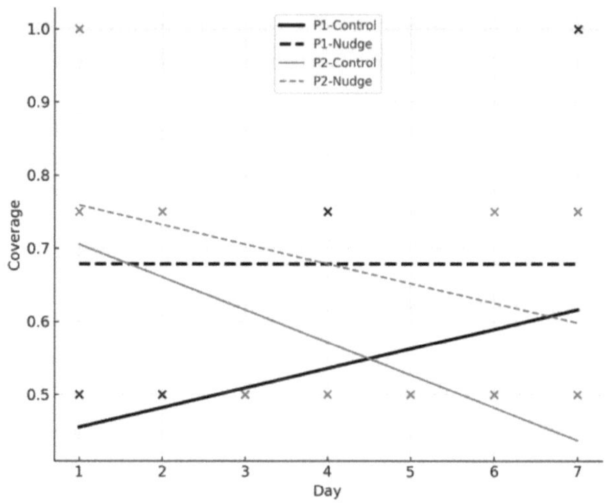

(a) Coverage

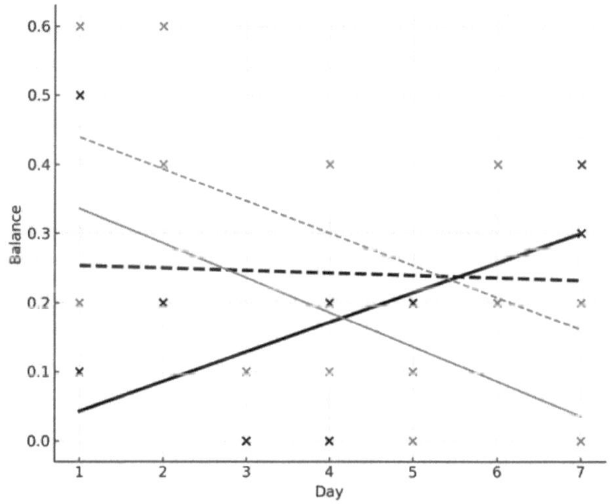

(b) Balance

Fig. 4. Transitions of coverage and balance over the 7-day period for LLM-based personas under Control/Nudge.

a wide range of perspectives, and to avoid focusing only on extreme opinions by instead viewing more moderate posts.

However, it is not necessarily the case that higher values for both metrics are always better. For example, even when reading extreme posts, users may maintain a neutral stance by viewing content from both ends of a particular perspective. In addition, depending on the context, it may be sufficient for users to focus on posts with a specific tendency for a certain period of time, rather than constantly seeking diverse viewpoints. Therefore, it cannot be concluded in a simplistic manner that higher coverage and balance are always preferable.

In this study, we examined changes over a one-week period using the specific keyword vaccination. In future work, we plan to investigate longer-term changes across a wider range of domains, including political, technological, and entertainment-related topics.

7.2 Using LLM-based Personas as Experimental Subjects

In this study, experiments using LLM-based personas were positioned as a preliminary step prior to evaluations with real human users. However, if it is found that evaluations based on LLM-based personas are similar to, or strongly correlated with, those conducted with human participants, such an approach could potentially serve as a practical alternative to large-scale user studies.

One advantage of using LLM-based personas is that they can be configured with a wide range of attributes, including not only nationality, gender, and age, but also occupation, hobbies, preferences, and cognitive tendencies (e.g., rigid or flexible thinking). Moreover, it is possible to generate an arbitrary number of such personas. This level of control is virtually impossible when recruiting human participants. Even in human-based studies, unless the sample size is extremely large and carefully designed, participant selection is likely to be biased toward certain characteristics. Therefore, evaluations using LLM-based personas may, in some cases, achieve a level of effectiveness comparable to those based on human participants.

Nevertheless, it is important to consider the technical limitations inherent in LLM-based personas [16, 17]. First, LLMs have structural constraints in terms of memory. Current LLMs perform inference only within a given context window and cannot accumulate long-term usage experiences as persistent internal states. As a result, long-term behavioral changes observed in human users, such as gradual familiarization with a UI or a reduction in operational errors through repeated use, cannot be fully reproduced.

Second, unlike humans, LLMs do not directly experience perceptual burdens such as poor visibility or the physical difficulty of interactions. Subtle stress caused by UI details, as well as irrational fluctuations in human behavior and decision-making, are difficult to simulate realistically.

Furthermore, it is known that the judgments and behaviors generated by LLMs may reflect statistical and cultural biases present in their training data. This raises the possibility that the intended persona attributes may not be accurately or consistently reflected in their responses.

Considering these factors, a hybrid approach that combines evaluations using LLM-based personas with studies involving human participants is currently the most realistic and promising direction.

8 Conclusion

This study investigated an interactive map-based SNS search system designed to mitigate filter bubbles through a preliminary evaluation using LLM-based personas as experimental subjects. The results suggest that providing a simple additional instruction, such as encouraging users to "observe the entire map broadly," has the potential to promote more diverse post browsing behavior.

In future work, we plan to expand the range of persona settings, search keywords, and experimental durations, and to conduct comparative evaluations involving real human participants. Through such comparisons, we aim to further examine the validity and limitations of the proposed evaluation approach.

Overall, this study indicates that persona-based evaluation using LLMs can serve as a promising method for assessing the initial effectiveness of interactive search systems, particularly in the early stages of system design and development.

Acknowledgments. This work was supported by JSPS KAKENHI Grant Number JP23K11205.

Disclosure of Interests. The authors have no competing interests to declare that are relevant to the content of this article.

References

1. Pariser, E.: The Filter Bubble: What the Internet Is Hiding From You. Penguin UK (2011)
2. Ruiz, C.D., Nilsson, T.: Disinformation and Echo Chambers: How Disinformation Circulates on Social Media Through Identity-Driven Controversies. J. Public Policy Market. **42**(1), 18–35 (2023). https://doi.org/10.1177/07439156221103852
3. Thurman, N.: Personalization of news. In: The International Encyclopedia of Journalism Studies. Wiley-Blackwell, Massachusetts, USA (2018)
4. Bozdag, E.: Bias in algorithmic filtering and personalization. Ethics Inform. Technol. **15**, 209–227 (2013). https://doi.org/10.1007/s10676-013-9321-6
5. M. D. Conover, J. Ratkiewicz, M. Francisco, B. Goncalves, A. Flammini, F. Menczer (2011): Political polarization on twitter, Proceedings of the Fifth International AAAI Conference on Weblogs and Social Media 5(1), 89–96
6. Kamba, T.: SNS search system that uses a large language model to display posts on an interactive map from various perspectives. In: HCI International 2025, LNCS, 16337. Springer (2026). https://doi.org/10.1007/978-3-032-12801-0_10
7. Faridani, S., Bitton, E., Ryokai, K., Goldberg, K.: Opinion space: a scalable tool for browsing online comments. In: Proceedings of CHI 2010, pp. 1175–1184 (2010). https://doi.org/10.1145/1753326.1753502
8. Palmonari, M., Uboldi, G., Cremaschi, M., Ciminieri, D., Bianchi, F.: DaCENA: Serendipitous News Reading with Data Contexts. In: ESWC (Satellite Events) 2015, pp. 133–137 (2015). https://doi.org/10.1007/978-3-319-25639-9_26
9. Thudt, A., Hinrichs, U., Carpendale, S.: The bohemian bookshelf: supporting serendipitous book discoveries through information visualization. In: CHI '12 Proceedings, pp. 1461–1470 (2012). https://doi.org/10.1145/2207676.2208607
10. Björneborn, L.: Serendipity dimensions and users' information behavior in the physical library interface. Inform. Res. **13**(1), 370 (2008)

11. McCay-Peet, L., Toms, E.: Measuring the dimensions of serendipity in digital environments. Inform. Res. **16**(3), 483 (2011) https://informationr.net/ir/16-3/paper483.html
12. Jasim, M., Collins, C., Sarvghad, A., Mahyar, N.: Supporting serendipitous discovery and balanced analysis of online product reviews with interaction-driven metrics and bias-mitigating suggestions. In: CHI '22 Proceedings, Article No. 9, pp. 1–24 (2022). https://doi.org/10.1145/3491102.3517649
13. Balog, K., Zhai, C.X.: User simulation in the era of generative AI: user modeling, synthetic data generation, and system evaluation. https://arxiv.org/abs/2501.04410. (2025). https://doi.org/10.48550/arXiv.2501.04410
14. Balog, K., Zhai, C.X.: User simulation for evaluating information access systems. In: SIGIR-AP '23, pp. 302–305 (2023). https://doi.org/10.1145/3624918.3629549
15. Jiang, H., Zhang, X., Cao, X., Breazeal, C., Roy, D., Kabbara, J.: Persona LLM: investigating the ability of large language models to express personality traits. In: Findings of the Association for Computational Linguistics: NAACL 2024, pp. 3605–3627. Association for Computational Linguistics, Mexico City, Mexico (2024)
16. Prpa, M., Troiano, G.M., Wood, M., Coady, Y.: Challenges and opportunities of LLM-based synthetic personae and data in HCI. In: CHI EA '24, No. 461, pp. 1–5 (2024). https://doi.org/10.1145/3613905.3636293
17. Lazik, C.K., et al.: The impostor is among us: can large language models capture the complexity of human personas? In: MuC '25, pp. 434–451 (2025). https://doi.org/10.1145/3743049.3743057

Seven Facets of the Facilitator Role in Co-Creation with Children: Insights from a Project in Danish Kindergartens

Caroline Louise Willer Kure(✉), Benedicte Fleron, and Morten Hertzum

Roskilde University, 4000 Roskilde, Denmark
clwk@ruc.dk

Abstract. User participation in design events is pivotal to Participatory Design and Co-Creation. For such participation to be effective and valuable, it must be carefully facilitated. While much research investigates the conditions for participation in general, less is concerned with the specific role of the facilitator. This study investigates the facets of the facilitator role in co-creation with children aged 3–6. Empirically, the study is based on interviews with facilitators in a project where children in Danish kindergartens were facilitated in the co-creation of a digital photo book aimed to increase their awareness of electricity consumption. Through a two-stage card-sorting analysis, we identified seven facets of the facilitator role and six groups of attributes that formed these facets. We contribute four findings: First, we describe and discuss the seven identified facets. Second, we point out differences in the facilitation of children vs. adults. Third, we discuss how the facets differ in temporal scope. Fourth, a distinct feature of our data is the co-presence of multiple facilitators and, thus, the presence of facets that concern facilitation as a collaborative activity.

Keywords: Facilitation · Co-Creation · Children · Participation

1 Introduction

Children are not just inheriting the world; they are active in creating it. Like adults, children must learn to act sustainably for us to succeed in the green transition. In this study, we take a co-creation approach to this learning process. Co-creation with children [1, 2] involves that adults facilitate children in contemplating and acting creatively on a specified issue. It differs from co-creation with adults by attending to the needs and prerequisites specific to children, such as how their developmental stage determines their capacity for thinking conceptually about, for example, sustainability. It also differs from co-design, which is about designers and users collaborating across the design process. Co-creation is broader; it refers to "any act of collective creativity" [3].

Co-creation hinges on facilitation. It is through facilitation that co-creation tools and artifacts are enacted and become concrete experiences for the participants [4]. In our empirical setting, it is a dedicated municipal employee and the kindergarten staff who

C. Stephanidis et al. (Eds.): HCII 2026, CCIS 3047, pp. 421–431, 2026.
https://doi.org/10.1007/978-3-032-30552-7_40

provide the facilitation. Their overarching move is to frame the co-creation activity as the joint creation of a book with photos of electricity-consuming objects and situations from the children's everyday life. This framing facilitates the children in engaging with the more abstract notions of electricity and sustainability through concrete action. However, the overarching framing must be communicated and reinforced through a range of instructions, explanations, and other supportive moves. In performing these moves, the municipal employee and kindergarten staff enact the facilitator role [5]. This study investigates the facets of this role and, thereby, seeks to answer the research question: *What are the facets of the facilitator role when co-creating with children?*

2 Related Work

To situate our analysis of facilitation, we draw on existing co-creation and participatory design (PD) research. User participation in design events is pivotal to PD [6–8] and co-creation [3, 9]. While this participation must be carefully facilitated, the facilitator role has not yet been adequately understood, though it is being studied [4, 5, 10, 11]. In one of these studies, Dahl & Sharma [5] identify six facets of the facilitator role, providing a structured account of how facilitators support, guide, and scaffold participation in PD activities. The six facets are the trust builder, the enabler, the inquirer, the direction setter, the value provider, and the user's advocate. For example, the enabler supplies the means for the participating users to express their ideas and reservations, and the direction setter keeps the activities on a course useful to the project [5]. Another study of the facilitator role is Carcani & Stigberg's [11] identification of four facilitator categories: the domain expert, the user expert, the PD expert, and the assistant facilitator. They often work together and, thus, combine their individual competencies with their relations to other facilitators, making contributions to different parts of the design process [11]. A feature shared by the studies mentioned above is, however, their focus on facilitating adult participants. Designing with children as participants is different [8, 12, 13]. As a result, the facilitator role must be reconsidered and adapted. Methods to engage children in co-creation include play-based design [14], cooperative inquiry [15], and material play [2]. These methods emphasize the PD pillars of empowerment [16] and trust [1, 13]. At the same time, Ponizovsky-Bergelson et al. [17] outline how the power dynamics in child-adult interactions can challenge these PD pillars and, thereby, the children's participation. To overcome such barriers, the facilitator must be especially sensitive and encouraging in interactions with children [17].

3 Method

This study explores the facilitator role when facilitating children aged 3–6 years in co-creation. To accomplish this, the authors analyze retrospective interviews with the facilitators of a series of co-creation events in Danish municipal kindergartens. Access to the research setting was obtained through the relation to a municipality as a joint partner in a broader research project. We used that collaboration to get in contact with a facilitating municipal employee who was experienced in conducting co-creation sessions with children and worked closely with municipal kindergartens. We joined two co-creation events in different kindergartens. Themed around electricity, the events concerned the development of a digital photo book. Using iPads, the children would take photos of electricity-consuming artifacts from their daily lives and save them in the book. Each event lasted about an hour and involved a group of 5–10 children. Multiple facilitators were involved as the municipal employee would work with 1–2 kindergarten staff members per event. The events consisted of activities in the full group and in smaller break-out groups of 2–4 children with a facilitating adult, being either the municipal employee, a kindergarten staff member, or on occasion the first author.

Our data consists of retrospective interviews with three facilitators after the co-creation events. Each interview lasted 15–30 min and followed a short, semi-structured interview guide. Two interviews took place in person, one via videocall. All three interviews were audio-recorded and transcribed, with the respondents' consent. The interviews concerned the informants' experiences and considerations as facilitators in the co-creation events. The interviews were supplemented with the first authors' field notes from observing the events. The observations were done in an observer-as-participant role [18], where the author participated as co-facilitator in selected activities while primarily focusing on observation. The field notes served to contextualize the interviews, rather than as primary empirical material. The research was IRB approved to ensure the ethical integrity of our work.

Table 1. The six attributes resulting from the first stage of the card sorting.

Attribute	Description	Number of cards
Facilitated	Cards related to the needs and requirements of the facilitated participants	53
Facilitators	Cards related to the necessary competencies and aspects of being a facilitator	56
Activity facilitation	Cards related to the facilitation of the activity	13
Planning	Cards related to the planning, considerations, and activities prior to the facilitated event	35
Facilitation space	Cards related to the experienced facilitation space and the prerequisites for its existence	25
Artifact/Activity	Cards related to artifacts or the activity in an objective sense	15

The authors conducted the analysis in collaboration. First, all three authors coded the three interview transcripts inductively for descriptive evidence of facilitation. Because the interviews were the facilitators' reflections on what it entailed to be a facilitator, the data reflected attributes, competencies, and activities associated with facilitation, rather than predefined facilitation facets. Second, the authors met to discuss their codes and reach a shared understanding of them. Third, two of the authors performed a digital open card sort of the inductively generated codes [19, 20]. For this card sort, the codes were copied onto individual cards in a Miro board, resulting in 130 cards. These cards were sorted into groups representing different attributes fundamental to the facilitation space. Some cards covered multiple attributes and were duplicated, with the copies assigned to the different attributes covered by the card. After duplication, there were 197 cards sorted into six attribute groups, see Table 1. Fourth, the cards were re-sorted. In this resorting, we focused on how the card contents related to the facilitation of practical co-creation events. Table 2 shows the seven facets of facilitation resulting from the resorting. Fifth, the cards were traced back to the corresponding interview excerpts to deepen the analysis and develop the final descriptions of the facets [20].

4 Results

Our analysis identified seven facets of the facilitator role and the six groups of attributes that formed them, see Table 2. The table provides definitions of the facets and gives the percentage distribution of the attributes. The analysis combines insights about the practical facilitation of children in co-creation events with attributes about the fundamental features of the facilitation space.

4.1 Enabler

The Enabler facet focuses on enabling participation by matching participants with event activities and by fitting the event to the participants, thereby ensuring their psychological safety and trust. This facet is represented by a total of 61 cards primarily from the Facilitated (43%) and Planning (26%) attributes, highlighting its focus on both preparation and execution. Regarding the execution of the event, the Enabler supported the children in feeling safe in the group to enable their agency. Another Enabler task was balancing the best interests of the group and the individual, setting clear boundaries that allowed the children to self-regulate their participation, for example by allowing children who got overwhelmed or bored to exit the activity. Because co-creation requires participation, it was central to the event preparations to minimize the risk of children withdrawing from the activities. An informant explained: "It is about finding children who are about equal in their development, so we can challenge them within their zone of proximal development. This way, everyone gets something from the activity." By matching the children with one another and with the event, the Enabler helped ensure that the children had a similar starting point. This enabled the children to participate in and gain from the co-creation process and reduced the risk of children withdrawing from the activity. The Enabler also emphasized the social makeup of the group of children, highlighting safe relationships and healthy social dynamics: "Yes, we look quite a bit at where they are, developmentally, and what their relationships are with one another. If they feel safe with the ones they are with, then it helps the activity and play."

4.2 Advocate

The Advocate focuses on advocating for the participants during the planning and execution of the co-creation event, either by supporting them in advocating for themselves or, if necessary, by advocating for them. This facet consists of 29 cards, mainly from

Table 2. The seven facets of the facilitator role.

Facet	Description	Attribute distribution
Enabler	Enabling participation by matching participants with activities and framing the activities to support and protect the participants.	Facilitated: 43% Facilitator: 8% Activity Facilitation: 10% Planning: 26% Facilitation Space: 8% Activity/Artifact: 5%
Advocate	Advocating for the participants and their needs, if/when/where they fail to advocate for themselves during the preparation and execution of the activity.	Facilitated: 45% Facilitator: 10% Activity Facilitation: 3% Planning: 24% Facilitation Space: 7% Activity/Artifact: 10%
Mentor	Mentoring the participants in developing capabilities that reach beyond the timeframe of the co-creation event.	Facilitated: 49% Facilitator: 25% Activity Facilitation: 5% Planning: 5% Facilitation Space: 5% Activity/Artifact: 9%
Guide	Guiding and supporting the participants during the activity with the purpose of ensuring the completion of the event.	Facilitated: 27% Facilitator: 32% Activity Facilitation: 11% Planning: 5% Facilitation Space: 8% Activity/Artifact: 16%
Delegator	Delegating responsibilities among the facilitators prior to the event, such that resource needs are met, competences are utilized, and everyone knows who should do what and when.	Facilitated: 7% Facilitator: 53% Activity Facilitation: 7% Planning: 20% Facilitation Space: 13% Activity/Artifact: 0%
Organizer	Supporting coordination and organizing among facilitators through a shared, situated understanding of the co-creation event.	Facilitated: 16% Facilitator: 45% Activity Facilitation: 6% Planning: 19% Facilitation Space: 13% Activity/Artifact: 0%
Transitioner	Supporting other facilitators in transitioning among facilitation facets during the co-creation event.	Facilitated: 12% Facilitator: 44% Activity Facilitation: 6% Planning: 15% Facilitation Space: 15% Activity/Artifact: 9%

the Facilitated (45%) and Planning (24%) attributes. The municipal facilitator provided an example of the Advocate during planning: "There are so many forms of expression. This is where the kindergarten staff provides a lot of knowledge because they know the child from their daily interactions: How does this child find it meaningful to express itself? There, they can contribute to what we arrive at, in the planning." The kindergarten staff influenced the central design artifact – the digital photo book – by advocating the children's need for multiple ways of expressing themselves in the co-creation process.

This highlighted how the Advocate, like the Enabler, benefited from being familiar with the children. While the Advocate has merit in single-facilitator scenarios, it was particularly apparent in our study due to its multiple facilitators with different main goals. The municipal facilitator focused on facilitating the event, whereas the kindergarten staff focused on advocating the children's needs. This became evident when our informants described how an activity proved poorly matched with the participants' age: "It was a little hard [for the children] to engage in this activity. It required just a little more. So, we could tell that the activity was probably not well adapted to their age." The kindergarten staff's pre-existing knowledge told them that the issue was not children unwilling to engage, but a poor match between the activity and the children's abilities, allowing the kindergarten staff to advocate for the children during the event.

4.3 Mentor

The Mentor focuses on mentoring the participants in their development of capabilities beyond the timeframe of the co-creation event, that is, on mentoring their long-term growth. This facet consists of 55 cards, predominantly from the Facilitated (49%) and Facilitator (25%) attributes. It focuses on providing active support, mentoring in the moment for the benefit of long-term development. The Mentor included things like supporting social development and fostering independence and self-confidence in the children by creating opportunities for them to challenge themselves and experience positive interactions. One of the facilitators from the kindergarten described their role during the event as being a role model for the children and "being curious with the children" while also being a source of safety as a familiar adult. To foster self-confidence and independence in the children, the kindergarten staff were first demonstrating "and then otherwise walking next to the children", to provide support without controlling the children in their design explorations. Another example of how the facilitators worked to empower the children and support their development was in how they aimed to foster interaction among the children: "This is where we really want to see some child-to-child learning. [...]. If you know this, why do I have to show you? Why are you not the one showing it to a friend, instead of the adult?" This way, the facilitators tell the children that they trust them, thereby supporting the children in developing their capabilities and self-efficacy in ways that reach beyond the timeframe of their participation in the co-creation event.

4.4 Guide

The Guide focuses strictly on supporting and guiding participation toward the successful completion of the co-creation event. Consisting of 37 cards, the Guide's main attributes are the Facilitator (32%) and Facilitated (27%). Concrete examples of the Guide supporting the participants were in helping them reach conclusions necessary to progress on an activity and in learning to use an required artifact. An informant highlighted the importance of providing guidance: "To begin with, we were a bit controlling [...] because the app was a bit complicated. You had to press the right things and such." If the children could not navigate the tool effectively, they could not participate effectively, hence the need for the Guide to help them. However, to guide the children in acquiring the skills needed for the activity, the facilitator must have those skills and be able to communicate them. A facilitator described how they felt a little outstripped by the children's ability to work with the digital elements of the activity, ascribing it to them being more digitally minded. While the children's own abilities compensated in this case, the example still illustrates the need for event-relevant skills and knowledge to serve as a Guide.

4.5 Delegator

The Delegator focuses on ensuring the practical performance of the event through the delegation of tasks and responsibilities and by sourcing needed resources. This facet consists of a total of 30 cards and is mainly rooted in the Facilitator attribute (53%). With the Planning attribute accounting for another 20%, this facet is also preparatory in nature. The Delegator facet involved how multiple co-present facilitators worked together during the event. A kindergarten facilitator described how they initially sat and "almost observed the children and needed to figure out what everything was about. Then, when we went out in the smaller groups, it was me who took over managing my small group". This division of tasks was pre-planned. That is, it was pre-planned that the kindergarten facilitators started as observers, like the children, while the municipal employee led everyone through the initial demonstrations, after which all the facilitators took the lead in a smaller group. This delegation of tasks and responsibilities supported the performance of the event by minimizing the risk of confusion and allowing the facilitators to be confident in their role throughout the event. Another example of the Delegator was that the iPads used for the co-creation event were supplied by the municipal employee because the kindergartens did not have enough on their own, thus supplying the equipment was delegated to someone with that resource.

4.6 Organizer

The Organizer focuses on coordinating and organizing among the facilitators during the event, through their shared understanding of the situation. It consists of 31 cards, 45% of which from the Facilitator attribute. The Organizer is particularly important in a setting with multiple facilitators who have different goals and outlooks. To perform the event, the facilitators needed to work together and exploit each other's strengths. The municipal facilitator gave an example: "When we have organized it from the beginning, that is when the kindergarten staff comes into the picture. [...] They define which children should work together. We have no knowledge about that, so we [leave that decision to them]." This shows how the municipal employee and kindergarten staff organized themselves during the event, understanding that the kindergarten staff had better prerequisites for grouping the children. In doing so, they relied on being able to read one another and understand when to release or take control of the situation. The municipal facilitator explained that despite his close relationship with the kindergartens, elements such as employee turnover and day-to-day practicalities in the kindergartens meant that he did not always know on arrival who he would be working with. These conditions made the Organizer facet and its focus on clear communication and organizing critical to the success of the co-creation event.

4.7 Transitioner

The Transitioner focuses on supporting facilitators in transitioning among the facilitation facets during the event. It consists of 34 cards with 44% of them from the Facilitator attribute. In their work, the facilitators frequently shifted from one facet to another. These frequent transitions were part of their role as facilitators. The Transitioner is about supporting the facilitators in these transitions. The municipal employee provided an example of this support: "I have talked with them [i.e., the kindergarten staff] about the idea of communicating [with the children] in different ways. Some of the children may struggle with one form of communication. If they get a new way to communicate… It is about giving some of these children an experience of success." Including a wider range of communication methods in the co-creation event was a way of enabling the children in their participation. By initiating this conversation, the municipal facilitator started shifting to the Enabler facet and by identifying additional communication methods, the kindergarten facilitators served as Transitioners helping him make the shift. Relatedly, the kindergarten facilitators described how the municipal facilitator initially demonstrated an activity for them and the children, thereby supporting them in subsequently guiding their own small groups. In this example, the municipal facilitator served as Transitioner by supporting the kindergarten staff in shifting to the Guide facet.

5 Discussion

The previous section presented the facets of the facilitator role when co-creating with children. In the following, we discuss three elements central to these findings: the children as the facilitated participants, the presence of multiple facilitators, and the extended temporal scope.

5.1 Children as the Facilitated Participants

We set out to explore the facilitators' role with child participants in a co-creation process. As each facet emerged from our data, it became clear how the facilitation of children shapes the facilitator role and its facets. This difference becomes visible when comparing our facets with those identified by Dahl & Sharma's [5]. Two share similar names across the studies: their Enabler and User's Advocate correspond to our Enabler and Advocate. However, while the facets share names, their analytical focus differs. Dahl & Sharma's Enabler centers on the participants as contributors, enabling their ability to express themselves for design purposes [5]. In contrast, our Enabler is concerned with supporting the children's overall ability to participate by matching the circumstances to the children's needs and abilities. A related perspective can be found in Carcani & Stigberg's [11] categories. Based on our descriptions, our Enabler appears similar to the User's Expert [11], a category that specifically is about the participating users. However, taking our research setting into account also reveals similarities with the Domain Expert [11], described as an expert on the context and setting of a project, with special insights on the user groups. In our research setting, the kindergarten staff function as experts on both the children and the kindergarten context. Elements of both the User's Expert and the

Domain Expert can therefore be identified across our Enabler and Advocate facets, as well as in Dahl & Sharma's Enabler and Advocate. Dahl & Sharma restrict their User's Advocate to post-session actions, supporting the participants by advocating for their contributions in the continued design process [5]. Our Advocate includes this aspect but also includes in-session support to advocate children's needs to other facilitators. This suggests that the Enabler and Advocate identified in our children context may also be relevant with adults, but often less visible.

5.2 Multiple Facilitators

Another central component to our study is the co-presence of multiple facilitators. This component is also central to Carcani & Stigberg [11], who map how PD processes involve a network of facilitators. They explore how the constellation changes throughout the process, along with the possible interprofessional tensions in such a collaboration. However, they do not explore in depth the practical articulation work involved in the collaboration itself. We identified three facets that concern how co-facilitators coordinate their collaboration and shift among facilitator facets: the Delegator, the Organizer, and the Transitioner. Carcani & Stigberg [11] identify how differing motivations, perspectives, and values cause tension in a facilitator group, thereby showing the value of facets that support facilitators in collaborating. However, it remains a topic for future research to determine how such facets are activated in practice. A potentially relevant study is Dahl & Sharma's [10] study of the skills needed to be an effective facilitator. While Dahl & Sharma [10] frame the six skills they identify (openness, patience, empathy, attentiveness, responsiveness, and adaptiveness) through the PD facilitator's relation to the participants, our facets also require these same skills in the interaction with co-facilitators. Both attentiveness and adaptiveness are relevant to the Organizer facet with its focus on shared, in-situ coordination among facilitators.

5.3 Long-term Temporal Perspective

The third central component in our findings is the long temporal perspective. It is perhaps unsurprising that developmental support and protection emerges as a central theme in the Facilitated attribute. Nonetheless, the kindergarten setting and the professional responsibilities of our respondents significantly shaped two of our facets: the Mentor and the Guide. While these two facets are related, and may often co-occur, their temporal focus differs. The Guide facet focuses exclusively on the limited time-frame of the co-creation events. The Mentor facet focuses on long-term impact. Studies on temporality exist in both PD [6, 13] and co-creation [1, 2] often focusing on trust building and long-term design projects involving repeated events with the same participants, some of them children [2, 13]. The Mentor's long temporal perspective differs from these studies because the kindergarten staff could not disconnect from their professional responsibilities when acting as facilitators in the co-creation event. Developmental perspectives on child participants exist in the literature, and Beeson [2] provides an example through material play in co-creation. This work shows how playful exploration can foster creativity, perspective, and practical skills as children grow up. Still, we find that making explicit the developmental support work involved in facilitating children provides further insight into the temporal scope of the facilitator role in the context of co-creating with children.

6 Conclusion

In this study, we explored the nature of the facilitator role when facilitating co-creation with children. From our analysis, we identified seven facets, each with its separate focus in the facilitation. Our findings suggest that the facilitator role, when facilitating children, can benefit from the influence of a developmental perspective. We contrast our findings with existing literature on the facilitator role, structured by three key elements in our findings: children as participants, co-presence of facilitators, and temporal scope. By foregrounding these key elements, we extend the existing understanding of the facilitator role in PD and co-creation literature. However, we acknowledge that our study is limited by the small amount of empirical data. As such, further research is needed, to investigate how these facets manifest across different contexts. Additionally, we propose that future work should explore the facilitator role in multi-facilitator constellations and the longer-term impact of facilitation on the participants.

Acknowledgments. This study was conducted as part of the Game For Green project, with funding by Innovation Fund Denmark (grant no. 2079-00034B).

References

1. Ligthart, M.E.U., Neerincx, M.A., Hindriks, K.V.: It takes two: using co-creation to facilitate child-robot co-regulation. ACM Trans. Hum. Robot. Interact. **12**, 42 (2023). https://doi.org/10.1145/3593812
2. Beeson, S.: The chair project: co-creation through material play. In: Place, Pedagogy and Play: Participation, Design and Research with Children, pp. 180–193. Routledge (2020). https://doi.org/10.4324/9780429023477
3. Sanders, E.B.-N., Stappers, P.J.: Co-creation and the new landscapes of design. CoDesign. **4**, 5–18 (2008). https://doi.org/10.1080/15710880701875068
4. Light, A., Akama, Y.: The human touch: participatory practice and the role of facilitation in designing with communities. In: PDC2012: Proceedings of the 12th Participatory Design Conference, pp. 61–70. ACM (2012). https://doi.org/10.1145/2347635.2347645
5. Dahl, Y., Sharma, K.: Six facets of facilitation: participatory design facilitators' perspectives on their role and its realization. In: Proceedings of the CHI2022 Conference on Human Factors in Computing Systems, p. 484. ACM (2022). https://doi.org/10.1145/3491102.3502013
6. Saad-Sulonen, J., Eriksson, E., Halskov, K., Karasti, H., Vines, J.: Unfolding participation over time: temporal lenses in participatory design. CoDesign. **14**, 4–16 (2018). https://doi.org/10.1080/15710882.2018.1426773
7. Simonsen, J., Robertson, T.: Routledge International Handbook of Participatory Design. Routledge, London (2012). https://doi.org/10.4324/9780203108543
8. Bonsignore, E. et al.: Embedding participatory design into designs for learning: an untapped interdisciplinary resource? In: CSCL 2013 Conference Proceedings, pp. 549–556. ISLS (2013). https://doi.org/10.13140/2.1.3961.7920

9. Ind, N., Coates, N.: The meanings of co-creation. Eur. Bus. Rev. **25**, 86–95 (2013). https://doi.org/10.1108/09555341311287754
10. Dahl, Y., Sharma, K., Svanæs, D.: Facilitation skills in participatory design. In: Proceedings of the CHI2025 Conference on Human Factors in Computing Systems, p. 802. ACM (2025). https://doi.org/10.1145/3706598.3713658
11. Çarçani, K., Stigberg, S.: Reflecting on collaboration in participatory design facilitation. In: Design, User Experience, and Usability. HCII 2023, pp. 66–77. Springer, Cham (2023). https://doi.org/10.1007/978-3-031-35699-5_6
12. Druin, A.: The role of children in the design of new technology. Behav. Inform. Technol. **21**, 1–25 (2002). https://doi.org/10.1080/01449290110108659
13. Spiel, K., Brulé, E., Frauenberger, C., Bailly, G., Fitzpatrick, G.: Micro-ethics for participatory design with marginalised children. In: PDC '18: Proceedings of the 15th Participatory Design Conference, pp. 1–12. ACM (2018). https://doi.org/10.1145/3210586.3210603
14. Superti Pantoja, L. et al.: Play-based design: giving 3- to 4-year-old children a voice in the design process. In: Proceedings of the CHI2020 Conference on Human Factors in Computing Systems, pp. 1–14. ACM (2020). https://doi.org/10.1145/3313831.3376407
15. Druin, A.: Cooperative Inquiry: developing new technologies for children with children. In: Proceedings of the CHI1999 Conference on Human Factors in Computing Systems, pp. 1–8. ACM (1999). https://doi.org/10.1145/302979.303166
16. Iversen, O.S., Smith, R.C., Dindler, C.: Child as protagonist: expanding the role of children in participatory design. In: IDC 2017 - Proceedings of the 2017 ACM Conference on Interaction Design and Children, pp. 27–37. ACM (2017). https://doi.org/10.1145/3078072.3079725
17. Ponizovsky-Bergelson, Y., Dayan, Y., Wahle, N., Roer-Strier, D.: A qualitative interview with young children: what encourages or inhibits young children's participation? Int J Qual Methods. **18**, 1–9 (2019). https://doi.org/10.1177/1609406919840516
18. Gold, R.L.: Roles in sociological field observations. Soc. Forces. **36**, 217–223 (1958). https://doi.org/10.2307/2573808
19. Spencer, D.: Card Sorting: Designing Usable Categories. Rosenfeld, New York, NY (2009)
20. Zimmermann, T.: Card-sorting: from text to themes. In: Perspectives on Data Science for Software Engineering, pp. 137–141 (2016). https://doi.org/10.1016/B978-0-12-804206-9.00027-1

An Exploratory Automated Analysis of UX Practitioners' Interviews: Structuring and Visualizing Cognitive Flows

Eunsol Lee and Myeong Heum Yeoun(✉)

Kookmin University, Seoul, Republic of Korea
yeounmh@kookmin.ac.kr

Abstract. In-depth interviews are a central method in user experience (UX) and design research, providing access to users' perceptions, reasoning, and contextualized experiences. However, the analysis of interview data remains labor-intensive, highly dependent on manual coding, and limited in scalability. Although conventional methods such as grounded theory and thematic analysis capture themes and concepts, they struggle to structurally represent cognitive transitions over time. To address these challenges, this study introduces an automated framework that segments interview data into cognitive units and visualizes reasoning flows to support more consistent and scalable qualitative analysis. We developed a Python-based analytical procedure consisting of four steps: semantic unit segmentation, clustering, cognitive tagging, and visualization. Six cognitive tags were defined, and a supervised classifier trained on manually labeled utterances automated the tagging process. Data collection comprised seven in-depth interviews with UX designers, product managers, and data scientists, resulting in 9.5 h of recorded material, approximately 110,000 characters of transcribed content, and 1,041 utterances for analysis. Sankey diagrams, heatmaps, and centrality analyses revealed recurring cognitive transitions and key nodes, allowing the structural characteristics of reasoning flows to be objectively identified. Implemented entirely with open-source Python tools, the method offers a pathway toward the standardization and scalability of qualitative analysis in UX and design research.

Keywords: Cognitive flow analysis · In-depth interview methods · Automated qualitative analysis · Structuring and visualization · UX research methodology · Data-driven design · Data-informed design

1 Introduction

In-depth interviews are widely recognized as a foundational method in user experience (UX) and design research, offering a powerful means of exploring users' experiences, perceptions, and problem-solving strategies. These methods provide access to users' cognitive reasoning, emotional progression, and contextual interpretation, and play a particularly critical role in the early stages of user-centered design, especially in framing problems and generating insights. Unlike structured questionnaires, in-depth interviews

C. Stephanidis et al. (Eds.): HCII 2026, CCIS 3047, pp. 432–442, 2026.
https://doi.org/10.1007/978-3-032-30552-7_41

encourage participants to recount their experiences as they naturally unfolded, enabling researchers to gain insights into users' reasoning, emotional dynamics, and the contextual factors that shape their perceptions.

Despite their value, the analysis of interview data remains heavily reliant on manual interpretation. Qualitative approaches such as grounded theory and thematic analysis are commonly used to code and organize user utterances, but these techniques are labor-intensive, time-consuming, and susceptible to inconsistencies due to individual analysts' subjective judgments (Glaser & Strauss, 1967; Braun & Clarke, 2006). Other auxiliary methods, including protocol analysis and affinity diagramming, also remain limited in their ability to structurally represent the temporal logic, shifts in judgment, and contextual linkages embedded in in-depth user narratives (Ericsson & Simon, 1993; Hanington & Martin, 2012). Recent studies have applied natural language processing (NLP), sentence embedding, clustering, and topic modeling to structure qualitative data, but most existing methods are optimized for short-form content and remain limited when applied to in-depth interview data (Petukhova et al., 2024; Min & Lee, 2023; Yoon et al., 2022; Park, 2020).

To address these limitations, this study proposes an automated procedure for the structural and quantitative analysis of in-depth interview data and explores its applicability within UX research contexts. The procedure segments interview transcripts into semantic units and applies a series of analytical processes, developed and executed in Python, to identify and visualize patterns in cognitive flow. Rather than focusing solely on the semantic content of user narratives, the proposed procedure adopts a structural, data-informed perspective to examine how user cognition unfolds over time. Ultimately, this study introduces a practical and accessible analysis framework that improves the consistency and repeatability of qualitative analysis while promoting the integration of structured, data-supported reasoning into UX research practice.

2 Research Procedure and Analytical Framework

2.1 Research Method

This study aimed to structure in-depth interview data into a format suitable for quantitative analysis and to design an automated procedure that supports the visual interpretation of cognitive flow. A Python-based framework was developed to transform qualitative data into analyzable structures and to visualize the progression and transitions of utterances (see Fig. 1).

To divide interview responses into cognitively meaningful segments rather than full The procedure consisted of semantic unit segmentation, utterance clustering, tagging of composite cognitive flows, and visualization and structural interpretation. Interview responses were segmented into cognitively meaningful units, clustered based on semantic similarity, tagged according to internal narrative structure and cognitive development, and visualized using Sankey diagrams, heatmaps, slope graphs, and radial plots.

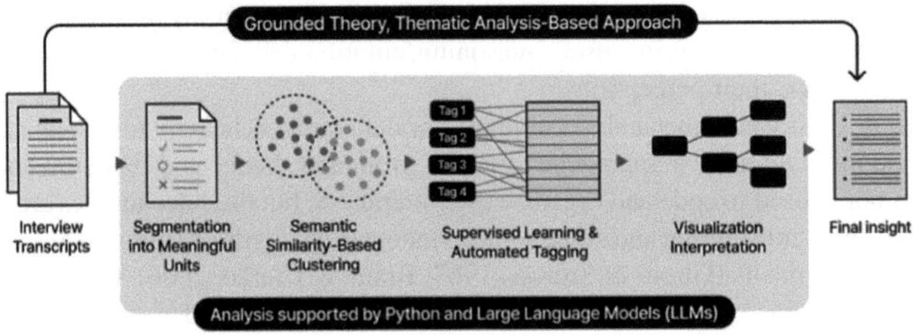

Fig. 1. From Intuitive Interpretation to Structured Automation: A Comparative Framework for Interview Data Analysis.

2.2 Interview Planning and Data Collection

The interview phase was initially designed to explore how data-informed design is implemented within real-world workflows, with a focus on problem framing, data interpretation, and cross-functional collaboration. However, participants' utterances were found to exhibit temporally sequenced reasoning patterns and recurring cognitive structures, and the interview transcripts were reinterpreted as experimental material for developing and validating an automated analysis method capable of structurally mapping and visualizing thought progression. The interview protocol was organized around three thematic domains: data in problem definition, challenges in data interpretation, and collaboration between design and data teams. A total of seven one-on-one, in-person interviews were conducted with UX/UI designers, product managers, and data scientists, all of whom had more than three years of professional experience and had worked on data-driven design projects (Table 1). A semi-structured interview format was adopted, and each interview lasted approximately 80 min, resulting in a total of 9.5 h of audio recordings and approximately 110,000 characters of transcribed content. The transcripts revealed that designers' cognitive approaches to data utilization unfolded in a structured and sequential manner, supporting the development of a methodology to automate the structuring and visualization of interview data (see Table. 3).

Table 1. Participants' Data-Related Design Work.

Code	Role	Experience	Domain
P1	UX Designer	5 years	Mobile Commerce
P2	Product Manager	7 years	Healthcare Platform
P3	UX/UI Designer	8 years	Content/Search
P4	UX Designer	11 years	B2B Solution (SI)
P5	UX Designer	5 years	B2B Solution (SI)
P6	Data Scientist	3 years	B2B Solution (SI)
P7	Product Manager	4 years	Mobile Commerce

2.3 Semantic Unit Segmentation and Preprocessing

To convert interview data into an analyzable format, utterances were segmented based not on grammatical sentences but on semantic units—discrete segments reflecting changes in cognitive flow and logical development. This study adopted semantic units as the minimal unit of analysis to more precisely represent the participants' thought processes. Semantic units were defined as interpretation-centered components that signify shifts in reasoning or rhetorical structure, and segmentation was guided by the presence of cognitive transitions, shifts in emphasis, and discourse markers.

The segmentation process was implemented in two stages. First, the interview transcripts were tokenized at the sentence level using Python's NLTK library. Next, a rule-based algorithm developed by the researcher restructured the data into semantic units by using discourse cues to determine whether to segment or merge clauses. After the initial segmentation, a length-based rule was applied to avoid excessively fragmented segments, and the researcher manually reviewed and revised 45 segments to ensure logical coherence and preserve causal relationships within the cognitive flow. These restructured semantic units formed the basis for all subsequent stages, including cognitive tagging, classifier training, clustering, and visualization, with negligible information loss during restructuring.

2.4 Utterance Clustering for Cognitive Pattern Structuring

After preprocessing the utterances into semantic units, each unit was transformed into a high-dimensional semantic vector using sentence embedding, and dimensionality reduction was applied using PCA and UMAP to examine semantic similarities among utterances and visualize the clustering structure in two-dimensional space. Cosine similarity was calculated to evaluate semantic closeness, and the results indicated a tendency toward forming two major clusters. The silhouette score peaked at 0.5008 when the number of clusters was set to K = 2, and the cosine distance between the two cluster centroids reached 2.000. Based on these findings, the number of clusters was finalized at two (see Fig. 2).

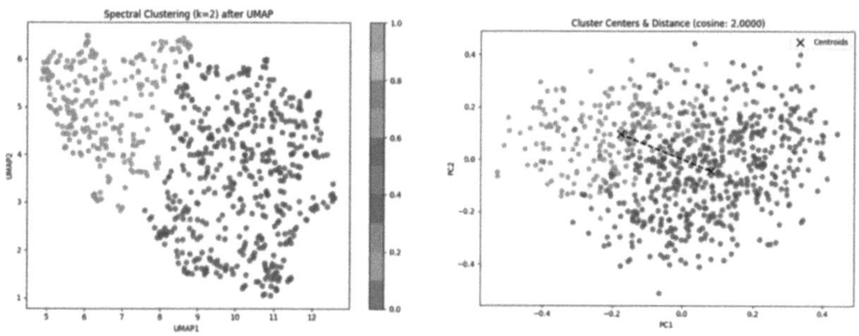

Fig. 2. Clustering Structure Visualization Using UMAP and PCA: Spectral Clustering Results and Inter-Centroid Relations.

To automatically classify each utterance into one of the two clusters, a supervised binary classification model was developed. Ten utterances were randomly selected from each cluster and manually labeled, creating a training dataset of 20 samples, and a logistic regression model was trained and applied to the full set of utterances. Approximately 60 utterances with confidence scores below 0.6 were manually reviewed and relabeled as necessary, resulting in 550 utterances assigned to Cluster 0 and 491 to Cluster 1, producing a final dataset of 1,041 utterances for analysis. To indirectly validate the semantic separation achieved by the automated classification model, representative keywords across the two clusters were compared using term frequency–inverse document frequency (TF-IDF). Cluster 0 featured user, problem, context, and coordination, whereas Cluster 1 was characterized by figures, data, and at this stage, illustrating that cognitive structures and data usage strategies can be distinguished based on utterance type. The classification served as a foundational framework for subsequent tagging-based flow analysis and visualization, highlighting its value as an analytical procedure for structuring and differentiating cognitive approaches (see Table 2).

Table 2. Comparison of TF-IDF Keywords and Utterances by Cluster.

Cluster	Number of utterances	Top TF-IDF keywords
Cluster 0	550	user, problem, limitation, context, coordination, etc.
Cluster 1	491	figure, data, at this stage, in some cases, frequently, etc.

2.5 Categorization Framework and Automated Analysis

Following the clustering of utterances into two distinct types, the study aimed to identify the cognitive flow embedded within each cluster. To achieve this, categorization criteria were developed to reflect the semantic structure of utterances, encompassing their communicative purpose, cognitive development, and decision-making logic. Emphasis was placed on both interpretability and applicability. Based on these criteria, composite tagging was performed by sequentially assigning tags to each transition point within the utterance, allowing the internal cognitive structure to unfold incrementally. This tagging method served as a practical analytical approach for structurally organizing qualitative utterances through automated tagging.

The categorization criteria were derived by combining the researcher's qualitative interpretations with suggestions from GPT-4 (OpenAI). For each sample utterance, both the researcher and the language model independently proposed tag labels. When interpretations aligned, the shared label was adopted. In cases of discrepancy, the researcher's categorization was prioritized, considering contextual coherence and interpretive reliability. This dual approach ensured a balance between semantic diversity and classification consistency (see Table 3).

Table 3. Comparison of TF-IDF Keywords and Utterances by Cluster.

Sample utterance	GPT-4 suggestion	Researcher tag	Agreement
"If you bring a hypothesis that data can support, they tend to listen more carefully."	Problem-Solving Strategy	Strategic Application	No
"Designers weren't really in a position to talk to developers about data integrity."	Situational Judgment	Situational Awareness	Yes (adopted)
"One of the limitations of data is that while it tells you what happened, it can't explain why it happened."	Strategic Error	Constraints & Limitations	Semantically aligned (adopted)

As a result, six final tag categories were confirmed. Their formal definitions and corresponding examples are detailed in Table 4.

Table 4. Final Tag Definitions.

Tag (Label)	Definition
Situational Awareness	Recognition of project context, constraints, or environmental conditions
Conceptual Clarification	Distinguishing concepts, ideas, or terminology
Strategic Application	Technical descriptions of data use, tools, or design tactics
Reflection & Insight	Personal reflection, lessons learned, or insights gained from experience
Perspective Shift	Efforts to reframe a problem from a different angle or expand one's perspective
Constraints & Limitations	Awareness of technical, organizational, or systemic limitations

These classification criteria enabled systematic analysis of the semantic progression within utterances and provided the foundation for subsequent structural comparisons of reasoning patterns. A total of 60 utterances—30 from each cluster—were manually tagged to form the training dataset, and the final number of tags was determined by the internal structure and progression of thought. Using these manually labeled samples, the model was trained for automatic tagging. Each utterance was embedded using the pre-trained KoSBERT model (jhgan/ko-sbert-nli), and the classification system employed a one-vs-rest architecture with logistic regression.

In addition to sentence embeddings, normalized utterance length was included as an input feature to adjust the number of predicted tags per utterance, allowing assignment of up to four tags per utterance. Approximately 57 utterances with confidence scores below 0.6 were manually reviewed and corrected to ensure tagging accuracy. Following this process, composite tagging was applied to the entire dataset, and approximately 65% of all utterances received two or more tags. Among the six categories, Strategic Application, Reflection & Insight, and Situational Awareness appeared most frequently (Table 5).

Table 5. Tag-Wise Frequency and Ratio.

Tag	Frequency (n)	Ratio (%)
Situational Awareness	388	37.3
Conceptual Clarification	211	20.3
Strategic Application	400	38.4
Reflection & Insight	406	39.0
Perspective Shift	134	12.9
Constraints & Limitations	282	27.1

Finally, the automated tagging results were visualized to examine internal cognitive flow and transitional structures within utterances. This approach supported the comparison of structural differences in thinking patterns across clusters and enabled a more nuanced interpretation of intercategory relationships within design cognition.

3 Results and Structural Validity of the Automated Analysis Framework

3.1 Visualization Results and Structural Validity

This study applied the proposed automated visualization analysis procedure to 1,041 qualitative interview utterances. Sankey diagrams were used to visualize directional transitions and frequency-based flows between cognitive functions within utterances, while heatmaps, slope graphs, and radial plots were used to examine co-occurrence patterns, centrality, and the overall distribution of functions across clusters. The results demonstrated the potential to quantitatively identify and visualize the structural characteristics of cognitive flow that are difficult to capture through conventional manual analysis. The integration of similarity-based clustering and automated tagging yielded two distinct clusters reflecting different characteristics of cognitive progression. Accordingly, Cluster 0 was labeled as Interpretation-Driven Cognition, while Cluster 1 was labeled as Execution-First Cognition (Figs. 3 and 4).

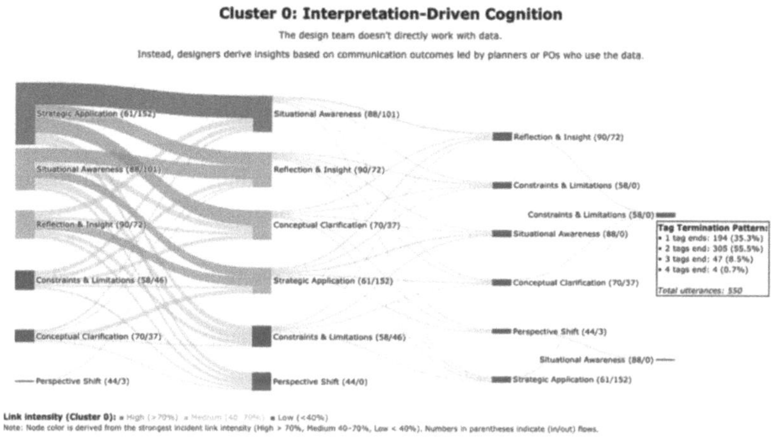

Fig. 3 Sankey Diagram of Cluster 0: Interpretation-Driven Cognition.

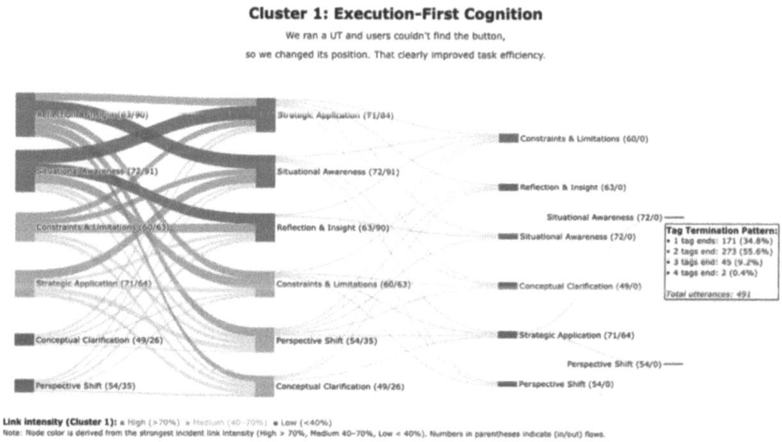

Fig. 4 Sankey Diagram of Cluster 1: Execution-First Cognition.

In the Interpretation-Driven Cognition cluster, the most frequent transition was from Strategic Application to Situational Awareness, followed by Situational Awareness → Reflection & Insight and Strategic Application → Conceptual Clarification, indicating a recurring pattern of cognitive preparation for interpretation. Strategic Application appeared as a major starting point in the flow, but centrality analysis revealed that Conceptual Clarification served as the most influential hub within this cluster, accounting for 25.9% of the total. This prominence was visually represented in the Sankey diagram by thicker orange connections, indicating its role as the core axis of cognitive progression in interpretation-driven cognition.

In the Execution-First Cognition cluster, transitions centered on lived executional experiences, with the most prominent pathway being Reflection & Insight → Situational Awareness, followed by Situational Awareness → Strategic Application and Situational Awareness → Constraints & Limitations. In terms of centrality scores, Situational Awareness emerged as the dominant hub within this cluster, accounting for 22.1% of the total, and this was reflected in the Sankey diagram through stronger blue connections. Centrality analysis further showed that, in the interpretation-driven cluster, Conceptual Clarification exhibited the highest centrality score, whereas in the execution-first cluster, Situational Awareness led, followed by Reflection & Insight and Conceptual Clarification. These results indicate that the hubs identified in the transition flow also align with structural centrality, enabling structural differentiation to be measured with greater objectivity and precision (Table 6).

Table 6. Centrality Scores and Proportions by Tag in Each Cognitive Type.

Tag	Centrality (C0)	Proportion (%)	Centrality (C1)	Proportion (%)
Conceptual Clarification	213	25.9	135	18.3
Situational Awareness	189	23.0	163	22.1
Constraints & Limitations	104	12.7	123	16.7
Perspective Shift	47	5.7	89	12.1
Strategic Application	107	13.0	75	10.2
Reflection & Insight	162	19.7	153	20.7

The results of the centrality analysis revealed that identical tags may assume markedly different roles depending on the type of cognitive flow (see Table 12). Conceptual Clarification held the highest centrality in interpretation-driven cognition at 25.9%, whereas its centrality decreased to 18.3% in execution-first cognition. In contrast, Situational Awareness was the most central tag in the execution-first cognition cluster, accounting for 22.1%. These findings suggest that centrality scores offer insights beyond mere frequency counts, elucidating the strategic positioning of each tag within the overall cognitive structure.

3.2 Supplementary Visual Analyses for Structural Comparison

While the Sankey diagram illustrated the sequential progression of cognitive flow tags, additional visualization methods were employed to interpret the multidimensional characteristics of cognitive structures and their quantitative differences across clusters. Heatmap analysis identified co-occurrence frequencies between cognitive flow tags, revealing distinct combinational patterns across clusters. In the interpretation-driven cognition cluster, Strategic Application – Conceptual Clarification frequently occurred, whereas the Execution-First Cognition cluster was dominated by Situational Awareness – Constraints & Limitations. This visual depiction of tag co-occurrence aided in quantifying the cohesion and convergence tendencies of cognitive structures (Fig. 5).

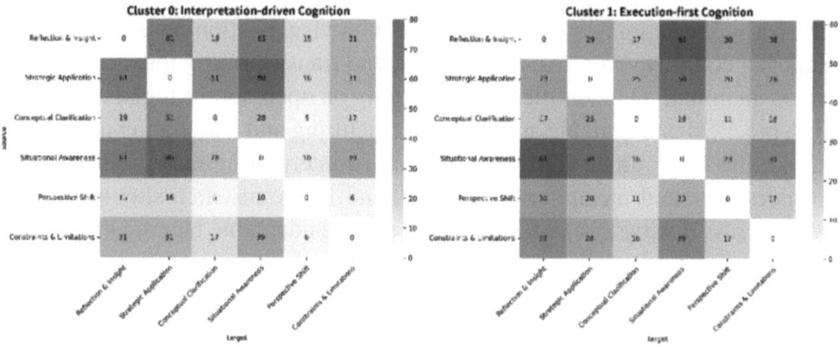

Fig. 5 Cluster-wise Heatmap of Cognitive Tag Co-occurrence Patterns.

The slope graph was employed to track changes in the centrality of each cognitive tag between clusters, showing that Strategic Application declined in the execution-first cluster, whereas Perspective Shift increased. A radial plot further showed that the interpretation-driven cluster exhibited a concentrated structure, while the execution-first cluster displayed a more dispersed structure. Additionally, a divergence bar chart supported intuitive comparisons of centrality scores across cognitive tags. Collectively, these complementary visualization techniques provided a multidimensional perspective on cognitive structure and enabled a more nuanced structural interpretation of cognitive flows (Fig. 6).

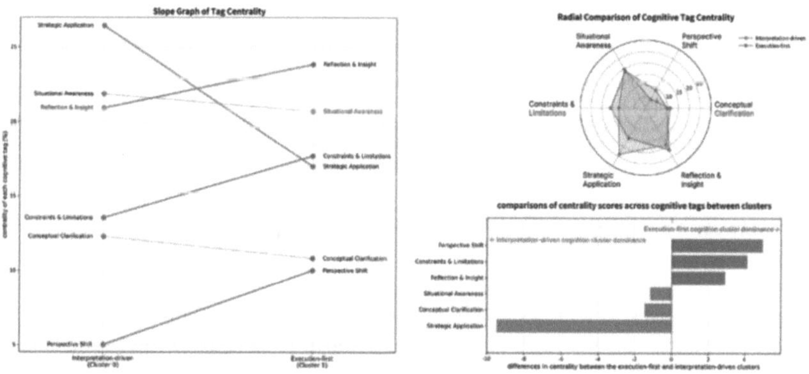

Fig. 6 Multimodal Visualization of Cognitive Tag Centrality Differences Between Clusters.

4 Discussion and Conclusion

This study introduced an analytical framework for the structured and visual analysis of cognitive flows based on qualitative interview data. By integrating the interpretive depth of qualitative methods with the systematic precision of quantitative analysis, the approach enabled a data-driven interpretation of designers' cognitive progression within UX research. Through a tagging system combined with visualization-based structural analysis, recurring cognitive patterns, central tags, and transition structures can be systematically and quantitatively identified. Built entirely on open-source tools, the framework supports a practical and scalable approach to structuring and automating qualitative UX research. At the same time, limitations remain in interpreting emotional expressions, implicit narratives, and metaphoric language, and future research should validate the framework across diverse contexts and develop more adaptable tagging systems.

References

Berg, B.L.: Qualitative Research Methods for the Social Sciences, 6th edn. Pearson Education (2007)

Braun, V., Clarke, V.: Using thematic analysis in psychology. Qual. Res. Psychol. **3**(2), 77–101 (2006). https://doi.org/10.1191/1478088706qp063oa

Ericsson, K.A., Simon, H.A.: Protocol Analysis: Verbal Reports as Data, Rev. edn. MIT Press (1993)

Glaser, B.G., Strauss, A.L.: The Discovery of Grounded Theory: Strategies for Qualitative Research. Aldine (1967)

Glaser, B.G., Strauss, A.L.: The Discovery of Grounded Theory: Strategies for Qualitative Research. Aldine Transaction (1999)

Hamza, K.M.: Disciplinary boundaries: a case study of constructing a relationship between the human body and electricity. Cult. Stud. Sci. Educ. **9**(2), 407–421 (2014). https://doi.org/10.1007/s11422-013-9516-z

Hanington, B., Martin, B.: Universal Methods of Design: 100 Ways to Research Complex Problems, Develop Innovative Ideas, and Design Effective Solutions. Rockport Publishers (2012)

Kvale, S.: InterViews: An Introduction to Qualitative Research Interviewing. Sage Publications (1996)

Min, J., Lee, H.: An analysis of user responses in the early stage of design thinking: a topic modeling approach based on YouTube comments. Korea Des. Forum. **45**, 43–54 (2023). https://doi.org/10.21326/kdf.2023.45.043

Nielsen Norman Group: User interviews. https://www.nngroup.com/articles/user-interviews/ (2017)

Park, J.: Exploring branding strategies of global design companies through SNS big data analysis. J. Digit. Des. Converg. **19**(2), 55–67 (2020). https://doi.org/10.37279/jdr.2020.19.2.55

Petukhova, A., Matos-Carvalho, J.P., Fachada, N.: Comparing embedding models and clustering methods for topic modeling on scientific and news text corpora. Inf. Process. Manag. **61**(1), 103328 (2024). https://doi.org/10.1016/j.ipm.2023.103328

APUB: An Adaptive Evaluation System for B2B User Experience

Dianyu Lin, Mengyan Guo, Jianpeng Li, Luping Wang, and Yao Cheng(✉)

Alibaba Cloud Computing, Hangzhou, China
{lindianyu.ldy,guomengyan.gmy,jiangpu.ljp,shushi.cy}@alibaba-inc.com, dopink@msn.com

Abstract. User experience (UX) evaluation in B2B context is often built on static and standardized metrics frameworks, which often assume stable evaluation dimensions. In practice, enterprise products evolve within shifting organizational strategies and lifecycle stages, and the relative importance of UX dimensions can change substantially over time. This paper proposes APUB (Adaptive Produc-User-Business): a conceptual framework and system architecture that uses automated data pipelines to (i) select context-appropriate UX metrics and (ii) adapt their weights based on product characteristics, user feedback signals, and business objectives. APUB combines a multi-layer metric classification scheme with a dynamic weighting mechanism to produce context-sensitive composite UX scores. To assess feasibility and organizational impact, we conducted exploratory semi-structured interviews with five senior practitioners from cross-functional B2B teams. Preliminary findings indicate broad recognition of APUB's comprehensiveness and adaptive capabilities, while also highlighting key implementation challenges, particularly the trade-offs between adaptability and cross-product comparability, and concerns about system interpretability. These insights provide guidance for framework optimization and lay the foundation for a more adaptive, data-driven UX evaluation system.

Keywords: UX evaluation · B2B · Adaptive benchmarking · Dynamic weighting

1 Introduction

User experience (UX) evaluation is a core component of HCI, helping teams identify user requirements and mitigate product failure risk [1]. This becomes especially important in B2B and enterprise contexts, where design work must account for complex organizational settings, cross-functional collaboration, and domain-specific workflows [2,3].

D. Lin, M. Guo, J. Li—These authors contributed equally.

C. Stephanidis et al. (Eds.): HCII 2026, CCIS 3047, pp. 443–453, 2026.
https://doi.org/10.1007/978-3-032-30552-7_42

However, three inherent characteristics of B2B enterprise products challenge traditional UX evaluation approaches:

(a) **Context complexity**. B2B products must accommodate diverse user roles and product types (e.g., tool-based vs. platform-based), and strategic priorities shift across different lifecycle stages (e.g., growth vs. maturity). One-size-fits-all metrics frameworks cannot capture this complexity [1,2,4].

(b) **Disconnect from user reality.** Traditional, infrequently updated metrics (e.g., annual surveys) often lag behind the fast pace of enterprise product deployment and iteration, failing to reflect real-time user pain points and perceptions [1,5,6].

(c) **Weak linkage to business value.** UX metrics are often isolated and fail to demonstrate a direct connection to key business outcomes such as customer retention or revenue, reducing organizational incentives to invest in continuous UX improvement [7–9].

Common UX evaluation approaches, including HEART and satisfaction/loyalty measures such as NPS, address parts of this problem but typically assume stable dimensions and weights [10,11]. To fill this gap, we propose Adaptive Produc-User-Business (APUB), a framework and system architecture that integrates UX and Information Systems (IS) constructs into a unified metric classification, then dynamically adjusts metric emphasis based on product context, user feedback signals, and business objectives.

This work contributes:

(1) **Comprehensive Adaptive UX Evaluation System.** APUB integrates product, user, and business dimensions to effectively address key evaluation challenges in B2B product environments.

(2) **Context-Sensitive Metric Aggregation Mechanism.** Introducing dynamic weighting logic, combined with exploratory qualitative research, reveals socio-technical challenges and organizational tensions in the evaluation process.

(3) **Theoretical and Practical Insights.** UX metrics are reconceptualized not as static truths but as contextually negotiated systems influenced by organizational priorities, providing practical guidance for developing adaptive UX evaluation models (UXEMs) and a reference for related research.

2 Related Work

2.1 Foundations and Limitations of UX Measurement

UX measurement has long centered on usability [12]. ISO 9241-11 defines usability in terms of effectiveness, efficiency, and satisfaction, while the System Usability Scale (SUS) operationalizes perceived usability through a standardized questionnaire [13,14]. Later instruments such as the User Experience Questionnaire (UEQ) expanded assessment beyond pragmatic qualities to include hedonic dimensions [15]. In industry practice, Google's HEART framework foregrounds outcome dimensions such as Happiness, Engagement, Adoption, Retention, and Task Success, while encouraging teams to define goal-relevant signals and metrics [10].

While these methods provide solid methodological foundations and some support for context-based adjustment of "what to measure," they leave the relative importance of dimensions to periodic manual judgment. They lack a theoretical framework for continuous, signal-driven reweighting as product context, user signals, and strategy evolve.

2.2 Information Systems Success and Business Alignment

Beyond usability, enterprise systems are frequently evaluated through organizational performance lenses. DeLone and McLean's Information Systems Success Model relates system quality, information quality, service quality, use, user satisfaction, and net benefits [16]. The Technology Acceptance Model (TAM) emphasizes perceived usefulness and perceived ease of use as drivers of adoption [17]. These models reinforce that evaluation should account for both user experience and organizational outcomes [18].

However, these traditions typically treat business impact as an endpoint rather than an input that can reshape what is measured and how strongly each construct is weighted [19,20]. This leaves room for further development in explaining how construct importance may evolve across different contexts.

2.3 Adaptive and Multi-criteria Evaluation Systems

Multi-Criteria Decision Analysis (MCDA) and weighted utility models offer formal approaches for aggregating heterogeneous criteria and have been widely used in decision-making and IS evaluation [21]. In UX research, related efforts have explored MCDA-style approaches to match evaluation methods to context characteristics, including constraints such as time, expertise, and project needs [22–24]. These efforts demonstrate the value of multi-criteria reasoning but also surface limitations relevant to B2B contexts: reliance on manual elicitation can amplify subjectivity; stakeholders may disagree on how to interpret "context"; and many applications remain one-off matching exercises rather than mechanisms that adapt continuously as products and organizations evolve [21,25–27].

Few UX frameworks explicitly support dynamic reconstruction of evaluation weights from ongoing signals (e.g., product features, feedback salience, strategic shifts). APUB addresses this gap by combining theory-informed metric selection with automated, signal-driven weight adaptation, while recognizing the organizational need to preserve comparability when required.

3 APUB Framework Design

3.1 Framework Overview

APUB is designed to address limitations of commonly used UX evaluation models in dynamic B2B environments. Many existing models apply fixed dimensions and weights, which can be insensitive to product archetype, lifecycle stage, and organizational strategy [10,15,16,25]. APUB instead conceptualizes UX benchmarking as a self-adjusting metric system: it combines theory-informed expectations, real user signals, and business-outcome alignment so that what is measured—and how strongly it is emphasized—can evolve with context.

The framework is illustrated in Fig 1, which summarizes its three-dimensional structure and adaptive evaluation process.

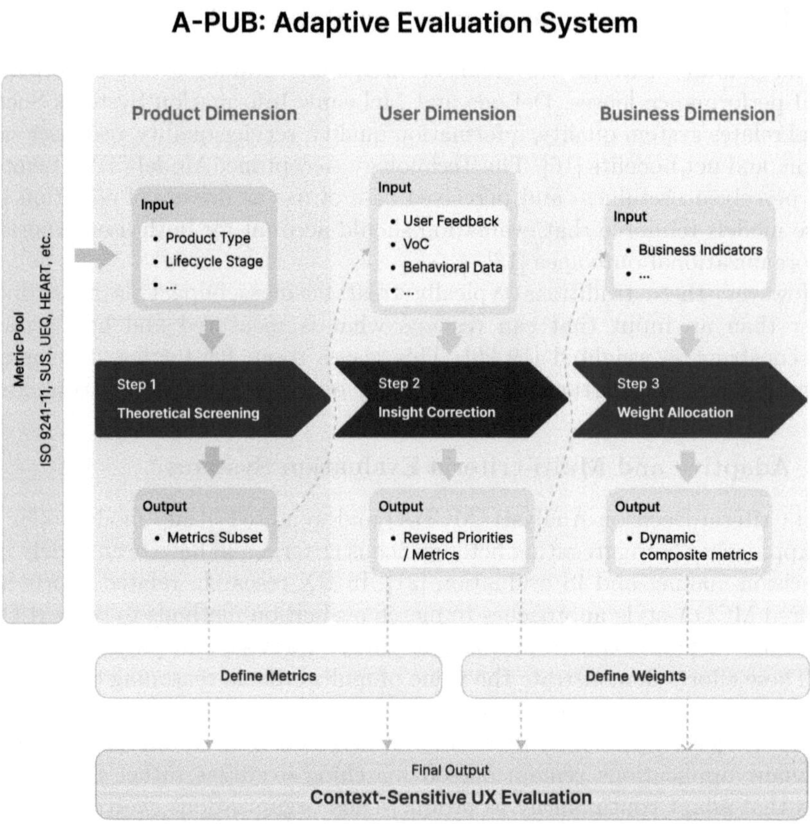

Fig. 1. APUB integrates the Product, User, and Business dimensions through three stages: Theoretical Screening, Insight Correction, and Weight Allocation, to generate dyamically weighted UX metrics aligned with product context, user feedback, and business objectives.

3.2 Three-Dimensional Analysis Logic

APUB operates by integrating three key dimensions to address major UX evaluation challenges:

(a) **Product Dimension.** Addresses contextual complexity by analyzing product archetypes (e.g., tool-based, platform-based) and lifecycle stages (e.g., growth, maturity) to establish theoretical baselines and strategic priorities.

(b) **User Dimension.** Mitigates disconnect risks by integrating multi-source unstructured user feedback (VoC) to identify core pain points and high-frequency issues, refining theoretical assumptions.

(c) **Business Dimension.** Addresses weak business linkage by quantifying statistical relationships between UX metrics and key business outcomes (e.g., renewal, retention), ensuring that the measurement system can directly drive business growth.

3.3 Metric System Construction Process

APUB generates the final evaluation output through a three-step process of theoretical screening, insight correction, and weight allocation, as illustrated in Fig. 1.

Step 1: Theoretical Screening (Product Dimension). APUB maintains a curated metric pool of established UX constructs (e.g., ISO 9241-11, SUS, UEQ, HEART), each stored with brief definitions and applicability cues. The system uses product context descriptors (e.g., archetype and lifecycle stage) to retrieve a relevant subset and form initial priority hypotheses. For example, a growth-stage, tool-oriented product might initially prioritize task efficiency and learnability, with performance and consistency treated as secondary. This step provides a principled starting point for what should matter in a given context.

Step 2: Insight Correction (User Dimension). : User feedback is analyzed (e.g., semantic analysis and clustering) to estimate the prominence of issues mapped to each UX dimension. When feedback diverges from theoretical assumptions, the system prioritizes adjustment based on user reality, ensuring the metric system reflects core user needs. For example, if "ease of use" concerns appear substantially more prominent than "task efficiency" concerns, the framework revises the initial prioritization so the evaluation better reflects current user reality.

Step 3: Weight Allocation (Business Dimension). Weights are adjusted based on the calculated correlations between each dimension and key business indicators. Under the guiding rule that dimensions with stronger business relevance and broader user pain tend to receive higher weight, APUB increases emphasis where improvements are more likely to support desired outcomes.

3.4 Output: Dynamic Composite Metrics

APUB produces a weighted composite UX metrics system, consisting of multiple quantifiable components (e.g., task success rate, load time, NPS), with dimension weights continuously adjusted through the above process. This allows enterprises to track long-term trends while focusing on the most critical growth levers at specific product stages.

4 Qualitative Evaluation: Value and Adoption Tensions

4.1 Method

To validate the concept and identify adoption risks, we conducted semi-structured interviews with five cross-functional B2B experts (each with more than five years of experience): Product Manager (P1), User Researcher (P2), Experience Designer (P3), Technical Account Manager (P4), and Software Engineer (P5). Interviews introduced APUB framework and then explored perceived validity, practical feasibility, potential benefits, concerns, and improvement directions. We analyzed transcripts using thematic analysis to identify recurring organizational dynamics and implementation tensions.

4.2 Findings: Perceived Value and Key Tensions

Overall, participants expressed moderate-to-high perceived conceptual validity (mean rating 5.5/7) and adoption willingness (mean rating 5.3/7) (Fig 2). Their feedback suggests that APUB's value is compelling at a conceptual level, while implementation raises predictable organizational frictions. We summarize results along two themes: perceived advantages and adoption tensions.

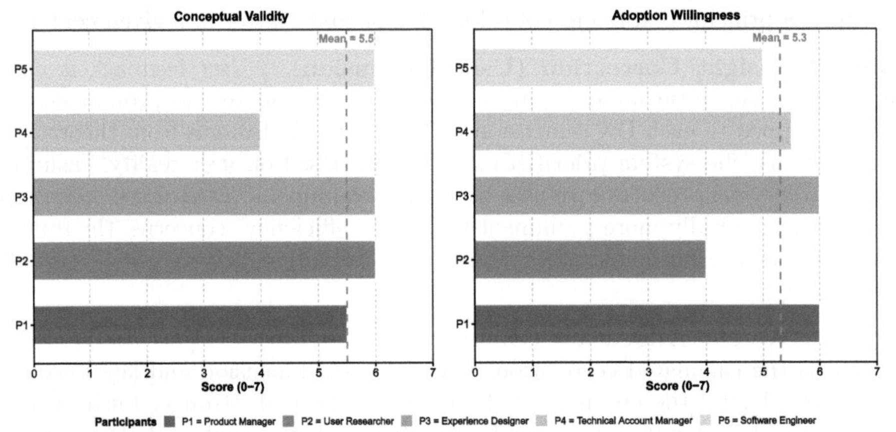

Fig. 2. Conceptual Validity and Adoption Willingness ratings from 5 corss-functional B2B experts (P1-P5).

Perceived Advantages: Dynamic, Multi-dimensional Alignment. Participants emphasized that APUB addresses rigidity and subjectivity in conventional metric practice.

Alignment with Lifecycle Change. P1 highlighted that the dynamic element matches how B2B products continuously evolve, noting, "The most valuable aspect is the dynamism... it aligns with the fact that product lifecycles are constantly iterating." They added that automation significantly improves efficiency in tracking these shifts.

More Comprehensive Evaluation Perspective. P3 noted that considering Product, User, and Business together is "relatively comprehensive," compared with single-axis reporting (e.g., only satisfaction or only business conversion).

More Defensible, Data-Informed Correction. P4 described APUB's value as providing "directional guidance and course correction," helping teams shift from relying on intuition to relying on data. Meanwhile, P2 observed that the approach can feel reliable when used for within-product diagnosis rather than cross-product ranking.

Adoption Challenges: Three Organizational Tensions. Despite enthusiasm, participants repeatedly surfaced three tensions that could impede real-world adoption.

Comparability Paradox. Dynamic weights can undermine the perceived fairness of horizontal comparisons across products or teams. Participants worried that if each product is evaluated under different weights, the results become less usable for management-level comparison and performance assessment. P2 highlighted this structural trade-off, observing that varying weights could challenge the ability to "score every product equally." Similarly, P1 questioned whether excessive variables would hinder uniform measurement, while P2 raised concerns about tracking longitudinal progress if benchmarks shift frequently.

Data–Reality Gap. Adaptive weighting presumes stable access to high-quality signals, yet teams often lack unified feedback channels or comparable data coverage across products. P4 noted that fragmented feedback channels often prevent access to a "single source of truth," a view supported by P3, who mentioned limited raw data dimensions for new products. P5 added that without unified inputs, there is a risk of the system amplifying noise rather than generating clear signals.

Trust Deficit and Explainability. Participants questioned how the system would justify weight changes, especially when rankings conflict with existing beliefs. They emphasized that the framework must provide interpretable rationale for adjustments, not only outputs. P5 echoed the need to verify the underlying mapping logic, while P3 suggested that trust would depend on transparency and proven success cases similar to established frameworks like HEART.

5 Discussion

5.1 Theoretical Perspective: UX Metrics as Organizationally Negotiated Constructs

Findings suggest that enterprise UX metrics function not only as technical measurement tools but also as social artifacts shaped by managerial structures and incentives [28, 29]. Static metric systems can obscure underlying value judgments, whereas adaptive weighting makes prioritization more explicit. Participant concerns that the "algorithm may be reliable but not suitable for horizontal scoring" point to a broader implication: APUB is simultaneously a measurement mechanism and a coordination device that reveals and formalizes shifting organizational priorities.

5.2 Design Implications: Balancing Adaptability with Stability

To respond to the tensions identified above, APUB's design should explicitly balance contextual sensitivity with organizational needs for stability and legitimacy.

Strategic Level: Dual-Track Evaluation. To address the comparability paradox, we propose a dual-track approach: **(i) Diagnostic mode** for improving a single product over time, where weights adapt fully so the metric system remains sensitive to lifecycle and user-signal changes.; and **(ii) Alignment mode** for cross-product comparison or performance reporting, using a stable core metric set with fixed or slowly changing weights. This separation preserves APUB's adaptive value while retaining a stable layer for organizational reporting.

System Level: Explainability and Phased Implementation. To address trust and data constraints, implementation should emphasize transparency and pacing [30]. In practice, this means providing dashboards that make weight distributions legible and maintain an audit trail of changes over time, validating outputs against external benchmarks where feasible to build credibility, and starting with a pilot product that has mature instrumentation and strong cross-functional alignment before scaling more broadly.

6 Limitations and Future Work

This study has several limitations. First, the interview sample is small (n=5) and may not represent the full diversity of B2B product organizations. Second, APUB remains a conceptual framework and has not yet been deployed at production scale; practical challenges of pipeline implementation, data quality management, and noise handling are not empirically evaluated here. Third, we do not yet understand the long-term effects of adaptive weighting on organizational culture, incentives, and product decision-making routines.

Future work will proceed along three directions: **(1) develop an APUB minimum viable product (MVP)** and run longitudinal field studies to measure quantitative impact; **(2) design explainable mechanisms** for weight generation with human-readable rationales; and **(3) study change-management strategies,** such as incentive design and communication practices, to mitigate resistance associated with the comparability paradox and support sustainable adoption [31–33].

7 Conclusion

This paper proposes APUB, a theory-informed adaptive UX evaluation framework for B2B enterprise products. By dynamically reconstructing metric weights using product context, user feedback signals, and business objectives, APUB shifts UX measurement from static benchmarking toward context-sensitive evaluation. Exploratory interviews suggest that practitioners value APUB's adaptability, comprehensiveness, and potential to reduce subjective decision-making, while also highlighting adoption challenges related to comparability, data readiness, and trust in explainability. Future UX evaluation systems should balance contextual validity with management stability, leveraging interpretability, benchmarking, and infrastructure support to ensure successful adaptive evaluation. More broadly, we argue that UX evaluation in organizations is best understood as an ongoing negotiation of priorities: one that adaptive metric systems can make visible and actionable rather than implicit and static.

References

1. Qiu, J. (2025). Dual-Track UX: A user experience evaluation method for identifying user requirements and mitigating the risk of product failure. In Proceedings of the CHI Conference on Human Factors in Computing Systems. Assoc. Comput. Mach. https://doi.org/10.1145/3706599.3719968
2. Roto, V., Lu, Y., Nieminen, H., Kaasinen, E., Seppänen, M.: UX expeditions in business-to-business heavy industry: lessons learned. In: Proceedings of the 2016 CHI Conference Extended Abstracts on Human Factors in Computing Systems. Association for Computing Machinery (2016). https://doi.org/10.1145/2851581.2851600
3. Raees, M., et al.: UX Challenges in Implementing an Interactive B2B Customer Segmentation Tool (2025)
4. Zdanowska, S., et al. (2022). A study of UX practitioners' roles in designing real-world enterprise ML systems. In: Proceedings of the 2022 CHI Conference on Human Factors in Computing Systems. Association for Computing Machinery. https://doi.org/10.1145/3491102.3517607
5. Nguyen, J., et al.: Closing the feedback loop between UX design, software development, and operations with telemetry data. In: Proceedings of the 31st Australian Conference on Human-Computer-Interaction. Assoc. Comput. Mach. (2019). https://doi.org/10.1145/3349266.3351420
6. Convertino, G., Frishberg, N.: Why agile teams fail without UX research. Commun. ACM **60**(9), 35–3 (2017). https://doi.org/10.1145/3126156
7. Campbell, J.L.: Balancing user needs and business goals for product and service success. In Proceedings of the 42nd ACM International Conference on Design of Communication. Assoc. Comput. Mach. (2024). https://doi.org/10.1145/3641237.3691676
8. Domingues, R.C., Silva, M.J., Marinho, M.: Low-code quality metrics for agile software development. In Proceedings of the Brazilian Symposium on Software Quality. Assoc. Comput. Mach. (2024). https://doi.org/10.1145/3701625.3701626
9. Jannach, D., Jugovac, M.: Measuring the business value of recommender systems . ACM Trans. Manage. Inf. Syst. **10**(4), Article 1 (2019). https://doi.org/10.1145/3370082

10. Rodden, K., Hutchinson, H., Fu, X.: Measuring the user experience on a large scale: User-centered metrics for web applications. In: Proceedings of the SIGCHI Conference on Human Factors in Computing Systems (pp. 2395–2398). Association for Computing Machinery (2010). https://doi.org/10.1145/1753326.1753687
11. Gao, X., Zhi, S., Wang, X.: Investigating the Relationship among Ease-of-Use, NPS, and Customers' Sequent Spending of Cloud Computing Products. In: HCI International 2021 - Posters (HCII 2021), Constantine Stephanidis, Margherita Antona, and Stavroula Ntoa (Eds.). Springer International Publishing, Cham, 417–42 (2021).https://doi.org/10.1007/978-3-030-78645-8_53
12. Frøkjær, E., Hertzum, M., Hornbæk, K.: Measuring usability: are effectiveness, efficiency, and satisfaction really correlated? In: Proceedings of the SIGCHI Conference on Human Factors in Computing Systems (pp. 345–352). Association for Computing Machinery (2000). https://doi.org/10.1145/332040.332455
13. International Organization for Standardization. Ergonomics of human-system interaction — Part 11: Usability: Definitions and concepts (ISO Standard No. 9241-11:2018). ISO (2018). https://www.iso.org/standard/63500.html
14. Brooke, J. (1996). SUS: A quick and dirty usability scale. In: Jordan, P.W., Thomas, B., McClelland, I.L., Weerdmeester, B. (Eds.), Usability evaluation in industry (pp. 189–194). Taylor & Franci https://doi.org/10.1201/9781498710411-35
15. Laugwitz, B., Held, T., Schrepp, M.: Construction and evaluation of a user experience questionnaire. In: Holzinger, A. (ed.) USAB 2008. LNCS, vol. 5298, pp. 63–76. Springer, Heidelberg (2008). https://doi.org/10.1007/978-3-540-89350-9_6
16. DeLone, W.H., McLean, E.R.: The DeLone and McLean model of information systems success: a ten-year update. J. Manage. Inf. Syst. **19**(4), 9–30 (2003). https://doi.org/10.1080/07421222.2003.11045748
17. Davis, F.D.: Perceived usefulness, perceived ease of use, and user acceptance of information technology. MIS Q. **13**(3), 319–34 (1989). https://doi.org/10.2307/249008
18. Wixom, B.H., Todd, P.A.: A theoretical integration of user satisfaction and technology acceptance. Inf. Syst. Res. **16**(1), 85–10 (2005). https://doi.org/10.1287/isre.1050.0042
19. Jeyaraj, A.: DeLone & McLean models of information system success: critical meta-review and research directions. Int. J. Inf. Manage. **54**, 10213 (2020). https://doi.org/10.1016/j.ijinfomgt.2020.102139
20. Ullah, A., Lai, R.: A systematic review of business and information technology alignment. ACM Trans. Manage. Inf. Syst. **4**(1), Article (2013). https://doi.org/10.1145/2445560.2445564
21. Cinelli, M., Kadziński, M., Gonzalez, M., Słowiński, R.: How to support the application of multiple criteria decision analysis? Let us start with a comprehensive taxonomy. Omega **96**, 10226 (2020). https://doi.org/10.1016/j.omega.2020.102261
22. Oliveira, S., Gadelha, B., Conte, T.: Smart UX method selection with UXNator. In: Proceedings of the XXXIX ACM/SIGAPP Symposium on Applied Computing (SAC '2024). Association for Computing Machinery (2024). https://doi.org/10.1145/3701625.3701694
23. Alves, R., Valente, P., Nunes, N.J.: The state of user experience evaluation practice. In Proceedings of the 8th Nordic Conference on Human-Computer Interaction: Fun, Fast, Foundational (NordiCHI '2014, pp. 93–102). Association for Computing Machinery (2014). https://doi.org/10.1145/2639189.2641208

24. Melo, P., Jorge, L.: Quantitative support for UX methods identification: how can multiple criteria decision making help? Univ. Access Inf. Soc. **14**(2), 215–229 (2014). https://doi.org/10.1007/s10209-013-0341-0
25. Lallemand, C., Koenig, V.: Measuring the contextual dimension of user experience: development of the User Experience Context Scale (UXCS). In: Proceedings of the 11th Nordic Conference on Human-Computer Interaction: Shaping Experiences, Shaping Society. Association for Computing Machinery (2020). https://doi.org/10.1145/3419249.3420156
26. Cinelli, M., Kadziński, M., Mousseau, V., Słowiński, R.: Recommending multiple criteria decision analysis methods with a new taxonomy-based decision support system. Eur. J. Oper. Res. **302**(2), 633–65 (2022). https://doi.org/10.1016/j.ejor.2022.01.021
27. Kuller, M., Beutler, P., Lienert, J.: Preference change in stakeholder group-decision processes in the public sector: Extent, causes and implications. Eur. J. Oper. Res. **308**(3), 1268–128 (2023). https://doi.org/10.1016/j.ejor.2022.12.001
28. Pine, K. H., Liboiron, M.: The politics of measurement and action. In: Proceedings of the 33rd Annual ACM Conference on Human Factors in Computing Systems (pp. 3147–3156). Association for Computing Machinery (2015). https://doi.org/10.1145/2702123.2702298
29. Mathur, A., Van den Broeck, W., Vanderhulst, G., Kawsar, F., Beresford, A. R., Lane, N.D.: Quantified workplace: Opportunities and challenges. In: Proceedings of the 2nd International Workshop on Personal Data Analytics in the Internet of Things (pp. 37–41). Association for Computing Machiner (2015). https://doi.org/10.1145/2753497.2753500
30. Springer, A., Whittaker, S.: Progressive disclosure: When, why, and how do users want algorithmic transparency information? ACM Trans. Interactive Intell. Syst. **10**(4). Article **32**, 1–3 (2020). https://doi.org/10.1145/3374218
31. Kim, S.S.Y., Watkins, E.A., Russakovsky, O., Fong, R., Monroy-Hernández, A.: Help Me Help the AI: Understanding How Explainability Can Support Human-AI Interaction. In: Proceedings of the 2023 CHI Conference on Human Factors in Computing Systems (2023). https://doi.org/10.1145/3544548.3581001
32. Kim, H.-W., Kankanhalli, A.: Investigating user resistance to information systems implementation: a status quo bias perspective. MIS Q. **33**(3), 567–58 (2009). https://doi.org/10.2307/20650309
33. Berente, N., Yoo, Y., Maurer, C., Lyytinen, K.: Institutional logics and pluralistic responses to enterprise system implementation: a qualitative meta-analysis. MIS Quarterly, **43**(3), 873–90 (2019). https://doi.org/10.25300/MISQ/2019/14214

Human–AI Collaboration in Resource Seeking: A Participatory Generative AI Design Study with Rural Foster Parents

Rachel Rodney(✉)

University of North Carolina, Chapel Hill, NC 27514, USA
rrodney@unc.edu

Abstract. This study examines how rural foster parents in North Carolina seek resources and how generative AI might support their information-seeking processes through human–AI collaboration. Using a participatory action research approach, the study was conducted in two phases: a diary and interview study mapping foster parents' resource-seeking behaviors, followed by participatory co-design workshops in which foster parents interacted with generative AI and designed resource-support tools. Preliminary findings suggest that foster parents view generative AI as useful for aggregating information, identifying local resources, and providing guidance for everyday caregiving situations, but not as a replacement for human support or decision-making. Participants emphasized the importance of centralized, up-to-date resource information and community-shared knowledge systems, and identified limitations of AI in handling complex, context-dependent situations. This work contributes to human–computer interaction research by examining human–AI collaboration in high-stakes social service contexts and demonstrates how participatory design with domain experts can inform the development of AI-supported information systems that complement existing human support networks rather than replace them.

Keywords: UX Research · Participatory Design · Generative AI

1 Introduction

Foster parents coordinate healthcare, education, therapy, legal requirements, and daily care for foster children—yet supporting information systems are fragmented and hard to navigate, especially in rural areas [6, 7, 15]. In rural North Carolina (NC), foster parents often must piece together information from multiple organizations, social workers, online groups, and informal networks to locate resources which are dependent on the county they reside in. When foster parents cannot access the resources they need, placement stability is threatened, which has direct consequences for child well-being and long-term outcomes [17, 18].

Despite the centrality of information access to foster parenting, limited research examines how foster parents seek and share information in their daily lives. This study addresses that gap by examining rural foster parents' resource-seeking behaviors to

C. Stephanidis et al. (Eds.): HCII 2026, CCIS 3047, pp. 454–460, 2026.
https://doi.org/10.1007/978-3-032-30552-7_43

inform the design of more effective information systems and support tools. Rather than primarily examining organizational or policy-level solutions to foster parent retention, this work investigates how foster parents find information in their day-to-day lives and how those processes might be redesigned. This study examines resource-seeking as a form of everyday information behavior within a complex socio-technical system, contributing to HCI research on human–AI collaboration, participatory design, and information systems for high-stakes social service environments.

2 Background

Foster parents must act as coordinators, advocates, and information managers while also providing daily care for children – all of which contributes to burnout and low foster parent retention. From an information science perspective, foster parenting involves complex information-seeking behaviors that include searching online, contacting social workers, consulting other foster parents, and navigating government systems. However, these information-seeking strategies are constrained by barriers such as limited local resources, long travel distances, and smaller support networks in rural areas [1].

Existing foster parent retention research largely focuses on personal characteristics, foster parent training, and organizational support structures [2, 7, 8, 11, 12]. As a result, there is a lack of actionable insight into how information systems and resource delivery mechanisms could be redesigned to better support foster parents in rural areas.

This research addresses that gap by examining foster parenting through the lens of information behavior and resource-seeking processes, with the goal of informing the design of more effective information systems and resource access tools.

2.1 Study Overview

This study was conducted in two phases using participatory action research (PAR) and grounded theory methods, guided by the following questions: (1) What barriers do rural North Carolina foster parents encounter when accessing resources for their foster youth? (2) How might foster parents' insights be used to redesign resource interactions to enhance access and usability to resources for foster youth?

Phase 1 of the study involved a diary study and semi-structured interviews with foster parents to map their resource-seeking processes and identify barriers. This study found that rural foster parents navigate a fragmented information environment in which access to resources depends on navigating multiple stakeholders with inconsistent knowledge and availability. These conditions create a recursive information-seeking process that produces a cumulative navigation burden. In rural counties, this burden is intensified by provider scarcity and geographic distance, leaving foster parents to develop informal strategies for accessing support. The recursive information seeking process was illustrated via process map, as seen in the following Fig. 1.

This figure emphasizes the complex information pathways foster parents navigate to find resources. There are many times where foster parents need to go back to different stakeholders, making it more time consuming.

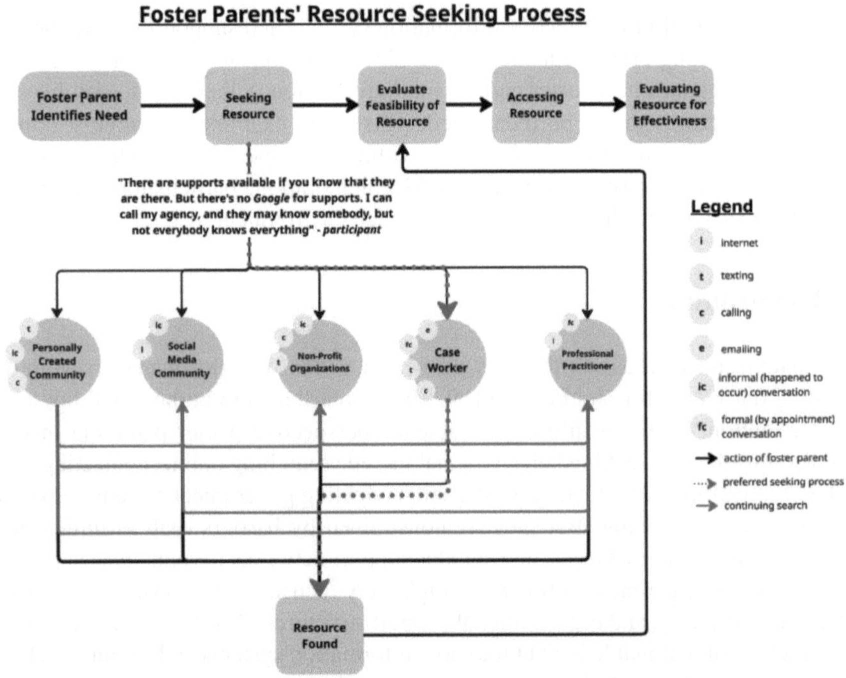

Fig. 1. Process map of foster parents seeking resources.

To target the application of foster parent needs in revisioning resource interactions, participants in the second phase of the study were asked to explore how they would have designed a resource seeking system for themselves [9, 13]. With the emergence of generative AI as a widely adopted information tool, this study incorporated inquiry into foster parent perceptions, uses, and potential applications of generative AI in their work as foster parents.

3 Co-Designing Information Seeking with Rural NC Foster Parents

Phase 2 expanded on Phase 1 findings with design thinking methods in supporting an iterative, user-centered process [3, 10, 11, 14]. Participants reflected on their information-seeking experiences, interacted with generative AI responses, and re-imagined how information systems could better support foster parents navigating complex resource environments.

3.1 Participants

NC presented a unique case study for this research due to the rurality of the state (70% of the counties are considered rural) and the county-administered system they use for foster care. Participants were recruited from rural NC counties through existing community partnerships and support organizations, using a snowball sampling approach to reach foster parents in hard-to-access populations [16]. Leveraging relationships with community partners built trust and supported recruitment through local networks. Eligible participants were required to have direct experience caring for at least one foster child and be licensed through a public or private foster care organization within the selected regions. Recruitment took place over a two-month period, with participants screened for eligibility prior to scheduling and participation.

A total of eight individuals reached out to participate, and six of these individuals proceeded to schedule studies. Each study was composed of two participants and the researcher, resulting in three co-design sessions.

3.2 Methods

Participants interacted with generative AI and engaged in co-design activities related to resource-seeking during a 90-min remote study. Workshops were conducted over video conferencing via Zoom, and included collaborative activities using Miro, a virtual whiteboard app. Each session began with an introduction to generative AI, including how prompt-based systems work, as well as discussions of limitations such as hallucinations and privacy concerns. This study used ChatGPT. ChatGPT was selected as the generative AI tool we would be testing because of its similarity to other generative AI tools and wide adoption. Participants generated resource-related questions they know first-year foster parents might have and transformed those questions ChatGPT by adding specificity and context to the prompts.

The group reviewed and discussed ChatGPT responses together, comparing the responses to how they would suggest seeking or sharing information. Following this evaluation, participants engaged in a co-design exercise in which they visualized a low-fidelity mockup of a tool, system, or process that would help a new foster parent locate resources in their area. The mockup artifacts and discussions were used to understand how foster parents envision improved information systems and the potential role of AI within resource-seeking workflows. The workshop structure allowed participants to reflect on their current information-seeking practices, critique AI-generated information, and redesign future interactions with resource-supporting tools grounded in their lived experiences.

Data Collection. Three forms of data were collected from the co-design studies. First, the workshops were audio-recorded to capture the conversations and evaluations participants had of ChatGPT responses. The audio recordings provided a way to understand foster parent perceptions of generative AI responses, and revealed insights into usability needs that must be prioritized. Secondly, this study gathered a question bank that participants brainstormed foster parents in their first year to have. These questions inform the understanding of what topics need to be prioritized for first year foster parents. Third, participants co-designed low-fidelity mock-ups of solutions to information seeking struggles they discussed during the workshop, resulting in artifacts that revealed design and information needs. The co-designed artifacts highlight core usability needs that foster parents seek in solutions.

Data Analysis. Phase 2 data was qualitatively analyzed using a grounded theory approach [4, 5] informed by Charmaz (2012) and Cunningham and Carmichael (2017).

Workshop recordings, chat transcripts, and co-design artifacts were coded using an iterative coding process. Initial coding focused on participants' interactions with ChatGPT, their evaluations of the responses, and their ideas during the co-design activities. This poster presents preliminary findings developed through initial coding.

4 Preliminary Findings

Preliminary findings from the co-design workshops suggest that foster parents viewed generative AI as *potentially* useful for resource navigation, but not as a *replacement* for human support or decision-making. There were two different forms of information-seeking that participants sought with ChatGPT. One form of inquiry was seeking what resources existed in the area. When evaluating AI-generated responses to resource-seeking questions, several participants noted that the information provided seemed accurate and helpful, particularly when responses included concise lists of organizations, contact information, or next steps. Participants compared this experience to using traditional search engines such as Google, explaining that searching for resources online often requires significant effort to visit multiple websites and "dig" for relevant information, whereas AI-generated responses reduced this effort by aggregating information into a single response. This suggests that one potential role for generative AI in this context is reducing the labor associated with information gathering and initial resource identification.

Another form of inquiry that participants sought was situational based information, where they would seek information about how to navigate certain situations. For example, one participant presented an experience they had where they did not know how to respond.

> It's the day-to-day stuff – things that you have to do in the house; that's the resources [we] need. Generative AI could be a really great tool for that, because if you ask it, 'how do I talk to this kid about, you know, [difficult topics]?' Because, I had to ask a social worker one time how to tell a child they were Black. [The foster child] didn't know.

The downside of needing to wait for a social worker's response is the time it takes. Social workers are already overburdened, some having up to thirty cases, and might not even know how to answer the foster parent. During the time where the foster parents are waiting for a response, they are also actively managing their relationship with the foster child to build trust with them. Waiting for a response from social workers on how to navigate difficult conversations isn't always the best for growing a genuine relationship with foster kids.

When evaluating ChatGPT's response to situations that required context, empathy, or knowledge of local systems, there were some limitations that highlighted the lack of a "human." Several participants noted that AI responses were often "technically correct" but did not reflect how systems operate in practice, especially in high-stress or time-sensitive situations. Participants expressed that new foster parents may not know what contextual details are important when asking questions, and AI systems currently do not ask relevant follow-up questions to clarify situations. As a result, participants felt that AI could be helpful for finding contact information or identifying general resources, but not for navigating complex interpersonal or case-specific situations that require human judgment and emotional support.

Another finding that emerged across workshops was the desire for centralized, up-to-date resource information. During co-design activities, participants frequently proposed systems that would function as a single, shared resource hub organized by region and maintained collaboratively by foster parents and community members. Participants described frustration with having to repeatedly search for the same information and felt that foster parents often "re-make the wheel" when trying to locate resources. The idea of crowdsourced or community-maintained information systems emerged as a preferred model, suggesting that foster parents value shared knowledge and collaborative information networks.

Overall, preliminary findings suggest that foster parents envision generative AI not as an authoritative system that replaces existing support structures, but as a tool that could support information organization and resource discovery. Participants consistently emphasized that human relationships, empathy, and contextual understanding remain essential in foster care support systems, indicating that future AI-supported resource systems should be designed to complement, rather than replace, human support networks.

5 Conclusion

This research identifies several directions for the design of AI-supported resource systems in foster care and similar social service contexts. First, findings suggest a need for systems that prioritize information aggregation and organization, enabling foster parents to quickly identify relevant resources without navigating multiple disconnected platforms. Second, participants' emphasis on shared knowledge highlights the value of community-informed and collaboratively maintained resource hubs that reflect local, up-to-date information. Third, the limitations identified in AI responses point to opportunities for designing systems that better support contextual inquiry, such as prompting users for additional details or integrating human support for complex situations.

6 Design Implications and Future Work

Future work will build on these findings by developing a design toolkit that translates co-design insights into actionable guidance for resource providers and system designers. Planned outputs include (1) a design guide outlining key barriers and opportunities in foster parent resource navigation, (2) prototype concepts for AI-supported resource systems that integrate community knowledge, and (3) training materials to support foster parents in effectively and critically using generative AI tools.

By centering foster parents' lived experiences in the design process, this work aims to inform the development of human–AI systems that reduce the burden of seeking, enhance access to resources, and strengthen existing support networks rather than displacing them.

Disclosure of Interests. The authors have no competing interests to declare that are relevant to the content of this article.

References

1. Balduf, M.: Barriers to resource access in rural communities. J. Rural Soc. Work. **28**(2), 145–162 (2023)
2. Brown, J.D.: Foster parent retention and support: the role of training and resources. Child Welfare. **87**(2), 45–63 (2008)
3. Buchanan, R.: Wicked problems in design thinking. Des. Issues. **8**(2), 5–21 (1992)
4. Charmaz, K.: Constructing Grounded Theory, 2nd edn. Sage, London (2012)
5. Cunningham, S., Carmichael, P.: Grounded theory. In: Rouse, W.B., Boff, K.R. (eds.) Organizational Simulation, pp. 213–226. Wiley, Hoboken, NJ (2017)
6. Engelhardt, A., et al.: Navigating fragmented systems: resource access in foster care. Child Youth Serv. Rev. **145**, 106–118 (2023)
7. Gouveia, R., et al.: Information challenges in social service systems: a foster care perspective. Soc. Sci. Comput. Rev. **39**(4), 567–583 (2021)
8. Larsen, M., et al.: Understanding foster parent experiences in support systems. Child Fam. Soc. Work. **25**(3), 678–689 (2020)
9. MacDonald, C.: Understanding participatory action research: a qualitative research methodology option. Can. J. Action Res. **13**(2), 34–50 (2012)
10. Mackenzie, C., et al.: Participatory design and community engagement methods. Des. Stud. **33**(4), 321–339 (2012)
11. MacGregor, T.E., et al.: Factors associated with foster parent retention. Child Welfare. **85**(6), 1005–1026 (2006)
12. Mancinelli, E., et al.: Supporting foster caregivers through system-level interventions. Child Youth Serv. Rev. **121**, 105–117 (2021)
13. McKenzie, P.J.: A model of information practices in accounts of everyday-life information seeking. J. Doc. **59**(1), 19–40 (2003)
14. Micheli, P., et al.: Design thinking: a review of the literature. Creat. Innov. Manag. **28**(2), 124–138 (2019)
15. Saarnik, S.: Information access and service fragmentation in rural welfare systems. J. Soc. Policy. **50**(3), 421–439 (2021)
16. Sadler, G.R., et al.: Recruitment of hard-to-reach populations via snowball sampling. Nurs. Health Sci. **12**(3), 369–374 (2010)
17. Simms, M.D.: The impact of foster care on child development. Pediatrics. **106**(5), 1145–1150 (2000)
18. Strijker, J., et al.: Placement stability and foster care outcomes. Child Youth Serv. Rev. **30**(2), 125–136 (2008)

HMI-Questionnaires: A Community-Driven, Open-Access Project for Human-Machine Interaction Scales

Moritz Schmidt(✉), Insa Schaffernak, Lara Watermann, Simone Kubowitsch, Sarah Hatfield, Eva Lermer, Alexandra Teynor, and Claudia Meitinger

Technical University of Applied Sciences Augsburg, Augsburg, Germany
{Moritz.Schmidt,Insa.Schaffernak,Lara.Watermann,Simone.Kubowitsch, Sarah.Hatfield,Eva.Lermer,Alexandra.Teynor,Claudia.Meitinger}@tha.de

Abstract. Questionnaires are essential tools in Human-Machine Interaction (HMI) research for evaluating human factors. However, two major challenges persist in this interdisciplinary field: first, the use of self-constructed and non-validated scales, which exacerbates the replication crisis; and second, the increasing development of new questionnaires, which makes it difficult for researchers to maintain an overview and choose appropriate questionnaires. Additionally, existing resources that aim to provide an overview of published questionnaires often fall short due to limited functionalities, e.g., lacking filtering options, being language-specific, missing questionnaires, or no contribution possibilities.

To address these challenges, we developed *HMI-Questionnaires*, an open-source, community-driven website designed to consolidate HMI scales for the interdisciplinary research field. The website features an intuitive design, for desktop and mobile, with searchable tables and filtering functions on different categories, e.g. available languages, subscales or questionnaire names. In addition to the overview table with filtering categories, a detailed view is available with further information, including reported reliability metrics. This enables researchers to efficiently identify and compare questionnaires tailored to their needs.

HMI-Questionnaires (https://tha-embedded-systems-lab.github.io/HMI-Questionnaires/.) represents a first step toward creating a comprehensive, community-driven baseline. We actively encourage people to share feedback, report problems or suggest improvements, leveraging the open design of the platform to expand quality criteria and improve the resource over time. By crowdsourcing contributions, the repository ensures continuous updates and peer validation, fostering collaborative methodological rigor.

Ultimately, *HMI-Questionnaires* bridges the gap between fragmented literature and practical research needs, empowering the interdisciplinary HMI community with a dynamic, accessible, and up-to-date tool for increasing the use of validated questionnaires in future publications.

C. Stephanidis et al. (Eds.): HCII 2026, CCIS 3047, pp. 461–470, 2026.
https://doi.org/10.1007/978-3-032-30552-7_44

Keywords: Human-Machine Interaction · Human-Robot Interaction · Psychometric Validation · Questionnaire Repository · Reproducibility · Open-Source

1 Background

Research in Human-Machine Interaction (HMI) predominantly addresses latent psychological constructs such as trust, acceptance, and anthropomorphism, which are central for understanding how humans perceive, evaluate, and interact with automated and robotic systems [4,8]. As these constructs are not directly observable, they are typically operationalized using standardized self-report questionnaires and rating scales. Questionnaires therefore constitute a core methodological instrument in HMI and Human-Robot Interaction (HRI) and form the primary link between theoretical concepts and empirical measurement [5].

Over the past decades, a large number of domain-specific questionnaires has been developed, for instance to assess trust in automation, perceived safety, anthropomorphism, or user acceptance (e.g. [6,10]). Systematic reviews illustrate both the breadth of available instruments and the central role of questionnaire-based measures in evaluating human factors in interaction with intelligent systems [4,8]. Consequently, the psychometric quality, theoretical grounding, and transparency of these instruments are crucial for the validity, comparability, and cumulative value of empirical findings. Recent work by Saad et al. [9] shows that more than half of all papers at major HRI venues rely on self-report scales, while at the same time many researchers lack formal training in psychometrics. Their guideline-based analysis of widely used instruments (e.g., Godspeed, RoSAS) demonstrates that popularity does not necessarily imply sufficient validation and that reporting of reliability, factor structure, and construct definition is often incomplete.

At the same time, HRI shares many characteristics with other behavioral science disciplines that are affected by the replication and confidence crisis. Leichtmann et al. [7] argue that HRI user studies exhibit similar structural problems, including small sample sizes, limited statistical power, heterogeneous operationalizations of core constructs, insufficient theoretical integration, incomplete reporting, and the frequent use of newly developed or weakly validated measures. These issues undermine the replicability of results and reduce confidence in the robustness and generalizability of empirical effects.

Beyond replicability concerns, recent meta-scientific evidence points to a more fundamental problem of construct and measure proliferation. Anvari et al. [1] demonstrate that psychological science is characterized by a rapid and continuing growth of constructs and questionnaires, with little convergence toward shared definitions or standardized measures. Most newly proposed scales are rarely reused, leading to a fragmented literature, redundancy, and jingle and jangle fallacies, where the same labels denote different constructs and different labels refer to the same construct. The lack of common taxonomies and agreed-upon measurement standards hampers the synthesis of results and the accumulation of knowledge.

These developments are particularly salient for the interdisciplinary field of HMI, where numerous partially overlapping scales exist for closely related concepts such as trust in automation, trust in robots, acceptance, social presence, or anthropomorphism. Survey work on evaluation methods in HRI further highlights the heterogeneity of subjective measures and questionnaires used across studies and domains, with little standardization and limited support for systematic comparison [11]. For researchers, this results in substantial practical challenges: identifying suitable validated instruments is time-consuming, comparing findings across studies is difficult, and there is a persistent risk of unnecessarily introducing new, insufficiently validated questionnaires. Existing repositories and databases of measurement instruments are often domain-unspecific, incomplete, outdated, or lack advanced filtering and community-driven updating mechanisms, leaving no central, structured, and HMI-focused overview of available scales.

2 Objective

In response to these challenges, the objective of the *HMI-Questionnaires* project is to provide a central, open, and curated platform that systematically collects and structures questionnaires relevant to HMI research. The project aims to support researchers in identifying established and validated instruments for key psychological constructs, thereby facilitating informed scale selection and reducing the need for redundant scale.

Fig. 1. Scan the QR code to access the *HMI-Questionnaires* repository on GitHub (left) and the *HMI-Questionnaires* website (right)

By making reliability indices, subscales, item counts, language versions, and conceptual assignments transparent, the project seeks to improve comparability across studies and to foster the use of psychometrically sound measures. In doing so, it directly addresses key factors contributing to the replication and confidence crisis, such as heterogeneous operationalizations and insufficient reporting, and supports cumulative and reproducible research practices, in line with recent calls for more rigorous scale evaluation and documentation in HRI [9].

Furthermore, the project aims to counteract construct and measure proliferation by structuring the existing landscape of questionnaires and making conceptual relations between scales explicit. Grouping instruments under higher-level constructs (e.g., trust, acceptance, social presence) and providing standardized metadata enables researchers to identify overlaps, redundancies, and gaps in current measurement practices, as well as to navigate the heterogeneous evaluation landscape described in recent HRI surveys [11].

A core design principle of *HMI-Questionnaires* is its community-driven approach. Instead of a static database, the platform is conceived as an open, continuously evolving resource that allows contributions, corrections, and extensions via issues and pull requests. This crowdsourced model supports long-term maintenance, transparency, and peer-based quality assurance, while keeping the platform up to date with newly published instruments and validation studies.

Overall, *HMI-Questionnaires* aims to bridge the gap between fragmented measurement practices and the practical needs of researchers by offering an accessible, structured, and collaborative infrastructure. By promoting the use of validated scales, enhancing transparency, and supporting conceptual integration, the project seeks to contribute to greater methodological rigor, comparability, and cumulative knowledge building in HMI and HRI research.

3 Characteristics

The HMI Questionnaire Application is a web-based platform designed to facilitate the discovery and selection of standardized questionnaires for HMI research by providing a centralized, searchable repository with rich metadata about each questionnaire's characteristics, psychometric properties, and practical constraints.

3.1 Architectural Approach

The system implements a single-page web application architecture that runs entirely in the user's browser. This design choice reflects several key trade-offs tailored to the needs of the research community:

Client-Side Processing vs. Server Infrastructure. Rather than implementing a traditional client-server architecture with a backend database, all questionnaire data is embedded directly in the application. This decision prioritizes:

- **Accessibility:** No authentication, no server costs for the hosting lab, no institutional barriers—any researcher can access the website immediately. Contributing requires a GitHub account.
- **Reliability:** No additional server downtime or maintenance windows that could disrupt research workflows other than the GitHub Server where the website is hosted.
- **Performance:** Instant filtering and search without network latency.
- **Sustainability:** Minimal technical infrastructure ensures long-term availability without ongoing funding.

The trade-off is a loss of dynamic features like user-contributed ratings or real-time updates. However, for a curated repository of standardized instruments, where new questionnaires are published relatively infrequently and undergo peer review, this limitation was assessed as acceptable.

Data as Code. The data structure supports versioning through standard software development practices, allowing community contributions through a transparent review process.

Questionnaire metadata is stored as structured data within the application codebase rather than in a separate database. This approach treats data with the same rigor as code: changes are version-controlled, peer-reviewed, and documented. This results in several advantages:

- Complete audit trail of all changes
- Ability to cite specific versions with persistent identifiers
- Community contribution through standard open-source workflows
- Type checking to prevent structural errors in metadata

3.2 Information Architecture for Questionnaire Metadata

Design Principles. The data model reflects the practical decision-making process researchers undergo when selecting measurement instruments. Each questionnaire entry captures information organized around four key questions:

1. **What does it measure?** Scales, constructs, and dimensional structure
2. **How well does it measure?** Psychometric properties, specifically reliability coefficients
3. **Can I use it?** Practical constraints including language availability, and length
4. **Where can I find the original?** References to original websites and links to papers

Multidimensional Metadata Structure. Each questionnaire is characterized by multiple dimensions of metadata:

Temporal Dimension. Questionnaires are classified by when they could be administered: pre-study (baseline measures), post-study (overall evaluation), or standalone requiring no accompanying experiment. This classification is critical for experimental design, as it affects both construct validity and practical feasibility.

Linguistic Dimension. The system tracks language availability for each questionnaire, recognizing that psychometric properties may not generalize across translations. Where available, language-specific validation data can be maintained separately, allowing researchers to assess whether a translated version has been properly validated for their target population.

Psychometric Dimension. For each scale within a questionnaire, reliability coefficients (Cronbach's alpha) and validation sample characteristics are recorded when available in the literature. This enables evidence-based instrument selection rather than selection by convention or familiarity.

Structured Flexibility. The data model balances standardization with flexibility. Core attributes are required for all entries, ensuring minimum viable information for filtering and comparison. Optional fields accommodate the heterogeneity of available validation literature—some questionnaires have extensive validation across multiple languages and populations, while others have limited published psychometric data despite widespread use.

3.3 User Interface and Interaction Design

Progressive Disclosure Strategy. The interface design addresses a fundamental tension in information presentation: researchers need access to rich, detailed metadata to make informed decisions, but presenting all information simultaneously creates cognitive overload. The solution employs progressive disclosure—displaying summary information in a scannable table format while providing detailed information on demand.

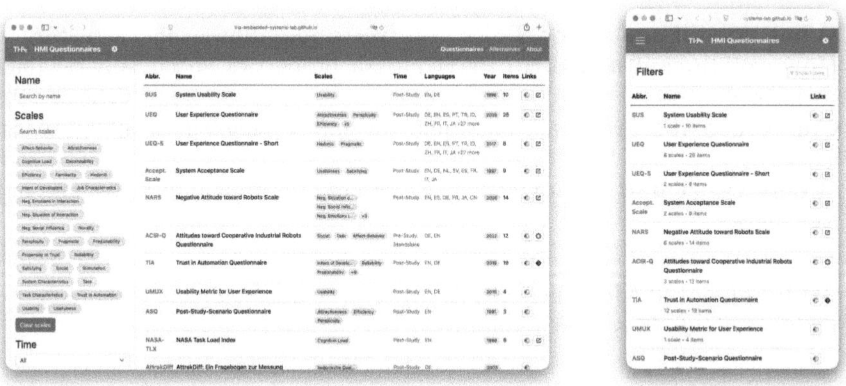

Fig. 2. The implemented website displayed on a desktop (left) and phone (right).

The main table view presents the minimum information needed for initial screening: questionnaire name and abbreviation, number of scales and items, administration timing, and available languages. Researchers can quickly scan questionnaires to identify candidates. Clicking a row opens a detailed modal with comprehensive psychometric information, validation study details, links to original sources, and notes.

Multi-criteria Filtering. The filtering interface supports the complex, multi-faceted decision process researchers employ when selecting instruments. Filters include:

- **Text search**: For researchers who recall partial names or abbreviations
- **Scale/construct selection**: For those seeking measures of specific constructs
- **Administration timing**: To ensure compatibility with study design
- **Language availability**: Ensuring the questionnaire is available in a language that is feasible for the target audience.

All filters operate on the complete dataset, providing immediate feedback. This supports exploratory browsing—researchers can iteratively refine criteria to discover instruments they might not have known to search for explicitly.

Responsive Design Considerations. The interface adapts to different contexts of use. On desktop displays with ample screen space, the filter panel remains persistently visible alongside the results table, supporting rapid iteration, see Fig. 2. On mobile devices, filters collapse into an expandable panel, prioritizing the results view while keeping filtering accessible. Similarly, the results table progressively hides less-critical columns on smaller screens, maintaining readability without horizontal scrolling, see Fig. 2.

This responsive design acknowledges that researchers may consult the tool in different contexts—at a desktop workstation during study planning, on a tablet during a lab meeting, or on a phone when reviewing options in transit.

4 Code and Usage Notes

HMI-Questionnaires is maintained as an open-source GitHub repository[1]. The project includes the full source code of the website, data files for questionnaire entries, and contribution templates. Usage is browser-based: users can search and filter questionnaires by key metadata (e.g., construct, language, sub-scales, number of items, and reported reliability) to identify candidate instruments for a specific study context. Contribution workflows and data-entry conventions are documented in the Contribution Guide[2]. This external documentation is continuously updated and therefore serves as the authoritative reference for installation, maintenance, and community contributions.

[1] https://github.com/THA-Embedded-Systems-Lab/HMI-Questionnaires.
[2] https://github.com/THA-Embedded-Systems-Lab/HMI-Questionnaires/blob/main/docs/ContributionGuide.md.

5 Discussion

The main strength of *HMI-Questionnaires* is broad accessibility: Researchers can quickly identify and compare instruments that would otherwise remain fragmented across domains and publication venues. At the same time, this breadth introduces methodological challenges.

First, construct ambiguity remains a core issue. Many scales use similar labels (e.g., trust, distrust, or propensity to trust) while measuring conceptually distinct phenomena. A purely name-based search is therefore useful for discovery but insufficient for conceptual precision.

Second, community-driven growth can introduce coverage bias. Highly cited scales (e.g., SUS [2] or NASA-TLX [3]) are likely to be overrepresented, whereas less visible or recently published questionnaires may be underreported. Continuous community contributions are necessary to reduce this imbalance.

Third, there is a deliberate trade-off between inclusiveness and strict quality selection. The platform is intended as a discovery and pre-selection tool, not as a substitute for a detailed psychometric evaluation. Researchers must still assess validity evidence, target population fit, translation quality, and study context before final instrument selection.

Overall, the repository supports methodological transparency and more informed questionnaire selection, while preserving researcher responsibility for rigorous final decisions.

6 Outlook/Conclusion

HMI-Questionnaires provides a practical baseline for more systematic and transparent questionnaire selection in HMI research. By combining open access, structured metadata, and community contribution mechanisms, the platform lowers the barrier to using validated instruments and supports reproducible study design.

Future work will focus on concept-level structuring across related scales, improved metadata completeness, and expanded international coverage. In particular, mapping questionnaires to higher-level constructs (e.g., trust in automation vs. trait trust propensity) can improve both search quality and theoretical alignment.

We invite the research community to contribute new entries, corrections, and quality annotations via GitHub issues and pull requests, see Fig. 1. Sustained community participation is essential to keep the repository current, representative, and methodologically useful over time.

Acknowledgments. This publication was created as part of the AI Production Network Augsburg research project funded by StMWK (H.6-M2126.5.2.2.1/1/1/1) at the Technical University of Applied Sciences Augsburg. This work also received funding from the Bavarian Ministry for Sciences and Art (project PSY-A-EYE) and the Bavarian Ministry of Economic Affairs, Regional Development and Energy (project DaTeam-VR). The authors thank all institutions for enabling this project.

Disclosure of Interests. The authors have no competing interests to declare that are relevant to the content of this article.

References

1. Anvari, F., et al.: A fragmented field: construct and measure proliferation in psychology. Adv. Methods Pract. Psychol. Sci. **8**(3), 25152459251360640 (2025). https://doi.org/10.1177/25152459251360642
2. Brooke, J.: SUS: a quick and dirty usability scale. Usabil. Eval. Ind. **189** (1995)
3. Hart, S.: Development of NASA-TLX (task load index): results of empirical and theoretical research. In: Advances in Psychology, vol. 52, pp. 139–183. Elsevier (1988). https://doi.org/10.1016/S0166-4115(08)62386-9,
4. Hoff, K.A., Bashir, M.: Trust in automation: integrating empirical evidence on factors that influence trust. Hum. Factors: J. Hum. Factors Ergon. Soc. **57**(3), 407–434 (2015). https://doi.org/10.1177/0018720814547570
5. Hornbæk, K., Law, E.L.C.: Meta-analysis of correlations among usability measures. In: Proceedings of the SIGCHI Conference on Human Factors in Computing Systems, pp. 617–626. ACM, San Jose California USA (2007). https://doi.org/10.1145/1240624.1240722
6. Körber, M.: Theoretical considerations and development of a questionnaire to measure trust in automation. In: Bagnara, S., Tartaglia, R., Albolino, S., Alexander, T., Fujita, Y. (eds.) IEA 2018. AISC, vol. 823, pp. 13–30. Springer, Cham (2019). https://doi.org/10.1007/978-3-319-96074-6_2
7. Leichtmann, B., Nitsch, V., Mara, M.: Crisis ahead? Why human-robot interaction user studies may have replicability problems and directions for improvement. Front. Robot. AI **9**, 838116 (2022). https://doi.org/10.3389/frobt.2022.838116
8. Pinto, A., Solovov, A., Simões, A.C., Menezes, P.: User acceptance in human-robot interaction: exploring the role of anthropomorphic mechanisms in manufacturing environments-a systematic literature review. J. Intell. Robot. Syst. **111**(2), 46 (2025). https://doi.org/10.1007/s10846-025-02248-x
9. Saad, L., Roesler, E., Phillips, E., Trafton, J.G.: Choosing the "perfect" scale: a primer to evaluate existing scales in HRI. ACM Trans. Hum.-Rob. .Interact. **15**(2), 1–29 (2026). https://doi.org/10.1145/3772066
10. Van Der Laan, J.D., Heino, A., De Waard, D.: A simple procedure for the assessment of acceptance of advanced transport telematics. Transp. Res. Part C: Emerg. Technol. **5**(1), 1–10 (1997). https://doi.org/10.1016/S0968-090X(96)00025-3
11. Wachowiak, L., Celiktutan, O., Coles, A., Canal, G.: A survey of evaluation methods and metrics for explanations in human-robot interaction (HRI). In: Explainable Robotics Workshop at IEEE International Conference on Robotics and Automation (ICRA) (2023)

From Self-report toSituated Behavior: Uncovering Information Evaluation Patterns ofAuthority-Dependent Users through System-Mediated Observation

Hyungwoo Song[1], Jeongha Kim[2], Minju Kim[2], and Hyunggu Jung[2](✉)

[1] Department of Intelligence and Information, Seoul National University, Seoul, Republic of Korea

[2] College of Nursing, Seoul National University, Seoul, Republic of Korea

Abstract. Prior research on authority-dependent users' information evaluation has relied primarily on self-report methods such as interviews, which may not fully capture how cognitive habits manifest during situated interaction. This study employs a two-phase investigative approach with North Korean defectors as an extreme case: qualitative inquiry first identified self-reported barriers (authority reliance, help-seeking inhibition, and conceptual gaps), and a need-informed prototype then served as an observational probe to surface behavioral patterns during information evaluation tasks. Scenario-based observation with six participants revealed three behavioral patterns not captured by self-report alone: persistent authority bias coexisting with private chatbot questioning, persona-mediated relief from social-behavioral inhibition, and conceptual misalignment rooted in divergent medical frameworks rather than vocabulary alone. These findings contribute an empirical characterization of authority-dependent evaluation at the behavioral level, demonstrate the utility of need-informed prototypes as observational probes, and offer design implications for multi-source information systems supporting users transitioning from closed to open information environments.

Keywords: Authority-dependent users · North Korean defectors · Multi-source information environments · Extreme user design

1 Introduction

Contemporary information systems present users with information from multiple sources of varying credibility, implicitly expecting autonomous evaluation of source reliability [20,21]. However, this capacity is not universally shared. For individuals socialized in authority-dependent information paradigms, information evaluation is shaped by prolonged reliance on singular, trusted authorities rather than comparative assessment across multiple sources [24,29]. North Korean defectors represent an extreme case of this transition, having lived under

C. Stephanidis et al. (Eds.): HCII 2026, CCIS 3047, pp. 471–481, 2026.
https://doi.org/10.1007/978-3-032-30552-7_45

one of the most tightly controlled information systems globally [7,31], and emergency medical contexts provide a particularly revealing domain for examining how such cognitive habits shape evaluation under time pressure.

Prior HCI research on displaced populations has focused largely on access-level barriers such as digital literacy [2,5,6], with less attention to how individuals evaluate credibility once encountered. Moreover, existing understanding of these populations' information challenges has been derived primarily from interview-based self-report [5,14,28]. Research on credibility evaluation has demonstrated discrepancies between self-reported and observed behavior: Flanagin and Metzger [12] found a negative relationship between self-reported and observed verification behavior, and interview-based approaches have been critiqued for capturing "not what people do, but what people say they think and do" [15].

To address this limitation, we employ a two-phase investigative approach with North Korean defectors as an extreme case [10]. We first conducted qualitative inquiry to identify self-reported barriers, including reliance on authoritative hierarchy, social-behavioral inhibition in help-seeking, and conceptual gaps in medical terminology. We then designed a multi-source emergency medical information prototype informed by these barriers and conducted scenario-based observations, using the prototype as an observational probe where participants' cognitive habits could be observed during actual information evaluation tasks.

Through this approach, we identified behavioral patterns that extended beyond what self-report alone had revealed: the co-occurrence of authority bias with private questioning, persona-mediated reduction of help-seeking inhibition, and conceptual misalignment rooted in divergent medical frameworks rather than vocabulary deficits alone. This study contributes an empirical characterization of authority-dependent evaluation at the behavioral level, a methodological demonstration of using need-informed prototypes as observational probes, and design implications for multi-source information systems supporting users transitioning from closed to open information environments.

2 Related Work

Research on online information credibility has established that users commonly rely on cognitive heuristics such as source reputation and authority cues rather than systematic evaluation [20,21,30]. For individuals whose information experience has been shaped by a single authoritative source, these heuristics may be particularly resistant to recalibration, reflecting default trust in testimony rather than calibrated trust through source variability [24,27]. However, these findings have been derived primarily from self-report methods [12,21]; Meinert and Krämer [19] noted that existing studies "merely give indications, for example, based on individuals' self-report" without testing behavioral prerequisites.

HCI research on displaced populations has expanded from addressing access barriers [2] to examining social and cultural dimensions of technology use [5,28], yet has largely focused on populations from partially open information environments. Recent work has begun to address North Korean defectors specifically, with Song et al. [26] identifying clinical consultation as a critical barrier in defectors' patient journeys due to difficulties in expressing symptoms and navigating language differences. Methodologically, however, this body of research has relied heavily on interviews [5,14]; Jacobsen and Landau [14] found that "in all the articles" they reviewed, "data collection methodologies relied on interviews of some kind." While Fisher [11] has advocated for participatory field methods, behavioral observation during situated information evaluation remains underutilized.

Prior work on culturally adaptive interfaces has advanced beyond surface-level translation [25], yet often leaves underlying assumptions about authority unexamined. The ACRL Framework's assertion that "Authority Is Constructed and Contextual" [3] underscores the need for designs that account for users whose understanding of authority differs fundamentally from dominant norms. Taken together, prior work leaves open how authority-dependent users evaluate multi-source information at the behavioral level of situated interaction.

3 Method

This study employed an exploratory approach grounded in extreme user design [10], structured in two sequential phases: (1) qualitative inquiry through semi-structured interviews to identify self-reported barriers, and (2) scenario-based observation through a need-informed prototype to surface behavioral patterns during situated information evaluation.

3.1 Participants

Six North Korean defectors participated (see Table 1), recruited through a community organization with purposive sampling for variation in age (20 s–60 s), gender (three male, three female), and duration of residence in South Korea (6–23 years). This sample size aligns with qualitative research guidelines for in-depth phenomenological investigation [9] and with extreme user design, which prioritizes analytical depth over statistical representativeness [10]. Extreme selection is warranted because individuals from fully closed information systems exhibit authority-dependent cognitive habits in their most pronounced form. Studying such individuals makes behavioral patterns observable that would otherwise be attenuated in populations with partial prior exposure to source plurality.

3.2 Procedure

Phase 1: Qualitative Inquiry (Weeks 1–3). Semi-structured interviews (60 min) addressed prior information experiences in North Korea, current emergency medical experiences in South Korea, and responses to hypothetical scenarios involving conflicting health information. All interviews followed trauma-informed protocols [13], including advance written topic disclosure, the option to pause without explanation, and post-interview debriefing with a trained support

Table 1. Demographics of participants.

ID	Age	Gender	Years in South Korea	Years in Transit
P1	30–40	Male	23	1
P2	30–40	Female	8	4
P3	50–60	Female	23	1
P4	30–40	Male	10	2
P5	20–30	Female	6	4
P6	50–60	Male	23	1

coordinator. This phase yielded three self-reported barriers: persistent reliance on authoritative hierarchy, social-behavioral inhibition in help-seeking due to perceived stigma, and conceptual gaps in South Korean medical terminology.

Phase 2: Prototype Design (Weeks 4–5). Based on the Phase 1 findings, we designed a multi-source emergency medical information prototype with two core components addressing the identified barriers: a multi-source evaluation interface informed by inoculation theory [18] to address authority reliance, and a chatbot with an informal persona to address help-seeking inhibition.

Phase 3: Expert Review (Week 6). Three HCI experts with an usability evaluation experience independently assessed the prototype against Nielsen's usability heuristics [22]. This review identified issues such as insufficient contrast between source labels and background, complex navigation for switching between the Guidelines and AI Assistant tabs, and ambiguous iconography for the timer function. These issues were resolved through refinements including high-contrast source labels, a persistent tab bar, and an explicit countdown display.

3.3 Prototype as Observational Probe

The evaluation task consisted of three emergency scenarios (cardiac arrest, severe allergic reaction, burn injury), each requiring participants to consult multiple information sources and select appropriate actions from 4–5 options under a five-minute countdown timer.

The interface comprised two primary tabs (Fig. 1). The Guidelines tab displayed information from multiple named sources, including official medical institutions, alternative sources, and anonymous community forums with varying institutional authority. Some authoritative-sounding sources contained deliberately incorrect information, while some informal sources provided accurate guidance, enabling observation of whether selection was driven by authority cues regardless of accuracy. The AI Assistant tab offered a chatbot employing Retrieval-Augmented Generation (RAG) [17], generating medically accurate responses grounded in Korean medical guidelines [8] and adapted through North Korean medical dictionaries [16]. The chatbot's informal persona was designed based on Phase 1 findings regarding help-seeking inhibition. After each scenario, a Feedback page explained the correctness of each action and its source.

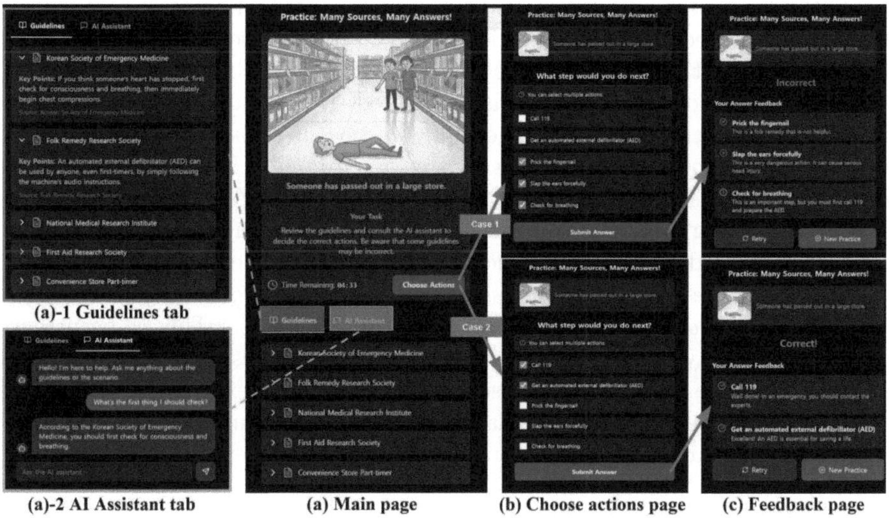

Fig. 1. Interface and system flow: (a-1) Guidelines tab showing multiple sources, (a-2) AI Assistant tab with conversational chatbot, (a) Main page with scenario description, (b) Choose actions page, (c) Feedback page with explanations.

Phase 4: Scenario-Based Observation (Weeks 7–8). Each participant completed three emergency scenarios in a single 45-minute session with counterbalanced order, followed by a 15-minute interview. The primary purpose was not to evaluate prototype effectiveness but to observe how self-reported barriers manifested as behavioral patterns during situated information evaluation.

3.4 Data Collection and Analysis

We collected think-aloud verbalizations, post-task interview transcripts, source consultation patterns (order and frequency), action selection accuracy, and chatbot interaction logs. Qualitative data were analyzed using reflexive thematic analysis [4], with two researchers independently coding and resolving disagreements through iterative discussion. Behavioral data were summarized descriptively as complementary evidence.

4 Findings

Scenario-based observation revealed three behavioral patterns that extend beyond what Phase 1 interviews alone had captured.

4.1 Pattern 1: Persistent Authority Bias with Private Questioning

Phase 1 interviews indicated general reliance on authoritative sources, consistent with participants' socialization in a single-authority information environment. However, observation revealed a more nuanced dual pattern: participants initially gravitated toward institutional sources but subsequently shifted their primary consultation to the private chatbot.

Five out of six participants initially selected the institutional source regardless of content accuracy. P3 explained: *"In North Korea, we were taught that the government's information is always correct. Even though I know South Korea is different, I still feel safer following the official source"*. Yet all six participants exhibited a strong preference for the chatbot when resolving uncertainty, reporting that it enabled private exploration of doubts without perceived judgment. P5 stated: *"With the chatbot, I can ask stupid questions without anyone knowing. If I asked a doctor this, they would think I am ignorant"*. This co-occurrence of initial authority adherence and subsequent private questioning suggests that authority reliance and information-seeking agency may coexist rather than being mutually exclusive, a distinction that self-report alone would be unlikely to capture. Table 2 summarizes source consultation patterns.

Table 2. Source consultation frequency across three emergency scenarios (N =6). "First consulted" indicates the source participants accessed first; "Most consulted" indicates the source accessed most frequently within each scenario.

Source Type	First Consulted	Most Consulted
Official medical institution	5/6 (83%)	3/6 (50%)
Chatbot (AI Assistant)	1/6 (17%)	4/6 (67%)
Folk/alternative source	0/6 (0%)	0/6 (0%)
Community forum	0/6 (0%)	1/6 (17%)

4.2 Pattern 2: Social-Behavioral Inhibition and Persona-Mediated Relief

Phase 1 interviews identified shame-based avoidance as a barrier to seeking medical help, with five out of six participants reporting reluctance to ask questions in clinical settings. Observation provided behavioral specificity: the chatbot's informal persona was associated with observable changes in questioning behavior, including reduced avoidance of questions, increased follow-up inquiries, and decreased pretense of comprehension.

P2 described: *"At the hospital, I pretend I understand because I do not want to look foolish. But with this chatbot, I asked the same question three times and it never made me feel bad"*. P6 contrasted: *"Korean doctors use difficult words, and when I ask them to explain, they look annoyed. The chatbot just explains again, more simply"*. Across scenarios, participants asked an average of 4.7 questions per scenario, with follow-up questions (requesting clarification or simpler explanations) accounting for 58% of all queries. This high proportion of follow-up questions, a behavioral indicator unavailable from interview data alone, suggests that the reduction in inhibition encouraged iterative engagement rather than superficial comprehension.

4.3 Pattern 3: Conceptual Misalignment Beyond Vocabulary

Phase 1 interviews framed terminology difficulty primarily as a vocabulary problem amenable to lexical translation. Observation revealed that the challenge extended to conceptual misalignment: cases where South Korean medical terms mapped onto fundamentally different explanatory frameworks in North Korean medical practice, rather than merely lacking equivalent lexical items.

P4 explained: *"I know the word 'defibrillator' now, but I do not understand why you would use electricity on someone whose heart stopped. In North Korea, we would try to warm the body"*. This example illustrates that the barrier is not the absence of a word but the incongruence between the biomedical rationale underlying the term and the participant's prior medical framework. Table 3 presents the types of comprehension errors observed. Conceptual misalignment was the most frequent error type (11 instances), exceeding simple vocabulary gaps (7 instances) and affecting all participants. This distribution indicates that cultural-linguistic adaptation requires addressing divergent explanatory frameworks, not merely substituting unfamiliar terms with familiar equivalents.

Table 3. Types of comprehension errors observed during scenario-based observation (N = 6, three scenarios per participant, 18 scenario instances total).

Error Type	Instances	Participants Affected
Vocabulary gap (unknown term)	7	4/6
Conceptual misalignment	11	6/6
Procedural confusion (action sequence)	5	3/6
Source misattribution	3	2/6

5 Discussion

The behavioral patterns identified through system-mediated observation extend the understanding of authority-dependent information evaluation in two respects. First, self-reported barriers do not fully predict the complexity of situated behavior; authority reliance coexists with active private questioning rather than precluding it. Second, dimensions such as the predominance of conceptual misalignment over vocabulary gaps are difficult to surface without structured interaction environments that elicit observable evaluation behavior.

5.1 Design Implications

DI1: Provide Conversational Mechanisms for Questioning Authoritative Information. The co-occurrence of authority bias and chatbot preference suggests that interfaces should offer low-pressure channels for questioning authoritative sources, such as side-by-side source comparisons with guided prompts, aligning with inoculation-based strategies [18].

DI2: Employ Persona-Based Interaction with Informal Conversational Styles. The observed changes (reduced avoidance of initial questions, increased follow-up inquiries, and decreased pretense of comprehension) suggest that persona design is a critical variable for populations acculturated to hierarchical communication norms. Design guidelines include using casual register, normalizing repeated questions through explicit reassurance (e.g., acknowledging that re-asking is expected), and avoiding evaluative or judgmental responses.

DI3: Implement Conceptual Framework Bridging Beyond Word-Level Translation. The prevalence of conceptual misalignment indicates that effective cultural adaptation requires first identifying users' prior explanatory frameworks and then providing bridging explanations that connect unfamiliar biomedical concepts to users' existing knowledge. This finding converges with Song et al. [26], who reported that language differences in clinical consultations constitute a persistent barrier for North Korean defectors beyond vocabulary-level difficulty. Because such conceptual bridging is inherently context-dependent, varying with the user's cultural background, the specific medical concept, and the situational demands, static dictionary-based translation is insufficient. Retrieval-Augmented Generation based systems are well suited for this purpose, as they can retrieve culturally grounded explanations from curated knowledge bases while maintaining factual accuracy through evidence-grounded generation [17].

5.2 Future Research Directions

Establishing causal relationships between design features and behavioral outcomes requires comparative studies with baseline conditions. Longitudinal studies are needed to examine whether sustained interaction fosters independent evaluation skills or reinforces system reliance. Future work could also explore adaptive persona styles and extend this approach to other authority-dependent populations transitioning from closed information environments, such as refugees from other authoritarian contexts, as well as to other information domains including financial and civic information.

6 Ethical Considerations and Limitations

This study received Institutional Review Board approval from Seoul National University. All participants provided written informed consent, with forms available in both standard and simplified language accommodating North Korean dialectal differences. Data were de-identified with particular attention to identity disclosure risks specific to the defector population [1,23]. The inclusion of deliberately incorrect authoritative sources was motivated by inoculation theory [18]; all incorrect information was identified and corrected during the feedback phase and post-session debriefing. We acknowledge a tension between fostering autonomous evaluation through controlled exposure to misleading sources and the risk of reinforcing distrust toward legitimate authorities, particularly for populations already navigating unfamiliar information environments. This tension warrants careful monitoring in future deployments.

Several limitations warrant consideration. First, the sample of six participants limits generalizability; findings should be treated as indicative patterns rather than established conclusions. Second, as the primary purpose was behavioral observation rather than effectiveness evaluation, the study lacks baseline comparisons; associations between design features and observed behaviors are suggestive rather than causal. Third, the emergency medical context and controlled setting may not generalize to real-world deployment conditions.

7 Conclusion

This study demonstrates the value of complementing self-report with system-mediated behavioral observation to investigate authority-dependent users' information evaluation in situated contexts. Using North Korean defectors as an extreme case, our two-phase approach (qualitative inquiry followed by scenario-based observation through a need-informed prototype) revealed three behavioral patterns that interviews alone did not surface: the dual structure of authority bias and private questioning, persona-mediated relief from social-behavioral inhibition, and conceptual misalignment rooted in divergent medical frameworks rather than vocabulary deficits alone. These findings provide empirical grounding for designing multi-source information systems that support users transitioning from closed to open information environments. As global displacement increases and authoritarian governance persists, understanding how cognitive habits shaped by closed information paradigms translate into situated evaluation behaviors becomes increasingly important for inclusive information system.

Acknowledgments. This work was supported by the New Faculty Startup Fund from Seoul National University. This work was also supported by the National Research Foundation of Korea (NRF) grant funded by the Korea government (MSIT) (No. RS-2024-00407105). During the preparation of this manuscript, the authors used a large language model for AI-assisted copy editing purposes, including grammar and readability improvements. The authors reviewed and edited all outputs and take full responsibility for the content of this publication.

Disclosure of Interests. The authors have no competing interests to declare that are relevant to the content of this article.

Data Availability Statement. The qualitative data generated during this study (interview transcripts, think-aloud verbalizations, and chatbot interaction logs) are not publicly available due to the heightened identity disclosure risks specific to the North Korean defector population [1,23]. Anonymized summary data supporting the findings are available from the corresponding author upon reasonable request.

References

1. Ahn, J.H., Kim, W.H., Choi, H.J., Jeon, J.Y., Song, I.G., Bae, J.N.: Stigma of mental illnesses as perceived by North Korean defectors living in South Korea. Psychiatry Investig. **12**(1), 9–15 (2015). https://doi.org/10.4306/pi.2015.12.1.9
2. Andrade, A.D., Doolin, B.: Information and communication technology and the social inclusion of refugees. MIS Q. **40**(2), 405–416 (2016). https://doi.org/10.25300/MISQ/2016/40.2.06
3. Association of College and Research Libraries: Framework for Information Literacy for Higher Education. American Library Association, Chicago (2015)
4. Braun, V., Clarke, V.: Using thematic analysis in psychology. Qual. Res. Psychol. **3**(2), 77–101 (2006). https://doi.org/10.1191/1478088706qp063oa
5. Bustamante Duarte, A.M., Degbelo, A., Kray, C.: A decade of international migration research in HCI: overview, challenges, ethics, impact, and future directions. ACM Trans. Comput.-Hum. Interact. **29**(2), 1–55 (2022). https://doi.org/10.1145/3502203
6. Caidi, N., Allard, D., Quirke, L.: Information practices of immigrants. Ann. Rev. Inf. Sci. Technol. **44**(1), 491–531 (2010). https://doi.org/10.1002/aris.2010.1440440119
7. Choi, J.: A comparative study on information control of mobile communication between North Korea and China/Vietnam. Korean J. Unification Affairs **34**(2), 197–238 (2022). https://doi.org/10.46561/KUA.2022.34.2.06
8. Choi, M., Kim, S.Y., Lee, Y.K.: Current status of clinical practice guidelines in Korea. J. Korean Med. Sci. **36**(6), e35 (2021). https://doi.org/10.3346/jkms.2021.36.e35
9. Creswell, J.W., Poth, C.N.: Qualitative Inquiry and Research Design: Choosing Among Five Approaches, 4th edn. Sage, Thousand Oaks (2018)
10. Djajadiningrat, J.P., Gaver, W.W., Fres, J.W.: Interaction relabelling and extreme characters: methods for exploring aesthetic interactions. In: Proceedings of the 3rd Conference on Designing Interactive Systems, pp. 66–71. ACM, New York (2000). https://doi.org/10.1145/347642.347664
11. Fisher, K.E.: People first, data second: a humanitarian research framework for fieldwork with refugees by war zones. Comput. Supported Coop. Work (CSCW) **31**, 237–297 (2022)
12. Flanagin, A.J., Metzger, M.J.: The role of site features, user attributes, and information verification behaviors on the perceived credibility of web-based information. New Media Soc. **9**(2), 319–342 (2007)
13. Isobel, S.: Trauma-informed qualitative research: some methodological and practical considerations. Int. J. Ment. Health Nurs. **30**(S1), 1456–1469 (2021). https://doi.org/10.1111/inm.12925
14. Jacobsen, K., Landau, L.: Researching refugees: some methodological and ethical considerations in an area of forced migration. New issues in refugee research, working paper no. 90, UNHCR (2003)
15. Jerolmack, C., Khan, S.: Talk is cheap: ethnography and the attitudinal fallacy. Sociol. Methods Res. **43**(2), 178–209 (2014)

16. Kim, Y.H.: Efforts to prepare inter-Korea medical consolidation: compilation of a medical dictionary for all of Korea. J. Korean Med. Assoc. **62**(10), 506–511 (2019). https://doi.org/10.5124/jkma.2019.62.10.506
17. Lewis, P., et al.: Retrieval-augmented generation for knowledge-intensive NLP tasks. In: Advances in Neural Information Processing Systems, vol. 33, pp. 9459–9474 (2020)
18. McGuire, W.J.: Resistance to persuasion conferred by active and passive prior refutation of the same and alternative counterarguments. J. Abnorm. Soc. Psychol. **63**(2), 326–332 (1961). https://doi.org/10.1037/h0048344
19. Meinert, J., Krämer, N.C.: How the expertise heuristic accelerates decision-making and credibility judgments in social media by means of effort reduction. PLoS ONE **17**(3), e0264428 (2022)
20. Metzger, M.J., Flanagin, A.J.: Credibility and trust of information in online environments: the use of cognitive heuristics. J. Pragmat. **59**, 210–220 (2013). https://doi.org/10.1016/j.pragma.2013.07.012
21. Metzger, M.J., Flanagin, A.J., Medders, R.B.: Social and heuristic approaches to credibility evaluation online. J. Commun. **60**(3), 413–439 (2010). https://doi.org/10.1111/j.1460-2466.2010.01488.x
22. Nielsen, J.: Heuristic evaluation. In: Nielsen, J., Mack, R.L. (eds.) Usability Inspection Methods, pp. 25–62. Wiley, New York (1994)
23. Noh, H., Yoon, S., Jo, H., Van Kleek, M., Kang, Y.: Starting a new life after crossing the tumen river: how north korean defectors use digital technology in transition. In: Proceedings of the 2024 CHI Conference on Human Factors in Computing Systems, CHI 2024. Association for Computing Machinery, New York (2024). https://doi.org/10.1145/3613904.3642892
24. Origgi, G.: Epistemic injustice and epistemic trust. Soc. Epistemol. **26**(2), 221–235 (2012). https://doi.org/10.1080/02691728.2011.652213
25. Reinecke, K., Bernstein, A.: Improving performance, perceived usability, and aesthetics with culturally adaptive user interfaces. ACM Trans. Comput.-Hum. Interact. **18**(2), 1–29 (2011). https://doi.org/10.1145/1970378.1970382
26. Song, H., et al.: "I should know, but I dare not ask": from understanding challenges in patient journeys to deriving design implications for North Korean defectors' adaptation. In: Proceedings of the 2026 CHI Conference on Human Factors in Computing Systems. CHI '26, Association for Computing Machinery, New York (2026). https://doi.org/10.1145/3772318.3790752
27. Sperber, D., et al.: Epistemic vigilance. Mind Lang. **25**(4), 359–393 (2010). https://doi.org/10.1111/j.1468-0017.2010.01394.x
28. Talhouk, R., et al.: Syrian refugees and digital health in Lebanon: opportunities for improving antenatal health. In: Proceedings of the 2016 CHI Conference on Human Factors in Computing Systems, pp. 331–342. ACM, New York (2016). https://doi.org/10.1145/2858036.2858331
29. Wang, C., Zhu, J., Zhang, D.: The paradox of information control under authoritarianism: explaining trust in competing messages in China. Political Studies (2024). https://doi.org/10.1177/00323217231191399
30. Wathen, C.N., Burkell, J.: Believe it or not: factors influencing credibility on the web. J. Am. Soc. Inform. Sci. Technol. **53**(2), 134–144 (2002). https://doi.org/10.1002/asi.10016
31. Williams, M.: Digital trenches: North Korea's information counter-offensive. Hrnk report, Committee for Human Rights in North Korea, Washington, D.C. (2019). https://www.hrnk.org/documentations/digital-trenches-north-koreas-information-counter-offensive/

Beyond the Lab: Capturing User Experience in the Wild with Psychophysiological Ambulatory Assessment

Magdalena K. Wekenborg[1(✉)], Christian Rominger[2], Elizabeth A. M. Michels[1], Isabella Wiest[1], Lonni Treiber[1], Andreas R. Schwerdtfeger[2], and Jakob N. Kather[1,3,4,5]

[1] Else Kroener Fresenius Center for Digital Health, Faculty of Medicine and University Hospital Carl Gustav Carus, TUD Dresden University of Technology, Dresden, Germany
magdalena.wekenborg@tu-dresden.de

[2] Institute of Psychology, University of Graz, Graz, Austria

[3] Department of Medicine I, Faculty of Medicine and University Hospital Carl Gustav Carus, TUD Dresden University of Technology, Dresden, Germany

[4] Medical Oncology, National Center for Tumor Diseases (NCT), University Hospital Heidelberg, Heidelberg, Germany

[5] Pathology & Data Analytics, Leeds Institute of Medical Research at St James's, University of Leeds, Leeds, United Kingdom

Abstract. Introduction: Digital workplace systems increasingly integrate automation and decision-support functionalities into workflows. Evaluating user experience (UX) under real-world conditions therefore requires methods that capture interaction as it unfolds in situ. However, most UX research remains confined to laboratory studies or retrospective self-reports, limiting ecological validity.

Objective: We aimed to empirically validate a multimodal ambulatory UX assessment toolkit for real-world work settings. Specifically, we tested (i) whether core UX components predict momentary system appraisal during actual use; (ii) whether real-time assessment adds explanatory value beyond retrospective questionnaires; and (iii) whether physiological measures provide incremental information beyond self-report.

Method: Of 25 recruited professionals, 22 completed an ambulatory protocol during routine interaction with a tumor documentation system, yielding 449 UX observations. The design combined randomized in-situ UX assessments, continuous wearable heart rate variability (HRV) monitoring, and a retrospective baseline questionnaire.

Results: Multilevel analyses showed that instrumental and non-instrumental quality independently predicted momentary system appraisal ($b = 0.27–0.66$, $p \leq 0.01$). Affective states showed neither significant direct nor mediating effects. Retrospective UX scores did not converge with ambulatory measures and explained substantially less variance in momentary system appraisal (overall evaluation $R^2m = 0.07$ vs. 0.29). HRV provided complementary but not incremental predictive information for system appraisal.

Supplementary Information The online version contains supplementary material available at https://doi.org/10.1007/978-3-032-30552-7_46.

C. Stephanidis et al. (Eds.): HCII 2026, CCIS 3047, pp. 482–492, 2026.
https://doi.org/10.1007/978-3-032-30552-7_46

Conclusion: Modeling UX during active interaction with a digital workplace system in real-world settings is feasible and informative. Despite contextual and sample limitations, our proposed ambulatory multimodal framework offers a scalable basis for evaluating increasingly automated workplace environments.

Keywords: User Experience · Ecological Momentary Assessment · Heart Rate Variability · Ambulatory Assessment

1 Introduction

Digitalization of work has accelerated rapidly over the past decade, reflected in the widespread integration of electronic health records, digital documentation systems, and decision-support tools into everyday professional routines. As these systems become deeply embedded in daily workflows, understanding how they are experienced during actual use becomes a central challenge for human-computer interaction (HCI). This study empirically validates a scalable psychophysiological toolkit for ambulatory user experience (UX) assessment in real work environments by integrating momentary self-reports with physiological data directly during HCI.

1.1 Related Work

Working conditions are increasingly recognized as a key determinant of mental health problems in working populations [1], with substantial costs for individuals, employers, and society [2, 3]. As digital systems become embedded in everyday professional routines, they constitute an integral part of these working conditions. Although such systems hold the potential to improve efficiency and coordination, their implementation is often experienced as an additional burden [4, 5]. For digital systems to genuinely contribute to improved working conditions, they must be aligned with the specific demands and constraints of concrete workflows. This, in turn, requires assessing UX within real-world work contexts. UX research offers established theoretical frameworks to guide such assessments. Approaches such as the Components of User Experience Model (CUE) [6], differentiate between instrumental quality, non-instrumental quality, and affect as determinants of overall system appraisal and provide validated measurement instruments [7]. However, these frameworks have predominantly been applied in leisure-oriented contexts rather than in real-world work contexts. As a result, UX research in work settings remains comparatively fragmented and limited in capturing how experience unfolds during ongoing interaction [8]. Beyond this limited focus on work contexts, existing research is also methodologically constrained. UX research has traditionally relied on laboratory studies and retrospective methods such as questionnaires and interviews, providing limited insight into how experience unfolds during actual HCI [9]. While laboratory studies offer experimental control, they sacrifice ecological validity, and retrospective methods are vulnerable to recall bias and cannot capture moment-to-moment fluctuations during use. Moreover, most approaches rely exclusively on self-report measures, despite theoretical accounts emphasizing the physiological dimension of UX [6], and a longstanding body of research indicating that self-reported and physiological indicators do not necessarily converge [10]. To address these limitations, ecological momentary assessment (EMA) offers a methodological bridge between the laboratory and the real world [9]. EMA captures self-report data in real time through brief, randomized prompts delivered to mobile devices [11]. Combined with wearable sensing, EMA enables multimodal assessment of UX as it unfolds during everyday workflows. Among physiological measures, heart rate variability (HRV) is particularly suited for ambulatory assessment, as it can be reliably captured during daily activities using wearable devices. Although its functional interpretation remains debated, HRV is generally understood as reflecting regulatory processes that complement self-report measures [12, 13]. Despite these methodological advances regarding psychophysiological EMA, comprehensive and scalable frameworks for assessing UX directly during real-world HCI remain underdeveloped. In particular, there is limited empirical evidence on how theory-driven, multimodal approaches can be implemented and validated within ongoing professional workflows.

1.2 Research Objectives and Hypotheses

The present study addresses this gap by empirically evaluating a theory-driven, multimodal ambulatory toolkit for assessing UX directly during routine HCI in a clinical workflow. Grounded in the CUE model, we examine whether its core UX components predict momentary system appraisal under real-world conditions, whether real-time assessment provides incremental value beyond established retrospective measures, and whether physiological monitoring contributes explanatory power beyond self-report. We test the following hypotheses:

H1: The CUE UX components (instrumental quality, non-instrumental quality, and affect) significantly predict momentary system appraisal during ambulatory assessment.
H2: Real-time EMA assessment provides stronger predictive validity for momentary system appraisal than retrospective baseline measures and captures additional within-person variance beyond between-person differences.
H3: Physiological monitoring using HRV provides incremental information beyond self-reported affect in predicting momentary system appraisal.

2 Method

2.1 Subjects and Procedure

Twenty-five professionals regularly using an EHR system in routine oncology care were recruited from a German university hospital (ethics approval: TU Dresden, AZ. BO ff (Mono)-EK-40012025). Eligibility required hospital employment, age > 18, regular EHR use, and no cardiovascular conditions or medication. After baseline assessment (meCUE 2.0, sociodemographics), participants were equipped with an EcgMove4 chest sensor (movisens GmbH, Karlsruhe, Germany) for continuous ECG recording, and were instructed on the EMA procedure. EMA prompts were delivered via the movisensXS app (movisens GmbH, Karlsruhe, Germany) on participants' own or a provided Android device. Up to eight prompts per shift assessed affect, with full UX assessments triggered during EHR use. Data collection continued until 50 prompts per participant were reached. The final sample comprised N = 22 (449 observations). For retrospective comparisons (H2), one participant was excluded due to missing baseline data (N = 21). HRV analyses included 342 observations from 18 participants after excluding cases with missing or insufficient ECG data. No data were imputed.

2.2 Measures

EMA UX and Affect. Momentary UX was assessed using ten adapted items from the meCUE 2.0 [7] capturing instrumental quality, non-instrumental quality, and system appraisal (i.e., consequences of use, overall evaluation). Affect was assessed with 8 items from the German Positive and Negative Affect Schedule (PANAS [14], 4 positive, 4 negative), chosen over the meCUE affect module because of its established psychometric properties in ambulatory research [15]. All EMA items used 5-point scales (1 = not at all, 5 = extremely). *Retrospective UX* was assessed at baseline using the full meCUE 2.0.

Heart Rate Variability. The EcgMove4 recorded a modified Einthoven II-lead ECG at 1024 Hz. HRV (root mean square of successive R-R interval differences, RMSSD) was derived from 5-min ECG segments preceding each prompt and log-transformed. Physical activity (MET) served as a covariate.

2.3 Statistical Analyses

The nested data structure (observations within participants) was analyzed using multilevel models in R (nlme package [16]; lme4 package [17]). Time-varying predictors were decomposed into within- and between-person components (ICCs in Supplementary Table S1). Model structures were determined based on fit criteria; random slopes were included only when supported by the data (Supplementary Table S2). Due to the small Level-2 sample in HRV analyses, models for H3 were estimated with random intercepts only.

H1 (CUE Model Validation). Instrumental quality, non-instrumental quality, and positive and negative affect were entered as simultaneous predictors of each system appraisal indicator (consequences, overall evaluation). Model comparisons tested the unique contribution of each component (main model). Mediation of affect between quality perceptions and appraisal was tested [18], with indirect effects evaluated via Monte Carlo simulation (10,000 replications [19]).

H2 (Real-time vs. Retrospective Assessment). Retrospective baseline meCUE 2.0 scores and EMA person-means were compared as Level-2 predictors of momentary system appraisal using marginal R^2, ensuring a comparison free from shared within-moment method bias. The additional within-person variance captured by EMA was quantified by comparing between-person-only and full EMA models. Affect was not included in H2, as retrospective and momentary assessments differed, making direct comparison inappropriate.

H3 (Physiological Monitoring). Convergence between self-reported affect and HRV was tested in a multilevel model predicting HRV from PANAS scores (controlling for MET). Incremental predictive value was assessed by comparing models with and without physiological data (HRV + MET) for each system appraisal outcome.

3 Results

The final sample comprised 22 participants (17 female, 5 male; mean age 41.0 years, SD = 8.5, range: 25–60).

3.1 Do Core UX Components Predict Momentary System Appraisal In Situ?

To test H1, we examined whether instrumental quality, non-instrumental quality, and affect independently predicted momentary system appraisal (consequences of use and overall evaluation), and whether affect mediated the relationship between product perception and system appraisal, as proposed by the CUE model. Both instrumental and non-instrumental quality independently predicted momentary system appraisal at the within-person level (Fig. 1).

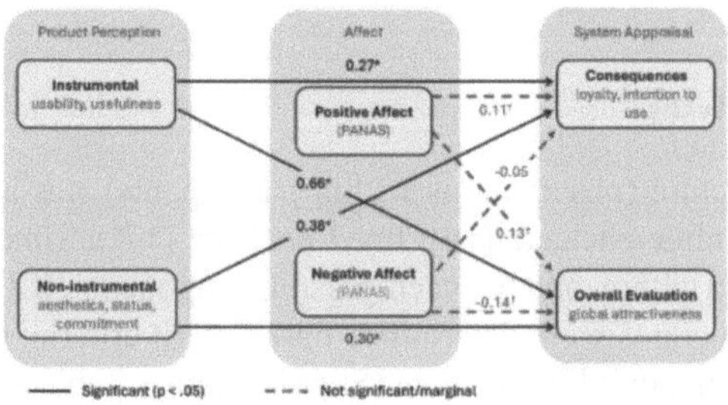

Fig. 1. Within-person associations between CUE model components and momentary system appraisal during routine EHR interaction (N = 449 observations, 22 participants). Solid lines: *$p < 0.05$; dashed lines: non-significant. Unstandardized multilevel estimates. † $p < 0.10$.

For consequences of use (ICC = 0.74), instrumental (b = 0.27, $p < 0.001$) and non-instrumental quality (b = 0.38, $p < 0.001$) were significant predictors, whereas neither positive nor negative affect reached significance. Model comparisons confirmed the unique contribution of both quality dimensions (both $p < 0.001$), while removing affect did not significantly worsen model fit ($p = 0.146$). For overall evaluation (ICC = 0.52), both instrumental (b = 0.66, $p < 0.001$) and non-instrumental quality (b = 0.30, $p = 0.001$) were again significant. Both positive and negative affect showed marginally significant associations (both $p = 0.054$), and removing affect marginally deteriorated model fit ($p = 0.071$). At the between-person level, non-instrumental quality was the only significant predictor of consequences (b = 0.75, $p = 0.005$), while instrumental quality was the only significant predictor of overall evaluation (b = 0.82, $p < 0.001$). Full model details are provided in Supplementary Table S3.

Multilevel mediation analyses showed no significant indirect (all Monte Carlo 95% CIs included zero; Supplementary Table S4), providing no evidence that affect mediated the link between quality perception and system appraisal. Direct effects remained virtually unchanged after including affect ($\Delta c' < 0.02$), indicating that affect did not account for the relationship between quality perception and system appraisal. Overall, H1 was partially supported. Instrumental and non-instrumental quality emerged as robust predictors of momentary system appraisal, whereas affect neither showed consistent direct effects nor mediated these relationships.

3.2 Does Real-Time Assessment Provide Incremental Predictive Value Over Retrospective Measures?

To address H2, we compared retrospective baseline measures and real-time EMA assessments in terms of convergence and predictive validity. Correlations between baseline meCUE 2.0 scores and EMA person-means were non-significant across all constructs (all $p > 0.21$; Supplementary Table S5), indicating a lack of convergence between retrospective and real-time assessments. Next, we compared their predictive validity by entering baseline scores and EMA person-means separately as Level-2 predictors of momentary system appraisal (Table 1). EMA person-means explained more between-person variance than retrospective scores: for consequences, $R^2m = 0.332$ (EMA) vs. 0.194 (baseline); for overall evaluation, $R^2m = 0.287$ vs. 0.074. Critically, these differences emerged despite both approaches capturing exclusively between-person variance, indicating that real-time EMA person-means carry information about stable individual differences in system appraisal that is not contained in retrospective baseline measures. Finally, we quantified the additional contribution of within-person fluctuations by comparing between-person-only EMA models with full EMA models. For consequences of use, explained variance increased from $R^2m = 0.332$ to 0.371 when within-person variability was added ($\Delta R^2 = 0.039$). For overall evaluation, the increase was substantially larger, rising from $R^2m = 0.287$ to 0.462 ($\Delta R^2 = +0.175$). Compared to retrospective baseline models, the full EMA model nearly doubled explained variance for consequences of use ($R^2m = 0.194$ to 0.371) and increased explained variance in overall evaluation more than sixfold ($R^2m = 0.074$ to 0.462), underscoring the added value of real-time assessment for capturing within-person dynamics. Taken together, these findings support H2, showing that real-time EMA substantially outperforms retrospective measures and captures additional within-person dynamics in system appraisal.

Table 1. Comparison of retrospective and real-time assessment approaches of UX components in predicting momentary system appraisal during routine EHR interaction (H2).

	Consequences of use		Overall evaluation	
	b (SE)	R^2m	b (SE)	R^2m
Baseline (retrospective, N = 21)		0.194		0.074
Instrumental quality (BP)	−0.37 (0.28)		−0.26 (0.24)	
Non-instrumental quality (BP)	0.39* (0.15)		0.23† (0.13)	

(continued)

Table 1. (*continued*)

	Consequences of use		Overall evaluation	
	b (SE)	R^2m	b (SE)	R^2m
EMA between-person (N = 22)		0.332		0.287
Instrumental quality (BP)	−0.18 (0.22)		0.75*** (0.18)	
Non-instrumental quality (BP)	0.81** (0.22)		0.21 (0.17)	
EMA full (BP + WP, N = 22)		0.371		0.462
Instrumental quality (BP)	−0.19 (0.22)		0.79*** (0.17)	
Non-instrumental quality (BP)	0.82** (0.22)		0.26 (0.16)	
Instrumental quality (WP)	0.28*** (0.05)		0.69*** (0.10)	
Non-instrumental quality (WP)	0.38*** (0.07)		0.30** (0.09)	

Note. Unstandardized coefficients (b) with standard errors in parentheses. BP = between-person; WP = within-person. Baseline: retrospective meCUE 2.0 scores; EMA BP: person-means of momentary ratings; EMA full: additionally includes person-mean-centered within-person deviations. Affect excluded (see text). R^2m = marginal R^2. † $p < 0.10$. * $p < 0.05$. ** $p < 0.01$. *** $p < 0.001$.

3.3 Does Physiological Monitoring Provide Incremental Value Beyond Self-Report?

To test H3, we first examined the convergence between self-reported affect and HRV. A multilevel model predicting HRV (lnRMSSD) from within- and between-person PANAS scores, while controlling for physical activity (MET), revealed no significant associations between HRV and any PANAS score (all ps > 0.604). The model explained only 1% of the variance at the fixed-effects level (R^2m = 0.010), indicating minimal convergence between subjective and physiological indicators of affect during system interaction. Next, we assessed incremental predictive value by comparing models with and without physiological data (HRV + MET) for each system appraisal outcome. Adding physiological data to the full CUE models showed a marginal trend toward improved prediction for consequences of use ($\chi^2(4) = 8.99$, $p = 0.061$, ΔR^2m = +0.03), but no improvement for overall evaluation ($p = 0.726$). Overall, H3 was not supported, as HRV showed no meaningful convergence with self-report and did not provide incremental predictive value for system appraisal.

4 Discussion

The present study provides first theory-driven evidence that a multimodal ambulatory toolkit can be implemented to assess UX directly during routine HCI in a clinical workflow. In this sense, the study extends prior CUE-based research from controlled and questionnaire-based settings [7, 20] to ambulatory real-world use. At the same time, it addresses a gap in UX-at-work research, where context-sensitive and workflow-integrated assessment approaches remain comparatively underdeveloped [8]. Across the three hypotheses, however, findings were mixed. In partial support of H1, instrumental and non-instrumental quality perceptions reliably predicted momentary system appraisal at the within-person level. This suggests that central perceptual components of the CUE framework remain empirically meaningful when assessed during ongoing interaction rather than retrospectively or under laboratory control. As these dimensions are directly addressable through interface design, their predictive role highlights their practical relevance for system refinement in applied settings. In contrast, affect neither showed direct effects on system appraisal nor mediated the relationship between quality perception and appraisal as assumed within the CUE framework [6]. Although relationships between affect and UX components have been reported [21], the specific mediating role assumed in the CUE framework has, to our knowledge, not yet been examined under ambulatory real-world conditions. The absence of mediation should be interpreted cautiously, as affect was operationalized using the PANAS, selected for its ambulatory validity [15], rather than the meCUE 2.0 affect module. Support for H2 was particularly strong. Retrospective baseline meCUE 2.0 scores did not converge with EMA person-means, indicating that retrospective and in-situ assessments capture different aspects of UX. Crucially, real-time assessment outperformed retrospective measures at every level of comparison, suggesting that system appraisal is not a stable retrospective judgment but a dynamic process shaped by moment-to-moment fluctuations during concrete workflow episodes. Methodologically, ambulatory assessment captures additional information beyond retrospective UX measures. Regarding H3, the hypothesis must be rejected, as HRV did not converge with self-reported affect and did not provide incremental predictive value for system appraisal. This may reflect the limited specificity of HRV as an indicator of affective states, as it has been linked to multiple and partly overlapping processes, including negative and positive affect as well as general regulatory and behavioral activation mechanisms [12]. Rather than serving as a direct predictor, HRV may nonetheless provide complementary information by indexing changes in cardiac arousal, for example as a passive indicator of critical interaction moments [22]. The present study has several limitations. First, the sample size was modest, and the HRV subsample was smaller still, limiting statistical power. Accordingly, more subtle effects, particularly for affective and physiological processes, may not have been detectable. Second, the study focused on a single EHR system within one clinical domain, restricting generalizability to other digital systems and work contexts. Third, affective responses were assessed using the PANAS rather than the meCUE 2.0 affect module, introducing conceptual differences.

4.1 Conclusion and Outlook

Overall, the study shows that multimodal ambulatory, theory-driven UX assessment in real-world work contexts is both feasible and informative. By capturing UX directly during HCI, the proposed toolkit makes visible within-person dynamics that remain largely hidden in retrospective evaluation. In this sense, the study provides one of the first theory-driven validations of multimodal ambulatory UX assessment within an active clinical workflow. The framework provides a basis for just-in-time evaluation of digital work systems and iterative, data-driven interface improvement under authentic conditions. Importantly, the present study does not evaluate AI-based systems directly, but establishes a methodological foundation for future in-situ evaluation of increasingly automated and AI-supported interfaces. The toolkit can be applied by UX researchers and practitioners to evaluate systems directly within ongoing workflows, for example before and after system implementation or interface changes. Future work should extend this approach to larger samples, diverse work contexts, and additional physiological and passive sensing modalities, combined with AI-based analysis to enable scalable and fine-grained UX evaluation, while ensuring strict data protection and privacy safeguards.

Acknowledgments. We thank Dr. Christine Hofbauer for her support, Laura Kaiser and Benjamin Petter for their assistance with data collection and organization, Julian Eder for statistical support, and all participants for their engagement. JNK is supported by the German Cancer Aid (DECADE, 70115166), the German Federal Ministry of Research, Technology and Space (PEARL, 01KD2104C; CAMINO, 01EO2101; TRANSFORM LIVER, 031L0312A; TANGERINE, 01KT2302 through ERA-NET Transcan; Come2Data, 16DKZ2044A; DEEP-HCC, 031L0315A; DECIPHER-M, 01KD2420A; NextBIG, 01ZU2402A; PROSURV, 01KD2509C), the German Research Foundation (DFG; as part of Germany's Excellence Strategy – EXC 2050/2 – Project ID 390696704 – Cluster of Excellence "Centre for Tactile Internet with Human-in-the-Loop" (CeTI) of Technische Universität Dresden, as well as through DFG-funded collaborative research projects TRR 412/1, 535081457 and SFB 1709/1 2025, 533056198), the German Academic Exchange Service (SECAI, 57616814), the German Federal Joint Committee (TransplantKI, 01VSF21048), the European Union's Horizon Europe research and innovation programme (ODELIA, 101057091; GENIAL, 101096312), the European Research Council (ERC; NADIR, 101114631), the National Institute for Health and Care Research (NIHR, NIHR203331) Leeds Biomedical Research Centre, and the Breast Cancer Research Foundation (BELLADONNA, BCRF-25-225). This work was funded by the European Union. Views and opinions expressed are however those of the author(s) only and do not necessarily reflect those of the European Union. Neither the European Union nor the granting authority can be held responsible for them. MKW is supported by the German Federal Ministry of Research, Technology and Space (BMFTR, 03ZU1210GA) and the German Research Foundation (DFG, WE 7072/2-1). During the preparation of this work, the authors used ChatGPT-4o (OpenAI) to perform a language check of the manuscript. After using this tool, the authors reviewed and edited the content as needed and take full responsibility for the content of the publication.

Disclosure of Interests. JNK declares consulting services for AstraZeneca, Bioptimus, Mindpeak, MultiplexDx, and Panakeia. He has participated in Advisory Boards for AstraZeneca, DoMoreDiagnostics, Owkin, and Panakeia. Furthermore, he holds shares in StratifAI, Synagen, Spira Labs, and Ignition Lab, has received institutional research grants from GSK and AstraZeneca, as well as honoraria from AstraZeneca, Bayer, Daiichi Sankyo, Eisai, Janssen, Merck, MSD, BMS, Roche, and Pfizer. He is a member of selected working groups of AACR, ESMO, EASL, and DGHO, and a board member at ESAC. ICW received lecture honoraria from AstraZeneca. No other potential conflicts of interest are reported by any of the remaining authors.

References

1. Rugulies, R. et al.: Work-related causes of mental health conditions and interventions for their improvement in workplaces. Lancet. **402**, 1368–1381 (2023). https://doi.org/10.1016/S0140-6736(23)00869-3
2. de Oliveira, C., Saka, M., Bone, L., Jacobs, R.: The role of mental health on workplace productivity: a critical review of the literature. Appl. Health Econ. Health Policy. **21**, 167–193 (2023). https://doi.org/10.1007/s40258-022-00761-w
3. Kelloway, E.K., Dimoff, J.K., Gilbert, S.: Mental health in the workplace. Annu. Rev. Organ. Psychol. Organ. Behav. **10**, 363–387 (2023). https://doi.org/10.1146/annurev-orgpsych-120920-050527
4. Klein, J., Bopp, E., Gilbert, S., Ditzen, B., Steinhäuser, J.L., Wekenborg, M.K.: The effects of information and communication technology (ICT) implementation on psychophysiological markers of stress: a systematic review. Behav. Inform. Technol., 1–26 (2025). https://doi.org/10.1080/0144929X.2025.2504511
5. Wekenborg, M.K., Harzbecker, J., Bechmann, N., Sbiera, S., Gilbert, S., Schwerdtfeger, A.R.: Effects of digital transformation on stress-relevant working conditions and employees' psychophysiological stress: a longitudinal, quasi-experimental control group study. Comput. Hum. Behav. Rep., 100839 (2025). https://doi.org/10.1016/j.chbr.2025.100839
6. Thüring, M., Mahlke, S.: Usability, aesthetics and emotions in human–technology interaction. Int. J. Psychol. **42**, 253–264 (2007). https://doi.org/10.1080/00207590701396674
7. Minge, M., Thüring, M.: The MeCUE questionnaire (2.0): meeting five basic requirements for lean and standardized UX assessment. In: Marcus, A., Wang, W. (eds.) Design, User Experience, and Usability: Theory and Practice, pp. 451–469. Springer International Publishing, Cham (2018). https://doi.org/10.1007/978-3-319-91797-9_33
8. Simsek Caglar, P., Roto, V., Vainio, T.: User experience research in the work context: maps, gaps and agenda. Proc. ACM HCI. **6**, 132:1–132:28 (2022). https://doi.org/10.1145/3512979
9. Wekenborg, M.K., Gilbert, S., Kather, J.N.: Examining human-AI interaction in real-world healthcare beyond the laboratory. npj Digit. Med. **8**, 169 (2025). https://doi.org/10.1038/s41746-025-01559-5
10. Mauss, I.B., Levenson, R.W., McCarter, L., Wilhelm, F.H., Gross, J.J.: The tie that binds? coherence among emotion experience, behavior, and physiology. Emotion. **5**, 175–190 (2005). https://doi.org/10.1037/1528-3542.5.2.175
11. Shiffman, S., Stone, A.A., Hufford, M.R.: Ecological momentary assessment. Annu. Rev. Clin. Psychol. **4**, 1–32 (2008). https://doi.org/10.1146/annurev.clinpsy.3.022806.091415
12. Laborde, S., Mosley, E., Thayer, J.F.: Heart rate variability and cardiac vagal tone in psychophysiological research - recommendations for experiment planning, data analysis, and data reporting. Front. Psychol. **8**, 213 (2017). https://doi.org/10.3389/fpsyg.2017.00213
13. Menuet, C. et al.: Redefining respiratory sinus arrhythmia as respiratory heart rate variability: an international expert recommendation for terminological clarity. Nat. Rev. Cardiol. **22**, 978–984 (2025). https://doi.org/10.1038/s41569-025-01160-z
14. Breyer, B., Bluemke, M.: Deutsche Version der Positive and Negative Affect Schedule PANAS (GESIS Panel). GESIS - Leibniz-Institut für Sozialwissenschaften, Mannheim (2016). https://doi.org/10.6102/zis242
15. Schwerdtfeger, A.R., Gerteis, A.K.S.: The manifold effects of positive affect on heart rate variability in everyday life: distinguishing within-person and between-person associations. Health Psychol. **33**, 1065–1073 (2014). https://doi.org/10.1037/hea0000079
16. Jose Pinheiro, D.B., DebRoy, S., Sarkar, D.: The R Developement Core Team: nlme: Linear and nonlinear mixed effects models R package version 3 (2013)

17. Bates, D., Mächler, M., Bolker, B., Walker, S.: Fitting linear mixed-effects models using lme4. J. Stat. Softw. **67**, 1–48 (2015). https://doi.org/10.18637/jss.v067.i01
18. Zhang, Z., Zyphur, M.J., Preacher, K.J.: Testing multilevel mediation using hierarchical linear models: problems and solutions. Organ. Res. Methods. **12**, 695–719 (2009). https://doi.org/10.1177/1094428108327450
19. Preacher, K.J., Selig, J.P.: Advantages of Monte Carlo Confidence Intervals for indirect effects. Comm. Method Meas. **6**, 77–98 (2012). https://doi.org/10.1080/19312458.2012.679848
20. Minge, M., Thüring, M., Wagner, I., Kuhr, C.V.: The meCUE Questionnaire: a modular tool for measuring user experience. In: Soares, M., Falcão, C., Ahram, T.Z. (eds.) Advances in Ergonomics Modeling, Usability & Special Populations, pp. 115–128. Springer International Publishing, Cham (2017). https://doi.org/10.1007/978-3-319-41685-4_11
21. Aranyi, G., van Schaik, P.: Testing a model of user-experience with news websites. JASIST. **67**, 1555–1575 (2016). https://doi.org/10.1002/asi.23462
22. Rominger, C., Schwerdtfeger, A.R.: Feelings from the heart part II: simulation and validation of static and dynamic HRV decrease-trigger algorithms to detect stress in firefighters. Sensors. **22**, 2925 (2022). https://doi.org/10.3390/s22082925

Accessibility and Inclusive Design

Interdisciplinary Perspectives on FinTech and Blockchain in Cryptocurrency Platforms: A Systematic Literature Review on Accessibility, Usability, and Digital Inclusion

Hugo Arias-Flores[1(✉)], Jose Luis-Chinchilla[2], Janio Jadán-Guerrero[1], and Tania Calle-Jimenez[3]

[1] Centro de Investigación de Ciencias Humanas y de la Educación (CICHE), Universidad Tecnológica Indoamérica, Av. Machala y Sabanilla, Quito EC170103, Ecuador
{hugoarias,janiojadan}@uti.edu.ec

[2] Maestría en Gestión y Dirección de Proyectos, Universidad Galileo, 4A Calle 7a. Avenida, Calle Dr. Eduardo Suger Cofiño, Cdad. de Guatemala 01010, Guatemala
14001431@galileo.edu

[3] Department of Informatics and Computer Science, Escuela Politécnica Nacional, Quito, Ecuador
tania.calle@epn.edu.ec

Abstract. According to recent studies, the application of agile methodologies in the development of cryptocurrency platforms can increase efficiency in improving accessibility and usability in digital financial systems by up to 35%. This study conducts a systematic literature review on the integration of FinTech and blockchain technologies, with a particular focus on accessibility and usability in digital platforms. Based on the PRISMA 2020 framework, indexed publications from the Scopus database published between 2021 and 2025 were analyzed. The results reveal a sustained growth in scientific output, especially during the period 2023–2025, with a notable concentration of publications from countries such as Malaysia, Spain, and Ukraine. The main contributing fields include business, computer science, and economics, reflecting the interdisciplinary nature of the topic. Furthermore, the findings highlight the role of FinTech and blockchain in modernizing financial services, improving transactional efficiency, and supporting the achievement of the Sustainable Development Goals (SDGs), particularly those related to environmental sustainability and digital inclusion. Finally, the study recommends expanding future research to include multiple databases and additional keywords in order to generalize the findings and deepen the understanding of the impact of these emerging technologies.

Keywords: FinTech · blockchain · digital accessibility · usability · financial innovation · sustainability · systematic review · technological transformation · Sustainable Development Goal 8 (Decent Work and Economic Growth)

C. Stephanidis et al. (Eds.): HCII 2026, CCIS 3047, pp. 495–503, 2026.
https://doi.org/10.1007/978-3-032-30552-7_47

1 Introduction

Cryptocurrency platforms emerged from the proposal of Bitcoin as a form of decentralized electronic cash, aimed at eliminating the involvement of traditional financial intermediaries and ensuring secure transactions through cryptographic mechanisms. These platforms are designed to facilitate the creation, exchange, storage, and management of crypto-assets by leveraging distributed ledger technologies, primarily blockchain. Since their inception, these platforms have evolved rapidly, giving rise to increasingly complex infrastructures and functionalities across financial, contractual, and computational domains (Nakamoto, 2009).

The rapid evolution of this technology has led to significant diversification in digital assets. While Bitcoin was originally conceived as a form of electronic money, subsequent platforms such as Ethereum enabled the execution of smart contracts, fostering the development of decentralized applications and new forms of digital interaction. This evolution resulted in a wide variety of cryptocurrencies, including Litecoin, Monero, Zcash, and Stellar, commonly categorized as alternative cryptocurrencies or "altcoins." Each of these assets presents distinct characteristics, purposes, and usage requirements (Buterin, 2015; Imamura & Omote, 2022).

Despite their rapid growth, these technologies pose significant development challenges, primarily due to their inherent complexity. Cryptocurrency platforms rely on advanced cryptographic techniques and often operate in the absence of a comprehensive regulatory framework for digital assets, which substantially limits access to these systems. In this context, several ethical considerations related to digital assets are discussed, including inclusion, data privacy, misuse, and environmental impact, underscoring the need to promote responsible digital asset development (Elsayed, 2025).

Although cryptocurrency platforms have gained widespread popularity, accessibility remains limited. The increasing functional diversity of these platforms has also intensified the complexity of their interfaces and interaction flows. To achieve broader cryptocurrency adoption, usability plays a crucial role in addressing user needs through simplified processes and tools that streamline interaction (Farrukh, Xu, Lim, & Nusrat, 2024).

To ensure easier access to blockchain-based platforms and applications, emphasis has been placed on developing interactive and engaging platforms that promote learning about this technology, particularly in educational contexts. This approach aims to enable users to access and explore these tools more comfortably and intuitively, thereby enhancing their overall experience and understanding of blockchain concepts (Asmawi, Saifulbahri, & Arifin, 2024).

In this context, usability and accessibility are determining factors for the sustained adoption of cryptocurrency platforms. Usability has become a key factor in software development, not only for evaluating the extent to which a system can be used by specific users, but also because it is strongly linked to the quality and ease with which a software product can be used. Accessibility, on the other hand, can be understood as a system property that enables users with diverse physical, sensory, and cognitive abilities to interact with the platform effectively and satisfactorily (Pailiacho, Garcés, & Balseca, 2022).

Consequently, this research aims to conduct an exhaustive review of the scientific literature on FinTech and blockchain platforms in order to assess the extent to which these technologies are being integrated.

The remainder of this study is structured as follows: Sect. 2 presents the background, Sect. 3 describes the research methodology, Sect. 4 presents the results, and Sect. 5 provides the discussion and conclusions.

2 Background

The evolution of blockchain technology can be divided into three stages (Tschorsch & Scheuermann, 2016; Idrees, Nowostawski, Jameel, & Mourya, 2021):

- The first stage, known as *Blockchain 1.0*, consists of a public ledger used to store cryptocurrencies within a distributed network.
- The second stage, *Blockchain 2.0*, incorporates trust management through smart contracts that are self-executing and operate without the involvement of third parties.
- The third stage, *Blockchain 3.0*, represents the present and future of the technology and encompasses a wide range of application domains, including decentralized finance, IoT, education, identity management, big data, artificial intelligence, and healthcare, among others.

In this regard, the financial industry has experienced a revolution with the rise of FinTech and the integration of technological platforms that leverage expertise to implement blockchain-based solutions (Belousova, Chichkanov, Gashnikov, Krayushkina, & Thurner, 2023; Salleh, Alwi, Rosnan, & Wahab, 2025). Some studies have focused on ensuring transaction security by integrating lightweight blockchain technologies with deep learning techniques (Darwish, EL-Naggar, & Elkaffas, 2026). Blockchain transparency enhances the clarity of banks' risk tolerance, reducing exposure to credit risk through improved information verifiability, cost-effective risk mitigation, and more accurate demand forecasting (He, Dong, Jiang, Chen, & Zhang, 2025).

Moreover, investment in blockchain creates a highly dynamic and open environment for employee innovation, allowing individuals to explore new ideas and test novel approaches more autonomously, without multiple layers of approval. FinTech effectively fosters workplace innovation and plays a mediating role in the relationship between blockchain investment and employee innovation (Wang & Gao, 2026).

3 Methodology

This study employed a systematic literature review methodology to comprehensively explore and synthesize existing research on FinTech and blockchain. Following established guidelines for systematic literature reviews, the PRISMA 2020 framework was adopted (Page et al., 2021). The Scopus database was selected as the sole source for literature retrieval due to its broad interdisciplinary coverage, standardized indexing, and advanced citation analysis capabilities.

An initial search was conducted using a structured keyword string incorporating Boolean operators and truncation symbols, constructed as follows: {(FinTech AND (blockchain OR block-chain) AND accessibility)}. Only open-access journal articles published between 2021 and 2025 and written in English were considered.

The PRISMA protocol guided each step of the selection and screening process, including identification, title and abstract screening, eligibility assessment through full-text review, and final inclusion. Following the PRISMA framework, the selection and screening process of this systematic literature review followed a transparent and rigorous approach (Fig. 1). The initial identification phase involved a targeted search within the Scopus database, which yielded 676 records relevant to the keywords *Fintech*, *blockchain*, and *block-chain*. The results were then filtered by applying a time window and the open-access criterion, resulting in 405 records. Subsequently, only journal articles were selected, reducing the dataset to 290 records, and further restricted to articles written in English, yielding 282 records. Finally, the records were refined using the term *"accessibility"*, which resulted in nine studies. Based on this process, the following research questions were formulated: Are publications related to Fintech and blockchain increasing? Which countries contribute the most to this field? Who are the main funding bodies supporting this research?

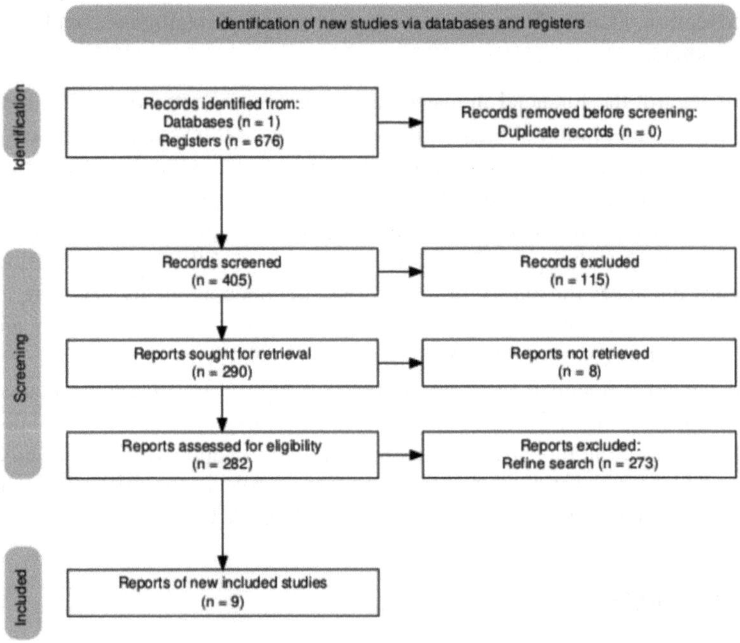

Fig. 1. PRISMA Flow Diagram.

4 Results

The volume of research related to FinTech and blockchain platforms has increased by 2025, indicating the growing integration of blockchain solutions with accessibility considerations (Fig. 2). Between 2023 and 2025, a total of nine studies were identified, six of which were published in the final year.

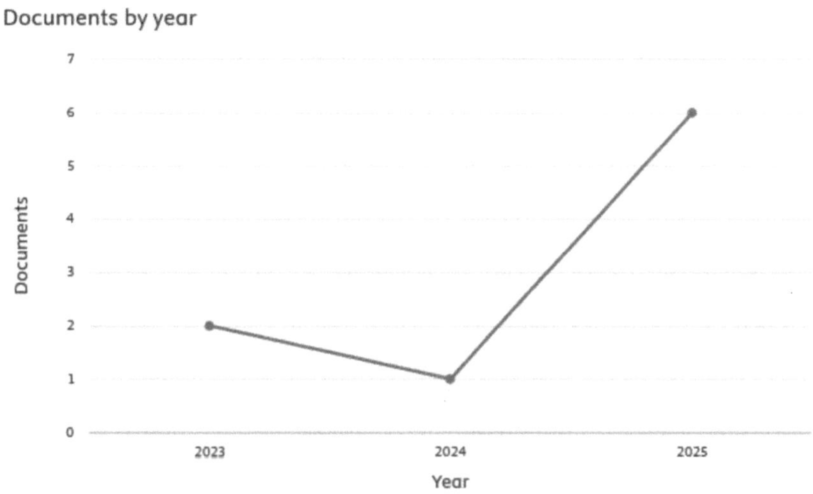

Fig. 2. Documents per year.

The highest number of published documents originated from countries such as Malaysia (Salleh, Alwi, Rosnan, & Wahab, 2025; Alrashdan, Aljabali, Alqudah, Jarah, & Alzoubi, 2025), Spain (Mohammed, De-Pablos-Heredero, & Montes Botella, 2023; Liu, Urquía-Grande, López-Sánchez, & Rodríguez-López, 2023), and Ukraine (Dzhereleyko, Pysarenko, Poltinina, Nesterenko, & Kolomiiets, 2025; Voloshyna-Sidei, Onishchenko, Zhydovska, Borodenko, & Abramova, 2025). Additional publications were identified from Greece (Varveris, Basdekidou, Basdekidou, & Xofis, 2025), Hungary (Mamun & László, 2025), India (Sharma et al., 2024) and Jordan (Alrashdan, Aljabali, Alqudah, Jarah, & Alzoubi, 2025), with one publication each, demonstrating a stronger contribution from European and Asian countries (Fig. 3).

Figure 4 illustrates the subject areas in which the reviewed studies were published. Approximately 47.4% of the results fall within three primary domains: "Business, Management and Accounting" (Dzhereleyko, Pysarenko, Poltinina, Nesterenko, & Kolomiiets, 2025; Voloshyna-Sidei, Onishchenko, Zhydovska, Borodenko, & Abramova, 2025; Liu, Urquía-Grande, López-Sánchez, & Rodríguez-López, 2023), "Computer Science" (Mamun & László, 2025; Varveris, Basdekidou, Basdekidou, & Xofis, 2025; Mohammed, De-Pablos-Heredero, & Montes Botella, 2023) and "Economics, Econometrics and Finance" (Mamun & László, 2025; Varveris, Basdekidou, Basdekidou, & Xofis, 2025; Dzhereleyko, Pysarenko, Poltinina, Nesterenko, & Kolomiiets, 2025). The areas of "Medicine" (Alrashdan, Aljabali, Alqudah, Jarah, & Alzoubi, 2025; Liu, Urquía-Grande, López-Sánchez, & Rodríguez-López, 2023), "Social Sciences" (Salleh, Alwi,

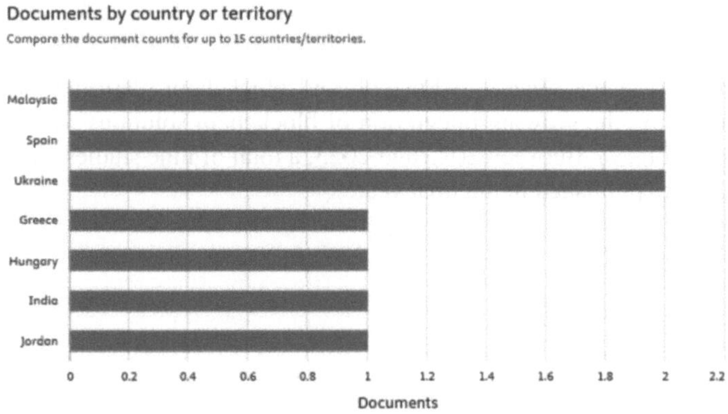

Fig. 3. Documents by country or territory.

Rosnan, & Wahab, 2025; Liu, Urquía-Grande, López-Sánchez, & Rodríguez-López, 2023) and "Environmental Science" (Salleh, Alwi, Rosnan, & Wahab, 2025; Sharma et al., 2024), account for 31.5% of the results, while the remaining 21.1% cover areas such as "Psychology" (Liu, Urquía-Grande, López-Sánchez, & Rodríguez-López, 2023), "Engineering" (Sharma et al., 2024), "Energy" (Salleh, Alwi, Rosnan, & Wahab, 2025) and "Decision Sciences" (Voloshyna-Sidei, Onishchenko, Zhydovska, Borodenko, & Abramova, 2025).

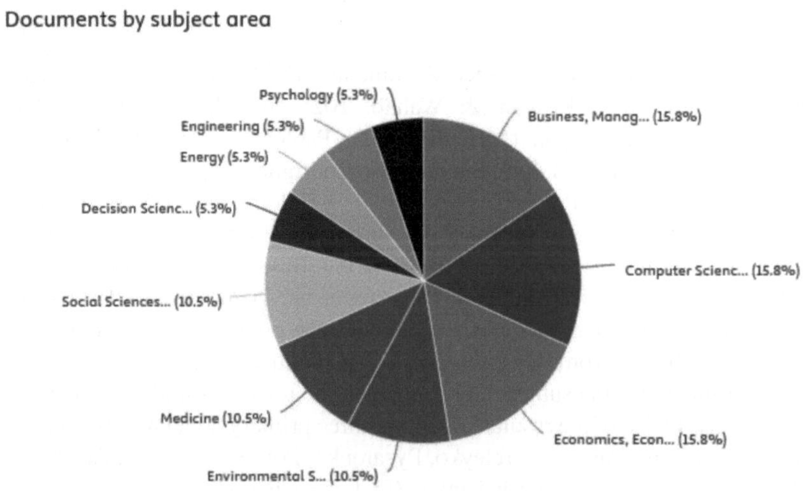

Fig. 4. Documents by subject area.

Only two funding sponsors were explicitly identified: the University of Debrecen, which funded the study in (Mamun & László, 2025), and Rey Juan Carlos University, which sponsored the research in (Mohammed, De-Pablos-Heredero, & Montes Botella, 2023) (Fig. 5).

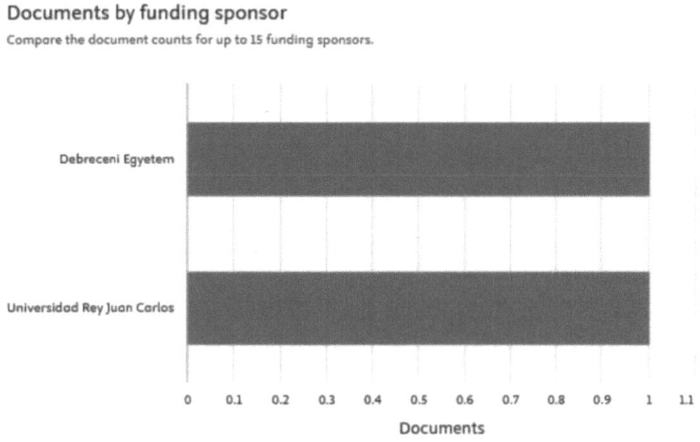

Fig. 5. Documents by funding sponsor.

5 Discussion and Conclusions

In this study, a total of nine samples were collected from the Scopus database following systematic review guidelines. Based on descriptive statistical analysis, trends in scientific production, contributing countries, influential knowledge fields, and funding sponsors were identified. First, an overall increase in the number of publications was observed in 2025.

Furthermore, the adoption of digital currencies is higher in countries with strong democratic institutions and effective governance (Mohammed, De-Pablos-Heredero, & Montes Botella, 2023). In this context, the implementation of artificial intelligence, blockchain, and API technologies to address systemic inefficiencies has improved transaction speed and security, transforming digital banking services by optimizing user interaction and operational processes (Voloshyna-Sidei, Onishchenko, Zhydovska, Borodenko, & Abramova, 2025).

By leveraging technology, FinTech has the potential to significantly contribute to achieving the SDGs and promoting a more equitable and sustainable future (Salleh, Alwi, Rosnan, & Wahab, 2025; Mamun & László, 2025). In particular, the integration of artificial intelligence with blockchain and the adoption of financial technologies for environmental projects offer substantial potential for advancing metaverse-based landscape architecture, intelligent forest monitoring, sustainable urban planning, and enhanced citizen participation in sustainable forestry initiatives (Varveris, Basdekidou, Basdekidou, & Xofis, 2025).

Since our sample is drawn from a single database, future research could expand the analysis to multiple databases to enable comparison and improve comprehensiveness. Another limitation of this study is that the sample size is restricted by the chosen search keywords. As a result, some relevant articles may have been omitted due to the exclusion of certain terms (e.g., *financial inclusion*). Therefore, future studies could enlarge the sample by incorporating additional keywords to enhance the generalizability of the findings.

Acknowledgments. The authors would like to thank the Universidad Tecnológica Indoamérica for its contribution to the development of this research through the project "Tecnología Educativa para Discapacidad- TEDI" of Centro de Ciencias Humanas y de la Educación - CICHE.

References

Nakamoto, S.: A Peer-to-Peer Electronic Cash System. [En línea]. https://bitcoin.org/files/bitcoin-paper/bitcoin.pdf (2009)

Buterin, V.: A next-generation smart contract and decentralized application platform. [En línea]. https://ethereum.org/es/whitepaper/ (2015)

Imamura, M., Omote, K.: Analysis of the features and structure behind availability in Blockchain using altcoin. IEEE Access. **10**, 98683–98699 (2022)

Elsayed, R.A.A.: Unveiling the black box: understanding digital assets' complexity. Fut. Bus. J. **11**(31) (2025)

Farrukh, M., Xu, S., Lim, W.M., Hasnain, M.F., Nusrat, S.: Cryptocurrency awareness, acceptance, and adoption: the role of trust as a cornerstone. Hum. Soc. Sci. Commun. **11**, 1–4 (2024)

Asmawi, A., Saifulbahri, E.M., Arifin, N.A.M.: Development of BlockScholar as an educational mobile application on blockchain technology. J. Adv. Res. Appl. Sci. Eng. Technol. **34**, 15–23 (2024)

Pailiacho, V., Garcés, E., Balseca, J.: Usabilidad del software: Una revisión sobre su evolución conceptual y parámetros de evaluación. In: Software Usability: A Review of Its Conceptual Evolution and Evaluation Parameters, pp. 121–134. Publicaciones en Ciencias y Tecnología (2022)

Tschorsch, F., Scheuermann, B.: Bitcoin and beyond: a technical survey on decentralized digital currencies. IEEE Commun. Surv. Tutor. **18**(3), 2084–2123 (2016)

Idrees, S., Nowostawski, M., Jameel, R., Mourya, A.: Security aspects of blockchain technology intended for industrial applications. Electronics. **10**(8), 951 (2021)

Belousova, V., Chichkanov, N., Gashnikov, G., Krayushkina, Z., Thurner, T.: Technology-intense service offerings in the light of economic complexity: establishing a holistic service ecosystem. Foresight STI Govern. **17**(1), 7–17 (2023)

Salleh, M.N.M., Alwi, S., Rosnan, H., Wahab, N.A.: Exploring the impact of FinTech on sustainable development in Malaysia: an interpretative phenomenological analysis. Discov. Sustain. **6**(1), 373 (2025)

Darwish, S., EL-Naggar, S., Elkaffas, S.: Securing financial transactions: exploring the role of lightweight blockchain-enabled deep learning for fraud detection in FinTech systems. Cybersecurity. **9**, 8 (2026)

He, Y., Dong, J., Jiang, C., Chen, B., Zhang, S.: Blockchain's impact on operation and finance decision: theoretical examinations across blockchain enabled inventory asset-based finance. Comput. Ind. Eng. **210**, 111491 (2025)

Wang, Y., Gao, X.: Blockchain investment, FinTech, and employee innovation. Financ. Res. Lett. **90**, 109297 (2026)

Page, M.J. et al.: The PRISMA 2020 statement: an updated guideline for reporting systematic reviews. BMJ. **372**, n71 (2021)

Alrashdan, M., Aljabali, A.M., Alqudah, M., Jarah, B.A., Alzoubi, M.: The impact of financial technology applications on the expansion of Islamic banking services in Jordan. Perinat. J. **33**, 293–300 (2025)

Mohammed, M.A., De-Pablos-Heredero, C., Botella, J.L.M.: exploring the factors affecting countries' adoption of blockchain-enabled central bank digital currencies. Fut. Internet. **15**, 321 (2023)

Liu, A., Urquía-Grande, E., López-Sánchez, P., Rodríguez-López, Á.: Research into microfinance and ICTs: a bibliometric analysis. Eval. Program Plann. **97**, 102215 (2023)

Dzhereleyko, S., Pysarenko, N., Poltinina, O., Nesterenko, O., Kolomiiets, V.: Digital economy and its effect on financial market structures: analyzing key trends and future opportunities. Int. J. Account. Econ. Stud. **12**, 747–759 (2025)

Voloshyna-Sidei, V., Onishchenko, S., Zhydovska, N., Borodenko, T., Abramova, M.: The influence of Fintech startups on the dynamics of innovative development of the financial market. Management (Montevideo). **3**, 218 (2025)

Varveris, D., Basdekidou, V., Basdekidou, C., Xofis, P.: Smart forest modeling behavioral for a greener future: an AI text-by-voice blockchain approach with citizen involvement in sustainable forestry functionality. FinTech. **4**(3), 47 (2025)

Mamun, A.Y., László, V.: Advancing sustainability through financial inclusion and sustainable finance: a systematic literature review. Digit. Financ. **7**(4), 853–870 (2025)

Sharma, A., Panse, C., Gupta, N., Dawar, S., Kudal, P., Sharma, M.: Adoption of cryptocurrency in India: an extended technology adoption model. Int. J. Saf. Sec. Eng. **14**, 1803–1816 (2024)

SoundWay: A BLE Multi-advertising System with Voice Interaction and Mobile Feedback for Indoor Orientation Assistance

Esteban Barracho(✉), Benedicte Tutekamukuta, Anas Damlakhi, Jonathan Kondolinkebi, and Arthur Smoos

Faculty of Computer Science, University of Namur, Namur, Belgium
{esteban.barracho,benedicte.tutekamukuta,anas.damlakhi, jonathan.kondolinkebi,arthur.smoos}@student.unamur.be

Abstract. Indoor and at-door navigation remain challenging for visually impaired individuals, especially in environments where GPS is unavailable and dedicated assistive infrastructure is costly. This paper presents SoundWay, a lightweight prototype that combines Bluetooth Low Energy (BLE) multi-advertising, RSSI-based proximity estimation, and multimodal interaction (voice and haptic feedback) to support non-visual orientation in corridor and entrance scenarios. The system relies on a Raspberry Pi configured as a BLE multi-advertising emitter and a cross-platform mobile application that performs signal smoothing and translates relative proximity into auditory guidance and vibration patterns. Preliminary technical trials in university corridors indicate that multi-advertising increases packet density and enables smoother proximity feedback compared to single advertising under similar settings. No structured user study has yet been conducted; future work will include participatory evaluations with visually impaired users and alignment with accessibility standards [8,19].

Keywords: Indoor navigation · Accessibility · Multimodal interaction · BLE · Voice interaction · Haptic feedback

1 Introduction

According to recent estimates by the World Health Organization, more than 43 million people globally are blind, and over 295 million live with moderate to severe visual impairments [18,20]. In Europe, these limitations directly impact autonomy, mobility, and access to public spaces [4]. Navigating indoor environments presents unique challenges: GPS is ineffective, dedicated assistive equipment remains costly, and BLE-based solutions often suffer from signal instability and limited integration with user-centric interfaces.

C. Stephanidis et al. (Eds.): HCII 2026, CCIS 3047, pp. 504–514, 2026.
https://doi.org/10.1007/978-3-032-30552-7_48

In response to these challenges, we introduce **SoundWay**, a prototype designed to assist visually impaired users through multimodal interaction. It consists of a Raspberry Pi emitting BLE signals, a mobile application interpreting these signals in real time, and a voice recognition interface through which users can control the application and receive haptic navigation guidance.

Rooted in Engelbart's vision of "augmenting the human intellect" [7], SoundWay does not attempt to replace the user's capabilities but seeks to enhance them by expanding access to spatial information through non-visual modalities. The system supports a multimodal interaction approach where voice commands, haptic cues, and spatial feedback are integrated into a single loop of perception and action.

This approach aligns with contemporary theories of augmented interaction, where digital tools are conceived not merely as computational devices, but as perceptual and cognitive extensions embedded in the environment. By distributing information across multiple sensory channels and anchoring feedback in spatial context, SoundWay promotes a more embodied and intuitive form of navigation.

This work explores lightweight, modular, and low-cost technologies that enhance orientation for users in both indoor and transitional outdoor settings, without requiring specialized hardware or complex installations.

2 Related Work

Assistive navigation systems for visually impaired individuals generally fall into three major categories:

Vision-Based Systems. These approaches use cameras and computer vision to provide environmental awareness. While they offer rich perceptual capabilities, they often require intensive computation, raise privacy concerns, and are sensitive to lighting conditions.

Sensing-Based Systems (e.g., Ultrasonic, LiDAR). These technologies enable accurate distance estimation and object detection. However, they depend on specialized hardware and are often less portable or more expensive to deploy at scale.

BLE-Based Systems. Bluetooth Low Energy (BLE) has emerged as a promising alternative due to its low power consumption, widespread availability on mobile devices, and ease of deployment. Prior research has explored:

- RSSI-based localization techniques [9],
- multimodal wearable devices for obstacle detection [11],
- mobile applications integrating haptic and auditory feedback [17].

Despite their potential, BLE-based systems often suffer from signal instability, limited advertising bandwidth, and weak integration with interactive user interfaces.

Recent trends emphasize the importance of multimodal, affordable, and infrastructure-light solutions for assistive navigation. A 2024 bibliometric review highlights rapid growth in wearable and mobile systems combining haptics and auditory feedback [21]. Several recent studies confirm BLE's continued relevance: high-precision indoor localization using low-cost beacons has achieved meter-level accuracy even in dynamic environments [14], while BLE-based navigation remains a key research avenue for visually impaired users [12,13]. Other innovations explore crowdsourced route mapping [15], or hybrid systems combining BLE and computer vision [10].

From a theoretical standpoint, foundational literature in Human-Computer Interaction (HCI) supports the shift toward embodied, multimodal designs. Dix et al.'s *Human-Computer Interaction* [6] and Preece et al.'s *Interaction Design* [16] emphasize how distributing interaction across sensory modalities can support non-visual interaction and improve robustness in real-world contexts. French-language research in interaction homme-machine (IHM) also conceptualizes interaction as a dynamic coupling between the user, the interface, and spatial context [5].

These principles directly inform the design of **SoundWay**, which leverages BLE sensing, haptic and audio cues, and voice interaction to deliver embodied guidance. In contrast to earlier BLE-based approaches, SoundWay introduces a novel use of simultaneous multi-advertising to improve signal density and integrates non-visual feedback within a mobile-first interaction model.

By addressing signal sparsity, interaction constraints, and sensory integration, SoundWay contributes to the development of accessible, low-cost navigation systems grounded in multimodal and situated interaction paradigms.

3 Methodology

The implementation of SoundWay follows a modular, bottom-up approach structured in four key components: BLE signal emission, distance estimation, voice interaction, and mobile interface integration. Each component was designed to maximize accessibility, responsiveness, and hardware simplicity (Fig. 1).

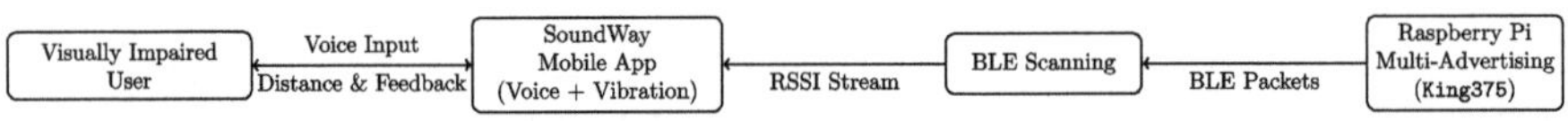

Fig. 1. System architecture of SoundWay. The Raspberry Pi emits multiple BLE advertisements, which are processed by the mobile application. RSSI streams are translated into multimodal feedback (voice and vibration) for the visually impaired user.

3.1 BLE Multi-advertising Emitter (Raspberry Pi)

We configured a Raspberry Pi as a BLE emitter using the BlueZ stack and the D-Bus interface [2,3]. The system was designed to:

- broadcast multiple BLE advertisements simultaneously under a shared identifier (`King375`),
- increase advertising frequency and mitigate packet loss,
- optionally leverage a USB Bluetooth dongle for enhanced signal stability and transmission power.

BLE was selected for its energy efficiency, native support on most smartphones, and low deployment cost. The Raspberry Pi provides a flexible and affordable platform for prototyping, with sufficient control over advertisement parameters and minimal hardware complexity. Compared to GPS or Wi-Fi, BLE enables finer-grained proximity estimation in short-range, obstacle-prone environments.

3.2 Mobile Application Interface

The smartphone application serves as the central interaction point. It features:

- authentication and profile management screens,
- a voice command interface,
- real-time proximity feedback based on RSSI,
- (experimental) map overlay using OpenStreetMap for spatial orientation.

The mobile application was developed using **React Native and Expo**, enabling cross-platform deployment while maintaining native performance and access to device capabilities. The backend infrastructure of the mobile application is implemented using **Firebase**, leveraging Firestore as a NoSQL database for storing building information, room descriptions, navigation instructions, and distance configuration data. This approach allows the mobile client to dynamically retrieve navigation-related data based on the detected environment.

Smartphones were chosen as the main platform due to their ubiquity and integrated capabilities (BLE, microphone, audio output, vibration motor). This design decision minimizes hardware requirements and enhances potential adoption. All interaction is conducted via standard components, ensuring accessibility and reducing the need for external devices or infrastructure.

3.3 RSSI-Based Distance Estimation

On the client side, the mobile application continuously scans for BLE advertisements and logs their received signal strength indication (RSSI). BLE scanning and RSSI acquisition on the client side rely on standard BLE APIs available in cross-platform toolchains; our prototyping also leveraged BLE client libraries such as Bleak for validation and debugging [1].

The processing pipeline includes:

- temporal smoothing via moving average,
- custom heuristics to filter noisy or inconsistent values,
- directional guidance logic based on signal flow analysis.

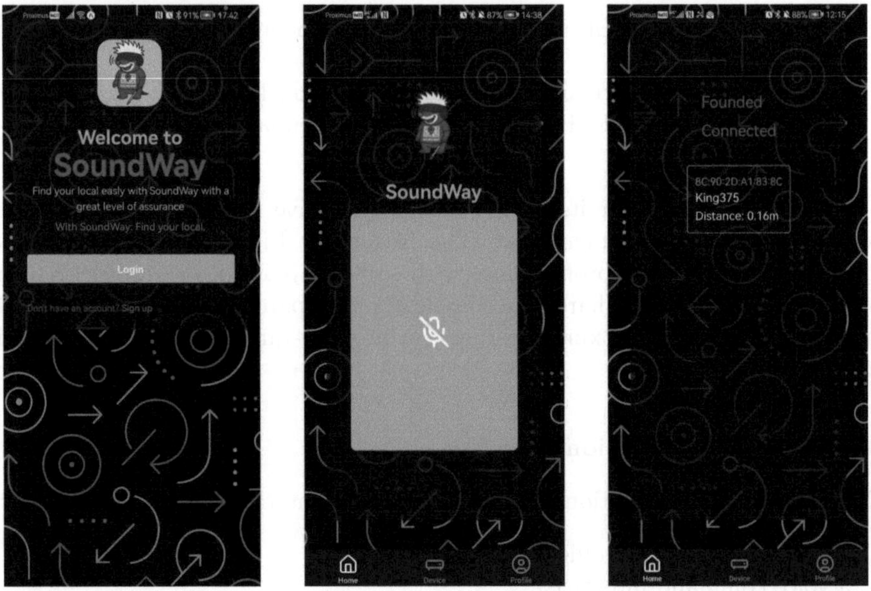

Fig. 2. Mobile interface of SoundWay: (a) login screen, (b) voice interaction module, and (c) real-time BLE proximity feedback showing detected device and estimated distance.

RSSI was chosen due to its ubiquity in BLE stacks and minimal computational overhead. Although its accuracy is limited by environmental factors, empirical testing showed that heuristic filtering and temporal aggregation yielded sufficiently stable feedback for basic orientation. The focus was on relative proximity (closer vs. farther) rather than absolute distance (Fig. 2).

3.4 Voice-Based Interaction

The mobile application integrates a speech-to-text module to support:

- hands-free system activation,
- simple directional queries and confirmations,
- multimodal interaction in non-visual contexts.

This mode of interaction is aligned with embodied and situated interaction paradigms, in which the user's perception, movement, and system feedback form a closed, dynamic loop. Voice input complements haptic and auditory outputs to support spatial decision-making in real time, particularly in environments where cues are absent or unusable.

The voice interaction system is implemented in the Expo React Native application via a dedicated **voice assistant provider**. This provider provides essential voice features, including voice capture, command recording, voice assistant status monitoring, and text-to-speech. The implementation is structured into three main components:

1. **Speech-to-Text (STT):** User voice commands are captured using Expo Speech Recognition and converted into text, which is then forwarded to the natural language processing (NLP) module.
2. **Natural Language Processing (NLP):** Command interpretation is handled by a Voice Command Manager that leverages Google Generative AI (Gemini Flash 2.5) to process user intent and determine the appropriate system response and the command to be executed.
3. **Text-to-Speech (TTS):** Processed commands and system feedback are communicated back to the user through synthesized speech using the Expo Speech library.

This modular architecture enables flexible voice interaction while maintaining clarity, responsiveness, and accessibility across different usage contexts.

3.5 Navigation Workflow

Navigation is implemented through a dedicated navigation provider within the mobile application. This provider manages navigation status, user progress, proximity information, and interaction with external services such as Bluetooth Low Energy (BLE) and the backend database.

When the user connects to a SoundWay-compatible environment, the system automatically detects the associated Bluetooth beacon. Once the connection is established, a request is sent to the Firestore database to retrieve the corresponding information about the building, including available rooms, navigation instructions, and proximity configuration settings. This allows the system to dynamically adapt the navigation behavior to the detected building.

Once the destination is specified, either by voice command or manual entry, the navigation provider queries the database for detailed room information and a sequence of navigation instructions. These instructions are then organized into a structured navigation session and are delivered to the user via voice guidance and haptic feedback.

Throughout the navigation process, the distance estimate based on BLE technology is continuously monitored. Changes in proximity are translated into vibration patterns that provide real-time spatial feedback as the user approaches their destination. The navigation service provider also manages state transitions, such as searching for a destination, active navigation, proximity-based arrival detection, and end of navigation.

This provider-based architecture ensures modularity, maintainability, and seamless integration between voice interaction, backend services, and proximity-based feedback mechanisms.

4 Contribution

SoundWay makes the following contributions to the field of assistive and embodied navigation:

1. **A BLE-based multi-advertising architecture** implemented on a Raspberry Pi, designed to increase signal density and enhance proximity estimation in indoor and outdoor transitional spaces.
2. **A voice-enabled mobile interface** that supports hands-free interaction and delivers multimodal feedback (auditory and haptic), enabling accessible navigation without relying on visual cues.
3. **A complete, low-cost end-to-end system pipeline**-from BLE signal emission to mobile interpretation and real-time user guidance-integrated into a portable and infrastructure-light prototype suitable for real-world deployment.

5 Evaluation

Evaluation Note. The following results are based on preliminary technical trials and informal walkthroughs; a structured user evaluation with visually impaired participants is part of future work.

The system was evaluated through a series of preliminary tests conducted in and around the corridors of the Faculty of Computer Science building. These tests aimed to assess the performance of BLE multi-advertising, the responsiveness of RSSI updates, and the usability of the voice interaction interface.

Signal Density. The use of simultaneous BLE advertisements significantly increased the frequency of received packets, resulting in smoother and more continuous signal acquisition. In comparison to a single advertisement setup, the multi-advertising approach reduced signal dropout and improved scan consistency, particularly in movement scenarios or near obstacles.

Responsiveness. RSSI updates on the mobile application were received with improved regularity. Averaging techniques and filtering heuristics contributed to perceptibly smoother distance estimations. While fluctuations remained, users were able to determine proximity changes within a 2–3 second response window.

Interaction Feedback. During informal walkthroughs performed by the project team, the voice-based interaction reduced the need for continuous touch input and the vibration patterns supported basic proximity and direction awareness in corridor and entrance scenarios. No structured user evaluation has yet been conducted.

Environmental Sensitivity. Despite the improvements, BLE signal reception remained susceptible to physical obstructions, device orientation, and body interference. Signal reflection in narrow corridors occasionally caused temporary RSSI inconsistencies, requiring users to pause for stabilization.

Summary. These preliminary tests confirmed that the system is viable for basic proximity-based navigation assistance. While not suitable for precise indoor localization, SoundWay successfully supports relative distance awareness and multimodal feedback in real time, using low-cost hardware and without requiring dedicated infrastructure.

6 Discussion

SoundWay demonstrates the feasibility of a lightweight, embodied navigation system that combines BLE multi-advertising, RSSI-based distance processing, and voice interaction in a cohesive, mobile-centric prototype. The system is particularly suited to transitional indoor/outdoor spaces where GPS is unreliable and full infrastructure is unavailable.

From a theoretical perspective, the system embodies principles of situated and embodied cognition. The BLE emitters serve as spatially embedded artifacts, transforming physical space into an interactive medium. User perception emerges not merely from signal reception, but from the continuous coupling between bodily motion, environmental feedback, and auditory/haptic cues. This reinforces the notion that navigation is a distributed cognitive process-situated within the interaction between user, device, and spatial context.

Implementation Difficulties: Several challenges emerged during development. Chief among them was the instability of RSSI readings, which were often affected by user orientation, obstacles, and multi-path reflections. Signal fluctuations frequently required waiting periods exceeding five seconds for measurements to stabilize. Similarly, the voice interaction module exhibited reduced reliability in acoustically noisy environments, limiting hands-free usability in some contexts.

Dependency Management Challenges: Another significant challenge arose from the fact that the mobile application depends on several third-party libraries for speech-to-text (STT) and text-to-speech (TTS) functionality. The ecosystem of React Native libraries for voice interaction is fragmented, with different packages requiring specific versions of React Native, Expo, or underlying native on Android often required extensive testing and version locking, sometimes resulting in temporary regressions or the need to completely change libraries. This experience highlights the complexity of integrating mobile-platform voice interaction into a rapidly evolving mobile development environment.

System Limitations: The prototype relies solely on RSSI for distance estimation, which inherently lacks accuracy due to BLE's sensitivity to environmental interference. Additionally, the current design provides only coarse directional feedback, without precise localization or spatial mapping. These limitations are acceptable within the scope of this prototype, whose goal is to support relative orientation rather than exact positioning. However, they represent clear barriers to long-term scalability or deployment in highly dynamic or cluttered spaces.

Natural Language Processing Limitations: The system's NLP module, responsible for interpreting user voice commands, occasionally produced unexpected outputs. For example, the model sometimes returned Markdown-formatted text instead of the expected JSON structure, leading to parsing errors and incorrect command execution. To mitigate this, a fallback response mechanism was implemented, providing a default prompt or error message to the user when command processing failed. This limitation highlights the challenges of relying on generative AI for real-time voice interaction and underscores the importance of robust error handling in navigation applications.

Accessibility and Participatory Design. While no formal accessibility compliance audit has been conducted, future iterations will be aligned with established accessibility guidance (e.g., WCAG and EN 301 549) [8,19] and evaluated through participatory methods involving visually impaired users (e.g., co-design sessions and structured usability studies).

Comparison with Existing Approaches. Compared to vision-based or dedicated sensing solutions, SoundWay focuses on low-cost BLE infrastructure and multimodal feedback, trading absolute localization accuracy for lightweight deployment and relative proximity guidance. Compared to typical BLE beacon approaches, the multi-advertising setup aims to increase packet density and stabilize proximity feedback after smoothing.

Future Work: Several enhancements are envisioned to improve the robustness, precision, and generalizability of SoundWay:

- **Filtering and Calibration:** Integration of advanced smoothing techniques such as Kalman filtering, along with a dedicated calibration phase to account for environmental variability.
- **Multi-emitter triangulation:** Deploying multiple BLE emitters to enable spatial triangulation and improve directional guidance accuracy.
- **User-centered evaluation:** Conducting participatory studies with visually impaired individuals to assess usability, comfort, and real-world accessibility impact.

Collectively, these avenues aim to transform SoundWay from a functional prototype into a scalable and reliable tool for inclusive navigation across multiple real-world settings.

7 Conclusion

This work has presented **SoundWay**, a functional prototype for augmented navigation that integrates BLE multi-advertising, mobile RSSI processing, and voice-enabled interaction. The system demonstrates that accessible, low-cost orientation support can be achieved using commodity hardware, without relying on dedicated infrastructure or visual feedback.

SoundWay contributes both technically and conceptually: it introduces a complete end-to-end pipeline for proximity-based navigation, and operationalizes key principles from embodied and multimodal interaction theory. By distributing guidance across auditory, haptic, and spatial modalities, the system enhances environmental awareness and user autonomy-particularly for individuals with visual impairments.

Although preliminary, the results confirm the feasibility of deploying BLE-based, feedback-rich navigation tools in real-world indoor and semi-outdoor settings. Future work will aim to extend SoundWay's scalability, robustness, and adaptability through sensor fusion, multi-emitter triangulation, and participatory user evaluations.

Ultimately, SoundWay illustrates how lightweight, human-centered technologies can meaningfully contribute to inclusive mobility in increasingly complex environments.

Acknowledgments. The authors would like to thank the Faculty of Computer Science at the University of Namur for their support.

Disclosure of Interests. The authors have no competing interests to declare that are relevant to the content of this article.

References

1. Bleak: Bluetooth low energy platform-agnostic client for python (2023). https://bleak.readthedocs.io/. Accessed 20 Oct 2025
2. Bluez: Official linux bluetooth protocol stack documentation (2023). http://www.bluez.org/documentation/. Accessed 20 Oct 2025
3. D-bus specification (2023). https://dbus.freedesktop.org/doc/dbus-specification.html. Accessed 20 Oct 2025
4. "don't invent for, invent with!" designing digital solutions inclusive of people with vision impairment (2023). https://www.who.int/europe/news-room/feature-stories/item/don-t-invent-for--invent-with!--designing-digital-solutions-inclusive-of-people-with-vision-impairment. Accessed 20 Oct 2025
5. Barthès, J.P., Martin, J.C.: Interfaces homme-machine. CNRS Éditions, Paris, France (2020). https://books.openedition.org/editionscnrs/30758
6. Dix, A., Finlay, J., Abowd, G., Beale, R.: Human-Computer Interaction, 3rd edn. Pearson Education, Harlow (2004)
7. Engelbart, D.C.: Augmenting human intellect: a conceptual framework. Technical report, Stanford Research Institute, Menlo Park (1962). aFOSR-3223 summary report
8. ETSI: EN 301 549: Accessibility requirements for ICT products and services (2019). https://www.etsi.org/deliver/etsi_en/301500_301599/301549/03.02.01_60/en_301549v030201p.pdf. Accessed 09 Feb 2026
9. Kammoun, S., et al.: Navigation and space perception assistance for the visually impaired: The navig project. IRBM **33**(2), 182–189 (2012). https://doi.org/10.1016/j.irbm.2012.01.009. SoundWay: BLE Multi-Advertising for Non-Visual Navigation 11
10. Li, B., et al.: Vision-based mobile indoor assistive navigation aid for blind people. IEEE Trans. Mob. Comput. **18**(3), 702–714 (2019). https://doi.org/10.1109/TMC.2018.2842751
11. Mekhalfi, M.L., Melgani, F., Zeggada, A., De Natale, F.G., Salem, M.A.M., Khamis, A.: Recovering the sight to blind people in indoor environments with smart technologies. Expert Syst. Appl. **46**, 129–138 (2016). https://doi.org/10.1016/j.eswa.2015.09.054
12. Mule, K., Shinde, J.V.: Smart approach for finding indoor navigation using BLE for visually impaired persons. Int. J. Comput. Sci. Eng. (IJCSE) **5**(3), 10492 (2018). https://www.ijcseonline.org/pub_paper/18-IJCSE-07624.pdf. bLE-based indoor navigation system designed to assist visually impaired users; Accessed 20 Oct 2025

13. Mule, K., Shinde, J.V.: Smart approach for finding indoor navigation using BLE for visually impaired person. Int. J. Adv. Res. Innov. Ideas Educ. **5**(3), 10492 (2019). https://ijariie.com/AdminUploadPdf/Smart_Approach_for_Finding_Indoor_Navigation_Using_BLE__for_Visually_Impaired_Person_ijariie10492.pdf
14. Mustafa, A., Sykes, E.R.: A high fidelity indoor navigation system for users in motion using BLE with beacons. In: Proceedings of the 2021 International Conference on Smart Computing (SmartComp 2021) (2021). https://ceur-ws.org/Vol-3097/paper13.pdf
15. Plikynas, D., Indriulionis, A., Laukaitis, A., Sakalauskas, L.: Indoor-guided navigation for people who are blind: crowdsourcing for route mapping and assistance. Appl. Sci. **12**(1), 523 (2022). https://doi.org/10.3390/app12010523
16. Preece, J., Rogers, Y., Sharp, H.: Interaction Design: Beyond Human-Computer Interaction, 4th edn. Wiley, Chichester (2015)
17. Sarfraz, M.S., Constantinescu, A., Zuzej, M., Stiefelhagen, R.: A multimodal assistive system for helping visually impaired in social interactions. Inform. - Spektr. **40**(6), 540–545 (2017). https://doi.org/10.1007/s00287-017-1077-7
18. Vision Loss Expert Group (VLEG): Vision loss expert group: Causes and prevalence of vision loss 1990–2020 (2021). https://www.iapb.org/wp-content/uploads/2021/02/Vision-Loss-Expert-Group-VLEG-Eye-Health-Report-2020.pdf. Accessed 20 Oct 2025
19. W3C: Web content accessibility guidelines (WCAG) 2.2 (2023). https://www.w3.org/TR/WCAG22/. Accessed 09 Feb 2026
20. World Health Organization: Blindness and vision impairment (2023). https://www.who.int/news-room/fact-sheets/detail/blindness-and-visual-impairment. Fact sheet, updated 10 August 2023; Accessed 20 Oct 2025
21. Zhang, X., Huang, X., Ding, Y., Long, L., Li, W., Xu, X.: Advancements in smart wearable mobility aids for visual impairment: a bibliometric narrative review. Sensors **24**(24), 7986 (2024). https://doi.org/10.3390/s24247986

PAVE A Guideline to Help Developers Produce Accessible Virtual Reality

Deborah Dantas[1(✉)], João Mello[1], Beatriz Gadelha[1], Marcos Melo[1], César Rennó-Costa[1], Alyson Souza[1], Luiza Cintra[2], Arlindo Galvão[2], Leina Yoshida[3], Gustavo Domingues[3], Thaynara de Jesus[3], Fabiana Peres[3], Pedro Mendes[4], William Ferreira[4], Marcio Soussa[4], and Ingrid Winkler[5]

[1] AKCIT, Instituto Metrópole Digital, Natal, Brazil
deboraharruda@hotmail.com, {cesar,alyson}@imd.ufrn.br
[2] AKCIT, Universidade Federal de Goiás, Goiânia, Brazil
cintraluiza@discente.ufg.br, arlindo@ufg.br
[3] Universidade Estadual do Oeste do Paraná, Cascavel, Brazil
{leina.yoshida,gustavo.domingues,thaynara.jesus, fabiana.peres}@unioeste.br
[4] Universidade SENAI CIMATEC, Salvador, Brazil
pedro.mendes@aln.senaicimatec.edu.br, william.f@ba.docente.senai.br
[5] AKCIT, CIMATEC, Caguas, Brazil
ingrid.winkler@fieb.org.br

Abstract. This paper details the early construction of PAVE (Producing Accessible Virtual Environments), a guideline geared towards virtual reality (VR) developers to assist them in creating more accessible VR environments for users with disabilities. Many people with disabilities (PWD), especially users with visually or auditory impairments, struggle to use VR, and rarely find use for the technology outside of treatment. To this end, PAVE seeks to find accessibility features that have been successfully tested by PWD users, and provide a roadmap for developers to alter or build VR software that is more inclusive. To this end, we have performed an initial systematic literature review (SLR) to analyze the current academic state of VR accessibility features, finding 35 research papers that fit our criteria, and developing them into the first version of PAVE. Future research will entail comparing a virtual environment with and without PAVE, and gathering feedback from developers and PWD to evolve PAVE.

Keywords: Virtual reality · Accessibility · Human-Computer Interaction · Sensory Substitution · Inclusion · Guideline

1 Introduction

The field of Virtual Reality (VR) has recently undergone a massive expansion since the 1990's, due to improvements in display technology and computational

C. Stephanidis et al. (Eds.): HCII 2026, CCIS 3047, pp. 515–525, 2026.
https://doi.org/10.1007/978-3-032-30552-7_49

power [2]. Millions of Head-Mounted Devices (HMD), such as Meta Quests, Oculus Rifts and Apple Vision Pros are sold every year, proving the field's growing popularity [29]. This technology has a wide array of uses that have helped increase interest, such as entertainment, education and gaming.

In spite of this, many people with disabilities (PWD) struggle to use VR for a variety of reasons, be it difficulty to see, hear, or move in a way that allows them to properly interface with HMDs. Research done by Mott et al. [30] shows that PWD want to use VR, but feel insecure given the lack of accessibility features that could help them. Many developers deeply understand the importance of implementing accessibility features in virtual reality, and have a desire to do so, but also convey that there is a lack of resources to help them understand what features to implement [21,43]. Resources are scarce and outdated, presumably due to the quick evolution of VR technology and the scope of pains to create solutions for, and most developers are unaware of such resources.

In order to address this gap, our research decided to tackle this issue with the following two-step approach: (1) performing a Systematic Literature Review (SLR) regarding VR and accessibility in major technological research publishers, and (2) analyzing the chosen literature and elaborating PAVE (Producing Accessible Virtual Environments), a guideline for developers to understand the best practices for developing accessible VR software. This guideline is meant to guide VR developers in the use of fully immersive HMDs. Augmented reality and semi-immersive VR are not covered, given the different ways those technologies allow the user to interact with the technology and the real world.

2 Related Works

In this section, (1) we explore therapeutic and educational studies of VR for PWD, (2) address the difficulties this community faces when using this kind of technology, and (3) discuss the motivation to create the development guideline.

2.1 VR's Potential for PWD

The ability of VR to create customizable scenarios opens doors for a variety of experiments for rehabilitation, therapeutic, and educational applications, which prove to be a great support tool for PWD. Within motor rehabilitation, studies such as Wijaya et al. [40] indicate that VR, particularly when combined with conventional therapies, improves motor function, balance, and quality of life for stroke patients. VR is also finding significant potential for education, especially for children with special educational needs (SEN). Stoev et al. [37] reinforces the potential of this technology to create personalized environments and be able to cater to people with special needs.

2.2 VR Usage Challenges for PWD

Despite the potential VR offers to PWD, there are still barriers that hinder or prevent them from using this technology, derived from the development of systems from users without impairments. Gerling & Spiel [12] criticize this tendency for its exclusion of a significant portion of users who could benefit from VR.

Some of these difficulties arise even before interacting with the systems. Mott et al. [30] identifies the setup of VR devices a concern for people with limited mobility, as it requires physical abilities that many users may not possess. Participants also found putting on an HMD difficult, and the design of certain models interfered with the headrest of wheelchairs, causing discomfort. In the same study, participants with upper limb impairments had difficulty or were unable to perform actions that required the simultaneous use of both controllers.

VR locomotion is extremely challenging for people with visual impairments, as shown by Ribeiro et al. [34]. Participants would accidentally stray from their intended direction, and alternate techniques such as Point & Teleport and Arm Swinging also proved difficult. A study by Kreimeier et al. [23] had similar results, requiring users with low vision to use a treadmill to move. Despite a highly satisfactory result, it is important to note that specialized equipment was necessary. Finally, it is important to note that while auditory feedback is crucial in addressing visual impairments in this group, a participant in the first study indicated that indiscriminate use of this feedback can lead to sensory overload.

People with autism spectrum disorder (ASD) also face several difficulties when using VR. Bozgeyikli et al. [5] points out several difficulties that these individuals face when immersed in virtual environments such as: controlling complex inputs can be tiring and frustrating; too much information and many interactions can leave users feeling overwhelmed; and very loud noises and breaks in immersion can cause irritation due to a feeling of lack of control.

2.3 Guideline Motivation and Current Resources

In light of these aspects about VR use by PWD, we sought to understand what developers face when trying to implement accessibility features in VR. Ji et al. [21] cites several challenges, such as a lack of a widely accepted guideline, development tools and example projects that might help a developer understand how to implement accessibility features, as well as difficulties in comprehending the perspectives of PWD, and how the VR software would need to be adapted.

Resources such as XR Accessibility User Requirements (XAUR) [1] and IEEE's Extended Reality (XR) Ethics and Diversity, Inclusion, and Accessibility [9], can help developers; however, as much as guidelines are needed, VR developers must also keep in mind the importance of testing their software with PWD if possible, to ensure that the features implemented are working properly, and that the user can use VR without difficulty. Peck et al. [33] highlights the importance of letting PWD participate in the development cycle.

In this context, we propose PAVE (Producing Accessible Virtual Environments), a guideline designed to detail accessibility features, how to implement them and who they are geared towards or can help.

3 Methodology

The methodology used to find articles for the guideline was a SLR, utilizing 4 technologically prominent databases: IEEE Xplore, ACM Digital Library, Springer and Scopus. The research string used to find articles relevant to the study was *[("Virtual Reality" OR VR) AND (accessibility OR disability OR impairment OR "assistive technology" OR "inclusive design")]*. Articles were filtered between 2020–2024, in order to ensure the most recent developments in VR technology, such as mass market HMDs, hand tracking, and a larger scale of software available to consumers. Inclusion criteria parameters were that the articles must be research or conference articles and in English. 3,861 articles were found.

After discussions, it was decided that the ideal article for the guideline needed to have 4 key elements: (1) it needed to focus solely on VR. Augmented reality, mixed reality (MR), and semi-immersive VR, would not be included in the study; (2) it needed to focus on improving the use of VR for PWD, such as recognizing difficulties and implementing or theorizing solutions; (3) the solution had to be reasonable for a developer to implement in their VR software; and (4) the feature must have been tested or vetted by PWD.

A first analysis of these articles' title and abstract was done, and articles that did not have any relation to virtual reality or accessibility and duplicate articles were removed from the study. A total of 1,151 articles remained.

The next round of analysis consisted of, still regarding the title and abstract, evaluating which articles were focused on VR use with PWD. Articles in this analysis regarding immersive technologies other than VR were removed. Articles that regarded the use of VR solely as an assessment or rehabilitation tool were maintained if the article discussed the PWD experience with VR as a technology, and the benefits and challenges it presented, and not solely the experience with it as a tool. A total of 106 articles remained.

The final analysis dove into the article's full text, and sought to eliminate articles that either did not discuss solutions, or whose solutions were difficult to implement, such as altering HMDs or external equipment that could not be obtained or developed easily (full body tracking, haptic equipment, among others). Some articles, while valuable, were removed given that they were part of a series of articles from a same research group, and repeated several solutions. A total of 35 articles remained to build the guideline.

4 Results

In an attempt to evaluate how developers might perceive the guideline, within the research team (composed by VR developers and researchers), the accessibility features received a ranking of development difficulty.

- 1: simple, with no software or hardware development needed
- 2: easy, open-source or easily reproducible software development
- 3: intermediate, software development that is hard to recreate

- 4: complex, hardware development required
- 5: difficult, both software and hardware development needed

4.1 Before Development and Good Practices

- *Interview users with disabilities to better understand what assistance is necessary:* 1. This step is crucial in ensuring accessibility and understanding what users with disabilities who will use your software will need [33].
- *Take into account user aids, and understand how to navigate using them with a head-set:* 4. This step may require alternate hardware, such as head straps that can accommodate cochlear implants, or controllers that users with limited movement or prosthetic limbs can use comfortably [18,35].

4.2 During Development

General Accessibility

- *Offer alternate control schemes and interaction types, such as hand controls and voice controls:* 3. While solutions to choose between standard controls and hand controls for HMDs with MR cameras are available, an alternate control scheme might have to be developed, and a voice recognition system will have to be implemented for voice controls [17,30,38,42].
- *Offer alternate movement types, such as teleportation:* 3. Some controls to activate movement types may not align with the controls being used, and may require further development (i.e.: teleportation using solely controls will have to be altered for hand or voice controls) [10].

Social/Multiplayer VR

- *Give the user the option to identify themselves as disabled, with signifiers and diverse player models:* 2. This will require developing and rigging player models, and adding signifiers to profile pages and gameplay [3,16,44].
- *Implement sign language interpretation:* 4. HMDs with MR cameras or support for haptic gloves can interpret a user's signing. Open-source solutions for this may be able depending the language being used, and adaptation to text-to-speech for visually impaired users should be considered [8].
- *Offer auditory cues for non-verbal interactions for visually impaired users:* 2. This will require tracking user positioning and making sure that these cues will not interfere with other audio sources such as communication and audio description [20,22,36].

Deaf/DHH Users

- *Offer close-captions when audio is active and display where the audio is coming from:* 2. This will require some attention so the close-captions do not prevent the user from seeing/interacting with objects [25,32].
- *Offer visual and haptic cues to substitute audio cues:* 3. Visual cues will be easier to implement than haptic cues, which will require controls or haptic devices such as gloves or vests [19].

Users with Mobility Impairments

- *Alter a player's height or movement type and reach:* 3. Movement will have to be tested to ensure that users don't get cybersickness or feel disoriented. Altered reach will also have to be tested with alternate controls, such as standard or hand controls [6,11,24,41].
- *Offer multimodal cues to improve balance and reduce cybersickness for users with gait issues:* 5. Haptic cues might be difficult to implement, while visual and audio cues, while being slightly less effective, will be easier, due to their nature integration in HMDs [26].

Visually Impaired Users

- *Offer features to correct distortion, enhance color and brightness, and magnify the image:* 2. The visual alterations should be applied to the user's field of vision [28].
- *Offer general and case-specific audio descriptions:* 3. Different audio descriptions will have to be made, depending on what the experience demands, and how the user would like to perceive it. The audio description should be developed so that it will not interfere with other audio sources such as diegetic sounds and audio cues [7,15,31].
- *Offer visual light transmission reduction for users with photophobia:* 2. This system will have to be implemented with caution, as light sources that are too intense or too weak might cause discomfort in a user [14].

4.3 After Development and During Testing

- *Call users with disabilities to participate in software testing:* 1. As mentioned earlier, understanding what a user with disabilities might want and need in VR is the most important step in ensuring inclusion. Ensure that the user feels safe during testing and that relevant feedback regarding comfort and user experience is collected [33].
- *Make information about the software's accessibility readily available both in the software and in publishing spaces:* 1. Several publishing stores do not have a specific place for this information to be inserted, however this can help users understand if they can properly use the software [39].

- *Offer assistance with setting up the VR system, such as putting on the HMD, and defining the play space, controls, and movement:* 1. Users may have a difficult time interacting with the HMD and its peripherals, such as controls and cables. Ensure that the testing space allows them to move freely, even if the experience does not require movement beyond head movement [30].
- *Offer alternate controls and head straps, to ensure the user's comfort:* 5. Many developers only have access to HMDs, and alternate accessories may not be available for all [4,13,45].
- *Offer haptic gloves, to assist with feedback for users with mobility and visual limitations:* 5. As mentioned previously, VR accessories are still hard to access for many developers, and haptic technology is still in its infancy. Integrating it with VR software is also a challenge, but the technology can assist users greatly [27].

4.4 Comparison with Other Guidelines and Noticeable Gaps

A comparison was made between the guideline we constructed and XAUR [1], created by the World Wide Web Consortium (W3C), and the Extended Reality (XR) Ethics and Diversity, Inclusion, and Accessibility [9], from the IEEE Standards Association. In this comparison, it was identified that a large part of the solutions compiled in our guideline were already addressed in some way in these pre-existing guidelines. However, it's crucial to acknowledge that the majority of these relationships were indirect. The points that these guidelines bring are mainly needs that the PWD public faces when using VR, along with broader solutions on how to solve these difficulties. In contrast, our guideline addresses functionalities both from this perspective and from a more specific one, where we bring techniques recently addressed in the literature to facilitate the use of VR by PWD. Thus, while the guides address the need for haptic feedback and alternative movement techniques for immersive environments, our study already brings examples such as haptic gloves, MR canes, and pointing, floating, and speech-based locomotion techniques. Furthermore, we were able to identify solutions that were not so evident in the comparison guides, such as techniques to improve users' balance, haptic feedback for non-verbal cues, light adjustments to reduce eye strain, and distortion correction. Thus, our work enhances and expands upon crucial guidelines previously addressed by the literature.

Some disabilities were underrepresented or not addressed in the chosen research papers, such as neurodivergence, wheelchair users and mild visual impairments, such as color-blindness. We hope to find more works in the future that cover a wider array of disabilities.

Accessibility in VR still has a long way to go, and as much as people without disabilities put in effort, it is erroneous to believe that they can be found without cooperation. As previously established, both VR developers and PWD wish for more accessibility in VR, and collaboration will help us reach that goal.

5 Limitations

The main limitation of this study resides in the absence of an empirical validation of the PAVE guideline with its intended users. Although the original project proposed the creation of adapted virtual environments for comparative tests, the focus of this research step was restricted to the theoretical foundation and the systemic structuring of the accessibility functionalities based on the literature. The practical efficacy of the identified functionalities still requires direct evaluation with PWD users and VR developers to measure their clarity and applicability in real development scenarios.

6 Conclusion

This study sought to understand the challenges faced by PWD in VR and by VR developers in order to develop a guideline entitled PAVE to help VR developers create more accessible VR. After a SLR, we found 35 articles detailing accessibility features not commonly included in guidelines and developed a guideline with the goal of helping VR developers to produce more accessible VR software. While the amount of research focusing on this topics has been increasing over the years, much more research is still needed on this technology regarding its accessibility for PWD to ensure that more robust and validated guidance can be developed to assist VR developers in implementing, using and improving these features. Future work will include testing the guideline in virtual environments and receiving feedback from developers and PWD VR users.

Acknowledgments. This work has been partially funded by the project 'Investigation of Immersive Technologies for the Development of New Experiences in the Arts', supported by the Advanced Knowledge Center in Immersive Technologies (AKCIT), with financial resources from the PPI IoT/Manufatura 4.0/PPI HardwareBR of the MCTI, through grant number 057/2023, signed with EMBRAPII. We would like to thank Instituto Metrópole Digital and Laboratório de Computação Gráfica (LabCG).

Disclosure of Interests. The authors have no competing interests to declare that are relevant to the content of this article.

References

1. XR Accessibility User Requirements — w3.org. https://www.w3.org/TR/xaur/. Accessed 12 Sep 2025
2. Ambrosio, A.P., Fidalgo, M.I.R.: Past, present and future of virtual reality: analysis of its technological variables and definitions. Cult. Hist. Digital J. e010–e010 (2020)
3. Angerbauer, K., et al.: Is it part of me? Exploring experiences of inclusive avatar use for visible and invisible disabilities in social VR. In: Proceedings of the 26th International ACM SIGACCESS Conference on Computers and Accessibility, pp. 1–15 (2024)

4. Barhoush, Y., Georgiev, G.V., Loudon, B.: Empathy and idea generation: exploring the design of a virtual reality controller for rehabilitation purposes. In: DS 105: Proceedings of the Sixth International Conference on Design Creativity, pp. 287–294. (2020) ICDC 2020
5. Bozgeyikli, L., Raij, A., Katkoori, S., Alqasemi, R.: A survey on virtual reality for individuals with autism spectrum disorder: design considerations. IEEE Trans. Learn. Technol. 133–151 (2017)
6. Cabrera-Araya, R.T., Rojas-Munoz, E.: INDYvr: towards an ergonomics-based framework for inclusive and dynamic personalizations of virtual reality environments. In: 2024 IEEE International Symposium on Mixed and Augmented Reality Adjunct (ISMAR-Adjunct), pp. 220–222 (2024)
7. Dang, K., Burke, G., Korreshi, H., Lee, S.: Towards accessible musical performances in virtual reality: designing a conceptual framework for omnidirectional audio descriptions. In: Proceedings of the 26th International ACM SIGACCESS Conference on Computers and Accessibility (2024)
8. Dudas, O., Nandra, C., Mocan, C.M., Gorgan, D.: Hand signal classification system for sign language communication in virtual reality. In: 2023 IEEE 19th International Conference on Intelligent Computer Communication and Processing (ICCP), pp. 177–183 (2023)
9. Fox, D., Thornton, I.G.: The IEEE global initiative on ethics of extended reality (XR) report-extended reality (XR) ethics and diversity, inclusion, and accessibility. In: The IEEE Global Initiative on Ethics of Extended Reality (XR) Report-Extended Reality (XR) Ethics and Diversity, Inclusion, and Accessibility, pp. 1–25 (2022)
10. Franz, R.L., Yu, J., Wobbrock, J.O.: Comparing locomotion techniques in virtual reality for people with upper-body motor impairments. In: Proceedings of the 25th International ACM SIGACCESS Conference on Computers and Accessibility, pp. 1–15 (2023)
11. Ganapathi, P., Thiel, F.J., Swapp, D., Steed, A.: Head in the clouds-floating locomotion in virtual reality. In: 2022 IEEE Conference on Virtual Reality and 3D User Interfaces Abstracts and Workshops (VRW), pp. 668–669 (2022)
12. Gerling, K., Spiel, K.: A critical examination of virtual reality technology in the context of the minority body. In: Proceedings of the 2021 CHI Conference on Human Factors in Computing Systems, pp. 1–14 (2021)
13. Gluck, A., Golba, E., Brinkley, J.: Development of a VR head-mounted display strap modification for use by individuals with a cochlear implant. In: Proceedings of the Human Factors and Ergonomics Society Annual Meeting, pp. 1541–1547 (2023)
14. Gluck, A., Huth, L.: Supporting individuals with photophobia in VR: a case study of VR shades, an accessible VR application feature prototype. In: 2024 IEEE Conference on Virtual Reality and 3D User Interfaces Abstracts and Workshops (VRW), pp. 311–315. (2024)
15. Gonzalez Penuela, R.E., Poremba, W., Trice, C., Azenkot, S.: Hands-on: using gestures to control descriptions of a virtual environment for people with visual impairments. In: Adjunct Proceedings of the 35th Annual ACM Symposium on User Interface Software and Technology, pp. 1–4 (2022)
16. Gualano, R.J., Jiang, L., Zhang, K., Shende, T., Won, A.S., Azenkot, S.: "i try to represent myself as i am": self-presentation preferences of people with invisible disabilities through embodied social VR avatars. In: Proceedings of the 26th International ACM SIGACCESS Conference on Computers and Accessibility, pp. 1–15 (2024)

17. Hombeck, J., Voigt, H., Heggemann, T., Datta, R.R., Lawonn, K.: Tell me where to go: voice-controlled hands-free locomotion for virtual reality systems. In: 2023 IEEE Conference Virtual Reality and 3D User Interfaces (VR), pp. 123–134. (2023)
18. Hsu, Y.H., Fang, I.K., Wang, C., Chen, J.C., Hu, M.C.: Integrating physical wheelchairs and virtual basketball for enhanced access and enjoyment in wheelchair basketball. In: 2024 IEEE International Conference on Artificial Intelligence and eXtended and Virtual Reality (AIxVR), pp. 80–84 (2024)
19. Jain, D., et al.: Towards sound accessibility in virtual reality. In: Proceedings of the 2021 International Conference on Multimodal Interaction, p. 80–91 (2021)
20. Ji, T.F., Cochran, B.R., Zhao, Y.: Demonstration of VRBubble: enhancing peripheral avatar awareness for people with visual impairments in social virtual reality. In: CHI Conference on Human Factors in Computing Systems Extended Abstracts, pp. 1–6 (2022)
21. Ji, T.F., Hu, Y., Huang, Y., Du, R., Zhao, Y.: A preliminary interview: understanding XR developers' needs towards open-source accessibility support. In: 2023 IEEE Conference on Virtual Reality and 3D User Interfaces Abstracts and Workshops (VRW), pp. 493–496 (2023)
22. Jung, C., et al.: Accessible nonverbal cues to support conversations in VR for blind and low vision people. In: Proceedings of the 26th International ACM SIGACCESS Conference on Computers and Accessibility, pp. 1–13 (2024)
23. Kreimeier, J., Karg, P., Götzelmann, T.: BlindWalkVR: formative insights into blind and visually impaired people's VR locomotion using commercially available approaches. In: Proceedings of the 13th ACM International Conference on PErvasive Technologies Related to Assistive Environments, pp. 1–8 (2020)
24. Franz, L., Junuzovic, R., Mott, S., M.: Nearmi: a framework for designing point of interest techniques for VR users with limited mobility. In: Proceedings of the 23rd International ACM SIGACCESS Conference on Computers and Accessibility, pp. 1–14 (2021)
25. Li, Z., Peiris, R.: Exploring the Soundvizvr plugin in the development of sound-accessible virtual reality games: insights from game developers and players. ACM Trans. Accessible Comput. 1–20 (2024)
26. Mahmud, M.R., Cordova, A., Quarles, J.: Multimodal feedback methods for advancing the accessibility of immersive virtual reality for people with balance impairments due to multiple sclerosis. IEEE Trans. Visual Comput. Graph. 7193–7202 (2024)
27. Masmoudi, M., et al.: Low-cost haptic glove for grasp precision improvement in virtual reality-based post-stroke hand rehabilitation. In: 2021 International Conference on Artificial Intelligence for Cyber Security Systems and Privacy (AI-CSP), pp. 1–3 (2021)
28. Masnadi, S., Williamson, B., González, A.N.V., LaViola, J.J.: VRiAssist: an eye-tracked virtual reality low vision assistance tool. In: 2020 IEEE Conference on Virtual Reality and 3D User Interfaces Abstracts and Workshops (VRW), pp. 808–809 (2020)
29. McCurdy, W.: Global VR Headset Shipments to Hit 9.6 Million in 2024 as Meta Leads — pcmag.com. https://www.pcmag.com/news/global-vr-headset-shipments-to-hit-96-million-in-2024-as-meta-leads (2024)
30. Mott, M., Tang, J., Kane, S., Cutrell, E., Ringel Morris, M.: "i just went into it assuming that i wouldn't be able to have the full experience" understanding the accessibility of virtual reality for people with limited mobility. In: Proceedings of the 22nd International ACM SIGACCESS Conference on Computers and Accessibility, pp. 1–13 (2020)

31. Oliveira, E.A.M.d., Silva, D.F.C., Filho, A.R.G.: Improving VR accessibility through automatic 360 scene description using multimodal large language models. In: Proceedings of the 26th Symposium on Virtual and Augmented Reality, pp. 289–293 (2024)
32. Orero, P., Brescia-Zapata, M., Hughes, C.: Evaluating subtitle readability in media immersive environments. In: Proceedings of the 9th International Conference on Software Development and Technologies for Enhancing Accessibility and Fighting Info-Exclusion, pp. 51–54 (2020)
33. Peck, T.C., McMullen, K.A., Quarles, J.: DiVRsify: break the cycle and develop VR for everyone. IEEE Comput. Graph. Appl. 133–142 (2021)
34. Ribeiro, R.A., et al.: Investigating virtual reality locomotion techniques with blind people. In: Proceedings of the 2024 CHI Conference on Human Factors in Computing Systems, pp. 1–17 (2024)
35. Sassi, V.F., Porcino, T., Clua, E.W., Trevisan, D.G.: Redefining redirected movement for wheelchair based interaction for virtual reality. In: 2023 IEEE 11th International Conference on Serious Games and Applications for Health (SeGAH), pp. 1–8 (2023)
36. Segal, J.I., et al.: SocialCueSwitch: towards customizable accessibility by representing social cues in multiple senses. In: Extended Abstracts of the CHI Conference on Human Factors in Computing Systems, pp. 1–7 (2024)
37. Stoev, S., Rasheva-Yordanova, K., Bankovska, M., Getova, I.: Analysis of the applicability of VR in the education of children with disabilities. In: 2024 47th MIPRO ICT and Electronics Convention (MIPRO), pp. 364–368 (2024)
38. Tian, J., et al.: Designing upper-body gesture interaction with and for people with spinal muscular atrophy in VR. In: Proceedings of the 2024 CHI Conference on Human Factors in Computing Systems, pp. 1–19 (2024)
39. Vlahovic, S., Skorin-Kapov, L., Car, Z.: An initiative toward an enhanced industry-reported comfort, accessibility, and safety rating system for VR applications. In: 2023 15th International Conference on Quality of Multimedia Experience (QoMEX), pp. 95–98 (2023)
40. Wijaya, Y., Ismail, R., Prahasto, T.: The effect of virtual reality-based on intervention in stroke patients: systematic review. In: 2023 IEEE International Biomedical Instrumentation and Technology Conference (IBITeC), pp. 34–39 (2023)
41. Yamagami, M., et al.: Two-in-one: a design space for mapping unimanual input into bimanual interactions in VR for users with limited movement. ACM Trans. Access. Comput. (2022)
42. Yildirim, C.: Designing with two hands in mind? A review of mainstream VR applications with upper-limb impairments in mind. In: Proceedings of the 16th International Workshop on Immersive Mixed and Virtual Environment Systems, pp. 29–34 (2024)
43. Zallio, M., Clarkson, P.J.: Designing the metaverse: a study on inclusion, diversity, equity, accessibility and safety for digital immersive environments. Telematics Inform. 101909 (2022)
44. Zhang, K., Deldari, E., Yao, Y., Zhao, Y.: A diary study in social virtual reality: impact of avatars with disability signifiers on the social experiences of people with disabilities. In: Proceedings of the 25th International ACM SIGACCESS Conference on Computers and Accessibility, pp. 1–17 (2023)
45. Zhang, L., Wu, K., Yang, B., Tang, H., Zhu, Z.: Exploring virtual environments by visually impaired using a mixed reality cane without visual feedback. In: 2020 IEEE International Symposium on Mixed and Augmented Reality Adjunct (ISMAR-Adjunct), pp. 51–56 (2020)

Specialized Design Heuristics that Optimize Interactions for Older Adults

Yonatan Kelemu Desta(✉) and Jerry Schnepp

Roosevelt University, Chicago, IL 60605, USA
ydesta@mail.roosevelt.edu, jschnepp@roosevelt.edu

Abstract. Social isolation among older adults represents a significant public health concern, and social media platforms offer an important but underutilized mechanism for fostering digital social participation in this population. This study formulates specialized user interface heuristics for older adults (65+) interacting with social media, using Instagram as a representative testbed due to its comparatively streamlined visual interface and widespread adoption. In Phase One, five participants performed guided tasks on the Instagram mobile interface using a think-aloud protocol followed by a questionnaire. Analysis revealed significant usability barriers including unfamiliar terminology, hidden features, scrolling challenges, and inconsistent icon placement. These findings, synthesized with Nielsen's established heuristics [5] and guidelines from Barros et al. [2], informed the development of seven specialized design heuristics prioritizing white space, color coding, shallow information architecture, explicit written labels, and consistent element placement. In Phase Two, these heuristics were applied to a high-fidelity Figma prototype and evaluated by four new participants using the same protocol. Results indicated modest improvements in task completion and navigational confidence. A key finding was a persistent discrepancy between researcher-observed and self-reported task completion rates, suggesting that even when older adults successfully navigate an interface, inadequate system feedback leaves them uncertain of their success. While limited by a small sample size, this research provides a qualitative, evidence-based framework for tailoring social media interfaces to support the digital inclusion of older populations.

Keywords: Older Adults · Heuristic Evaluation · Interface Research · Social Media Usability · Universal Access

1 Background

Social isolation among older adults is an established public health concern, associated with increased rates of depression, cognitive decline, and premature mortality [9]. Social media platforms offer a meaningful mechanism for mitigating this isolation: they allow older adults to maintain existing social ties, access community support, and participate in civic and cultural life regardless of physical mobility. Research confirms that digital social engagement can measurably reduce perceived isolation and improve subjective well-being in this population [9, 10]. However, the potential of social media to support

C. Stephanidis et al. (Eds.): HCII 2026, CCIS 3047, pp. 526–534, 2026.
https://doi.org/10.1007/978-3-032-30552-7_50

older adults is contingent on those adults being able to use these platforms effectively. Despite growing smartphone ownership among adults aged 65 and older, adoption of social media by this group remains markedly lower than in younger cohorts [11]. Critically, this gap is not simply a matter of motivation or access: it reflects the failure of interface design to account for the diverse cognitive, sensory, and experiential profiles of older users [1, 3]. Instagram was selected as the platform of study for two reasons. First, its comparatively streamlined visual interface—centered on image and video content rather than the complex multi-feature layouts of platforms such as Facebook—makes it a tractable and well-scoped testbed for evaluating core navigation heuristics [12]. Second, Instagram is among the most widely adopted visual social media platforms globally, with meaningful penetration among adults aged 60 and above [10]. This combination of relative simplicity and real-world prevalence makes it an appropriate context in which to develop and validate age-specific design heuristics. The following sections review three interconnected bodies of work that together motivate this study: research on age-specific usability heuristics, evidence from user-centered design (UCD) studies with older populations, and precedents for developing specialized heuristics in adjacent domains.

1.1 Age-Specific Design Heuristics

There is considerable discourse surrounding usability for older adults. Chisnell et al. [1] question the effectiveness of Jakob Nielsen's traditional heuristics [5] when applied to aging populations. They identified the lack of consensus on what age a person is considered an "older adult". Further, they argue that chronological age should be considered alongside other factors such as physical health, which includes eyesight, prior computer experience, and cognitive ability. These factors were characterized into four dimensions: age, ability, attitude, and aptitude, and codified in the AARP model. Eight personas representing a set of variations of the factors were tested against fifty websites. Results revealed that traditional heuristics often failed to account for the diverse interaction patterns of older users. This early study established that features like larger fonts and clickable buttons improve usability. However, it relied on persona-based simulations rather than real-world field testing with users. These limitations motivated the shift toward empirically grounded, user-centered approaches examined in the following section.

1.2 User-Centered Design

Recent studies have moved toward more evidence-led, user-centered design (UCD) processes. Barros, A. C. et al. [2] repurposed an application designed to test gait as an online dancing game. The study identified critical pain points: participants were unfamiliar with the interaction mechanisms, and commands were misunderstood, as were hidden features, scrolling, and contrast. Placing all items on the home page eliminated the need to search for hidden items, improving usability as measured by time-on-task, which dropped from 1 min 17 s to 10 s. Adding contrasting colors further improved usability. Despite these successes, the authors still observed problems with participants' understanding of the interface information architecture and navigation expectations.

Participants also struggled to distinguish between different types of input interactions, indicating that the number of required interactions should be reduced. Task completion reached 100% compared with the prior interface.

The key interface design takeaways were:

- Use wordings that suit older adults' semantic field.
- Provide generous spacing between items.
- Use icons along with text when designing buttons
- Be cautious about the positioning of interactive elements towards the edge of the screen.
- Use the home screen menu as a safe point of return,
- Display all of the application's main categories on the start screen
- Use the back button as a safeguard.
- Take advantage of scrolling if the application requires it.

Okafor & Akcay [3] utilized semi-guided interviews and iterative prototyping to identify misalignments between user needs and mobile health (mHealth) applications. Their research mirrors the pipeline used in this study, where qualitative data from user interactions directly informs the creation of new prototypes. However, their research focuses on the specific application of telemedicine and targets broader age groups, leaving a gap in generalized heuristics for social media platforms for older users. The final strand of prior work examines whether heuristics developed for one population can serve as a model for creating analogous tools for another.

1.3 Specialized Heuristics

Alsumait, A. & Al-Osaimi, A [4]. set forth a new set of heuristics for assessing and analyzing an educational application that was used to instruct kindergarten. The data was gathered by experts from the government body for education in Kuwait. The researchers evaluated three sets of usability heuristics: Nielsen's heuristics for evaluation, the E-learning Usability Heuristics [6], and the Child Usability Heuristics [7]. Out of the three, the Child Usability Heuristics closely mirrored real-life results. This research demonstrates that specialized heuristics may be more effective for assessing digital interfaces than generalized ones.

Despite the growing body of work, there remains a critical need for qualitative analysis that addresses the unique motivations and behaviors of older adults in the social media domain. Existing studies have either relied on simulated personas rather than real users [1], focused on non-social-media applications [2, 3], or examined populations other than older adults [4]. This study addresses that gap by formulating specialized heuristics through direct field testing with older adult users of Instagram, with the aim of producing design principles that can support more inclusive social media interfaces.

2 Methodology

This study was conducted in two phases. Phase one utilized an observed user test, the think-aloud protocol [8], and field observations combined with a questionnaire to collect data about older adults' interactions with a social media interface. Participant recruitment was facilitated through a targeted poster campaign designed to attract individuals 65 and older. Participants were recruited from community settings including a local church and public spaces such as parks and the Lake Michigan shoreline, yielding a geographically and socially diverse sample. After a brief introduction the principal investigator (PI) provided an explanation orally to potential participants. All participants demonstrated their working comprehension of English, read a consent form, and had the opportunity to ask clarifying questions before signing it.

This study was conducted in accordance with the ethical standards of the Roosevelt University Institutional Review Board (IRB Project No. 2025–053, approved July 15, 2025, expiring July 15, 2026). The study title as registered with the IRB is "Heuristics specialized to evaluate and assess digital products for older adults." Prior to participation, all individuals were provided with a written informed consent form explaining the study's purpose, procedures, and their right to withdraw at any time without penalty. Participants were advised that their involvement was entirely voluntary and that all data would be anonymized. No personally identifiable information was collected or retained.

To ensure data protection and participant anonymity, participants were provided with a "dummy" account that was created by the PI using a name and email address not associated with any participant. All media content used for task-based uploads was standardized and provided by the PI. The participants were asked to perform a list of tasks on Instagram. They were instructed to think aloud while they performed the tasks. The investigator recorded both observational notes and performance metrics throughout these sessions, noting specific interaction failures and successes. Upon completion of the tasks, participants provided subjective feedback via a questionnaire. These data sets were subsequently analyzed using thematic and categorical methods to prioritize the most frequent pain points and calculate task completion percentages.

In Phase two, the identified pain points were synthesized with existing heuristic standards to derive a new set of specialized design heuristics. These heuristics prioritized design modifications, including the expansion of white space, the implementation of a shallow information architecture, enhanced color coding, and the inclusion of explicit written labels alongside icons. These principles guided the development of a high-fidelity mockup of the Instagram interface created within the Figma design environment. A second cohort of older adults was recruited to evaluate this redesign, following the same sequence of observed tasks and think-aloud protocols utilized in the initial phase. Finally, the results from this validation phase were compared against the baseline data from Phase one to determine if the specialized heuristics successfully reduced interaction friction, increased positive user feedback, and improved task completion rates.

3 Results

This section presents findings from both phases of the study. Phase One findings document the specific usability barriers encountered by older adults interacting with Instagram's native interface; these barriers served as the empirical basis for deriving the specialized heuristics. Phase Two findings evaluate the effectiveness of those heuristics when applied to a redesigned prototype. Taken together, the two phases constitute a complete evidence-to-heuristic-to-validation pipeline, in which participant behavior directly informs the design principles, which are in turn tested with a new cohort.

3.1 Phase One: Exploratory Investigation

The initial phase involved five participants aged 65 or older, consisting of four women and one man. These subjects were recruited from various public and community locations in Chicago, including a local church and the Lake Michigan shoreline. One participant was unable to perform any of the assigned tasks but verbally explained that the experience was enjoyable. Many of the respondents chose to have the researcher fill out the information in the survey while they dictated.

Observations revealed that some of the terms for actions were not familiar to the participants such as "log-in" and "opening a feed". This led to instances where participants were unaware that they had successfully completed a task. This lack of familiarity directly impacted the accuracy of self-reported performance, necessitating the use of investigator observations to augment the data. Differences in the observed levels of success and reported level of success are the consequences of that factor.

The persistence of usability barriers was further highlighted by qualitative feedback from the community. One individual noted that frequent application updates often relocate essential action items, forcing older users to repeatedly relearn the interface. This observation was confirmed during testing when a participant failed to identify a task as completed because an icon was not in its expected location. Despite these challenges, participants generally expressed enjoyment when interacting with visual content like images and videos. Table 1 summarizes the self-reported and researcher-observed task completion rates for each phase one participant, alongside their qualitative feedback.

Table 1. Phase one participant task completion summary.

Participant Number	Age (years)	Self-reported Task Completion	Observed Task Completion	Notes
1	>65 (unspecified)	50%	90%	Remarked that he needed to spend more time learning
2	65	50%	50%	Was unsure what could make the interface easier
3	65	75%	50%	
4	83	30%	40%	Wanted written instructions to follow
5	85	0%	0%	

The data in Table **1** reveal a consistent and noteworthy discrepancy between self-reported and researcher-observed task completion. Across most participants, observed completion rates exceeded self-reported ones—most strikingly in the case of Participant 1, who reported 50% completion despite the researcher recording 90%. This pattern indicates that participants sometimes succeeded at tasks without recognizing their own success, a finding attributable to insufficient system feedback and unfamiliar terminology in the native Instagram interface. The exception is Participant 3, whose self-reported rate (75%) exceeded the observed rate (50%). This suggests an additional layer of complexity in which some participants might believe they had completed tasks they had not, underscoring the bidirectional nature of the feedback gap.

3.2 Development of Specialized Heuristics

Following the analysis of phase one, a set of specialized heuristics was derived by synthesizing the observed pain points with existing standards from Nielsen [5] and Barros et al. [2]. The results suggested that labelling, naming and otherwise indicating elements of the interface greatly improve the findability of tools. Additionally, the literature review revealed that shallow information density and color coordination also improve the usability of the interfaces for older adults. The synthesized heuristics prioritize the reduction of cognitive load and the enhancement of visual clarity. They are:

1. Establish a safe point of return and provide user control.
2. Reduce information depth to a shallow stratum and minimize scrolling.
3. Utilize explicit labeling, markers, to maintain system status visibility.
4. Utilize color to distinguish between elements and create contrast.
5. Maximizing the use of white space.
6. Utilize standardized, labeled symbols.
7. Maintain consistent placement of elements.

3.3 Phase Two: Heuristic Evaluation

In phase two, a high-fidelity mock-up of Instagram was made in Figma following the insights learned during phase one. This prototype was field tested with older adults. Revisions to the interface included simplification by removing unnecessary icons and symbols, using color coding to emphasize the primary tools, increasing white space, using bigger fonts, and labelling the featured tools. The information architecture depth was also reduced to a very shallow level. Below are some images of the mock-up tested with participants. Figure 1 presents side-by-side comparisons of six key screens: the main feed, profile view, comments, messaging, reels, and login. The figure shows the original Instagram interface alongside the corresponding redesigned prototype.

Across all screens, the redesign is characterized by the elimination of decorative or ambiguous icons, the addition of explicit text labels on all interactive elements, increased padding and white space between components, and a reduced navigation depth that surfaces key actions directly on each screen. Color is used purposefully in the prototype to differentiate primary actions from secondary ones, addressing the contrast and discoverability issues identified in Phase One.

Four participants aged 65 or older were recruited for Phase Two. As in Phase One, the sample was predominantly female, reflecting the continued reluctance of older male adults to take part. Table 2 presents their self-reported and researcher-observed task completion rates on the redesigned interface.

Validation testing with a new cohort of older adults indicated that while labeling tools and providing success notifications yielded measurable improvements, a degree of

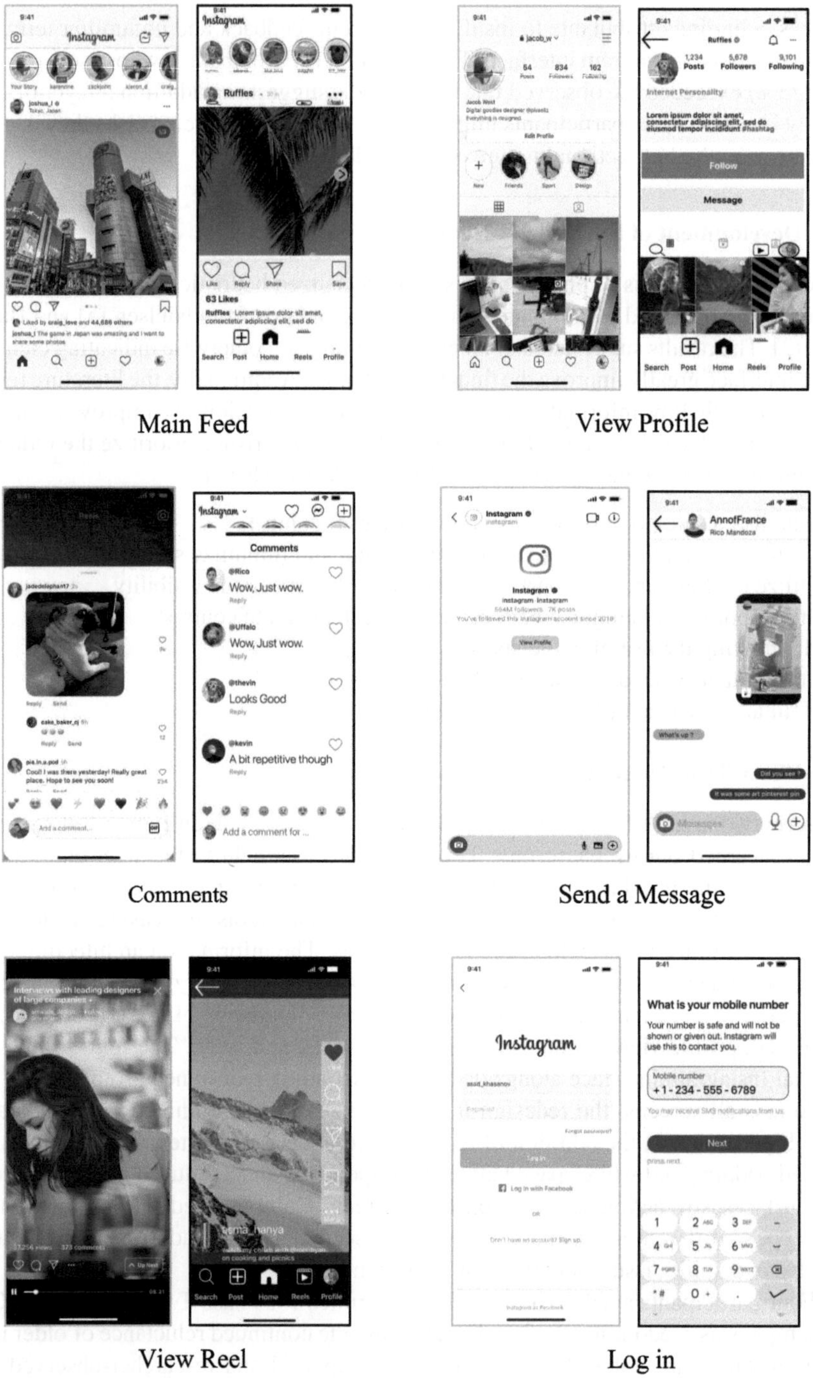

Fig. 1. Screenshots juxtaposing the original Instagram interface on the left and the corresponding redesigned prototype screen on the right.

Table 2. Phase two participant task completion summary.

Participant Number	Age (years)	Self-reported Task Completion	Observed Task Completion	Notes
6	73	70%	70%	Remarked that he needed to spend more time learning
7	>65	30%	60%	Was unsure what could make the interface easier
8	65	70%	70%	
9	>65	30%	30%	Wanted training

uncertainty regarding task completion remained. Notably, Table 2 shows a narrowing of the gap between self-reported and observed completion rates compared to Phase One: Participants 6 and 8 achieved full alignment (70% self-reported, 70% observed), suggesting that clearer system feedback in the redesign helped users more accurately gauge their own success. However, Participant 7's continued underestimation of their performance (30% self-reported vs. 60% observed) indicates that the feedback gap, while reduced, had not been fully resolved.

4 Conclusion and Limitation

This study set out to formulate interaction heuristics for older adults (65+) within the context of social media platforms. It collected qualitative data in two phases. In the first phase it identified the pain points of an existing social media interface (Instagram), The results were used to formulate a set of design heuristics which guided the redesign of the Instagram interface in a high-fidelity mockup. The findings in the first phase confirmed that many older adults encounter recurring usability barriers, including jargon and unfamiliar semantics, inconsistent icon placement, and insufficient feedback on completed actions. These insights led to development of heuristics that prioritize labelling, shallow information stratum, increased white space, and color-coded elements.

The second phase yielded modest improvements in user performance and confidence. Specifically, informing users of successful completion of tasks and providing labels for tools along with icons were found to be effective in reducing cognitive load and increasing navigational confidence. However, the results also suggested a persistent gap between user perception and interface reality, as some participants remained uncertain of their success despite measurable performance gains. Furthermore, the study reinforced existing literature suggesting that older adults may not always perceive significant personal value in social media platforms, which can affect their motivation to overcome minor usability hurdles. Nevertheless, the testing strongly suggests that some heuristics such as those addressing visibility of system status and control were effective tools for reducing cognitive load and increasing navigational confidence.

Several significant limitations must be acknowledged, which impact the generalizability of the results. The participant pool was notably small and exhibited a significant gender imbalance, with most respondents being female. The reluctance of older adults, particularly men, to participate in the study restricted the quantitative reliability of the findings. Despite these constraints, the study provides valuable qualitative evidence that specialized, age-specific heuristics can significantly reduce interaction friction for older users. By demonstrating the effectiveness of design elements like visibility of system status and enhanced control, this research contributes to a framework for more inclusive digital design. Ultimately, these heuristics could be instrumental in shaping accessible interfaces across various domains, fostering greater digital participation and inclusion for the aging population.

Acknowledgments. The authors would like to express their gratitude to the participants who shared their time and experiences during the two phases of this study. Additionally, we thank Roosevelt University for its institutional support of this research.

Disclosure of Interests. The authors declare that they have no competing financial or personal interests that could have appeared to influence the work reported in this paper.

References

1. Chisnell, D., Redish, J., Lee, A.: New heuristics for understanding older adults as web users. Tech. Commun. **53**(1), 39–59 (2006)
2. Barros, A.C., Leitão, R., Ribeiro, J.: Design and evaluation of a mobile game for older people. In: Proceedings of the 12th International Joint Conference on Computer Vision, Imaging and Computer Graphics Theory and Applications (VISIGRAPP), vol. 6, p. 288. GRAPP, 295. SCITEPRESS (2017)
3. Okafor, E.J., Akcay, E.: Applying user-centered design methods to improve the experience of the NHS app. Qeios. (2024). https://doi.org/10.32388/BYAENM
4. Alsumait, A., Al-Osaimi, A.: Usability heuristics evaluation for child e-learning applications. J Softw. **5**(6), 654–661 (2010)
5. Nielsen, J.: Usability Engineering. Morgan Kaufmann, San Francisco, CA (1994)
6. Squires, D., Preece, J.: Predicting quality in educational software: evaluating for learning, usability and the synergy between them. Interact. Comput. **11**(5), 467–483 (1999)
7. Hanna, L., Risden, K., Alexander, K.: Guidelines for usability testing with children. Interactions. **4**(5), 9–14 (1997)
8. Ericsson, K.A., Simon, H.A.: Protocol Analysis: Verbal Reports as Data, Revised edn. MIT Press, Cambridge, MA (1993)
9. Sen, K., Prybutok, G., Prybutok, V.: The use of digital technology for social wellbeing reduces social isolation in older adults: a systematic review. SS – Popul. Health. **17**, 101020 (2022)
10. Ribeiro, R.M., et al.: Beyond isolation: social media as a bridge to well-being in old age. Int. J. Environ. Res. Public Health. **22**(6), 882 (2025)
11. Vogels, E.A.: Older Americans and Technology. Pew Research Center, Washington, DC (2022) https://www.pewresearch.org/internet/2022/01/13/digital-technology-and-older-adults/
12. Gomez-Hernandez, M., Ferre, X., Moral, C., Villalba-Mora, E.: Design guidelines of mobile apps for older adults: systematic review and thematic analysis. JMIR Mhealth Uhealth. **11**, e43186 (2023)

Inclusive Design Principles Based on an Evaluation Structure Analysis of Inclusive Products

Tomomi Hatano[1(✉)], Tomomi Takezawa[1,2], Fan Zhang[1], Ruigang Ge[1], Hideto Motomura[1], Noriko Nagata[1], Ryohei Yuasa[3], Shun Kitagata[3], and Hiroya Tanaka[3]

[1] Kwansei Gakuin University, 1 Gakuen Uegahara, Sanda, Hyogo 669-1330, Japan
hatano@kwansei.ac.jp
[2] Otemae University, 6-42 Ochakashocho, Nishinomiya, Hyogo 662-8552, Japan
[3] Keio University, 5322 Endo, Fujisawa, Kanagawa 252-0882, Japan

Abstract. This study examines inclusiveness as an experiential and participatory concept that builds on Universal Design (UD). Using the Evaluation Grid Method (EGM), we analyze how users and one playground equipment designer perceive inclusiveness through the case of playground equipment, treated as an interactive environment that mediates human activities and social interaction. The results reveal a layered value structure in which Universal Design conditions form the foundation of inclusive experiences. Based on this structure, five Inclusive Design (ID) principles centered on the "potential for action" are derived. Their practical relevance is further examined through the design and exhibition of playground equipment at EXPO 2025 Osaka, Kansai, Japan, where visitors' evaluation structures were analyzed. These findings provide a perspective for designing physical environments that support diverse forms of participation and interaction.

Keywords: Inclusiveness · symbiotic society · potential for action

1 Introduction

The concept of a symbiotic society is essential for achieving both prosperity (well-being) and sustainability (SDGs), and inclusiveness is considered a key concept supporting this goal [1–4]. Inclusiveness often refers to a condition in which diverse individuals can participate across contexts. Although social understanding of this concept is still developing, various practical reports have demonstrated its effectiveness [5–8].

For example, in business contexts, inclusive practices have been reported to improve internal organizational environments and promote innovation [5, 8]. These findings suggest that inclusiveness may contribute not only to accessibility and diversity but also to community activity and value creation.

Interest in inclusiveness is also increasing in design and manufacturing. One relevant approach is Inclusive Design. In Japan, this term often refers to design methods that involve users who have previously been excluded as minorities from the earliest

C. Stephanidis et al. (Eds.): HCII 2026, CCIS 3047, pp. 535–545, 2026.
https://doi.org/10.1007/978-3-032-30552-7_51

stages of the design process [8–10]. Participation by users with extreme experiences can provide designers with new perspectives and generate value. Julia Cassim reports that such participation has led to the creation of new products and services while also fostering community development [9, 10]. These effects are not temporary and can lead to sustained co-creation.

This study focuses on the possibility that inclusiveness contributes to qualitative development of communities. Inclusive design (ID) is positioned as a mediator of this process, and this study attempts to clarify its structure. In this framework, not only design processes but also products and services perceived as inclusive are regarded as ID. Products or services that evoke inclusiveness may function as mediating contexts that connect individuals and communities and encourage participation.

Examples include inclusive playground equipment, which naturally facilitates play among children and adults [11], and community fridges, which address food issues while rebuilding community relationships [12]. Public space has also been discussed as a designable context that can foster social interaction and cohesion [13].

Universal Design (UD) can be considered a foundational framework for inclusive design. UD aims to remove barriers to participation and defines basic product attributes such as safety, appropriate scale, perceptibility, and low physical effort [14]. These attributes are articulated as the seven principles of Universal Design (Table 1). UD provides a fair starting point for all individuals and ensures accessibility. While UD may support social activation, its primary aim is equitable access rather than the creation of new communal value. Inclusive Design therefore builds upon UD by focusing on participation and value creation.

Table 1. The Seven Principles of Universal Design (UD1–UD7).

UD1	Equitable Use
UD2	Flexibility in Use
UD3	Simple and Intuitive Use
UD4	Perceptible Information
UD5	Tolerance for Error
UD6	Low Physical Effort
UD7	Size and Space for Approach and Use

If we assume that inclusive design contains Kansei (affective) value, the value generated by diverse participation may be structurally clarified. Kansei refers to cognition involving emotion, and its evaluation can be organized hierarchically [15, 16]. Previous studies have shown that emotions, impressions, and physical characteristics can be structured into causal relationships [17]. This approach has been applied not only to physical objects such as T-shirts and tourist sites [18, 19] but also to abstract concepts such as sustainability [17].

To structure Kansei value, this study employs the evaluation grid method [20]. This method visualizes causal relationships among evaluation items as a hierarchical diagram called an evaluation structure diagram. It is a semi-structured interview technique that identifies evaluation factors by comparing evaluation objects.

In this study, inclusive playground equipment is used as objects because it represents diverse physical designs intended for inclusive use. Playground equipment is placed in public spaces and designed for users of different ages, abilities, and backgrounds. Therefore, it must provide diverse benefits while meeting safety requirements and supporting community activity.

Furthermore, this study examines evaluation structures of both non-experts and experts. Non-experts are university students who have experience using playground equipment and can articulate their impressions. The expert is a playground equipment designer who makes professional judgments considering design constraints and social values. Comparing these perspectives allows the study to clarify how inclusiveness is structured and interpreted.

Accordingly, this study aims to clarify the structure of inclusiveness associated with inclusive playground equipment using the evaluation grid method. Study 1 selects evaluation objects, Study 2 identifies the evaluation structure among users, and Study 3 investigates the structure among designers. Based on these structures, the study proposes principles of Inclusive Design. Study 4 then examines their validity by applying these principles as design hints in the creation of playground equipment and analyzing users' evaluations through evaluation grid interviews.

2 Study 1: Selection of Evaluation Objects

2.1 Method

Eleven adults participated. A total of 251 photographs of playground equipment were collected from publicly available web sources as evaluation objects. Only images of actual equipment that clearly showed size without overlapping structures were included; photographs with overlaid text or minor variations of the same product series were excluded. Participants classified similar photographs using a free-sorting method with custom software.

2.2 Results and Discussion

Distances between photographs were calculated based on participants' classifications. Cluster analysis (Ward's method) was applied, and a 28-cluster solution was selected based on the dendrogram.

Clusters were mapped using multidimensional scaling (PROXSCAL). Photographs closest to each cluster centroid were selected as representatives. After discussion among three researchers, 28 photographs were chosen for subsequent studies to ensure representativeness and minimize selection bias.

3 Study 2: Evaluation Structure of University Students

3.1 Method

Thirty-six university students participated. Twenty-eight photographs of playground equipment selected in Study 1 were used as evaluation objects.

Participants first categorized the 28 photographs on their own computers into three folders labeled high, medium, and low inclusiveness. The photographs were initially placed in the medium folder. Before the task, participants were briefly informed that the term "inclusiveness" is often used to refer to something that can be used by anyone. No formal definition or evaluation criteria were provided, and participants classified the playground equipment according to their own understanding of inclusiveness.

Next, participants formed pairs and interviewed each other using the evaluation grid method [20]. They explained why playground equipment judged as high was more inclusive than that judged as medium, and why medium was more inclusive than low, describing the reasons or specific examples in one sentence. This process continued until no further responses were obtained. Each interview lasted about 20 min per interviewee, and interviewers were switched after each interview. Interview results were recorded using EGi-Visualizer [18, 21], which visualizes evaluation grid interview data as evaluation structure diagrams. Additionally, in EGi-Visualizer, Katz centrality can be set as a threshold, allowing only evaluation items above that value to be visualized. Katz centrality is a network metric based on graph theory, corresponding to the importance of evaluation items. Setting it to zero displays all nodes, while setting it high displays only important nodes. In practice, the threshold is adjusted to maintain interpretability of the evaluation structure while avoiding excessive visual complexity.

3.2 Results and Discussion

Figure 1 shows the evaluation structure derived from the interview results. The threshold was set to 0.06. Boxes in the diagram represent evaluation items, and lines indicate causal relationships, with the right side representing causes and the left side representing results. For example, the connection between "simple shape" and "simple structure" indicates that structures are evaluated as simple because their shapes are simple. Evaluation items categorize responses with identical meanings; for instance, "simple shape" includes responses such as "not complex in shape" and "simple form."

From the evaluation structure in Fig. 1, evaluation items related to Universal Design (UD) appear mainly in the lower layers. The items shown in blue boxes correspond to the seven principles of UD listed in Table 1 [14]. For example, "can be used regardless of disability" corresponds to UD1: Equitable Use, and "allows various ways of play" corresponds to UD2: Flexibility in Use. Other items can also be interpreted as reflecting UD3–UD7. The lower-level concepts supporting these items refer to concrete physical properties and specifications; for example, the evaluation "less risk of injury" is associated with characteristics such as "low in height." These results suggest that features of Universal Design function as a foundation for Inclusive Design.

Evaluation items related to states and emotions appear in the higher layers of the structure. Items shown in yellow boxes represent states, while those in red boxes represent emotions. These are derived from Universal Design conditions. For example, "less risk of injury" (UD5) and "can be used regardless of disability" (UD1) lead to feelings such as safe and reassuring. Meanwhile, "allows various ways of play" (UD2) connects not only to the feeling that the equipment is fun, but also to the perception that anyone can play and that communication may increase.

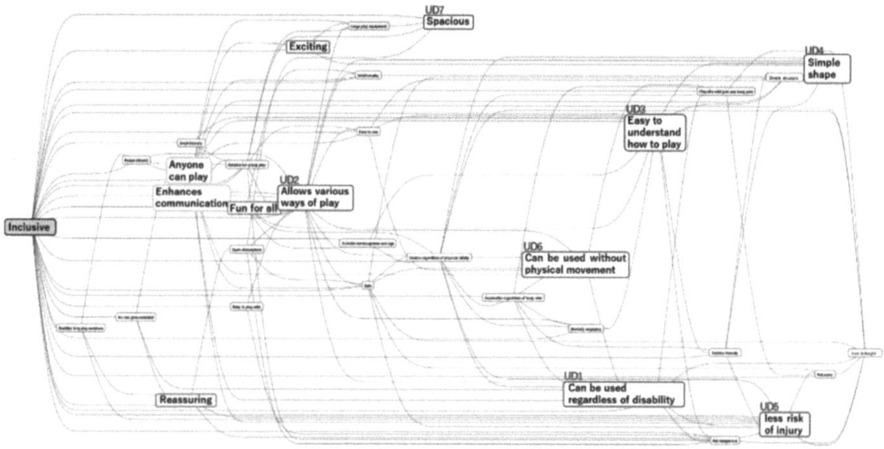

Fig. 1. Evaluation structure for inclusiveness (University Students).

These results suggest that university students, as users of playground equipment, tend to focus on whether the equipment satisfies Universal Design conditions as tools or facilities. Inclusiveness is then perceived through the states and emotions generated by those conditions.

4 Study 3: Evaluation Structure of Experts

4.1 Method

One playground equipment design specialist participated. The participant is a designer at a Japanese manufacturer specializing in playground equipment and inclusive play products and has long been involved in developing inclusive play environments. Given the exploratory aim of this study—to articulate candidate principles of Inclusive Design rather than achieve statistical generalization—an in-depth interview with a practitioner directly engaged in inclusive equipment design was considered appropriate.

Twenty-eight photographs of playground equipment selected in Study 1 were used as evaluation objects. The participant's inclusive evaluation structure was investigated using the evaluation grid method. The interview was conducted by the researcher (second author). The participant first sorted printed cards of the evaluation objects into three groups (high, medium, and low inclusiveness). While observing these groups, the participant was asked to explain in one sentence the reasons or conditions underlying the differences in inclusiveness. This process continued until no further responses were obtained. As in Study 2, no formal definition of inclusiveness was imposed; the expert evaluated the playground equipment according to his own professional understanding.

4.2 Results and Discussion

Figure 2 shows the evaluation structure derived from the interview regarding high inclusiveness. The threshold was set to 0.01 to retain sufficient evaluation items for interpreting the structure. Responses were not categorized and were recorded as directly as possible.

Because the student and expert models differed in network size and response patterns, a single fixed threshold was not appropriate. In the student model, repeated responses across participants produced higher centrality values for shared evaluation items, whereas the expert model produced more distributed and generally lower centrality scores. Therefore, the threshold was adjusted in each case to maintain interpretability of the network structure.

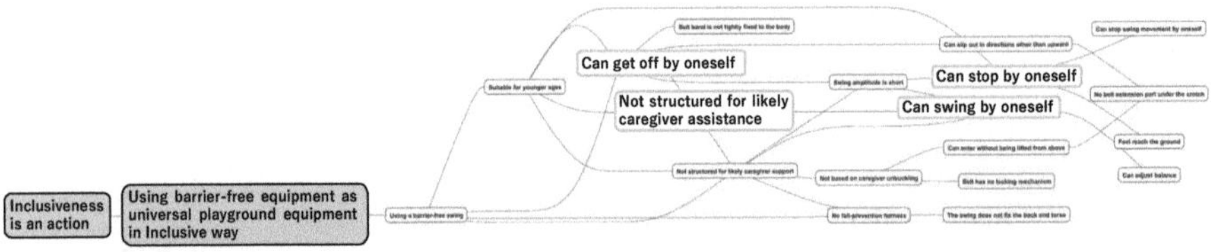

Fig. 2. Evaluation structure for inclusiveness (Playground Equipment Designer).

From the evaluation structure in Fig. 2, evaluation items concerning the potential for action appear frequently. The evaluation items in yellow boxes indicate states and reflect the view that high inclusiveness requires maintaining the possibility of independent behavior—the "potential for action"—without assuming assistance from caregivers. Statements such as "making barrier-free play equipment into universal play equipment for inclusive use" and "inclusiveness is an act" suggest that Universal Design enables this potential for action, with value emerging through the user's engagement.

Figure 3 shows the evaluation structure derived from the interview regarding low inclusiveness. The threshold was set to 0, and all evaluation items were displayed. Responses were again recorded in their original wording. Several evaluation items negate this potential for action. For example, playground equipment designed for single-user play leads to "limits who can use it," "lose the chance to become friends someday," and "unable to enjoy group activities even when they'd be more fun together."

These results suggest that playground equipment designers implicitly assume Universal Design principles while focusing on users' potential for action and preserving this potential. In other words, the participant refers to various states (potentials) and appears to consider the loss of these states as leading to a lack of inclusiveness.

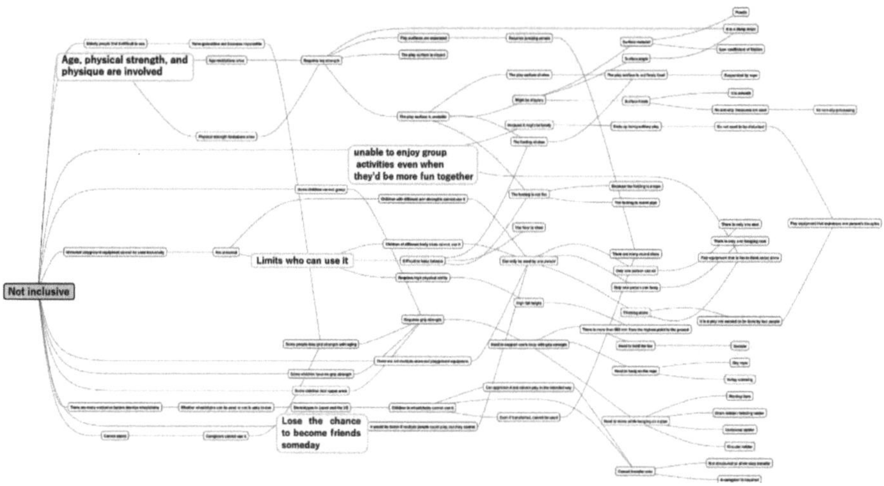

Fig. 3. Evaluation structure for non-inclusiveness (Playground Equipment Designer).

5 Proposal for Inclusive Design Principles

Based on Study 2 and Study 3, the evaluation structure of inclusive playground equipment can be interpreted as layered. First, whether the tools and facilities are appropriate functions as a basic condition; for playground equipment, Universal Design serves as the standard. On this foundation, the potential for action becomes important. For example, even if safety (UD5 in Table 1) is ensured, if the potential for self-directed activity is lost, the value that should follow is also lost and inclusiveness is undermined (Fig. 3). In other words, Inclusive Design can be understood as providing and preserving the potential for action.

Based on this interpretation, this study proposes five Inclusive Design Principles grounded in the potential for action (Table 2), hereafter referred to as ID1–ID5.

Table 2. The Five Principles of Inclusive Design (ID1–ID5).

ID1	Doing Things in One's Own Way
ID2	Engaging with Others
ID3	Sharing Joyful Experiences
ID4	Authentic Participation
ID5	A Place for Everyone

First, Fig. 2 suggests the importance of enabling independent, self-directed play without relying on caregiver assistance, which is defined as ID1: Doing Things in One's Own Way.

Second, the statement "Lose the chance to become friends someday" in Fig. 3, together with "Enhances communication" in Fig. 1, indicates the possibility of connecting with others; this is defined as ID2: Engaging with Others.

Third, the statement "unable to enjoy group activities even when they'd be more fun together" highlights the importance of shared enjoyment within human relationships, defined as ID3: Sharing Joyful Experiences.

Fourth, the statement "Age, physical strength, and physique are involved" suggests that participation should not be constrained by individual characteristics; this is defined as ID4: Authentic Participation.

Finally, statements such as "Anyone can play" (Fig. 1) and "Limits who can use it" (Fig. 3) indicate the importance of a place where diverse users feel able to participate, defined as ID5: A Place for Everyone.

These principles are intended as exploratory guidelines rather than fixed rules. Inclusive design requires continuously considering what kinds of potential for action are created or constrained in a given environment.

However, the principles proposed above were derived primarily from interviews and analyses of evaluation structures. To examine whether they meaningfully inform actual design practice, it is necessary to investigate how they function when applied to real artifacts and real play experiences. Therefore, in the next step of this research, we tested the validity of the proposed principles by designing and creating playground equipment using the five Inclusive Design Principles as design hints and conducting evaluation grid interviews with people who actually played with it.

6 Study 4: Validation through Playground Equipment Implementation

6.1 Method

Playground equipment was designed and created using the five Inclusive Design Principles as design hints (Fig. 4). The equipment was produced from plant-based resin with a large-scale 3D printer. The object was placed on the ground and allowed movements such as sitting and rocking. However, its use was intentionally left open-ended: visitors were free to decide how to interact with it, including moving or overturning it.

Fig. 4. Exhibition at EXPO 2025 Osaka, Kansai, Japan.

The playground equipment was exhibited at EXPO 2025 Osaka, Kansai, Japan, where evaluation grid interviews were conducted with visitors who used it. Among the users,

303 individuals who agreed to participate in the interview were included as participants. They first interacted freely with the playground equipment. Their experiences were then elicited and analyzed using an AI-based automated evaluation grid interview system [22]. In addition, each participant's evaluation structure diagram was generated and displayed in real time at the exhibition site (Fig. 4). These on-site diagrams were simplified visualizations, while detailed analysis and visualization were conducted separately for research purposes.

6.2 Results and Discussion

Figure 5 shows the evaluation structure derived from the responses of participants who considered the exhibited playground equipment to be more inclusive than conventional playground equipment. As shown in the figure, items related to Universal Design (UD) appear in the lower layers of the structure, similar to the evaluation structure obtained from university students in Study 2 (Fig. 1). This suggests that UD functions as a foundational condition that supports the emergence of inclusive experiences.

Several evaluation items in the upper layers can be interpreted as corresponding to the five Inclusive Design Principles proposed in this study. For example, "Can be used as you wish" corresponds to ID1, and "Usable for sharing" corresponds to ID2. Taken together, these results suggest that inclusiveness is perceived through experiential values that emerge when the foundational conditions provided by UD enable the potential for action described by the ID principles. They also indicate that the characteristics described by the ID principles are reflected in why the created playground equipment was perceived as inclusive, suggesting that the principles are useful for design.

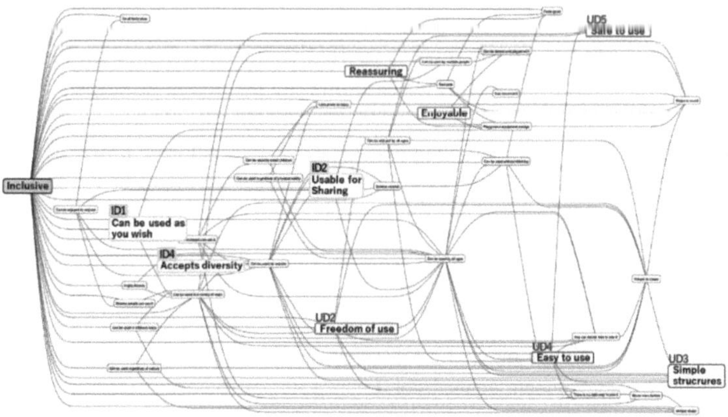

Fig. 5. Evaluation structure for perceived inclusiveness.

7 Conclusion

This study aimed to clarify the structure of inclusiveness in design and to propose principles of Inclusive Design using the evaluation grid method. Using inclusive playground equipment as the evaluation context, the study examined how inclusiveness is perceived by users and interpreted by designers.

Interviews with university students showed that evaluation items related to Universal Design (UD) appeared mainly in the lower layers of the evaluation structure, suggesting that inclusiveness is often recognized through conditions created by accessibility, safety, and flexible use. In contrast, the playground-equipment designer emphasized preserving users' potential for action, indicating that inclusiveness involves maintaining opportunities for self-directed activity and interaction.

Based on these findings, this study proposed five Inclusive Design Principles (ID1–ID5) grounded in the concept of potential for action. Their practical relevance was examined by designing playground equipment using these principles as design hints and analyzing the evaluation structures of participants who experienced the equipment at EXPO 2025 Osaka, Kansai, Japan. The results showed that items corresponding to the ID principles appeared in the upper layers of the structure, while UD-related items appeared in the lower layers. This layered structure suggests that inclusive experiences emerge when the foundational conditions provided by UD support the potential for action described by the ID principles.

Several limitations should be noted. Study 3 involved only one playground equipment designer, and Study 2 included only university students, which may limit the generalizability of the findings. In addition, Study 2 relied on photographs rather than actual interaction with playground equipment. Although Study 4 examined real-world experiences, the interviews were simplified in order not to interfere with play experiences, and the causal relationships among evaluation items may therefore not be fully represented. Future studies should involve more diverse participants, multiple designers, and field-based investigations to further examine the proposed principles.

Acknowledgments. This work was supported by JST Grant Number JPMJPF2111 and JSPS KAKENHI (grant number 23K24936).

References

1. Costanza, R. et al.: Modelling and measuring sustainable wellbeing in connection with the UN sustainable development goals. Ecol. Econ. **130**, 350–355 (2016)
2. Gupta, J., Vegelin, C.: Sustainable development goals and inclusive development. Int. Environ. Agreem.: Politics Law Econ. **16**(3), 433–448 (2016)
3. Helne, T., Hirvilammi, T.: Wellbeing and sustainability: a relational approach. Sustain. Dev. **23**(3), 167–175 (2015)
4. Rammelt, C.F., Gupta, J.: Inclusive is not an adjective, it transforms development: a post-growth interpretation of inclusive development. Environ. Sci. Pol. **124**, 144–155 (2021)
5. Li, T., Tang, N.: Inclusive leadership and innovative performance: a multi-level mediation model of psychological safety. Front. Psychol. **13**, 934831 (2022)

6. Otsuki, H., Nakadai, S., Tanaka, H., Yamazaki, R., Fushimi, Y.: Creative reuse. Millegraph. (2013) (in Japanese)
7. Rojas-Pernia, S., Sanahuja-Gavaldà, J.M., Macho de Cos, I., Montero-Camacho, M.: Opening the doors: inclusive creative projects and community engagement in Spanish museums. Front. Educ. **10** (2025)
8. Sato, T.: Integration of program management and inclusive design in collective impact practice. Int. J. P2M. **14**(1), 141–155 (2019) (in Japanese)
9. Cassim, J., Dong, H.: Interdisciplinary engagement with inclusive design–the challenge workshops model. Appl. Ergon. **46**, 292–296 (2015)
10. Lee, Y., Cassim, J.: How the inclusive design process enables social inclusion. Int. Assoc. Soc. Des. Res. **2009**, 1–10 (2009)
11. James, M.E., Jianopoulos, E., Ross, T., Buliung, R., Arbour-Nicitopoulos, K.P.: Children's usage of inclusive playgrounds: a naturalistic observation study of play. Int. J. Environ. Res. Public Health. **19**(20), 13648 (2022)
12. Jo, J., Xie, J., Aiyer, P., Knearem, T., Carroll, J.M.: Infrastructuring community fridges for food commoning. Proce. ACM Hum-Comput. Interact. **8**, 1–27 (2024)
13. Qi, J., Mazumdar, S., Vasconcelos, A.C.: Understanding the relationship between urban public space and social cohesion: a systematic review. Int. J. Community Well-Being. **7**(2), 155–212 (2024)
14. Center for Universal Design: The principles of universal design, Version 2.0. https://design.ncsu.edu/research/center-for-universal-design/, last accessed 2026/3/20
15. Katahira, K., Mutō, K., Hashimoto, S., Tobitani, K., Nagata, N.: The hierarchical approach to the semantic differential model: the equivocality of "evaluation" factor in the EPA structure. Trans. Jpn. Soc. Kansei Eng. **17**, 453–463 (2018) (in Japanese)
16. Miyai, S., Katahira, K., Sugimoto, M., Nagata, N., Nikata, K., Kawasaki, K.: Hierarchical structuring of the impressions of 3D shapes targeting for art and non-art university students. In: HCII 2019, CCIS, p. 1032 (2019)
17. Toga, M. et al.: Visualizing and classifying Kansei values: a study on the comfort of washing in electronic bidet seats. In: Proceedings of the 7th ACM International Conference on Multimedia in Asia, pp. 1–7. ACM, Kuala Lumpur (2025)
18. Sugimoto, M., Yagi, Y., Nagata, N.: How different tourist sites evoke different emotions: investigation focusing on the urban and rural sites in Japan. In: International Conference on Human-Computer Interaction, pp. 332–343. Springer, Copenhagen (2023)
19. Zhu, Y., Takahashi, N., Shoji, H.: Comparison of evaluation of T-shirts between Japanese and Chinese based on hierarchical Kansei model. Int. J. Affect. Eng. **23**(2), 169–181 (2024)
20. Sanui, J.: Interview research for product planning: present status and issues to be solved. J. Jpn. Soc. Qual. Control. **33**(3), 13–20 (2003) (in Japanese)
21. Takezawa, T. et al.: Structure of psychological stress during the COVID-19 pandemic and effects of essential oil odor exposure. J. Hum. Interf. Soc. **23**, 337–348 (2021) (in Japanese)
22. Sugimoto, M., Zhang, F., Nagata, N.: EGinterview: a tool for enhancing the evaluation grid method with big data and generative AI. In: Proceedings of the 7th ACM International Conference on Multimedia in Asia, vol. 18, pp. 1–7. ACM, Kuala Lumpur (2025)

Towards an Inclusive User Experience Evaluation Framework for E-Government Mobile Applications

Emmy Hossain[1,2](✉), Noris Mohd Norowi[1], Azrina Kamaruddin[1], and Hazura Zulzalil[1]

[1] Faculty of Computer Science and Information Technology, Universiti Putra Malaysia, 43400 Serdang, Selangor, Malaysia
gs67916@student.upm.edu.my

[2] Faculty of Computer Science and Information Technology, Universiti Malaysia Sarawak, 94300 Kota Samarahan, Sarawak, Malaysia

Abstract. With the growth of smartphone adoption, governments are expanding public services delivery via e-government mobile applications, highlighting the need for user experience (UX) that is inclusive across diverse cultural, digital literacy, Internet access and user abilities contexts. Current UX evaluations for these applications predominantly employ usability evaluation approaches, which is insufficient to account for other UX aspects, and aspects specific to e-government applications. This study presents an ongoing PhD research aimed at developing a UX evaluation framework tailored for e-government mobile applications, with a specific focus on the state of Sarawak in Malaysia. The proposed framework's conceptual structure consisting of pragmatic, hedonic, mobile-specific, government-specific and inclusive access dimensions, and the basis for these dimensions in the framework are presented in this study. The development of this framework is motivated by Sarawak's rapid digitalization in the recent years, and the recognition that e-government mobile applications must be evaluated in ways that considers multicultural user population, differences in digital literacy, Internet access, age, and abilities. The framework incorporates an inclusive access dimension for these considerations. Potential use scenarios for the framework such as expert- or inspection-based evaluations and design reviews, are also indicated. The framework is intended to support evaluators in assessing relevant UX dimensions are addressed in the applications, and to strengthen UX evaluation practices for e-government mobile applications, towards a more meaningful evaluation that leads to inclusive UX for the users.

Keywords: User experience evaluation · UX evaluation · e-government mobile applications · inclusive UX

C. Stephanidis et al. (Eds.): HCII 2026, CCIS 3047, pp. 546–555, 2026.
https://doi.org/10.1007/978-3-032-30552-7_52

1 Introduction

E-government is broadly referred to as the use of information and communication technologies for the access and delivery of public services and information, communication among governments, citizens and stakeholders, and internal administrative operations. With the increasing ownership of smartphones, e-government mobile applications have emerged as an important medium for this purpose, allowing users the convenient access through their smartphone devices. It is essential that these mobile applications are designed and evaluated to provide users with meaningful engagement and to ensure positive user experience. User experience (UX) is broadly understood as all facets of users' interactions with product service, including emotions, perceptions, and reactions, throughout the usage lifecycle [1–4].

UX significantly impacts users' trust, satisfaction and continued use of digital public services such as e-government mobile applications. It is essential for e-government mobile applications to have positive UX in order for users to benefit from what the government intended to provide and share though the e-government mobile applications and avoid facing difficulties during usage, missing out on information, frustration, and abandonment [2, 5]. Users facing challenges associated with Internet access, digital literacy, age and abilities, may also encounter exclusion. Hence, conducting UX evaluation, which is the process of collecting and analyzing data about the UX of users or prospective users when interacting with the product or service [4], is one of the steps that can be undertaken to support the provision of positive UX in the e-government mobile application.

Research that investigates UX evaluation for e-government mobile applications is constrained, with most of existing studies rely on usability evaluation approaches that focused more on task and performance and may overlook aspects beyond usability, which is just one of UX's many components. Existing works on UX evaluation for e-government mobile applications also employ general UX evaluation approaches meant for evaluation across any domain or technological environment, which may not address the e-government mobile application's specific requirements. Along with this, factors that can affect UX and how users interact with the mobile applications, such as cultural diversity, digital literacy levels, Internet access, age and abilities, have received little attention in these existing works.

To address the gaps identified, this study proposes an inclusive UX evaluation framework for e-government mobile applications with dimensions addressing pragmatic and hedonic UX, as well as dimensions specific to the mobile platform, e-government domain and inclusive access as the main contribution. The proposed framework has a specific focus on the Malaysian state of Sarawak, motivated by the state's rapid digitalization and transformation of public services, and its unique multicultural user population with different levels of digital literacy, Internet access, age and abilities.

The rest of this paper is organized into the following sections. Section 2 reviews the related works, Sect. 3 details the method, Sect. 4 presents the proposed framework, Sect. 5 provides the discussion, and Sect. 6 concludes the paper.

2 Related Works

UX evaluation has been studied across a range of domains. Generally, existing works generally focus on the pragmatic and hedonic components of UX, based on the established UX model by [6]. This is often represented through dimensions such as attractiveness, efficiency, learnability, usability, usefulness, visual aesthetics [7, 8]. These works enable the systematic approach in evaluating UX of digital systems.

Existing research on UX evaluation can be broadly categorized into two categories: general and domain specific. General UX evaluation approaches are applicable across different domains, while the domain-specific approaches are designed for the domain. Commonly used UX evaluation approaches include the User Experience Questionnaire [8] which has six scales for attractiveness, perspicuity, efficiency, dependability, stimulation and novelty. [7] proposed the Modular Evaluation of Key Components of User Experience, currently in its second version (meCUE 2.0), which has five modules on perception of instrumental and non-instrumental qualities, user emotions, consequences of use, and overall evaluation. [9]'s Mobile Application User Experience Checklist (MAUX-C), based on the UX Honeycomb, is another general approach built to assess UX of mobile applications. While general UX evaluation approaches offer useful insights, they may not capture specific requirements unique to particular domains.

In response to this limitation, several existing works have proposed domain-specific UX evaluation approaches. [10] presented EDUGX, a UX evaluation framework for educational games, with education- and games- specific dimensions such as knowledge improvement, learning goals, game usability, player context, and flow. Subsequently the EDUGX framework was extended to include mobile educational games by [11], resulting in mobile educational games UX evaluation model (MEGUX) that considers mobility for the mobile games context. [12]'s UX for Business Intelligence Visualization (UXBIV) framework demonstrated domain-specific requirements consideration, in the incorporation of decision-making experience dimensions of decision complexity, decision quality and auxiliary importance. These studies illustrate the significance and possibility of including domain-specific requirements in UX evaluation. Prior research also supports UX evaluation incorporating domain-specificity to capture unique characteristics, user needs, and contextual requirements as different domains, user contexts, and technological environments involve different user expectations, interaction patterns, and evaluation priorities [12–14].

Within the e-government domain, current UX evaluations for e-government mobile applications predominantly employ usability evaluation approaches, which is insufficient to account for other UX aspects, and aspects specific to e-government applications [4, 9, 14–16]. In contrast, only a small number of works adopt general and domain-specific UX evaluation approaches for e-government mobile applications. [17, 18] employed meCUE 2.0, while [19] used the UEQ, to evaluate the UX of various Indonesian e-government mobile applications. Only one study was found within the retrieved studies, [20] incorporated domain-specific considerations in their evaluation of Chinese e-government mobile applications by having the dimensions of professional authority, participation in politics, and freedom of complaint. For e-government websites, prior work generally adopted the domain-specific approach. [21] proposed the AIT2-UX framework to evaluate the Brazilian Federal Reserve Bureau website. [21] built the E-government

Portal Assessment Method (EPGAM) to evaluate Kuwait's Ministry of Public Works portal. [21] designed their own questionnaires to evaluate Malaysian and Nigerian e-government websites respectively; [21] also used the think aloud method together with their questionnaire. [22, 23] interviewed respondents with specific questions to evaluate Kenya and India's e-government websites.

As mobile applications are typically used in dynamic and on-the-go environments with limited or smaller screen input sizes, touch-based interaction, and varying levels of connectivity, mobile applications have unique challenges compared to websites. E-government applications have domain-specific requirements that are different from applications in other domains such as healthcare, commercial, education, and games. Prior work has shown that users' background and capabilities in terms of diverse cultures, digital literacy levels, Internet access quality, age and abilities play a role in their interaction and experience with digital systems [9, 24–28]. All these calls for consideration of the mobile- and government- specific and inclusive access dimensions in UX evaluation. However, research in this area remains underexplored. Therefore, there is a lack of comprehensive framework that incorporates general UX with mobile-specific, government-specific, and inclusive access considerations for e-government mobile applications. This gap calls for a structured approach developed for e-government mobile applications, which is addressed by the framework proposed in this study.

3 Method

This study is conducted using a traditional literature review approach to support the development of the UX evaluation framework for e-government mobile applications. Studies on UX evaluation of e-government mobile applications are examined to identify and synthesize recurring themes and UX dimensions. Because of the limited availability of mobile-specific studies, studies on UX evaluation of e-government websites are examined to provide additional insights. Databases such as Scopus, ACM Digital Library, and IEEE Explore are used to retrieve relevant studies. The searches are guided by various combined keywords related to user experience (e.g. "user experience", "UX"), evaluation (e.g. "evaluation", "assessment"), domain-specific terms (e.g. "e-government", "electronic government" "e government", "m-government", "mobile government", "digital government", and platforms (e.g. "mobile applications", "mobile app", "website"). Studies are selected based on the following criteria: relevance to the scope of study, written in English language, and published in journals and conference proceedings. Backward and forward reference searches are employed to identify and include a wider body of studies. The selected studies are then reviewed to identify the existing approaches and considerations in UX evaluation of e-government mobile applications. Following this, the reviewed studies are organized in a tabular format to facilitate comparison across the studies that results a set of recurring evaluation aspects, domain-specific considerations, and gaps within the studies. Subsequently, a framework base that comprise of five dimensions was established based on the insights from the literature reviewed. The dimensions are pragmatic, hedonic, mobile-specific, government specific, and inclusive access. The first two dimensions, pragmatic and hedonic, are frequently recognized in UX research [6]. The mobile-specific and government-specific dimensions are incorporated to reflect the domain-specific characteristics of e-government mobile applications, in line with prior research that emphasize the importance of including domain-specific characteristics in UX evaluation [12–14]. The inclusive access dimension accounts for considerations for culturally diverse users, digital literacy levels, Internet access, age and abilities.

4 Proposed Framework

This study proposes a UX evaluation framework for evaluating the UX of e-government mobile applications, intended to be used by evaluators prior to user testing. The proposed framework presents a structured approach for evaluating UX during the early stages of development of the application, allowing for detection of potential UX issues before user testing, formal evaluation, or deployment. Conducting evaluation at this stage assists designers and developers address the UX aspects earlier and potentially mitigates later-stage revisions. The proposed framework is designed to account for general UX, domain-specific and inclusive access relevant to mobile platforms, government services and local user context. There are five dimensions that form the base of this proposed framework that collectively account for the functional, experiential, domain-related and inclusive access related to the UX of e-government mobile applications. Figure 1 illustrates the structure of the proposed framework.

The pragmatic dimension pertains to the relevant functionality and goal-oriented aspects of UX, focusing on helping users achieve their goals when using the application [6]. This dimension is a core component of UX according to [6], a widely recognized UX model, and reflects usability-related qualities, ensuring users are able to carry out tasks in the application. Examples of tasks include accessing information and services, payment transactions, service applications and submissions, communicating with the government, scheduling appointments and reporting issues. Efficiency, effectiveness, usefulness, learnability, findability and consistency are some of the key aspects of the pragmatic dimension.

The hedonic dimension addresses the non-functional and experiential aspects of UX, that contributes to how users interact with the application beyond task completion and functional requirements [6]. Both the pragmatic hedonic dimensions form the established UX model by [6]. The hedonic dimension supports improvements in user engagement and encourages the continued use of the application. Some key aspects of the hedonic dimensions include visual appeal, attractiveness, satisfaction, and pleasant user journey.

The mobile-specific dimension is associated with UX aspects specific to mobile features and interactions, concerned with considerations unique to mobile applications instead of websites [29–31]. The mobile-specific dimension is included in the framework to reflect the framework's focus on mobile application. Interaction and input (touch usability), screen size and layout (interface size), performance and responsiveness, and navigation simplicity are among the key aspects of this mobile-specific dimension.

The government-specific dimension deals with UX aspects unique to government platform, focusing on features and requirements that differentiate government applications from commercial ones [32–34]. This government-specific dimension is incorporated in the framework to make this framework domain-specific to e-government, aligning with prior works' call for domain-specific considerations in UX evaluations.

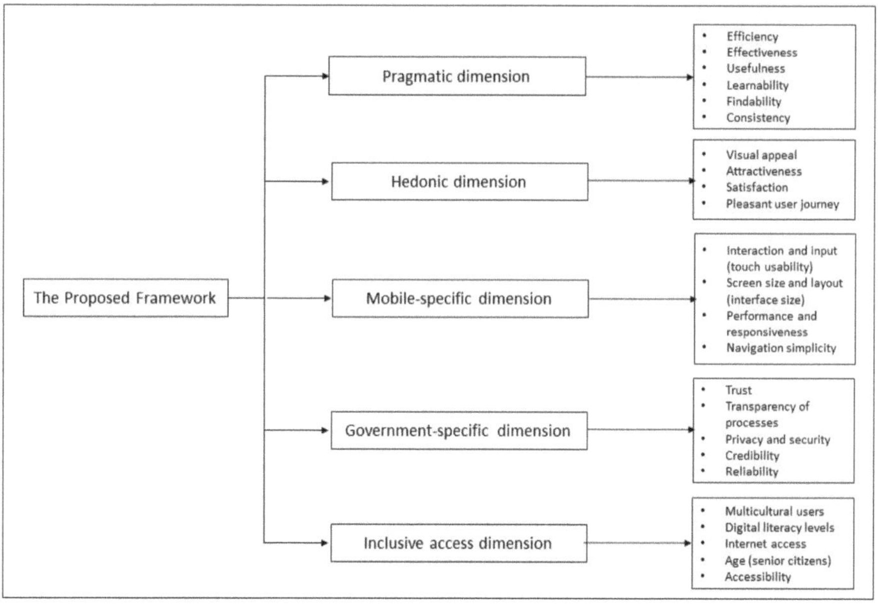

Fig. 1. The proposed framework.

The key aspects in this dimension comprise of trust, transparency of processes, privacy and security, credibility, and reliability.

The inclusive access dimension encompasses the considerations for the users for whom the e-government applications are for. While the aspects in this dimension are not strictly UX aspects, these aspects influence the overall user experience and therefore needs to be considered. These aspects are multicultural users, digital literacy levels, Internet access, age (senior citizens) and different abilities (accessibility) [24–26, 35, 36]. The users in this context are citizens of the state of Sarawak. The key contribution of this work lies in the integration of this inclusive access dimension, to address the gap in the existing literature.

In this proposed framework, the combination of general UX dimensions (pragmatic and hedonic), domain-specific dimensions (mobile and government), and contextual considerations (inclusive access dimension) provides a comprehensive structure for evaluating e-government mobile applications. the five dimensions of this proposed framework presents a holistic UX evaluation approach. Notably, this proposed framework is intended to support pre-user testing UX evaluation by evaluators, enabling early assessment of potential UX issues by designers and developers and subsequently more efficient development process and improved quality the application.

5 Discussion

The proposed framework responds to the gaps in current research, which largely rely on usability-focused evaluations, with relatively few addressing UX evaluation in e-government mobile applications. The proposed framework provides a comprehensive and holistic approach for evaluating UX of e-government mobile applications by bringing together the five dimensions that make up the framework: pragmatic, hedonic, mobile-specific, government-specific, and inclusive access dimensions. The incorporation of the inclusive access dimension, which accommodates the considerations for multicultural users, digital literacy levels, Internet access, age (senior citizens) and different abilities (accessibility), is a key contribution of this proposed framework. These considerations are often overlooked in prior work. The considerations of these aspects enable the e-government mobile applications to be more accessible and inclusive to diverse user groups.

Motivated by rapid digitalization and government efforts to transform public service [37] and the recognition that e-government mobile applications must be evaluated in ways that considers cultural diversity, differences in digital literacy, age and abilities, as well as Internet access, this framework is tailored with a specific focus on the Bornean state of Sarawak, the largest state in Malaysia. Sarawak, largest state in Malaysia, is characterized by a multicultural user population with diverse levels of digital literacy, age, and abilities, alongside uneven Internet access qualities across urban and rural areas. Notably, smartphones or mobile phones are often the primary medium for accessing the Internet and digital services in rural areas is the smartphone or mobile phone. Therefore, there is a need for evaluation approaches that reflect real-world usage with user population characteristics taken into consideration. The proposed framework addresses this through the inclusive access dimension.

The proposed framework is also adaptable for use in other states or countries, government service types, and technological environments. Such adaptation can be achieved by adjusting the dimensions to align with local characteristics, service context, and requirements. The proposed framework is intended to be used before user testing, which enables UX issues to be identified early by designers and developers, through approaches such as expert- or inspection- based evaluations as well as periodical design reviews. Through this, a more efficient development process, less need for costly redesign works, and improved overall quality of e-government mobile applications, can be achieved.

However, this proposed framework comes with several limitations. The framework is developed via a literature-driven approach and has not undergone validation. Future works will include expert validation, empirical testing, and evaluation with practitioners to assess its applicability and usefulness. Further refinement may additionally be needed to improve the framework.

6 Conclusion

This study proposed an inclusive UX evaluation framework for e-government mobile applications, with a specific focus on the state of Sarawak in Malaysia. Five base dimensions, hedonic, mobile-specific, government-specific, and inclusive access, are integrated to form this proposed framework that presents a comprehensive and holistic UX evaluation approach in respond to the gaps in existing works. The framework is intended to be used by designers and developers to evaluate the UX of e-government mobile applications before user testing, to assist in identifying potential UX issues earlier and reducing the need for revision at later stages. Future works will include validating this conceptual framework as it is has not undergone validation. The framework aims to support the development of inclusive and accessible e-government mobile applications, especially in contexts of culturally diverse user population with varying levels of digital literacy, Internet access, age and abilities. Ultimately, this study contributes to the advancement of inclusive UX evaluation practices, especially for digital government services.

Acknowledgments. The authors extend their appreciation to Universiti Malaysia Sarawak, the Ministry of Higher Education Malaysia, and Universiti Putra Malaysia for their continued support in this study.

Disclosure of Interests. The authors have no competing interests to declare that are relevant to the content of this article.

References

1. Norman, D., Nielsen, J.: The Definition of User Experience (UX). https://www.nngroup.com/articles/definition-user-experience/, last accessed 2025/05/01
2. Yusof, N., Hashim, N.L., Hussain, A.: A conceptual user experience evaluation model on online systems. Int. J. Adv. Comput. Sci. Appl. (2022). https://doi.org/10.14569/IJACSA.2022.0130153
3. Hashim, N.L., Yusof, N., Pulau, P.B., Hussain, A., Ibrahim, M.: User experience dimensions for E-procurement: a systematic review. J. Inf. Commun. Technol. **21**, 465–494 (2022). https://doi.org/10.32890/jict2022.21.4.1
4. Hossain, E., Norowi, N.M., Kamaruddin, A., Zulzalil, H.: User experience evaluation in government applications: a systematic review. Int. J. Adv. Comput. Sci. Appl. **16**, 726–735 (2025)
5. Rogers, Y., Sharp, H., Preece, J.: Interaction Design: Beyond Human-Computer Interaction. Wiley (2023)
6. Hassenzahl, M.: The thing and I: understanding the relationship between user and product. Springer International Publishing (2018). https://doi.org/10.1007/978-3-319-68213-6_19
7. Minge, M., Thüring, M., Wagner, I.: Developing and validating an English version of the meCUE questionnaire for measuring user experience. Proc. Hum. Fact. Ergon. Soc., 2056–2060 (2016). https://doi.org/10.1177/1541931213601468
8. Schrepp, M., Hinderks, A., Thomaschewski, J.: Construction of a benchmark for the user experience questionnaire (UEQ). Int. J. Interact. Multimed. Artif. Intell. **4**, 40 (2017). https://doi.org/10.9781/ijimai.2017.445
9. Richardson, B., Campbell-yeo, M., Smit, M.: Mobile application user experience checklist: a tool to assess attention to Core UX principles mobile application user experience checklist: a tool to assess attention to Core UX. Int. J. Hum.-Comput. Interact., 1–8 (2021). https://doi.org/10.1080/10447318.2021.1876361
10. Nagalingam, V., Ibrahim, R., Yusoff, R.C.M.: EDUGXQ: user experience instrument for educational games' evaluation. Int. J. Adv. Comput. Sci. Appl. **11**, 562–569 (2020). https://doi.org/10.14569/ijacsa.2020.0110170
11. Syed Yasin, S.N.H., Ibrahim, R.: A review on user experience model in mobile educational games evaluation. Open Int. J. Informatics. **11**, 165–178 (2023). https://doi.org/10.11113/oiji2023.11n2.286
12. Liu, S., Zhang, H., Yang, Z., Kong, J., Zhang, L., Gao, C.: UXBIV: an evaluation framework for business intelligence visualization. IEEE Access. **11**, 92391–92415 (2023). https://doi.org/10.1109/ACCESS.2023.3300418

13. Jang, H., Han, S.H.: User experience framework for understanding user experience in blockchain services. Int. J. Hum. - Comput. Stud. **158**, 102733 (2022). https://doi.org/10.1016/j.ijhcs.2021.102733
14. Zheng, Q. et al.: EvAlignUX: Advancing UX Evaluation through LLM-Supported Metrics Exploration (2025). https://doi.org/10.1145/3706598.3714045
15. Lyzara, R., Purwandari, B., Zulfikar, M.F., Santoso, H.B., Solichah, I.: E-Government usability evaluation: insights from a systematic literature review. In: Proceedings of the 2019 2nd International Conference on Software Engineering and Information Management, ICSIM 2019, pp. 249–253. ACM International Conference Proceeding Series, Bali, Indonesia (2019). https://doi.org/10.1145/3305160.3305178
16. Bastardo, R., Pavão, J., Rocha, N.P.: Methodological quality of user-centered usability evaluation of digital applications to promote citizens' engagement and participation in public governance: a systematic literature review. Digital, 4740–4761 (2024)
17. Darmawan, A.K., Arifin, I., Anwari, A.: Exploring user experience and user interface of Indonesian e-health PeduliLindungi mobile-apps with MeCUE 2.0 framework. J. Sisfokom (Sistem Inf. dan Komputer). **12**, 244–253 (2023). https://doi.org/10.32736/sisfokom.v12i2.1657
18. Darmawan, A.K., Setyawan, M.B., Bakir, B., Walid, M., Hamzah, M.A., Asir, A.: Assessing and enhancing an existing user experience (UX) of smart regency mobile-apps service with meCUE 2.0 Framework. In: 2021 9th International Conference on Cyber and IT Service Management (CITSM 2021), pp. 1–6 (2021). https://doi.org/10.1109/CITSM52892.2021.9587917
19. Hendrian, A., Hamzah, M.L., Zarnelly, A., Ansyar, T.K.: Evaluation of user experience in mobile applications using user experience questionnaire and user centered design methods. In: 2024 International Conference on Circuit, Systems and Communication (ICCSC 2024), pp. 1–6 (2024). https://doi.org/10.1109/ICCSC62074.2024.10616867
20. Zhu, J., Hou, H.: Research on user experience evaluation of Mobile applications in government services. IEEE Access. **9**, 52634–52641 (2021). https://doi.org/10.1109/ACCESS.2021.3070365
21. Souza, K.E.S.D. et al.: An evaluation framework for user experience using eye tracking, mouse tracking, keyboard input, and artificial intelligence: a case study. Int. J. Hum. Comput. Interact. **38**, 646–660 (2022). https://doi.org/10.1080/10447318.2021.1960092
22. Kamau, G., Njihia, J., Wausi, A.: E-government websites user experience from public value perspective: case study of iTax website in Kenya. In: 2016 IST-Africa Conference on IST-Africa 2016, pp. 1–8 (2016). https://doi.org/10.1109/ISTAFRICA.2016.7530631
23. Kumar, R., Sachan, A., Mukherjee, A.: Qualitative approach to determine user experience of e-government services. Comput. Hum. Behav. **71**, 299–306 (2017). https://doi.org/10.1016/j.chb.2017.02.023
24. Vergari, F., Eriksson, Y., Sjölinder, M.: Navigating Cultural Diversity in UI/UX Design of Mobile Applications: A Design Approach. (2024).
25. Horn, C., Rennie, E.: Digital access, choice and agency in remote Sarawak. Telemat. Inform. **35**, 1935–1948 (2018). https://doi.org/10.1016/j.tele.2018.06.006
26. Ubam, E., Hipiny, I., Ujir, H.: User Interface/user experience (UI/UX) analysis design of mobile banking app for senior citizens: a case study in Sarawak, Malaysia. Proc. Int. Conf. Electr. Eng. Inform., 1–6 (2021). https://doi.org/10.1109/ICEEI52609.2021.9611136
27. Alias, N.A.N., Abu Hassan, A.A., Azan, Z.: Evaluating the Accessibility of E-Government Services Usage in, pp. 1–10 (2023)
28. Husin, H., Hakim, L., Huda, C.: From digital literacy to public trust: the strategic role of E-government service quality, 4 (2026)

29. Standardization, I.O. for: ISO/IEC 25010:2011: Systems and software engineering—Systems and software quality requirements and evaluation (SQuaRE)—System and software quality models. https://www.iso.org/standard/35733.html
30. Roto, V., Obrist, M., Väänänen-Vainio-Mattila, K.: User experience evaluation methods in academic and industrial contexts. In: Interact 2009 Conference User Experience Evaluation Methods in Product Development, pp. 1–5 (2009)
31. Kushchu, I., Kuscu, M.H.: From E-government to M-government: Facing the Inevitable. In: Proceeding of the 3rd European Conference on eGovernment, pp. 1–13 (2004)
32. Anthopoulos, L., Reddick, C.G., Giannakidou, I., Mavridis, N.: Why e-government projects fail? An analysis of the Healthcare.gov website. Gov. Inf. Q. **33**, 161–173 (2016). https://doi.org/10.1016/j.giq.2015.07.003
33. Affairs, U.N.D. of E. and S.: United Nations E-Government Survey 2022. United Nations. https://desapublications.un.org/publications/un-e-government-survey-2022
34. Weerakkody, V., Omar, A., El-Haddadeh, R., Al-Busaidy, M.: Digitally-enabled service transformation in the public sector: the lure of institutional pressure and strategic response towards change. Gov. Inf. Q. **33**, 658–668 (2016). https://doi.org/10.1016/j.giq.2016.06.006
35. Hofstede, G., Hofstede, G.J., Minkov, M.: Cultures and Organizations: Software of the Mind. (2010).
36. (W3C), - World Wide Web Consortium: Mobile Accessibility: How WCAG 2.0 and Other W3C/WAI Guidelines Apply to Mobile. https://www.w3.org/TR/mobile-accessibility-mapping/
37. Goi, C.L.: The next frontier towards digital sarawak. In: Almunawar, M.N., Islam, M.Z., de Pablos, P.O. (eds.) Digital Transformation Management: Challenges and Futures in the Asian Digital Economy, pp. 247–265. Routledge (2022). https://doi.org/10.4324/9781003224532

Development and Evaluation of a Radio Calisthenics Learning System for the Visually Impaired, Using BlazePose and Sound Feedback

Keishin Komuro(✉), Tota Mizuno, Naoaki Itakura, and Kazuyuki Mito

The University of Electro-Communication, 1-5-1 Chofugaoka, Chofu, Tokyo, Japan
keishin.komkom99@gmail.com

Abstract. Visually impaired individuals face difficulties learning how to perform exercises. This is because they lack visual feedback and cannot independently judge whether their movements are correct or incorrect. Even movements they have learned cannot be reviewed on their own, making mastery time-consuming and labor-intensive. We developed systems for verifying the correctness of movements and enabling movement relearning, targeting Radio Calisthenics First (taught in many Japanese schools for the blind). Designed for implementation in educational settings and homes, we adopted BlazePose, a skeleton estimation algorithm developed by Google, for movement assessment. For each of the 13 exercises included in Radio Calisthenics First, key postures are established, and the system evaluates the correctness of them. When the user performs the posture correctly, the system provides sound effects. An experiment involving 10 sighted participants wearing blindfolds confirmed that this system is effective for users to verify the accuracy of their own movements. After that, three visually impaired children used it, and reported it was easy to understand to check their own movement accuracy and the sound effects made performing the exercises enjoyable. Then, we developed systems for relearning movements, targeting three exercises identified as prone to errors. Performing key postures in the correct sequence, it provides audio feedback, enabling users to learn the movement accurately. We conducted experiments comparing the learning effectiveness of the systems with that of "Radio Calisthenics Learning Videos" available on YouTube, using sighted participants wearing blindfolds. The results clearly showed that using the system enabled more accurate learning.

Keywords: to support visually impaired · learning exercise · gamification

1 Introduction

Visually impaired individuals experience difficulty learning physical movements by observing and imitating an instructor's demonstration. Consequently, motor skills are typically taught through verbal instruction, in which the instructor explains the movement orally and the learner attempts to execute it based on the explanation. However, verbal instruction alone is often insufficient for effective motor learning. Previous research

C. Stephanidis et al. (Eds.): HCII 2026, CCIS 3047, pp. 556–564, 2026.
https://doi.org/10.1007/978-3-032-30552-7_53

on verbal instruction in mat exercises has reported that visually impaired children frequently perform movements that differ from what the instructor intended [1]. In such cases, instructors physically guide the learner by directly manipulating the learner's body to correct erroneous movements, enabling gradual acquisition of the target skill [2]. Nevertheless, this approach requires considerable time and effort, even for the acquisition of a single movement. Furthermore, the absence of visual feedback poses challenges not only during instruction at school but also during practice at home. Because visually impaired learners cannot visually monitor their own movements, they are unable to verify whether the movements practiced at home are performed correctly. As a result, when the instructor later evaluates the learner's performance at school, the movement may have deviated from the intended form. In such cases, as in the initial learning phase, the instructor must again physically guide the learner and correct the movement through direct bodily manipulation. Consequently, a substantial amount of time is required for learners to acquire a single movement accurately. To address these challenges, it is necessary to establish an environment in which visually impaired individuals can independently evaluate the correctness of their movements and identify and correct errors on their own.

Miyajima et al. proposed motor learning support systems for visually impaired individuals using wearable devices such as gyroscope sensors and a Wii Remote [3, 4]. These systems captured upper-limb movements and provided auditory and vibrotactile feedback to facilitate the learning of aerobic exercises. Experimental results indicated that users were able to understand the correspondence between movements and auditory signals within a short period of time. However, movement recognition accuracy from auditory patterns was approximately 70%, with notable individual differences. In addition, the system required wearable sensors and involved high equipment costs, which limited its practicality and accessibility.

Therefore, this study aims to develop a system that enables visually impaired individuals to verify the correctness of learned movements using only video captured by a standard web camera available in home and educational settings. In addition, the study seeks to develop systems that facilitate the relearning of movements that have been incorrectly acquired. Unlike previous wearable sensor–based approaches, the proposed system relies solely on a standard web camera, enabling low-cost and easily deployable motor learning support in both home and educational environments.

2 System Overview

2.1 System for Verifying the Correctness of Movements

In this study, Blaze Pose [5], a machine learning–based pose estimation framework developed by Google, was employed to estimate body posture using the built-in camera of a PC or tablet device. For each exercise, predefined key postures that must be passed through were specified. The system determines whether an exercise is successfully performed based on whether the user achieves these postures within the designated movement duration of *Radio Calisthenics No. 1*. Figure 1 illustrates the evaluation process for Exercise 1 ("Stretching Exercise").

For Exercise 1, the following two postures were defined as required checkpoints:

- **Posture 1:** Raising both arms straight overhead (Fig. 1-②)
- **Posture 2:** Extending both arms straight out to the sides (Fig. 1-③)

Successful detection of both postures is regarded as completion of one repetition of the exercise.

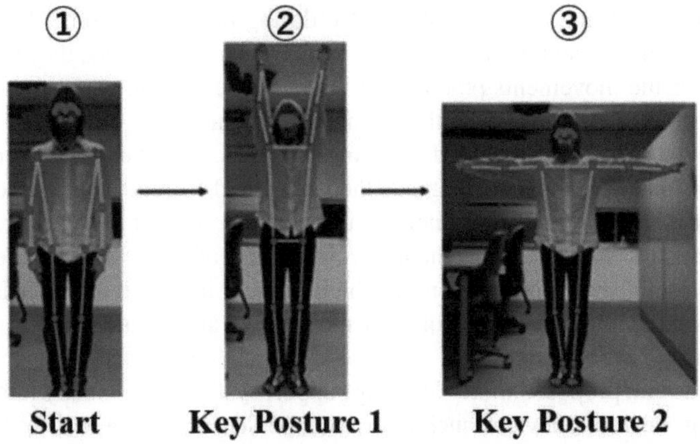

Fig. 1. Process for Exercise 1

The predefined postures for each movement were determined in accordance with the official instructional video and descriptions of *Radio Calisthenics No. 1* provided by Kampo Life Insurance. Exercise evaluation is initiated only when the participant's full body is visible in the camera frame, including both wrists even when the arms are fully extended. Users perform the exercises in synchronization with the official audio track, and a sound effect is played when a movement is successfully completed. After finishing the session, users can press a button to receive auditory feedback regarding the total score and the number of successful repetitions for each exercise.

2.2 Relearning System

The systems were also designed using BlazePose. Based on the results of the experiment using the correctness verification system, three exercises with relatively low success rates were selected: Exercise 4, Exercise 6, and Exercise 10. A relearning system was developed for each of these exercises.

The system consists of two modes: a learning mode and a practice mode. In the learning mode, users learn the key postures of each exercise. The key postures were defined based on the video "Radio Calisthenics No. 1: Learn by Listening" provided by the Simple Insurance Subscribers Association [6]. When a user performs a correct posture, a sound effect is presented to indicate success. The system then proceeds to the explanation of the next key posture, allowing users to learn the movements while confirming their correctness. In the practice mode, a chord is generated when the user follows the key postures in the correct order. Figure 2 shows the relationship between the key postures (①–③) in Exercise 4 and the generated sounds.

① Stand with the feet shoulder-width apart and cross the arms in front of the chest.
② Stand with the feet shoulder-width apart and extend the arms horizontally to the sides.
③ Stand with the feet shoulder-width apart and raise the arms diagonally upward.

If the exercise is performed correctly, the notes C3, E3, G3, and C4 are played at each key posture, forming a chord.

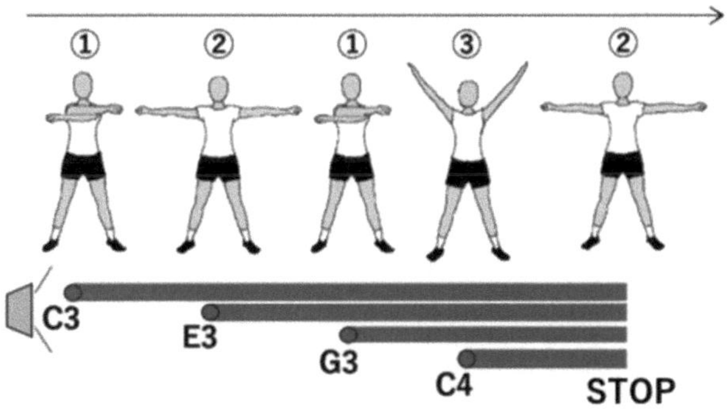

Fig. 2. Image of Sound and Postures.

3 Experiment

3.1 Experiment for System for Verifying the Correctness of Movements

An experiment was conducted with 10 sighted participants and 3 visually impaired participants. As the system is intended for use by visually impaired individuals, the sighted participants performed the movement evaluation while wearing blindfolds. The camera was fixed at a height of 90 cm, and participants stood 240 cm away from the camera before starting the movement evaluation of *Radio Calisthenics No. 1*. After completing the experiment, participants were asked to respond to a questionnaire (Table 1).

3.2 Experiments for Relearning System

An experiment was conducted with ten sighted participants (male and female, age: 22.9 ± 1.85 years). The participants wore eye masks to simulate the use of the system by visually impaired individuals. The participants performed each exercise ten times using the system, and their performance was scored. The participants were then divided into two groups (Group A and Group B), each consisting of five participants, so that the scores for each exercise were balanced between the groups. Group A learned the exercises by moving their bodies while listening only to the audio from the video "Radio Calisthenics No. 1: Learn by Listening" [6]. Group B learned the exercises while moving their bodies using the proposed system. After the learning phase, the participants again performed each exercise ten times using the system, and their performance was scored to evaluate the learning effect of proposal system.

Table 1. Questionnaire.

Item	Response Format
Q1. Please indicate the total score assigned by the system for your overall performance.	0–100
Q2. Please rate your own performance on a 100-point scale.	0–100
Q3. Did you feel that the criteria for determining successful movements were strict?	1 (Very lenient) – 5 (Very strict)
Q4. Among the 13 exercises, which exercise did you feel had particularly strict evaluation criteria?	Multiple choice
Q5. Was the auditory feedback indicating movement success easy to understand?	1 (Very difficult) –5 (Very easy)
Q6. Please provide any comments or suggestions for improving the system.	Open-ended

4 Results

4.1 Results of Experiments for System for Verifying the Correctness of Movements

The results of the questionnaire (excluding Q6) are summarized in Table 2, obtained from 10 sighted participants. A comparison of Q1 and Q2 revealed that many participants rated their own performance higher than the score assigned by the system. Regarding Q3, nine participants selected a score of 4 or higher, indicating that they perceived the criteria for successful movement detection as strict. In Q4, eight participants identified Exercise 10 ("Large Body Rotation") as having particularly strict evaluation criteria. In contrast, for Q5, all participants selected a score of 4 or higher, suggesting that the auditory feedback for successful movements was generally perceived as easy to understand.

Table 3 summarizes the questionnaire responses (excluding Q6) obtained from the three participants with visual impairments. According to the results, none of the participants rated their own performance lower than the score provided by the system. Regarding the strictness of the evaluation criteria, only Participant K selected "4 (strict)," while the other participants selected "2 (lenient)." As for the sound-effect feedback, two participants (K and M) responded that it was "very easy to understand."

Table 2. Questionnaire Results (Sighted Participants).

Participants	Q1	Q2	Q3	Q4	Q5
A	55	70	4	6,10	5
B	60	90	4	6.10,13	5
C	85	100	4	10,13	5
D	65	70	5	6,10	4

(continued)

Table 2. (*continued*)

Participants	Q1	Q2	Q3	Q4	Q5
E	90	100	4	10	5
F	60	58	4	8,11	5
G	70	80	4	10,13	5
H	90	85	4	10	5
I	40	40	4	8,10	4
J	50	30	2	–	5
Mean	66.5	72.3	3.9	–	4.8

Table 3. Questionnaire Results (Visually impaired Individuals).

participants	Q1	Q2	Q3	Q4	Q5
K	40	60	4	1	5
L	60	60	2	–	3
M	70	90	2	10	5
Mean	56.7	70	2.7	–	4.3

4.2 Results of Experiments for Relearning System

A Wilcoxon signed-rank test with a significance level of 5% was conducted to compare the success rates before and after learning. Table 4 shows the mean success rates, standard deviations, and p-values for each group.

Table 4. Mean Success Rates before and after learning.

Group	Exercise No	Success rates (%)		p-value
		Before	After	
A	4	16 ± 32	48 ± 43	0.108 (ns)
	6	36 ± 7.5	48 ± 29	0.414 (ns)
	10	26 ± 25	40 ± 26	0.102 (ns)
B	4	14 ± 28	100 ± 0	0.034 (*)
	6	40 ± 11	78 ± 12	0.042 (*)
	10	18 ± 18	58 ± 7.5	0.067(ns)

*$p < 0.05$, ns: not significant

For all three exercises, Group B showed higher success rates after learning compared with Group A, and the increase in success rates from before to after learning was larger. In addition, the standard deviations of the post-learning success rates were smaller in Group B, indicating less variation in performance among participants.

Furthermore, no significant differences were observed in Group A, whereas significant improvements were found in Exercises 4 and 6 in Group B.

5 Discussion

5.1 System for Verifying the Correctness of Movements

Both sighted participants wearing eye masks and visually impaired participants tended to rate their own performance higher than the system score. The difference between the system score and self-evaluation tended to be larger for visually impaired participants. For example, while only one sighted participant showed a difference greater than 20 points, two out of three visually impaired participants showed a difference of around 20 points. This discrepancy may be related to differences in body image formation. Previous studies have reported that visually impaired individuals tend to have greater difficulty forming body images [7]. Because the proposed system evaluates movements based on factors that require an internal representation of body posture, such as joint angles and the coordinates of estimated body points, it may have been more difficult for visually impaired participants to accurately assess their own movements.

The results of Q3 suggest that visually impaired participants tended to perceive the evaluation criteria as less strict than the sighted participants. One possible reason is the difference in experience in evaluating body movements. Sighted individuals often rely on visual information to judge the accuracy of their movements, and the system's posture-based evaluation may therefore have been perceived as stricter than their own expectations. In contrast, visually impaired individuals may rely more on external feedback when evaluating their movements, which may have led them to accept the system's evaluation more readily. This tendency is also reflected in the results of Q4: sighted participants identified five different exercises as having particularly strict evaluation criteria, whereas visually impaired participants identified only two. However, because the number of visually impaired participants was small, further investigation with a larger sample size is required.

The results of Q5 indicate that the sound-effect feedback was generally easy to understand for the participants. In addition, one participant commented in Q6 that they consciously tried to perform the movements so that the sound feedback would be triggered, which resulted in performing the exercises with greater intensity than usual. This suggests that the sound feedback may have encouraged participants to move more actively and pay closer attention to their movements during exercise.

Although the sound feedback was positively evaluated, several limitations of the system were also identified. In Q6, some participants commented that they wanted to know which part of their movement was incorrect when the exercise was not judged as successful. Because the current system only provides success or failure feedback, it may be difficult for users to understand how to correct their movements. Therefore, a system that can support the relearning of incorrect movements is required.

5.2 Relearning System

Comparing the mean success rates after learning, the results suggest that learning with the proposed system was more effective than learning using only the audio from "Radio Calisthenics No. 1: Learn by Listening" [6]. In addition, the comparison of standard deviations indicates that the proposed system resulted in less variation in learning outcomes among participants. One possible reason is that the sound feedback was triggered when the correct posture was achieved, which may have helped participants interpret the instructions in a more consistent manner. For example, posture ③ in Exercise 4 required the angle formed by the estimated points of the waist, shoulder, and elbow (θ) to be greater than 140°. When participants learned the movement using only audio instructions, some participants did not raise their arms high enough, as shown by Group A in Fig. 3. In contrast, when sound feedback was provided, the target arm position became clearer, and all participants were able to perform the movement correctly, as shown by Group B in Fig. 3.

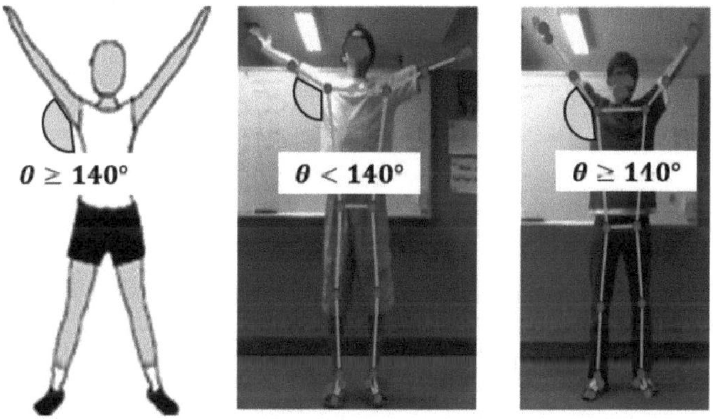

Model Posture **Group A** **Group B**

Fig. 3. Comparison of Point Posture③.

On the other hand, some participants in Group B were not able to immediately perform the correct posture after hearing the explanation of the key posture (Fig. 3). These participants appeared to move their bodies while recalling the instructions and tried to determine how to trigger the sound feedback through trial and error. A similar situation may occur when the system is used by visually impaired individuals. In addition, visually impaired individuals tend to have more difficulty performing movements such as "raising the arms" or "extending the elbows" compared with sighted individuals. Therefore, even when using the proposed system, the learning process may require additional time. To further improve the effectiveness of the proposed system, it is necessary to introduce a feedback function that informs users which part of their movement is incorrect.

6 Conclusion

In this study, we developed a system that enables visually impaired individuals to check the correctness of learned movements using only a web camera. The system evaluates body movements based on posture estimation and provides sound feedback to indicate successful execution.

In addition, we proposed a relearning system that helps users practice key postures of radio calisthenics exercises. An experiment comparing audio-based learning and learning with the proposed system showed that the proposed system improved success rates and reduced variation in performance among participants.

These results suggest that the proposed approach can support the learning and relearning of physical movements for visually impaired individuals.

In future work, it will be necessary to conduct experiments with visually impaired users and to improve the system by providing more detailed feedback on incorrect movements.

Acknowledgments. The authors would like to thank the students and staff of a school for the visually impaired for their cooperation in the experiments.

Disclosure of Interests. The authors declare that they have no conflict of interest.

References

1. Kawasaki, M.: A teaching of mat exercises for visually impaired children. Jpn. J. Sport Movem. Behav. **21**, 19–32 (2008)
2. Koda, Y.: Coaching and support for sports for the visually impaired. J. Soc. Biomech. Jpn. **38**(2), 117–122 (2014)
3. Miyajima, Y., Murasaki, K., Izuhara, R., Nagase, H.: Development of aerobics study support system that uses motion capture for visually handicapped person. J. Soc. Des. Art Fus. Sci. Technol. **51**, 48–49 (2009)
4. Miyajima, Y., Izuhara, R., Nagase, H.: Development of aerobics learning support system with Wii remote for blind. J. Soc. Des. Art Fus. Sci. Technol. **54**, 46–47 (2010)
5. Google.dev. https://ai.google.dev/edge/mediapipe/solutions/guide?hl=ja, last accessed 2026/3/10
6. Raji ch. https://www.youtube.com/channel/UCSQ_2ZrxYK3UGEkEK43Daeg, last accessed 2026/3/10
7. Chebel, N.A., Gaunet, F., Chavet, P., Assaiante, C., Bourdin, C., Sarlgna, F.: Does visual experience influence arm proprioception and its lateralization? Evidence from passive matching performance in congenitally-blind and sighted adults. Neurosci. Lett. **810**, 137335 (2023)

A Review of Exoskeleton Developments to Meet User Needs

Martin Maguire(✉)

School of Design and Creative Arts, Loughborough University, Leicestershire LE11 3TU, UK
m.c.maguire@lboro.ac.uk

Abstract. An exoskeleton is a wearable, external mechanical frame that supports, assists, or enhances a person's physical abilities. The paper describes some of the application areas that exoskeletons can be applied to and the technical developments that make this possible. Key developments include smart sensor technology to track movement and identify and correct poor posture or causes of fatigue, the use of AI to learn user movements for the system to adapt to, and lightweight materials to improve comfort and portability. A high-level description of the human factors process is also described so that an exoskeleton system can be developed to meet user needs. The acceptance of exoskeletons by users and organizations is also discussed. It is concluded that exoskeletons have the potential to revolutionize both the industrial and healthcare sectors by significantly reducing work-related musculoskeletal injuries, enhancing worker productivity, and enabling individuals with physical limitations to regain mobility and independence.

Keywords: Exoskeleton · Wearable robot · Human augmentation · Bionic support · Smart material · Smart clothing

1 Introduction

A robotic exoskeleton is a wearable device that supports, amplifies, or assists human movements to boost strength, endurance, and mobility. Unlike a simple orthopedic device, it integrates motors, sensors, and sometimes artificial intelligence to anticipate and facilitate the user's movements.

It may be used to help workers lift heavy objects (strength augmentation) or perform repetitive tasks with less strain and fatigue using motors, sensors, and AI (Artificial Intelligence) to move with the user's body. Exoskeletons may also support activities like walking, running, or crawling, to be carried out for longer periods with less effort and improved endurance. They are also useful for medical rehabilitation for people with paralysis or recovering from injury.

As described by [1], there are two types of exoskeletons. *Passive exoskeletons* are designed to support and enhance user movements without the aid of power sources. Instead, support is provided by mechanical elements such as elastomers or spring systems. *Active exoskeletons* sense the initiation of the user's movement and then trigger integrated actuators to assist or enhance the movement. Passive and active systems have

C. Stephanidis et al. (Eds.): HCII 2026, CCIS 3047, pp. 565–571, 2026.
https://doi.org/10.1007/978-3-032-30552-7_54

comparative advantages and disadvantages regarding support performance, weight, flexibility, complexity, and operating time, so the choice of exoskeleton type depends on the application area, context of use and task type being supported.

Once considered a laboratory curiosity or military equipment, exoskeletons are now becoming accessible products for practical use [2]. Example current systems include:

- Help lift the heel and stabilize each step, making walking smoother and less tiring, especially for people with mild mobility limitations.
- AI based and trained on real human movements to optimize in real time the amount of force, posture, and assistance for walking or lifting.
- Lightweight assistance for elderly people or those with daily mobility needs, with potential impact on quality of life with reduced fatigue, longer walking distances, and prevention of chronic pain. They can allow walkers to make extended outings (up to 25 km) while adapting to different terrains and activities.
- Modular architectures where different segments (hip, knee) can be adapted for specific uses from hiking to medical assistance to sports activities.

2 Application Areas

The Table 1 shows different application areas for exoskeletons and the kinds of activity that can be supported.

Table 1. Exoskeleton application areas.

Application Area	Uses for Exoskeletons
Logistics and warehousing	Assisting workers to lift and carry heavy loads, reduce fatigue, and minimize musculoskeletal injuries.
Industrial production	Providing lifting and postural assistance, alleviating pressure on the body and reducing the risk of chronic injuries during repetitive or demanding tasks.
Construction	Lifting and carrying significant loads on a building site such as bricks, cement, plaster, paint, tools, etc.
Defense and security	Aiding with performing battlefield tasks such as running, crawling, lifting, carrying reloading.
Healthcare	In hospitals or care facilities, assisting with patient rehabilitation through movement or repositioning to improve safety for both caregivers and patients.
Leisure, domestic	Assisting people with different levels of mobility to perform leisure or sports activities such as walking, carrying; climbing or running, as well as domestic tasks such as cooking, cleaning, gardening; and shopping.

However, while all these activities can be supported with exoskeleton technology, user research and requirements analysis is needed to ensure that a suitable product is developed that will help the user to be assisted effectively. For example, after a review of the use of exoskeletons in the defense industry, it was found that while promising evidence is available for exoskeletons' capacity to assist with load carriage, manual lifting, and working with tools in general, more detailed use case scenarios are needed to be able to run controlled tests in defense and security contexts [3].

3 Development Trends and Innovations

The following trends and innovations in exoskeleton technology will play an important role in the design of future products to be successful in use and give an improved user experience.

- **Smart Sensor Technology:** Exoskeletons now integrate inertial, position, and pressure sensors to track movement and identify and correct improper posture or fatigue to prevent injury. Advances in small body-worn sensors and their integration with wearable devices can help reveal biological mechanisms to enable optimized control. Ultrasound imaging has been used with a soft exosuit to reduce the metabolic cost of walking by detecting instantaneous changes in muscle function. Similar technologies could enable wearable devices to quickly adapt to individual wearers or unknown environments [4]. They could also offer a metric of user effort and provide insight into how wearable devices can offload stress on soft tissue.
- **Use of Artificial Intelligence:** Exoskeletons are using AI to learn user movements, providing personalized, intuitive, and smoother assistance. They can also predict movements and adjust to challenging situations like stairs or uneven ground. AI analyzes movements and biomechanics in real time, adjusts the force applied by the motors, prevents risky motions, and learns the user's habits to provide personalized and smooth support. This self-optimization capability is crucial for making these systems usable by a diverse population from industrial workers to medical caregivers. In the medical field, machine-learning approaches may be applied to help clinicians prescribe a type of exoskeleton or a particular mode of assistance to improve walking for an individual user. Work is also being done on more efficient power sources and batteries, and smarter control systems that use AI to adapt in real-time to the user's intent and environment.
- **Soft Exosuits and Lightweight materials:** To improve comfort and portability, development has moved towards soft, textile-based structures or lightweight rigid-soft hybrids e.g. using carbon fiber that is less bulky and provides higher comfort and flexibility. The pneumatic structures also mimic natural muscle function so that they are easier to wear under clothes and less bulky.
- **Medical rehabilitation:** Lower-limb exoskeletons are focused on "assist-as-needed" (AAN) controllers, which can adapt support to the patient's individual functional level rather than forcing a fixed movement pattern.
- **Modular Architectures:** There is interest in modular designs, allowing for customization across different tasks and activities. Future devices are likely to harness emerging innovative technology such as 3D printing to develop bespoke, lightweight devices based on individual body size and shape [4].

- **Working with Robots:** As more industries adopt automation and smart technologies, exoskeletons are likely to become tools that work alongside robots. These systems can help workers perform their jobs more safely and efficiently, combining human skills with robotic precision.
- **Ergonomics:** Designing exoskeletons that fit and feel good will ensure that they enhance, rather than hinder, a worker's natural abilities.
- **Digital Twin Technology:** An emerging trend is where a virtual replica of the exoskeleton can be used to simulate and optimize performance in real time to analyze and improve design in a more efficient way.

The main aim is the development of products which are functionally useful, safe, and go noticed by an observer or are simply widely accepted.

4 Meeting User Needs

A review was conducted of 124 studies related to hand exoskeletons [5]. The authors found that more studies aim for rehabilitation than assistance and the dominant form of assessment is system validation. Wearability, comfort, portability, adaptability, affordability, and safety were the most frequently targeted user-centered criteria. 38 articles reported assessment of designs with human subjects, the majority being functional tests followed by usability tests. The authors offer user-centered design directions and methodological suggestions for user involvement to improve the usability and acceptability of the exoskeleton systems. They also discuss the necessity for restructuring the engineering design strategy for better adaptability.

A further study reviewed 34 studies that reported the development of exoskeleton adopting user-centered design (UCD) methods in healthcare and community settings [6]. From the review, the authors felt that there was a need for better collaborations both between and within disciplines involved in the exoskeleton design process. Greater involvement of stakeholders to help meet their needs and to promote acceptance was also required. A tool to assess and manage multidisciplinary collaboration is described.

To meet user needs, it is necessary to identify and understand the range of physical and cognitive activities that the user would perform to achieve their goals as well as the environmental conditions in which they would operate. Each activity should then be broken down into actionable steps that the user carries out. This creates an understanding of what the system (exoskeleton) might need to do to support these activities.

In analyzing the context of use to assist with the selection or design of an exoskeleton, the following human factors should be considered:

- Task description
- Area of the body affected
- Physical effort requirement, stress and strain levels on the body
- Mental or cognitive effort requirement
- Period-of-time carried out
- Number of repetitions that might be undertaken
- Risks associated with the activity or task
- Potential benefits that an exoskeleton could provide

Requirements for an exoskeleton can then be specified as a basis for developing different design solutions, either based on existing products or the development of new ones. Evaluation of potential products on the market or of prototype designs is needed under laboratory and then field conditions before a final design is created (or an existing product is selected). These user-centered design activities can be specified more formally within [7]. Organizations wishing to use exoskeletons may need to decide whether to utilize an existing product or to partner with a design company to produce an exoskeleton customized to their needs. To support this, there is a need for standardized testing protocols and safety guidelines so that it is possible to compare devices and ensure long-term safety.

Beyond technical function, consideration needs to be given to understanding psychological and social factors, such as the potential for stigmatization and the need for personalized devices that empower, rather than hinder, the user. Key areas of focus include:

- **Comfort and Ergonomics:** User studies highlight that minimizing weight and skin contact pressure is critical. Some systems are optimized for all-day comfort and mobility.
- **Donning/Doffing Time:** A key user requirement for personal use is the ability to put on/take off the device without assistance, which remains a challenge for heavier powered devices.
- **Task-Specific Support:** Industrial users prioritize shoulder and back support for static postures, while rehabilitation users need gait assistance that improves symmetry and speed.
- **Independence:** Some devices enable users with limited movement to stand and walk independently, addressing the need for autonomy.

Users' ideas about their needs can be influenced by their expectations about the capability of technology. A survey of was conducted of participants (company representatives and students) attending an exoskeleton information event to investigate this [1]. It was found that participants would expect to plan for a short to medium term future (1–2 years) instead of the long term (5 years), showing that the introduction of exoskeletons is a current issue in their minds, rather than looking ahead to when exoskeleton capabilities may increase. They also found that the introduction of exoskeletons is expected, by both participant groups, to bring benefits in terms of improving the ergonomics of workstations and reducing absenteeism, as well as enabling staff to work for longer. In terms of lifting loads, both groups considered moderate loads of between 5–20 kg to be where assistance is needed rather than lighter or heavier loads. This may be due to the perception that support from an exoskeleton is unnecessary or may not be sufficient outside of this range.

5 Challenges for User and Organization Acceptance

An important issue is the acceptance of exoskeletons by users and organizations. Only if they recognize and understand the advantages of these systems, will they be motivated to employ them. A literature review was conducted to see if there was a consensus on user perspectives of exoskeleton technology [8]. It was noted that for some individuals with neurological impairment, exoskeletons would provide their first opportunity to be mobile without their wheelchair. However, not all potential users, such as wheelchair users, were motivated to use exoskeletons as a satisfactory alternative to the independence afforded by their wheelchairs. Issues related to acceptance include [2]:

- **Cost:** Exoskeletons remain relatively expensive. High-end powered models remain unaffordable for many small businesses and individuals, limiting widespread adoption.
- **Battery/equipment weight, life and portability:** Exoskeletons carry batteries, actuators, and sensors, so may be too heavy for comfort (or perceived as such). Limited battery life can reduce appeal for all-day use either in industrial or daily life. Maximizing assistance with portability is a delicate balance for manufacturers to achieve.
- **Social and ergonomic acceptance:** Wearing an exoskeleton is not yet natural for many users. Bulky and visible devices can lead to user discomfort in public settings, driving the need for more discrete, "clothing-like" designs. Ergonomics, comfort, and aesthetics are key to large-scale adoption.
- **Need for long-term studies:** While short-term laboratory trials show benefit, long-term field studies are required to show effectiveness in real-world environments.

6 Future Outlook and Conclusions

Future developments of exoskeletons are predicted to focus on:

- Sustainable and wearable materials (3D printing, carbon fiber).
- IoT Integration for capturing data and offering customized functional capability.
- Cross-discipline collaboration (e.g. between engineers, therapists, and users) to ensure the design meets actual user needs.

It is also important that the long-term effects of exoskeletons on the health and well-being of employees are investigated as there is still a knowledge gap in this area. By integrating smart sensor technology, data can be collected so that the effects on employees can be visualized and understood.

Improving the acceptance of exoskeletons requires a user-centered approach, focusing on comfort, ease of use, and demonstrable physical relief. Key strategies include early user involvement in design, tailored training, reduced device weight, and clear, practical demonstrations of benefits to build trust.

As more industries adopt automation and smart technologies, exoskeletons are likely to become tools that work alongside robots. These systems can help workers perform their jobs more safely and efficiently, combining human skills with robotic precision. Focusing on ergonomics and designing exoskeletons that fit and feel good will ensure that they enhance, rather than hinder, a worker's natural abilities. Future devices are likely to harness emerging innovative technology such as 3D printing to develop bespoke, lightweight devices based on an individual's body size and shape.

The evolution of exoskeletons is redefining the boundaries of assisted mobility, workplace ergonomics and functional rehabilitation as well as pushing the boundaries of what technology can do to assist, augment, and improve human physical capability and well-being. With the use of smart sensors, AI, and advanced materials, they have the potential to evolve into functional, intelligent, personalized systems that deliver significant benefits to their users.

References

1. Pupkes, B., Petzolt, C., Freitag, M.: User expectations, requirements, and applications of exoskeletons: insights from a survey. In: Proceedings of 58th CIRP Conference on Manufacturing Systems (2025). https://doi.org/10.1016/j.procir.2025.01.100
2. Louis, C.C.: Exoskeletons 2026: when robotics gives "superpowers" to walking, Robot Mag. (March 2026). https://www.robot-magazine.fr/en/exoskeletons-2026-when-robotics-gives-superpowers-to-walking/
3. Farris, D.J. et al.: A systematic literature review of evidence for the use of assistive exoskeletons in defence and security use cases. Ergonomics. **66**(1), 61–87 (2023). https://doi.org/10.1080/00140139.2022.2059106
4. Siviy, C. et al.: Opportunities and challenges in the development of exoskeletons for locomotor assistance. Nat. Biomed. Eng. **7**(4), 456–472 (2023). https://doi.org/10.1038/s41551-022-00984-1
5. Süner-Pla-Cerda, S., Şahin, B., Arikan, K.B.: User requirements and involvement methods in the development of hand exoskeletons: a review. ACM Trans. Hum.-Robot Interact. **14**(1) (2024). https://doi.org/10.1145/36982
6. Cheng, C.Y.M., Lee, C.C.Y., Chen, C.K., Lou, V.W.Q.: Multidisciplinary collaboration on exoskeleton development adopting user-centered design: a systematic integrative review. Disabil. Rehabil. Assist. Technol. **19**(3), 909–937 (2024). https://doi.org/10.1080/17483107.2022.2134470
7. ISO 9241-210:2019: Ergonomics of Human-System Interaction, Part 210: Human-Centred Design for Interactive Systems. International Organization for Standardization, Geneva, Switzerland (2019)
8. Hill, D., Smitham, P., Holloway, C.S., Ramirez, D.F.M., Pappas, Y.: What are user perspectives of exoskeleton technology? A literature review. Int. J. Technol. Assess. Health Care. **33**(2), 160–167 (2017). https://doi.org/10.1017/S0266462317000460

Reimagining the Augmented Reality Accessibility Ecosystem for Deaf Students: Service Provider Perspectives in Experiential Learning

Roshan Mathew(✉) and Roshan Peiris

Accessible and Immersive Realities Lab, Rochester Institute of Technology, Rochester, NY, USA
{rm1299,roshan.peiris}@rit.edu

Abstract. In experiential learning environments, Deaf and Hard of Hearing (DHH) students often experience *"split attention,"* dividing their focus among tasks, instructors, and access providers. Augmented Reality (AR) has been proposed as a means to centralize communication access within the student's field of view; however, little is known about how such systems affect the instructors, interpreters, and captioners who support access in these settings. We present a formative, expert-based evaluation of ARRAE, an AR-mediated communication access ecosystem, examining the experiences of an instructor, an American Sign Language (ASL) interpreter, and a real-time captioner in a simulated laboratory environment. Comparing in-person, traditional remote, and AR-mediated access, our findings suggest that AR reconfigures accessibility labor and interactional practices by redistributing communication, attention, and awareness across participants. While AR-mediated access supported integrated, in-situ communication and enhanced contextual awareness, it also altered interactional feedback mechanisms, such as gaze coordination and pacing, that support shared understanding during instruction. These observations highlight trade-offs between access, control, and coordination, and suggest that AR-mediated systems may be most effective when considered as part of a broader, hybrid ecosystem rather than as standalone replacements for existing modalities. This work contributes initial insights into how AR reshapes communication access in experiential learning and informs the design of systems that support coordinated, multi-user interaction in hands-on educational contexts.

Keywords: Augmented Reality · Deaf and Hard of Hearing · Experiential Learning · Accessibility Ecosystems · Remote Interpreting · Remote Captioning

1 Introduction

Accessibility in higher education is typically framed as a service delivered to a student. However, in practice, it is a complex orchestration of labor involving

C. Stephanidis et al. (Eds.): HCII 2026, CCIS 3047, pp. 572–584, 2026.
https://doi.org/10.1007/978-3-032-30552-7_55

multiple stakeholders: the instructor managing the pedagogy, the interpreter or captioner translating the content, and the student synthesizing it. This coordination becomes fragile in experiential learning environments, such as chemistry laboratories, where visual attention is a scarce resource. In these settings, DHH students face the *"split-attention effect,"* forcing a choice between looking at their experimental task, a potential safety hazard, and an interpreter [19]. While recent work has explored Augmented Reality (AR) smart glasses to overlay access services directly into the student's field of view [16,18], these interventions are almost exclusively evaluated through the lens of the end user's user experience. However, access technologies do not exist in a vacuum. If a system reduces the student's cognitive load but increases the cognitive burden on the interpreter or disconnects the instructor from their instructional rhythm, the ecosystem fails.

Our work presents a formative, expert-based evaluation of ARRAE (Augmented Reality Real-Time Access for Education) that centers the accessibility provider ecosystem. Through an analysis of the experiences of an instructor, an American Sign Language (ASL) interpreter, and a real-time captioner in a simulated laboratory setting, we make the following contributions: (1) A qualitative account of how AR-mediated communication access reshapes accessibility labor and interactional practices among instructors, interpreters, and captioners during hands-on laboratory tasks, in comparison to in-person and conventional remote access; and (2) An articulation of key usability, workflow, and design considerations that emerge when deploying AR-mediated communication access in experiential higher education settings.

2 Method

2.1 ARRAE Platform Implementation

We developed ARRAE, a platform that connects support personnel to deaf students wearing optical see-through (OST) smart glasses [7]. The platform provides distinct interfaces for students and support personnel. Students use a streamlined heads-up display (HUD) to receive live video of the interpreter or captioning within their line of sight, while support personnel use a web-based interface to manage real-time access services.

Access for DHH Students. For deaf students, ARRAE functions as a receiver, overlaying either a live video feed of an interpreter or a scrolling text stream of captions directly into the student's line of sight. This design follows the spatial contiguity principle [4], allowing students to remain visually engaged with the task while receiving access to spoken instruction.

The Support Ecosystem. Unlike traditional remote access solutions, where support personnel may see only a limited webcam view of the student, ARRAE instruments the lab with three Pan-Tilt-Zoom (PTZ) cameras: a Workstation

Camera (workbench view), an Observation Camera (wide-angle view of the student's signing space), and an Instructor Camera (instructor view). These feeds are streamed via WebRTC to a browser-based dashboard with sub-second latency.

Interpreting Workflow. Interpreters broadcast their video feed directly to the student's smart glasses display. Their dashboard shows all active lab feeds simultaneously, allowing interpreters to monitor both the student's workbench and signing space to support context-aware interpretation. The architecture also supports team interpreting standards [3,9].

Captioning Workflow. Captioners operate through a view integrated with a TypeWell ingestion server [6]. This interface supports rapid text entry and delivery while also displaying the PTZ camera feeds, providing visual context for task-relevant actions that may not be evident from audio alone.

Instructor Monitoring. While students view only their selected access service to reduce cognitive load, the instructor's dashboard aggregates all active feeds, supporting situational awareness during hands-on experiments.

2.2 Study Design

We conducted a formative, expert-based evaluation of ARRAE in a simulated laboratory setting. The study was approved by the institutional review board, and all participants provided informed consent. The broader study involved 12 deaf student participants: six in the interpreting study and six in the captioning study. Deaf student perspectives are reported in a separate study [17]. This paper focuses on the qualitative experiences of three expert participants: one Science, Technology, Engineering, and Mathematics (STEM) instructor (10–15 years of experience), one certified ASL interpreter (3–5 years of Video Remote Interpreting (VRI) experience), and one professional captioner (5–10 years of real-time captioning experience). The instructor participated in both studies, which were run separately; the interpreter participated only in the interpreting study, and the captioner only in the captioning study.

An expert review approach was used to identify interactional barriers, workflow demands, and role-specific design requirements relevant to early-stage system development. Three service delivery conditions were compared: (1) In-Person Access, (2) Remote Access (traditional VRI/captioning via tablet), and (3) AR-Mediated Access (ARRAE).

Study Environment and Instrumentation. To simulate remote service delivery, the study utilized two distinct locations.

Location A: Simulated Lab. A workstation with a biosafety cabinet was used to approximate a STEM laboratory environment (Fig. 1). The space was instrumented with an OBSBOT Tail Air 4K Pan Tilt Zoom (PTZ) camera for the workbench [1] for the workbench, an overhead Tenveo 10× Zoom PTZ camera [5] for the student's wider signing space, and an OBSBOT Tiny 4K webcam [2] for the instructor. All feeds were streamed to the ARRAE dashboard. PTZ cameras were chosen based on the findings from a prior study where interpreters reported a preference for PTZ cameras in remote interpreting contexts [15].

Location B: Remote Support Hub. During the Remote and ARRAE conditions, the interpreter and captioner worked from a separate room equipped with a laptop and external monitor (Fig. 2), allowing them to view the lab feeds and stream interpretation or captions back to the student.

Procedure. The interpreting and captioning studies were conducted separately. Each study included six sessions with six different deaf student participants, segregated according to their preference for the primary access modality. In each session, the student completed three hands-on laboratory tasks (making artificial snow using an instant snow polymer) guided by spoken English instructions, experiencing all three access conditions. Condition order and task order were counterbalanced across sessions. Sessions were moderated by deaf researchers, and students received smart-glasses training before beginning the tasks. The same instructor participated across all conditions in both studies.

Data Collection and Analysis. The qualitative analysis reported here focuses on the three expert participants. After each session, the instructor and the relevant access provider completed open-ended surveys reflecting on the three access conditions. After all six sessions in each study, a brief follow-up semi-structured interview was conducted with the expert participant, and the moderator recorded interview notes. The present analysis draws on the expert participants' survey responses and interview notes.

These data were analyzed inductively by the study researchers using reflexive thematic analysis [8]. The researchers iteratively reviewed the survey responses and interview notes, generated initial codes, and developed themes across participants and modalities to identify recurring barriers, facilitators, and design implications in the in-person, remote, and AR-mediated conditions. Given the exploratory and expert-based nature of the study, the analysis focused on identifying recurring patterns across sessions and conditions rather than achieving thematic saturation or generalizable findings.

3 Findings

We report findings across themes, focusing on how AR-mediated communication access reshapes accessibility labor and interactional practices among the instructor, interpreter, and captioner in hands-on learning environments.

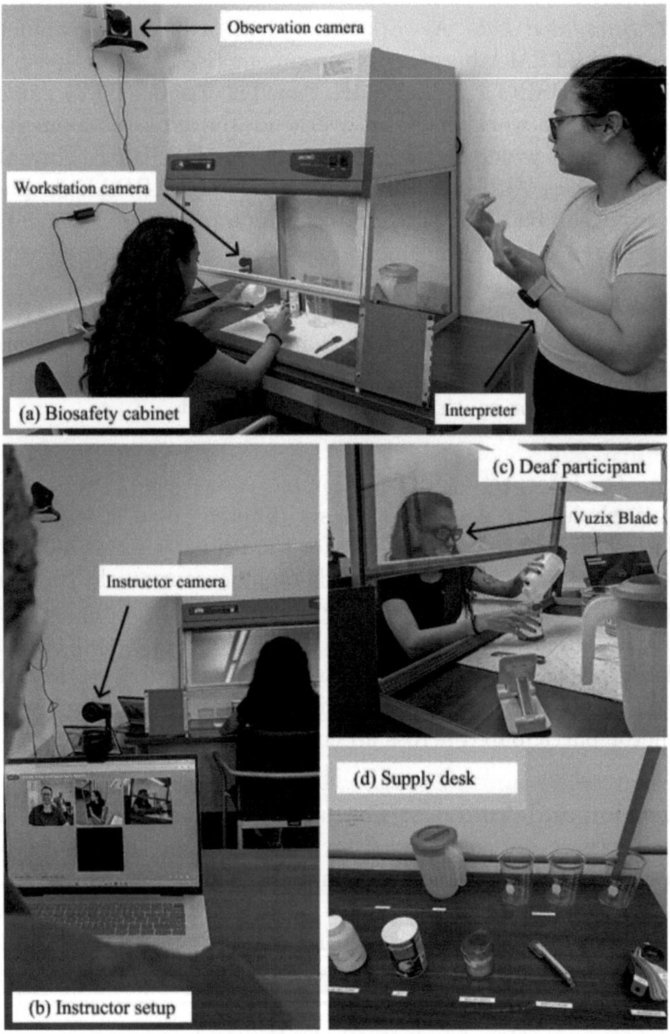

Fig. 1. ARRAE study setup at Location A. (a) Biosafety cabinet with workstation and observation cameras. (b) Instructor setup. (c) Deaf participant wearing Vuzix Blade smart glasses. (d) Supply desk for student participants.

3.1 Familiarity vs. Mediated Access

In-person condition was consistently described as the most natural and reliable. The instructor noted that in-person interpreting *"feels the most familiar,"* while the interpreter described it as *"least cognitively demanding."* The captioner similarly characterized in-person captioning as *"effortless and highly familiar."* However, this condition limited visibility and introduced spatial constraints. The instructor reported, *"I cannot see the student's face or work station so I don't*

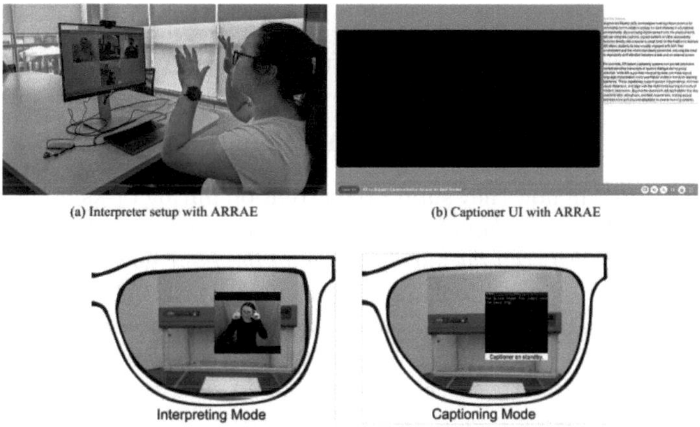

(a) Interpreter setup with ARRAE

(b) Captioner UI with ARRAE

(c) ARRAE modes viewed through smart glasses

Fig. 2. ARRAE interfaces. (a) Interpreter setup at Location B. (b) Captioner user interface. (c) Smart glasses view illustrating interpreting and captioning modes.

know when they are confused or what step they are on in the experiment. That's a big disadvantage." The instructor also emphasized that *"having another body in the room is always difficult in a science lab."* The interpreter also experienced line-of-sight issues. Remote and AR-mediated modalities reduced these physical constraints but introduced technological mediation. Remote interpreting was described as *"impersonal,"* while Zoom captioning was described as frustrating, with the captioner noting, *"I definitely do not prefer to type into Zoom. It just doesn't feel that great typing into the tiny window and then having my captions disappear."* ARRAE balanced these trade-offs by improving access while retaining some mediation challenges.

3.2 Visual Awareness and Task Coordination

Across all roles, visual access to the student, workspace, and communication stream was key to effective coordination. Remote Access and ARRAE conditions improved instructor awareness. The instructor explained, *"I really enjoy being able to see the student's face...limited view of the student's workstation...and also the interpreter. I can see when the student is confused or needs further clarification. I can also see what part of the task the student is working on. This helps me with pacing of giving directions."* ARRAE further enhanced this through multi-camera views: *"Multiple camera views is very helpful, especially when I'm able to see what the student is doing. This helps with how I pace my instructions."* The interpreter and the captioner similarly emphasized contextual awareness. The captioner noted, *"I also liked how there were multiple camera angles that allowed me to see what the student was working on, which just gave me some more context which helps with captioning."* However, visibility remained fragile. In remote setups, occlusion from materials disrupted communication, and similar issues persisted in ARRAE. These findings highlight that robust, multi-perspective visibility is essential but not fully resolved.

3.3 Attention Integration and Interactional Flow

Conditions differed in how they supported attention during tasks. Remote Access setups required attention shifts or movement. The instructor observed that students had to *"move between the supply desk and the fume hood"* to communicate, and Zoom captions required looking away from the task. ARRAE reduced this overhead by integrating communication into the student's field of view. The instructor noted, *"the student was able to continue working while still watching the interpreter through the glasses instead of needing to shift [their] gaze to the iPad [as in the case with Zoom]."* Similarly, *"[They were] able to work while reading the captions simultaneously and as an instructor, I thought that was efficient."* The interpreter also reported reduced reliance on gaze alignment. However, ARRAE introduced coordination challenges. The instructor noted difficulty initiating interaction, requiring coordination with both interpreter and camera positioning. This suggests a need for better attention signaling mechanisms.

3.4 Instructor Awareness and Control of Communication

Instructor awareness of communication processes was critical for pacing and clarity. In remote captioning, the instructor valued seeing captions: *"I like being able to see the captions...so I know if I need to slow down."* Similarly, visibility of the student and interpreter supported comprehension monitoring. In ARRAE, this awareness was reduced. The instructor noted, *"I wish I could see the captions myself so that I know instructions are being conveyed correctly and if I need to slow down my pacing."* While AR improved student access, it limited instructor oversight. In-person setups provided indirect awareness through environmental cues (e.g., *"seeing/hearing the captionist type helped me with my pace"*). Overall, these findings indicate a trade-off between optimizing student experience and maintaining instructor control.

3.5 Usability and Workflow Constraints

Technology-mediated modalities introduced usability and reliability challenges. Remote Access setups were affected by audio capture issues, setup complexity, and platform limitations. For example, the instructor described the setup as cumbersome: *"Making sure everyone except the instructor is muted and that the captioner is granted manual caption ability is just extra stuff to have to take care of before 'class' starts."* ARRAE improved audio quality, contextual awareness, and interface ergonomics. The captioner noted, *"Setup and delivery was pretty seamless. The audio was much more clear than Zoom as well."* However, ARRAE introduced new challenges, including system instability (*"freezing of the video feed"*), limited interface flexibility, and hardware constraints. These findings highlight the need for reliable, low-friction setup and ergonomic design in AR systems.

3.6 Persistence of Information for Task Continuity

Persistence of communication content was critical in multi-step lab tasks. In-person captioning supported this through stable text displays. As the instructor noted, *"Everything went smoothly, I noticed that the student was able to refer back to the iPad screen to verify [they] had gotten all of [their] supplies. On Zoom and with the smart glasses, there wasn't enough text that remained on the screen for [them] to do so."* In contrast, Zoom captions were transient: *"The captions...disappear quickly."* ARRAE improved persistence by keeping captions visible within the student's field of view. The instructor observed, *"I noticed that the student was able to refer back to the captioning text still visible on the glasses while [they] gathered all of [their] required materials."* These findings highlight the importance of persistent, integrated access to communication in supporting task continuity.

Overall, these findings reveal consistent trade-offs across modalities. In-person access offers reliability but limits visibility and scalability. Remote approaches improve awareness but introduce fragmentation and technical challenges. AR-mediated access integrates communication into ongoing activity and enhances contextual awareness, but currently limits instructor oversight and presents usability constraints. A summary of these trade-offs across modalities is provided in Table 1.

Table 1. Comparison of Communication Access Modalities Across Key Themes

Themes	In-person	Remote Access	ARRAE
Familiarity & Reliability	High, no tech issues	Moderate, platform dependent	Moderate; emerging, some instability
Visual Awareness	Limited, restricted line-of-sight	Improved; single view of student/workspace	High; multi-camera views, richer context
Attention & Interaction	Direct, requires co-location	Requires gaze shifts and repositioning	Integrated into task; reduced gaze shifts
Instructor Awareness	Indirect cues only	High; can see captions/interpreter	Limited; cannot see captions directly
Usability & Setup	Simple, no setup	Moderate complexity; audio, roles, setup	Higher complexity; multi-camera positioning
Information Persistence	High; stable display	Low; transient captions	Moderate–high; persistent in-view captions
Space Constraints	High (extra body in lab)	Low	Low

4 Discussion

Our findings suggest that AR reconfigures how communication, attention, and awareness are distributed across the instructor, interpreter, captioner, and student, rather than simply improving access. We interpret these findings below.

4.1 Communication Access as Distributed Awareness

A key contribution of this work is the reframing of communication access as *distributed awareness*. Within the context of this study, effective instructional coordination depended on how well the instructor, interpreter or captioner, maintained awareness of student activity, communication flow, and task progress. In-person condition supported ecological awareness through co-presence, enabling the interpreter and the captioner to access environmental cues with minimal effort. However, this came at the expense of instructor awareness as it limited the instructor's ability to monitor comprehension and progress.

Remote and AR-mediated modalities redistributed awareness through video streams. ARRAE, in particular, expanded awareness by providing simultaneous views of the student, workspace, and communication channels, supporting more informed instructional pacing. However, this redistribution was uneven. While AR improved student-facing access and provider awareness, it reduced instructor's visibility into communication outputs, particularly captions. This asymmetry highlights that increasing visibility for one role may reduce it for another, suggesting that communication access systems must be understood as shared, multi-user awareness environments rather than individual assistive tools.

4.2 Embodied Interaction and Integration of Communication

The findings also point to a shift in how communication is integrated into embodied activity. In traditional configurations, communication and task execution are spatially separated, requiring students to alternate attention between the task and the communication channel. This introduces interactional overhead, particularly in dynamic environments such as laboratory settings. AR-mediated access reduces this separation by embedding communication within the student's perceptual field. From a distributed cognition perspective, this integration reduces the need for explicit coordination but introduces new interactional challenges. The interpreter reported reduced dependence on gaze alignment, while the instructor experienced difficulty initiating interaction without shared physical cues. These findings suggest that while AR supports continuous access, it alters the mechanisms through which participants establish attention and coordination.

4.3 Trade-Offs Between Access, Control, and Coordination

The findings reveal persistent trade-offs between improving access, maintaining instructional control, and supporting coordination. First, enhancing student access through AR can reduce instructor control over communication processes. In contrast to remote captioning, where the instructor could monitor captions directly, ARRAE limited this visibility. This suggests a tension between student-centered access and instructor oversight of communication accuracy and pacing. Second, while AR enhances contextual awareness through multi-perspective views, it introduces coordination overhead. Participants reported challenges related to camera positioning, system setup, and managing occlusions. This reflects a broader pattern where technological augmentation redistributes coordination work rather than eliminating it. Third, the persistence of information played a key role in supporting task continuity. In-person captioning enabled students to revisit information easily, while Zoom captions were described as transient. ARRAE addressed this by allowing captions to remain visible within the student's workspace, supporting continuous engagement without repeated clarification. However, this was limited by the space available in the captioning container seen within the AR view.

4.4 Implications for Experiential Learning Contexts

Collectively, the findings from this study offer initial insights into technology-mediated interaction in experiential learning environments. In laboratory settings, where perception, action, and communication are tightly coupled, our findings suggest that AR-mediated systems may support this coupling by integrating communication into ongoing activity and enhancing contextual awareness. At the same time, the effectiveness of such systems appears to depend on how well they align with the social and spatial organization of the classroom. Within the context of this study, AR-mediated access did not function as a replacement for existing modalities, but rather as part of a hybrid configuration in which different approaches afforded different forms of awareness, control, and interaction.

5 Limitations and Future Work

This work should be interpreted as an exploratory study of AR-mediated communication access in experiential higher education. The study involved a single instructor, interpreter, and captioner, enabling a close examination of expert workflows and modality-specific trade-offs, but not supporting statistical generalization. The findings are therefore intended to inform early-stage design and theory-building for communication access in hands-on instructional settings. Replication with multiple professionals in longitudinal studies is needed to assess whether the observed patterns hold across different instructors and access service providers over time, and how increasing familiarity may reshape coordination demands, usability, and instructional fit. Additionally, some challenges observed in the ARRAE condition may reflect the current maturity of the prototype, as well as the broader demands of AR-mediated communication access.

Future work should also move beyond technical feasibility toward professional efficacy in experiential learning environments. Key priorities include addressing the fractured interactional feedback reported in AR-mediated conditions, particularly reduced access to non-verbal and backchanneling cues used to gauge comprehension, pacing, and communicative alignment-and refining the system in line with the requirements identified in this study. These include role-specific visual views, shared awareness features for instructors, improved persistence and review of captioning content, more flexible interface controls, and more dependable audio and video performance. Future studies should further examine these issues across a broader set of instructors, students, interpreters, and captioners, and across diverse experiential tasks, to assess how these patterns generalize under varied user demands and whether AR-mediated access can become dependable in routine practice.

Finally, as a broader future direction, we plan to explore the presentation of additional elements of speech, such as affective captions, which have been shown to enhance user experience [10–14, 20]. However, it is critical to examine how these features can be effectively delivered from a service-provider perspective, as well as their impact on users' experiences. Accordingly, our future work will investigate both the design and implications of such approaches.

6 Conclusion

Accessibility in experiential higher education is not simply a matter of delivering communication access; it also depends on how that access supports relationships among students, instructors, and access providers during active task work. This exploratory study suggests that AR-mediated support can help restore forms of spatial and contextual awareness that are often diminished in conventional remote access. In particular, ARRAE showed promise in improving shared visual awareness, reducing gaze shifting, and better integrating interpreting and captioning into hands-on laboratory activity. At the same time, in-person support remained the most familiar and dependable modality, while the AR condition introduced new demands related to positioning, interface flexibility, and system reliability. Overall, these findings suggest that AR-mediated access in experiential higher education may be most effective when designed not simply as a wearable replacement for traditional interfaces, but as a shared system that supports the distinct yet interconnected needs of students, instructors, interpreters, and captioners through shared awareness, feedback loops, and reliable coordination.

Acknowledgments. The contents of this paper were partially developed under a grant from the National Institute on Disability, Independent Living, and Rehabilitation Research (NIDILRR grant number 90IFRE0083). NIDILRR is a Center within the Administration for Community Living (ACL), Department of Health and Human Services (HHS). The contents of this paper do not necessarily represent the policy of NIDILRR, ACL, or HHS, and you should not assume endorsement by the Federal Government. The authors thank Ms. Wendy Dannels for her guidance and valuable contributions to the development of this study.

References

1. OBSBOT Tail Air: AI-Powered 4K PTZ Streaming Camera. https://www.obsbot.com/obsbot-tail-air-streaming-camera
2. OBSBOT Tiny 4K - AI-Powered AI Tracking PTZ 4K Webcam. https://www.obsbot.com/obsbot-tiny-4k-webcam
3. Resources - registry of interpreters for the deaf, inc. https://rid.org/resources/#fortheinterpreter
4. Spatial contiguity principle. In: Mayer, R.E. (ed.) Multimedia Learning, pp. 135–152. Cambridge University Press, 2 edn. https://doi.org/10.1017/CBO9780511811678.010, https://www.cambridge.org/core/books/multimedia-learning/spatial-contiguity-principle/B9B79EDC777C375C7ED410B82EF80247
5. TEVO-VHD10U USB HDMI 10X optical Zoom Conference Camera. https://www.tenveo.com/product/ptz-camera/418.html
6. TypeWell — real-time transcription services and professional training for accessibility. https://typewell.com/
7. Vuzix blade 2™ smart glasses. https://www.vuzix.com/products/vuzix-blade-2-smart-glasses
8. Braun, V., Clarke, V.: Using thematic analysis in psychology **3**(2), 77–101. https://doi.org/10.1191/1478088706qp063oa
9. Hoza, J.: Team interpreting. In: Stone, C., Adam, R., Müller de Quadros, R., Rathmann, C. (eds.) The Routledge Handbook of Sign Language Translation and Interpreting, pp. 162–177. Routledge, New York (2022). https://doi.org/10.4324/9781003019664-14
10. de Lacerda Pataca, C.a., et al.: Tactile emotions: multimodal affective captioning with haptics improves narrative engagement for d/deaf and hard-of-hearing viewers. In: Proceedings of the 2025 CHI Conference on Human Factors in Computing Systems. CHI '25, Association for Computing Machinery, New York, NY, USA (2025). https://doi.org/10.1145/3706598.3713304
11. de Lacerda Pataca, C.a., Hassan, S., Tinker, N., Peiris, R.L., Huenerfauth, M.: Caption royale: exploring the design space of affective captions from the perspective of deaf and hard-of-hearing individuals. In: Proceedings of the CHI Conference on Human Factors in Computing Systems. CHI '24, Association for Computing Machinery, New York, NY, USA (2024). https://doi.org/10.1145/3613904.3642258
12. de Lacerda Pataca, C.a., Patterson, S., Peiris, R., Huenerfauth, M.: Fuzzy feelings: arousal's interpretive noise and the case for acoustic-based haptics. In: Proceedings of the CHI Conference on Human Factors in Computing Systems. CHI '26, Association for Computing Machinery, New York, NY, USA (2026). https://doi.org/10.1145/3772318.3793421
13. de Lacerda Pataca, C.a., Watkins, M., Peiris, R., Lee, S., Huenerfauth, M.: Visualization of speech prosody and emotion in captions: Accessibility for deaf and hard-of-hearing users. In: Proceedings of the 2023 CHI Conference on Human Factors in Computing Systems. CHI '23, Association for Computing Machinery, New York, NY, USA (2023). https://doi.org/10.1145/3544548.3581511
14. Pataca, C. et al.: Comparative analysis of customized captioning between north american and south korean d/deaf and hard-of-hearing users. In: Proceedings of the 27th International ACM SIGACCESS Conference on Computers and Accessibility (ASSETS 2025). ACM, New York, NY (2025). https://doi.org/10.1145/3663547.3746400

15. Mathew, R., Dannels, W.: Improving the user experience for sign language interpreters in remote interpretation for small group settings. In: Proceedings of the 22nd International Web for All Conference, pp. 51–62. W4A '25, Association for Computing Machinery. https://doi.org/10.1145/3744257.3744261
16. Mathew, R., Mak, B., Dannels, W.: Access on demand: real-time, multi-modal accessibility for the deaf and hard-of-hearing based on augmented reality. In: Proceedings of the 24th International ACM SIGACCESS Conference on Computers and Accessibility, pp. 1–6. ASSETS '22, Association for Computing Machinery. https://doi.org/10.1145/3517428.3551352
17. Mathew, R., Peiris, R.L.: Evaluating the feasibility of augmented reality to support communication access for deaf students in experiential higher education contexts. In: Proceedings of the 23rd International Web for All Conference. W4A '26, Association for Computing Machinery. https://doi.org/10.1145/3800424.3800450
18. Miller, A., Malasig, J., Castro, B., Hanson, V.L., Nicolau, H., Brandão, A.: The use of smart glasses for lecture comprehension by deaf and hard of hearing students. In: Proceedings of the 2017 CHI Conference Extended Abstracts on Human Factors in Computing Systems, pp. 1909–1915. CHI EA '17, Association for Computing Machinery. https://doi.org/10.1145/3027063.3053117
19. Smith, S.B., Ross, A.D., Pagano, T.: Chemical and biological research with deaf and hard-of-hearing students and professionals: Ensuring a safe and successful laboratory environment **23**(1), 24–31. https://doi.org/10.1016/j.jchas.2015.03.002
20. Wang, Y., Li, Z., Chelladurai, P.K., Dannels, W., Oh, T., Peiris, R.L.: Haptic-captioning: using audio-haptic interfaces to enhance speaker indication in real-time captions for deaf and hard-of-hearing viewers. In: Proceedings of the 2023 CHI Conference on Human Factors in Computing Systems. CHI '23, Association for Computing Machinery, New York, NY, USA (2023). https://doi.org/10.1145/3544548.3581076

Relationship Between Tactile Pictogram Relief Method and the Identifiability of the Tactile Map for the Visually Impaired

Kazuyuki Mito(✉), Naoto Takayama, Natsuki Sano, Tota Mizuno, and Naoaki Itakura

The University of Electro-Communications, 1-5-1 Chofugaoka, Chofu, Tokyo, Japan
k.mito@uec.ac.jp

Abstract. This study aims to develop a tactile map using pictograms for visually impaired users. To clarify the relationship between tactile pictogram relief methods and the identifiability of tactile maps. This study used 10 kinds of pictograms (30 × 30 mm). The tactile pictograms were created by a 3D printer following three relief methods: a) uniformly raised form (Type 1), b) varying the raised height for each component (Type 2), and varying the raised height for each element and applying curved surfaces according to the characteristics of the elements (Type 3). Ten subjects with an eye mask evaluated the discriminability of the tactile map and three relief methods in learning and recall tests. In the learning test, the learning time of Types 2 and 3 was shorter than for Type 1. And the understandability of Types 2 and 3 was significantly higher than for Type 1. In the recall test, the results showed that the recall time for Types 2 and 3 was significantly shorter than for Type 1. Furthermore, the accuracy rate and understandability for Types 2 and 3 were significantly higher than for Type 1. In conclusion, varying component heights in tactile pictograms improves the identifiability of the tactile map for the visually impaired.

Keywords: Tactile Pictogram · Tactile Map · Visually Impaired

1 Introduction

Tactile maps with tactile symbols and Braille are installed in public facilities and public transport to support the movement of the blind and visually impaired. Its map is recognizable using convex lines, convex or concave surfaces, tactile marks, Braille, and raised characters [1]. Typically, Braille letters describe the location information of tactile guide maps, such as toilets, elevators, and railway stations. However, since the literacy rate of Braille is only about 10% in the United States [2] and Japan [3], other methods of information transfer using the sense of touch should be considered. Therefore, we focused on tactile pictograms for visually impaired people with difficulty understanding Braille [4, 5]. A pictogram is a graphical symbol for guidance that conveys information through visual graphical symbols, and a tactile pictogram is a raised pictogram. However, since standard pictograms are designed to be easily recognizable visually, it is necessary to

C. Stephanidis et al. (Eds.): HCII 2026, CCIS 3047, pp. 585–590, 2026.
https://doi.org/10.1007/978-3-032-30552-7_56

consider pictograms that are easily recognizable by touch. The previous studies [6] have shown that it is difficult to tactually identify pictograms that contain "people" or complex figures including curves. In a previous study on the stereoscopic method, it was found that the average identification time was shorter for a multi-valued representation (relief representation) that highlights the form of the object in three dimensions than for a binary representation that uniformly highlights the silhouette of a grape or an apple. The purpose of this study is to apply the stereoscopic method to tactile pictograms and to clarify the relationship between the stereoscopic method and the ease of tactile identification.

2 Methods

2.1 Tactile Map Design

This study used ten pictograms seized 30 mm in length and width shown in Fig. 1. The tactile pictograms were created by a 3D printer (snapmaker 2.0 A350T) following three relief methods: a) uniformly raised form (Type 1), b) varying the raised height for each component (Type 2), and varying the raised height for each element and applying curved surfaces according to the characteristics of the elements (Type 3) as shown in Fig. 2. Learning and recall experiments were conducted using four types of tactile maps (each measuring 116–227 mm on a side) featuring 4 to 8 of these tactile pictograms as shown in Fig. 3.

2.2 Procedure

Subjects were 9 healthy adult males and 1 female aged 21 to 34, for a total of ten subjects (clear-sighted persons). The subjects wore an eye mask to simulate the use by a visually impaired person. The index finger of the dominant hand was used to touch tactile maps. The subjects' hands were filmed during the experiment.

The experiment was conducted in two stages: a learning experiment and a recall experiment. In the learning experiment, a total of 30 tactile pictograms (10 types × 3 relief methods) were presented to the participants one at a time in random order for them to learn. The names and characteristics of the tactile pictograms were explained before the learning phase began. After learning, participants were asked to rate the ease of understandability (1: difficult to understand to 5: easy to understand) on a 5-point scale. In addition, the time taken to learn the pictograms was measured as 'learning time'.

In the identification experiment, 12 tactile maps were presented to participants in random order for them to explore by touch. Whenever a participant identified a tactile pictogram during exploration, they were asked to rate the pictogram's name and perceptibility on a 5-point scale (1: difficult to 5: easy). In addition, the time elapsed from the moment participants began touching a tactile pictogram on the map until they provided their response was measured as the identification time.

2.3 Data Analysis

All values in the text and figures are presented as means and standard error (SE). The Steel-Dwass test was used in the multiple-group comparisons. Differences were assessed with two-sided tests, with an alpha level of 0.05.

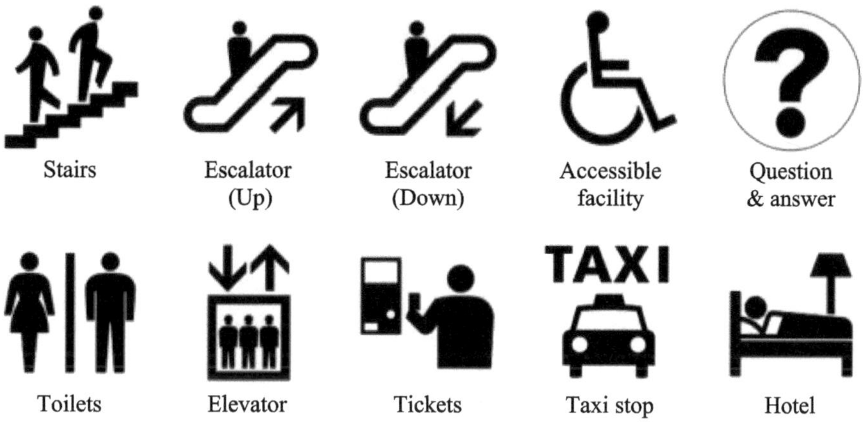

Fig. 1. Pictograms used in this experiment.

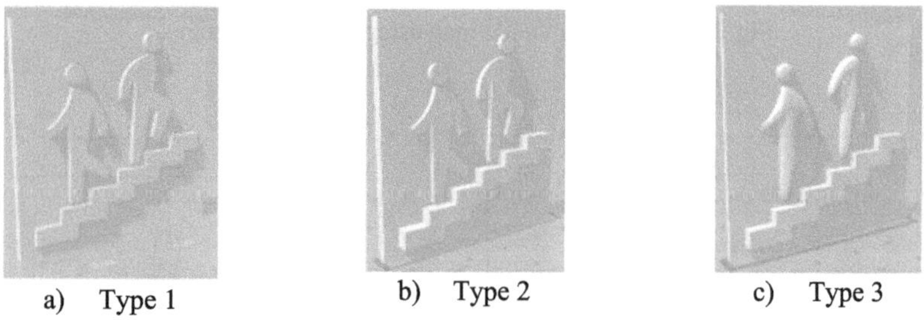

Fig. 2. Tactile pictograms by three relief methods.

3 Results and Discussions

Figure 4 shows the results of the learning experiment. Learning time (Fig. 4a) was shortest for Type 3 than for the other types, and understandability (Fig. 4b) was highest for Type 3 than for the other types.

Figure 5 shows the results of the recall experiment. Correct answer rate (Fig. 5a) was over 99% in Type 2 and Type 3. Recall time (Fig. 5b) was shortest for Type 3, and perceptibility (Fig. 5c) was highest for Type 3 than for the other types.

These results suggest that changes in embossing height facilitate the identification of pictograms on tactile maps and contribute to the formation of mental maps and improved understanding of the maps. Furthermore, Type 2 and Type 3 also made it easier to distinguish between the background of the tactile map and the pictograms.

However, no differences were observed between Type2 and Type 3 in either the learning or recall experiments. Therefore, it is considered that curving certain elements is not as effective as varying the relief height in improving the comprehension of tactile maps.

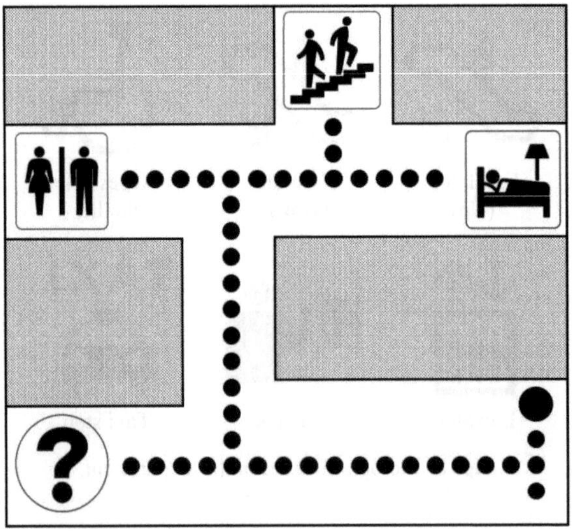

Fig. 3. Example of tactile map using tactile pictograms.

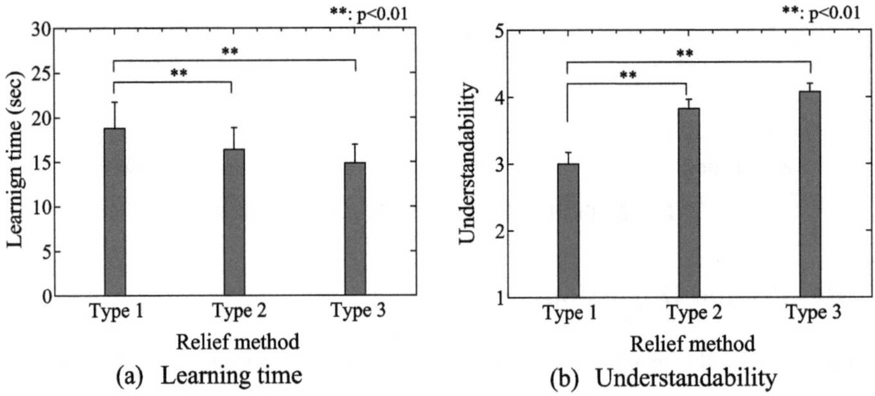

Fig. 4. Results of learning experiment.

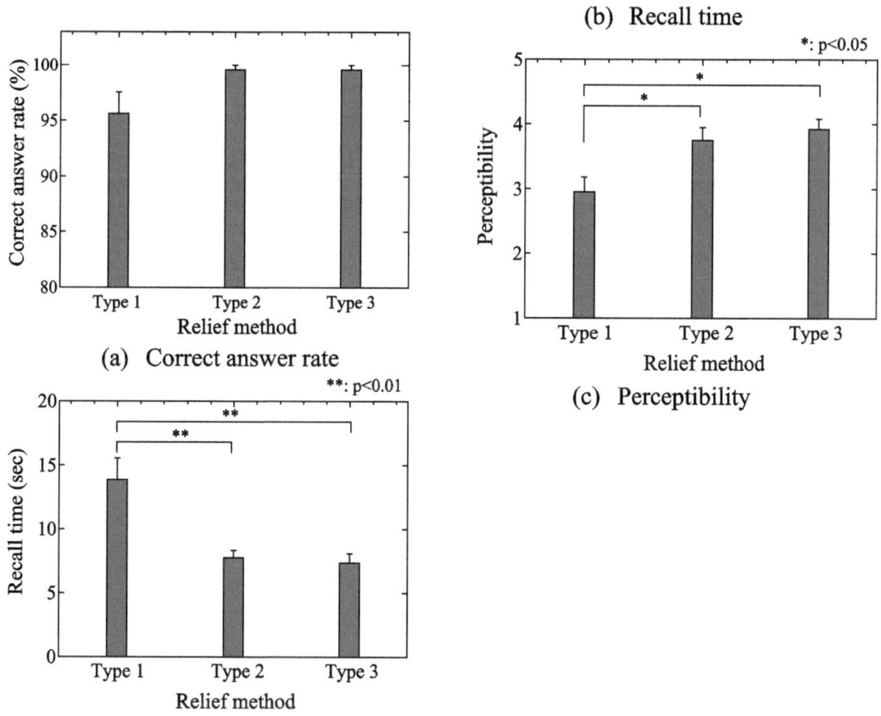

Fig. 5. Results of recall experiment.

4 Conclusions

This study aims to develop a tactile map using pictograms for visually impaired users. To clarify the relationship between tactile pictogram relief methods and the identifiability of tactile maps. It was suggested that varying the height of the raised areas for each component or applying curved surfaces according to the characteristics of the elements would improve the ease of identification of tactile diagrams and may contribute to the formation of mental maps.

Acknowledgments. This work was supported by JSPS KAKENHI Grant Number JP24K07945. The authors have no competing interests to declare that are relevant to the content of this article.

References

1. ISO 19028:2016(en) Homepage. https://www.iso.org/standard/63761.html, last accessed March 2024
2. National Federation of the Blind: The Braille Literacy Crisis in America: Facing the Truth, Reversing the Trend, Empowering the Blind (2009)
3. Ministry of Health, Labor and Welfare of Japan Homepage (in Japanese). https://www.mhlw.go.jp/toukei/saikin/hw/shintai/06/index.html, last accessed 3 March 2024

4. Ueda, A., Sawada, Y., Murakami, T., Saito, M., Tsutsui, S.: Preliminary investigation of the optimal size on tactile pictogram for visually impaired persons. Bull. Jpn. Soc. Sci. Des. **63**(3), 29–36 (2016)
5. Fukita, Y., Shirai, A., Mizuno, T., Itakura, N., Mito, K.: Evaluation of discriminability of tactile pictogram for visually impaired person. J. Jpn. Soc. Welfare Eng. **22**(1), 16–23 (2020)
6. Shimizu, Y., Shinohara, M., Nagaoka, H.: Recognition of tactile patterns in a graphic display: evaluation of presenting modes. J. Vis. Impair. Blind. **94**(7), 456–491 (2000)

Evaluating Accessibility in Games Across Platforms: A Guideline-Based Comparative Study

Anastasia Ntagianta[1], Stavroula Ntoa[1(✉)], and Constantine Stephanidis[2]

[1] Institute of Computer Science, Foundation for Research and Technology - Hellas (FORTH), Heraklion, Crete, Greece
{dagianta,stant}@ics.forth.gr

[2] Department of Computer Science, University of Crete, Heraklion, Crete, Greece
cs@ics.forth.gr

Abstract. Motivated by the need to identify cross-platform game accessibility guidelines and explore their horizontal applicability, this work presents a comparative accessibility evaluation of PC, mobile, and VR games using a consolidated guideline-based framework derived from existing industry and academic accessibility recommendations. A curated set of accessibility guidelines was synthesized and organized across six accessibility categories, namely auditory, physical, visual, speech, cognitive-learning-neurological, and general accessibility. The framework was applied through expert-based heuristic evaluations of three commercially available games representing different platforms, namely computer, mobile device, and virtual reality device. The findings reveal common themes and differences in accessibility implementation across platforms, as well as persistent limitations related to customization, interface scalability, interaction flexibility, and alternative input support. Based on the findings, the study identifies recurring platform specific accessibility challenges and emphasizes the need for accessibility by design in games.

Keywords: Game accessibility · accessibility guidelines · cross-platform games · mobile game accessibility · virtual reality game accessibility

1 Introduction

Digital games constitute one of the most widespread forms of interactive entertainment, attracting increasingly diverse audiences. Beyond their traditional role as a source of entertainment, games are now widely employed in a variety of domains and application contexts, including education, training, healthcare, rehabilitation, public awareness, cultural heritage, and social advocacy. Today, games have expanded from traditional desktop platforms to contemporary devices, such as smartphones, tablets, augmented reality (AR), and virtual reality (VR) devices, creating new opportunities and challenges for interaction design. Among the key challenges is game inclusivity, enabling players with diverse abilities to access gameplay experiences and equitably enjoy the associated benefits [1].

C. Stephanidis et al. (Eds.): HCII 2026, CCIS 3047, pp. 591–606, 2026.
https://doi.org/10.1007/978-3-032-30552-7_57

Digital accessibility refers to the design of games that can be played by people with diverse sensory, motor, cognitive, learning, and communication abilities [2]. Accessibility barriers in games may arise from multiple sources, including lack of support for assistive technologies, inaccessible audiovisual stimuli, or interaction techniques requiring high physical precision [1, 3]. Such barriers can significantly restrict participation and negatively affect player experience, autonomy, and inclusion. Consequently, accessibility is increasingly recognized not merely as a technical requirement but as a fundamental component of user-centered and inclusive game design.

Over the last decade, substantial efforts have been devoted to establishing accessibility guidelines and recommendations for digital games. Several guidelines have been produced, while academic research has proposed accessibility strategies and games for specific disability groups, platforms and gameplay contexts, including visual impairments, motor disabilities, cognitive impairments, and aging populations [4–12]. Despite these advances, games remain inaccessible, while universal accessibility is considered challenging or even unrealistic [1, 2]. Furthermore, there is limited work investigating how research and guidelines translate into practice as design and evaluation instruments, especially in cross-platform games.

Motivated by this gap, the current study investigates accessibility practices across PC, mobile, and VR games through a comparative guideline-based evaluation approach. First, a consolidated accessibility framework was developed by synthesizing accessibility recommendations from established industry and academic sources. The framework was then applied to three commercially available games, praised for their accessibility, representing different technological platforms: OXENFREE II: Lost Signals (PC), Minecraft (mobile), and Moss (VR). The study aims to examine how accessibility support differs across platforms and to identify recurring strengths, limitations, and design challenges associated with contemporary game accessibility practices.

This paper is organized as follows. Section 2 introduces the game accessibility guidelines on which the consolidated list was developed, while Sect. 3 elaborates on the methodology followed. Section 4 presents the results from the three games studied. Conclusions and avenues for future work are provided in Sect. 5.

2 Background and Related Work

An important role in promoting game accessibility has been played by guidelines developed by researchers and associations [13]. This section introduces well-established guidelines, particularly those that were used in the context of the described work.

Game Accessibility Guidelines (GAG). The Game Accessibility Guidelines (GAG) were developed in a 'collaborative effort between a group of studios, specialists and academics, to produce a straightforward developer-friendly reference on how to avoid unnecessarily excluding players, and ensure that games are equally fun just as fun for as wide a range of people as possible' [14, 15]. Guidelines are organized per targeted disability (motor, cognitive, vision, hearing, speech, and general), as well as per conformance level (basic, intermediate, and advanced). In more detail:

- Basic guidelines recommend low-effort but high-impact features, such as subtitles, scalable text, and colourblind-friendly palettes.

- Intermediate guidelines require more planning, such as remappable controls and UI scaling.
- Advanced guidelines reflect cutting-edge practice, including real-time text-to-speech and saving accessibility profiles.

This tiered system is widely recognized for its clarity and adaptability, making it customizable according to the developers' needs.

IGDA Game Accessibility Guidelines. The International Game Developers Association (IGDA), through its Game Accessibility Special Interest Group (GASIG), has proposed a list of guidelines, organized per player disability [16]. Currently, they maintain the full list available for archival purposes and also provide their top ten guidelines, organized in the form of questions.

Platform-Specific Guidelines. Several platforms have developed their own accessibility guidelines. Microsoft's Xbox Accessibility Guidelines provide detailed requirements across categories such as input, visuals, audio, and documentation. These guidelines are integrated into Microsoft's certification processes, ensuring a baseline of accessibility compliance for Xbox titles [17]. Ultraleap has produced its own set of guidelines for accessible VR experiences [18]. The World Wide Web Consortium (W3C) has also produced recommendations for accessible XR environments [19]. Mobile accessibility guidelines have also been provided by W3C, but became later subsumed by the Web Content Accessibility Guidelines [20].

Research-Oriented Guidelines. Academic research has played an essential role in providing theoretical grounding for accessibility. Following an evaluation of 50 games chosen for their sales data, Brown and Anderson [4] propose a list of recommendations for accessible game design, while Yuan, et al. [21] surveyed the state of the art in game accessibility and produced a list of game accessibility strategies per disability type. Several other efforts have focused on providing guidance for game accessibility for a specific target user group, such as for people with visual impairments [22, 23], with motor impairments [24, 25] with cognitive impairments [26], or for older adults [27].

3 Methodology

The methodology adopted in this study was designed to ensure a systematic, transparent, and replicable approach to assessing game accessibility conformance. Its primary aim was to identify, adapt, and apply accessibility guidelines across multiple platforms (PC, mobile, and VR), while also assessing their practical applicability through iterative evaluations.

To support the accessibility assessment of games across multiple platforms, a curated list of guidelines applicable to PC, mobile and VR platforms was created. Initially, the guidelines list for PC was created – by extracting information from the aforementioned sources, which also served as the basis upon which the remaining two guidelines' lists were built. The PC guidelines list was treated as a universal or general guidelines list, which was expanded with additional platform-specific items for mobile and VR [28].

The guidelines consolidated were organized per user category and difficulty level, adopting two levels for simplicity purposes, namely basic and advanced. The accessibility categories the guidelines were divided into were: auditory, physical, visual, speech, cognitive-learning-neurological, and general. Besides their detailed analysis in the sections that follow, a more 'glanceable' guidelines list has been developed (as illustrated in Fig. 1).

Auditory Accessibility Guidelines

All platforms		Mobile		VR		Level
Provide subtitles for all important speech	☐		☐	Masked characters or private data are not read aloud without the user's allowance	☐	Basic
Provide separate volume controls or mutes for effects, speech, and background / music	☐		☐		☐	
Ensure no essential information is conveyed by sounds alone	☐		☐		☐	
If any subtitles / captions are used, present them in a clear and easy-to-read way	☐		☐		☐	
Avoid or keep background noise to minimum during speech	☐		☐	Use surround sound	☐	Advanced
Use distinct sound/music design for all objects and events	☐		☐		☐	
Provide captions or visuals for significant background sounds	☐		☐		☐	
Provide a visual indication of who is currently speaking	☐		☐		☐	
Allow subtitle/caption presentation to be customized	☐		☐		☐	
Provide a stereo/mono toggle	☐		☐		☐	

General Accessibility Guidelines

All platforms		Mobile		VR		Level
Allow gameplay to be fine-tuned by exposing as many variables as possible	☐	Elements that trigger changes should be sufficiently distinct to be clearly distinguishable from non-actionable elements	☐	Make interactive elements that require accuracy stationary or prevent using them	☐	Basic
Offer a wide choice of difficulty levels	☐	Provide instructions for custom touchscreen and device manipulation gestures	☐		☐	
Provide details of accessibility features on packaging and/or website	☐	When multiple elements perform the same action or go to the same destination (e.g., link icon with link text), these should be contained within the same actionable element	☐		☐	
Provide details of accessibility features in-game	☐		☐		☐	
Ensure that all settings are saved/remembered	☐		☐		☐	
Solicit accessibility feedback	☐		☐		☐	
Players can confirm or reverse choices they have made	☐		☐		☐	Advanced
Where possible software shall use the settings (colour, contrast, font) of the platform and native screen readers or voice assistance	☐		☐		☐	
Allow the user to set a "safe place" - quick key, shortcut or macro and a time limit with a clear start and stop	☐		☐		☐	

Fig. 1. Example of the glanceable guidelines

This consolidated set of guidelines aims to serve as a resource for researchers and game developers, in both printed and online formats, to support the accessibility assessment of games across the three platforms. To validate the applicability of the curated guidelines in practice, three games were selected for evaluation, one for each platform, specifically *OXENFREE II: Lost Signals*[1] for PC, *Minecraft*[2] for mobile and *Moss*[3] for VR. These titles were selected because they were either designed with accessibility in mind or were explicitly promoted as accessible [29–31] within their respective platforms, allowing the guidelines to be evaluated against strong existing examples. The selection of three different games was intentional, since the study focuses on platform-specific accessibility considerations and currently there is no single title that offers equally strong accessibility support across all platforms.

OXENFREE II: Lost Signals is a narrative-driven horror/mystery adventure game, where players control Riley, the main character, investigating mysterious ghostly signals in her coastal hometown. The players experience the game through third-person Point of View (PoV) in a 2D world setup. The game can be played by using a keyboard, a mouse, or a gamepad, while players can switch seamlessly between the interaction methods during gameplay, without the need to indicate or select a preferred method of playing, since the game adapts automatically to the players' style.

Minecraft is a 3D sandbox game offering players a large amount of freedom to explore and create their version of a virtual world on a seemingly infinite terrain. Through a boxy and pixelated art style, the players can extract materials and use them to build items, tools, and structures. Additionally, there are available modes for the players to choose from, such as 'survival mode' (where players aim to build their world with the raw material they extract from the terrain and maintain their health) or 'creative mode' (where players have unlimited resources to build their world).

Moss is a virtual reality (VR) adventure game, presented both in first- and third-person perspectives. In the game, the player, presented as a masked face with orbs for hands, meets Quill, a young mouse, and helps her navigate the kingdom where she lives, in order to save her captured uncle. The player can use either hand holding the controller to manipulate the environment for Quill to navigate through, or control her in battling enemies. On the other hand, Quill uses American Sign Language (ASL) to communicate with the player for puzzle hints or emotions. Although the game can be played while seated, the player can choose to change positions by leaning or standing up to view the world from different perspectives and discover hidden collectables.

The evaluation was conducted following an expert-based approach, involving two researchers with experience in accessibility and Human–Computer Interaction. Using the consolidated set of accessibility guidelines, each evaluator independently carried out an accessibility audit for the selected games. For each game, the evaluators engaged in multiple gameplay sessions covering core gameplay mechanics, menus, tutorials, interaction systems, audiovisual feedback, settings, and accessibility options and independently recorded their observations. Following the independent evaluation phase, a consolidation process was conducted to compare findings, discuss disagreements, and resolve inconsistencies through discussion and re-examination of the games where necessary.

[1] https://nightschoolstudio.com/oxenfree-ii

[2] https://help.minecraft.net/hc/en-us

[3] https://www.polyarcgames.com/games/moss

4 Results

4.1 Accessibility Evaluation Results of OXENFREE II: Lost Signals

The accessibility evaluation of the game shows generally positive results across most categories, with some limitations that affect inclusivity. Overall, the design reflects thoughtful choices, especially in presentation and simplicity, but lacks flexibility and user control in key areas.

Auditory accessibility demonstrated a particularly high level of success. A distinctive design choice is the consistent use of colour to represent each character, which is also reflected in dialogue presentation. This, combined with subtitles in speech bubbles, improves speaker identification and comprehension, particularly for players relying less on audio cues. The availability of subtitle customization further strengthens this category (Fig. 2).

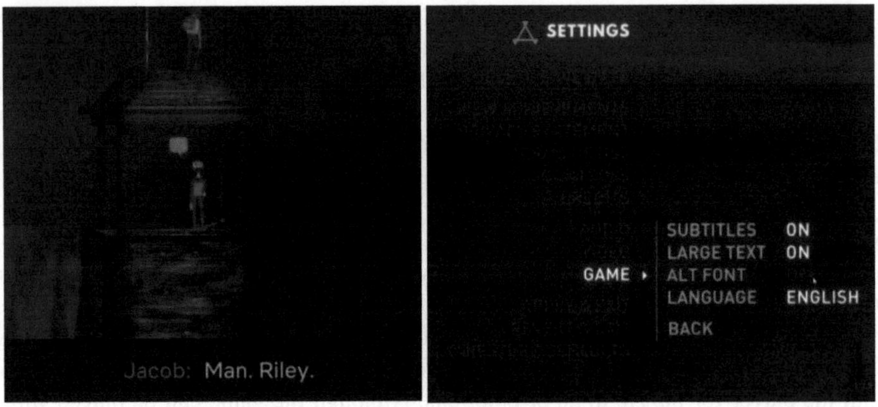

Fig. 2. Character and color association (left) and customizable subtitles (right)

In terms of physical accessibility, the game balances simplicity with limited adaptability. The controls were assessed as intentionally minimal and easy to learn, with all interface elements being accessed using the same input method. Another notable feature was that interactive elements are appropriately sized and well-spaced, supporting ease of interaction. Furthermore, the game reduces complexity by offering straightforward mechanics and limited input requirements. However, the absence of control remapping functionality constitutes a clear limitation, even if its practical impact is minimized by the simplicity of the controls. Similarly, while the game partially addresses time constraints, players are still required to select dialogue options within a limited timeframe. Although these choices do not affect gameplay outcomes and only provide additional narrative context, they may still pose challenges for some users. The lack of options to adjust interface layout or precision of input further limits flexibility.

The results for visual accessibility were largely positive, indicating careful attention to readability and presentation. The game successfully avoids conveying information through colour alone, uses clear and readable default font sizes, and applies simple text formatting. Subtitles are generally well-designed, adhering to recommended practices in terms of length and structure, and the game also supports font size adjustments and speech output. However, while most text elements, such as subtitles, include a darker background to improve contrast, certain in-game elements, such as shop signs, do not, resulting in only partial success in contrast-related guidelines. Additionally, the absence of options to further enhance contrast, enable zoom, or support sonification slightly limits accessibility for users with visual impairments.

Regarding speech accessibility, the game's design renders most related guidelines inapplicable, as it does not include online multiplayer or voice communication features. Consequently, this category does not significantly influence the overall accessibility outcome.

Fig. 3. Short tutorial and interaction prompts to show players how to interact with the game

Cognitive, learning, and neurological accessibility demonstrated good performance in basic guidelines but weaker results in advanced ones. The game benefits from a simple structure, clear language, and interactive tutorials that support player understanding of new mechanics (Fig. 3). The minimal user interface further contributes to reducing cognitive load. However, some dialogue sequences progress automatically without user input, which can disrupt pacing, even if they do not affect the storyline. Additionally, contrast issues in certain text elements remain present in this category. The timed dialogue selection mechanic also appears here as a partial limitation; although sufficient time is generally provided, the presence of any time constraint can pose challenges for some players. Moreover, the lack of UI customization options and the inability to adjust contrast for gameplay-critical elements contribute to the low performance in advanced guidelines. The presence of flickering or repetitive visual patterns, without an option to disable them, further impacts accessibility for certain users.

Finally, the game scored relatively low in general accessibility practices, despite some positive elements. On the one hand, the game ensures that settings are saved and provides in-game information about accessibility features, while also including assistive options such as gameplay bypass mechanisms and autosave functionality. On the other hand, it lacks several important features, including a wide range of difficulty levels, a manual save option, and clear communication of accessibility features outside the game. Additionally, the absence of mechanisms to solicit accessibility feedback limits opportunities for user-driven improvements.

4.2 Accessibility Evaluation Results of Minecraft

The accessibility evaluation of the mobile game produced a well-balanced result, combining extensive support for customization and interaction flexibility with persistent challenges in readability and interface scaling. The results suggest a system that is thoughtfully designed in terms of functionality and player control, yet occasionally constrained by aesthetic and design decisions.

Auditory accessibility achieved a high success rate, reflecting strong support for players who rely on non-auditory cues. Subtitles are consistently provided for essential speech, audio channels can be independently adjusted, and no critical information is conveyed exclusively through sound. Additional support, such as captions for significant background audio, further strengthens this category. However, the absence of subtitle customization options and the lack of a stereo/mono toggle are two limitations that remain present. These omissions become more apparent when considered alongside the readability issues of the default font, slightly weakening an otherwise robust auditory accessibility framework.

In the domain of physical accessibility, the game performs well across most guidelines, offering a flexible and inclusive interaction model. Players benefit from remappable controls, adjustable sensitivity, simplified input schemes, and multiple control methods, including support for alternative interaction styles (Fig. 4). Time constraints and input demands are also appropriately minimized, contributing to a more accessible experience. Despite this, many touch targets fall below the recommended minimum size and lack sufficient spacing, a mobile-specific issue. This introduces a layer of precision difficulty, particularly for users with limited fine motor control, creating a contrast between the system's conceptual flexibility and its practical usability on touchscreens.

The evaluation of visual accessibility revealed the most significant challenges. While the game succeeds in areas such as avoiding reliance on colour alone, maintaining adequate contrast in many interface elements, and offering options to adjust or disable visual effects, it underperforms in scalability and readability. The inability to resize text or interface components, combined with limited support for system-level font scaling and screen magnification, significantly restricts accessibility for users with low vision. The stylized, pixel-based font, although consistent with the game's visual identity, further reduces legibility. Additionally, several guidelines related to subtitle clarity, zoom functionality, and element sizing are not met, reinforcing the conclusion that visual accessibility is the most constrained aspect of the experience.

On the contrary, speech accessibility stands out as a particularly strong category. The game not only avoids requiring speech input but also provides a rich set of communication alternatives for multiplayer interaction (Fig. 5). These include full support for text chat, visual communication mechanisms, and player preferences regarding voice chat participation. This layered communication ecosystem allows players to tailor their interaction style, fostering inclusivity in socially interactive contexts.

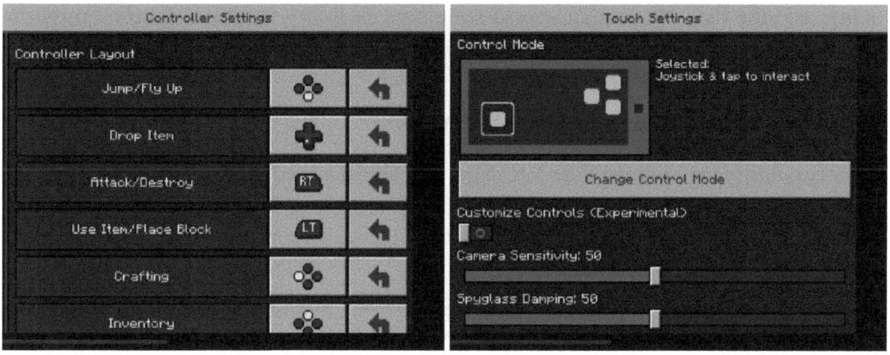

Fig. 4. Remappable controls, adjustable sensitivity, simplified input schemes

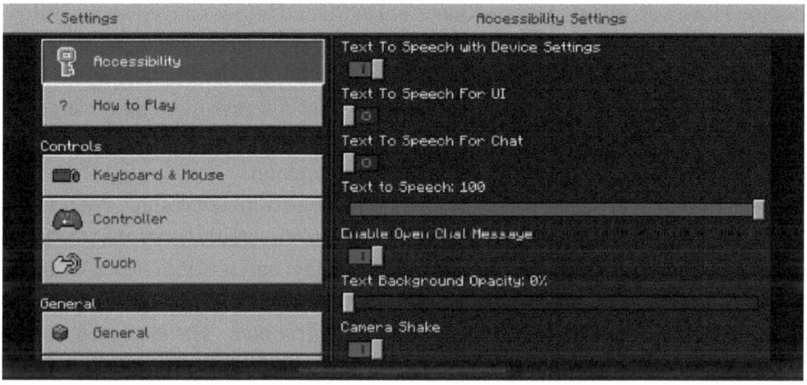

Fig. 5. Accessibility settings exposing many customizable variables

The results for cognitive, learning, and neurological accessibility indicated a generally high level of support, with the majority of guidelines successfully implemented. The game promotes accessibility through clear language, consistent layouts, minimal navigation complexity, and the ability for players to control the pacing of text progression. It also avoids disruptive visual stimuli and reduces both time pressure and input complexity. However, several shortcomings persist, primarily linked to previously identified visual and physical issues. The default font size and style remain difficult to read, and small interactive elements can increase cognitive load by demanding greater attention and precision. Additionally, the absence of interactive tutorials and the lack of interface customization options limit the game's adaptability to diverse user needs.

Finally, the assessment of general accessibility practices highlighted a largely positive picture. The game provides extensive information about its accessibility features both in-game and externally, supports multiple difficulty levels, includes assistive modes, and ensures that user settings are preserved. Autosave functionality is also implemented, supporting uninterrupted gameplay. However, two notable gaps remain: the absence of a manual save option, which can be important for players requiring greater control over pacing, and the lack of mechanisms to solicit accessibility feedback. These omissions suggest missed opportunities for user empowerment and continuous improvement.

4.3 Accessibility Evaluation Results of Moss

The accessibility evaluation of the VR game revealed a varied profile, where strong foundational design choices are evident, particularly in presentation and spatial interaction, yet are accompanied by notable limitations in customization, flexibility, and advanced accessibility support.

Auditory accessibility achieved full success in all basic guidelines, indicating a solid and reliable auditory foundation. The game consistently provides subtitles for important speech, ensures that no critical information is conveyed through audio alone, and allows for independent control of different audio channels. Additionally, distinct sound design and the effective use of surround sound contribute positively to spatial awareness and immersion. However, this strong baseline is not extended into advanced accessibility support. The absence of visual indicators for identifying the current speaker, along with the lack of subtitle customization options, reduces flexibility for diverse user needs. Furthermore, captions for significant background sounds are not provided, and a stereo/mono toggle is missing. While background noise during speech is present, it remains at low levels, resulting in only a minor impact on comprehension.

In terms of physical accessibility, the game presented mixed results, balancing intuitive interaction with limited adaptability. On the positive side, controls are generally simple, consistent, and integrated within the gameplay, and most interface elements are accessible using the same input methods. Interactive elements are also adequately sized and spaced, supporting usability within the VR environment. The system does not rely heavily on strict body positioning, and most interactions are within reach, accommodating a range of users to some extent. However, several important limitations persist. The game does not support control remapping, sensitivity adjustment, or alternative input methods, and it does not provide solutions for reducing simultaneous or complex inputs. Additionally, certain interactions require physical movement, such as tilting the body, which may not be comfortable or feasible for all players. The absence of options to adjust interface layout or input precision further constrains accessibility, particularly for users with motor impairments.

The results for visual accessibility were strong in the basic guidelines, achieving a complete success rate. The game demonstrates careful attention to readability, contrast, and visual clarity, while also avoiding common VR discomfort triggers. Text elements are generally clear and well-formatted, and interactive components are easy to identify and engage with. The positioning of essential information within the player's field of view further enhances usability. However, similar to other categories, limitations emerged in the advanced guidelines. While subtitles are readable in terms of font and contrast, their placement within the 3D environment, often tilted or anchored to dynamic elements, introduces additional effort for reading (Fig. 6). Moreover, the absence of customization options, such as adjustable font size, zoom functionality, or contrast enhancement for critical elements, reduces accessibility. Additional shortcomings include the lack of support for sonification, limited color accessibility options, and no ability to customize cursor or crosshair properties.

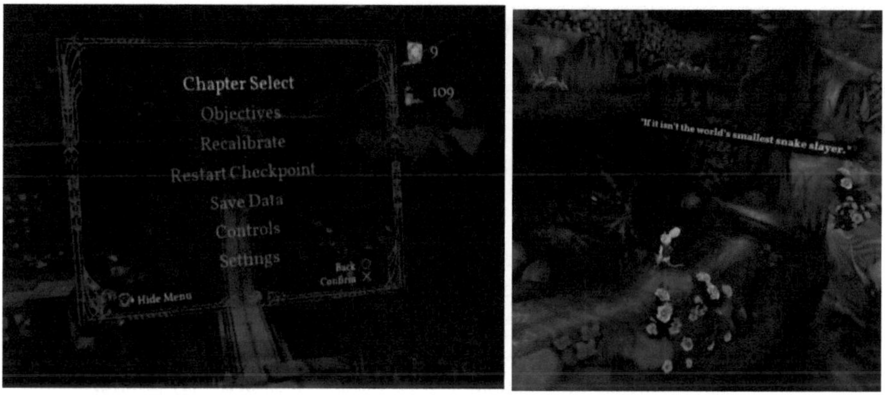

Fig. 6. Readable font in terms of size and contrast, but tilted placement in the 3D environment introduces additional effort

Regarding speech accessibility, the game does not include multiplayer functionality, so most advanced guidelines were not applicable. Importantly, speech input is not required at any stage, ensuring that players are not dependent on voice-based interaction.

The evaluation of cognitive, learning, and neurological accessibility indicated generally positive results, particularly in the basic guidelines. The game benefits from clear language, readable text, and a relatively straightforward structure that avoids unnecessary complexity. It also includes interactive tutorials at the beginning, supporting initial player onboarding, although these do not cover all interaction types. Visual comfort is further supported by the avoidance of flickering or disruptive patterns. However, several limitations affect overall accessibility. Not all interactive elements are clearly indicated, which may lead to uncertainty during gameplay. More significantly, the game imposes time constraints in certain interactions without offering options to adjust or extend them, resulting in multiple 'Fail' outcomes. Players are also unable to control the pacing of all text or narrative elements, as some cannot be paused or replayed. The lack of customization options for contrast and interface elements further contributes to increased cognitive load in more demanding scenarios.

Finally, the assessment of general accessibility practices presented a varied picture. The game allows a degree of fine-tuning and ensures that user settings are retained, while also successfully addressing certain VR-specific interaction requirements, such as stabilizing precise interactive elements. However, several important gaps remain. The game does not provide sufficient information about its accessibility features, either in-game or externally, and does not include mechanisms for collecting user feedback. Additionally, it lacks assistive modes, options to bypass non-essential gameplay segments, and features such as customizable safe spaces. While a manual save feature is available, which supports flexible gameplay pacing, the overall lack of broader accessibility support and transparency limits the effectiveness of these positive elements.

Table 1. Platform-specific accessibility challenges in contemporary games

Platform	Accessibility challenges	Underlying causes
PC	Balancing accessibility customization with narrative pacing and gameplay immersion	Narrative-driven experiences often rely on timed interactions, cinematic pacing, and fixed interface structures that may conflict with flexibility
	Limited accessibility personalization in otherwise simple interaction systems	Developers may assume that simplified controls eliminate the need for advanced accessibility options
	Inconsistent readability of environmental information	Decorative or immersive visual design choices may prioritize aesthetics over readability and contrast
Mobile	Small touch targets and interaction precision requirements	Limited screen size and dense interface layouts constrain element spacing and touch accessibility
	Limited interface and text scalability	Fixed UI layouts and stylized visual identities may reduce support for system-level accessibility scaling
	Readability issues caused by stylized fonts and visually dense interfaces	Aesthetic consistency and brand identity may take precedence over accessibility considerations
	Increased cognitive load from complex multi-layer interfaces	Mobile games frequently integrate extensive menus, overlays, and contextual interactions within limited screen space
VR	Physical fatigue and movement-related accessibility barriers	VR interaction frequently depends on embodied movement, reachability, posture changes, and sustained physical engagement
	Spatial readability challenges in three-dimensional interfaces	Text and interface elements positioned in 3D environments may require head movement, refocusing, or awkward viewing angles
	Limited support for alternative interaction methods	VR systems often rely on controller-specific gestures and motion-based interaction paradigms
	Increased risk of sensory overload and cognitive fatigue	Immersive audiovisual environments and simultaneous spatial interactions can increase attentional demands

(*continued*)

Table 1. *(continued)*

Platform	Accessibility challenges	Underlying causes
	Balancing immersion with accessibility flexibility	Accessibility accommodations may be perceived as conflicting with immersion or realism goals
Cross-platform	Limited accessibility transparency and feedback mechanisms	Many games provide insufficient information regarding available accessibility features and rarely solicit user feedback

5 Conclusions

The findings of this study reveal that contemporary digital games increasingly incorporate accessibility-oriented design practices across PC, mobile, and VR platforms, yet substantial differences remain in the extent, maturity, and consistency of accessibility support among platforms and accessibility categories. As summarized in Table 1, PC games primarily face challenges related to balancing accessibility with narrative pacing and immersive gameplay design. Mobile games, on the other hand, are more strongly affected by interface-related accessibility issues, particularly small touch targets, limited scalability, and readability problems caused by dense layouts and stylized visual elements. The evaluation further showed that VR games introduce additional accessibility concerns associated with embodied interaction and spatial interfaces. Physical movement requirements, interaction precision, and the positioning of interface elements within three-dimensional environments can significantly affect accessibility and usability. Across all platforms, customization and adaptability appeared to be key factors influencing accessibility quality. Games that allowed players to modify controls, pacing, interface settings, and communication methods generally provided a more inclusive experience. Conversely, limited personalization options consistently reduced accessibility support for users with diverse sensory, motor, and cognitive needs. The evaluation process highlighted the usefulness of the developed set of guidelines, which supported a structured evaluation procedure across the three platforms and helped identify both shared and platform-specific accessibility issues. The practical usefulness of the curated guidelines set is also evidenced by the fact that, despite the fact that the assessed games were appreciated for their accessibility features, several defects were identified. In particular, the guidelines made it easier to detect recurring problems related to customization, readability, interaction methods, and interface design across different types of games and environments. Overall, the results emphasize the importance of integrating accessibility considerations early in the game design process and treating accessibility as a core component of game design rather than as an optional feature set, and highlight the important role of well-curated guidelines in this regard.

Acknowledgments. Part of this work has received funding from the European Union (GA no. 101061496). Views and opinions expressed are those of the author(s) only and do not necessarily reflect those of the European Union or the Research Executive Agency. Neither the European Union nor the granting authority can be held responsible for them.

Disclosure of Interests. The authors have no competing interests to declare that are relevant to the content of this article.

References

1. Aguado-Delgado, J., Gutiérrez-Martínez, J.-M., Hilera, J.R., de-Marcos, L., Otón, S.: Accessibility in video games: a systematic review. Univ. Access Inf. Soc. **19**(1), 169–193 (2020). https://doi.org/10.1007/s10209-018-0628-2
2. Ntoa, S., Margetis, G., Adami, I., Balafa, K., Antona, M., Stephanidis, C.: Digital accessibility for users with disabilities. In: Designing for Usability, Inclusion and Sustainability in Human-Computer Interaction. CRC Press (2024)
3. Porter, J.R., Kientz, J.A.: An empirical study of issues and barriers to mainstream video game accessibility. In: Proceedings of the 15th International ACM SIGACCESS Conference on Computers and Accessibility, pp. 1–8. ACM, Bellevue Washington (2013). https://doi.org/10.1145/2513383.2513444
4. Brown, M., Anderson, S.L.: Designing for disability: evaluating the state of accessibility design in video games. Games Cult. **16**(6), 702–718 (2021). https://doi.org/10.1177/1555412020971500
5. Hassan, L.: Accessibility of games and game-based applications: a systematic literature review and mapping of future directions. New Media Soc. **26**(4), 2336–2384 (2024). https://doi.org/10.1177/14614448231204020
6. Valakou, A., Margetis, G., Ntoa, S., Stephanidis, C.: A framework for accessibility in XR environments. In: Stephanidis, C., Antona, M., Ntoa, S., Salvendy, G. (eds.) HCI International 2023 – Late Breaking Posters Communications in Computer and Information Science, vol. 1958, pp. 252–263. Springer Nature Switzerland, Cham (2024). https://doi.org/10.1007/978-3-031-49215-0_31
7. Simantiraki, I., Ntoa, S., Margetis, G., Sykianaki, E., Stephanidis, C.: Supporting motor skill rehabilitation in autism spectrum disorder through an augmented reality piano exergame. In: Stephanidis, C., Antona, M., Ntoa, S., Margetis, G., Salvendy, G. (eds.) HCI International 2025 – Late Breaking Papers Communications in Computer and Information Science, vol. 2771, pp. 300–310. Springer Nature Switzerland, Cham (2026). https://doi.org/10.1007/978-3-032-12764-8_27
8. Ntoa, S., Adami, I., Prokopiou, G., Antona, M., Stephanidis, C.: A-cross: an accessible crossword puzzle for visually impaired users. In: Stephanidis, C. (ed.) Universal Access in Human-Computer Interaction. Users Diversity Lecture Notes in Computer Science, vol. 6766, pp. 342–351. Springer Berlin Heidelberg, Berlin, Heidelberg (2011). https://doi.org/10.1007/978-3-642-21663-3_37
9. Grammenos, D., Savidis, A., Georgalis, Y., Stephanidis, C.: Access Invaders: Developing a Universally Accessible Action Game Lecture Notes in Computer Science, pp. 388–395. Springer Berlin Heidelberg, Berlin, Heidelberg (2006). https://doi.org/10.1007/11788713_58
10. Abdoulqadir, C., Loizides, F.: Mobile game accessibility guidelines for users with dual concurrent disabilities: a systematic literature review. Int. J. Hum.-Comput. Interact., 1–49 (2026). https://doi.org/10.1080/10447318.2026.2651346
11. Scardovelli, T.A., Frère, A.F.: The design and evaluation of a peripheral device for use with a computer game intended for children with motor disabilities. Comput. Methods Prog. Biomed. **118**(1), 44–58 (2015). https://doi.org/10.1016/j.cmpb.2014.10.002

12. Gerling, K.M., Schulte, F.P., Smeddinck, J., Masuch, M.: Game design for older adults: effects of age-related changes on structural elements of digital games. In: Herrlich, M., Malaka, R., Masuch, M. (eds.) Entertainment Computing - ICEC 2012 Lecture Notes in Computer Science, vol. 7522, pp. 235–242. Springer Berlin Heidelberg, Berlin, Heidelberg (2012). https://doi.org/10.1007/978-3-642-33542-6_20
13. Westin, T., Ku, J.J., Dupire, J., Hamilton, I.: Game accessibility guidelines and WCAG 2.0 – a gap analysis. In: Miesenberger, K., Kouroupetroglou, G. (eds.) Computers Helping People with Special Needs Lecture Notes in Computer Science, vol. 10896, pp. 270–279. Springer International Publishing, Cham (2018). https://doi.org/10.1007/978-3-319-94277-3_43
14. Ellis, B., et al.: Game Accessibility Guidelines. [Online]. https://gameaccessibilityguidelines.com/full-list/. Accessed Sep 23 2025
15. Chiasson, A., et al.: SIG top ten. IGDA Game Accessibility SIG. [Online]. http://igda-gasig.org/how/sig-top-ten/. Accessed Sep 23 2025
16. Bierre, K., et al.: IGDA Accessibility in Games: Motivations and Approaches. [Online]. https://igda-gasig.org/wp-content/uploads/2011/10/igda_accessibility_whitepaper.pdf. Accessed May 12 2026
17. Microsoft: Xbox Accessibility Guidelines - Microsoft Game Dev. [Online]. https://learn.microsoft.com/en-us/gaming/accessibility/guidelines. Accessed Sep 23 2025
18. Wilk, J.: VR Accessibility Recommendations. [Online]. https://docs.ultraleap.com/ultralab/vr-gaming-accessibility-recommendations.html. Accessed Sep 23 2025
19. World Wide Web Consortium (W3C): XR Accessibility User Requirements. World Wide Web Consortium, 2021. [Online]. https://www.w3.org/TR/xaur/
20. Patch, K., Spellman, J., Wahlbin, K.: Mobile Accessibility: How WCAG 2.0 and Other W3C/WAI Guidelines Apply to Mobile. [Online]. https://www.w3.org/TR/mobile-accessibility-mapping/. Accessed Sep 23 2025
21. Yuan, B., Folmer, E., Harris, F.C.: Game accessibility: a survey. Univ. Access Inf. Soc. **10**(1), 81–100 (2011). https://doi.org/10.1007/s10209-010-0189-5
22. Garcia, F.E., de Almeida Neris, V.P.: Design guidelines for audio games. In: International Conference on Human-Computer Interaction, pp. 229–238. Springer Berlin Heidelberg, Berlin, Heidelberg (2013)
23. Teixeira Borges, O., Damasio Oliveira, J., De Borba Campos, M., Marczak, S.: Fair play: a guidelines proposal for the development of accessible audiogames for visually impaired users. In: Antona, M., Stephanidis, C. (eds.) Universal Access in Human-Computer Interaction. Methods, Technologies, and Users Lecture Notes in Computer Science, vol. 10907, pp. 401–419. Springer International Publishing, Cham (2018). https://doi.org/10.1007/978-3-319-92049-8_29
24. Hernandez, H.A., Ye, Z., Graham, T.C.N., Fehlings, D., Switzer, L.: Designing action-based exergames for children with cerebral palsy. In: Proceedings of the SIGCHI Conference on Human Factors in Computing Systems, pp. 1261–1270. ACM, Paris, France (Apr. 2013). https://doi.org/10.1145/2470654.2466164
25. Paraskevopoulos, I.T., Tsekleves, E., Craig, C., Whyatt, C., Cosmas, J.: Design guidelines for developing customised serious games for Parkinson's disease rehabilitation using bespoke game sensors. Entertain. Comput. **5**(4), 413–424 (2014)
26. Malinverni, L., Mora-Guiard, J., Padillo, V., Valero, L., Hervás, A., Pares, N.: An inclusive design approach for developing video games for children with autism spectrum disorder. Comput. Hum. Behav. **71**, 535–549 (2017)
27. Marston, H.R.: Design recommendations for digital game design within an ageing society. Educ. Gerontol. **39**(2), 103–118 (2013). https://doi.org/10.1080/03601277.2012.689936
28. Heilemann, F., Zimmermann, G., Münster, P.: Accessibility guidelines for VR games-A comparison and synthesis of a comprehensive set. Front. Virt. Real. **2**, 697504 (2021)

29. Matlock, M.: Oxenfree 2: Lost Signals accessibility review. Can I Play That? [Online]. https://caniplaythat.com/2023/09/18/oxenfree-2-lost-signals-accessibility-review/. Accessed Sep 23 2025
30. Minecraft: Accessibility Settings for Minecraft: Bedrock Edition | Minecraft Help. Minecraft.net. [Online]. https://www.minecraft.net/hc/en-us. Accessed Sep 23 2025
31. Can I. Play That?: Deaf Game Review – Moss. Can I Play That? [Online]. https://caniplaythat.com/2019/01/29/deaf-game-review-moss/. Accessed Sep 23 2025

Optimizing Sensory Substitution Training: The Role of Structure and Intervention in VSST Skill Acquisition

YunKyung Park(✉), Kyeongdeok Moon, Mooseop Kim, and Chi Yoon Jeong

ETRI, 218 Gajeong-ro, Yuseong-gu, Daejeon 34129, South Korea
{parkyk,kdmoon,gomskim,iamready}@etri.re.kr

Abstract. Visual-to-auditory Sensory Substitution Technology (VSST) transforms image data into sound, enabling users to perceive visual information through hearing. Acquiring this novel perceptual ability demands a continuous and highly efficient training process, analogous to the sensory development that occurs after birth. This research directly addresses the challenge of optimizing this skill development, aiming to enhance the effectiveness of VSST training methodologies through systematic structuring and dynamic intervention strategies.

This study designed two sequential experiments to evaluate the core factors influencing training efficacy. The first experiment assessed the impact of structured training by comparing an experimental group following a detailed training protocol against a control group that received only simple, repetitive practice. The second experiment analyzed the impact of intervention on training effectiveness by classifying instructor intervention types into four categories. The results showed that the experimental group achieved 82.75% in accuracy, compared to 78.94% for the control group, representing a statistically significant difference ($p < 0.05$). Similarly, groups receiving intervention achieved an accuracy of 82.67%, compared to 78.83% for those without, while qualitative assessments revealed that metacognitive intervention was the most effective among the four types.

This research provides a basis for establishing methodology-oriented training systems beyond a technology-centered approach. It will serve as a crucial foundation for the real-world application of sensory substitution systems and for improving learning efficiency in the future.

Keywords: Visual-to-Auditory · Sensory Substitution · Training Method · Evaluation · Level of Difficulty

1 Introduction

Sensory substitution technology, which converts visual signals into auditory stimuli, has achieved remarkable technical progress. However, the process of perceiving visual information through hearing requires high-level neurological adaptation to forge new cognitive pathways in the brain. Interpreting sounds as visual forms is by no means an intuitive experience; rather, it necessitates a sustained and sophisticated learning process analogous to innate sensory development.

C. Stephanidis et al. (Eds.): HCII 2026, CCIS 3047, pp. 607–616, 2026.
https://doi.org/10.1007/978-3-032-30552-7_58

In this study, to evaluate the effectiveness of structured training, the experimental group underwent systematic training while the control group performed simple repetitive practice. For the systematic training, materials were categorized by their auditory characteristics and organized according to difficulty levels. Moving beyond simple repetitive playback, training activities were provided that included principle comprehension, comparison, and contrast. The training was designed using a cumulative approach and was implemented through a spaced repetition protocol to enhance memory retention. The experimental group showed a statistically significant increase in accuracy compared to the control group.

The second experiment focused on the role of instructor intervention as a form of dynamic scaffolding to support the acquisition of VSST skills. To investigate how different support mechanisms influence learning outcomes, the intervention was classified into four distinct categories. The results demonstrated that groups receiving intervention achieved higher accuracy compared to those without such support, indicating that the presence of instructor guidance positively impacted training performance.

In Sect. 2, we review visual-to-auditory transformation technologies and their evaluation metrics. Section 3 describes the experimental design conducted to evaluate the effectiveness of structured training and intervention strategies. Section 4 evaluates the core results of the experiments conducted to improve the efficiency of the sensory substitution training program. The paper concludes with Sect. 5, which synthesizes the study's implications and outlines a roadmap for future investigations.

2 Related Works

Early research in sensory substitution focused primarily on the direct mapping of physical image properties. However, recent trends have evolved toward enhancing recognition accuracy and practicality by integrating deep learning and virtual environments. This chapter examines representative conversion algorithms widely utilized in the field.

vOICe is a sensory substitution algorithm that converts visual information into auditory signals. This algorithm scans images captured by a camera from left to right, translating brightness into sound volume and vertical position into pitch. This allows users to 'hear' and interpret visual information through sound. In experiments, participants trained to recognize grayscale images by converting them into sound demonstrated the ability to perceive shapes, positions, and other features of objects through this system [1, 2]. Additionally, using the vOICe system, it was found that participants could recognize edges, shapes, depth, and even some color information through the converted auditory signals. The findings also suggested that long-term use of the system could enhance visual perception abilities [3].

The vOICe-based VBTones is a system that converts visual information into auditory signals to assist visually impaired individuals in perceiving their environment. Additionally, by removing unnecessary information and applying filters during the image-to-sound conversion, more refined sounds were generated, improving recognition accuracy. Both visually impaired and sighted participants demonstrated high accuracy in the tests [4]. A method has also been proposed that maps visual environmental elements (e.g., coordinates, object types, sizes) to audio features related to musical tones (e.g., frequency, temporal duration, note variations). In this study, a Convolutional Neural Network (CNN) was employed to remove the background and recognize objects, which were then converted into audio signals based on specific timing and pitch. This method demonstrated higher training time efficiency compared to VBTones and achieved an average accuracy of 88.05% in real object recognition [5].

3 Design and Implementation of the Experiment

The experiments were conducted in accordance with the ethical standards set by the respective Institutional Review Boards (IRB). The research protocol for Experiment 1 was reviewed and approved by the IRB of Korea University (Approval No. KUIRB-2023-0301-01). For Experiment 2, the protocol was reviewed and approved by the IRB of Yonsei University (Approval No. 7001988-202408-HR-2367-02).

3.1 VSST Algorithm

Visual stimuli were converted into auditory signals using the vOICe algorithm. This system functions by scanning images column-by-column, effectively translating spatial coordinates into acoustic parameters: vertical positions are represented by frequency, while horizontal positions are defined by timing. The visual field was digitized into a 64 × 64 grid, with each column's 64 pixels assigned to frequencies between 80 and 7,600 Hz. The scanning speed was fixed at 1.05 s per frame, with all pixels within a single column synthesized simultaneously into a composite sound to maintain spatial coherence. Brightness was encoded through 16 levels of gray, where intensity directly dictated the loudness. Additionally, transient click sounds were employed as temporal markers to indicate the start and end of each conversion period [6, 7].

3.2 Experiment Design

Stimulus Configuration and Classification. In this study, black-and-white shapes were selected as training materials, with the difficulty of each shape determined based on accuracy rates from previous research. The shapes were arranged in order of increasing difficulty and organized into six modules according to the similarity of their sound patterns. While Experiment 1 utilized 23 shapes, Experiment 2 was composed by adding 2 additional shapes to the initial experimental set.

Module 1 is comprised of shapes where a consistent interval is maintained between high and low pitches. Module 2 features shapes where one pitch remains constant while the other changes in a consistent direction. Module 3 encompasses shapes where one pitch remains constant while the other changes in one direction and then reverses. Module 4 involves shapes where one pitch remains constant while the other changes in the opposite direction, creating a sound pattern where the interval between the pitches increases linearly and then decreases. Regarding the multi-axial variations, Module 5 includes shapes in which the pitch changes simultaneously along both the horizontal and vertical axes. Specifically, Experiment 1 utilized five shapes with simultaneous pitch changes along the horizontal axis, whereas Experiment 2 was expanded by incorporating two additional shapes characterized by simultaneous changes along the vertical axis, as indicated by the dotted lines in Table 1. Lastly, Module 6 contains shapes characterized by auditorsty patterns that either converge toward the midpoint of the frequency range or diverge toward the upper and lower extremes. Table 1 summarizes the overall classification of these shapes based on the similarity of their auditory patterns.

Table 1. Categorization of shapes based on sound pattern similarity.

Module	Shape	Module	Shape
1	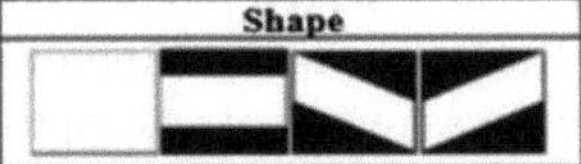	4	
2	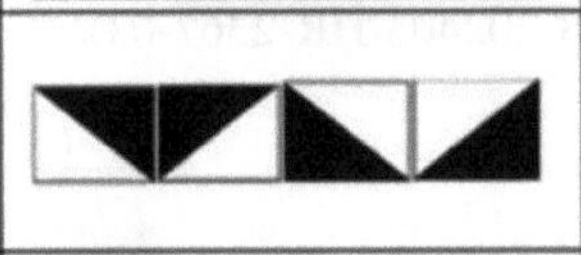	5	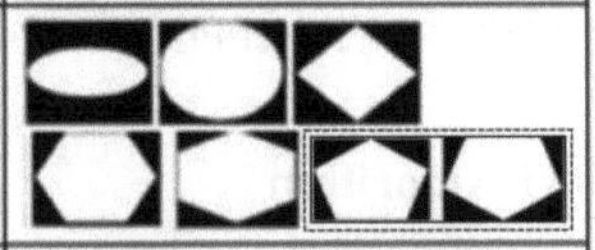
3		6	

Design of Training Activities. The training activities for both experiments were designed to facilitate the acquisition of visual-to-auditory mapping rules. In Experiment 1, the training protocol consisted of the sequential playback of auditory representations, the comparison and contrast of sound patterns between different shape pairs, and structured quizzes and reviews. Experiment 2 incorporated the same training activities as Experiment 1 but added a partial playback feature, enabling participants to focus on localized geometric details that might otherwise be obscured during the playback of the full sound.

Training Procedure for the Experiments. The training procedure was designed to enable step-by-step learning and cumulative repetitive training. To verify the effectiveness of the training, the operational methods for the experimental and control groups were differentiated for each experiment as follows. In Experiment 1, the experimental group performed periodic repetitive training using structured materials, while the control group performed simple repetitive training for the same number of sessions to identify the effects of the structured training. In Experiment 2, the experimental group received direct intervention and feedback from an instructor during the training process. In contrast, the control group performed simple repetitive training for the same total duration as the experimental group without any instructor intervention. The training procedures provided to each experimental group are presented in Table 2.

Musical ability was assessed using the Micro-PROMS. The Micro-PROMS is a validated assessment tool developed to evaluate musical perceptual abilities and is available for online administration [8]. Quizzes and tests were administered throughout the experiment. During the assessment, participants listened to sounds corresponding to geometric shapes and were asked to select the correct image from four provided options. A pre-test

Table 2. Training Procedure for Experimental Group (Experiment 1, 2).

Day	Session	Experiment1		Experiment2	
		Procedure	Playback	Procedure	Time(Min) Total/Intv.
1	1	• Music Ability Test • Pre-test		• Music Ability Test • Pre-test	25
		• Training(Modules 1–2) • Test(Modules 1–2)	168	• Training(Modules 1–2) • Test(Modules 1–2) • Review(Incorrect Only)	55/10
2	2	• Review(Modules 1–2) • Training(Modules 3–4) • Test(Modules 3–4)	208	• Training(Modules 3–4) • Test(Modules 3–4) • Mid-term Test(Modules 1–4) • Review(Incorrect Only)	55/15
	3	• Review(Modules 1–2) • Review(Modules 3–4) • Mid-term Test(Modules 1–4)	208	• Training(Modules 5) • Test(Modules 5) • Mid-term Test(Modules 1–5) • Review(Incorrect Only)	78/28
3	4	• Review(Modules 3–4) • Review(Modules 1–6) • Training(Modules 5–6) • Test(Modules 5–6)	187	• Training(Modules 6) • Test(Modules 6) • Post-Test(Modules 1–6)	78/38
	5	• Review(Modules 1–6) • Post-Test(Modules 1–6)	211	• Delayed Post-Test (Modules 1–6)	20
4	6	• Delayed Post-Test(Modules 1–6)	53		

Note. Intv. = Intervention duration. Values are presented as Total/Intv.

was conducted to evaluate the participants' foundational abilities, followed by quizzes to review training content, a midterm test, a post-test, and a delayed post-test. The post-test was carried out to finalise the evaluation of training performance, while the delayed post-test was performed to assess the degree of long-term memory retention. In Experiment 2, interventions (scaffolding) were provided to enhance participants' understanding and engagement. Four types of interventions—conceptual, strategic, metacognitive, and motivational support—were implemented, and the specific objectives and examples for each type are presented in Table 3.

Table 3. Types and Purposes of Intervention Strategies.

Type	Purpose	Example Instruction/Sentence
Conceptual	To facilitate a clear understanding of visual-to-auditory conversion principles and shape-sound correspondence.	"Consider the relationship between the spatial features of the shape and the resulting sound. Which auditory characteristic matches the shape's specific edge?"
Strategic	To assist in developing and applying problem-solving strategies for accurate shape-sound matching.	"While listening to the sound patterns, try to mentally or physically trace the pitch and direction to visualize the corresponding shape."
Metacognitive	To enhance self-reflection and monitoring abilities regarding the learner's own understanding and assessment process.	"If you were to design a system to convert this pentagon into sound, what logic would you use to represent its vertices?"
Motivational	To sustain learning engagement and confidence by providing emotional support and goal-oriented feedback.	"It might be challenging at first, but your accuracy is improving as you get used to the patterns. Let's reach the goal for this session."

3.3 Experiment Implementation

The study was conducted on adults with no visual or auditory impairments, who were randomly assigned to either the experimental or control group. In Experiment 1, 32 participants were initially assigned to each group; however, following the attrition of one participant, the final sample consisted of 31 individuals in the experimental group and 32 in the control group. In Experiment 2, while 24 participants were originally allocated to each group, the final analysis included 21 participants in the experimental group and 24 in the control group.

4 Assessment of Experimental Results

Quizzes and tests were administered throughout the experiment. During the assessment, participants were presented with sounds corresponding to specific geometric images and were asked to select the correct image from four provided options. To evaluate the participants' baseline performance, the study included a pre-test, followed by quizzes to review the training content, a mid-test, a post-test, and a delayed post-test. The post-test was conducted to evaluate training outcomes, while the delayed post-test was used to measure long-term memory retention.

4.1 Analysis of Systematic Training Effects

Accuracy Assessment Based on Correct Response Rates. The results of Experiment 1 revealed that both the experimental and control groups exhibited higher accuracy rates compared to the pre-test (Fig. 1). Specifically, relative to the pre-test scores, the accuracy rate improved in both the experimental and control groups. Figure 2 illustrates the accuracy rates for each group across the tests.

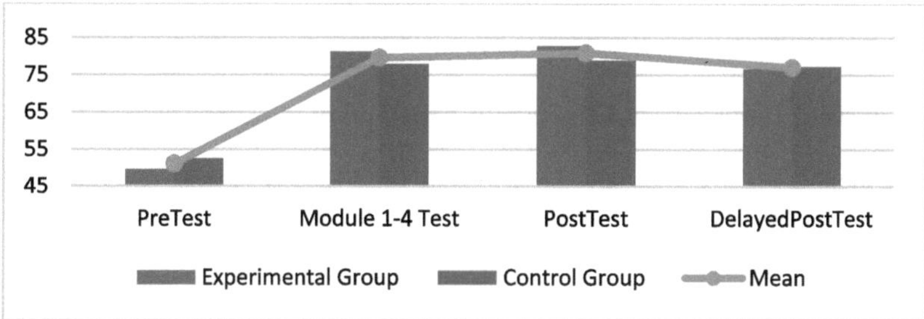

Fig. 1. Accuracy Rates by Group.

Validation of Statistical Significance and Reliability of Experimental Results Using Regression Analysis. Multiple regression analysis was conducted to isolate the impact of the training on the comprehension of auditory information by controlling for extraneous variables. Specifically, the model incorporates treatment, musical ability score, pre-test score, age, gender(female) ratio, undergraduate ratio, and STEM major ratio to achieve a more refined assessment of the program's effectiveness.

$$Y = \beta 0 + \beta 1 Treatment + \beta 2 MusicalAbility + \beta 3 PreTestScore + \\ \beta 4 Age + \beta 5 GenderRatio + \beta 6 UGRatio + \beta 7 STEMMajorRatio + \in \tag{1}$$

The treatment improved outcomes in the post-test (Estimate = 0.5727, p = 0.0132), confirming its immediate impact. Nevertheless, this effect failed to persist in the delayed post-test (Estimate = 0.2523, p = 0.2833). This indicates that although the structured training is effective for immediate skill acquisition, its benefits may not naturally extend to long-term retention. These regression results are summarized in Table 4.

Table 4. Regression Analysis Results.

Metric		Post-test	Delayed Post-test
F-statistic		5.609	4.695
F-statistic p-value		7.84E-05***	0.000403***
R-square		0.435	0.3919
Adjusted R-squared		0.3574	0.3084
Treatment	Estimate	0.5727	0.2523
	Std. Error	0.2229	0.2327
	t-value	2.569	1.084
	p-value	0.0132*	0.2833

Note. * $p < 0.05$, ** $p < 0.01$, *** $p < 0.001$

4.2 Analysis of Intervention Effects and Satisfaction by Type

In Experiment 2, the pre-test results showed that both groups recorded similar scores, confirming their homogeneity. Subsequently, both the experimental and control groups showed improved scores in the post-test, proving the overall effectiveness of the program. Notably, as the difficulty of the learning tasks increased, the experimental group achieved higher performance than the control group, suggesting that the provided intervention (scaffolding) offered substantial support in performing high-difficulty tasks. Overall, the experimental group not only achieved higher scores in the post-test but also demonstrated superior retention with a gentler decline in the delayed post-test. Consequently, it is analyzed that the experimental group yielded more positive outcomes in terms of difficulty overcoming ability and long-term learning retention compared to the control group.

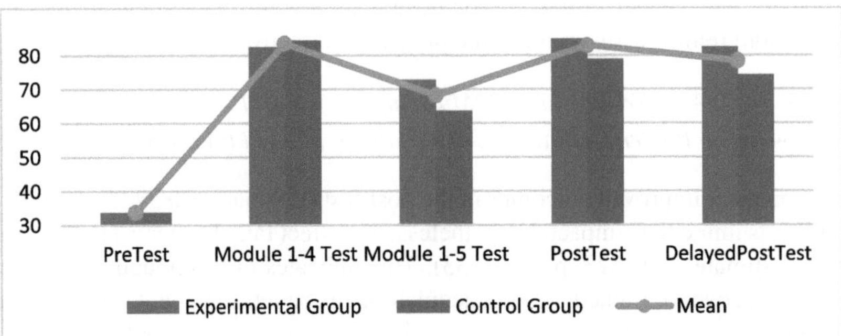

Fig. 2. Comparison of Training Accuracy: With vs. Without Intervention.

This study utilized a 16-item, 5-point Likert scale survey to evaluate how 21 participants perceived the effectiveness of four intervention(scaffolding) types across four key educational dimensions: educational effectiveness, long-term memory effectiveness, application to difficult levels, and sound pattern recognition. Among the 4 types of scaffolding, metacognitive scaffolding demonstrated the highest overall effectiveness (M = 4.54), particularly excelling in long-term memory retention. Conceptual scaffolding was found to be most effective for sound pattern recognition (M = 4.76), while motivational scaffolding played a crucial role in overall educational effectiveness and assisting learners during difficult tasks. Detailed results are presented in Table 5.

Table 5. Comparison of Intervention Effects by Type.

Scaffolding Type	Educational Effectiveness	Long-term Memory Effectiveness	Application to Difficult Levels	Sound Pattern Recognition	Total Average
Conceptual	4.57	4.43	4.29	4.76	4.51
Strategic	4.52	4.05	4.10	4.14	4.20
Metacognitive	4.57	4.57	4.43	4.57	4.54
Motivational	4.62	4.38	4.48	4.48	4.49
Category Average	4.57	4.36	4.32	4.49	4.43

5 Conclusion

This study validated the effectiveness of structured training and intervention in sensory substitution education through Experiments 1 and 2. The structured training process significantly improved overall achievement, proving that a structured learning path is universally effective for skill acquisition. Notably, timely scaffolding reduced cognitive load in high-difficulty tasks, leading to superior performance compared to the control group. This intervention further facilitated the transfer of knowledge to long-term memory, ensuring high performance even in delayed post-tests. In conclusion, maximizing the efficiency of sensory substitution training requires a combination of systematic task organization and strategic cognitive support.

Based on the findings of this study, future research should focus on two primary directions. First, it is essential to conduct practical studies that apply and validate this training model in real-world environments beyond controlled laboratory settings. Second, further investigation is required into specific methodologies to maximize and improve long-term memory retention, ensuring that acquired sensory substitution skills are consolidated as enduring capabilities for daily use.

Acknowledgments. This work was supported by the Electronics and Telecommunications Research Institute (ETRI) grant funded by Korean government [26ZR1200, Research on Autonomous Vision Augmentation and Extension Technologies].

Disclosure of Interests. The authors have no competing interests to declare that are relevant to the content of this article.

References

1. Peter, B.L.: Meijer: an experimental system for auditory image representations. IEEE Trans. Biomed. Eng. **39**(2), 112–121 (1992)
2. Haigh, A., Brown, D., Meijer, P., Proulx, M.J.: How well do you see what you hear? The acuity of visual-to-auditory sensory substitution. Front. Psychol. **4**, 330 (2013). https://doi.org/10.3389/fpsyg.2013.00330
3. Ward, J., Meijer, P.B.L.: Visual experiences in the blind induced by an auditory sensory substitution device. Conscious. Cogn. **19**(1), 492–500 (2010)
4. Riahi, N., Mirhoseini, S.F., Mehrbani, E.: VBTones: a visual to auditory device for the blind. Int. J. Adv. Comput. Res. **7**(33), 233–243 (2017)
5. Mehrbani, E., Mirhosseini, S.F., Riahi, N.: A novel mapping for visual to auditory sensory substitution. arXiv preprint https://arxiv.org/abs/2106.07448. (2021). https://arxiv.org/abs/2106.07448
6. Kim, M., Park, Y., Moon, K., Jeong, C.Y.: Impact of device and environment on visual-auditory sensory substitution: a comprehensive behavioral analysis using the vOICe algorithm. IEEE Access. **12**, 90501–90510 (2024)
7. Kim, M., Park, Y., Moon, K., Jeong, C.Y.: Deep learning-based optimization of visual–auditory sensory substitution. IEEE Access. **11**, 14169–14180 (2023)
8. Strauss, H., Reiche, S., Dick, M., Zentner, M.: Online assessment of musical ability in 10 minutes: development and validation of the micro-PROMS. Behav. Res. Methods, 1–16 (2023)

AI for All? Inclusive Learning Environments With and Through AI in Early Elementary Education

Anna Plohmer(✉) and Sarah Désirée Lange

Chemnitz University of Technology, Chemnitz, Germany
{anna.plohmer,sarah.lange}@zlb.tu-chemnitz.de

Abstract. The aim of this paper is to identify the learning-promoting potential and key success factors of Artificial Intelligence (AI) for and in inclusive early elementary education. To this end, an intervention was designed and continuously refined over the course of three rounds (spanning 18 months) with the aim of promoting AI literacy among young children. Methodologically grounded in Design-Based Research (DBR), the intervention was implemented at an elementary school in Chemnitz/Germany with 41 children and was continuously refined. The intervention consists of three modules (how AI works; applications of AI; reflections on AI) and is outlined as an example in this paper. As part of the intervention's development, the AI-related conceptions of elementary school children were assessed through group discussions and individual ebooks throughout the learning process. The results highlight the specific learning potential that the created learning environment as they illustrate that the participating children developed a basic understanding of AI, view AI as a digital-technical system, and describe AI using overarching concepts. The childen's conceptions of AI can be charaterized by their view of AI as a learning system and described in contrast to (intelligent) humans. Furthermore, AI is viewed on the one hand as a knowledge-dispensing system, while on the other hand it is described as a flawed system. The results are discussed in relation to existing concepts for inclusive digital learning environments and framework models for AI literacy, which need to be adapted for elementary school children. The resulting intervention and the empirical findings on the children's conceptions will serve as the basis for developing a Concept Inventory on AI literacy adressing elementary school children in early education.

Keywords: AI literacy · inclusive education · elementary school · design-based research

1 Background

The level of diversity among elementary school children is high and is considered the norm in elementary school classrooms [9, 11]. From an elementary education perspective, particularly significant are dimensions of diversity relevant to learning – such as language proficiency [20, 23]. The pedagogical response to early elementary school

C. Stephanidis et al. (Eds.): HCII 2026, CCIS 3047, pp. 617–627, 2026.
https://doi.org/10.1007/978-3-032-30552-7_59

children with varying prior experiences, developmental levels, and prior knowledge is to design inclusive education. This refers to open learning environments and tasks that allow children with individual learning prerequisites and diverse support needs to work on the same subject matter as independently as possible, with different learning objectives and various support options [14, 24]. The design of inclusive learning environments in early elementary education (grades 1 and 2) therefore requires a balance between individual learning needs and shared learning processes [27]. This challenge is increasingly being discussed in connection with the potential of Artificial Intelligence (AI) to support inclusive teaching and learning in (elementary) schools [2, 16, 17].

AI-supported tools are believed to have the potential to fundamentally transform the design of inclusive learning environments by enabling individualized support for all children and thus helping to reduce educational disadvantages [4, 8, 20]. AI opens up a wide range of possibilities for further individualizing learning processes, taking different needs into account, and promoting the participation of children with diverse learning requirements through features such as multimodality, interactivity, and adaptability [17]. In addition, functions such as text, image, and speech translation to help reduce language-related discrimination in the classroom [22]. This gives multilingual children more opportunities to apply their language skills in ways that support their learning [20, 21, 23]. A solid foundation for a reflective and effective approach to AI should therefore be established as early as elementary school [16].

In contrast, there are ongoing discussions – particularly in the realm of education policy (including in Germany) – regarding the appropriate age or grade level at which AI tools should be introduced in formal education [29, 36, 40]. Regardless of these discussions, it is up to elementary school teachers themselves to use their pedagogical freedom of decision-making in class to employ AI tools as learning aids in a targeted-oriented manner, to an appropriate extent, and embedded in didactically structured learning environments. In doing so, the decision to incorporate AI must be made in accordance with the available guidelines of the respective education system – based on subject-specific and pedagogical arguments and with focus on the children's learning needs [6, 29].

The aim of this paper is to present the results of a Design-Based Research project in which we investigate how AI can be meaningfully integrated into early elementary education in inclusive learning environments that support the learning of all children regardless of their individual learning needs.

2 Theoretical Context: AI in Inclusive Education

Computer science education should be viewed as an interdisciplinary, ongoing task for elementary schools, as an understanding of fundamental computer science concepts can be identified as a prerequisite for future-oriented, real-world-relevant education [12, 34]. Accordingly, the importance of a critical and reflective approach to AI is growing as both a requirement and a task for elementary schools. In this context, it is increasingly important to understand AI as an integral part of fundamental digital competencies and to expand existing concepts of basic digital education to include AI literacy [16]. Based on a framwork for digital-technological education in Germany (Dagstuhl Triangle/„Dagstuhl Dreieck"), the technological perspective, the technological perspective

(How does it work?), the application-oriented perspective (How do I use it?), and the socio-cultural perspective (What effect does it have?) are emphasized as prerequisites for a self-determined approach to technological developments [12]. With the uprise of AI in the world of education, digital-technical frameworks have been used as guiding principles and concepts with a specific AI focus were developed. On the one hand, existing concepts such as the DPACK model are being expanded to include the AI perspective in order to create a framework for AI-related digital competencies [21, 38]. The aim is to develop AI knowledge, AI pedagogical knowledge, AI content knowledge, and AI pedagogical content knowledge. On the other hand, also frameworks are being developed that specifically address AI literacy. Following the OECD framework [32], the AILit Framework for building AI literacy comprises three basic levels: (1) "How AI and Machine Learning Work" (functional aspects); (2) "Human Skills to Emphasize for Successful Collaboration with AI Tools" (application-oriented); (3) "AI's Effects on Individuals, Society, and the Environment" (societal context) as well as the four dimensions: Engaging with AI, Creating with AI, Managing AI, and Designing AI. There are various approaches to developing AI literacy in schools, and there is an increasing awareness to also focus on elementary schools and young children [42–44]. In particular, this includes how AI literacy can be promoted in inclusive education and how AI can transform or support the implementation of inclusive education [17, 36, 39].

AI literacy refers to the development of competencies that enable individuals to critically evaluate AI technologies, communicate and collaborate effectively with AI, and use AI as a tool [25]. AI literacy in elementary education is predominantly understood as a bundle of knowledge about basic AI principles, application-oriented skills, and reflective or ethical attitudes, which, however, are operationalized differently depending on the research [1, 3, 44]. This multi-perspective approach is also evident in the concepts and models. It is important not only to focus on the scope of application (e.g., prompting), but also to consider the teaching of the underlying fundamental concepts of computer science, their reflective use, and their socio-cultural implications [31, 41].

What do we know about the knowlede, competences, concepts an percetions children have regarding AI? To date, only a few empirical studies exist which survey children in early elementary education. Initial findings indicate that elementary school children tend to have a limited understanding of AI and describe AI in terms of everyday phenomena, usually without specific technical references to how AI works [13, 15]. Chang et al. [5] were able to demonstrate in their study with elementary school children aged 7 to 9 that children depict AI as human- or animal-like figures. They emphasize that anthropomorphism poses a major challenge in teaching AI concepts to young children. Children primarily understand AI as a supportive aid and tool in everyday life that assists their individual actions [5, 15]. Recent studies show that in some instances elementary school children are already aware of fake news generated by AI [13, 18].

Overall, it can be concluded that AI literacy among elementary school children is a relevant and rapidly expanding field of research. While initial teaching and learning formats are now available, there is a need to develop long-term, inclusive, and empirically validated competency models for elementary education. Concepts for inclusive early elementary education that take into account the three perspectives (technical, application-oriented, and societal) are a desideratum.

The focus on the perspectives of young elementary school children and, in particular, on inclusive early education represents a research need. Existing work on AI literacy, as well as AI perceptions, concepts, and understanding, primarily focuses on older children and is particularly geared toward cognitive-conceptual learning objectives, while questions regarding the quality of inclusive education – specifically concerning accessibility, differentiation, and participation for children with varying learning prerequisites and divers linguistic backgrounds – remain largely unaddressed. This study addresses these research gaps.

3 Methodological Approach

The results reported below provide an overview of the children's learning process with regard to the conceptual development of AI and served, within the DBR approach (see Sect. 5), as the basis for the continuous revision and design of the learning environment. The data was collected on an ongoing basis as a part of an extracurricular program at a German elementary school between February 2025 and February 2026 with three different groups of children. A total of 14 group discussions were conducted with 41 children. The children also designed digitale books, which were used to support the learning process within the individualized, inclusive setting with young children. At the time of the study, the children were between five and eight years old and attended preschool, first, and second grade. The present analyses are based primarily on three particularly in-depth and extensive group discussions involving a total of 15 children at the end of the final round of the intervention and the ebooks that were used to support the process.

The aim of the data analysis was to assess how children describe AI and what their AI-related conceptions are. The following research questions are addressed:

1. How do elementary school children describe AI?
2. What AI-related conceptions do elementary school children have?

The data was analyzed inductively-deductively by qualitative content analysis; the categories developed were refined within the research team [19].

4 Empirical Findings on Young Elementary School Children's Conceptions Regarding AI

In the following section the findings regarding elementary school children's conceptions of AI are reported; they are illustrated with exemplary statements made by the children. The results highlight the specific learning potential that this learning environment can offer.

4.1 How Do Elementary School Children Describe AI?

The analysis shows that a majority of the children developed a basic conceptual understanding of AI through the tasks offered in the developed learning environments. This is initially evident in the fact that the children can correctly define the abbreviation 'AI' as 'artificial intelligence' *("I already know that AI is a kind of artificial intelligence."; EB1).* Although the conceptual definition often remains at the level of naming, it is nevertheless clear that an initial entry point addressing the subject area has been established.

When attempting to describe AI in more detail, the children predominantly draw on more abstract concepts. AI is often understood as part of science or at least closely associated with scientific practices *("And AI is/has a lot to do with science"; EB1).* Furthermore, the children describe AI as the result of technological developments built upon existing computer science and technical foundations *("and they kept developing that until something like this came out"; GD1,132).* In this context, analogies are drawn to familiar artifacts such as computers or robots, thereby placing AI within existing interpretive frameworks. In some cases, AI is also characterized as a kind of database *("Those are databases, computers, and much, much more"; EB1).*

Overall, the children construct AI as a digital-technical system. This understanding is evident, among other things, in their identification of prerequisites such as electricity or physical connections (e.g., cables) as necessary for AI to function *("some electrical things have AI, but not all"; GD2, 25–26).* At the same time, initial conceptions hint at the complexity of such systems by describing AI as a system that *"consists of many cables and networks" (EB1).* The results thus indicate that the children were able to develop basic – yet still rather vague and simplified – conceptualizations of AI that build on existing every day and prior knowledge.

4.2 What AI-Related Conceptions Do Elementary School Children Have?

The results could be summarized into the following key concepts, which describe the children's understanding of AI:

1. *AI as a learning system:* The children's statements show that many children were able to develop a basic understanding of AI, characterized by the description of machine learning as a mode of operation of AI. The children emphasize that AI is a system that is programmed and, for example, *"learns from data" (EB4)* or *"learns from people (…) by us teaching it" (EB3).* Some statements emphasize that AI are learning systems *("they're taught things, and they have to remember what they're taught"; GB2, 48–49).*
2. *AI in contrast to humans:* In the children's descriptions of AI, 'humans' – and thus characteristic human traits such as experiencing emotions and acting irrationally – play a major role. A key role in the children's descriptions plays the comparison between AI and the human brain, which is frequently used to distinguish between artificial and human intelligence. Thus, AI is described as the brain of robots *("that it's, so to speak, the brain of robots"; EB1)* and is sometimes referred to as *"AI (…) also [being] very smart" (GD3, 123).* On the other hand, it is emphasized that AI does not have a brain and cannot think for itself, but is an executive system that requires humans *("Artificial intelligence. Umm... (..) that carries out commands"; GD1, 148).*
3. *AI as a voice output:* The children describe AI based on the possibilities they can be realized with it. AI is predominantly described as a knowledge system *"that tells us a lot of things" (EB1)*, and the linguistic 'abilities' of AI are emphasized *("AI*

can speak all languages"; EB4). It is noticeable that the children have little concrete understanding of the possibilities AI can open up, which is why they also describe it in very general terms *("[AI can] do much, much more"; EB1).*

4. *AI as a flawed system:* In some statements, the children adopt a critical and reflective stance when describing AI. It is described as a flawed system which statements must be verified *("So AI can also make mistakes. You can't always believe everything AI says."; GD2, 76–77; "Yes, but what a robot says doesn't always have to be right. You always have to check whether it can even be true" GD2,69–70).* At a basic level, aspects such as bias are also addressed. Additionally, sustainability aspects are raised, since *"AI needs a lot of electricity and also a lot of water for cooling" (EB4).*

5 Intervention: AI for All – Inclusive Learning Environments for Early Elementary School Children

The aim is to design an intervention focused on AI literacy that aims to enhance and foster elementary school childrens' conceptual understanding of AI, with the ultimate aim of developing an conceptual inventory – to assess the conceptual understanding of early elementary school children.

Methodologically, the development of the intervention is guided by the Design-Based Research (DBR) approach, with which the aim is followed to continuously optimize teaching concepts by linking theory, empirical evidence, and practice [28]. The key starting point of DBR is the recognition of a discrepancy between theoretical aspirations and their implementation in educational practice [35]. To address this, the theoretically grounded intervention was designed co-constructively and continuously refined. Characteristic of DBR are iterative cycles in which development, testing, and evaluation are repeatedly carried out [10].

Since February 2025, themodules have beend esigned, developed, implemented, and continuously adapted incollaboration with the participating children (aged5–8). The learning environments were implemented weekly over a four-month period in extra curricular education settings and have been conducted three times to date. The AI-based learning environments presented below were developed over three rounds, during which a weekly 60-min afternoon program on robotics and AI was conducted with a group of approximately 15 elementary school children. Many of the developed tasks were tested, refined, and revised throughout the process, as it became apparent during implementation that the initial versions did not meet the requirements of an inclusive learning environment. Often, technical limitations or usability issues also necessitated the further development of tasks within the learning environments. For this continuous development process, assessing the children's conceptions in group discussions and through learning journals were very helpful.

Based on current concepts regarding (inclusive) AI literacy frameworks and quality criteria for inclusive education [25, 32, 39], as well as on an analysis of misconceptions and conceptual understanding of AI among the participating elementary school children (see Sect. 4), modules were designed to promote AI literacy. In the presented modules, AI is chosen as the subject of study, and learning environments were developed to examine AI in inclusive early elementary school education from three perspectives that enable a multi-perspective AI literacy [12, 32]: (1) technological perspective; (2)

application-oriented perspective; (3) socio-critical perspective. AI plays a dual role in the teaching modules, functioning both as a subject of study (learning about AI) and as a learning assistant (learning through AI) [36]. With the developed modules the aim is followed to enable participation and autonomy in a digitally shaped world for all children [30]. The focus is on integrating AI into and for inclusive education [17, 24, 39], by creating individual and cooperative learning environments [26]. To build AI literacy, particularly among younger children, unplugged materials are also used, in which children understand AI processes through role-playing, card-sorting tasks, or 'embodied' algorithms [7, 8, 37]. However, child-friendly digital media, such as robotics environments or platforms like ScratchJr!, are also used [7, 38].

Module 1: How AI Works. The first module focuses on the educational and technical aspects of computer science. It covers what AI is, how AI works, how AI is programmed using machine learning, and the role of neural networks. Data and data sorting are also covered in detail.
The aim is for children to acquire the following skills, among others:

- Children can explain the concept of AI based on its characteristic features.
- Children can describe the function of neural networks.
- Children understand machine learning as a method for programming AI and can use it to train AI systems.
- Children can explain how AI makes decisions using the example of the wool perceptron.

Module 2: Applications of AI. The second module focuses on the application-oriented perspective. It addresses how AI can be utilized in various fields and applied within the school environment. For instance, AI can be used for creative and design projects (e.g. image generation) or integrated as a learning aid (e.g. AI assistance systems). Application-oriented skills such as effective prompting, which are fundamental for successful work with AI tools, are required.
The aim is for children to acquire the following skills, among others:

- Children understand the criteria for effective prompting and can compose functional instructions for AI in the form of prompts.
- Children can use AI tools for creative, design-oriented processes.

Module 3: Reflection on AI. The third module focuses on a socially critical and reflective perspective. The aim is to understand the prerequisites for a successful and data-protection-compliant use of AI – such as the impact of AI on children's lives (individual, society, environment dimension).
The aim is for children to acquire the following competencies, among others:

- Children can assess the opportunities and limitations of incorporating AI.
- Children can critically reflect on the use of AI.
- Children are aware of the socio-cultural impacts of AI.

Ebooks as learning guides and support: Ebooks are used as learning guides throughout the three modules. The potential of digital learning journals for the support of inclusive early education can be seen in their multimodal and individualized learning opportunities [20, 24]. Children can create content in their ebook using text, audio, images, or videos; this variety of modal opportunities can be particularly helpful for children with varying language proficiency levels. Even without prior experiences in using iPads for learning tasks, the children quickly developed a routine in using the digital tools through continuous practice throughout the modules. In addition, the created ebooks enable flexible, individualized, and collaborative task completion [26], thereby also promoting social learning.

6 AI Literacy for Young Children: Discussion of Potentials and Key Success Factors

To discuss the present empirical results and the designed intervention, we will address below what the children were able to learn in the learning environments based on the results of the learning process monitoring, and what insights we draw for the design of the inclusive learning environments. Subsequently, limitations will be described, and an outlook on the follow-up study will be presented.

Lessons for the Design of Inclusive Learning Environments. The results show that children often equate AI with robots on the one hand, and on the other hand overgeneralize AI as 'everything'. This highlights the need to develop conceptually appropriate and simultaneously accessible conceptions of AI that are grounded in the children's everyday lives. Furthermore, fostering critical-reflective skills is essential, particularly with regard to the error-prone nature, provisionality, and data dependency of AI systems. From a didactical perspective, the combination of digital and unplugged approaches, as well as action-oriented learning arrangements, has proven particularly effective [7] in demystifying AI for young children [42, 44].

The analyses reveal that while children show a high level of interest, they also have limited prior knowledge and pronounced misconceptions, particularly in the form of anthropomorphism [33]: AI is often described as human-like and closely linked to human intelligence or the brain. This is attributable, on the one hand, to the design of accessible AI systems and, on the other hand, to the conceptual dominance of the term 'intelligence'. From this, we can derive the need to work on targeted didactical interventions aimed at developing robust conceptual understandings and reflecting on simplistic interpretive patterns.

Limitations. In line with the Design-Based Research approach, both the learning modules and the empirical results were developed iteratively. It should be noted that the assessment tools used, particularly the open formats group discussion was only partially suitable for gathering valid data on the children's prior knowledge. Building on that, the assessment tool is currently further developed into a concept inventory, which aims to be a child-friendly and adapted knowledge test that can be used to assess the AI-related conceptual knowledge from young children. The results should therefore be interpreted as part of an iterative development process.

Outlook. The findings raise further questions regarding the design of inclusive learning environments in the field of AI, with the aim of developing learning environments and validating their outcomes at the children level. Inclusive learning environments are needed that both build on children's prior experiences and specifically contribute to reflection and the reduction of misconceptions. These questions will be systematically explored by the authors.

Disclosure of Interests. The authors declare that the research was conducted in the absence of any commercial or financial relationships that could be construed as a potential conflict of interest.

References

1. Almatrafi, O., Johri, A., Lee, H.: A systematic review of AI literacy conceptualization, constructs, and implementation and assessment efforts (2019–2023). Comput. Educ. Open. **6**, 1–20 (2024). https://doi.org/10.1016/j.caeo.2024.100173
2. Arranz García, O., Romero García, M.d.C., Alonso-Secades, V.: Perceptions, strategies, and challenges of teachers in the integration of artificial intelligence in primary education: a systematic review. J. Inf. Technol. Educ. **24**, Article 6 (2025). https://doi.org/10.28945/5458
3. Atias, O., Mawasi, A.: Conceptualizing AI literacies for children and youth. Comput. Educ.: Artif. Intell. **9**, 1–17 (2025). https://doi.org/10.1016/j.caeai.2025.100491
4. Beudt, S., Feichtenbeiner, R., Blanc, B., Pinkwart, N.: Inklusion durch künstliche Intelligenz? In: Gondlach, K., Brinkmann, B., Brinkmann, M., Plath, J. (eds.) Regenerative Zukünfte und künstliche Intelligenz, pp. 143–161. Springer, Wiesbaden (2024). https://doi.org/10.1007/978-3-658-44852-3_12
5. Chang, X., Yan, Z., Wong, G.K.W.: Young children's understanding of arifilicial intelligence. Br. J. Educ. Technol. **57**(1), 346–372 (2026). https://doi.org/10.1111/bjet.70022
6. Chiu, T.K.F., Chai, C.-S.: Sustainable curriculum planning for artificial intelligence education. Sustainability. **12**(14), 5568 (2020). https://doi.org/10.3390/su12145568
7. Dai, Y.: Integrating unplugged and plugged activities for holistic AI education. Educ. Inf. Technol. **30**(5), 6741–6764 (2024). https://doi.org/10.1007/s10639-024-13043-w
8. Darabipourshiraz, H., Bhat, M., Long, D.: Introducing AI without computers. In: CHI EA '25: Proceedings of the Extended Abstracts of the CHI Conference on Human Factors in Computing Systems, Artikel, p. 353. ACM, New York, NY (2025). https://doi.org/10.1145/3706599.3719876
9. Decristan, J., Fauth, B., Kunter, M., Büttner, G., Klieme, E.: The interplay between class heterogeneity and teaching quality in primary school. Int. J. Educ. Res. **86**, 109–121 (2017). https://doi.org/10.1016/j.ijer.2017.09.004
10. Easterday, M.W., Rees Lewis, D.G., Gerber, E.M.: The logic of design research. Learn.: Res. Pract. **4**(2), 131–160 (2018). https://doi.org/10.1080/23735082.2017.1286367
11. Gabaldón-Estevan, D.: Heterogeneity versus Homogeneity in Schools. Educ. Sci. **10**(11), 335 (2020). https://doi.org/10.3390/educsci10110335
12. Gesellschaft für Informatik [GI] (eds.): Dagstuhl-Erklärung (2016). https://dagstuhl.gi.de/dagstuhl-erklaerung
13. Götz, M., Holler, A.: Zu schön, um wahr zu sein. Televizion. **37**(2), 23–27 (2024)
14. Hardy, I., Stern, E.: Anspruchsvolle Lernaufgaben. In: Götz, M., Hartinger, A., Heinzel, F., Kahlert, H., Miller, S., Sandfuchs, U. (eds.) Handbuch Grundschulpädagogik und Grundschuldidaktik, 5th edn, pp. 410–418. Klinkhardt, Bad Heilbrunn (2024)

15. Heeg, D.M., Avraamidou, L.: Young children's understanding of AI. Educ. Inf. Technol. **30**(8), 10207–10230 (2024). https://doi.org/10.1007/s10639-024-13169-x
16. Irion, T., Lange, S.D., Pohlmann-Rother, S.: Künstliche Intelligenz in der Grundschule (2025). https://www.dgfe.de/fileadmin/OrdnerRedakteure/Sektionen/Sek05_SchPaed/GFPP/Positionspapier_KI-in-der-GS.pdf
17. Julien, G.: How artificial intelligence (AI) impacts inclusive education. Educ. Res. Rev. **19**(6), 98–103 (2024). https://doi.org/10.5897/ERR2024.4404
18. Kosoy, E., Jeong, S., Sinha, A., Gopnik, A., Kraljic, T.: Children's mental models of generative visual and text based AI models. (2024). https://doi.org/10.48550/arXiv.2405.13081
19. Kuckartz, U., Rädiker, S.: Qualitative Inhaltsanalyse, 6th edn. Beltz Juventa, Weinheim (2024)
20. Kuzu, T.: Using ChatGPT and 'multilingualism cards' in multilingual classrooms. In: Bernhard, G., Grassinger, R., Immerfall, S., Kürzinger, A., Kuzu, T., Schnebel, S. (eds.) Heterogenität gestalten – starke Grundschulen entwickeln, pp. 185–206. Waxmann, Münster/New York, NY (2025). https://doi.org/10.31244/9783818850340
21. Kuzu, T., Bay, W., Irion, T.: AI-based task development in teacher education. Educ. Inf. Technol. **30**(10), 1–35 (2025). https://doi.org/10.1007/s10639-025-13673-82025
22. Lange, S.D., Alhallak, Z., Lüssenhop, M.: Addressing multilingual students by primary school teachers from a linguistic-critical perspective. In: Gross, B., Montero-Sieburth, M. (eds.) Beyond Diversity Equity, and Inclusion in Education – Towards Belonging and Societal Transformations. Springer, Wiesbaden (2026) /in press
23. Lange, S.D., Pohlmann-Rother, S.: Didaktische Funktionen zum lernförderlichen Nutzen von Familiensprachen im Grundschulunterricht – Perspektiven aus grundschultheoretischer Sicht. Zeitschrift für Pädagogik. **71**(4), 509–529 (2025). https://doi.org/10.3262/ZP2504509
24. Lindner, K.-T., Schwab, S.: Differentiation and individualisation in inclusive education: a systematic review and narrative synthesis. Int. J. Incl. Educ. **29**(12), 2199–2219 (2020). https://doi.org/10.1080/13603116.2020.1813450
25. Long, D., Magerko, B.: What is AI literacy? In: CHI '20: Proceedings of the 2020 CHI Conference on Human Factors in Computing Systems, pp. 1–16. ACM, New York, NY (2020). https://doi.org/10.1145/3313831.3376727
26. Long, D., Padiyath, A., Teachey, A., Magerko, B.: The role of collaboration, creativity, and embodiment in AI learning experiences. In: Proceedings of the 13th Conference on Creativity and Cognition, pp. 1–10. ACM, New York, NY (2021)
27. Macartney, B., Morton, M.: Kinds of participation: teacher and special education perceptions and practices of 'inclusion' in early childhood and primary school settings. Int. J. Incl. Educ. **17**(8), 776–792 (2013). https://doi.org/10.1080/13603116.2011.602529
28. McKenney, S., Reeves, T. C.: Conducting Educational Design Research. Routledge, London (2012) doi:https://doi.org/10.4324/9780203818183
29. Miao, F., Cukurova, M.: AI Competency Framework for Teachers, vol. 7. UNESCO, Paris (2024). https://doi.org/10.54675/ZJTE2084
30. Michaeli, T.: Künstliche Intelligenz ist kein Werkzeug. Schule post digital. **2**, 6–11 (2025)
31. Michaeli, T., Romeike, R., Seegerer, S.: What students can learn about artificial intelligence. In: Keane, T., Lewin, C., Brinda, T., Bottino, R. (eds.) Towards a Collaborative Society Through Creative Learning, vol. 685, pp. 196–208. Springer, Cham (2023). https://doi.org/10.1007/978-3-031-43393-1_19
32. Organization for Economic Cooperation and Development [OECD]: Empowering Learners for the Age of AI (2025). https://ailiteracyframework.org/wp-content/uploads/2025/05/AILitFramework_ReviewDraft.pdf
33. Placani, A.: Anthropomorphism in AI: hype and fallacy. AI Ethics. **4**, 691–698 (2024). https://doi.org/10.1007/s43681-024-00419-4

34. Pohlmann-Rother, S., Joacham, T., Schmid, U., Lange, S.D., Gärtig-Daugs, A.: Informatische Bildung in der Grundschule. Kohlhammer, Stuttgart (2026). https://doi.org/10.17433/978-3-17-040749-7
35. Reinmann, G.: Was macht Design-Based Research zu Forschung? Educ. Des. Res. **6**(2), 1–22 (2022). https://doi.org/10.15460/eder.6.2.1909
36. Scheiter, K., Bauer, E., Omarchevska, Y., Schumacher, C., Sailer, M.: Künstliche Intelligenz in der Schule (2025). https://www.empirische-bildungsforschung-bmbfsfj.de/img/KI_Review.pdf
37. Seegerer, S., Lindner, A., Romeike, R.: AI unplugged. In: Pasternak, A. (ed.) Proceedings der 18. GI-Fachtagung Informatik und Schule, pp. 325–334. GI, Bonn (2019). https://doi.org/10.18420/infos2019-c18
38. Seyferth-Zapf, C., Mikula, L., Ehmann, M.: Förderung KI-bezogener Kompetenzen bei Lehramtsstudierenden. J. für allgemeine Didaktik. **13**(13), 109–134 (2025). https://doi.org/10.25656/01:34255
39. Song, Y., Weisberg, L.R., Zhang, S., Tian, X., Boyer, K.E., Israel, M.: A framework for inclusive AI learning design for diverse learners. Comput. Educ.: Artif. Intell. **6**, 100212 (2024). https://doi.org/10.1016/j.caeai.2024.100212
40. Ständige Wissenschaftliche Kommission [SWK] (eds.): Large Language Models und ihre Potenziale im Bildungssystem (2024). https://www.swk-bildung.org/content/uploads/2024/02/SWK-2024-Impulspapier_LargeLanguageModels.pdf
41. Touretzky, D., Gardner-McCune, C., Seehorn, D.: Machine learning and the five big ideas. Int. J. Artif. Intell. Educ. **33**(2), 233–266 (2023). https://doi.org/10.1007/s40593-022-00314-1
42. Yang, W., Hu, X., Yeter, I.H., Su, J., Yang, Y., Lee, J.C.-K.: Artificial intelligence education for young children. J. Comput. Assist. Learn. **40**(2), 465–477 (2023). https://doi.org/10.1111/jcal.12892
43. Yeter, I.H., Yang, W., Sturgess, J.B.: Global initiatives and challenges in integrating artificial intelligence literacy in elementary education. Fut. Educ. Res. **2**(4), 328–402 (2024). https://doi.org/10.1002/fer3.59
44. Yim, I.H.Y., Su, J.: Artificial intelligence literacy education in primary schools: a review. Int. J. Technol. Des. Educ. **35**(5), 2175–2204 (2025). https://doi.org/10.1007/s10798-025-09979-w

A Formative Design Evaluation System for Deaf and Hard-of-Hearing Students Reflecting Professional Assessment Processes

Takuya Suzuki(✉)

Tsukuba University of Technology, Tsukuba-shi, Ibaraki, Japan
suzukit@a.tsukuba-tech.ac.jp

Abstract. Deaf and Hard-of-Hearing (DHH) students often face significant barriers in obtaining timely and continuous formative feedback during iterative design processes, particularly in online and hybrid learning environments. Delays in communication and increased cognitive load associated with multimodal interaction can limit opportunities for spontaneous clarification and reflection. Prior research in Human–Computer Interaction (HCI) has highlighted the lack of immediacy in learning support systems as a major challenge for DHH learners.

To address this issue, we present a web-based formative design assessment system that operationalizes professional assessment processes commonly used by design educators. The system enables instructors to configure assessment criteria in advance through a layered structure consisting of a global shared prompt and task-specific analysis settings. The shared prompt establishes a consistent assessment baseline, while task-specific configurations adapt feedback to the goals of individual assignments.

In addition, students explicitly specify their design intentions by selecting which aspects of their work they aimed to emphasize. This input is incorporated into the feedback generation process, allowing the system to assess how stated intentions are reflected in the artifact rather than applying one-size-fits-all criteria. This design is particularly valuable for DHH students, as it reduces reliance on real-time instructional dialogue and makes assessment conditions explicit and accessible.

We demonstrate the technical feasibility of the proposed approach through a proof-of-concept implementation and an illustrative example using an existing student recruitment poster. While no formal user study has been conducted at this stage, the system illustrates how intention-aware, instructor-configured formative feedback can be delivered on demand. This work lays the groundwork for future empirical studies and contributes to the design of more inclusive and responsive iterative design learning environments. More broadly, the study positions AI not as an autonomous evaluator, but as a medium through which professional assessment reasoning can be externalized, structured, and made accessible to learners.

Keywords: Formative Assessment · Deaf and Hard-of-Hearing Students · Design Education · Instructor-Configurable AI

C. Stephanidis et al. (Eds.): HCII 2026, CCIS 3047, pp. 628–635, 2026.
https://doi.org/10.1007/978-3-032-30552-7_60

1 Introduction

1.1 Background and Motivation

Formative feedback plays a critical role in design education, where students iteratively develop ideas through cycles of making, reflection, and revision. However, for Deaf and Hard-of-Hearing (DHH) students, obtaining timely and continuous formative feedback remains challenging. In particular, real-time instructional dialogue is often constrained by delays introduced through interpretation or textual mediation, as well as by the cognitive load associated with multimodal information processing.

These challenges are amplified in online and hybrid learning environments, where opportunities for spontaneous clarification and informal feedback are limited. As a result, DHH students may receive feedback that is delayed, fragmented, or overly dependent on synchronous instructor availability. Prior work in Human–Computer Interaction (HCI) has identified the lack of immediacy and accessibility in learning support systems as a significant barrier for DHH learners, underscoring the need for alternative approaches to formative assessment.

Recent advances in AI-based feedback systems offer new possibilities for supporting iterative learning. However, when students rely on general-purpose AI tools, feedback quality depends heavily on how questions are formulated, which can create an additional barrier for DHH students. To address this issue, we explore a system design that makes professional assessment criteria explicit, configurable, and accessible within the design workflow.

Prior studies have emphasized the importance of formative assessment and reflective practice in design education [1, 2, 5, 8], as well as the challenges faced by Deaf and Hard-of-Hearing (DHH) students in accessing timely instructional feedback [3, 4, 6]. This research asks how professional assessment reasoning can be structured through AI to support accessible formative learning.

1.2 Contributions

This paper makes the following contributions:

1. An instructor-configurable formative design assessment system that operationalizes professional assessment reasoning into a structured AI feedback framework.
2. A layered assessment configuration model that separates global assessment principles from task-specific analysis settings, ensuring both consistency and flexibility in formative feedback.
3. An intention-aware formative feedback mechanism that incorporates student-stated design intentions into the assessment process.
4. A proof-of-concept implementation demonstrating the feasibility of intention-aware, instructor-configurable AI feedback in design education.

2 Related Work

This work builds on prior research in three main areas: learning support for Deaf and Hard-of-Hearing (DHH) students, formative assessment in design education, and AI-based feedback systems.

Learning Support for DHH Students. Previous HCI and accessibility research has documented the challenges DHH students face in educational settings, particularly with respect to real-time communication, information accessibility, and cognitive load. Studies have shown that delays introduced by interpretation or captioning can disrupt the flow of interaction and limit opportunities for spontaneous feedback. While various technologies have been proposed to improve accessibility, many approaches still rely on synchronous interaction or place additional demands on learners to actively request support.

Formative Assessment in Design Education. Formative feedback is widely recognized as a core component of design education, supporting iterative learning through critique and revision. Prior work has explored digital tools for supporting critique, peer feedback, and reflection in design contexts. However, much of this research assumes the availability of timely instructor feedback or focuses on peer-based mechanisms, leaving open questions about how professional assessment processes can be made continuously accessible, particularly for students who face communication barriers. Foundational work on formative assessment emphasizes the importance of making assessment criteria explicit and enabling learners to engage with those criteria through structured feedback processes [8].

AI-Based Feedback Systems. Recent advances in generative AI have led to increased interest in automated feedback for learning and creative tasks. Existing systems have demonstrated the potential of AI to provide rapid feedback, suggestions, and assessments. However, the quality and relevance of such feedback often depend heavily on how users formulate prompts or questions. This reliance can disadvantage learners who have difficulty articulating evaluative queries or who are unfamiliar with professional assessment criteria.

In contrast to prior work, our approach focuses on operationalizing professional assessment reasoning through instructor-configurable assessment structures and intention-aware feedback. By making assessment criteria explicit and accessible, the proposed system aims to complement existing accessibility technologies and support formative learning without requiring continuous synchronous interaction.

3 Design Goals

Based on the challenges identified for Deaf and Hard-of-Hearing (DHH) students, we derived the following design goals to guide our system development.

G1: Provide Timely Feedback Without Synchronous Interaction. The system should enable students to receive formative feedback on demand without real-time instructional dialogue. This goal addresses situations where synchronous communication is delayed, fragmented, or inaccessible, particularly in online and hybrid learning environments.

G2: Make Professional Assessment Criteria Explicit and Configurable. Rather than relying on implicit or ad hoc evaluation, the system should allow instructors to externalize professional assessment reasoning as configurable structures. By making assessment criteria explicit and consistently applied, the system aims to reduce ambiguity and ensure alignment with instructional intent.

G3: Support Diverse Design Intentions Without One-Size-Fits-All Assessment. Design assignments often allow multiple valid approaches, such as emphasizing several aspects of a concept or focusing on a single key feature. The system should support this diversity by enabling students to specify their design intentions and by generating feedback that assesses how well those intentions are reflected in the artifact.

G4: Reduce Cognitive and Communicative Burden for DHH Students. The system should minimize the need for students to formulate complex evaluative questions or negotiate assessment conditions during feedback interactions. By structuring both assessment criteria and student input, the system aims to lower cognitive load and improve accessibility.

These goals emphasize formative support, transparency in assessment, and accessibility, and provide the basis for the system design described in the following sections.

4 System Overview

The proposed system is a web-based formative design assessment platform designed to support iterative learning without requiring continuous synchronous interaction. The system consists of three main components: an instructor configuration interface, task-specific analysis forms, and an AI-driven feedback generation module (Fig. 1).

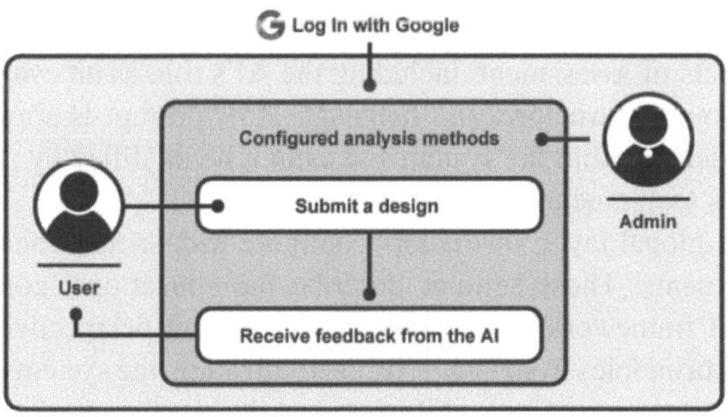

Fig. 1. Overview of the formative design assessment workflow.

1. Instructors configure global assessment settings and task-specific criteria.
2. Students submit design artifacts and specify their design intentions.
3. The system integrates instructor criteria and student intention to generate intention-aware formative feedback without synchronous interaction.

Instructors first configure assessment settings through an administrator interface. These settings include a global shared prompt that defines the AI's evaluative role, feedback tone, output structure, and language. This shared configuration functions as a foundational assessment layer and is automatically applied to all analyses conducted within the system. Instructors also create task-specific analysis forms for individual assignments, specifying the educational context, analytical frameworks, and expected assessment perspectives.

Students interact with the system through task-specific analysis forms. When submitting a design artifact, students upload their work and provide structured input regarding their design intentions, such as which aspects of the assignment they aimed to emphasize. This input does not alter the instructor-defined assessment criteria but serves as a condition for how the feedback is generated.

Once a submission is made, the system combines the global shared prompt, the task-specific analysis configuration, and the student-provided intentions to generate formative feedback using a selected AI model. The resulting feedback is returned to the student in a structured format that highlights strengths, areas for improvement, and suggestions for next steps. Throughout this process, students are not required to formulate evaluative questions or negotiate feedback conditions, allowing them to focus on reflection and revision within the design workflow.

5 Instructor-Configurable Assessment

A key characteristic of the proposed system is that formative assessment is configured by instructors rather than inferred implicitly by the AI or determined through ad hoc student interaction. This design reflects professional assessment practices in design education, where instructors apply stable evaluative perspectives across student work.

The system adopts a layered configuration structure consisting of a global shared assessment prompt and task-specific analysis settings. The global shared prompt defines foundational aspects of assessment, including the AI's role as an evaluator, the overall feedback stance, output structure, and language. This prompt is applied uniformly to all analyses conducted within the system and cannot be modified by students, ensuring consistency across assignments and submissions.

On top of this global layer, instructors configure task-specific analysis settings for individual assignments. These settings describe the educational context of the task, relevant analytical frameworks, and expected assessment perspectives. By separating global assessment principles from task-level customization, the system allows instructors to maintain a consistent assessment philosophy while adapting feedback to the learning goals of each assignment.

6 Student-Specified Design Intent

In design education, multiple interpretations and strategies are often valid for a single assignment. For example, students may choose to communicate a broad overview by presenting multiple features, or they may intentionally focus on a single aspect to create a strong impression. Applying uniform assessment criteria without considering such intent can result in feedback that is misaligned with students' design goals.

To address this issue, the proposed system allows students to explicitly specify their design intentions at the time of submission. Through structured input fields, students indicate which aspects of the assignment they aimed to emphasize in their design. These inputs do not function as self-evaluation or justification, nor do they alter the instructor-defined assessment criteria. Instead, they provide contextual information that conditions how feedback is generated.

This design enables intention-aware formative feedback. Rather than evaluating what is absent or underrepresented according to a fixed checklist, the system assesses how effectively the selected intentions are reflected in the artifact. For instance, when a student chooses to focus on a single key feature, the feedback emphasizes clarity, coherence, and strength of expression for that feature, rather than penalizing the omission of other aspects.

This mechanism is particularly important for Deaf and Hard-of-Hearing (DHH) students. By making assessment conditions explicit and selectable, the system reduces ambiguity and the need for students to infer implicit assessment expectations. Students are not required to negotiate their design rationale through real-time dialogue or to formulate complex evaluative prompts. Instead, they can communicate intent through simple, structured interaction, supporting more accessible and equitable formative assessment.

7 Proof of Concept and Example Output

To examine the feasibility of the proposed approach, we implemented a proof-of-concept system and applied it to an existing student-created recruitment poster for a design assignment. The goal of this demonstration is not to evaluate learning outcomes, but to illustrate how instructor-configured criteria and student-specified intent are integrated in practice.

Figure 2 illustrates both the student input interface and the generated formative feedback. The left image shows the student-facing analysis interface. Students are first presented with a brief explanation of the assessment purpose and assumptions, including the fact that prior analytical work has already been completed. They then upload a design artifact and specify their design intentions by selecting relevant aspects through structured input fields. This interaction requires minimal free-text input and avoids the need for students to formulate evaluative questions.

The right image presents an excerpt of the formative feedback generated by the system. The feedback reflects the instructor-configured assessment structure and is conditioned by the design intentions selected by the student. Rather than enumerating missing elements according to a fixed checklist, the feedback focuses on how effectively the stated intentions are reflected in the artifact, while offering suggestions for refinement and future improvement.

8 Limitations and Future Work

This work has several limitations that should be acknowledged. First, the proposed system is presented as a proof of concept, and no formal user study has been conducted at the time of writing. The example described in this paper is intended to demonstrate

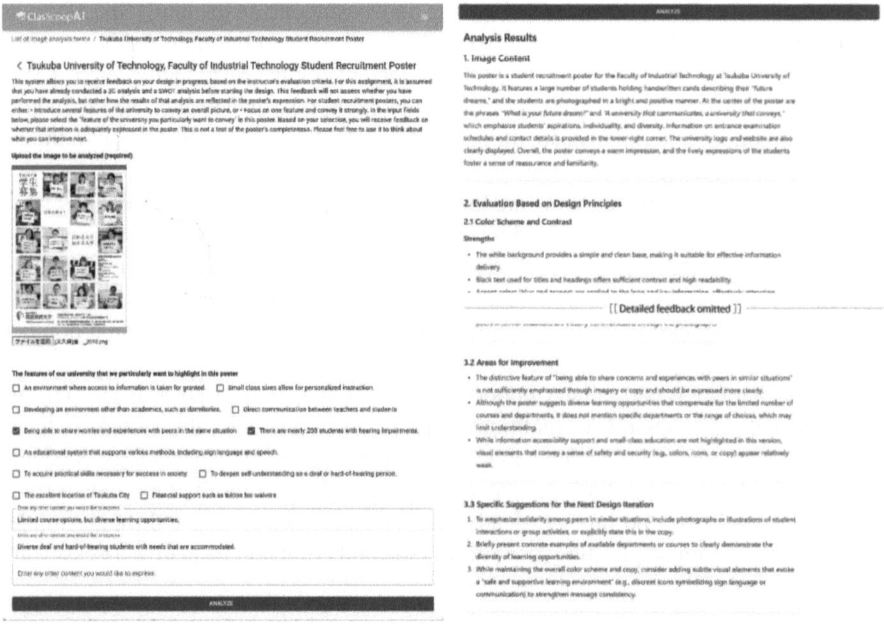

Fig. 2. Student input and generated formative feedback. The left image shows the student-facing input interface for specifying design intention and submitting an artifact, while the right image shows the structure of the generated formative feedback, with detailed content abbreviated.

technical feasibility and design rationale rather than to provide empirical evidence of learning effectiveness.

Second, the current demonstration is based on an existing student artifact and has primarily been used to validate workflow consistency and output structure. While the generated feedback illustrates how instructor-configured criteria and student-specified intent can be integrated, the system's impact on learning processes, usability, and student experience—particularly for Deaf and Hard-of-Hearing (DHH) students—remains to be evaluated in authentic educational settings.

Future work will involve deploying the system in actual design courses with DHH students and conducting qualitative and quantitative studies to examine its educational value. Planned evaluations include classroom use over multiple iterations, analysis of student reflections and revisions, and feedback from instructors regarding workload and assessment consistency. In addition, future extensions may explore the refinement of assessment templates, support for collaborative critique, and adaptation to other domains of creative and project-based learning.

Despite these limitations, this work establishes a foundation for instructor-configurable, intention-aware formative feedback systems and highlights the potential of operationalizing professional assessment processes to support more accessible and inclusive design education.

Acknowledgments. This work was supported by JSPS KAKENHI (grant number JP25K06562).

Disclosure of Interests. The author declares that there are no competing interests relevant to the content of this article.

References

1. Black, P., Wiliam, D.: Assessment and classroom learning. Assess. Educ.: Princ. Policy Pract. **5**(1), 7–74 (1998)
2. Nicol, D.J., Macfarlane-Dick, D.: Formative assessment and self-regulated learning: a model and seven principles of good feedback practice. Stud. High. Educ. **31**(2), 199–218 (2006)
3. Lang, H.G.: Higher education for deaf students: research priorities in the new millennium. J. Deaf. Stud. Deaf. Educ. **7**(4), 267–280 (2002)
4. Marschark, M., Spencer, P.E. (eds.): The Oxford Handbook of Deaf Studies, Language, and Education. Oxford University Press, Oxford (2010)
5. Schön, D.A.: The Reflective Practitioner: How Professionals Think in Action. Basic Books, New York, NY (1983)
6. Yang, Q., Steinfeld, A., Rosé, C.P.: Re-examining whether, why, and how human–AI interaction is uniquely difficult to design. In: Proceedings of the CHI Conference on Human Factors in Computing Systems (CHI 2020), pp. 1–13. ACM, New York, NY (2020)
7. Zamfirescu-Pereira, J.D., Wong, R.Y., Hartmann, B., Yang, Q.: Why Johnny can't prompt: how non-AI experts try (and fail) to design LLM prompts. In: Proceedings of the 2023 CHI Conference on Human Factors in Computing Systems (CHI '23). ACM, New York, NY (2023)
8. Sadler, D.R.: Formative assessment and the design of instructional systems. Instr. Sci. **18**, 119–144 (1989)

A Comparative Study of Automated Accessibility Checker Tools and Manual Evaluation on Rwanda's E-Government Portals: Towards a Hybrid Framework for Digital Inclusion

Pauline Uwase and Edith Talina Luhanga(✉)

Carnegie Mellon University Africa, Kigali, Rwanda
{puwase,eluhanga}@andrew.cmu.edu

Abstract. Automated web accessibility checker tools provide evidence of compliance with the World Content Accessibility Guidelines (WCAG). However, there is very limited research comparing how well these programs work in assessing websites against expert evaluators in Sub-Saharan African contexts. This research study will compare 3 different automated evaluation programs (EqualWeb, WAVE, and AChecker) against expert evaluations of the five most frequently visited government portals in Rwanda (Irembo, Rwanda Revenue Agency, Rwanda Development Board, Rwanda Social Security Board, and the Ministry of Public Service and Labour); and will assess them against all 13 WCAG guidelines as defined by the four "POUR" categories. The average accessibility compliance of the five e-government portals obtained with the use of the automated tools was approximately 58.6%. Comparatively, the human experts had determined that the same five portals were compliant at a rate of approximately 32%. The automated tools were able to detect an average of 76% of the non-compliant items identified by the expert evaluators (with WAVE achieving an even higher rate of 95.6% agreement and EqualWeb achieving an 86.7% agreement). The automated tools reported 47 false-positive findings and did not detect 24% of compliant items (most notably dynamic content, keyboard interactions, and usability issues related to screen reader usage, which are generally context-dependent). The inter-rater reliability between the experts was substantial (Fleiss' $\kappa = 0.678$). Given the results of this research study, we can conclude that automated tools are an excellent tool for complementing and supporting expert evaluators; however, they should not replace expert evaluators when it comes to conducting accessibility compliance reviews of the many digital platforms that provide service to the public. This study is the first research study to provide an empirical assessment of the e-government infrastructure in Rwanda, and offers a framework for hybrid evaluations to improve inclusive digital governance.

Keywords: Web accessibility · Automated tools · WCAG 2.1 · E-government · Rwanda · Human evaluation

C. Stephanidis et al. (Eds.): HCII 2026, CCIS 3047, pp. 636–646, 2026.
https://doi.org/10.1007/978-3-032-30552-7_61

1 Introduction

About 1.3 billion people, which is 16% of the world's population, live with some form of disability [1]. In Africa, there are an estimated 60–80 million people with disabilities, most of whom live in Sub-Saharan countries [2]. An increasing number of countries in the Sub-Saharan Africa (SSA) region now offer public services through digital platforms, so it is critical to ensure these platforms are accessible for people with disabilities, in order to ensure equal participation in society. In Rwanda, e-government platforms like Irembo have grown quickly, with over 2.2 million registered users. However, the accessibility of these systems remains largely unexplored [3].

The Web Content Accessibility Guidelines (WCAG) provide recommendations that, if followed correctly, provide accommodations for a variety of disabilities, including low vision and blindness, deafness and hearing loss, limited mobility, speech impediments, and some accommodations for cognitive and learning disabilities. Accommodations promote accessibility on any device [4]. The latest version, WCAG 2.2 contains 87 success criteria [4]. Analyzing websites' compliance with these guidelines on websites is a time consuming endeavor that requires human experts, and in recent years automated checker tools such as WAVE [5] have been widely adopted to allow comprehensive website evaluations. The WebAIM Million project, for example, has used WAVE to analyze the accessibility of the top 1,000,000 webpages yearly since 2019, providing valuable insight on accessibility improvements and remaining gaps (in 2025, the top 1,000,000 webpages had 10.3% less errors than in 2024, but they still had an average of 51 accessibility errors per page) [6] However, the coverage and accuracy of these tools can vary significantly [7, 8]. To promote better coverage and accuracy, it is prudent to use multiple checkers at a time or to pair human evaluators with automated checkers. The latter is preferable for low-resource contexts, where such collaboration can also build local capacity, as practitioners learn iteratively from AI feedback [9], a model with growing empirical support.

In this paper, we present a comparative evaluation of Rwandan experts vs. automated checkers in detecting web accessibility violations in Rwandan e-government websites. We make two main contributions of relevance to the global HCI community: (1) we add to the body of work providing empirical assessments of accessibility of e-government websites in low- and middle- income countries; (2) by presenting evidence on areas where automated tools and human experts complement each other, informing the design of hybrid evaluation frameworks suited to low-resource contexts.

2 Related Work

2.1 Automated vs. Human Accessibility Evaluation

The tension between automated and manual accessibility evaluation is well established in the literature. Brajnik [4] demonstrated through a comparative tool study that automated checkers identify false positives and miss context-dependent issues, establishing that tool performance varies substantially across criteria types. Vigo et al. [5] validated automated tools against expert evaluations and found that tools perform reliably on syntactic issues (e.g., missing alt text, color contrast) but struggle with semantic and interaction-level problems. Abduganiev [6] conducted a systematic comparison across multiple automated tools and concluded that no single tool covers more than 40% of all possible WCAG success criteria, reinforcing the need for complementary evaluation methods.

The WebAIM Million project, which uses WAVE to analyze the top 1,000,000 web pages annually, provides large-scale evidence of persistent accessibility failures: in 2025, pages averaged 51 errors each, even after a 10.3% year-on-year improvement [10] and found that a typical home page now has 1,257 elements and has increased by 61% since 2019. Approximately 4.1% of the elements found on a typical home page have a detectable accessibility error, indicating that individuals with disabilities will likely experience an issue with accessibility with one in every 24 of the home page's elements. The increasing level of complexity of the home page means that it will become progressively more difficult to ensure compliance to accessibility principles. The results support the need for evaluating accessibility on every government service portal; government systems are primarily used for citizens seeking access to public services.

Ferrara et al. [13] conducted a multi-site comparison of WAVE, Axe and TAW and found that using multiple tools increases the rate at which problem types are detected by as much as 30%, providing further evidence to support the use of multiple tools. Yesilada et al. [14] proposed a unified web evaluation methodology (UWEM) which explicitly combines automated scanning with manual expert review and serves as the foundation for Hybrid models.

Similarly, Bühler et al. [15] proposed evaluation guidelines that position automated tools as first-pass filters, followed by structured expert walkthrough for issues requiring human judgment. Despite these limitations, automated checkers can be beneficial in resource-constrained settings, where accessibility and user experience design experts may be in short supply.

2.2 E-Government Accessibility in Sub-Saharan Africa

The most thorough examination of e-government websites in Sub-Saharan Africa has been undertaken by Verkijika and De Wet [11]. Their audit revealed significant non-compliance, even at the most basic WCAG Level A standards. The most common issues were found in the areas of alternative text, keyboard accessibility, and color contrast. Country-specific assessments reinforce this picture: Elisa [16] found accessibility problems across all Tanzanian government sites examined, while Adepoju et al. [17] has identified many violations of different types of Nigerian governmental platforms. Kuzma [18] has described four types of barriers that recur across UK e-government sites and shows that even highly resourced governments have difficulty achieving simple compliance with the law. Furthermore, there are some unique contextual matters within the e-government environment of Rwanda. For example, the use of both the English and Kinyarwanda languages, an increase in the number of people using technology rapidly, and the estimated 200,000+ citizens with disabilities in Rwanda are all related to the complexity of and urgency of accessible services [19]. The current study will address the lack of any previously completed accessibility audit of the digital government resources of Rwanda.

3 Methodology

This research used a mixed-methods approach, combining automated accessibility assessment tools with expert human evaluation. This was done to assess the accessibility compliance of Rwandan eGovernment platforms. The study consisted of five distinct stages: website selection, automated tool selection, automated accessibility assessment, human expert evaluation, and comparative analysis.

3.1 Website Selection

We analyzed the websites of the top five e-government platforms returned in Google searches in Rwanda, namely (1) Irembo, (2) Rwanda Social Security Board (RSSB) (3) Ministry of Public Service and Labour (Mifotra), (4) Rwanda Revenue Authority (RRA), and (5) Rwanda Development Board (RDB). The search terms used were ""the most used ranked websites in Rwanda" and "Rwanda government online services platforms." Irembo is a one-stop website offering over 100 civic services including applications for birth, death, and marriage certificates, applications for visas and residency, applications for land permits, and applications for police clearance certificates. To date, over 25 million applications have been processed, saving citizens more than 100 million hours of time each year through automation and reduced service delivery time from five days to twenty-four hours. So far Irembo has generated greater than RWF 350 billion (around US $239.9 million) in revenue due to the streamlined services provided [21, 22]. RSSB manages pension contributions for hundreds of thousands of employees and employers through digital platforms, while Mifotra provides online labor-related services such as E-recruitment services, employment regulations and acts as a one-stop platform for many services related to public servants. RRA manages online tax declaration and payment services used by thousands of taxpayers annually, while RDB provides online business registration services that allow entrepreneurs to register a business in less than 24 h [3].

This study was carried out in March 2025 and analysis was limited to the homepages of the selected websites because the homepage is often the main entry point of the website and several studies emphasize analyzing core pages (often starting with homepages) to identify pervasive issues such as missing alt text, contrast problems, heading structure, and keyboard navigation barriers [23, 24]. Additionally, many of the secondary pages in the selected websites require form filling or authentication to access.

3.2 Automated Tool Selection and Rationale

We searched for academic publications comparing automated web accessibility tools and for the top ranked (in search results) automated tools. The keywords used include: "WCAG automated accessibility checker", "web accessibility evaluation tools", and "WCAG compliance testing tools" were used to identify frequently used tools for assessing web sites for automated and practical accessibility compliance. A shortlist of the identified tools was created based on three criteria: (1) WCAG 2.1 accessibility evaluation standards; (2) proven efficacy and reliability in past empirical studies of automated accessibility evaluation tools; and (3) free and easily implemented as browser extensions or web-based platforms. Using these criteria, the following three tools were selected:

EqualWeb, WAVE, and AChecker. EqualWeb was selected due to its ability to identify common types of critical accessibility barriers (i.e. colour contrast and ARIA implementation problems) that are considered to be high impact barriers to accessibility [25]. WAVE was selected for its breadth of WCAG 2.1 AA coverage and due to its abundance of use by researchers in large scale automated accessibility evaluation studies [26–28] AChecker was included to derive percentage compliance scores the only tool in the set that produces a normalized compliance metric and for its prior use in comparative accessibility studies [4, 6]. Using three tools with overlapping but distinct detection methods follows best practice established by Ferrara et al. [9], who showed that tool combination substantially increases violation detection rates.

3.3 WCAG Guidelines Evaluation Framework

WCAG 2.1 is structured around four accessibility principles: Perceivable, Operable, Understandable, and Robust (POUR) comprising 13 guidelines and 61 testable success criteria across three conformance levels: Level A (minimum), Level AA (recommended), and Level AAA (enhanced).

This study adopted the 13 WCAG guidelines as the primary evaluation framework, assessing applicable success criteria within each guideline against the homepage interfaces of the selected e-government platforms. The guideline level structure follows approaches used in previous e-government accessibility studies [7, 12, 13] enabling systematic comparison across websites while maintaining alignment with WCAG's principle based organization. The 13 guidelines span the four POUR principles as follows: Perceivable (4 guidelines), Operable (5 guidelines), Understandable (3 guidelines), and Robust (1 guideline). The evaluation focused on Level A and Level AA success criteria, which represent the minimum and recommended accessibility standards for public sector websites. Level AAA criteria were excluded, as they represent advanced accessibility requirements that are often difficult to achieve across entire websites and are not typically mandated for government digital services.

Within each guideline, only success criteria applicable to a static homepage interface were assessed. Criteria requiring multi page workflows, time based media, or multimedia elements not present on the evaluated pages were marked as Not Applicable (N/A). Each criterion was evaluated by accessibility experts using a standardized assessment form, where compliance was recorded using Pass, Fail, or N/A ratings based on WCAG 2.1 requirements.

3.4 Evaluation Procedure

To perform accessibility assessments, the URLs of each platform's homepage were submitted through verification using the selected accessibility checker tools [16] in March 2025. The tools provided a quantitative overall accessibility score along with breakdowns of the scores along each of the four POUR categories and a summary of how to fix the issues. combined the three accessibility reports into one comprehensive report to ensure we retained the widest possible coverage of POUR violations.

3.5 Expert Review and Inter-Rater Reliability Analysis

We asked three human experts to conduct a manual review of the five homepages and categorize all instances of WCAG 2.1 AA noncompliance into the four POUR categories. The three experts had backgrounds in user interface design and digital accessibility. Calculated the inter-rater agreement achieved by the experts using Fleiss' kappa as a measurement of inter-rater reliability [20].

3.6 Comparative Analysis: Automated Tools vs. Expert Review

To determine how automated vs. human experts performed, we compared the reports of the POUR violations generated by the tools and by the experts and identified which accessibility issues were flagged by both groups and which accessibility issues were only flagged by one of the two. We categorized the results into three key groups:

- True Positives: Issues that were identified by the automated tools and the expert reviewers were identified and agreed on. These show that the tool does identify actual accessibility violations
- False Positives: issues that were flagged in the automated tools but the expert reviewers found were not violations, or they simply disregarded. These represent possible over-reporting or misreading by the automated tools.
- False Negatives: issues that the expert reviewers noted but were not detected by the automated tools. These are most concerning because they are real access barriers missed by the automated processes.

4 Results

4.1 POUR Violations Flagged by Automated Accessibility Tools

The three tools collectively identified 297 POUR principle violations across the five homepages (Fig. 1). Perceivable violations dominated at 186/297 (62.6%), followed by Operable (30.7%), Robust (18.1%), and Understandable (16.8%). Figure 2 presents the distribution of the POUR violations across all five websites in a pie chart while Table 1 summarizes the POUR violations by webpage.

RSSB had the highest number of violations across all four POUR categories (n = 99), while RRA had the least (n = 28).

Six WCAG criteria were violated by all five platforms, indicating systemic rather than site-specific failures: 1.1.1 (Non-text Content), 1.3.1 (Info & Relationships), 1.4.3 (Contrast), 2.4.1 (Bypass Blocks), 2.4.4 (Link Purpose), and 4.1.2 (Name, Role, Value). The most frequent violation categories were contrast errors (79 violations), missing alternative text (74), non-descriptive links (48), improper interactive element labeling (40), and poor document structure (33).

Overall compliance scores varied widely per platform. According to the AChecker tool, scores ranged from 23% (RSSB) to 72% (RRA) all below the 80% threshold considered acceptable in government accessibility standards [14]. Scores for the other webpages were: 64% for Irembo, 52% for RDB, 47% for Mifotra, and 3% for RSSB (not compliant). The average compliance score for the five platforms was 58.6%.

Table 1. POUR Principle Violations by Platform.

Website	Perceivable	Operable	Understandable	Robust	Total
Irembo	36	12	2	12	62
RRA	13	7	3	5	28
RDB	45	7	2	5	59
RSSB	53	34	1	11	99
MIFOTRA	39	1	2	7	49
Total	**186**	**61**	**10**	**40**	**297**

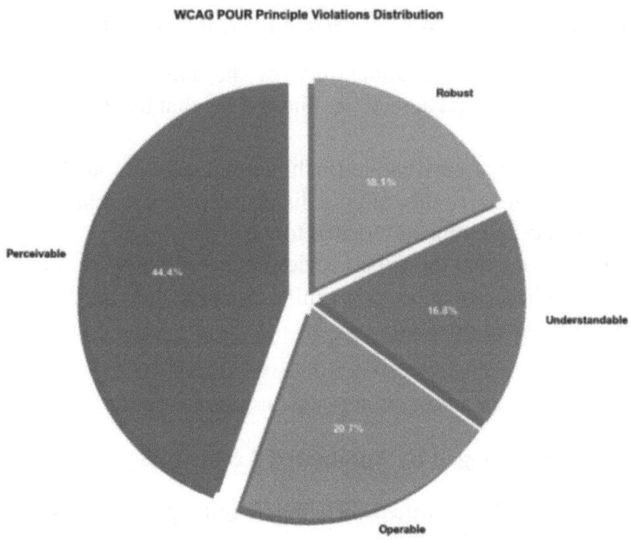

Fig. 1. WCAG POUR principle violations distribution.

4.2 Expert Evaluation and Inter-Rater Reliability

Experts reported an average overall compliance rate of 32% compared with those of automation tools which is 58.6%, which confirms the expected pattern of over-estimation previously documented in [4, 5]. Across all guidelines and sites, Fleiss' Kappa = 0.678, which indicates substantial agreement between expert consensus as a ground truth benchmark for reference. The per guideline Kappa values ranged from 0.524 (1.4 Distinguishable: resizing of text) to a maximum of 0.893 (1.4 Distinguishable: contrast); Higher Kappa values were associated with the objective, measurable criteria associated with the evaluation process and lower Kappa values were associated with the dependent criteria, example focus order (2.4 Navigable).

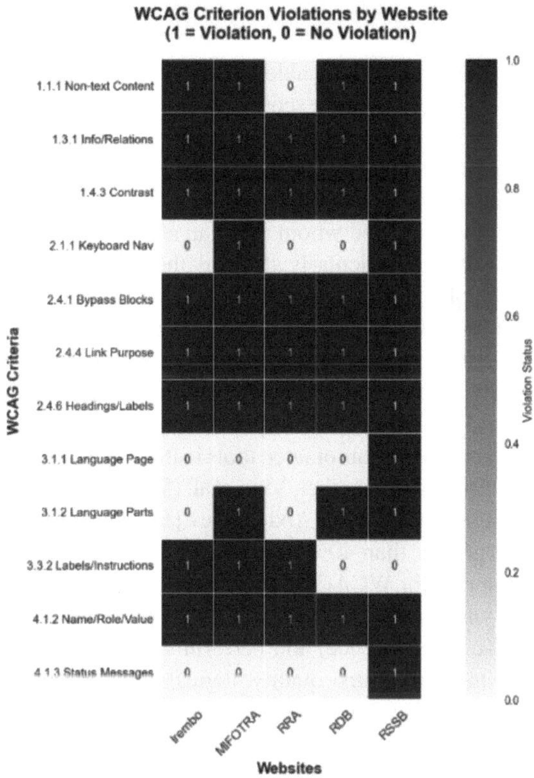

Fig. 2. WCAG criterion violations by website (1 = violation, 0 = no violation).

4.3 Automated Tools vs. Expert Consensus

When comparing the outputs of the two tools against. According to the consensus view of experts, WAVE achieved 95.6% agreement (43/45) with the expert group and EqualWeb had 86.7% (39/45). In total, both automated tools found 76% (188) of the violations identified by the experts. The remaining 24% (59) of violations were missed by these tools (false negatives), with the majority occurring in the areas of dynamic content, keyboard navigation sequences, and screen reader interaction, all of which can only be tested at runtime or in context. Accessibility checker tools generated 47 false positive findings, which could have a negative impact on development teams or testing teams while testing using automation only because they were flagged and yet are correctly implemented ARIA elements and resizing text as violations. Automated tools do not detect the accessibility menus, for example: RRA has an accessibility menu, and before Human evolution it was well flagged with different violations including contrast, text sizing. Experts opened the accessibility menu and all the issues where not technically there cause on the menu you can change the contrast, resize the text. The false positives aspect was also reported from research previously conducted by Brajnik [4].

5 Discussion

None of the platforms evaluated were able to comply with the WCAG 2.1 AA standards for accessibility. The compliance scores for the platforms evaluated in this study ranges between (23%–72%) and were similar reported by Verkijika and De Wet [7] for e-Government in sub-Saharan Africa and were substantially below the 80% compliance threshold; meaning that the non-compliance rates were much higher than expected. Looking at the violations found and whom they can affect. The high percentage of Perceivable violations (62.6%) is particularly affecting the people with visual impairments, which are around 0.8% of Rwanda's population according to census data, and that the Rwanda Union of the Blind has publicly flagged digital exclusion as a priority concern [19]. Operable violations (30.7%) affect users with mobility impairments, who constitute approximately 35% of persons with disabilities in Rwanda [15] making keyboard accessibility failures a significant barrier to public service access.

The detection rate achieved by automated tools in this study aligns with prior research contribution made by different researcher, Vigo et al. [5] found tool detection rates of 30–70% depending on criterion type, also, Abduganiev [6] determined that while no single tool will ever achieve greater than 40% of all WCAG criteria, when used in combination, the total detection rate for WCAG can be extraordinarily high. Overall, automated tools perform best at syntactically defined violations (example: contrast ratios, language declarations, alternative text presence) and perform worst at semantically defined violations (example: meaningful alt text quality, logical structure to navigation, usability of interactive components). The difference between "syntactic" and "semantic «interaction" barrier types as classified in Yesilada et al. [14] provides a logical framework for comparing the different ways in which tools perform: essentially, they are very good for detecting syntactic barriers, but very poor in terms of detecting semantic & interaction barriers.

Research confirms that hybrid structure of Accessibility evaluation includes the three components of the hybrid structure are: (1) Automated continuous monitoring of accessible compliance; (2) Regular expert evaluations performed; and (3) User testing (with individuals with disabilities).

6 Limitations and Future Work

This research has limitations with three being the primary one. Firstly, research has only been done at the homepage level and so examining the entire user experience and all other evaluated criteria would help to portray a better picture of the level of compliance. Secondly, this study used five different websites which was good for an exploratory type of research, however, five websites is not enough to generalize any inferential statistics. Therefore, this study's findings should be viewed as empirical baseline data for collating an accurate picture of e-governance in Rwanda. Thirdly, no direct testing was completed with the users who have a disability therefore the use of the screen reader and keyboard by the evaluators was only accomplished through proxy and cannot replace the feedback of someone who has lived the experience of using the website. Future research should conduct analysis of complete service delivery processes, assess additional evaluation criteria, include testing with people that utilize assistive technologies, and provide longitudinal studies to assess compliance as they apply to updates of the website over time.

7 Conclusion

The accessibility of Rwandan e-government platforms was evaluated for the first time in an extensive study that included both automated tool assessments and human expert reviews based on the internationally accepted WCAG 2.1 AA guidelines. All five reviewed platforms failed to meet the baseline levels of compliance established by the WCAG; a total of 297 violations were identified with the majority impacting the accessibility of the platforms for users experiencing visual impairments. Of the 297 violations, identified by experts, 76% were also detected by automated tools but 47 false positives were identified and 24% of context-dependent barriers were missed by automated tools indicating that automated tools are useful for some aspects of accessibility evaluation, but cannot be relied upon solely to conduct a comprehensive evaluation of e-government platform accessibility. Agreement amongst the expert evaluators (Fleiss' $\kappa = 0.678$) supports the expert evaluations used as the evaluation ground truth. The hybrid framework presented in this paper, based on empirical data and previous methodological literature, provides an actionable plan for government digital teams wishing to improve the accessibility of their platforms in a systematic and resource-constrained manner. The authors recommend that immediate policy priorities include requiring compliance with WCAG 2.1 AA, providing developers with systematic training in and resources for accessibility, and including the disability community in the design process of e-government platforms.

References

1. World Health Organization: Disability and Health. WHO, Fact Sheet (2019) https://www.who.int/news-room/fact-sheets/detail/disability-and-health
2. Lombardi, A.: How living with hope is helping people with disabilities in Africa. The Borgen Project. https://borgenproject.org/people-with-disabilities-in-africa/ (2022)
3. Umutoni, N.: Digitisation of government services in Rwanda: lessons from the data. Cenfri. https://cenfri.org/articles/digitisation-of-government-services-in-rwanda-lessons-from-the-data/ (2024)
4. Brajnik, G.: Comparing accessibility evaluation tools: a method for tool effectiveness. Univ. Access Inf. Soc. **3**, 252–263 (2004)
5. Vigo, M., Brown, J., Conway, V.: Benchmarking web accessibility evaluation tools: measuring the harm of sole reliance on automated tests. In: Proceeding of the W4A 2013, pp. 1–10. ACM, New York, NY (2013)
6. Lazar, J., et al.: Exploring WHO communication during the COVID-19 pandemic through the WHO website based on W3C guidelines: accessible for all? Int. J. Environ. Res. Public Health. **17**(16), 5663 (2020). https://doi.org/10.3390/ijerph17165663
7. Abduganiev, S.: Towards automated web accessibility evaluation: a comparative study. Int. J. Inform. Technol. Comput. Sci. **9**, 18–44 (2017). https://doi.org/10.5815/ijitcs.2017.09.03
8. Abu Doush, I., Sultan, K., Al-Betar, M., Almeraj, Z., Alyasseri, Z., Awadallah, M.: Web accessibility automatic evaluation tools: to what extent can they be automated? CCF Trans. Pervasive Comput. Interact. **5**, 288–320 (2023). https://doi.org/10.1007/s42486-023-00127-8

9. Gwandu, F.B., et al.: Strengthening the Capacity of Agricultural Extension Agents towards Supporting an Inclusive and Sustainable Cassava Seed System in Tanzania (2025).
10. Abduganiev, S.G.: Towards Automated Web Accessibility Evaluation: a Comparative Study, vol. 9, pp. 18–44. I.J. Inform. Technol. Comput. Sci. (2017)
11. Verkijika, S.F., De Wet, L.: A usability assessment of e-government websites in sub-Saharan Africa. Int. J. Inform. Manag. **39**, 20–29 (2018)
12. WebAIM: The WebAIM Million—2025 report on the accessibility of the top 1,000,000 home pages. https://webaim.org/projects/million/ (2025)
13. Ferrara, A., et al.: Measuring web accessibility: which tools for what? In: Proceeding of the W4A 2021. ACM, New York, NY (2021)
14. Yesilada, Y., Harper, S. (eds.): Web Accessibility: a Foundation for Research. Springer, London (2008). https://doi.org/10.1007/978-1-84800-050-6
15. Bühler, C., Heck, H., Perlick, O., Nietzio, A., Ulltveit-Moe, N.: Interpreting results from large scale automatic evaluation of web accessibility. In: Stephanidis, C. (ed.) UAHCI 2006 LNCS, vol. 4556, pp. 184–193. Springer, Heidelberg (2007)
16. Elisa, N.: Usability, accessibility and web security assessment of e-government websites in Tanzania. Int. J. Comput. Appl. **164**(5), 42–48 (2017). https://doi.org/10.5120/ijca2017913632
17. Adepoju, S.A., Shehu, I.S., Bake, P.: Accessibility evaluation and performance analysis of e-government websites in Nigeria. J. Adv. Inform. Technol. (2016)
18. Kuzma, J.M.: Accessibility design issues with UK e-government sites. Gov. Inf. Q. **27**(2), 141–146 (2010)
19. Access to Finance Rwanda: FinScope 2020 Persons with Disabilities Thematic Report. AFR, Kigali (2020) https://afr.rw/downloads/finscope-2020-persons-with-disabilities-thematic-report/
20. SEMrush: Most visited websites in Rwanda 2025. https://www.semrush.com/trending-websites/rw/all (2025)
21. Pool, J.R.: Accessibility metatesting: comparing nine testing tools. In: Proceeding of the W4A '23. ACM, Austin (2023)
22. Nielsen, J.: Usability Engineering. Academic Press, Boston, MA (1993)
23. Top Africa News: Rwanda Union of the Blind urges greater digital accessibility for the visually impaired. https://www.topafricanews.com/2025/05/23/rwanda-union-of-the-blind-urges-greater-digital-accessibility-for-the-visually-impaired/ (May 2025)
24. W3C Web Accessibility Initiative: Web Content Accessibility Guidelines (WCAG) 2.1. https://www.w3.org/TR/WCAG21/ (2018)
25. Irembo: Platform outcomes and impact statistics. https://irembo.com (2024), last accessed 2025/03/01
26. DIAL: Rwanda Digital Government Services Case Study. DIAL Global, Washington, DC (2024) https://dial.global/wp-content/uploads/2024/08/rwanda-final.pdf
27. Cahill, K., Cornish, S.: How well do Ontario library web sites meet new accessibility requirements? Partnership. Can. J. Libr. Inform. Pract. Res. **7**(1) (2012). https://doi.org/10.21083/partnership.v7i1.1613
28. Holloway, A., et al.: Digital accessibility gaps of U.S. higher education websites: insights from a multi-institution automated accessibility audit. Preprint (2024). https://doi.org/10.21203/rs.3.rs-7611216/v1
29. Jap, B., et al.: Accessibility design issues in ophthalmology diagnostic platforms. RISTI. **57**, 19–38 (2024). https://doi.org/10.17013/risti.57.19-38
30. Kaur, S., Mahajan, R., Sharma, A.: Banking websites in India: an accessibility evaluation. CSI Trans. ICT. **2**(2–4), 91–98 (2014). https://doi.org/10.1007/s40012-014-0040-x

Building an Adaptive Planner for Neurodivergence

Annabel Wen(✉), Sarah To, Sara Downing, Madelyn Isaacs, and Crisrael Lucero

California State Polytechnic University, Pomona, Pomona, CA 91768, USA
{amwen,sarahto,sddowning,misaacs,cmlucero}@cpp.edu

Abstract. Many tools exist that assist with planning, both physical and digital. Common productivity strategies include making use of physical calendars, planners, journals, and to-do lists, digital calendars or notes applications, or a combination of both physical and digital resources. Our survey found that many people struggle with procrastination and time management, with a tendency to focus on short-term goals. With such a wide variety of possible productivity tools and strategies, it may be difficult for people to find a solution that aligns with their needs. Studies show that digital applications can beneficially impact certain aspects of Attention-Deficit/Hyperactivity Disorder (ADHD) [1]. Our goal is to develop a planning system that helps manage challenges associated with executive dysfunction and ADHD, including difficulties planning and organizing events or finishing tasks. By implementing an AI-based adaptive approach, we individualize and personalize user experiences, allowing users to achieve long-term productivity goals.

Keywords: Scheduling · Artificial Intelligence (AI) · Attention-Deficit/Hyperactivity Disorder (ADHD)

1 Introduction

There is growing research on building technology for neurodivergence in the Human-Computer Interaction (HCI) field, but many focus on fixing weaknesses, rather than a holistic approach supporting both strengths and weaknesses [1]. Additionally, the majority of ADHD studies focus on solutions for children, with a lack of research on ADHD applications assisting teenagers and adults [2]. We introduce a mobile application that aims to improve upon planning solutions for individuals diagnosed with ADHD, assisting in impacted areas of planning and organization. The application features a scrollable timeline calendar that allows the user to add events, tasks, and goals and receive personalized pre-work suggestions. These suggestions provide users with related tasks or events to consider while planning around the ones they input. By implementing real-time adaptive methodologies [3], our productivity app focuses on helping people engage with their executive dysfunction effectively, increasing user satisfaction through a user input feedback loop [4].

C. Stephanidis et al. (Eds.): HCII 2026, CCIS 3047, pp. 647–653, 2026.
https://doi.org/10.1007/978-3-032-30552-7_62

2 Background and Related Works

One analysis covering eleven HCI publications on neurodivergence in workplace settings explores definitions of neurodiversity in medical and biopsychosocial fields, and compares how neurodivergence is seen in the context of HCI fields versus in the workplace. The papers included in the analysis focused on research pertaining to ADHD (as our planning solution is), autism, and dyslexia, in technical or office work contexts. They discuss two separate research approaches: one aiming to establish neurotypical norms by reducing neurodivergent behaviors, and one centered on improving access and quality of life for neurodivergent workers. The authors summarize the kinds of technology used to address workplace barriers associated with neurodivergence, however, emphasize that these tools have limitations with their approaches to addressing these barriers and with what type of work settings they can be applied to. They also discuss areas for future work, including expanding the workplace tasks and situations that are studied from the lens of neurodivergence and designing comprehensive solutions that take both strengths and weaknesses associated with neurodivergence into account [1].

Another study covers ADHD and reviews papers that explore the role of technology in providing assistance with challenges associated with ADHD. It sorts and views different methods of design based on the specific ADHD-related challenge that the study focuses the most on. Out of these challenges, executive functioning is the most relevant to our research as it involves time management and goal planning. One design researchers reviewed was of a time management wristband made for school age children with ADHD called Takt. The results of this study revealed that students wanted personalized control of the system, such as different vibrational haptic feedback or colors for different events [2]. In our planning system, customization and personalization features will be emphasized in order to increase user satisfaction and our application's effectiveness.

Audemy[1], an adaptive audio-based educational learning platform, integrates AI to utilize feedback from blind and visually impaired students and educators. The difficulty of each question is adjusted to increase engagement, and the speed at which content is delivered varies based on how often students use the repetition function. Their development process featured an iterative design cycle, where the application was modified to improve accessibility and user engagement based on input from educators. Through interviews with teachers, the researchers compiled key considerations for accessible learning tools. These tools should focus on user engagement, through gamification (as our planning solution will) or through other means, and keep users motivated through positive reinforcement. Additionally, applications should work with previous assistive technologies and be designed with minimalistic and accessible interfaces to allow students to use the tool on their own. Their work also discusses future research, such as greater personalization and empathy in AI responses, and data privacy concerns, such as encrypting user data and limiting in what ways it can be used [3]. Our planning

[1] audemy.org.

solution uses takeaways from this paper, as we utilize an iterative design process and use user feedback to personalize the application and improve its results.

Another work introduces a "human-in-the-loop" feedback system for autonomous vehicles, using dynamic preferences that are adjusted based on user expectations and feedback. The approach used for their feedback system relies more heavily on recent feedback, as in cases of autonomous driving, it is possible that preferences change frequently based on different driving scenarios. Their system focuses on user dissatisfaction, as this kind of feedback better contrasts what users expect and how the system behaves [4]. In our planner tool, a feedback system is used to explicitly gather feedback. Certain features of the application, such as pre-work generation, will be modified based on this data to better fit user expectations.

Prior research such as the adaptive audio-based learning platform for BVI students [3] and "human-on-the-loop" feedback system for autonomous vehicles [4] integrated their application's AI to adapt to user preferences and feedback, making their application more personalizable. Our application will also utilize the advantage of real-time adaptive technology to help users who struggle with executive function plans for tasks, goals, and events. We plan to use this adaptive technology to assist users by breaking down tasks into subtasks and events into pre-work to make them more manageable. We also plan to include a human-on-the-loop mechanism to make suggested pre-work adapt to how an individual user completes tasks. This expands the research in support tools in the neurodivergence landscape and introduces a new concept of pre-work within digital planning tools and calendars.

3 Methodology

An initial mockup was created on Figma, utilizing concepts from preexisting research (with a focus on gamification). After creating the initial mockup, user surveys were administered online to a small group of 12 participants, all college students within the age range of 18–21. (This group of user surveys did not focus on participants formally diagnosed with ADHD due to time constraints; however, future rounds of user interviews and trials will target neurodivergent participants.) Surveys were conducted in one-on-one meetings, and the gathered data was anonymized. Each individual was asked about their productivity strategies and tools (both successful and unsuccessful), their approaches to achieving goals (short- and long-term), and specific day-to-day tasks that require planning. Results were then aggregated.

Results from the survey (see Appendix A) indicate the use of a variety of planning methods, including digital and physical tools such as Google Calendar, Notion, note-taking apps, and planners. Most participants mention organizing activities such as schoolwork, chores, work, and meetings. The majority also focused on short-term goals rather than long-term ones, prioritizing deadlines that were sooner. Several factors can influence whether participants meet a deadline, including sleep deprivation, interest, clarity of instructions, and mental health. The results also reveal a common struggle with procrastination or time management. Paywalls, high friction, and unintuitive interfaces are frustrating features that can deter individuals from using an application. Contrary to our original hypothesis, the survey results suggest that functionality outweighs personalization in determining whether to use an application, particularly applications designed to boost productivity.

We plan to conduct 1-on-1 user-experience interviews to compare several Figma mockups, using the findings to inform further frontend prototypes. Once implemented, A/B testing is incorporated to track the effectiveness of our "pre-work" solution, which generates suggestions for prerequisite tasks based on a user-submitted task or event. Our model tracks pre-work progress; upon task completion, the user can provide feedback, which is combined with performance metrics to help users address challenges in task initiation and time estimation (Fig. 1).

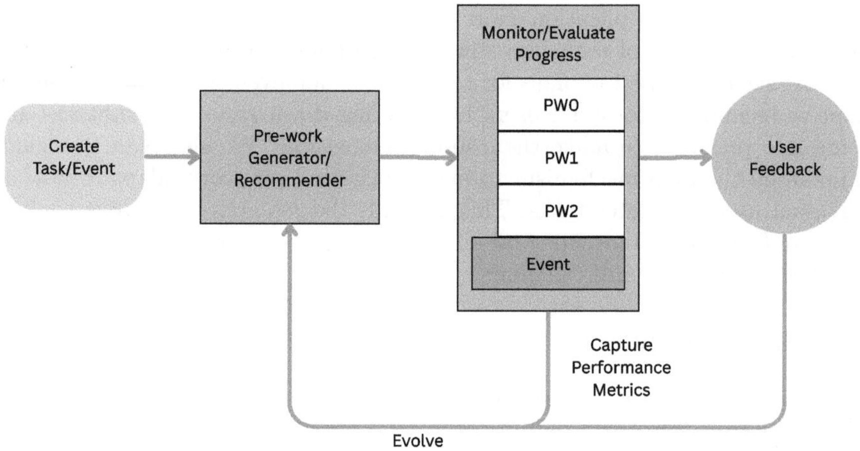

Fig. 1. After a task/event is created, task progress and user feedback affect future pre-work generation.

3.1 Adaptive Strategies

The goal of the pre-work feature is to allow users to plan and block out the time needed to prepare for a task or event. During the task-creation process, users are given the option to input or generate pre-work. Pre-work is generated by calling a Large Language Model (LLM), using the task title and description as input, along with a premade prompt. Once pre-work is generated, users can choose what pre-work tasks to accept or delete. Additionally, users can manually add their own pre-work tasks at any time by typing a list, separated by commas, into the pre-work field. Both generated pre-work tasks (along with information on whether the task was accepted or deleted) and manual pre-work tasks will be added into a database used for Retrieval-Augmented Generation (RAG). Common tasks/events/goals are clustered using Natural Language Processing (NLP), and their accompanying (accepted) pre-work tasks are stored in a vector database for RAG.

Users can also offer feedback directly through a feedback form, which can be submitted daily. This feedback is processed with NLP and is weighted more heavily than passively gathered feedback. Such as discussed in [4], there is a psychological tendency that suggests people have more prominent reactions to negative experiences. Whether positive or negative, users that provide feedback voluntarily likely have strong opinions, indicating that this data should be considered with greater weight.

Experimentation Setup. A group of participants will be randomly selected from a pool of interested Cal Poly Pomona students for the study. Participants use the mobile app for a two-month period, with check-ins after one week, one month, and two months. To test the effectiveness of the user feedback system, participants spend the first month without inputting user feedback. Participants spend the second month engaging with the user feedback system. At the end of the study, participant feedback is used to refine the application. Check-ins consist of users rating their experiences, including ease of use, motivation level, and ease of task completion. Other success metrics include time spent on the app, the ratio of accepted LLM-generated pre-work tasks to user-generated pre-work tasks, etc.

4 Future Work

Future work largely consists of continuing to implement application functionality and iterate on UI designs. A variety of models will be tested for the pre-work and user feedback systems. User input will continue to influence the implementation of the UI through A/B testing. Additionally, testing the application with a wider group of participants (including neurodivergent individuals/people with ADHD) will provide greater feedback and insights into the effectiveness of specific, user-focused features, such as event and task pre-work generation. Getting a larger group of participants, particularly from outside the student and young adult demographic, will assist in improving and refining these features as well as the overall app design and functionality. Once the pre-work and user feedback systems are in place, gamification can be introduced. Features for personalization, such as collecting themes or customizing an avatar or virtual pet, are intended to reward timely task completion.

Disclosure of Interests. The authors have no competing interests to declare that are relevant to the content of this article.

A Appendix

B Survey Questions and Aggregated Results

Table 1. Survey Questions and Aggregated Responses

#	Survey Question	Aggregated Top Responses
1	How do you keep track of things you need to do?	Digital: Google Calendar, Google Docs, Notion, Notes apps, Canvas; Physical: paper calendar, journal/planner, Post-It notes, memory.
1a	Can you describe the types of activities you typically need to organize?/What kinds of tasks do you usually plan for in your day-to-day life?	Homework, studying, classes, exam prep; chores; events; work; (job) applications; emails; club meetings; hobbies/personal projects; personal tasks
2	When planning your work, do you focus more on short-term goals, long-term goals, or both?	Majority: short-term. More tangible and easier to get done. Minority: both. Focus on short-term goals, leading up to tracked long-term goals; break long-term goals into short-term.
3	How do you usually manage your time when working towards deadlines?	Focus on deadlines in order due; easier tasks first. May procrastinate and be motivated closer to the deadline.
3a	Does this change when given a larger project/further deadline versus a shorter deadline?	Some respondents try to plan or space out work before the deadline, while others continue to procrastinate.
3b	How do you manage your time when working on a project/task without a clear deadline?	Some respondents block out work time, while others use their free time. The deadline may be worked on slowly, easy parts first, or when motivation strikes.
4	In your experience, what factors influence whether or not you meet a deadline?	Sleep, interest/motivation, current workload, importance (effect on overall grades), mental health, clarity on project or its due date
5	When starting a task (an assignment, chore, etc.), what do you struggle the most with?	Figuring out how to start a task (what to do? motivation, getting into the flow), distractions
6	What time management or productivity tools/strategies have you used in the past?	Google Calendar, Notes App, Paper planner/journal, Notion, Canvas, Post-it notes, timers, Pomodoro, Tick Tick, YPT, CoStudy
6a	What [time management or productivity tools/strategies] worked and what didn't work?	Most tools and strategies had mixed results, depending on the person.
6b	What features make you stop using an app? Do you find any features frustrating or annoying?	Too much effort to use the app, too costly, complicated UI/UX, lack of desired functionality
6c	Are there any features you wish these apps had?	Easy input (voice, photo parsing to fill in calendar), clear functionality and UI, reminders, gamification/motivation, smart (AI) features, integration with other apps, no paywalls
7	How important is personalization or customization in the apps you use? (particularly productivity apps)	Some respondents say personalization motivates them to use the app, while others prefer that the app is functional

References

1. Burtscher, S., Gerling, K.: Neurodivergence and work in human-computer interaction: mapping the research landscape. In: CHIWORK '24: Proceedings of the 3rd Annual Meeting of the Symposium on Human-Computer Interaction for Work (2024)
2. Hussain, F.: Investigating Current State-of-The-Art Applications of Supportive Technologies for Individuals with ADHD. https://arxiv.org/pdf/2005.09993 (2020)
3. Yang, C., Taele, P.: AI for Accessible Education: Personalized Audio-Based Learning for Blind Students. https://www.arxiv.org/abs/2504.17117 (2025)
4. Zhang, M., Li, J., et al.: Adaptive preferences: pivoting through user complaints. ACM Trans. Auton. Adapt. Syst. (2025). https://doi.org/10.1145/3727621

Author Index

C. Stephanidis et al. (Eds.): HCII 2026, CCIS 3047, pp. 655–658, 2026.
https://doi.org/10.1007/978-3-032-30552-7

MIX
Papier aus verantwortungsvollen Quellen
Paper from responsible sources
FSC® C105338

If you have any concerns about our products,
you can contact us on
ProductSafety@springernature.com

In case Publisher is established outside the EU,
the EU authorized representative is:
Springer Nature Customer Service Center GmbH
Europaplatz 3, 69115 Heidelberg, Germany

Printed by Libri Plureos GmbH
in Hamburg, Germany